THEORIES
OF
MATHEM
LEAR

THEORIES
OF
MATHEMATICAL
LEARNING

General Editors
LESLIE P. STEFFE
University of Georgia
PEARLA NESHER
Haifa University

Section Editors
PAUL COBB
Vanderbilt University
GERALD A. GOLDIN
Rutgers University
BRIAN GREER
Queen's University

LAWRENCE ERLBAUM ASSOCIATES, PUBLISHERS
1996   Mahwah, New Jersey

Lawrence Erlbaum Associates, Inc., Publishers
10 Industrial Avenue
Mahwah, New Jersey 07430

Library of Congress Cataloging-in-Publication Data
Theories of mathematical learning / general editors, Leslie P. Steffe
. . .[et al.].
  p. cm.
 Proceedings of a working group on theories of learning
mathematics, presented at the Seventh International Congress on
Mathematical Education, held at Université Laval, Québec, Canada.
 Includes bibliographical references (p. –) and index.
 ISBN 0-8058-1661-5 (cloth : alk. paper). — ISBN 0-8058-1662-3
(paper : alk. paper)
 1. Mathematics—Study and teaching—Congresses. I. Steffe,
Leslie P. II. International Congress on Mathematical Education (7th
: 1992 : Québec, Québec)
QA11.A1T47 1996
510'.71—dc20   96-19730
                CIP

Books published by Lawrence Erlbaum Associates are printed on acid-free paper,
and their bindings are chosen for strength and durability.

Printed in the United States of America
10 9 8 7 6 5 4 3 2 1

Contents

Preface

On each fourth year, an International Congress on Mathematical Education (ICME) is held under the auspices of the International Commission on Mathematical Instruction. The seventh ICME[1] was held in Québec City, Québec, Canada, at Université Laval. The International Program Committee for ICME-7 established 23 Working Groups as a part of their organizational pattern. Each Working Group comprised a subconference within ICME-7 and each was allocated four 1½-hour time slots on the program. This volume contains the proceedings of Working Group 4 (WG4), Theories of Learning Mathematics.

I was asked by Pearla Nesher, Chief Organizer of WG4, to be a consultant to the working group. Advisory Team Members were Nicolas Balacheff, Erik de Corte, and Hans-Georg Steiner. Little did I realize then that my acceptance of this invitation would lead to 3 years of intensive activity culminating in the publication of this book. Much of the credit for the proceedings is due to Dr. Nesher, who provided the leadership, vision, and organization for the working group. She organized WG4 into three subgroups: sociological and anthropological perspectives on mathematics learning, contributions of constructivism to the learning of mathematics, and cognitive science theories and their contribution to the learning of mathematics. Paul Cobb organized the first subgroup, Gerald Goldin the second, and Brian Greer the third. Their efforts are only indicated by the sections of the book which they edited, because many of the contributions of WG4 took place during the lively discussions and debates that transpired in the meetings of the subgroups. Nevertheless, this volume contains revisions of initial contributions that were written prior to ICME-7 and chapters by the three subgroup organizers that reflect many of the issues that were raised at the time of the Congress. So the reader has the advantage of a considerable amount of postconference editing and writing activity. Nevertheless, we editors make no claim that the postconference writing and editorial activity adequately capture what transpired in WG4.

Upon reading the various chapters in this book, the reader will be impressed by the lack of agreement among the authors concerning what constitutes mathe-

---

[1]Gaulin, C., Hodgson, B. R., Wheeler, D. H., & Egsgrad, J. C. (Eds.). (1994). *Proceedings of the 7th International Congress on Mathematical Education*. Sainte-Foy, Québec: Les Presses de l'Université Laval.

matical learning. Even though their world views dramatically influence what they consider mathematical learning to be, I believe that the chapters are only snapshots, or indications, of the authors' understanding of mathematical learning. Through observing and participating in the mathematical learning of others, I have come to believe that much of what constitutes mathematical learning remains unaccessible to consciousness. Thus, coupled with my attempts to talk and write about mathematical learning, I have come to understand the extreme difficulty in communicating what I might mean by the phrase. Although I can distinctly remember my first understanding that a^{-1} does not necessarily mean $1/a$, I have no access to how I might have come to this understanding, and what I understand about induction and deduction does not shed any light on the matter. In our search to understand how a human being might construct meaning for things like a^{-1}, my belief is that we must at the very minimum participate in bringing forth the construction of such meaning by others. In this, I concur with Davis' (Chapter 16, this volume) observation that chemists could not have gotten very far if they only worked with their chemicals. They needed explanatory models of what was going on "inside" their elements of experience. And so it is with those elements of our experience that we regard to be mathematical learning. We need explanatory models of what constitutes the phenomena that we might point to and say, "Yes, that is one thing I mean by mathematical learning."

Some of the authors provide examples, or images, of mathematical learning. However, upon reading the chapters written by the three subgroup organizers (Cobb, Greer, and Goldin), one realizes the force of the book is directed toward elaborating theoretical principles that might undergird making the kind of models called for by Davis. In my opinion, these elaborations reflect the progress that has been made in the field over the past 20 years and represent starting points for understanding mathematical learning today.

The chapters in Part IV were presented in a plenary session of WG4. This explains why they are set apart from the rest of the book. The chapter by Dörfler presents his views on representation and remains unchanged from its original version. I find Dörfler's way of thinking about mathematical objects quite useful when trying to explain the mathematical knowledge of another person and regard his chapter as a valuable contribution to anyone interested in making a model of mathematical learning. In fact, in the chapter by Wiegel and myself, we try to indicate how Dörfler's thinking about mathematical objects is compatible with our understanding of the mathematics of children.

There is no substitute for being at Québec City and participating in the work of WG4. Because that experience was limited to participating in one of the three subgroups, this book is first and foremost for the participants of WG4 as they carry on with their work. However, the fundamental necessity to improve mathematics learning worldwide should make the book of interest to anyone concerned with that enterprise. The book represents the hard work, the understanding, and the time of many people and the resources of many institutions. In particular, I thank the Department of Mathematics Education at the University of Georgia for supporting my efforts in the production of this book. All of the editors wish to express our gratitude to the people at Lawrence Erlbaum Associates for publishing this book and for their patience and competence during its preparation and publication.

Leslie P. Steffe

SOCIOLOGICAL AND ANTHROPOLOGICAL PERSPECTIVES ON MATHEMATICS LEARNING

Paul Cobb, Editor

1 Emergent and Sociocultural Views of Mathematical Activity

Paul Cobb
Vanderbilt University

Barbara Jaworski
Oxford University

Norma Presmeg
Florida State University

Taken together, the six plenary chapters presented in this section indicate that a wide range of approaches fall under the rubric of sociological and anthropological perspectives. These contributions all reflect the contention that knowing and doing mathematics is an inherently social and cultural activity. This claim does not merely mean that social interaction serves as a catalyst for otherwise autonomous cognitive development. In the view of each of the contributors, social and cultural influences are not limited to the process of learning but also extend to its products, increasingly sophisticated mathematical ways of knowing. Consequently, in describing their own positions, the contributors each challenge the assumption that students' mathematical activity can be adequately accounted for solely in terms of individualistic theories such as constructivism or information-processing psychology. Three of the contributors, Voigt, Stigler et al., and Saxe and Bermudez, develop analyses that complement psychological constructivism. In contrast, the perspectives developed by van Oers, Forman, and Crawford are proposed as alternatives to psychological theories that focus on the individual.

In this commentary, we first consider the key assumptions of these two groups of theorists, giving particular attention to the role they attribute to individualistic theories. We then contrast their differing treatments of a variety of key issues and conclude by discussing possible ways in which their perspectives might be complementary.

EMERGENT PERSPECTIVES

Voigt, Stigler et al., and Saxe and Bermudez use differing theoretical constructs to address a diverse range of issues. In our view, this diversity belies several areas of compatibility in their treatment of students' mathematical activity in classroom situations.

Voigt's work is premised on the assumption that mathematical learning and teaching are linked via classroom interaction. His work can therefore be viewed as an attempt to transcend individualistic analyses of either students' or the teacher's activity (cf. Romberg & Carpenter, 1986). One of his central concerns is to clarify the processes by which the teacher and students develop a basis for mathematical communication. He approaches this issue by analyzing their negotiation of taken-as-shared meanings. It is important to appreciate that Voigt's use of the term *negotiation* is derived from symbolic interactionist theory (Blumer, 1969). In this view, social interactions involve subtle shifts and slides of meaning that frequently occur outside the participants' awareness. Thus, when Voigt speaks of the negotiation of meaning, he declares a theoretical interest—that of analyzing the evolution of mathematical meaning in interaction. His overall goal is to develop a theoretical framework within which to analyze the interrelationships between the teacher's and students' activities. The sample episodes he discusses indicate that this framework is not tied to any particular instructional approach. Instead, the theoretical constructs he employed are intended to be applicable to any mathematics classroom, regardless of how desirable or undesirable the instruction might appear.

Voigt's notion of negotiation can be contrasted with Richards' use of the term in his contribution. For Richards, negotiation occurs only when the teacher actively listens and consciously adapts to students' mathematical activity. He contrasts interactions of this type with those that characterize traditional classrooms and argues that, in the latter case, the teacher is a conveyer of information and the students are the recipients. This distinction between desirable and undesirable instructional practices is motivated at least in part by the pragmatic concern to reform traditional American instructional practices. Thus, Richards argues that the teacher should be a trained negotiator whose goal is to initiate students into the consensual domain of mathematically literate adults.

Voigt's and Richards' notions of negotiation are clearly in conflict. For example, Richards argues that interactions in which students merely adopt the teacher's language do not involve negotiation. However, Voigt would contend that even the most draconian teachers necessarily adapt to their students' activity. The issue for Voigt is not to ascertain whether the teacher and students negotiate meanings, but to understand how they do so by analyzing the microprocesses of their interactions. One way to resolve this conflict is to differentiate between *implicit negotiation* and *explicit negotiation* (Cobb & Yackel, 1993). This distinction highlights Voigt's claim that students' mathematical learning is frequently indirect and occurs as they participate in implicit negotiations that are outside their own and the teacher's awareness. For his part, Richards proposes that classroom interactions should involve the explicit negotiation of mathematical meanings in which the teacher encourages students to articulate their mathematical problems, interpretations, and solutions.

Although Voigt focuses on collective meanings, he takes care to emphasize that taken-as-shared meanings do not displace analyses of individual, personal meanings. Indeed, the references he makes to constructivist psychological analyses in his chapter indicate that these and interactionist analyses can be complementary. We can clarify the relationship between the two types of analyses by taking as an example an interaction between a researcher and one student. To the extent that a constructivist psychological analysis takes account of the interaction, the focus is on the student's interpretations of the teacher's actions. An analysis of this type is made from the perspective of the researcher, who is inside the interaction and is concerned with the ways in which the student modifies his or her activity. In contrast, an interactional analysis is made from the outside, from the point of view of an observer rather than that of a participant in the interaction. From this perspective, the focus is on the obligations the researcher and the student attempt to fulfill, and on the taken-as-shared meanings that emerge between them, rather than on the student's personal interpretations. As Voigt makes clear, these taken-as-shared meanings are not cognitive elements that capture the partial match of individual interpretations, but are instead located at the level of interaction. The complementarity between the two theoretical perspectives becomes apparent when it is noted that taken-as-shared meanings emerge as the teacher and students attempt to coordinate their individual activities. Conversely, the teacher's and student's participation in the establishment of these taken-as-shared mathematical meanings both supports and constrains their individual interpretations.

This complementarity between interactionist and psychological constructivist perspectives implies that the link between the social and psychological aspects of mathematical activity is indirect. Thus, although it is not possible to deduce individual students' cognitions from interactional analyses, such analyses can inform cognitive analyses. For example, one can infer from an interactional analysis what, minimally, students need to know and do in order to fulfill their obligations and thus be effective as they participate in classroom interactions. Further, one can infer the conceptual constructions that students might make as they participate in the evolution of such patterns of interaction. Inferences of this type reflect the view that students have to reorganize their own activity in order to learn. As a consequence, Voigt rejects the notion that the social dynamics of the classroom determine students' mathematical development. He instead analyses how students' participation in specific patterns of interaction might support their mathematical development by identifying possible learning opportunities.

At first glance, Voigt's interactionist approach might seem unrelated to the problem of accounting for differences in Japanese and American students' mathematics achievement. However, the framing of the issue by Stigler et al. focuses attention on the quality of classroom social interactions. Stigler et al. contend that there are cultural differences in what it means to teach and learn mathematics in the two countries, and that these differences constitute two distinct traditions of classroom practice. The goal of their analysis is to identify aspects of these two cultural traditions by comparing representative lessons from each country. Thus, Stigler et al. link the macrosociological and microsociological levels of analysis by treating the microcultures established in particular classrooms as manifestations of broader cultural phenomena. This enables them to address a cultural-difference issue by focusing on teacher–student classroom interactions.

It should be noted that whereas Voigt attempts to tease out hidden interactional regularities, Stigler et al. analyze the teacher's routines and explore the consequences for students' mathematical learning. In doing so, Stigler et al. repeatedly hint at the interdependency of the teacher's and students' activity, thereby establishing a point of contact with Voigt's work. For example, on one occasion, they describe an interaction in which an American fifth-grade teacher asked his students for the area of a right triangle that has been divided into square units. The teacher anticipated that the students would find it difficult to count the squares because fractional parts of square units lined the hypotenuse. However, the students persisted in their attempts to count the squares. On three occasions, the teacher attempted to motivate the need for an alternative method by capitalizing on the students' solution attempts. Thus, when a student called the fractional parts halves, the teacher asked, "Are they halves? This one is not a half, is it? This one is not a half, this one is way more than a half." The students ignored these interventions and persisted with their counting approach until they jointly developed a viable solution and arrived at the correct answer. It was only at this point that the teacher introduced a planned demonstration that involved placing two triangles together to make a square. Clearly, the teacher felt obliged to follow his scripted lesson plan. This is a key aspect of the American tradition of school mathematics identified by Stigler et al. However, the authoritarian way in which the teacher eventually introduced the demonstration can only be understood by taking account of the students' unanticipated persistence. The teacher's role as an authority who controlled the mathematical agenda can therefore be seen to have emerged in the course of the interaction.

Stigler et al. relate their analysis of classroom episodes to students' mathematical learning by identifying the opportunities that arise for thinking and reflection. Thus, like Voigt, they leave room for psychological analyses of individual students' cognitions. The characterization of mathematical learning they offer is that of a process of individual construction that occurs in social interaction within a cultural tradition of practice. Given the relationship they propose between classroom processes and broader cultural phenomena, it can in fact be argued that the teacher and students in each country are regenerating culturally specific traditions of practice as they interact in the classroom.

Saxe and Bermudez's work complements that of Stigler et al. by emphasizing the culturally situated nature of mathematical activity. In their chapter, they illustrate how their Emergent Goals model can be used to analyze the mathematical environments that emerge for children as they participate in classroom activities. Saxe (1991) clarifies that this model was originally developed to account for the mathematical learning that occurs as individuals participate in nonschool cultural practices such as selling candy in the street. The central problem addressed by Saxe (1991) was that of explaining how individuals' personal goals become interwoven with the socially organized activities in which they participate. The solution he proposed involves the explicit coordination of two theoretical perspectives—a constructivist treatment of children's mathematical activity and a sociocultural treatment of cognition. Thus, like Voigt and Stigler et al., Saxe's theoretical work complements psychological constructivist analyses of individual children's mathematical activity.

The four parameters incorporated into the Emergent Goals model deal with the cultural aspects of mathematical activity (activity structures and artifacts), the interactional aspects (social interactions), and the individual psychological aspects (prior understandings). The view of mathematical learning offered by Saxe and Bermudez is therefore similar to that implicit in the Stigler et al. analysis: a constructive process that occurs while participating in a cultural practice, frequently while interacting with others. It can also be noted that Saxe and Bermudez follow Voigt and Stigler et al. in using the notion of learning opportunities to link the cultural and social aspects of mathematical activity to conceptual development. In effect they propose that learning opportunities and thus the mathematical knowledge constructed are relative to the socially and culturally constrained goals that an individual attempts to achieve.

The sociocultural treatment of cognition that Saxe and Bermudez incorporate into the Emergent Goals model draws heavily on Leont'ev's (1981) activity theory. For example, Saxe (1991) follows Leont'ev in arguing that an individual's actions are necessarily elements of a broader sociocultural system and cannot be adequately understood unless this relation is explicated. Further, he notes that the term *activity* in activity theory refers to this broader system of practice and to its associated motive (cf. Crawford, Chapter 9, this volume). In the case of Saxe's prior work with Brazilian street vendors, the activity was that of candy selling and the motive was that of economic survival. In line with Leont'ev's theory, Saxe analyzed the structure of the candy-selling activity by decomposing it into a cycle of goal-directed actions (i.e., purchase boxes of candy, price candy for sale, sell candy, and select new boxes for purchase). The Treasure Hunt game that Saxe and Bermudez describe was developed to provide a classroom simulation of mathematically productive out-of-school activities such as candy selling. In this case, the activity is that of playing the game, and the associated motive is to win the game by accumulating treasure. As before, the structure of the activity is delineated by identifying a sequence of goal-directed actions (i.e., challenge, rent, purchase, region, and check).

Despite these commonalities in Saxe's analyses of mathematical activity in streets and in school, he and Bermudez modified their theoretical framework when they moved from out-of-school practices to the classroom. For example, the notion of an activity structure was relatively unproblematic when Saxe analyzed individuals' participation in practices such as candy selling. In contrast, he and Bermudez explain that they found it necessary to distinguish between the intended and the actual activity structure when they analyzed children's game-playing activity. They further clarify that the intended structure of the game corresponds to the developers' understanding, and that the actual structure implicit in a child's activity corresponds to that child's understanding. Thus, in making the transition from out-of-school practices to the classroom, Saxe and Bermudez transformed the sociocultural construct of activity structure into a personal construct. In this regard, they note that the children were often engaged with different mathematical environments even though they were ostensibly playing the same game, using the same materials, in the same classrooms.

In their chapters, Yackel and Schliemann and Carraher identify points of contact between Voigt's and Saxe and Bermudez's analyses. Yackel notes that the Emergent Goals model treats students' mathematical environments as dynamic worlds that unfold as they play the Treasure Hunt game. Similarly, Voigt argues that the topic of classroom discourse changes through the negotiation of meaning and is like a river that finds its own bed. Each of these accounts is consistent with Varela, Thompson, and Rosch's (1991) emergent approach wherein cognitive capacities are considered to be "inextricably linked to histories that are lived, much like paths that exist only as they are laid down by walking" (p. 205). Varela et al. contended that the emergent view of cognition constitutes "a middle path between the Scylla of cognition as the recovery of a pregiven outer world (realism) and the Charybdis of cognition as the projection of a pregiven inner world (idealism)" (p. 172). Schliemann and Carraher, in commenting on the Emergent Goals model, explicate an implication of this view when they question the all too prevalent assumption that students are engaged in the cognitive task intended by the researcher (cf. Newman, Griffin, & Cole, 1989). Voigt, for his part, observes that there is a hermeneutical "uncertainty relation" inherent in interviewing students because their cognitive processes are specific to their participation in the interview as a social event.

Thus far, we have highlighted several commonalities in Voigt's and Saxe and Bermudez's positions. However, it is important to acknowledge that there is one significant difference in their views. Saxe and Bermudez stress that students' goals are interwoven with the properties of the artifacts they use. Further, they appear to treat these properties as unambiguous, objective features of the artifacts. Voigt would presumably acknowledge that Saxe and Bermudez make an important contribution when they draw attention to the influence of artifacts. However, he also contends that every object and event in human interaction is ambiguous and plurisemantic. This implies that the meaning and use of artifacts are negotiated by the teacher and students. Thus, for Voigt, artifacts are emergent interactional accomplishments that can differ from one classroom to another.

In summary, we have identified several areas of compatibility in the frameworks that Voigt, Stigler et al., and Saxe and Bermudez propose and have suggested that they all take an emergent approach to mathematical meaning. We have also suggested that their treatments of the social and cultural aspects of mathematical activity complement rather than displace psychological constructivist analyses. In addition, we have illustrated that they all use the notion of learning opportunities to relate these social and cultural aspects to psychological analyses. Finally, we have noted that they all developed their theoretical frameworks to understand various aspects of teachers' and students' classroom activity.

SOCIOCULTURAL PERSPECTIVES

In their chapters, van Oers, Forman, and Crawford each develop a sociocultural perspective by drawing on either Vygotsky's work or activity theory. They all view mathematics as a cultural practice and treat learning either as a process of enculturation or as an apprenticeship. Further, they all contend that individual cognitive processes are derived from social and cultural processes. In this regard, they follow Vygotsky (1979) arguing that "the social dimension of consciousness is primary in time and in fact. The individual dimension of consciousness is derivative and secondary" (p. 30).

van Oers notes at the beginning of his contribution that he takes an explicitly Vygotskian point of view. He subsequently clarifies his position by distancing it from constructivist analyses of the social and cultural aspects of mathematical activity. In constructivist approaches, students are assumed to construct their own conceptual understandings as they participate in cultural practices, frequently while interacting with others. From this point of view, participation in social and cultural processes enables and constrains but does not determine individual development. We have seen that Voigt, Stigler et al., and Saxe and Bermudez all propose an indirect linkage of this type. In contrast, van Oers contends that the link between the sociocultural and cognitive domains is direct: The qualities of students' thinking are generated by the organizational features of social activities. On the basis of this assumption, van Oers attempts to deduce how, ideally, classroom activities should be organized during mathematics lessons.

In addressing this goal, van Oers first clarifies the nature of mathematics as a cultural practice. To this end, he examines both histories of mathematics and self-observational literature written by mathematicians to identify characteristics of the activity that are taken for granted by most mathematicians. In taking this approach, van Oers follows Davydov (1988) in assuming that mathematicians are the custodians of students' intellectual inheritance—mathematics viewed as a historically evolving sociocultural activity. He continues this line of reasoning by arguing that classroom learning activities should be modeled after the process of knowledge production in the discipline. This leads him to argue that the motive of classroom activities should be the deliberate, constructive production of mathematical knowledge, and that the learning activities should involve problem solving, negotiation and communication, mental organization, symbol formation, and construction. We note in passing that van Oers' approach bears a certain resemblance to that of Lampert (1990) in that both draw on the discipline to clarify both the process and the product of mathematical learning. However, van Oers focuses on general characteristics of mathematical practices whereas Lampert derived a specific model for the nature of classroom discourse.

Vygotskian learning theory comes to the fore when van Oers considers how instruction should be organized so that the identified aspects of the discipline are realized in the classroom. As Forman notes in her chapter, the two primary issues addressed by Vygotsky concern the nature of classroom social interactions and role of semiotic activity involving written and spoken symbols. van Oers deals with the first of these issues by suggesting that students should imitate culturally established mathematical practices when they interact with the teacher or a more capable peer. Help should then be gradually withdrawn so that the students take over functions they could not initially perform, thus interiorizing the cultural activity. This account instantiates Vygotsky's frequently cited general genetic law of cultural development: "Any higher mental function was external and social before it was internal. It was once a social relationship between two people. . . . We can formulate the general genetic law of cultural development in the following way. Any function appears twice or on two planes. . . . It appears first between people as an intermental category, and then within the child as an intramental category" (Vygotsky, 1960, pp. 197–198). It is here that the characterization of learning as apprenticeship is most apparent in van Oers' analysis (cf. Rogoff, 1990).

van Oers addresses the second major aspect of Vygotsky's sociohistorical theory, that concerning the role of symbols, when he discusses the process of interiorization. In van Oers' view, symbols are carriers of meaning and therefore constitute the primary vehicles of the enculturation process. This does not, of course, imply a transmission view of communication wherein conventional mathematical symbols are considered to carry meaning directly from the teacher to the students. Instead, the fundamental claim is that symbols serve as carriers of meaning from one generation to the next when students use them while engaging in a sociocultural activity. Thus, when Vygotsky called symbols "objective tools," he was referring to symbols-in-practice, not to symbols per se (cf. Bauersfeld, 1990).

The crucial role that van Oers attributes to symbols is apparent in his statement that the process of symbol formation is identical with the process of concept formation. In particular, the appropriation of a symbol is synonymous with the interiorization of an action. For example, an external action such as that of combining two collections of two objects might first be related to the symbol string "$2 + 2 = 4$." The action is then transformed to the mental level, and eventually it becomes coincidental with the act of reading the symbol string. As van Oers notes, this account of interiorization implies that conceptual development in mathematics involves mastering mathematics as a written language and appropriating the spoken mathematical register.

Given the underlying metaphor of apprenticeship and the close relationship that van Oers sees between symbol and concept formation, it follows that one of the teacher's major responsibilities is to insert culturally approved insights into discussions, particularly by introducing conventional spoken and written symbols. Thus, the teacher is characterized as a representative of mathematical culture who supports students' discursive reconstruction of culturally approved meanings. This view of the teacher's role leads to a treatment of negotiation that is partially at odds with Voigt's interactionist account of communication. For Voigt, negotiation is a process of mutual adaptation that gives rise to shifts and slides of meaning as the teacher and students attempt to coordinate their individual activities. However, from the sociocultural perspective, negotiation is a process of mutual appropriation in which the teacher and students continually coopt or use each other's contributions (Newman et al., 1989). The teacher is therefore expected to insert culturally approved insights that students can coopt, and to appropriate students' actions into the wider system of mathematical practices that they are to reconstruct. In this account, the teacher negotiates with students in order to mediate between personal and cultural meanings. Voigt, however, takes the local classroom community rather than the mathematical practices institutionalized by wider society as his primary point of reference. In his view, the teacher negotiates with students in order to initiate and guide both students' individual constructions and the evolution of taken-as-shared mathematical meanings so that they become increasingly compatible with culturally approved meanings. Thus, whereas van Oers frames instructional issues in terms of the transmission of mathematical culture from one generation to the next, Voigt focuses on the emergence of mathematical meaning in the classroom.

The issue that Forman addresses in her chapter is that of using sociocultural theory to develop a hypothetical connection between proposed changes in instructional processes and the desired goals of current American reform recommendations. Thus, like van Oers, Forman proposes that there is a direct link between sociocultural processes and mathematical learning. Further, she emphasizes the two key aspects of Vygotsky's sociohistorical theory discussed by van Oers—social organizational processes and semiotic mediation. Forman's primary contribution is to introduce recent American revisions of sociocultural theory. In commenting on Forman's chapter, we therefore have the opportunity to consider the implications of these developments.

Forman uses Lave and Wenger's (1991) notion of legitimate peripheral participation to analyze mathematical learning. In such an approach, learning is considered to be synonymous with increasing participation in socially-situated activities. Lave and Wenger in fact took the relatively radical position of attempting to avoid any reference to the mind in the head. In doing so, they went beyond van

Oers' Vygotskian position. As van Oers makes clear, Vygotsky was a developmentalist who attempted to account for qualitative change in internal psychological processes. His fundamental contention was that these changes are generated by social and cultural processes. Lave and Wenger challenged all theories that acknowledge an internal psychological domain. Further, they took issue with Vygotsky's claim that the mind is formed as an individual participates in a community of practice and instead contended that learning is increasing participation in communities of practice. In doing so, they dispensed with Vygotsky's notions of mental organization and internalization because, in their view, there is no internal domain into which intermental processes can be internalized. Forman illustrates an implication of this approach by arguing that indices of learning are as much present in classroom discourse as in individual problem solving protocols, and that the establishment of a community of practices should be taken as evidence of learning.

Forman introduces a second construct, that of classroom discourse, to address the issue of semiotic mediation. Like van Oers, Forman stresses that discourse is not limited to spoken language but includes written symbols. She further contends that discursive activity goes beyond concept learning to involve the mastery of specialized speech genres such as the mathematics register. This claim appears to parallel van Oers' argument that symbols are carriers of meaning. In addition, just as van Oers equates concept formation and symbol formation, Forman suggests that the process of learning mathematics is synonymous with mastering the mathematics register. Forman therefore appears to treat mathematical learning almost exclusively as a process of enculturation. In her view, the teacher's role is to support students' appropriation of the mathematics register by engaging them in instructional conversations that interweave this register with the everyday register. It can be noted that this interweaving corresponds to the process of mathematization that Voigt discusses in his chapter. The contrast between Forman's and Voigt's interpretations of this process is symptomatic of the differing premises that underpin sociocultural and emergent perspectives. For Forman, mathematization is accounted for in terms of the mastery of a preestablished, culturally specific form of discourse. For Voigt, it is a collective activity of the classroom community and is accounted for in terms of the evolution of thematic patterns of interaction.

In contrast to Forman, Crawford includes psychological processes in her theoretical scheme. Her overriding purpose is to investigate how changes in the quality of the sociocultural contexts for learning influence learning outcomes. The way in which Crawford formulates this issue implies a direct link between sociocultural and cognitive processes, with the former having priority over the latter. In support of this position, Crawford notes that Vygotsky viewed conscious behavior as a reflection of the sociocultural environment in which an individual functions. Thus, like van Oers and Forman, she stresses the influence of social relations on development. However, semiotic mediation and associated notions such as the mathematical register do not play a prominent role in her analysis. Further, Crawford draws more heavily on Leont'ev's activity theory than she does on Vygotsky's work. The contrast between Crawford's approach and that taken by van Oers and Forman allows us to identify two general positions within sociocultural theory.

Crawford explains that in Leont'ev's theory, internal cognitive activity is derived from external, object-related activity. In particular, in the course of development, collective or joint practical activity is internalized to form the plane of internal, conscious thought. Kozulin (1986, 1990) and van der Veer and Valsiner (1991) both argued that there is a significant discontinuity between Vygotsky's and Leont'ev's theories in that Leont'ev downplayed social and semiotic mediation in favor of practical activity or labor. Further, Kozulin and van der Veer and Valsiner both accounted for this discontinuity by focusing on the sociopolitical setting in which Vygotsky and Leont'ev worked. Thus, they observed that from 1931 "the Party culture, with its fear of dissenting opinions and its demand for a strictly uniform world-view, was being imposed on scientific debates. More and more frequently, researchers were forced to demonstrate their loyalty to the latest ideological point of view" (van der Veer & Valsiner, 1991, p. 375). In this intellectual climate, Vygotsky had to cope with a series of systematically organized attacks that commenced in 1932 and continued until his death in 1934. His critics focused particularly on the pivotal role he attributed to semiotic mediation because this deviated from the official ideology, which dictated that material production or labor should take precedence.

It was against this background that Leont'ev developed

> a theory of psychological activity based on the paradigm of material production as it is interpreted in traditional Marxism. In Leont'ev's psychological theory, human motives and objects of activity are determined by the division of labor of society, while more concrete actions are related to practical goals. . . . Leont'ev and his followers also seem to have been determined to show that human interpersonal relations and communication are derivatives of the activity of material production (Kozulin, 1990, p. 121)

Accounts of psychological development formulated on this basis therefore emphasize the child's activity as it relates to objective, sociohistorically developed reality rather than to his or her interpersonal and semiotic interactions.

Crawford develops this relation between students' activity and objective, culturally determined reality by drawing on Lave's (1988) notion of activity setting. In Crawford's formulation, the relationship between students as acting individuals and the classroom viewed as a cultural arena influences the quality of students' cognitive processes and thus their learning outcomes. Crawford illustrates her analytical approach by discussing the difficulties that arise for Australian aboriginal students as a consequence of inconsistencies in their cultural experiences at home and in school. Her central point is that the relation between aboriginal students' activity and the classroom arena differs from the relation for most other Australian students. As a consequence, there are significant differences in aboriginal and nonaboriginal students' cognitive processes when they engage in the same instructional activities in the same classrooms. This in turn leads to differences in the students' learning outcomes.

Crawford supplements her focus on the classroom as a cultural arena with a concern for the ways in which learners are positioned by the authoritative expert. The discussion of the social and cultural dimensions of aboriginal students' school experiences indicates, for example, that they and nonaboriginal students are typically positioned differently by the teacher. Crawford also clarifies the distinction between Vygotskian approaches and activity theory when she contrasts two interpretations of the zone of proximal development. She notes that this construct has generally been interpreted in terms of the expert's role in supporting students' learning. We have seen that van Oers proposed a definition of this type when he elaborated his Vygotskian point of view. Although Crawford does not deny the importance of such support, she argues that the notion of zone of proximal development should be extended to take account of the quality of the arena for joint activity and the positioning of the learner.

Crawford makes it clear that her theoretical framework is designed to account for situations where there is a conflict or tension in individuals' needs, expectations, and goals. She notes that these situations are not limited to those that involve a clash between home and school experiences, but include attempts to reform instruction. In the latter case, the tension is between the needs, expectations, and goals of the innovators and the teachers, or between those of the teacher and the students. Innovation can in fact be interpreted as an attempt to change both the arena of the classroom and the positioning of the students. Thus, although Crawford indicates that the teacher and students can remake the cultural arena in which they act, she also emphasizes the difficulties involved in this process due to deeply entrenched expectations and values. In many ways, the classroom arena is, for her, culturally given. This perspective can be contrasted with Voigt's contention that the teacher and students necessarily create the classroom microculture in the course of their ongoing interactions. Thus, for Voigt, the classroom arena is a local phenomenon, whereas for Crawford it is a more general cultural phenomenon.

The distinction between sociocultural and emergent perspectives can be further clarified by considering Crawford's and Saxe and Bermudez's analyses of small-group activity. Both observe that students' actions, needs, goals, and expectations differ even though, at a superficial level, all take part in the same collaborative activities in the same classrooms. Crawford accounts for these differences by focusing on the ways in which students position themselves in relation to the tasks and to each other. In her view, these positionings are derived from students' various experiences outside school. Thus, differences in students' classroom activities are traced to the social and cultural dimensions of their experiences at home. In contrast, Saxe and Bermudez analyze differences in the mathematical environments that emerge for students when they play the Treasure Hunt game by documenting their rules, values, and routines. It is apparent from the sample episodes that the rules are established jointly by two children and that the values and routines are relatively idiosyncratic and differ from student to student. Saxe and Bermudez take care to describe the influence of the intended activity structure, the artifacts used to play the game, the students' interactions, and their prior understandings on the emergence of rules, values, and routines. However, in doing so, they treat the mathematical environments that emerge for students in the course of small-group activity as richly varied local phenomena. Thus, in their view, these environments are generated by individual and collective processes located at the classroom level, whereas for Crawford they are derivatives of broader sociocultural processes. We argue next that this difference in focus typifies the distinction between emergent and sociocultural perspectives.

SUMMARY

We have witnessed a burgeoning interest in the social and cultural dimensions of mathematical activity in the last decade. Taken together, the six plenary chapters indicate that it is essential to consider these aspects of activity even when one's goal is to account for the mathematical development of a single student. In the course of the discussion, we have contrasted two major approaches to social and cultural issues in mathematics education and have suggested that these perspectives reflect differing assumptions about the relation between individual activity and sociocultural processes.

Sociocultural theorists contend that the individual dimensions of experience are subsidiary to the social and cultural dimensions. They therefore attempt to account for students' mathematical learning by focusing almost exclusively on their participation in sociocultural practices either in school or at home. Within this scheme, social interaction is treated as the medium by which historically developed mathematical ways of knowing are transmitted from one generation to the next. For their part, emergent theorists propose that the individual dimensions of experience are on a par with the social and cultural dimensions. In this view, both the process and the products of mathematical development are social through and through. However, by the same token, social and cultural processes are continually regenerated by actively cognizing individuals. Thus, whereas sociocultural theorists see individuals-in-social practice, emergent theorists argue that individuals jointly create interactional routines and patterns as they adapt to each other's activity. From this latter perspective, the link between sociocultural and cognitive processes is indirect and is accounted for in terms of the opportunities for conceptual construction that arise as students participate in classroom activities. Further, individual and collective meanings are seen to evolve in the course of classroom interactions. The teacher's role is therefore considered to be that of guiding the emergence of mathematical meanings in the classroom so that they become increasingly compatible with those established by wider society. This can be contrasted with sociocultural accounts in which the teacher's primary responsibility is that of mediating directly between students' personal meanings and culturally established mathematical meanings.

REFLECTION

In light of the contrasts between sociocultural and emergent perspectives, it is tempting to argue that one side or the other has got the relation between individual and community right. However, we find that each of the two groups of theorists has much to say that is of value. We therefore believe that it is more constructive to consider the problems and issues that might be profitably addressed from each perspective. In this regard, it can be noted that Vygotsky developed his sociohistorical theory while addressing issues of cultural diversity and change. More specifically, he seems to have been committed to the notion of "the new socialist man" and to have viewed education as a primary means of bringing about this change in Soviet society (Kozulin, 1990; van der Veer & Valsiner, 1991). Further, much of his empirical research focused on differences in the activity of members of different cultural groups in the Soviet Union. The vantage point from which he analyzed psychological development therefore appears to be that of an observer located outside the cultural group. From this point of view, thought and activity within a cultural group appear to be relatively homogeneous when compared with the differences across groups. An issue that then comes to the fore is that of accounting for the social and cultural basis of personal experience. Vygotsky's theory of development can in fact be interpreted as a response to this problem (Kozulin, 1990; Wertsch, 1985). From this outsider's perspective, it is reasonable to emphasize the relation between developing individuals and the sociocultural practices in which they participate. Learning then appears to be primarily a process of enculturation that is supported both by interactions with more knowledgeable others and by the use of cultural tools.

In contrast to Vygotsky's focus on cultural diversity and change, emergent theorists seek to identify the patterns, routines, and intersubjective meanings created by specific local communities in the course of their ongoing interactions. From this point of view, "learning is characterized by the subjective reconstruction of societal means and models through negotiation of meaning in social interaction" (Bauersfeld, 1988, p. 39). Here, it is the practices of the local community rather than those of wider society that are taken as the point of reference. The vantage point of the emergent theorist is, in effect, that of an observer located outside the local community but inside the broader cultural community. The thought and activity of members of a local community such as that constituted by the teacher and students in a classroom then appear to be relatively heterogeneous. An issue that therefore comes to the fore is that of understanding how these mutually adapting individuals jointly create their local microculture. Thus, whereas sociocultural theorists attempt to account for the social and cultural basis of personal experience, emergent theorists analyze the constitution of social and cultural processes by actively interpreting individuals.

In our view, both research traditions are progressive and have much to contribute to the problems and issues of mathematics education. We therefore conclude this commentary by exploring how they might complement each other. To this end, we consider two possible coordinations. The first possible coordination stems from the contrast between van Oers' and Saxe and Bermudez's analyses. The direct link that van Oers proposes between sociocultural and psychological processes allows him to be relatively prescriptive. Thus, he argues that students who participate in particular learning activities that involve the use of symbols will develop particular thought processes. However, Saxe and Bermudez's analysis indicates that there is frequently a considerable discrepancy between the learning activity intended by the theorist and actual learning activity as it is realized in any particular classroom. Further, we note with Bauersfeld that "everything in social interaction can be loaded with meaning and thus develop into a socially taken-as-shared 'mediator'" (1990, p. 5). This insight suggests that it can be useful to differentiate between the intended symbolic meanings and the actual symbolic meanings jointly established by the teacher and students. Taken together, Saxe and Bermudez's and Bauersfeld's observations indicate the value of conducting an emergent analysis when investigating the viability of instructional recommendations derived from a sociocultural perspective such as that outlined by van Oers. In particular, explanations of the students' learning appear to be problematic unless one documents the obligations they attempt to fulfill in the classroom, the actual learning activities in which they engage, and the meanings they establish for symbols. An analysis of the type we propose can in fact be viewed as an attempt to "unpack" van Oers' internalization process by analyzing what goes on between the teacher and students in the course of their interaction in the classroom.

A second possible coordination of the two perspectives draws on Crawford's analysis of her work with preservice teachers. In Crawford's view, prospective teachers need to unlearn because they internalized undesirable expectations, knowledge, attitudes, and beliefs while participating as mathematics students in the traditional practices of schooling. This explanation in which the preservice teachers are viewed as "carriers" of a complex of culturally based understandings accounts for the general observation that teachers typically teach as they were taught. However, from the emergent perspective, the internalization that Crawford speaks of ignores the intricacies of the process by which teachers induct their students into particular interpretive stances with regard to mathematics, learning, and teaching. In their analysis of Japanese and American classrooms,

Stigler et al. illustrate a situation where it is useful to "unpack" this internalization process. The sample episodes they provide are, in effect, snapshots of Japanese and American students' enculturation as it occurs in interaction.

In making this comparison of the work of Crawford and of Stigler et al., we do not mean to imply that it is always productive to "unpack" internalization processes. Crawford's discussion of the difficulties aboriginal students encounter at school exemplifies a situation where it is useful to view individuals as "carriers" of culturally based understandings. Instead, our point is that internalization can be viewed as a shorthand for a complex of processes that occur at the level of interaction. Sociocultural and emergent theorists both might object that we have violated some of their basic assumptions. However, the challenge for us is to capitalize on the insights of the various perspectives by exploring possible coordinations. This task is worth pursuing in our view, given that the various perspectives together span the individual student, the classroom community, and broader communities of practice.

REFERENCES

Bauersfeld, H. (1988). Interaction, construction, and knowledge: Alternative perspectives for mathematics education. In T. Cooney & D. Grouws (Eds.), *Effective mathematics teaching* (pp. 27–46). Reston, VA: National Council of Teachers of Mathematics and Lawrence Erlbaum Associates.

Bauersfeld, H. (1990). *Activity theory and radical constructivism—What do they have in common and how do they differ?* Bielefeld, Germany: University of Bielefeld, Institut für Didaktik der Mathematik, Occasional Paper 121.

Blumer, H. (1969). *Symbolic interactionism: Perspectives and method.* Englewood Cliffs, NJ: Prentice Hall.

Cobb, P., & Yackel, E. (1993, October). *A constructivist perspective on the culture of the mathematics classroom.* Paper presented at the Conference on The Culture of the Mathematics Classroom, Osnabrück, Germany.

Davydov, V. V. (1988). Problems of developmental teaching (part I). *Soviet Education, 30*(8), 6–97.

Kozulin, A. (1986). The concept of activity in Soviet psychology: Vygotsky, his disciples and critics. *American Psychologist, 41,* 264–274.

Kozulin, A. (1990). *Vygotsky's psychology. A biography of ideas.* Brighton, England: Harvester Wheatsheaf.

Lampert, M. (1990). When the problem is not the question and the solution is not the answer: Mathematical knowing and teaching. *American Educational Research Journal, 27,* 29–63.

Lave, J. (1988). *Cognition in practice: Mind, mathematics and culture in everyday life.* Cambridge, MA: Cambridge University Press.

Lave, J., & Wenger, E. (1991). *Situated learning: Legitimate peripheral participation.* Cambridge, MA: Cambridge University Press.

Leont'ev, A. N. (1981). Chelovek i kul'tura [Man and culture]. In A. N. Leont'ev, *Problemy razvitiia psikhiki* [Problems of the development of mind] (4th ed., pp. 410–435). Moscow: Moskovskogo Universiteta.

Newman, D., Griffin, P., & Cole, M. (1989). *The construction zone: Working for cognitive change in school.* Cambridge, MA: Cambridge University Press.

Rogoff, B. (1990). *Apprenticeship in thinking: Cognitive development in social context.* Oxford: Oxford University Press.

Romberg, T. A., & Carpenter, T. P. (1986). Research on teaching and learning mathematics: Two disciplines of scientific inquiry. In M. C. Wittrock (Ed.), *Handbook of research on teaching* (3rd ed., pp. 850–873). New York: Macmillan.

Saxe, G. B. (1991). *Culture and cognitive development: Studies in mathematical understanding.* Hillsdale, NJ: Lawrence Erlbaum Associates.

van der Veer, R., & Valsiner, J. (1991). *Understanding Vygotsky: A quest for synthesis.* Cambridge, MA: Blackwell.

Varela, F. J., Thompson, E., & Rosch, E. (1991). *The embodied mind: Cognitive science and human experience.* Cambridge, MA: MIT Press.

Vygotsky, L. S. (1960). *Razvitie vysshikh psikhicheskikh tunktsii* [*The development of the higher mental functions*]. Moscow: Akad. Ped. Nauk. RSFSR.

Vygotsky, L. S. (1979). Consciousness as a problem in the psychology of behavior. *Soviet Psychology, 17*(4), 3–35.

Wertsch, J. V. (1985). *Vygotsky and the social formation of mind.* Cambridge, MA: Harvard University Press.

2 Negotiation of Mathematical Meaning in Classroom Processes: Social Interaction and Learning Mathematics

Jörg Voigt
Institut für Didaktik der Mathematik, Universität Bielefeld, Germany

> *Rigor alone is paralytic death, but imagination alone is insanity.*
> —Gregory Bateson, *Mind and Nature*

In this chapter, teaching and learning mathematics are viewed as linked in the local processes of classroom interaction. The special interest is in how mathematical meanings are negotiated and become taken to be shared in the classroom discourse. In the first section, general aspects of mathematics learning in a cultural context are discussed with regard to different schools of thought. Is mathematical meaning really a matter under negotiation? Why are social aspects intrinsic to learning mathematics? In the second section, several specific findings and theoretical concepts of the negotiation of mathematical meaning are presented. Why is ambiguity an essential feature of discourse in mathematics lessons? Through which regularities can knowledge be taken to be shared in spite of the teacher's and the students' different background understandings? In the third section, relations between mathematics learning and social interaction are discussed. Is learning mathematics an effect of social regulations or does it occur when overcoming the entanglement in the regulations? In all sections, several classroom scenes and specific findings of ethnographical studies are used to illustrate abstract statements.

SOME LINKS BETWEEN MATHEMATICS, CULTURE, AND COGNITION

In several countries, there is a growing body of research demonstrating the relevance of social activities to learning mathematics. In Brazil, Carraher, Car-

21

raher, and Schliemann (1985) and Saxe (1991) studied relations between cultural activities and cognitive development by comparing the children's mathematical thinking outside and inside the culture of school. In Great Britain, Bishop and Geoffrey (1986) and Walkerdine (1988) analyzed the social constitution of mathematical meaning during classroom processes. In France, Balacheff and Laborde (1988) developed experimental situations in which students interactively constituted mathematical solutions. In Italy, Bartolini Bussi (1990) introduced phases of mathematical discussions into classrooms and explored the learning processes taking place during the discussions. In the United States, Cobb, Wood, and Yackel (1991) analyzed how the change of social norms in the classroom affected the students' learning. In Germany, Bauersfeld, Krummheuer, and Voigt (1988) investigated relations between social characteristics of interaction processes and the students' or teacher's thinking.

Although the list is not complete, it gives an impression of the change of many mathematics educators' foci of attention. In the decades before, in order to understand the individual student's thinking, clinical interviews were preferred. Nowadays cultural and social dimensions are not excluded or neglected, but they are taken into account by undertaking "ethnographical" case studies in order to understand mathematics learning in context. The basic assumption is that cultural and social dimensions are not only peripheral conditions of learning mathematics but are intrinsic to learning mathematics.

This view has to be justified because mathematics is often seen as a domain of rationality which is free of social dynamics and cultural influences. Other reasons against the emphasis on social aspects are given by child-centered conceptions that stress the autonomy of the learner. First, I justify that mathematical meanings are matter under negotiation. Epistemological considerations are emphasized that support the relevance of the concept of negotiation of mathematical meaning. The claim is not declaring what mathematics "really" is. Second, the theoretical focus on the individual child is contrasted with the theoretical focus on the social context. Finally, I give reasons for the decision to go along with the interactionist perspective.

Social Aspects of School Mathematics

Traditional philosophies like platonism or intuitionism assume that mathematics expresses eternal relationships between objects that are intuitive as well as objective. Tymoczko (1986) called such theories "private theories" because, in the ideal situation, a single isolated mathematician discovers or creates mathematical knowledge. Diverging from these perspectives, other philosophers, such as Lakatos (1976) and Wittgenstein (1967), considered mathematics to be also a product of social processes. Using the literary form of classroom discussions, Lakatos described how mathematical concepts are stabilized or changed over time through processes of agreement and refutation. From this philosophical point of view, the truth of mathematical statements is not absolute. The statements are only (justified) conjectures, which can fail in the future when new problems are created.

Wittgenstein explained the inexorableness of mathematical argumentation in our experience by his concept of "language game."

> The indelible nature of numbers and figures and the certainty of proving procedures are not expressions of the ideal existence of mathematical objects nor of the absolute validity of the procedures. Because we needed such a rigid language game for various purposes we invented it along with its grammar and its dovetailing with practice [see Glatfeld & Schröder (1977, p. 153) about Wittgenstein's viewpoint]. The mathematician is an inventor not a discoverer. (Wittgenstein, 1967, p. 99)

The image of the mathematician as an inventor corresponds to the statement that mathematics is a product of social processes because individual inventions have to be accepted in order to become official mathematics.

The dispute is very old: Is mathematics invented, and thus man-made, or is mathematics discovered, and thus pregiven? Although philosophers can make rigid and universal assumptions about "the nature of mathematics," it seems to be helpful here to make distinctions between different components of mathematics. In his dialogues about mathematics, the mathematician Rényi offered a distinction (1967)—the mathematician invents concepts and discovers theorems. Rényi compared the mathematical researcher with a seafarer who discovers unknown islands:

> If a seafarer intends to sail into a region into which nobody before has sailed he has to be also an inventor. The seafarer has to construct a ship that is more stormproof than the ships of his predecessors. I would like to say that the new concepts which a mathematician puts forward are like ships of a new type. These ships take the seafarer who is out for discoveries faster and faster over the stormy sea into new regions. (p. 28)

By using epistemological arguments, Burscheid and Struve (1992) came to a similar conclusion. The learning of "theoretical concepts" in school cannot be explained sufficiently by focusing on the individual learner who would discover concepts. Burscheid and Struve emphasized the necessity of "social impulses" in school so that the learner constructs theoretical concepts as wanted.

Working at the forefront of research, the mathematician has a relative freedom to invent concepts or to change concepts given. However, the learner is not as free to introduce new concepts into the discipline. In Protocol 1, two students extended the concept of an even number to fractions (Harvey, Kerslake, Shuard, & Torbe, 1982). Although the construction fits several mathematical inferences, it is excluded by definition in regular mathematics.

Protocol 1

David:	Fifteen's odd and a half's even
Interviewer:	Fifteen's odd and a half's even? Is it?
David:	Yes.
Interviewer:	Why is half even?
David:	Because, erm, a quarter's odd and a half must be even.
Interviewer:	Why is a quarter odd?
David:	Because it's only three.
Interviewer:	What's only three?
David:	A quarter.
Interviewer:	A quarter's only three?
David:	That's what I did in my division.
Robert:	Yes, there's three parts in a quarter like on a clock. It goes five, ten, fifteen.
Interviewer:	Oh, I see.
Robert:	There's only three parts in it.

The pupils had possibly learned that every whole number is odd or even. Later on, they learned that fractions are numbers, too. Also, the students drew the conclusion correctly that the sum of two odd numbers is an even number. Now, there is the need of negotiation of meaning so that, on the one hand, the students confirm their correct inferences and, on the other hand, are supported in imaging the contradictions evoked by their extension of the definition of oddness. (For example, the teacher may puzzle the students by stating that the addition of two halves makes one, an odd number.)

In the following, I want to argue against the assumption that social interaction is not intrinsic for the learning of mathematics because single mathematical meanings would be given self-referentially through their interrelations in a mathematical theory (cf. Steinbring, 1991). Mathematics is often understood as a body of knowledge that is relatively autonomous. It is often viewed as a closed system that is not mixed up by meanings from other domains of experience (except in application of mathematics).

In the scene described, the students make sense of oddness and evenness of fractions by links to units of time represented on clocks. In school, it is typical that mathematical meanings are related to domains of experience outside pure mathematics. Although the modern mathematician (in Hilbert's sense) considers concepts to be variables whose meanings are given self-referentially through the system of the mathematical theory (especially through the network of concepts), the epistemological status of school mathematics is not so definite. Struve (1990) analyzed several domains of school mathematics by epistemological means. He summarizes his findings as follows: "Mathematical knowledge taught in school does not consist of clear-cut mathematical facts but of rather complex structures of different epistemological status, viz. of empirical and normative character"

(p. 118). In the classroom, mathematical knowledge is intertwined with meanings of objects outside "pure" mathematics.

For example, in elementary classrooms, the validity of the statement $3 + 4 = 7$ is not explained by inferences from Peano's axioms. At first, adults regulate the children's use of fingers or chips coordinated with sequences of words. Addition is explained as counting forward or as increasing the number of concrete things. Later, sophisticated argumentations come nearer to the autonomous characteristics of mathematical activities, for example, "$3 + 4 = 7$, therefore $13 + 4$ has to be 17." During introduction to negative numbers, addition can not successfully be interpreted as synonymous with increasing the amount of concrete things like apples: Addition should become an operation with more abstract objects.

In classroom life, the meanings of mathematical concepts and the validity of mathematical statements are socially accomplished. Only when the mathematical meanings are enriched so that they mutually support each other as a system, does the socially regulated "borrowing" of experience from outside mathematics become less important for further learning; for example, then the student handles negative numbers by thinking of mathematical interrelations of numbers rather than imagining (missing) apples.

Nevertheless, whereas the expert can experience an element of the topic as an element to be discovered by reasoning, the learner cannot experience "it" if the learner does not realize at least the outlines of the expert's theory. There is the need of negotiation of meaning if the topic of discourse is to be meaningful for the learner and if the learner is to avoid confusing mathematical meanings with divergent everyday meanings of clocks, fingers, apples, and so forth. My claim is not that students should learn mathematics in Hilbert's sense. My point is that, especially in introductory situations, we cannot presume that the learner would ascribe specific meanings to the topic by themselves—meanings that are compatible with the mathematical meanings the teacher wants the student to learn.

The Focus on the Individual

Up to this point, in my use of the term "mathematical meaning," I have mixed the observer's point of view with the sense-making of the individual observed. In this, there is the danger of identifying objective validity with subjective conviction. The ambiguous meaning of "mathematical meaning" arises from the fact that it can be understood with regard to an epistemological theory of mathematics as well as with regard to a psychological theory of subjective sense-making processes. The following discussion restricts the meaning of meaning to the latter issue.

For a long period of time, research in mathematics education has been profoundly influenced by Piaget's genetic epistemology and developmental psychology. Many researchers focused their attention on the cognitive development of individual children (e.g. Steffe, von Glasersfeld, Richards, & Cobb, 1983). The child's mathematical knowledge is viewed as the product of the individual's conceptual operations. Nowadays, this perspective is well known as radical constructivism (von Glasersfeld, 1987). From this point of view, the individual's knowledge can be at best viable; that is, if the student's knowledge is compatible with new experiences subjectively interpreted, the student's knowledge is confirmed without necessarily being true or intended by the teacher. In this perspective, there is no place for the idea of transmission of knowledge from the teacher to the student or for the idea of reading reality as it is. (In order to describe learning processes that are specific to situations, I do not take care of developmental processes as radical constructivists might expect.)

In Protocol 2, the students construct meanings of sequences of numbers. Although the teacher poses questions in order to elicit definite meanings that he intends, the students interpret the problem differently. The students (aged 13 to 14) experience their first lesson in probability. In a preparatory situation, several students had thrown a die each 100 times. The outcomes of the casts are written on the blackboard.

1	2	3	4	5	6
15	13	19	14	19	17
23	15	18	12	12	20
14	14	13	19	18	22
20	15	11	21	20	13
18	21	15	18	10	18
15	15	15	20	15	20
19	15	14	15	14	21

The teacher wants the students to look at the outcomes, to see the variations of the outcomes, and to trace the variations to the concept of randomness.

Protocol 2

Teacher: What do you notice about these outcomes? Martina.
Martina: The outcomes are all above ten.
Teacher: (drawling way of speaking) Yes, Achim.
Achim: I wanted to say it, too.
Teacher: Does anybody notice something else? Michael.
Michael: It's obvious that the outcomes are different.
Teacher: Why didn't you expect that all outcomes are the same?
Michael: 100 cannot be divided by 6. [The teacher shows surprise.]

Nothing of the table is conspicuous by itself. Realizing something in the givens, that is not readily apparent, depends on corresponding expectations. Presumably, the students' actual constructions of meaning are influenced by their

previous experiences in situations in which similarities of numbers or calculations were relevant. In contrast to it, the teacher's intention (fixed introduction in
probability) influences his construction of meaning of the table as well as his
interpretation of Michael's thinking. Presumably, the teacher sees Michael on the
right track toward the meaning of randomness. Later on, the teacher will give a
suggestive hint so that the students offer the catchword "random."

The problem of misunderstanding between the adult and the student can be
reconstructed not only during frontal teaching but also during clinical interviews.
Varying Piagetian experiments, Donaldson (1978) and Hundeide (1988) showed
that a student's ability displayed in an interview can depend on the interview
situation. Neglecting the relevance of the social and empirical context supports
the illusion that the subject's thinking can be explained sufficiently by developmental processes inside the person.

Although the sociological aspects in Piaget's research are underspecified,
Piaget remarked that "social interaction is a necessary condition for the development of logic" (Piaget, quoted by Doise & Mugny, 1984, p. 19). In Genevé,
Piaget's followers (Doise & Mugny, 1984; Perret-Clermont, 1980) took Piaget's
developmental psychology as a basis of their work, and they explored social
interactions between children and conflicts between the children's perspectives
as conditions of mental reorganizations. However, they conceptualized social
interaction as an external variable with regard to developmental processes inside
the learner. Solomon (1989, pp. 109–119) criticized this extension of Piaget's
work because only the learning of knowledge and not the knowledge itself is
viewed as socially conditioned. If we do not assume innate organizers, how can
we think of intersubjective meanings when each individual constructs his or her
own meanings? The cultural aspects of mathematical practices in school have to
be taken into account. "Acculturation and the institutionalisation of mathematical
practices are . . . a necessary aspect of children's mathematics education. Analyses that focus solely on individual children's construction of mathematical
knowledge tell only half of a good story" (Cobb, 1990, p. 213; see also Bauersfeld, 1980).

The Focus on Culture

Bruner is well known for emphasizing children's discoveries and for criticizing
the teacher's guidance. In 1986, he remarked on a development in his own work:
"I have come increasingly to recognize that most learning in most settings is a
communal activity, a sharing of the culture" (p. 127). As early as during the
dispute about the concept of discovery, Bruner stated: "Culture, thus, is not
discovered; it is passed on or forgotten. All this suggests to me that we have
better to be cautions in talking about the method of discovery, or discovery as the
principal vehicle of education" (Bruner, 1966, p. 101). Edwards and Mercer
(1987) increased the importance of culture as the point of reference in education-

al research: "The child-centered ideology needs to be replaced with one that emphasizes the socio-cultural and discursive bases of knowledge and learning" (p. 168). Instead of the individual person, now, the social group is the basic element of interest. Before the appropriateness of this change is discussed, the implications of a one-sided concentration on culture are roughly outlined.

In contrast to locating rational argumentation in the private realms of individual experience, Harré (1984) understood rationality as "a feature of public-collective discourses to which there may have been several individual contributions" (p. 120). "To say that someone is rational is not to congratulate them on their private cognitive processes but to praise them for their contributions to the collective discourse" (p. 119). Like Wittgenstein, Harré and other social constructivists looked for the roots of (mathematical) competence in social activities. Correspondingly, Solomon (1989) claimed that cognitive development is "the progressive socialization of the child's judgements" (p. 118). In mathematics lessons, "learning is the initiation into a social tradition" (p. 150).

Many researchers are inspired by Vygotsky's work (1978) when they are studying social events in order to explore links between culture and cognition. Vygotsky assumed that the characteristics of adult-guided interactions are internalized by the learner during the learner's development: "Any function in the child's cultural development appears twice, or on two planes. First it appears on the social plane, and then on the psychological plane. First it appears between people as an interpsychological category, and then within the child as an intrapsychological category. . . . All higher mental functions are internalized social relationships" (Vygotsky, 1981, p. 163–164). Vygotsky characterized the learner's development in terms of shifts in control or responsibility. The possibility of shifts is given in the "zone of proximal development," that is, the difference between a learner's actual development as determined by independent problem solving and the higher level of "potential development as determined through problem solving under adult guidance or in collaboration with more capable peers" (Vygotsky, 1978, p. 86). The more competent participants guide the interactions so that the learners can participate in activities that they could not manage by themselves. More and more, in these interactions learners increase their control and responsibility.

In comparison to the emphasis on the autonomy of the individual's cognitive processes, theories inspired by Vygotsky tend to take the student as an object of the teacher's activities or as a rather passive participant of the classroom processes. The classroom culture seems to be pregiven, the students' unusual and unexpected actions could be evaluated as mere deviations, and differences among individuals' developments are rather unexplained. However, the learner's active role in the constitution of a classroom culture becomes more relevant if microprocesses of classroom discourse are investigated (see the section on the negotiation of mathematical meanings).

The Focus on Interaction—A Chance of Mediating Between the Foci on the Subject and on Culture?

Several theoretical approaches with regard to mathematics learning through inter-action have already been mentioned. Roughly compared, two antithetical strands can be reconstructed: individualism versus collectivism. With reference to Piaget (especially in von Glaserfeld's interpretation), learning mathematics is viewed as structured by the individual's attempts to resolve what he or she finds problematic in the world of his or her experience. With reference to Vygotsky (especially in Leont'ev's interpretation), the environment given seems to direct the individual's learning of mathematics. On the one hand, the individual is the actor ("subject"), and mathematical knowledge is constructed by it. On the other hand, the subject is the object of cultural practices, and mathematical knowledge given is internalized. I think it does not happen by chance that the former school of thought has been established as prominent in the Western part of the world, whereas the latter school is rooted in the Eastern part.

Of course, the comparison gives a crude contrast of opposing tendencies. Either school has produced sophisticated ideas to answer questions posed from the other side (Bauersfeld, 1990). But which basic alternatives should a mathematics educator pursue? The statement that we should follow both orientations is avoiding an answer even though one perspective is more appropriate to the microlevel of classroom processes and the other to the macrolevel of school culture (cf. Knorr-Cetina & Cicourel, 1981). Bauersfeld (1988, pp. 38–40) and Cobb (1990, pp. 213–15) stressed the complementary character of the theories. If mixing incompatible theories is unsatisfactory and if the juxtaposition of theories shifts the problem of integration to the practitioner, normative considerations may help.

Personally, I take the emphasis on the subject as the starting point in order to understand the negotiation of meaning and the learning of mathematics in classrooms. The main reason is that concepts like "socialization," "internalization," "initiation into a social tradition," and so forth do not (directly) explain what I think is the most important objective of mathematics education: *Bildung*. Bildung is a main claim in the German tradition of thinking about education. Immanuel Kant, the German philosopher of Enlightenment, criticized what appeared to be habitual or natural. The individual should act on rational grounds in the individual's mind without relying on the other's guidance. (Today, we would comment that reason (*Vernunft*) is not innate but emerges when the subject becomes a member of our culture.) The prominent objective of mathematics education is not that the students produce objectively solutions to mathematical problems but that they do it insightfully and by reasonably thinking. What on the behavioral level does in fact not make a difference should be an important subjective difference. Do the students act as desired because they intend to fulfill the teacher's expectations in order to participate successfully, or because they draw conclusions in order to solve a mathematical problem in their experiential world?

Accordingly, the following discussion about social interaction stresses the reasoning and sense-making processes of subjects that interactively constitute mathematical meanings. An interactionist approach is preferred because it emphasizes the individual's sense-making processes as well as the interaction processes. It does not deduce the individual's learning from the social interaction as suggested by theories of socialization and of internationalization. From the interactionist point of view, social interaction does not function as a vehicle that transforms "objective" knowledge into subjective knowledge. But social interaction makes possible that subjective ideas become compatible with culture and with intersubjective knowledge like mathematics.

In the following section, a network of theoretical concepts is outlined. First, a possible conflict between the reader's expectation and the author's intention should be taken into account. The term *negotiation of mathematical meanings* is used with regard to a theoretical perspective on mathematics classrooms. Its use could be misunderstood in a normative sense, as if negotiation of meaning happens only in a liberal classroom culture. From the theoretical point of view of symbolic interactionism, negotiation of meanings happens in every social interaction. Of course, in a specific classroom situation, the negotiation could be more explicit or implicit. The application of the theoretical concept to a specific classroom situation could be more or less helpful in order to understand what happens in the classroom. Nevertheless, in this chapter, theoretical considerations give reasons for the relevance of the concept.

NEGOTIATION OF MATHEMATICAL MEANINGS

This section presents an interactional approach to classroom processes. The approach is based on microsociology; it is particularly influenced by symbolic interactionism (Blumer, 1969; Goffman, 1974) and ethnomethodology (Garfinkel, 1976; Mehan, 1979). However, the sociological concepts have been modified in order to deal with teaching and learning of mathematics (Bauersfeld et al., 1988).

Ambiguity and Interpretation

According to folk beliefs, the tasks, the questions, the signs, and so on of mathematics lessons have definite, clear-cut meanings. These beliefs have to be questioned in order to realize the relevance of negotiation. Of course, for the reader I am charging an open door. If one looks at microprocesses in the class

FIG. 2.1. Picture problem taken from a schoolbook for first graders.

room carefully, things seem to be ambiguous and call for interpretation. What is the meaning of "5" to young children in a specific situation? Is the meaning bound to concrete things (e.g., "the little finger of my left hand"), does the sign remind the student of previous activities (e.g., "a difficult number to write"), does it evoke specific emotions (e.g., "my favourite number"), is its meaning related to other numbers (e.g., "equal to 2 plus 3, 1 and 4, 0 and 5"), and so on?

Another example is given by the interpretations of a picture which is presented as a supposed unambiguous task in a regular German schoolbook for first graders (Fig. 2.1). Several children were asked to give the correct number sentence. Solutions are:

$2 + 3 = 5$ ("sum of the bananas")
$5 - 2 = 3$ ("the keeper gives two bananas to the ape")
$1 + 1 = 2$ ("the keeper and the ape")
$3 - 2 = 1$ ("the keeper has one banana more than the ape")
$5 - 4 = 1$ ("one banana more than hands, the keeper will lose the middle one")

One of the findings of a research project (Neth & Voigt, 1991) was that, in principle, such pictures, text problems, games, and stories have multiple meanings if the interpreting children are not familiar with the specific type of the task. Nevertheless, many textbook authors and mathematics teachers, as well as the students, assume that these pictures have unambiguous meanings with respect to solutions. The processes of mathematicization taken for granted turn out to be problematic when the situations are interpreted by subjects who are (still) not members of the classroom culture.

According to one of the interactionist assumptions, every object or event in human interaction is plurisemantic ("indexical;" Leiter, 1980, pp. 106–138). In order to make sense of it, the subject uses a background knowledge and forms a context of sense for interpreting the object. For example, a first grader can interpret the picture as the invitation to tell a personal experience of a zoo; or, the

FIG. 2.2.   Dice.

teacher can take the picture as the opportunity for motivating students to apply subtraction. The subject does not necessarily experience the ambiguous object as plurisemantic but as factual if the background understanding is taken for granted. With reference to Goffman's frame analysis (1974), Krummheuer (1983) reconstructed different background understandings ("framings") between the teacher and the students of an algebra class over a longer period of time. Comparing the interactions during collaborative learning with the interactions during frontal class teaching, he demonstrated that "misunderstandings" between the teacher and the students are quite usual without the participants being aware of it. Steinbring's epistemological study (1991) explained why the disparity between the teacher's and the students' background understandings exists necessarily. In order to learn new mathematical concepts that the teacher introduces, the students change their background understandings.

The ambiguity of tasks, question, and so forth does not have to be evaluated as a disaster so that we would try to minimize it. The following problem situation (Wittmann & Müller, 1990) makes explicit use of different possibilities of interpreting a problem. In Fig. 2.2, the teacher has thrown three dice without the students seeing the outcomes. The teacher announces the sum of the spots: __ + __ + __ = 11. The students have to jointly ascertain the number of spots of each die. In the classroom discourse the students are free to ask clever questions, to guess, to consider the probability of singular outcomes (if the sum is very small or large), or to calculate. Thus, there are more or less advanced ways to interpret the problem depending on the students's dispositions. The matter of interaction needs attention if we consider reactions to students who are always guessing even though the first two numbers of spots are known.

Social Interaction

From the point of view of symbolic interactionism, interaction is more than a sequence of actions and reactions. A participant of an interaction monitors his action in accordance with what he assumes to be the other participants' background understandings, expectations, and so on, whereas the other participants make sense of the action adopting what they believe to be the actor's background understandings, intentions, and so on. The following actions of the other participants are interpreted by the former actor with regard to his expectations and can prompt a reconsideration, and so on. For example, the student can interpret the teacher's reaction as a specific evaluation of his own thinking even though the teacher's reaction might have been only the expression of amusement at a particular moment during the student's action. Using his background knowledge of the teacher's supposed emotion and being ashamed, the student might search for more advanced ways to interpret the problem at hand and to solve it. Experiencing a similar situation, another student might cope by pleasing the teacher superficially. Of course, the teacher could react differently according to his background knowledge of the two students' different dispositions.

It is not only important that the teacher and the students attempt to understand each other. A third thing, the accomplishment of intersubjective meanings taken as mathematical ones, is essential in mathematics teaching and learning. The point is not that teacher and students "share knowledge." From the symbolic interactionist and the radical constructivist point of view, only mathematical meanings "taken to be shared" can be produced through negotiation.[1] The participants take meanings to be shared if they neglect that they could interpret the signs differently. Krummheuer (1983, with reference to Goffman) and Cobb (1990, with reference to von Glasersfeld) used the terms *working interim* and *consensual domain,* respectively, in order to describe that the participants interact as if they interpret the mathematical topic of their discourse equally. However, one can never be sure that two persons are thinking the same even if they collaborate without conflict, especially if they agree about formal statements and processes. One of the characteristics of formal mathematics is that people can coordinate their actions smoothly while they are actually ascribing different meanings to the objects.

Cobb, Wood, and Yackel documented the following scene in a classroom teaching experiment. The students Josh and Joey are solving several tasks:

1. $50 - 9 = \underline{41}$
2. $60 - 9 = \underline{51}$
3. $60 - 19 = \underline{41}$
4. $41 + 19 = \underline{60}$
5. $31 + 29 = \underline{60}$
6. $31 + 19 = \underline{50}$
7. $32 + 18 = \underline{}$

We don't know how both students solved the first six tasks because the videotape begins when the students are solving the seventh task. In the classroom a variety of ways of solving was allowed, such as counting by ones, using the hundreds board, or relating a new problem to a previously solved one (Wood & Yackel, 1990).

---

[1]In this chapter, the terms *taken as shared* and *taken to be shared* are used synonymously. It may be that a participant is convinced that a meaning is shared as well as that a participant knows that it is an assumption for the time beeing.

The videotape begins when Josh makes a statement.

Protocol 3

Josh:	Uh-huh, that's 18, not 19.
Joey:	Yeah, but that's 32 not 31.
Josh:	Oh yeah!
Joey:	They're the same thing.
Project member:	What's the same thing?
Joey:	These two [points to 31 + 19 = 50 and 32 + 18 = __].
Project member:	Hang on, I was asking Josh. Which ones? We've got 31 and 19.
Josh:	Makes 50.
Project member:	Yeah.
Josh:	And, look 32 and 18. See, it's just one more than that [points to the tasks], and that's one higher than that.

Later on in the interview, Josh and Joey indicated that they solved the fifth task by adding the tens and the ones $31 + 29 = 30 + 20 + 1 + 9 = 50 + 10 = 60$. The sixth task was solved by comparing the second summands of the sixth and the fifth task. So the students were able to combine two tasks that did not differ in one summand. But the fifth task, which differs in both summands from the preceding task, was solved as an isolated one.

When the students solve the seventh task a new way of solving emerges in the course of interaction. From the interactionist point of view, the meaning of this task is interactively constituted as one in which the increase of one number compensates the decrease of the other. At the beginning, either of the students focused his attention to the change of one summand and points to it. Either alters his attention stimulated by his partner and accepts the partner's statement. The students gain a tacit agreement without checking whether they "share" a common knowledge in fact. Through this negotiation, a meaning of the task is constituted, without which we have to suppose that one student would have constructed this meaning if working alone or that one student would take over the responsibility for the solution alone. (Nevertheless, the students would have had to construct a related knowledge individually during or after the collaborative work so that the negotiation would satisfy the educator.)

In the classroom, the participants interactively constitute taken-to-be-shared meanings. What is referred to taken-to-be-shared meaning emerges during processes of negotiation. From the observer's point of view, the meaning of "taken-to-be-shared" is not a partial match of individuals' constructions, nor is it a cognitive element. Instead, it exists at the level of interaction. "Symbolic interactionism views meaning . . . as arising in the process of interaction between people. The meaning of a thing grows out of the ways in which other persons act toward the person with regard to the thing. . . . Symbolic interactionism sees meanings as social products" (Blumer, 1969, p. 5). In the scene just described, the meaning of the seventh task emerges when the students interact. The task is taken as the "same thing" compared with the sixth task. When the project member and the students interact, this meaning is stabilized between them.

In the course of negotiation, the teacher and the students (or the students among themselves) accomplish relationships of mathematical meanings taken to be shared. From the observer's point of view, I call these relationships of meanings a mathematical *theme*. In the scene described, the theme is the comparison of two tasks because the participants seem to pay attention to differences and correspondences of the tasks.

During frontal teaching, the students can originally contribute to the theme. Thus, the theme may not be a representation of the mathematical content which the teacher intended to establish (cf. Protocol 2: Initiated by the students, the theme "regularities of sequences of numbers" does not fit directly with the intention of the teacher, who wants to deal immediately with randomness). Realizing his or her intentions, the teacher is dependent on the students' indications of understanding and, reciprocally, the students are dependent on the teacher's acceptance of their contributions. Thus, the theme is not a fixed body of knowledge. As the topic of discourse, it is interactively constituted and it is changed through the negotiation of meaning.

If the teacher does not direct and evaluate the students rigidly, step by step, and if a dialogue is not established in the old normative sense, the theme can be described as a river that produces its own bed. The result of the dialogue is not clear in advance. In the scene described, Joey and Josh are not forced to solve the task using a compensation strategy. But if they solved several tasks in a similar way and if they justified this way successfully, the observer might expect that the comparison of tasks will be a common theme between Josh and Joey in future problems.

Because people usually are obliged to take care of the thematic coherence of discourse (except small talk) and because mathematical discussions are constrained by specific rigid obligations, the theme gains stability often as time is spent in a discussion. In cases of conflict, the participants clarify what is taken as the theme. A participant could be accused of straying from the theme or could be forced to justify the relevance of his or her divergent contribution, or a change in the theme may need metacommunicative remarks or markers (Luhmann, 1972).

From an epistemological point of view, the stability of a theme corresponds to the self-reference of mathematical knowledge (cf. Steinbring, 1991). For example, an observer could state that Josh's and Joey's way of solving expresses the use or the discovery of mathematical laws in a theory of numbers. The fit of this description to the students' sense-making processes can be clarified if we interview them about their reasoning or if we ask them whether subtraction tasks can be solved analogously: $31 - 19 \overset{?}{=} 32 - 18$.

Provisionally summarized, in the classroom situation, objects are ambiguous. But the individuals experience the objects as unambiguous by using a background understanding taken for granted. The objective appearance of the individual's knowledge is the accomplishment of subjective activity. Because of the disparity of their background knowledge, the teacher and the students have to negotiate mathematical meanings. When constituted, the relations between meanings form a theme.

In the following, the objective appearance of the taken-to-be-shared knowledge is described as the accomplishment of the interaction between individuals.

Stability and Regulations of the Negotiation of Meaning

In time, the negotiation of meaning forms commitments between the participants with respect to stable expectations on the individual's side. In smooth interactions a background knowledge is taken to be shared. What was before constituted explicitly, now remains implicit. Cobb called this process the institutionalization of knowledge (1990, pp. 211–213). Studying everyday life, ethnomethodologists point out that knowledge is to be shared and to be given using descriptive "accounting practices": "The stories that people are continually telling are descriptive accounts. . . . To construct an account is to make an object or event (past or present) observable and understandable to oneself or to someone else. To make an object or event observable and understandable is to endow it with the status of an intersubjective object" (Leiter, 1980, pp. 161–162). In the scene described earlier, Joey and Josh made the compensation observable and understandable between themselves; they took for granted that the results of the sixth and the seventh task are the same. They endowed their solution with the status of intersubjectivity, which has to be established once more when the project member joins them.

The ambiguity of a single object is reduced by relating its meaning to a context that is taken to be shared. At the same time, the context is confirmed by constituting the meaning of the single object. The context and the singular meaning elaborate each other. From the ethnomethodological point of view, meanings are not given by the context (of school mathematics or of the classroom culture), which would exist independently of the negotiation of meaning, but the context is continually constituted. Ethnomethodologists call this relationship *reflexivity* (Leiter 1980, pp. 138–156). For example, first graders experience that apples, coloured blocks, chips, and so forth are used differently in the mathematics classroom than at home. The members of the classroom ascribe mathematical meanings to the things. At the same time, the meaning of what is called "math" becomes clearer to the first graders. One has to compare apples and other things numerically.

If the observer looks at the classroom life as an ethnographer who investigates a strange culture, the observer may be surprised by what is taken for granted by the participants: The use of fingers is taken as an explanation, a picture is taken as a calculation task, and so on. However, in the treadmill of everyday life, the participants would say that they know what mathematics or the classroom practice really is. In everyday classroom situations, the teacher and the students often constitute the context routinely, without being aware of this ongoing accomplishment, so that the context seems to be pregiven. In everyday classroom practice, the teacher and the students assume that the context is known, but it is in fact taken to be shared, diffuse, and vague.

For example, describing a specific method of solving as "simple" does not only ascribe meaning to the method but at the same time gives meaning to the context of mathematical argumentation. In the classroom mentioned earlier, the participants use the term "simple" in the sense of "mathematically elegant" (and not as cognitively easy). For example, Josh's and Joey's way would be evaluated as simple. This positive evaluation supports the students in orienting their activities toward this advanced mathematical argumentation. The students can be assured that the construction and use of complex thinking strategies and abstract considerations are characteristics of mathematics classrooms. Nevertheless, from a distance, the ethnographer can think of traditional classrooms with different characteristics. In traditional classrooms, the teacher sets a standard how to solve a task; the students have to obey step by step.

To close this section, I would like to sketch several findings of micro-ethnographical projects that explore hidden regularities of interaction in mathematics classrooms. In Germany, educational reformers have been disappointed when comparing their ideal conceptions with the usual teaching styles. Disillusionment about the period of educational reform in the 1960s and 1970s has provided a motive for understanding the stability of the regularities of everyday classroom life (Maier & Voigt, 1992).

Because of the ambiguity and different background understandings in the classroom, on principle, the negotiation of meaning in the microsituation is fragile. There is a permanent risk of collapse and disorganization of the interactive process, but "routines" function to minimize this risk. In several case studies, teachers' and students' routines, through which a smooth functioning of the classroom discourse proceeds and through which mathematical meanings are interactively constituted, have been reconstructed (the teacher's "open" questions to which one definite answer is expected, the suggestive hint, the decomposing of a solving process in small pieces of subsequent actions, the student's routine of verbal reduction, i.e., restricting utterances to numbers or catchwords, the trial-and-error routine in order to meet the teacher's expectation, etc.; Voigt, 1989).

The routines are connected by interactional "obligations." The obligations become more obvious in cases of conflict. In the following scene (Voigt, 1985), a student violates an obligation and the teacher takes care to maintain the sense of normality and the image of the classroom orientated toward the folk ideal of discovery learning. The conflict happens in the probability class from which another scene was taken earlier ("100 cannot be divided by six"):

Protocol 4

Teacher: That is enough for the moment. We cannot write down all the results, don't you think. Does anybody notice anything?

Student: What am I supposed to notice?

Teacher: What are you supposed to notice? That's something you ought to know your-self. Björn, have you noticed anything?

The teacher's activities are also under obligations. For example, in traditional classrooms, the students often expect the teacher to present an official algorithm of solving "problems" step by step without the need for reflection ("What to do next?"). So the students are not only the "victims" of the microculture but are also the "culprits."

The network of routines and obligations can be described as "patterns of interaction" (Bauersfeld, 1988; Jungwirth, 1991; McNeal, 1991; Voigt, 1985). The patterns of interaction are considered as regularities interactively constituted by the teacher and the students: "What is presented is a level on which processes remain processes and do not coagulate into entities, to which the very process from which they were abstracted is assigned to as effect" (Falk & Steinert, 1973, p. 20).

For example, the "elicitation pattern" (Voigt, 1985) hints at the contradictory combination of two claims. The idea of eliciting a clear-cut body of mathematical knowledge is juxtaposed with the claims of a liberal and child-centered class-room. In the pattern, three phases can be distinguished:

- The teacher proposes an ambiguous task, and the students offer different answers or solutions, which the teacher evaluates.
- If the students' contributions are too divergent the teacher guides the stu-dents toward one definite argument, solution, and so forth. Believing that it will help the students, the teacher poses small questions and elicits bits of knowledge.
- The teacher and the students reflect and evaluate what has been done.

Jungwirth (1991) reconstructed gender-specific routines by which boys con-tribute to the elicitation pattern and activities by which girls modify the ordinary pattern. In the classrooms analyzed, the boys participated more successfully in the smooth accomplishment of the pattern. Therefore, they might (erroneously) appear to the teachers to be more mathematically competent.

When educators study classroom processes by microethnographical means (Voigt, 1990), the stability of traditional regularities is astonishing. Expected to be structured by rational argumentation, the mathematical discourse comes out to be highly socially structured. Even in classroom situations that are expected to be designed with regard to modern educational claims, traditional patterns are reconstructed. For example, students' group work is realized in order to overcome the bad features of frontal teaching. Bauersfeld (1982) used the concept *habitus* in order to explain the persistence of students' routines during group work. He demonstrated that, in one group, the students constituted patterns and ways of solving the mathematical problem that partly appeared as copies of traditional frontal teaching. The change of the formal social organization of classroom life (replacing frontal teaching by group work) does not guarantee the immediate change of hidden and stable regularities in the microprocesses. The resistance of the regularities to change has to be taken into account when changing the microculture of mathematics classrooms.

Voigt (1991) pointed out that teachers do not realize that traditional patterns of interaction are still alive in their classrooms and that they contradict the teachers' intentions. The tradition of "Socratic catechism" still has an effect in the microculture today (Maier & Voigt, 1992). In context of preservice teacher training, examined "under the microscope," ideal teaching styles in part merely seem to be staged in "holiday lessons" (Andelfinger & Voigt, 1986). Presumably, in everyday classroom processes, teachers reproduce routines and background understandings that have been developed during their schooldays and behind the back of their intentional orientation.

Therefore, Yackel, Cobb, Wood, Wheatley, and Merkel (1990) influenced classroom life, for example, by encouraging teachers to change specific social norms in the classroom discourse. Voigt (1991) developed teacher training courses where teachers videotape their own teaching and analyze the tapes. Nevertheless, it must be taken into account that in everyday classroom life routines and patterns cannot all be eliminated. Because of the permanent ambiguity we want assurance, relief, implicit orientation, and reliability. "We like to settle down like in a familiar nest, the nest of everyday life" (duBois-Reymond & Söll, 1974, p. 13).

At the beginning of the section on negotiation of mathematical meanings, an ambiguous illustration was presented (ape, keeper, and bananas). With regard to such a picture, it was typical of the observed elementary class that a definite solution was established step by step. When the teacher was confronted with divergent interpretations ("one more banana" or "you have to add," etc.) the teacher asked a sequence of questions: How many bananas has the keeper brought ("5")? Which sign has to be written if something is taken away ("−")? How many bananas does the keeper give to the ape ("2")? How many bananas does the keeper have left over ("3")? Through this procedure, the picture comes out to be a specific arithmetical task, and a "number sentence" comes out to be the solution. Details of the picture are clearly related to mathematical signs. The sequence of questions goes along with writing the sentence. Accordingly, nearly all pictures of the textbook are so stereotyped that a subtraction intended is indicated by the picture of persons or things leaving the picture at the right-hand side. In the course of lessons, the students learn so that they mathematize such pictures as expected.

This procedure is an example of a pattern of interaction that I name *direct mathematization*. The pattern of direct mathematization is a "thematic pattern (procedure)" because it is specific to mathematics classrooms (Voigt, 1989). Producing a thematic pattern, the teacher and the students constitute the theme routinely. The variety of options on how to continue the theme is reduced by specific conventions. If a thematic pattern is ritualized as in the presented case there is the danger that the students learn to participate effectively in complying with didactical conventions without realizing the mathematical coherence. For example, if the last question of the sequence is replaced by "How many more bananas does the keeper have than the ape?" the student might answer all questions correctly but contribute a mathematically incorrect statement: $5 - 2 = 1$.

Although the (thematic) patterns of interaction take over functions for the institution of school (e.g., definiteness for examinations), they are not pregiven but constituted by the participants. Therefore, the regularities could change at every moment. The following event may serve as an example.

In an elementary classroom observed (Neth & Voigt, 1991, pp. 105–107), the negotiation of meaning of multiplication has run into conflict when the discussion has focussed on mathematical signs. The teacher feels herself under the obligation to relate the meaning of multiplication to concrete materials, which seem to stand for the rock bottom of the knowledge taken to be shared. She holds up three packs each containing ten pens. In the lessons before, a thematical pattern was established so that these materials definitely implied "3 times 10."

Protocol 5

Teacher: To these packs, please, find a multiplication task.
Natalie: 10 times 3.
[The students become noisy, the teacher calls them to order.]
Teacher: Yeah, but, is this really correct?
Student A: No!
Teacher: Do you all agree?
Student B: No.
Student C: That's the same like a swap task.
            [known by the student in the context of addition, e.g., $3 + 4 = 4 + 3$]
Teacher: That's a swap task. If I empty the packs and if I line them up in threes, then this is 30, too. In lines of three! But to these packs (points to the three original packs) you would really have to write 3 times 10 ("müßtet ihr eigentlich schreiben"). And then you have the same amount of all pens.

Natalie at first does not fulfill the teacher's expectation of the mathematization, that the first factor represents the amounts of packs. Presumably, Natalie's mental representation conflicts with the official mathematization constituted in the lesson before. The teacher seems to elicit a negative evaluation of Natalie's answer from the students. Considering the "weaker" students, perhaps, the teacher wants to avoid the risk of ambiguity. However, Student C hints at the mathematical identity of the different forms and the teacher is now under the obligation to consider the swap task that implies the commutative law. She mentions that the difference between the orders of pens does not affect the total amount. Implicitly, the teacher points out that, at the level of the concrete things, the different terms have something in common. The obligation, that the students undertake only a specific mathematization, seems to be weakened. Also, the teacher uses the subjunctive mood "irrealis"—that is, the German phrase "müßtet ihr eigentlich schreiben" is sometimes used to express an expectation on which one does not insist any longer. The former thematic pattern implied that each number of a product is represented unambiguously by specific materials. But in this scene, the mathematization is not rigid but open to change because a child introduces a level of argumentation that the teacher didn't expect but accepts.

The theoretical considerations of this section can be summarized as follows. In the negotiation of mathematical meaning, the single meaning and the context of meaning elaborate each other. The potential conflicts of the negotiation are minimized through routines and obligations. As they are constituted, the relations between routines and obligations form (thematic) patterns of interaction. Through the (thematic) patterns, the teacher and the students arrive at mathematical meanings taken to be shared. In everyday classroom life, there is the danger that the processes degenerate into poor rituals. However, on the microlevel, the regularities are not pregiven, and the negotiation could be improvised by the participants themselves.

INDIRECT RELATIONS BETWEEN SOCIAL INTERACTION AND MATHEMATICS LEARNING

Before proceeding further, I would like to stress that the interactionist does not view relations between interaction and learning as relations between variables in the technological sense. Using ethnographical methods and examining individual's sense-making as closely as possible, the interactionist constructs more and more interpretations of what the student is actually thinking. Maier (1991) described this experience the interpreter has as a hermeneutical "uncertainty relation." Also, using interview methods, the interactionist's attention is caught by the interviewer's influences on the individual interviewed, so there is no clear access to the privacy of the individual's thinking and learning. Furthermore, in classroom discourses, the mutual influences between the teacher and the students have become more subtle through their history. Comparing detailed reports of classroom processes of the last centuries with transcripts of present mathematics classroom, Maier and Voigt (1989) realized that today the interactional regularities seem to be more hidden and complex. The regularities of microprocesses are not methods that the participants would intentionally apply. Taking the modern educational claims of the autonomy of the learner into account, Luhmann and Schorr (1982) gave reasons for the fact that, in education, there exists a "deficit" of technology on principle. That is, there is no hope to find methods that "make" the students learn.

Several approaches to the relation between interaction and learning have been mentioned earlier. One chain of thought assumes that some aspects of the social interaction are transformed into the learner's mind when learning occurs. Bruner (1976) and Vygotsky (1981) described how other-regulation results in self-regulation. Referring to Bruner, Krummheuer (1991) analyzed mathematics classrooms. He reconstructed specific patterns of interaction, "formats of argumentation," which are initiated by the teacher and which imply obligations for the students. The more the students participate successfully in the formats, the more the teacher lets the students take responsibility, so that, at the end, the students gain the ability to argue independently.

Another line of theories stresses the individual's sense-making processes. Saxe (1991) and Saxe, Guberman, and Gearhart (1987) criticized the Vygotskian studies in that sufficient attention is not given to the learner's point of view and to the learner's active role as a participant in social interaction. The basic assumption is that learners construct mathematical understandings in their efforts to achieve mathematical goals; these goals emerge partly through adjustments of the participants to each other in the interaction. In empirical studies of the practice of street-vending and of mother–child interaction, the learner's goals are reconstructed by a developmental analysis, the official goals are reconstructed by a cultural analysis, and the shifts and emergings of goals are reconstructed by a social interactional analysis.

Furthermore, several researchers take interactional conflicts as a condition of learning. For example, learning is viewed as arising from the learner's attempts to resolve conflicting points of view. The conflicts are indicated as contradictions between arguments in the interaction between individuals (Perret-Clermont, 1980). These socioconflicts result in a contradiction of oneself, which leads to mental reorganization. Also, Kumagai (1988) stressed that the differences of perspectives between the interacting individuals form a helpful prerequisite of learning mathematics. Because the observer's realization of an interactional conflict does not suffice to engender a learning process, Balacheff (1986) suggested considering an existing contradiction between persons as essential if the learner could experience it.

From the interactionist point of view, the negotiation between the teacher and the students is a fascinating unit of analysis because of the differences between the participants. The teacher represents mathematical claims and the tradition of mathematics education, whereas the student has a different background knowledge. The negotiation of meaning is a necessary condition of learning if the students' background knowledge differs from the knowledge the teacher wants the students to gain. The difference (no deficit) of knowledge characterizes discourses especially with ambiguous topics where the students erroneously assume that they understand mathematically according to the teacher's intentions. "Thus, instead of making entries on a blank slate, teaching in school seems to be involved in erasing entries from a too full slate" (Griffin & Mehan, 1981, p. 212).

Nevertheless, the student is not a minor partner at all. In Protocol 5, for example, Student C proposed a solution to a conflict between interpretations by using a mathematical argument. Opposed to it, the teacher stated arguments in a very concrete domain of meanings. If mathematics teachers have the opportunity to look at videotapes of their lessons and to analyze the students' contributions in a leisurely way, there is the chance that the teachers can experience their students as being more knowledgeable than expected and as influencing the teacher's activities more than experienced during teaching (Voigt, 1991). Thus the students' contributions to the mathematical theme have to be considered as an essential aspect in the theory: The student's thinking and the mathematical theme develop reflexively, and the student's learning contributes to the evolution of the theme that contributes to the student's learning.

Cobb, Wood, and Yackel (1991) conducted an year-long teaching experiment in which the mathematical themes were highly influenced by the students. The students worked on tasks that could be solved in very different ways. The students had to work in pairs, and they knew that they were expected to attempt to understand each other's thoughts and to make themselves understandable. The students were obliged to explain and to justify their ways of solving to the partner and to the whole class. These conditions contributed to classroom situations in which the students constituted themes by themselves.

For example, two different representations of a number are implied in the missing adding task of Fig. 2.3: How many do you have to add to [picture] to make 73?

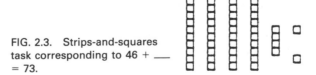

FIG. 2.3. Strips-and-squares task corresponding to 46 + ___ = 73.

The students know that the strips and squares are representations of multilinks and that they can use the concrete materials to solve the task. Analyzing several lessons I reconstructed two relatively stable thematic patterns:

Thematic pattern of counting materials (T_1)	Thematic pattern of calculation with two-digit numbers (T_2).
Working together some students interpret the signs as representations of concrete materials. They compare the bars and cubes separately. A typical solution would be: Add 3 bars and take away 3 ones.	Working together some students interpret the signs as representations of numbers. The difference is calculated within a system of numbers. A typical solution would be: 46, 56, 66 are 20, and 4, and 3, it's 27.
Quantities of materials are thematized.	The application of arithmetical rules is thematized.

In the classroom, the participation in a thematic pattern facilitates the cognitive development of a corresponding aspect of the concept of number, and vice versa. Moreover, in the classroom, several occasions have been reconstructed in which the patterns are not constituted purely. In these situations, the theme is improvised: In some cases, the teacher transforms the statements from the students' comparison of material objects to the calculation with numerals, and vice versa. In other cases, the students make contributions that the observer can take as relations between the different domains of meaning, such as "but 20 take away 3 more is 17." By these improvisations, different aspects of the number concept are combined. The improvisations offer the opportunity for students to change their individual interpretation of the task. The dealing with squares and bars is combined with the calculation of two-digit numbers. From a developmental point of view, the thematic transition from T_1 to T_2 supports the students' construction of numbers as "abstract composite units" and not longer as figurative objects (Cobb & Wheatley, 1988).

Although the students' participation in the thematic pattern can facilitate the students' learning, the inference is problematic that the teacher should force the students to participate in specific patterns because the students can bypass the regulations enforced by the teacher.

In German classrooms, a specific diagram shown in Fig. 2.4 is used as an aid to training students in crossing the ten: $7 + 8 =$ ___. In the diagram, 8 should be split up into 3 (in order to fill 7 up to 10) and 5. The students are expected to fill the diagram out, marking the left array with "+ 3" and the right array with "+ 5" and noting the solution at last. Instead, many students solve the arithmetical task by own methods in their head, and they fill out the right square. Then they mark the arrays because they know that the teacher wants them to do so.

Mead (1934) described the subject's identity as a dynamic balance between the "I" and the "Me." The student has to keep a balance between what she experiences as expected to do, what she wants to do, what she can do, and what

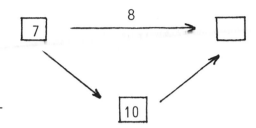

FIG. 2.4. Schematic representation of crossing the ten.

she experiences the others do. As in the last example, there can be a difference
between the student's private sense-making and the student's causes for doing
something. Therefore, the emphasis on the negotiation of mathematical meaning
seems to be more promising than the tradition of ritualized classroom interaction
controlled by the teacher step by step.

Up to this point, interactional regularities as well as the subject's creativity
have been described as prerequisites of learning mathematics. "So, what we have
here are neither automatic rituals—repeated endlessly and mechanically, nor
instantaneous creations,—emerging uniquely upon each occasion of interaction.
These are negotiated conventions—spontaneous improvisations on basic patterns
of interaction" (Griffin & Mehan, 1981, p. 205).

On the one hand, the conventions are useful insofar as they enable the participants to collaborate even if the individual backgrounds of knowledge differ. In
analyzing mathematical discussions, Walther (1982) and Lampert (1990) took
the conventions as means of negotiation of mathematical meaning. Both authors
described how teachers took care of conventions constituted upon the students'
contributions. Here, the teacher acts as a mediator between students' individual
knowledge and school mathematics.

On the other hand, unnoticed conventions of school mathematics could be
established incidentally and could become a burden on the learner. In an elementary class observed, first graders experienced that the numbers always stand for
the amounts of several things or persons. Some months later, the teacher presented several columns filled with different stickers, with uniform stickers in
each column. At the top of each column the price of one sticker is written, for
example "4¢." The teacher wants the students to fictitiously buy several stickers
in order to arrive at addition problems. However, the students protest vehe-
mently. They call for a change of the numbers at the top of the columns. They
argue that a number written has to correspond to the quantity of stickers of the
column. Although the teacher explains her intention, a student engages in a long
and excited negotiation of meaning. If a student really went shopping one would
not expect a similar conflict.

Students have to learn to distinguish between mathematical arguments and
those conventions that are established in order to make the negotiation of mathematical meaning easier. This is a difficult point, because mathematics itself is full

of conventions invented to make mathematical communication easier. Nevertheless, in school mathematics there are many conventions that educators developed because of didactical reasons and that have a short life during teaching mathematics. Thus, the student's skeptical attitude toward the routine participation in regularities is reasonable. The student should share the responsibility to negotiate mathematical meanings of the objects of the classroom discourse.

The arguments of this section have been developed starting from theories that take learning as the effect of interaction and moving to an interactionist view that takes the student as an actor who orientates himself instead of merely being regulated. In order to describe a relation between the student's self-orientation and interaction, a final case is presented. The protocol is taken from the teacher experiment of the group of Cobb, Wood, and Yackel.

Working in pairs, the students solved the following tasks:

$27 + 9 =$
$37 + 9 =$
$47 + 9 =$
$47 + 19 =$
$48 + 18 =$
$49 + 17 =$
etc.

Many students solved the tasks by using fingers, tally marks, multilinks, or the hundreds board. Some students compared the tasks and made use of previous solutions in order to solve the next ones. Next, during a whole class discussion, different ways of solving were compared. The teacher accepted all correct explanations. It is important to note that the teacher evaluated the correct explanations differently. If the offered way of solving seemed to be demanding (e.g., use of the compensation strategy), the teacher outlined the mathematical structure or she asked the students to explain their methods while requesting the other students to listen. Furthermore, the teacher explicitly characterized the way as an insightful way one or she expressed delight ("Aha!").

By her evaluations, the teacher indicated mathematical claims implicitly. It was up to the students to decide whether or not they would orientate their activities toward these claims. Usually, the students expect the teacher to represent the culture of the mathematical discipline. In the classroom observed, several students accepted the intellectual challenge. Looking at the fourth, fifth, and sixth tasks, Jonathan said, "I made two discoveries . . . the beginning numbers go 47, 48, and 49 . . . then it was 17 the bottom one then 18 . . . 19 . . . so it's all the same answer." And Matt, who realized that the fourth solution has to be 10 more than the third one, announced, "I found a discovery." In this lesson, the students' contributions form the basis of the theme. The teacher influences the development of the theme so that the students can orientate their activities toward more advanced mathematical arguments.

Stressing the negotiation of mathematical meaning in classroom processes, I have attempted to relate theoretical ideas to concrete examples. But I did not present concrete proposals to tell teachers what to do. Rather, I have tried to build an appreciation of problems with regard to the microculture of the classroom. Hopefully, the considerations form a contribution to the understanding of what we want to improve.

ACKNOWLEDGMENTS

Several aspects discussed in this chapter were elaborated in the course of discussions with Heinrich Bauersfeld, Götz Krummheuer, and Angelika Neth (Germany) and with Paul Cobb, Terry Wood, and Erna Yackel (USA). I especially thank John Richards, Analúcia Dias Schliemann, Leslie Steffe, and Erna Yackel for their written reactions to an earlier version presented at ICME-7.

The research reported in this chapter was supported by the Spencer Foundation. The opinions expressed do not necessarily reflect the views of the foundation.

REFERENCES

Andelfinger, B., & Voigt, J. (1986). Holiday lessons and everyday classroom practice—Preservice teacher training for secondary mathematics teachers. *Zentralblatt für Didaktik der Mathematik, 1*, 2–9.

Balacheff, N. (1986). Cognitive versus situational analysis of problem-solving behaviors. *For the Learning of Mathematics, 6*(3), 10–12.

Balacheff, N., & Laborde, C. (1988). Social interactions for experimental studies of pupils' conceptions: Its relevance for research in didactics of mathematics. In H.-G. Steiner & A. Vermandel (Eds.), *Foundations and methodology of the discipline of mathematics education*, Proceedings of the 2nd TME Conference (pp. 189–195). Bielefeld: IDM.

Bartolini Bussi, M. (1990). Mathematics knowledge as a collective enterprise. *Proceedings of the 4th SCTP Conference* in Brakel, West Germany (pp. 121–151). Bielefeld: IDM.

Bauersfeld, H. (1980). Hidden dimensions in the so-called reality of an mathematics classroom. *Educational Studies in Mathematics 11*, 23–41.

Bauersfeld, H. (1982). Analyses of communication in the mathematics classroom. In H. Bauersfeld, H. W. Heymann, G. Krummheuer, J. H. Lorenz, & V. Reiss (Eds.), *Analyses of classroom practice* (pp. 1–40). Köln: Aulis.

Bauersfeld, H. (1988). Interaction, construction, and knowledge—Alternative perspectives for mathematics education. In T. Cooney & D. Grouws (Eds.), *Effective mathematics teaching* (pp. 27–46). Reston, VA: National Council of Teachers of Mathematics.

Bauersfeld, H. (1990). *Activity theory and radical constructivism—What do they have in common, and how do they differ.* Occasional Paper 121. Bielefeld: IDM.

Bauersfeld, H., Krummheuer, G., & Voigt, J. (1988). Interactional theory of learning and teaching mathematics and related microethnographical studies. In H.-G. Steiner & A. Vermandel (Eds.),

Foundations and methodology of the discipline mathematics education (pp. 174–188). Antwerp: University of Antwerp.

Bishop, A. J., & Goffrey, F. (1986). Classroom organisation and dynamics. In B. Christiansen, A. G. Howsen, & M. Otte (Eds.), *Perspectives on mathematics education,* (pp. 309–365). Dordrecht: Reidel.

Blumer, H. (1969). *Symbolic interactionism: Perspective and method.* Englewood Cliffs, NJ: Prentice Hall.

Bruner, J. (1966). Some elements of discovery. In L. S. Shulman & E. R. Keisler (Eds.), *Learning by discovery: A critical appraisal* (pp. 101–113). Chicago: Rand McNally.

Bruner, J. (1976). Early rule structure: The case of peek-a-boo. In R. Harré (Ed.), *Life sentences* (pp. 55–62). London: Wiley & Sons.

Bruner, J. (1986). *Actual minds, possible worlds.* Cambridge, MA: Harvard University Press.

Burscheid, H. J., & Struve, H. (1992). Integrating psychological and social elements of the learning process. *Beiträge zum Mathematikunterricht* (pp. 133–136). Hildesheim: Franzbecker.

Carraher, T. N., Carraher, D. W., & Schliemann, A. D. (1985). Mathematics in the streets and in schools. *British Journal of Developmental Psychology, 3,* 21–29.

Cobb, P. (1990). Multiple perspectives. In L. P. Steffe & T. Wood (Eds.), *Transforming children's mathematical education: International perspectives* (pp. 200–215). Hillsdale, NJ: Lawrence Erlbaum Associates.

Cobb, P., & Wheatley, G. (1988). Children's initial understanding of ten. *Focus on Learning in Mathematics, 10*(3), 1–28.

Cobb, P., Wood, T., & Yackel, E. (1991). A constructivist approach to second grade mathematics. In E. von Glaserfeld (Ed.), *Constructivism in mathematics education* (pp. 157–176). Dordrecht: Kluwer.

Doise, W., & Mugny, G. (1984). *The social development of the intellect.* Oxford: Pergamon.

Donaldson, M. (1978). *Children's mind.* Glasgow: Fontana.

duBois-Reymond, M., & Söll, B. (1974). *Neuköllner schoolbook* (Vol. 2). Frankfurt: Suhrkamp.

Edwards, D., & Mercer, N. (1987). *Common knowledge. The development of understanding in the classroom.* London: Methuen.

Falk, G., & Steinert, H. (1973). The sociologist constructing reality, the essence of social reality, the definition of social situations, and methods for coping with these situations. In H. Steinert (Ed.), *Symbolic interaction. Works in reflexive sociology* (pp. 13–46). Stuttgart: Klett.

Garfinkel, H. (1967). *Studies in ethnomethology.* Englewood Cliffs, NJ: Prentice Hall.

Glatfeld, M., & Schröder, E. C. (1977). Induction and learning mathematics. In M. Glatfeld (Ed.), *Learning mathematics. Problems and chances.* (pp. 140–175). Braunschweig: Vieweg.

Goffman, E. (1974). *Frame analysis—An essay on the organization of experience.* Cambridge, MA: Harvard University Press.

Griffin, P., & Mehan, H. (1981). Sense and ritual in classroom discourse. In F. Coulmas (Ed.), *Conversational routine* (pp. 187–214). The Hague: Mounton.

Harvey, R., Kerslake, D., Shard, H., & Torbe, M. (1982). *Teaching and learning, 6, Mathematics.* London: Ward Lock Educational.

Harré, R. (1984). *Personal being. A theory for individual psychology.* Cambridge, MA: Harvard University Press.

Hundeide, K. (1988). Metacontracts for situational definitions and for presentation of cognitive skills. *Quarterly Newsletter of the Laboratory of Comparative Human Cognition, 10*(3), 85–91.

Jungwirth, H. (1991). Interaction and gender—Findings of a microethnographical approach to classroom discourse, *Educational Studies in Mathematics, 22,* 263–284.

Knorr-Cetina, K., & Cicourel, A. V. (Eds.). (1981). *Advances in social theory and methodology— Toward an integration of micro- and macro-sociologies,* Boston: Routledge & Kegan Paul.

Krummheuer, G. (1983). Algebraic transformations at secondary school—Final report of a research project. *Materials and studies* (Vol. 31). Bielefeld: IDM.

Krummheuer, G. (1991). Argumentationsformate im Mathematikunterricht. In H. Maier & J. Voigt (Eds.), *Interpretative unterrichtsforschung* (pp. 57–78). Köln; Aulis

Kumagai, K. (1988). Research on the "sharing process" in the mathematics classroom—An attempt to construct a mathematics classroom. *Tsukaba Journal of Educational Study in Mathematics Japan, 7,* 247–257.

Lakatos, J. (1976). *Proofs and refutations—The logic of mathematical discovery.* London: Cambridge University Press.

Lampert, M. (1990). Connecting inventions with conventions. In L. P. Steffe & T. Wood (Eds.), *Transforming children's mathematics education* (pp. 253–265). Hillsdale, NJ: Lawrence Erlbaum Associates.

Leiter, K. (1980). *A primer on ethnomethodology.* New York: Oxford University Press.

Luhmann, N. (1972). Simple social systems. *German Journal for Sociology, 1*(1), 51–65.

Luhmann, N., & Schorr, K. E. (Eds.). (1982). *Between technology and self-reference. Questions directed to pedagogy.* Frankfurt: Suhrkamp.

Maier, H. (1991). Analyzing students' understandings in classroom processes. In H. Maier & J. Voigt (Eds.), *Interpretative classroom research* (pp. 117–151). Köln: Aulis.

Maier, H., & Voigt, J. (1989). Teacher's question in the mathematics classroom, Part I. *Mathematica Didactica, 12*(1), 23–55.

Maier, H., & Voigt, J. (1992). Teaching styles in mathematics education. *Zentralblatt für Didaktik der Mathematik, 7,* 249–253.

McNeal, M. G. (1991). The social context of mathematical development. Doctoral dissertation, Purdue University.

Mead, G. H. (1934). *Mind, self and society.* Chicago: University of Chicago Press.

Mehan, H. (1979). *Learning lessons.* Cambridge, MA: Harvard University.

Neth, A., & Voigt, J. (1991). Staging the life-world. The negotiation of mathematical meanings of story problems. In H. Maier & J. Voigt (Eds.), *Interpretative research in classrooms* (pp. 79–116). Köln: Aulis.

Perret-Clermont, A.-N. (1980). *Social interaction and cognitive development in children.* London: Academic Press.

Rényi, A. (1967). *Dialogues about mathematics.* Basel: Birkhäuser.

Saxe, G. B. (1991). *Culture and cognitive development: Studies in mathematical understanding.* Hillsdale, NJ: Lawrence Erlbaum Associates.

Saxe, G. B., Gubermann, S. R., & Gearhart, M. (1987). *Social processes in early number development.* Monographs of the Society for Research in Child Development 52(2).

Solomon, Y. (1989). The practice of mathematics. London: Routledge.

Steffe, L. P., von Glasersfeld, E., Richards, J., & Cobb, P. (1983). *Children's counting types: Philosophy, theory, and application.* New York: Praeger Scientific.

Steinbring, H. (1991). Mathematics in teaching processes. The disparity between teacher and student knowledge. *Recherches en Didactique des Mathématiques, 11*(11), 65–108.

Struve, H. (1990). Analysis of didactical developments on the basis of rational reconstructions. *Proceedings of the 2nd Bratislava International Symposium on Mathematics Education,* Bratislava (pp. 99–119).

Tymoczko, T. (1986). Making room for mathematicians in the philosophy of mathematics. *The Mathematical Intelligencer, 8*(3), 44–50.

Voigt, J. (1985). Pattern and routines in classroom interaction. *Recherches en Diactique des Mathématiques, 6*(1), 69–118.

Voigt, J. (1989). Social functions of routines and consequences for subject matter learning. *International Journal of Educational Research, 13*(6), 647–656.

Voigt, J. (1990). The microethnographical investigation of the interactive constitution of mathematical meaning. *Proceedings of the 2nd Bratislava International Symposium on Mathematics Education,* Bratislava (pp. 120–143).

Voigt, J. (1991). Interactional analyses in teacher education. *Zentralblatt für Didaktik der Mathematik, 5,* 161–168.

von Glasersfeld, E. (1987). *Knowledge, language, and reality. Works in radical constructivism.* Braunschweig: Vieweg.

Vygotsky, L. S. (1978). *Mind in society.* Cambridge, MA: Harvard University Press.

Vygotsky, L. S. (1981). The genesis of higher mental functions. In J. V. Wertsch (Ed.), *The concept of activity in Soviet psychology* (pp. 144–188). Armonk, NY: Sharpe.

Walkerdine, V. (1988). *The mastery of reason.* London: Routledge.

Walther, G. (1982). Acquiring mathematical knowledge. *Mathematics Teaching, 101,* 10–12.

Wittgenstein, L. (1967). *Remarks on the foundations of mathematics.* Oxford: Blackwell.

Wittmann, E. C., & Müller, G. N. (1990). *Handbook of productive arithmetic problems* (Vol. 1). Stuttgart: Klett.

Wood, T., & Yackel, E. (1990). The development of collaborative dialogue in small group interactions. In L. P. Steffe & T. Wood (Eds.), *Transforming children's mathematics education* (pp. 200–215). Hillsdale, NJ: Lawrence Erlbaum Associates.

Yackel, E., Cobb, P., Wood, T., Wheatley, G., & Merkel, G. (1990). The importance of social interaction in children's construction of mathematical knowledge. In T. J. Cooney (Ed.), *Teaching and learning mathematics in the 1990s* (pp. 12–21). Reston, VA: National Council of Teachers of Mathematics.

3 Emergent Mathematical Environments in Children's Games

Geoffrey B. Saxe
Teresita Bermudez
University of California, Los Angeles

In their daily lives, children engage in a wide range of cultural practices: They play games, participate in sports, and sell goods. For many, such activities are the staples of childhood, and much of what has come to be called out-of-school mathematics learning occurs through children's participation in such practices.

What kinds of environments emerge in everyday cultural practices in which children engage in mathematics learning? The question presents difficult problems for analysis. We know that learning environments are not presented to individuals and thus directly observable by analysts; rather, they are constructed by individuals in activity. Further, such constructions are deeply interwoven with historical achievements as well as cultural values and norms. Much of the existing research on children's learning environments have not produced adequate coordinations of these epistemological and cultural issues in descriptions of learning environments in practices.

Sociological approaches often skirt efforts to analyze practices entirely. Instead, such approaches often use distal features of children's environments (social class, economic organization), properties of individuals (race, gender), or small-group organization in classrooms (e.g., reward structures) to analyze effects of these "proxy" variables on children's achievements. Although such distal variables as social class or reward structure may be predictive of children's accomplishments (e.g., Johnson, Johnson, & Stanne, 1985; Slavin, 1980, 1983), such approaches can provide little insight into the learning environments that emerge in children's practices.

Social-interactional approaches have offered useful fine-grained analyses of children's turn-for-turn exchanges in terms of categories of questions and expla-

51

nations (Webb, 1982, 1991) or social conflicts (Ames & Murray, 1982; Botvin & Murray, 1975; Doise & Mugny, 1984) and how these variables affect children's achievement. However, we do not find critical analyses of mathematics in these analyses or the way in which aspects of culture are interwoven with individuals' mathematical environments.

Ethnographic approaches often point to cultural aspects of children's activities as ingredient to children's learning environments (Clark, 1983; Eckert, 1989). Although such approaches are more sensitive to the cultural features of practices, they do not offer frameworks for the systematic analysis of mathematical environments nor how such environments might come to be represented in individuals' activities.

In this chapter, we describe a framework for the analysis of children's learning environments in which a core construct is children's *emergent goals* (Saxe, 1991). To illustrate the approach, we focus on our recent work on children's play of a game in which children become engaged with mathematical problems.

SOME CORE ASSUMPTIONS OF THE EMERGENT GOALS FRAMEWORK

Central to our work is the view that an understanding of the mathematical environments that emerge in the game requires the coordination of two analytic perspectives (Saxe, 1991). The first is a constructivist treatment of children's mathematics: We take as a core assumption that children's mathematical environments cannot be understood apart from children's own cognizing activities (Piaget, 1952, 1977; Saxe, 1991; Steffe, von Glasersfeld, Richards, & Cobb, 1983; von Glasersfeld, 1992). Indeed, mathematical environments take form as children construct and accomplish goals and subgoals that are grounded in their prior understandings. Such goals may be relatively elementary, such as those that a child constructs in counting a collection of objects, or relatively sophisticated, such as those that an adolescent constructs in creating a geometrical proof. Regardless, mathematical environments become constituted only as individuals structure mathematical goals.

The second perspective derives from sociocultural treatments of cognition (e.g., Laboratory of Comparative Human Cognition, 1986; Rogoff, 1990; Saxe, 1991). Children's construction of mathematical goals and subgoals is interwoven with the socially organized activities in which they are participants; whether computing batting averages or making change for lemonade, children construct goals that are framed by cultural artifacts (e.g., currency or number systems), activity structures (e.g., the rules and objectives of playing Monopoly), and social interactions.

The game that is the focus of our analysis was designed specifically to favor

the emergence of particular kinds of mathematical goals in children's peer interactions.[1] Through analyses of videotapes of children's play, our aim was to
provide some insight into children's emergent mathematical environments.

TREASURE HUNT AND THE EMERGENT
GOALS FRAMEWORK

The game of Treasure Hunt is depicted in Fig. 3.1. To play the game, children
assume the roles of treasure hunters in search of "gold doubloons," gold-painted
base-10 blocks in denominations of 1, 10, 100, and 1000. In play, children
collect their gold in treasure chests that consist of long rectangular cards organized into thousands, hundreds, tens, and ones columns, and children report their
quantity of gold on their gold register with the number orthography. The child
who acquires the most gold wins the game.

The game has a turn-taking structure. Children take turns rolling a die on a
large rectangular playing board that consists of six islands (see Fig. 3.2). A roll
shows how many islands a player hops until landing. Each island contains a
trading post where a player may purchase supplies and four geographical regions
where players receive messages that offer opportunities either to use their supplies to gain additional gold or to protect their existing gold. An enlargement
of Snake Island—its trading posts and its geographical regions—is given in
Fig. 3.3. At the end of each turn, players must report the quantities of their gold
in their treasure chest on their gold register; players are subject to "challenges"
from their opponents for inaccurate reports (e.g., reporting 9 hundreds, 8 tens,
and 15 ones [9(100) + 8(10) + 15(1)] as "9815"[2]).

Emergent Goals in the Play of Treasure Hunt

A basic assumption of the Emergent Goals Framework is that goals are not fixed
or static constructions, but rather take form and shift as children participate in
practices. In this process, goals are necessarily interwoven with cognitive and

---

[1]Members of the peer interaction research group at UCLA participated in the development and/or
analysis of the game. These individuals included Joseph Becker, Teresita Bermudez, Kristin Droege,
Tine Falk, Steven Guberman, Marta Laupa, Scott Lewis, Anne McDonald, David Niemi, Mary
Note, Pamela Paduano, Laura Romo, Geoffrey Saxe, Rachelle Seelinger, and Christine Starczak.

[2]Henceforth, we use the following notation to indicate quantities of blocks: We indicate in
parentheses the denominational value of a block; for instance, a block of value 100 is denoted as
(100), and a block of value 10 is denoted as (10). We indicate the number of blocks of a specified
denomination by an integer to the left of the block denomination. Thus, 9 blocks of value 10 are
denoted by the expression, "9(10)".

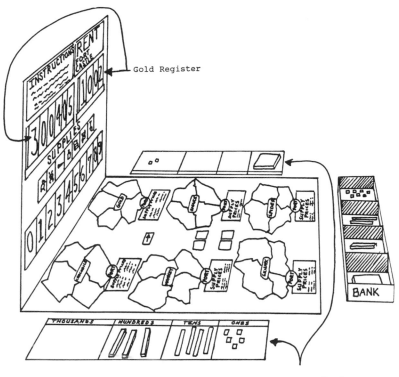

Gold Register

BANK

Treasure Chest

FIG. 3.1.   The Treasure Hunt game.

socio-cultural aspects of children's functioning. The Emergent Goals Framework targets four principal parameters (see Fig. 3.4): activity structures, social interactions, artifacts/conventions, and prior understandings. Next, we sketch these parameters, pointing to the way in which they serve as a frame for an analysis of emergent goals in Treasure Hunt.

Parameter 1: Activity Structures

In our analyses of the activity structure (Parameter 1) of Treasure Hunt, we distinguish between an *intended structure* and an *actual structure*. The intended structure consists of the rules, objectives, and organization of play as prescribed by the designers of Treasure Hunt. The actual structure, in contrast, is the game that emerges as children play. Each serves an important function in our analyses: Our specification of the intended structure provides a schema of the organization of play as presented to children, whereas our analyses of the actual structure provides a description of the transformation of this structure in the play of children. In our empirical analyses of play, a central concern is with the way the

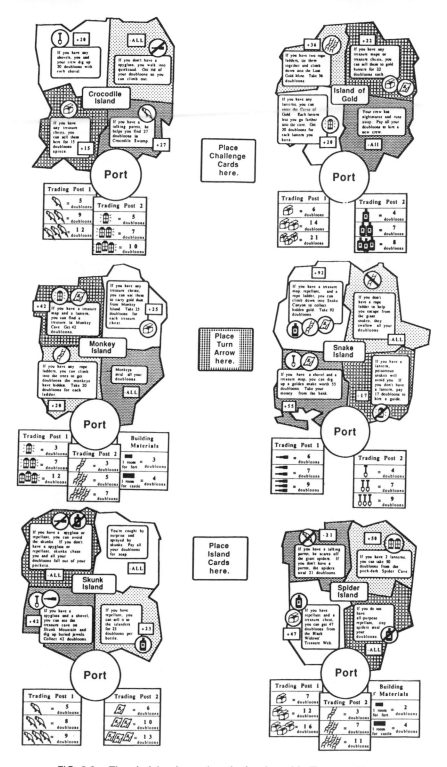

FIG. 3.2. The six islands on the playing board in Treasure Hunt.

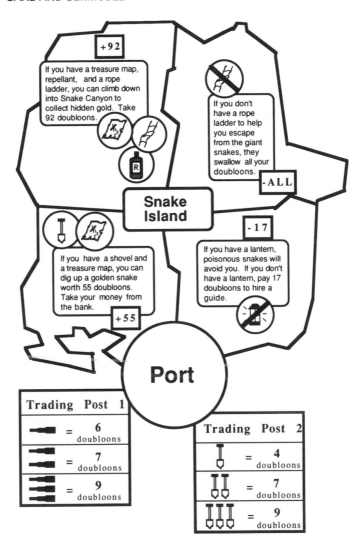

FIG. 3.3. An enlargement of Snake Island.

actual structure of play—the emergent rules by which children play, the values that they form in play, and their own particular routines by which they play—is interwoven with children's emergent mathematical goals.

The Intended Structure. Our prescribed objective for players of Treasure Hunt is to acquire gold, and the rules of the game specify a routine turn-taking organization. Each player begins the game with a specified quantity of gold (players generally started with 9 hundreds, 5 tens, and 6 ones blocks [9(100),

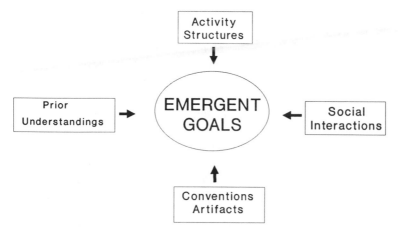

FIG. 3.4. The four parameters of the Emergent Goals model.

5(10), and 6(1)]). This quantity is both contained in each player's treasure chest and represented in numeric form on each player's gold register. Play begins when the first player rolls the die and moves his or her ship to one of the six islands as a function of the roll.

After moving to the appropriate island, a player's turn consists of an ordered sequence of five routine phases (see Fig. 3.5). In the first phase, the *challenge*, the player has the option of questioning whether the opponent's numeric repre-

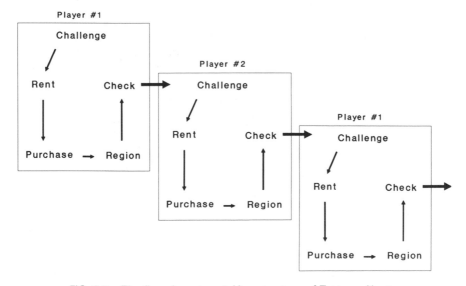

FIG. 3.5. The five-phase turn-taking structure of Treasure Hunt.

sentation in the opponent's gold register actually reflects the appropriate quantity of gold in the opponent's treasure chest. To initiate a challenge, the player draws a challenge card from the center of the playing board. The card contains a number, indicating how many doubloons the player will receive from the bank if the player's challenge to the opponent is, in fact, appropriate (as determined by player–opponent negotiation). The second phase of a turn, the *rent*, occurs if the player lands on an island on which the opponent has placed a fort or castle (previously purchased and positioned by the opponent). If so, the player is obligated to pay the opponent a specified amount of gold. The *purchase* phase follows; the player now has the option of purchasing supplies using the two or three menus contained at the port of the player's island (see Fig. 3.3). Next, the player draws a colored card that initiates the *region* phase, in which the player moves—as a function of the color on the card—to one of four colored regions of the island. At the colored region, the player receives a printed message indicating whether the player may trade some of the specified supplies to either gain gold or to avoid losing gold (see Fig. 3.3). Finally, after a purchase is complete, the player, in a *check* phase, adjusts the gold register (numeric representation of quantity) to adequately reflect the amount of gold in the treasure chest (see Fig. 3.1). Once the phase is completed, the player turns an arrow on the center of the game board toward her opponent, signaling that the turn is completed.

The intended structure of Treasure Hunt has various implications for children's emergent mathematical goals in play. In the purchase phase, for instance, players should buy supplies at island trading posts, attempting to add or multiply supply values and then subtract the sum from their gold, and perhaps even attempt to accomplish price-ratio comparisons. In the region phase, players draw island cards that send them to particular island areas where, depending on the particular region, they must add gold to their chests in exchange for certain supplies, or they must pay for gold if they lack certain supplies by subtracting a value of gold from their treasure chest. Later, in the check phase, children compare their gold and gold registers to make sure that their gold registers (orthographic representations) adequately represent their quantities of gold (base-10 block representations); this cross-representation comparison goal is supported by their opponents' license to challenge, the phase that begins the opponent's turn. Thus, the intended structure of the game—the objective to acquire gold, the rules of play, and the cyclical phase organization—was designed to support the emergence of various kinds of mathematical goals.

Actual Structure.   The actual structure of play is a principal target of empirical analysis. In play, children transform the intended structure—an external definition of how to play—into their own rules, values, and routines. Although the intended rules are presented as external prescriptions, the actual rules are the ones that define for them what is legitimate and important in play. Similarly, while the intended objectives (e.g., to acquire more gold) are defined externally for children, in play children form their own values that guide their own objectives. Finally, although we present a routine structure of play (e.g., our five phases), children in the course of play form their own idiosyncratic routines. Thus, the intended structure of play defines a potential organization of play that is realized in different ways by children in activity. Children's emergent mathematical goals take form in relation to this emergent activity structure.

We sketch next three additional parameters, each of which is necessary for the analysis of children's emergent mathematical goals. These consist of the artifacts and conventions that may become interwoven with children's mathematical activities, the social interactions during play that may either constrain or enable children's construction of mathematical goals, and the prior understandings that form the cognitive basis of children's construction of mathematical goals.

Parameter 2: Artifacts, Conventions

There are several artifacts and conventions (Parameter 2) that are intrinsic to play that influence the character of children's mathematical goals. These include the price-ratio menus, base-10 blocks (gold doubloons, Fig. 3.6), and the numerals for representing gold. During play, children's mathematical goals are interwoven with properties of these artifacts. Consider, for instance, an arithmetical problem that may emerge in the purchase of supplies and the implications for accomplishing the purchase using two different sets of artifacts. First, the player must sum the prices of the specified number of supplies, keeping tallies of prices and number of supplies as prescribed by the different price ratios (a form of addition linked to the price ratios). Then, in the purchase of supplies, a player needs to accomplish a subtraction problem; the child's goals will differ as a function of whether the child calculates using the base-10 blocks or using the standard orthography. For instance, to perform the subtraction in gold doubloons, the player may generate goals and subgoals involving equivalence trades of larger blocks for smaller blocks in order to accomplish the subtraction; in

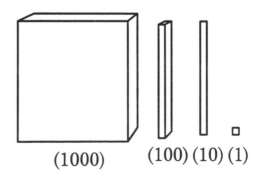

FIG. 3.6.   Exemplars of the four denominations of base-10 blocks used as gold doubloons.

(1000)   (100) (10) (1)

contrast, with the orthography, the player may apply the school-linked column subtraction procedure with borrowing.

Parameter 3: Prior Understanding

The prior understandings (Parameter 3) children bring to Treasure Hunt have implications for the mathematical goals that emerge in play. For Treasure Hunt, prior understandings may include children's knowledge of board games as well as their knowledge of basic arithmetic operations. For instance, some children have difficulty understanding the denominational structure of the blocks. They may treat all blocks with a value of unity, not conceptualizing blocks with reference to their many-to-one equivalence relations [e.g., 10(1) is equivalent to 1(10)]. As a result, when faced with a problem that requires payments when one does not have exact change to pay [e.g., paying 14 when one has only 8(100) 1(10)], a child will structure different kinds of subgoals in the formation and accomplishment of the arithmetical problem. Thus, goals are rooted in children's conceptual constructions, and analyses of processes of goal formation must be grounded in a treatment of children's understandings.

Parameter 4: Social Interactions

Children's goals often shift and take form as individuals participate in practice-linked social interactions (Parameter 4). For instance, in the purchase of supplies that cost 14 doubloons without exact change, a child who has difficulty accomplishing the payment may receive assistance with the more difficult aspects of the problem from his or her opponent. Such assistance may have the effect of reducing the complexity of the arithmetical goals that the child structures and accomplishes in the problem. Rather than conceptualizing the trade of a large for middle doubloon values, the trade may be accomplished by the opponent, and the player may merely need to form and accomplish goals of paying the exact amount (adding single or multidenominational doubloon pieces).

The Emergent Goals Framework and Children's Mathematical Environments

The view put forth here is that the mathematical environment known by the child is no more than the process of mathematical goal and subgoal formation and accomplishment. From this perspective, the Emergent Goals model provides a basis for the analysis of the mathematical environments children structure in practices. In analyzing aspects of the mathematical environments that emerge in Treasure Hunt, we guide our analyses by the three principal constructs that define the actual structure of play—children's rules, values, and routines.

Rules

Rules are warrants that are used to define what is and what is not legitimate in play. In this section, we point to the way rules, an aspect of the actual activity structure of play, are interwoven with children's emergent mathematical goals and how rules themselves may emerge and take new forms in the course of play.

In the design of Treasure Hunt, we developed a rule structure that we believed would involve students in sustained play and at the same time lead them to structure some rich mathematical environments. Recall that rules of play were linked to each phase of the game. For instance, in the purchase phase, children could buy supplies using prices from the menus of the island that they had landed on. They could buy as many supplies as they liked, drawing gold from their own treasure chests and depositing the payment in the bank. In actual play, some children embellished the rules, others simplified the rules, and still others played more or less faithfully by them. In the interactions discussed next, we focus on some of the emergent purchase-phase rules and the way these rules were interwoven with the emergence of children's mathematical environments.

Like most children, in their play Monica and Jackie frequently made use of base-10 blocks, the principal artifact of play (Parameter 2). We know from observations of their play and prior assessments that Monica and Jackie had difficulty understanding denominational transformations [like 1 one hundred block is equivalent to 10 ten blocks, $1(100) = 10(10)$ (Parameter 3)]: Whenever they were "running low" on ones and tens doubloon pieces in supply purchases, they merely drew a challenge card and then collected from the bank the amount indicated on the card.[3] Through their invented rule, Monica and Jackie, through a negotiated process (Parameter 4), created a means of preempting the emergence of base-10 block problem that would require them to make an equivalence transformation [e.g., trade $1(10)$ for $10(1)$ or $1(100)$ for $10(10)$]. Now, they merely counted single-unit blocks (or a combination of single- and multiunit blocks) to pay for a supply purchase. Thus, the mathematical environment for these children emerged as adding units, or multiples of units, to produce a particular sum.

Toni and Veronica's play, described next, presents an interesting instance in which children's emergent rules led them to construct more complex goals. In the prescribed rules of play, children were allowed to buy supplies sold only on the island on which they had landed, a rule that Toni and Veronica chose to ignore early in their first session of the game:

Toni landed on Skunk Island and indicated to Veronica that she wanted to purchase spyglasses. Indicating that no spyglasses were sold on the island, Veronica then proceeded to look at other island supply menus to determine on which island they were sold (with Toni's tacit agreement that this was a legitimate activity.) Veronica located a spyglass menu on Snake Island, and quoted Toni the price (6 doubloons for 1 spyglass), whereupon Toni paid and took the supplies.

---

[3]As indicated earlier, the intended use of these cards was that they be drawn when players questioned their opponents report (in numerals) of their gold (base-10 blocks).

In this interaction, Veronica and Toni reached an implicit agreement about a new rule: You can buy any supply regardless of where it is sold. The new rule led to Toni's formulation of a subtraction goal—to pay 6 from her treasure chest. Thus, the new rule (Parameter 1) in conjunction with the interaction between players (Parameter 4) framed the emergence of the problem. Further, the representational embodiment of the goal was set in the context of the base-10 blocks, a principal artifact of play (Parameter 2), and the cognitions entailed in formulating and accomplishing the goal necessarily involved an understanding of base-10 block arithmetical transformations (Parameter 3).

Values

Children came to value some aspects of the game over others. Children's emergent game-linked values were central in their creation of their own objectives of the game. Like emergent rules, we found that children's values varied and that they could enhance as well as limit the complexity of children's goals. We next consider two emergent values during play: a value linked to obtaining a "best buy" in the purchase of supplies, and a value linked to acquiring the "thousands" block.

Finding a "Best Buy."   Consider an interaction during a purchase phase in Toni and Veronica's last session of play.[4] Toni constructs the goal to compare ratios and the appropriate subgoals that allow her to accomplish this comparison successfully:

> Toni says: "I wanna buy two chests and two . . . " [points to the ladders and says] "and that's it, 'cause two of these over here" [Spider Island] "is seven and two over here" [Monkey Island] "is five, so I'll get them over there."

During her turn, Toni compared the price for two ladders at two different islands, and decided not to buy them where she had landed because they cost more. Toni formulated the goal of ratio comparison: two for seven doubloons versus two for five doubloons, reaching the conclusion that two ladders for seven doubloons is a more expensive price than two for five doubloons. Then during Veronica's turn, Toni advised Veronica what to purchase based upon her comparison of price ratios, further evidence that she has come to value best buys.

It is instructive to compare this example in which Toni guides her activity by her value to find a "best buy" with the prior example in which Toni and Veronica formed a new implicit rule. Toni and Veronica's earlier rule-linked interaction consisted of an across-island search for supplies. The search occurred because

---

[4]After 2½ months of playing, they were no longer playing by the new rule they had created during the first session but were abiding by the prescribed rules.

Toni wanted to find spyglasses (a single supply). The across-island search and the discovery that the same supplies were sold for different values on different islands could well have provided a context for Toni's construction of a new value—obtaining a "best buy." The value led her to form ratio comparison goals, conceptually more complex goals than other children formed when they were making purchases.

The 1000 Piece.   A more common value than obtaining a "best buy" was that of acquiring enough doubloons to obtain a 1000-doubloon piece, the largest denomination used in the game. In observing Jorge play with Felix, we found that Jorge came to value obtaining a 1000 block and that his value resulted in more complex mathematical goals.

Prior to showing evidence that he regarded the 1000 block in any special way, Jorge had not formed goals that involved equivalence transformations of his blocks, despite sanctions we built into the game to encourage doubloon equivalence trades.[5] Indeed, Jorge had left the gold in noncanonical form—more than 9 units of a single denomination [e.g., 12(1) instead of 1(10) + 2(1) pieces]. With the emergence of the concern to get the 1000 block (a new value), Jorge formed goals of trading across denominations in order to obtain the valued block. In the following excerpt, we observe an instance of the import of the 1000 block for Jorge's emergent goals.

Jorge has just purchased two parrots and two lanterns and then draws an orange region card (if you have a parrot, collect 27 doubloons). He looks through his supplies and finds one parrot. His opponent gives him 2(10)s and 7(1)s, and Jorge now has 9(100)s, 8(10)s and 20(1). He once again expresses a desire of "getting one like that" (referring to the 1000). He counts his ones up to ten, then ten more. Then says, with sudden realization, "Twenty, twenty. I change, I change, I wanna change!" He trades, saying: "I change for a thousand."

As the excerpt shows, Jorge became involved in a trading problem that involved forming and accomplishing several consecutive many-to-one correspondence goals. When he counted his 20 ones, he realized that it would result in his total of 1000: We infer that he calculated a series of trades—20 ones could be traded for 2 tens; those 2 tens would be added to his already existing 8 tens to form a total of 10 tens; those 10 tens could be traded in for an additional hundred block, which together with his existing 9 hundreds would total 10 hundreds; in

---

[5]Some messages on the geographical regions required that children deposit in the bank all of their one-doubloon pieces (see, e.g., the upper right region on Snake Island in Figure 3.3). This requirement was designed to encourage children to trade ones pieces for tens pieces, so as to minimize possible losses. For example, having 11(1) as opposed to 1(1) + 1(1) would subject a child to risk of losing 11 doubloons as opposed to a risk of losing only 1 doubloon.

turn, those 10 hundreds could be traded for the 1000 block. Jorge did not physically accomplish every trading step; he was able to mentally work out the equivalence of 9 hundreds, 8 tens, and 20 ones, to 1000.

In a subsequent game, we noted Jorge's interest in the 1000 block leading to new kinds of arithmetical goals. Rather than simply trading to determine whether he could obtain a 1000 block, Jorge became concerned with anticipating through additions and subtractions how much gold he would have to add to his treasure chest in order to obtain a 1000 block. For instance, at one point Jorge had 9(100) + 8(10) + 7(1), and he stated to his opponent that he needed two more tens to have 1000. Later in play, Jorge had 9(100) + 9(10) + 3(1) and stated the he needed "one more [ten]."

In contrast to Jorge and his opponent, Ralph's play illustrates how valuing the 1000 block could limit the complexity of emergent mathematical goals. On one occasion, we observed that Ralph's doubloons approached 1000 (he had 993). In order to keep his doubloons, Ralph reduced his supply purchases, since every payment for supplies would further deplete his treasure chest, taking him further from his targeted 1000 block. As a result, Ralph reduced the complexity and frequency of emergent mathematical goals. Unfortunately, there was some irony to his strategy. Over the course of the game, Ralph never did acquire the appropriate supplies that would allow him to garner additional gold to obtain his targeted block.

In the examples just cited related to finding best buys and obtaining the 1000 block, we find that the mathematical environments that emerged in play are constituted by children's emergent mathematical goals and interpretable from the perspective of the Emergent Goals model. In all cases, children's values (Parameter 1) were the basis for structuring problems in which mathematical goals emerged, whether they involved ratio comparisons or block trades and computations. These goals were shaped by the principal artifacts of play (Parameter 2), price ratios, and base-10 blocks, and the goals took form in the context of the give-and-take exchanges with their opponents (Parameter 4). Finally, both the ratio comparison goals and the computations involving the thousand block necessarily involved at least an incipient understanding of the mathematics involved in these concepts (Parameter 3).

Routines

Children's idiosyncratic routines were organizing schemas that, like rules and values, had implications for the emergence of children's mathematical goals. Common classes of routines were related to purchasing and to challenging. The purchase routines varied from regular purchases of large quantities of supplies to regular purchases of only one or two items for exact change. Sometimes purchase habits became shared by players, usually by mutual imitation, and thus we found large-scale purchasers playing with one another (and, reciprocally, small-scale purchasers playing with one another). Challenging routines included challenging after every change in gold and regular warnings by opponents of possible upcoming challenges. We next consider the way both kinds of routines were related to children's emerging mathematical goals.

Routines Involving Purchases.   The routine of purchasing multiple supplies was shared by Ramiro and David. This routine led both players to structure arithmetical problems of addition, subtraction, and multiplication (successive additions), equivalence trades, and translations of base-10 blocks into the standard number orthography. The following excerpt illustrates well the complexity of goals that can emerge when children routinely buy large quantities of supplies.

> On his turn, Ramiro lands at the port on Monkey Island, reads the price menus, and decides to buy all of the castle rooms available—19—at a cost of 4 doubloons each. He pays with one one hundred piece and takes change, trades to put his gold in canonical form, and then changes his gold register. Next, he draws a colored island card which sends him to Monkey Island's white region. The crux of the region message reads, ". . . if you have a ladder, collect 20 doubloons." Being well-stocked with supplies, Ramiro presents 3 ladders, takes 6 tens from the bank and uses an additional 4 tens in his treasure chest to trade for a 100 doubloon piece, changing his gold register, accordingly, to 900.

As a part of his routine purchase of large quantities of supplies (buying 19 castle rooms at 4 doubloons each), Ramiro led himself down a path in which he came to structure the goal of adding 4, 19 times. During payment, he then formed a complex subtraction goal—to subtract 86 from his 916 in gold. After collecting change, he formed and accomplished two additional mathematical goals: He transformed his gold into canonical form by trading 10(1) for 1(10), and then represented his gold in the standard orthography in his gold register. During his turns, David engaged in similar purchasing behavior, buying, for example, all of the available fort rooms. Although some of their calculations were incorrect, in this process of mathematical goal formation and accomplishment they were constructing complex arithmetical environments.

Like Ramiro and David, Fanny and Carla also shared a purchasing routine in their play. However, unlike David and Ramiro, their routine led to emergent goals of quite a different order. Fanny and Carla would buy only those supplies for which they had exact change; further, when they did make a purchase, they would only buy one kind of supply at a time. An excerpt provides a typical example of this type of transaction routine:

> Fanny had 9(100) 4(10) 1(1) in her treasure chest when she found herself at the at the port on Monkey Island. The cost of items at the port were three, four, five, seven, and twelve doubloons. She could not pay any of those amounts with exact change, and chose not to purchase anything.

The routine of purchasing only when exact change was available clearly limited the emergence of addition and subtraction goals because it reduced the instances in which Fanny and Carla could purchase and pay.

Routine and Nonroutine Challengers.   All children were told about rules linked to challenges—that they could challenge only at the beginning of their turn, and that they needed to change their gold register at the end of their turn to avoid being challenged by their opponent. Despite children's knowledge of the challenge rules, many children routinely declined to challenge. Others, however, developed some interesting routines linked to challenging that led to the emergence of particular kinds of mathematical goals.

Jose and Guni played together and developed a shared routine. After Guni challenged Jose a few times early in the game, both of these players came to challenge each other with great regularity. To defend against one another's challenges, both players did not wait until the end of their respective turns to change their register. Instead, both changed their registers whenever the amount of gold was altered in their treasure chests.

Due to their routine and frequent challenges, both players came to form goals linked to translating the base-10 block representations of gold doubloons into the standard number orthography quite regularly in their play. Perhaps due to the routine challenges, Jose and Guni showed more efficient means of maintaining accurate correspondences: Sometimes they performed the math (adding or subtracting) directly on the gold register. In such cases, they changed their gold registers prior to their gold transactions, representing in the orthography the anticipated outcome of their forthcoming gold transaction.

In the examples cited involving purchase and challenge routines, we find mathematical environments constituted by children's emergent mathematical goals, goals linked to each of the four parameters. Children's routines (Parameter 1) were the basis for structuring the complexity levels of arithmetical and representational problems in purchases and base-10 block translations into the standard orthography. These goals were shaped by the principal artifacts of play (Parameter 2), base-10 blocks, and the standard number orthography, and the goals took form in the context of the sometimes heated interactions of challenging their opponent or buying from their opponent (Parameter 4). Finally, the arithmetical and representation goals necessarily involve at least an incipient understanding of the mathematics involved in these activities (Parameter 3).

CONCLUDING REMARKS

In our analyses of Treasure Hunt, we found that despite the fact that children were ostensibly playing the same game, using the same materials, and participating in the same classrooms, children were often engaged with different mathematical environments. Indeed, in our analyses of emergent goals we found that the structure of Treasure Hunt emerged over play, with children structuring varying rules, values, and routines. We found that sometimes children's emergent rules, values, and routines served to limit the potential complexity of the mathematical environments children structured in play, as when children adopted a new purchase-phase rule that allowed them to circumvent the construction and accomplishment of goals entailed in subtraction problems involving trades; at other times, children's rules, values, and routines enhanced the mathematical complexity, as when a child came to value best buys, leading to incipient ratio comparison goals. Although rules, values, and routines were central constructs for understanding the dynamic activity structure of play, to capture the character of children's emergent mathematical goals required us to anchor our analyses in the other three parameters of the Emergent Goals model. Indeed, whether we considered the emergent goals linked to best buys or to simplifying subtraction problems with trades, children's mathematical goals could not be well understood without coextensive analyses of the artifacts in play (base-10 blocks, numerals, price ratios), the mathematical understandings children brought to the game (e.g., their understanding of part–whole relations in denominational structures), and emergent social interactional processes (e.g., conflicts, negotiations, agreements).

In closing, the issues that we confronted in our analyses are fundamental ones for research addressed to the representation of social and cultural processes in children's mathematics. Children's learning environments, whether in or out of school, can only be adequately understood insofar as we can document the goals with which children are engaged. Understanding how particular practices support and limit children's goal-directed activities is both a critical feature of sociocultural analyses of children's learning and key to the design and modification of educational practices.

ACKNOWLEDGMENTS

This chapter was presented as a paper at the 1992 Meetings of the International Congress of Mathematics Education, Montreal, Canada. The research described was supported by grants from the Spencer Foundation (M890224) and the National Science Foundation (MDR-8855643), although the opinions expressed are not necessarily those of the funding agencies. Appreciation is extended to the students, teachers, and staff at Seeds University Elementary School and Westminster Elementary School for participation and help in the conduct of the study described, and to Maryl Gearhart, Steven Guberman, and Anne McDonald for comments on an earlier draft of the chapter.

REFERENCES

Ames, G., & Murray, F. (1982). When two wrongs make a right: Promoting cognitive change by social conflict. *Developmental Psychology, 18,* 894–897.

Botvin, G. J., & Murray, F. B. (1975). The efficacy of peer modeling and social conflict in the acquisition of conservation. *Child Development, 46,* 796–799.

Clark, R. M. (1983). *Family life and school achievement: Why poor black children succeed or fail.* Chicago: University of Chicago Press.

Doise, W., & Mugny, G. (1984). *The social development of the intellect.* Oxford, England: Pergamon.

Eckert, P. (1989). *Jocks and burnouts: Social categories and identity in high school.* New York: Teachers College.

Johnson, R. T., Johnson, D. W., & Stanne, M. B. (1985). Effects of cooperative, competitive, and individualistic goal structures on computer-assisted instruction. *Journal of Educational Psychology, 77,* 668–678.

Laboratory of Comparative Human Cognition. (1986). Culture and cognitive development. In W. Kessen (Ed.), *Manual of child psychology: History, theory and methods,* (pp. 295–356). New York: Wiley.

Piaget, J. (1952). *The child's conception of number.* New York: Norton.

Piaget, J. (1977). *The development of thought: Equilibration of cognitive structures.* New York: Viking.

Rogoff, B. (1990). *Apprenticeship in thinking: Cognitive development in social context.* New York: Oxford University Press.

Saxe, G. B. (1991). *Culture and cognitive development: Studies in mathematical understanding.* Hillsdale, NJ: Lawrence Erlbaum Associates.

Slavin, R. E. (1980). Cooperative learning. *Review of Educational Research, 50,* 315–342.

Slavin, R. E. (1983). When does cooperative learning increase student achievement? *Psychological Bulletin, 94,* 429–445.

Steffe, L. P., Glasersfeld, E. von, Richards, J., & Cobb, P. (1983). *Children's counting types: Philosophy, theory, and application.* New York: Praeger.

von Glasersfeld, E. (1992). *A constructivist approach to experiential foundations of mathematical concepts.* Unpublished manuscript, Amherst, MA.

Webb, N. M. (1982). Student interaction and learning in small groups. *Review of Educational Research, 52,* 421–445.

Webb, N. M. (1991). *Task-related verbal interaction and mathematics learning in small groups.* Unpublished manuscript, University of California, Los Angeles.

4

Negotiating the Negotiation of Meaning: Comments on Voigt (1992) and Saxe and Bermudez (1992)

John Richards
BBN Labs, Cambridge, Massachusetts

Jörg Voigt sent me a copy of his 1992 paper, writing that he looked forward to meeting in Quebec to continue "negotiating the negotiation of meaning." Such then is the topic of my chapter. I focus on Voigt's paper first, because it is an attempt to provide a theoretical framework for looking at classroom behaviors and interactions. In the spirit of negotiation, I submit that there is much that we hold in common, but will focus almost entirely on the fuzzy edges where ambiguity rears its ugly head.

I examine how Voigt places his interactionist framework within the context of current epistemological positions. I then focus more directly on the concept of negotiation, and on how it enters into mathematical communication. Finally, I turn to the extended example in Saxe and Bermudez and evaluate it from this perspective.

EPISTEMOLOGICAL CONCERNS

Describing the current situation in mathematical education research, Voigt (1992) wrote about a change in the *focus of attention*. In the radical constructivist tradition there is a "focus" on the individual learner; in the social constructivist tradition there is a "focus" on group dynamics; and for his interactionist perspective there is a "focus" on the reasoning and sense-making processes of subjects who "interactively constitute mathematical meanings" (p. 11). The different traditions each use a different methodology: clinical interviews, ethnographical case studies, and "microsociology, especially symbolic interactionism and ethnomethodology" (p. 11), respectively.

Although this division seems straightforward and clear, I do not believe that it is accurate. This is largely because these theories are about different things. Radical constructivism is an epistemological theory. Social constructivism is largely a set of research methodologies and, in its more "radical" forms, even antiepistemological (cf. Gergen, 1995). Interactionism seems to build on the two, in the sense that it has adopted the implications of the epistemological sophistication of radical constructivism, yet maintains the important methodological contributions of the social approaches. In fact, I would argue, it is much closer to the radical constructivist position than Voigt would admit. The earliest application of the radical constructivist epistemology to mathematics education did indeed use clinical interviews, but these were used in the context of the teaching experiment (cf. Steffe, von Glasersfeld, Richards, & Cobb, 1983). That is, from the very beginning, there was an integration and awareness of the Vygotsky, social, perspective, with the individual, Piagetian perspective.[1] This is not to discard the methodological differences. These are indeed significant, and there is much to share. Rather, the caricature of radical constructivism as never moving beyond the individual underestimates the theory's contributions.

There is an awkward point here that is not easy to make. Voigt argued that recent research has assumed that cultural and social dimensions are "intrinsic to learning mathematics," and that this is to be contrasted with the "child-centered conceptions" that stress the autonomy of the learner. Although I agree that both observations are correct, and there is indeed a contrast in methodology, or approach, there need not be a fundamental epistemological conflict. Moreover, radical constructivism is extremely comfortable with a Lakatos-type analysis of mathematics as an evolving and changing discipline, subject to cultural and metaphysical stresses. If one thinks of mathematics as being built up in each individual, the critical point for radical constructivism is not how mathematics diversifies, but rather how mathematics, as a tradition, converges at all. For radical constructivism, how is it possible to communicate with any other individual, and to become a member of any community? Radical constructivism begins with the individual, but takes seriously the need to establish an epistemological basis for interaction and communication. If all knowledge is constructed by an individual, how do we share knowledge, and how do we create knowledge in common? Most important, for educators, how can one individual, a teacher, act to change another individual, a student? The answer ties very much to the notion of language and social development, as argued in Maturana (1978), Winograd and Flores (1986), and Richards (1991).

---

[1]The early writings of the group did focus on the individual construction, but there was a serious research effort to account for language and for social constructions (particularly the historical/social construction of mathematics and science). This is not meant to deny the tremendous impact that ethnomethodology has had on the program.

The current debate is about whether knowing is an individual act or a social act. Framed in this way it is a relatively uninteresting question. In particular, it seems impossible to construct a theory of knowledge that ignores the perspective of the knowing subject. Similarly, it also becomes clear that the "rational" individual is a social construct, and insofar as thinking and argument are useful to an analysis, we must see the individual as a participant in society. In the terms of Michael Oakeshott (1962), education is the process of initiation into the conversation that began in the primeval forests. Even from the radical constructivist perspective it remains an interesting question of how an individual, in the course of a 13-year precollege education, reconstructs the mathematics that civilization has produced over the last five to ten thousand (or more) years. Thus, I object to Voigt's claim that "there is no place for the idea of transmission of knowledge from the teacher to the student" (1992, p. 6) on several grounds. First, I reject the notion of transmission of knowledge in the first place, but more importantly, I believe that there is a place for communication between students and teachers, and for learning and teaching. The important contribution of the radical constructive perspective is that learning, teaching, and communicating do not happen magically—that is, they are important questions that need to be addressed.

The point is, questions regarding the nature of individual mathematical construction must be integrated with questions concerning the initiation of that individual into the mathematical community. In the process of teaching we need to understand that each individual must, ultimately, construct his or her own mathematics. (In Voigt's paired example [p. 15], we still want to know whether Joey knows the compensation strategy—as opposed to the Joey–Josh construct). At the same time, we must understand that students construct their own mathematics in a social context. These are not contradictory statements, and I believe, with Bauersfeld, Cobb, and others, that these are not incompatible theories. I do not believe that this is avoiding an answer.

NEGOTIATION

How does taking these two theories as, in some important ways, mutually supportive contribute to education? I believe a piece of the answer lays in the negotiation of meaning that is the focus of the rest of my chapter.

I begin by asking a seemingly unrelated question that I have been intrigued with for some time, namely, what is unique to mathematical communication? That is, how does the negotiation of meaning in a mathematical discussion distinguish that discussion from any other type of discussion? A related but separate issue is to consider what is the implicit agenda in a mathematics classroom. Thus, in contrast to Voigt, ambiguity is not "an essential feature of discourse in mathematics lessons" (1992, p. 1)—at least, it is not more so than in any other human communication. From the perspective of radical constructivism, ambiguity is an essential feature of all discourse. Nevertheless, we do communicate, and we do so by building up a consensual domain (cf. Maturana, 1978). While ambiguity is intrinsic to human communication, it is perhaps more evident in teaching situations. Why would this be the case? The very nature of the teaching situation—whether it be mathematics, science, or social studies—is that there is an individual (the teacher) with knowledge and a world view that are different from the other participants in the conversation (the students). The very nature of the teaching situation is that, when it is successful, there is a foundation of trust established that allows the individuals to build up a consensual domain. This point can be trivialized through bad teaching. For example, one study shows that there are more new vocabulary words taught in high school science than in teaching a foreign language. But the main point here is that the initiation into the field requires a negotiation in meanings. This is not merely a matter of the students adapting to the teacher's language. If the teacher is to talk to the students and listen to the students then this negotiation must be bidirectional.

But we have in the Voigt paper a further set of distinctions that are seen as critical from the student's perspective. In the classrooms described we see students and teachers actually negotiating mathematical meaning with one another. This bothers me because it is succeeding too well. That is, I believe we have a confusion between "is" and "ought"—between description and prescription. We are told that mathematics classes consist of negotiations of meaning. In fact, I would argue, this occurs rarely, and only in special classes such as those described by Voigt.[2] This is an ideal for which one strives. Mathematics classes ought to involve a negotiation of meaning. What then is happening in mathematics classes? How do we understand the " 'misunderstandings' between the teacher and the students" (Voigt, 1992, p. 13) that are so common in the standard classroom?

These are critical questions that evolve around the nature of communication in a mathematics classroom. To begin with, not all mathematics classrooms are the same. To make this clearer, I refer to some distinctions I have drawn (cf. Richards, 1991) between different types of mathematical discussions:

1. Research math—the spoken mathematics of the professional mathematician and scientist. Professional mathematicians share much of their dis-

---

[2]In a trivial sense it is indeed true that all classes require negotiation of meanings, but I wish to draw a normative distinction parallel to one I drew in 1991. In that paper I argued that communication only occurs when a consensual domain has been established, and that much that is popularly characterized as "communication" is better characterized as talking. In the previous paper I argued that, for communication to occur, both participants must have the potential for change. This becomes even clearer if we look at the meaning of negotiation. Without the potential for change, it seems ludicrous to speak of "negotiation."

course structure with other research communities in that the language is technical and makes many assumptions regarding the underlying content area. The mathematical research community discourse is structured according to a "logic of discovery" (cf. Popper, 1959) stressing the actions of making conjectures and refutations. This underscores the constant negotiation of meanings at the edge of a discipline. The characteristic that distinguishes mathematicians from other research communities is their subtle reliance on notions regarding the nature of proof.

2. Inquiry math—mathematics as it is used by mathematically literate adults. This approximates but is still distinct from the language of the "mathematical research community." The language of mathematical literacy includes participating in a mathematical discussion, and acting mathematically—asking mathematical questions; solving mathematical problems that are new to you; proposing conjectures; listening to mathematical arguments; and reading and challenging popular articles containing mathematical content.

3. Journal math—the language of mathematical publications and papers. The emphasis is on formal communication, at a distance or across time, where there is no opportunity to clarify ambiguities. This language is very different from the spoken language of the research community; that is, it is very different from a logic of discovery. Papers and publications are based on a "reconstructed logic" that makes mathematical discoveries more palatable for public consumption (cf. Richards, 1988).

4. School math—the discourse of the standard classroom in which mathematics is taught. This discourse does not differ much from "school science" or "school English." Viewed as discourse structure, classroom lessons mostly consist of "initiation–reply–evaluation" sequences (cf. Mehan, 1979). What is learned is useful for solving habitual, unreflective, arithmetic problems. In many ways, this discourse does not produce mathematics, or mathematical discussions, but rather a type of "number talk" that is driven by computation. There is little negotiation of mathematical meanings.

There are steps that a teacher can take toward setting up an inquiry math classroom. These become clearer if we focus on the underlying assumptions that allow both the students and teacher to negotiate meanings, in general, and to engage in mathematical discussions where they can negotiate mathematical meanings.

First, a teacher must listen to the students, and students must listen to each other. Traditional classrooms, where the teacher is the conveyor of information and students the recipients, do not involve negotiation. In negotiation there are at least two sides, and they must both listen to the other. This general perspective requires a classroom atmosphere that supports risk taking, and allows for mistakes and blind starts.

Second, a teacher must be able to hear what the students are saying. That is, the teacher needs to be able to place the student's questions and ideas in a broader mathematical context. This helps in giving meaning to the student's mathematics. When a teacher cannot understand the larger mathematical picture that provides a context for the student's questions, it is very difficult to hear the question being asked.

Third, the classroom must be established in such a way as to support mathematical discussions. There are rules for argument and understanding in mathematics discussions that are based in the notion of proof.

These last two points bring us back to the question of the uniqueness of mathematical communication. The point is, the difference between the teacher and the student ought to be that the teacher has an agenda. The teacher is a trained negotiator, who has the goal of brining the student into the mathematical consensual domain (cf. Richards, 1991). The teacher's role is to represent the mathematical community in the negotiations. It is only with the teacher's guidance and understanding that a student can reconstruct contemporary mathematics by the time he or she is 18.

RULES AND PERSPECTIVES

The Saxe and Bermudez paper (1992) fits very much in the same framework. They too place themselves in the cross between the need for understanding the "children's own cognizing activities" (p. 3) and the way it is "interwoven with the socially organized activities in which they are participants" (p. 3). The critical notion that shows up in their paper is gained when one contrasts the teacher's perspective or curriculum developer's perspective with the child's perspective. The obvious social construction created a meaningful context for children to interact. Within this context the children were constrained by their own knowledge and values. It is this interaction that the social constructionists deny. As Saxe and Bermudez argued, "despite the fact that children were ostensibly playing the same game, using the same materials, and participating in the same classrooms, children were often engaged with different mathematical environments" (p. 14).

The interesting piece of the Saxe and Bermudez paper is not only that the children created their own mathematical environments, interactively, but that, in contrast with most mathematical classrooms, recognizing multiple perspectives is an intrinsic part of the classroom.

FINAL THOUGHT

In both papers, the interesting analyses benefited from looking at the social context, from thinking about the individual's construction, and from taking communication seriously, rather than as a given. It is this ability to change perspectives that provides the basis for a fuller analysis. I believe that radical constructivism provides the epistemological foundation for examining the individual's construction and for analyzing the nature of communication. It is also clear that the methodological contributions of social constructionism are necessary for analyses of the complex social constructs of the mathematics classroom.

REFERENCES

Gergen, K. (1995). Social construction and the educational process. In L. Steffe & J. Gale (Eds.), *Constructivism in education* (pp. 17–40). Hillsdale, NJ: Lawrence Erlbaum Associates.

Maturana, H. (1978). Biology of language: The epistemology of reality. In G. A. Miller & E. Lenneberg (Eds.), *Psychology and biology of language and thought* (pp. 27–64). New York: Academic Press.

Mehan, H. (1979). *The competent student*. Sociolinguistic Working Paper 61. Austin, TX: Southwest Educational Development Laboratory.

Oakeshott, M. (1962). The voice of poetry in the conversation of mankind. In *Rationalism in politics*. New York: Basic Books.

Popper, K. (1959). *Logic of scientific discovery*. English translation of *Logik der Forschung*. London: Hutchinson. (Original work published 1934)

Richards, J. (1988). Epistemology and mathematical proof. *Methodologia, 3*, 73–121.

Richards, J. (1991). Mathematical discussions. In E. von Glasersfeld (Ed.), *Radical constructivism in mathematics education* (pp. 13–52). Dordrecht: Kluwer.

Saxe, G. B., & Bermudez, T. (1992, August). *Emergent mathematical environments in children's games*. Quebec: ICME.

Steffe, L., von Glasersfeld, E., Richards, J., & Cobb, P. (1983). *Children's counting types*. New York: Praeger.

Voigt, J. (1992, August). *Negotiations of mathematical meaning in classroom processes: Social interaction and learning mathematics*. Quebec: ICME.

Winograd, T., & Flores, F. (1986). *Understanding computers and cognition*. Norwood, NJ: Ablex.

5 Negotiating Mathematical Meanings in and out of School

Analúcia D. Schliemann
Tufts University, Medford, MA

David W. Carraher
Universidade Federal de Pernambuco, Recife, Brazil and TERC, Cambridge, MA

If ever there was a subject matter that was deceptively clear and straightforward, it is mathematics and, in particular, arithmetic. Kant used the problem "7 + 5 = 12" as a demonstration that mathematical knowledge was a priori, that is, not dependent on prior experience in order to be known to be true. Such a view can no longer be sustained under the weight of 20th century studies of learning and psychological development. There is now overwhelming evidence that arithmetical knowledge depends on prior experience beginning in early childhood, well before children have studied the addition and subtraction of numbers. In a remarkable series of investigations, Piaget and his collaborators and followers amassed evidence that the child's understanding of arithmetic stems from acting upon physical quantities and reflecting upon the effects of her actions. Whether or not one accepts the structuralist framework within which the findings were interpreted, great strides were made in advancing our understanding of how children come to acquire mathematical knowledge.

But approaches from developmental psychology tend to have a blind spot with regard to the social processes involved in the construction of mathematical knowledge, treating mathematical knowledge as though it were the product of the individual child's interaction with the physical world and reflections thereon. We know that this cannot be the case because much of children's mathematical knowledge entails the appropriation of symbols and symbolic systems that have evolved over centuries. Understanding how students come to understand mathematics requires an approach sensitive to issues of learning and development within a social and cultural context. We became convinced of this years ago when we discovered (Carraher, Carraher, & Schliemann, 1982, 1985) that youths who had considerable difficulty in solving arithmetic problems in school-

77

like contexts solved "the same" problems in their work as street vendors in Brazil. Much of our own work (D. Carraher, 1991; T. Carraher, 1986; Nunes, Schliemann, & Carraher, 1993; Schliemann, 1985; Schliemann & Carraher, 1992; Schliemann & Acioly, 1989; Schliemann & Magalhães, 1990; Schliemann & Nunes, 1990) has been devoted to clarifying the similarities and differences between mathematics learned in and out of school.

Voigt's and Saxe and Bermudez's presentations (chapters 2 and 3, this volume) aim at clarifying how mathematical ideas are meaningfully constituted by means of the social interaction between children in the context of a game, or between children and teachers in school contexts. In this chapter, we try to relate their work to what we have learned about mathematical knowledge acquired in and out of school. Then we raise a few issues that remain to be addressed in the field, especially in what concerns how mathematical instruction could be improved in schools.

Saxe and Bermudez's analysis of children's activities while they play the game is mainly aimed at exemplifying the appropriateness of his emergent goals model for the development of mathematical knowledge and constitutes an important contribution to the analysis of how mathematical knowledge is constructed in real everyday situations. The distinction between the intended structure and the actual structure expresses the idea that "what is going on" can always be interpreted in at least two ways. Were Treasure Hunt included in a mathematics curriculum, the intended structure would conform closely to what the curriculum planner had in mind in designing the learning activity. In Saxe and Bermudez's words, "the intended structure of the game—the objective to acquire gold, the rules of play, and the cyclical phase organization—was designed to support the emergence of various kinds of mathematical goals" (chapter 3). Situations are set up in such a way that children, for example, must perform certain mathematical actions, such as adding or subtracting amounts of money, in order to proceed to the next step of the game. Saxe and Bermudez's intended rules are constitutive insofar as they constitute what are legal and desirable moves in the game. Actual rules define what is legal and desirable from the student's perspective. Actual rules will englobe strategic rules (e.g., finding the best buy) as well as values. Saxe and Bermudez note, for example, that several children were observed to work toward acquiring monetary units corresponding to 1000 doubloons. Nothing inherent in the rules of play requires them to do so. This goal emerges from the values that they bring into the game. What Saxe and Bermudez appear to be arguing is that when one observes students engaged in mathematical activity, it is insufficient to interpret their behavior merely as "doing mathematics" because their actions are guided by goals and rules that go beyond the traditional, narrow view all too prevalent of "subjects engaged in a cognitive task." Mathematical activity in the game situation is at the service of overarching goals, including those of a social nature (playfulness, ostentation—display of one's cleverness, "wealth," creativity, etc.).

We have known for years (Carraher, Carraher, & Schliemann, 1982, 1985; Lave, 1977) that the development of mathematical knowledge may occur, and does occur, in out-of-school situations. What we have not yet been able to document is how it occurs. The environment Saxe and Bermudez created provides a setting that seems to be appropriate to perform such an analysis. After all, nothing is more part of children's everyday activities than games. In this environment, as in out-of-school settings, mathematics is used as a tool to solve meaningful problems. Previous knowledge children bring to the game and interaction with others play important roles in shaping the different levels of activities or, in Saxe's terms, in determining the subject's emergent goals and the construction of mathematical knowledge.

Voigt's chapter (chapter 2) provides an insightful review of theories and studies on individual and social contributions for the construction of mathematical knowledge and shows the difficulties children and teachers have to cope with in order to reach mathematical meanings through classroom interactions. For Voigt, the meaning of mathematical concepts is accomplished by the pupil through social interaction with the teacher. It is "negotiated" in the sense that neither the student nor the teacher determines meaning, independently of the other. In general, the pupil's understandings become increasingly compatible with the mathematical meanings aimed at by the teacher, but this is a slow and nonlinear process. According to Voigt (chapter 2, this volume),

> The ambiguity of single objects is reduced by relating its meaning to a context taken to be shared. At the same time the context is confirmed by constituting the meaning of the single object. The context and the singular meaning elaborate each other. From this ethnomethodological point of view meanings are not given by a cultural context that would exist independently of the negotiation of meaning, but the cultural context is continually constituted.

Voigt notes as examples how colored blocks, chips, and pictures are used and interpreted in schools as opposed to at home. The overall thrust of such examples is to characterize the child as being socialized into a community where initially ambiguous situations are made less and less ambiguous through the establishment of conventions, that is, shared interpretations. This occurs through the teacher's deployment of "interactional obligations." Part of learning mathematics in traditional classrooms entails coming to learn what the teacher has in mind in presenting an example. A question such as "Björn, have you noticed anything?" makes clear that it is not sufficient for the student to have an opinion. He should be noticing those aspects of the situations that the teacher views as relevant to the issues at hand. To use Saxe and Bermudez's terminology, we might say that not just any "emergent goals" emerge. Although teachers may have to treat as legitimate unforeseen interpretations made by students, over the long run interpretations championed by teachers will win out.

In both chapters we find analysis of children's development of mathematical knowledge through interaction with others. Both proposals recognize the role of the subjects as well as the essential role of social interactions in the construction of knowledge. There are, however, important differences between the two descriptions of how knowledge develops through interaction.

In Saxe and Bermudez's analysis the interaction takes place in the context of a game where children compete with each other in order to win the game. Saxe and Bermudez stress the importance of interactions in the establishment of children's own goals, which will allow the construction of new mathematical concepts. These goals are different from those intended by the general structure of the game, but they constitute the pathway for the development of mathematical concepts. No discussions about the meaning of concepts needs to take place, and therefore ambiguities and negotiation in this context does not refer to the meaning of concepts. Instead they focus on the goals themselves. Voigt's analysis focuses on interactions among children or among children and teachers that take place in schools. He stresses the ambiguity concerning the meaning of mathematical concepts found in classroom situations, as well as the need for and the role of negotiation among partners in the constitution of common mathematical meanings. In schools, as in the examples provided by Voigt, children are mainly reflecting upon mathematical properties and relations by themselves, and not as means to reach external goals. While Saxe and Bermudez's emergent goals model fits the game situations well, Voigt's analysis provides an account of what happens in classrooms and in situations where the ultimate goal is to look at mathematics as an object, and not as a tool (see Douady, 1985, for a discussion on mathematics as tool and as object).

Another important difference between the two analyses appears when we consider the types of ambiguities and conflicts that take place in the two environments. Voigt focuses his analysis on ambiguities that are bound to appear when teachers and pupils discuss on the basis of the previous different meanings each attributes to the tasks they deal with. From his description it seems to us that ambiguities and conflicts are more frequent between teachers and pupils than between pupils working together. They also seem to be more evident in tasks where the goals to be reached are not clear for the pupil from the start. A frequent feature of the teacher/pupil interactions seem to be questions and answers that have to do with what is it that the teacher wants the pupil to notice. It is possible that such ambiguities also occur in games or in everyday situations where mathematical knowledge occurs. However, the fact that the general goals of the tasks in these contexts are established from the beginning may prevent the appearance of such ambiguities. But we have to keep in mind that, even in nontraditional classrooms, we are dealing with teachers and students who were, most likely, educated in traditional educational environments where the teachers always had the last word and where it was their duty to tell children whether they were right or wrong. With the onset of new educational views, many of them adopt the new proposals and verbally express this adoption.

But it is one thing to embrace a new educational view and a very different one to put it into practice. Some of the ambiguities and conflicts documented by Voigt and by recent studies on the impact of constructivistic or interactional views in classroom activities could be, at least in part, a cultural artifact or a result of teachers and students previous experiences in traditional classroom contexts. Certain types of ambiguities and misunderstandings in interactional classroom contexts could be not an essential characteristic of classroom interactions and school learning situations, but a result of the transitional period we are now going through. Studies on the development of knowledge in other cultural environments should help to clarify the issue. Cross-cultural studies comparing, for instance, interactional activities in Japanese or in French classrooms with those in American schools would be specially helpful in clarifying these issues. The Japanese tradition emphasizes interaction in the solution of well-structured problems in the classroom. In this case the goals seem to be established from the beginning and the teachers are experienced in coping with children's different views in the classroom. The French didactical engineering approach gives emphasis to the structure of the task to be discussed and a careful step-by-step plan is followed by the teacher and pupils in their interactions toward common mathematical understanding. Would ambiguities and conflicts in these environments occur in the same way as described by Voigt in traditional and in transitional teaching environments? Comparative analysis would be helpful in the generalization of Voigt's model and could also provide useful insights for the improvement of classroom interactional activities.

Given the differences between school and out-of-school contexts, a question that immediately comes into mind is whether or not mathematical concepts developed in such different environments, with different aims, differ. In our previous work (Carraher, Carraher, & Schliemann, 1985; Nunes, Schliemann, & Carraher, 1993) we showed that, despite the different strategies they use to solve problems in out of schools contexts, children develop an understanding of the mathematical models and concepts they use as tools in their everyday activities. Although using different symbols and applying mathematics to different situations, children who learn mathematics in out of school environments display understanding of the same logical invariants that are at the base of school mathematics (see Vergnaud, 1985, for his analysis of concepts as invariants, symbols and situations). Our studies also show that meaning plays an important role in the solution of problems in everyday activities, whereas school problem-solving activities focus more on the use of algorithmic rules. As a result (see Schliemann, 1985; Schliemann & Nunes, 1990; Nunes, Schliemann, & Carraher, 1993) strategies and solutions to problems that appear in real-life contexts are usually meaningful and correct, whereas in schools, rules are used without understanding and absurd errors are not detected by children.

But our analyses of school mathematics were based on data collected among pupils who were participating in traditional mathematics classrooms, where conceptual understanding and meaning were usually neither the focus nor the aim of teaching activities. In order to get a clearer picture of the types of mathematical understandings children develop in different interactive activities, we need detailed analysis about the concepts and strategies they develop in environments such as the one provided by Saxe and Bermudez's game or in the interactive classroom settings described by Voigt. This should constitute our next step toward relevant analysis for a better mathematical education. For this we need to have, in future studies of mathematical knowledge in games or in classroom settings, a clear picture of the previous mathematical understandings and concepts children bring to the task and detailed analysis about which new pieces of knowledge they develop as a result of different interactional activities. We need to know which mathematical invariants children construct during their activities, which new rules, concepts, or modes of representations they adopt, which new relations or structures they discover. We also have to analyze the role that information and conventions provided by the others play. Such analyses are needed not only to provide suggestions for better mathematics education but also to contribute to a better understanding of the psychological issues related to how new knowledge comes to be constructed, discovered, and used by children.

REFERENCES

Carraher, D. W. (1991). Mathematics in and out of school: A selective review of studies from Brazil. In M. Harris (Ed.), *Schools, mathematics and work* (pp. 169–201). London, Falmer.

Carraher, T. N. (1986). From drawings to buildings: Working with mathematical scales. *International Journal of Behavioural Development, 9,* 527–544.

Carraher, T. N., Carraher, D. W., & Schliemann, A. D. (1982). Na vida, dez; Na escola, zero: Os contextos culturais de Educação Matemática [In life, ten; in school, zero: The cultural contexts of mathematics education]. *Cadernos de Pesquisa, 42,* 79–86.

Carraher, T. N., Carraher, D. W., & Schliemann, A. D. (1985). Mathematics in the streets and in schools. *British Journal of Developmental Psychology, 3,* 21–29.

Douady, R. (1985). The interplay between different settings: Tool object dialectic in the extension of mathematical ability. In L. Streefland (Ed.), *Proceedings of the IX International Conference for the Psychology of Mathematics Education.* Noordwijkerhout, Holland, pp. 33–52.

Lave, J. (1977). Cognitive consequences of traditional apprenticeship training in Africa. *Anthropology and Educational Quarterly, 7,* 177–180.

Nunes, T., Schliemann, A. D., & Carraher, D. W. (1993). *Street mathematics and school mathematics.* New York: Cambridge University Press.

Schliemann, A. D. (1985). Mathematics among carpenters and carpenters apprentices: Implications for school teaching. In P. Damerow, M. Dunckley, B. Nebres, & B. Werry (Eds.), *Mathematics for all* (pp. 92–95). Science and Technology Education Document Series, Paris, UNESCO, No. 2562.

Schliemann, A. D., & Acioly, N. M. (1989). Mathematical knowledge developed at work: the contributions of practice versus the contribution of schooling. *Cognition and Instruction, 6(3),* 185–221.

Schliemann, A. D., & Carraher, D. W. (1992). Proportional reasoning in and out of schools. In P. Light & G. Butterworth (Eds.), *Context and cognition* (pp. 47–73). Hemel Hempstead: Harvester-Wheatsheaf.

Schliemann, A. D., & Magalhães, V. P. (1990). Proportional reasoning: From shops, to kitchens, laboratories, and, hopefully, schools. *Proceedings of the XIV International Conference for the Psychology of Mathematics Education.* Oaxtepec, México, pp. 67–73.

Schliemann, A. D., & Nunes, T. (1990). A situated schema of proportionality. *British Journal of Developmental Psychology, 8,* 259–268.

Vergnaud, G. (1985). Concepts et schemes dans une théorie opératoire de la réprésentation. *Psychologie Française, 30*(3–4), 245–252.

6 Social Interaction and Individual Cognition

Erna Yackel
Purdue University Calumet

The contrasting starting points for the chapters by Voigt and by Saxe and Bermudez (chapters 2 and 3, this volume) indicate the breadth of investigations in mathematics education that fall within sociological and anthropological perspectives. On the one hand, Voigt gives a detailed theoretical development of social interaction and mathematics learning based on analyses of classroom practice. On the other hand, Saxe and Bermudez provide an extensive study of children's mathematical activity in a street selling setting (Saxe, 1991). The latter chapter illustrates how an analytic framework developed in an out-of-school setting is useful for making sense of children's mathematical activity while engaged in a school-type task. Despite their different starting points, the authors of both chapters attempt to coordinate the perspectives of social interaction and individual cognition.

REACTION TO VOIGT'S CHAPTER

Voigt's chapter exemplifies the importance of careful attention to theoretical underpinnings. He sets out to accomplish three main purposes. First, he argues for the need to consider cultural and social dimensions of learning; second, he outlines various theoretical positions regarding mathematics learning in cultural context; and third, he explains the potential of social interactionism for coordinating a focus on the subject with a focus on culture. His selection of examples from classrooms in two different countries and from both traditional and reformed instructional practice indicates the potential of the developed theoretical constructs for clarifying contemporary issues in mathematics education. Two of these issues have been selected for discussion here. The first is the nature of mathematics, and the second is the idea of Bildung.

The Nature of Mathematics

In order to make the case for the importance of cultural and social dimensions to mathematics learning, Voigt engages the reader in a discussion about nature of mathematics, both of school mathematics and mathematician's mathematics. In this discussion he refers to the distinction between "creation" and "discovery" and argues for the importance of the social dimension of school mathematics because "we cannot presume that the learner would ascribe specific meanings to the topic by themselves—meanings which are compatible with the meanings the teacher wants the student to ascribe" (Voigt, chapter 2, this volume). The implication is that the social dimension serves a function of validation, as in the example of the student's attempt to extend the concepts of even and odd to fractions. It could be argued that the notion of validation itself implies a view of mathematics as a body of (external) knowledge that a learner should come to know.

This same view is implied by the distinction between creating concepts and discovering laws. An alternative interpretation is that "mathematical objects" like all other "objects" are social creations (Blumer, 1969) and as such become "objects" for individuals in the classroom through the process of social interaction. For example, rings, ideals, fields, integral domains, and mappings are not things that we can point to and "see" in the world around us. Yet in the mind of the mathematician they are real mathematical objects. At the level of elementary school mathematics, we might talk about "the ten" in 15, as though it is an object that can be pointed at. Voigt elaborates this view himself later in the chapter at some length while discussing the development of taken-as-shared meanings through the process of negotiation. As Voigt says, "the accomplishment of inter-subjective meanings taken as mathematical ones is essential in mathematics teaching and learning" and "The participants interact as if they interpret the mathematical topic of their discourse equally" (Voigt, chapter 2, this volume). Thus, he seemingly presents two views of mathematics. On the one hand, taken-as-shared meanings are developed through the process of negotiation. On the other hand, the mathematician's mathematics is an external body of knowledge that the learner should approximate. Voigt deals with this difficulty by noting that the meaning of "mathematical meaning" is ambiguous. He distinguishes between mathematical meaning as understood "with regard to an epistemological theory of mathematics" and mathematical meaning "with regard to a psychological theory of subjective sense-making processes." This difficult issue deserves further clarification because it is the source of much misunderstanding among mathematics educators and between mathematics educators and mathematicians.

Bildung as the Goal of Mathematics Education

Voigt introduces the notion of Bildung from the German tradition of education to explain his rationale for taking the individual as the starting point and consequently taking an interactionist approach as opposed to alternative approaches to social interaction. In the current climate where much research is based on attempts to apply social interaction theories to mathematics education, Voigt's careful attention to selecting which theory to use based on specific goals is refreshing. As Voigt explains, his selection of symbolic interactionism is based on its potential for mediating between the foci on the subject and on culture. This is, in turn, based on the purpose of mathematics education. According to Voigt, "The prominent objective of mathematics education is not that the students produce objectively solutions to mathematical problems but that they do it insightfully and by reasonably thinking" (chapter 2, this volume). This objective, which derives from the German notion of Bildung, captures the spirit of the American reform as outlined in the *Curriculum and Evaluation Standards for School Mathematics* (NCTM, 1989) and is consistent with the Piagetian notion of autonomy (Kamii, 1989). It therefore provides a rationale for other researchers as well for using a symbolic interactionist approach to social interaction. Voigt's decision to use symbolic interactionism is a pragmatic decision rather than an essentialist claim and in this sense itself indicates a constructivist way of working.

REACTION TO THE CHAPTER BY SAXE AND BERMUDEZ

The chapter by Saxe and Bermudez (chapter 3, this volume) discusses and illustrates an analytic framework for linking social processes and mathematics cognition that was first developed in the course of studying the candy-selling practices of Brazilian children. In this sense, the chapter illustrates the potential utility of analyses at one level and in one setting for guiding analyses at another level and in a different setting. The framework, which was developed in the course of analyzing mathematical cognition and cultural practices, is now used at the level of investigating classroom activity.

Inferences About Students' Goals

The "emergent goals" model is designed to emphasize the dynamic nature of children's experience as they engage in mathematical activity. The notion of "emergent mathematical environment" is consistent with a hermeneutical interpretative stance (Mehan & Wood, 1975). Individuals engage in interpretation, but once they do so the interpretation becomes part of their understanding. Their now altered "world" appears to them as their "autonomous reality" (Mehan &

Wood, 1975, p. 193). It is this autonomous reality that emerges for a student as he or she engages in a particular task—in this case, in the Treasure Hunt Game—that Saxe and Bermudez call the student's mathematical environment. This autonomous reality is similar to Cobb's notion of context (Cobb, 1990). Bauersfeld (1991) described it as follows:

> [Mathematics] problems [are] always problems forming. . . . And every step and every decision taken in the process of dealing with "the problem" changes the issue. What in the end the problem has been for the individual is open to an interpretative reconstruction from step to step in retrospect only. It is a kind of biography of this "problem" related to this specific "solver." (p. 17)

In the discussion of goals, it would be useful for Saxe and Bermudez to distinguish between goals in the mind of the observer, in this case the researcher, and the goals that the children have as they play the Treasure Hunt Game. For example, the authors refer to the emergence of addition and subtraction goals or to the lack of their emergence due to certain routines enacted by some of the children: "The new rule led to Toni's formulation of a subtraction goal—to pay 6 from her treasure chest" (Saxe & Bermudez, chapter 3, this volume). It could be argued that Toni's goal may have been simply to complete the transaction and then represent her gold in the standard orthography in her gold register. She could be acting much like a customer who enters a store, pays the clerk the amount of the item(s) purchased, and then, after the transaction is complete, counts his money to figure out how much he has now. In that case we would not say that the customer had a subtraction goal, but rather a goal of completing the transaction and figuring out how much money was left. One of the values of microsociological analyses is that it allows the investigator to make distinctions such as this because the intentions of the actors are taken into account. It is understood, of course, that the investigator is making inferences based on the actor's activity.

Caution also needs to be exercised when inferring students' cognitive activity. For instance, in the example in which Jorge had 9(100)s, 8(10)s, and 20(1)s and realized that he could trade for 1000, the inference is made that he calculated the following series of trades: 20 ones for 2 tens, the resulting 10 tens for a hundred, and the 10 hundreds for a thousand. However, without confirming evidence of such trades, we might also infer that he used a purely numerical approach, 980 and 20 is 1000, without thinking of trading at all.

The Role of Values

A final observation on the chapter relates to the role of values. In their analysis Saxe and Bermudez use rules, values, and routines to describe what they call the "actual activity structure" of the game, but describe what they call the "intended structure" by stating the objective, rules, and the cyclic phase of organization. It is important to realize that the intended structure is based on values as well, values that guided the developers, perhaps unintentionally. For example, an implicit assumption underlying the challenge phase of the game is that it is important to not make errors. When playing the game, before a player completes a turn he or she should have everything right because the effect of making an error is that the challenge of the player's partner will result in the partner gaining gold. This implicit emphasis on being correct is consistent with the value that is placed on not making errors in an overwhelming number of American mathematics classrooms. It would be interesting to see the game altered to omit this phase and instead be structured to encourage students to help each other when they have difficulty with transactions and with recording results. This apparently subtle difference is precisely the type of issue that Saxe and Bermudez intend to take into account when considering interactions between the social and cultural dimensions and children's emerging mathematical environment. This example affords researchers the opportunity to become aware that there are implicit assumptions underlying their own activity, including the activity of developing instructional tasks. In this sense, Saxe and Bermudez have illustrated the point they wish to make, namely, that one's values influence one's interpretation of a task and consequently one's activity.

CONCLUDING REMARKS

These two chapters illustrate the potential for using approaches to study students' mathematical development that account for both social interaction and individual cognition. Both chapters stress the dynamic nature of a learning situation, as students interpret a task and/or the comments of a teacher or peer. The notions of emergent mathematical environments and negotiation of mathematical meaning that are elaborated in these chapters illustrate the complexities that arise when attempting to coordinate sociological and psychological perspectives.

REFERENCES

Bauersfeld, H. (1991, October). *Integrating theories for mathematics education.* Invited address at the Thirteenth annual meeting of the North American Group for the Psychology of Mathematics Education. Blacksburg, VA.

Blumer, H. (1969). *Symbolic interactionism: Perspective and method.* Englewood Cliffs, NJ: Prentice Hall.

Cobb, P. (1990). Multiple perspectives. In L. P. Steffe & T. Wood (Eds.), *Transforming children's mathematics education: International perspectives* (pp. 200–215). Hillsdale, NJ: Lawrence Erlbaum Associates.

Kamii, C. (1989). *Young children continue to reinvent arithmetic second grade: Implications of Piaget's theory.* New York: Teachers College Press.

Mehan, H., & Wood, H. (1975). *The reality of ethnomethodology.* New York: John Wiley.

National Council of Teachers of Mathematics. (1989). *Curriculum and evaluation standards for school mathematics.* Reston, VA: NCTM.

Saxe, G. B. (1991). *Culture and cognitive development: Studies in mathematical understanding.* Hillsdale, NJ: Lawrence Erlbaum Associates.

7 Learning Mathematics as a Meaningful Activity

Bert van Oers
Vrije Universiteit, Amsterdam

MATHEMATICS EDUCATION AND THE QUEST FOR MEANING

In the past decade increasing demands have been placed on individuals' mathematical skills. Concurrently, however, educationalists have come to acknowledge to an increasing extent the shortcomings of most traditional forms of mathematics instruction. There is now wide agreement among educationalists and teachers that mathematics education should not consist in cramming pupils' heads with mathematical facts, nor should it consist in merely teaching (sophisticated) mathematical techniques or general cognitive skills. This criticism has been expressed worldwide and in a variety of ways (Fischer, 1990; Freudenthal, 1978; Greer & Mulhern, 1989, to name just a few).

In a counterreaction to the situation criticized here, mathematics is portrayed as a "way of knowing" (Bishop, 1988), as a culturally developed activity meant for the structuring of a person's experience. In its capacity as a structuring device, great successes have been attributed to mathematics in Western thinking. Probably as a result of its achievements, mathematical activity could make history and has become a part of the cultural legacy of our community.

From this view point, mathematics education has to be conceived of as a form of *enculturation* in which the young generation is prompted to appropriate (in some honest and meaningful form) this cultural legacy. Mathematical enculturation, then, is the pupils' and teachers' pursuit of making sense of mathematics as it is embodied (formally or informally) in various practices in the surrounding world. Bruner (1986) described such enculturation as a process of constant negotiation and recreation of cultural meanings. He wrote (p. 123), "a culture is constantly in process of being recreated as it is interpreted and renegotiated by its members. In this view, a culture is as much a *forum* for negotiating and renegotiating meaning and for explicating action as it is a set of rules or specifications for action." In Bruner's view education is a constant quest for meaning. In the wake of this view, I conceive of mathematics learning as a process of making sense of mathematics as it is brought to us by cultural history (see also Bishop, 1988; Cobb, 1990). A theory of mathematical learning must be able to account for this process of meaning formation within the context of the school. In my opinion, such a theory must be basically a psychological theory. Although presumably not all mathematical educationists will agree with me on the relevance of such a psychologically oriented approach toward mathematics education (see, e.g., Freudenthal, 1978), my approach here is, nevertheless, mainly psychological. In this chapter, I expound a theory of meaningful mathematics learning from a Vygotskian point of view (be it only sketchily), by way of applying Vygotskian principles for the domain of mathematics education.

I put my argument along the following line. After my analysis of the kinds of meaning, I explain my view on mathematics. Subsequently, I focus on my general theory of learning. A theory of mathematics learning then is described as a specification of this general learning theory, constrained by a view on mathematics. In a final section I reflect briefly on the assessment of the value of this theory, concentrating on the new issues that this theory can contribute to this domain of study and that probably would remain beyond the scope of a purely mathematical–didactical approach. In order to put my argument into a conceptual framework, I first sketch a few starting points of a Vygotskian approach to education.

GENERAL CHARACTERISTIC
OF A VYGOTSKIAN APPROACH

In the elaborations of the Vygotskian cultural–historical view of human development, the process of meaningful appropriation of culture is generally considered to be essential (see, e.g., Rogoff, 1990; Wardekker, 1991; Wertsch, 1991). Education for Vygotsky was basically a process of enculturation (see Yaroshevski, 1989), in which children are encouraged and assisted in the appropriation of a broad range of fundamental knowledge and understanding, combined with a humanistic cast of mind. The main aim of education is the personal and cultural development of the individual. However, culture should not be imposed upon pupils. Instead, pupils should be assisted by representatives of the community (parents, teachers) in the attempt to reconstruct (reinvent) valuable cultural elements in a meaningful way. The Vygotskian cultural–historical approach thus entails a concept of education in which meaningful learning is made dependent on the pupils' opportunity to evaluate their own insights and ideas in critical comparison with culturally available concepts, norms and methods.[1]

One of the basic tenets of the Vygotskian approach to education is the assumption that individual learning is dependent on social interaction. However, it should be clear from the outset that this is not merely a statement of correlation between individual learning and social context. This thesis should be interpreted in its strongest possible form, proposing that the qualities of thinking are actually generated by the organizational features of the social interaction. When we want some mental function (like reflection, evaluation, logical memory, etc.) to emerge in the developing child, the educative interactions with the child must be organized in such a way that the fulfillment of this function is provided for already at the social level (in a public way) by one of the participants. This means that one of the participants must actually take the role of a public "reflector," "evaluator," "supplier of new and contrasting viewpoints," or whatever mental function we want to develop in the participating children (see Cole, 1990; Wertsch, 1985). The availability of these psychological functions (at the social or individual level) will subsequently influence the quality and content of specific (mathematical) concepts.

Thus, the distinctive properties of the interactions among adults and children can be said to have a strong impact on the quality of educational results. By embedding new actions, roles, or social functions into a socially shared activity, new learning processes can be promoted. It is this kind of learning that will promote the child's development, according to Vygotsky (1978). The systematic attempt to provide this kind of learning in school is referred to here as *developmental teaching* (see Davydov, 1988).

TWO KINDS OF MEANING

Two kinds of meaning are involved in the process of education. According to Leont'ev (1975), we have to distinguish *cultural meaning* (značenie) from *personal meaning* (sense; smysl') in the process of enculturation. Cultural meaning refers to the generalized knowledge and skills for dealing with the world that have been built up throughout cultural history. Cultural meanings are represented by symbols, mostly language, but as Leont'ev (1975, pp. 140–141) stated, "Although language is the carrier of meanings, it is not itself the creator of meanings. Behind lexical meanings lie the culturally developed methods of acting, with which man can change and cognize the world." Broadly speaking, we can conceive of cultural meaning as a body of cultural knowledge (including

---

[1]Similiar concepts of education have been described in western literature as well. See Young's (1989) "critical education," Jackson's (1986) "transformative approach to teaching," or Fenstermacher and Soltis's (1986) "liberationist view" on education.

both declarative and procedural knowledge), embodied in the historically approved and symbolically codified actions and methods of acting in a certain domain of human activity.

On the other hand, Leont'ev distinguished another kind of meaning, one that is related to the sphere of human motives. This personal meaning (sense) is based on the attribution of personal value to the actions and goals as actually generated within an activity (in relation to some problem or task) from the perspective of one's personal motives. As such, "sense" expresses the personal significance that an individual attaches to actions and goals within a cultural activity, considering its motives, its perceived position in the world or society, and its ambitions and aim in life (see Leont'ev, 1975, pp. 149–158).

It is important not to confuse these two kinds of meaning. Cultural meaning can be transformed into curriculum content and, as such, it can be taught. Personal meaning (sense), however, cannot be taught directly; it can only be built up by involvement in an educative relationship (Leont'ev, 1975, p. 286). However, these two kinds of meaning should not be treated as independent phenomena, as Leont'ev pointed out. Education for personal meaning obviously requires some object (cultural meaning) to attach values to, whereas the teaching of cultural meanings somehow or other becomes intermingled with personal sense. The attempt to transmit cultural meaning without allowing pupils to attach personal sense to it—as is often the case in traditional instruction—generally ends up in formal rote learning. According to Leont'ev, such learning actually results in dehumanizing the individual.

Considering the curriculum and the issue of school learning, we can now conceptualize the meaningfulness of the learning process in terms of the two kinds of meaning. On the one hand, the meaningfulness refers to the subject matter. It should be defined as the culturally developed and approved meanings occurring within some sociocultural activity. On the other hand, the meaningfulness of the learning process refers to the process of attaching personal sense to the actions, rules, methods and values as provided by a school subject (discipline). Learning as a process of appropriation of culture, then, is meaningful as far as it encompasses both kinds of meaning. Hence, the learning of mathematics as a meaningful activity refers both to the process of technically mastering mathematics as an historically developed activity and to the process of attaching personal meaning to the actions, methods, and results involved. Only then can this learning promote the personal and cultural development of the individual.

MATHEMATICS AS A CULTURAL ACTIVITY

To begin with, let me unequivocally state the intention of this section. I do not make any attempt to define the essence of mathematics. As far as defining mathematics is concerned, I think this is a job that mathematicians have to accomplish among themselves. And in fact they do, as history teaches us. The history of mathematics can be characterized as a long series of lively debates among mathematicians about what is to be accepted as valid mathematics. What rules of proof are to be followed in order to find certain, uncontestable results? What assumptions can be adopted as valid? Which results produced by mathematicians are to be accepted in the body of mathematical knowledge? There are more questions like these. Obviously, not all proposals put forward by mathematicians have been accepted immediately and with great enthusiasm by the mathematical community. Some mathematical terms still testify to the original judgements and feelings of the mathematicians. One need only take a look at such terms as "irrational numbers" and "negative numbers" (see Struik, 1990).

This sketchy picture provides a basis for an educationally relevant conception of mathematics as it really is. "Real mathematics" is conceived of here as the historically developing human pursuit of making sense of the quantitative and relational aspects of our physical and cultural world by way of reasoning, discourse, and judgements regarding to what is or is not to be accepted as "mathematical."

As psychologists we do not necessarily have to get mixed up in this mathematical tête-à-tête. Rather, we should analyze the opinions of historically influential mathematicians and observe, listen to, and speak with living mathematicians and mathematics users. Relying on that information, I have tried to figure out what is meant when people claim to employ mathematics or to carry out mathematical activity. From those observations, a more specified picture of "real" mathematical activity can be put together. I take this picture as a normative basis for instructional practice in the domain of mathematics education.

There is a rich literature about the history of mathematics, showing how mathematics has developed through the ages (Barabašev, 1983; Dijksterhuis, 1990; Struik, 1948, 1990; Wilder, 1968). In addition, there are also several very informative narratives about mathematics as an intellectual endeavor, written by mathematicians on the basis of self-observations (Freudenthal, 1973; Hadamard, 1945; Lamon, 1972; Otte, 1974).

The picture that arises as a result of such observations is evidently historical. As I said, the image of mathematics that has evolved through the ages is continually developing as a result of debates and negotiations among mathematicians regarding the nature of mathematics. Most interesting for the present argument, however, is the fact that there are characteristics that are generally taken for granted by most (if not all) mathematicians. For the sake of brevity, I mention only those characteristics that are most important for my argument and educational purposes:

- Mathematicians agree that mathematics is based on the curiosity for structures in human thought; as such it is concerned with the process of reasoning with variables and their relations.

- Mathematics is not to be confused with the results of mathematical labour as presented in books and journals. Mathematics is the activity of mathematicians and mathematics users. This activity is rule bound, but never completely determined by one homogeneous set of rules. Being a problem-solving activity, mathematics is to be characterized as an "untidy activity," as Griffith once put it: It is "sometimes wrong, often based on guesswork, or on folk theorems with no public proof, and expressed in various languages and notations" (Griffith, 1978, p. 16). Expressive examples of the "untidy activity" in the mathematical workplace are given by Lakatos (1976). For the use of mathematics in everyday thinking, see Lave (1988).

- Mathematics is a means for the organization of mental or empirical experiences. Mathematics has an instrumental value. Freudenthal (1973, p. 16) wrote, "Mathematics started as a useful activity and today it is more useful than it ever was. This is, however, an understatement. One should say: if it were not useful, mathematics would not exist."

- Mathematics depends on the use of symbols. In a certain sense, the history of mathematics can be characterized as a struggle for adequate symbols (notations) for the expression and communication of (new) mathematical ideas. According to the well-known historian of mathematics Struik (1948, 1990), the importance of symbols can hardly be underestimated in the development of mathematical activity. All great breakthroughs in mathematical thinking are accompanied by the invention of new symbolic instruments (notations).

In this characterization of mathematics as an historically developing socio-cultural activity, several aspects are articulated (e.g., problem solving, negotiation and communication, mental organization, symbol formation, construction). Any psychological theory of mathematics learning should be able to deal with these issues. However, before we can discuss this theory in greater detail, we have to take a sidestep to a general theory of learning.

LEARNING AS A MEANINGFUL ACTIVITY

Learning in the Zone of Proximal Development

As Vygotsky once wrote, "Human learning presupposes a specific social nature and a process by which children grow into the intellectual life of those around them" (Vygotsky, 1978, p. 88). More specifically, Vygotsky showed that people obtain access to their cultural environment through participating as an apprentice in sociocultural activities. As explained earlier in this chapter, the organizational features of this interaction actually determine the qualities of the resulting mental functions.

In the beginning children can accomplish only a minor part of this common activity. They have to be assisted by their parents or older children, who carry out those parts of the activity that the young children cannot perform themselves. When this cooperative activity is repeated and the young child is adequately helped, we can observe that the child gradually takes over most or all of the functions he or she could not perform at first. Imagine, for instance, how a child learns to ride a bike. At first the child eagerly wants to ride a bike. However, the child can only ride a bike when someone else (or some material device) helps the child to balance, steer the bike, and move forward. Gradually, we can observe that the child takes over the functions of balancing, steering, and pedaling. To put this example in Vygotskian terms, actually the child imitates the cultural activity of riding a bike, and it can do so because it is helped by an older person or a more capable peer. The child gradually interiorizes all the functions it could not perform initially.

Imitating a sociocultural activity with the help of others constitutes the essence of what Vygotsky called the *zone of proximal development* (see Vygotsky, 1982, p. 248; Vygotsky, 1978). According to Vygotsky, the zone of proximal development is the activity setting in which the child can learn with the greatest developmental effects. This zone is constructed in the cooperation between the child and the adult (parent, teacher) on the basis of what the child wants and the actions the child actually can carry out, as well as the help the child gets from the adult. It is the adult's task to look for ways to communicate with the child in such a way that the latter can participate at least in a minimal way within the sociocultural activity and can eventually come to define the task setting in a new, culturally more appropriate way, or even perform the task in a more proficient way (see also Lave & Wenger, 1991; Wertsch, 1985, pp. 67–76).

Learning within the zone of proximal development obviously makes sense for the child, because the need for this learning emerges from the activity the child wanted to be involved in. What the child learns within this sociocultural activity setting is significant for the child's ongoing activity because it contributes to his or her abilities to participate. However, the zone of proximal development does not generate learning automatically; it is only a sense-supporting context for learning. As Bruner once put it, it is "a scaffold" (Bruner, 1985) that helps the child move (or better: struggle) upward along the line of cultural development.

An Action-Psychological Approach to Learning

The Vygotskian approach to learning and development is intrinsically related to an action-psychological theory (see Davydov & Radzikhovskii, 1985; van Oers, 1990; Zinchenko, 1985). On the basis of the research of van Parreren (1954, 1978), Leont'ev (1975), and Gal'perin (1969), we can define an *action* as an attempt to change some (material or mental) object from its initial form into another form. Sawing a plank is obviously an action, because it changes the plank into pieces of wood; by the same reasoning we can say that striking a match and tying a shoelace are actions. Moreover, it is possible to perform actions on a mental level too. Transforming on the mental plane the formula 2 + 2 into another form (e.g., 4 or 5 − 1) is also an action, as well as working out a definition for "friendship" or making a plan for a letter.

A characteristic aspect of human action is that humans can reflect on the execution of their actions and subsequently can improve or even radically change their performance. This reflection part of an action (in advance or afterwards) is called *orientation*. It is focused on the object-related actions, on the method of changing this object, and on how to evaluate the results. Orientation is meant for finding a reasonable action in a given situation. In this orientational act people often employ available cultural instruments (knowledge, rules, approved methods, concepts) in a personally reasonable way in order to estimate the situation and to plan the actions so as to reach optimal results. It should be clear that this is not a purely rational decision procedure.

In this view learning is conceived of as a process of qualitative change of an action or an activity. At least two variants can be distinguished here (see also van Oers, 1990, in press):

1. Extension: The repertoire of available actions is enlarged by the addition of a new action; within the current activity the child can perform an action he could not do before.

2. Microgenetic development: The way an action is performed changes into a new—often more proficient—form. The action can become more fluent, abridged, transferrable to other situations, automatized, and so on. The child can now perform an old action in a qualitatively new way.

An important moment in a learning process is the moment an action becomes related to a sign or symbol. From that moment on, the action is a part of the meaning of that sign or symbol. It then becomes possible to evoke that action with the help of the sign, to communicate about that action or to store it consciously in the memory. As Gal'perin (1969; see also Sabel'nikov, 1982) showed, an action can become interiorized (transformed onto a mental level) and abridged. In that case, some parts of the action have been erased or combined into one new form. As a result, the action becomes more and more condensed, eventually collapsing into a momentary event coincidental with the sight or the hearing of the sign (symbol). In this microgenetic process the original action has been transformed into a psychological event, immediately occurring upon the appearance of the sign, without even evoking the subjective experience of an action. Paradoxically, it now becomes possible to "perform" the original action without actually performing it, but only by thinking about it or referring to its sign (see van Parreren & Carpay, 1980; van Oers, 1987, in press). As we have tried to explain elsewhere, this process of abbreviation is very important in the development of mathematical thinking (see van Oers, 1990).

Through the ages, teachers have tried all kinds of strategies to promote learning (changes of actions or activity). Reasoning from a cultural-historical perspective, Davydov (1988) contended that this strategy of teaching is itself culturally developing, often in close relationship with a theory of learning. Only in this century have we come to recognize that the orientational part of an activity is the basic concern in the teaching–learning process. In the wake of this insight, the activity of deliberate, constructive knowledge production was acknowledged as a valuable strategy of learning in school. This "learning activity" (as Davydov calls it) must be modeled after the activity of knowledge production in the sciences. In fact, this kind of learning is also a cultural-historically developed activity. Pupils should be exposed to it in due time in order to get them involved in an activity of scholarly learning. As I have argued elsewhere (van Oers, in press), the basis of this learning activity is the negotiation of meanings, the exchange and comparison of a pupil's meanings in relation to some problem at hand with the meanings of others (including the teacher). Hence we call this form of learning *discursive learning activity* (see also Roegholt, 1993, for further elaborations). Actually, this learning can be considered as a sociocultural form of orientation on future activity.

It is important to note here that the discursive character of this learning activity implies two kinds of discussion. On the one hand it requires discussions (negotiations of meaning) with actually present people (adults, pupils), trying to find out jointly what can validly be said about the subject at hand. We can call this kind of discussion *dialogue*. On the other hand there is need for discussions (in a more metaphorical sense) with historical agents trying to figure out the value of their ideas regarding to the problem at hand. Discursive learning activity encompasses both kinds of discussions. In this case we speak (with Davydov, 1988) of *polylogue*. From a cultural-historical point of view dialogue is mostly too much restricted to the insights accidentally available here and now. Discursive learning in the full cultural-historical sense requires polylogue. Ultimately, humans can only understand themselves when they have tested their words (symbols-in-use) on all possible others, both contemporary and historical others (see also van Oers, in press).

Children are then assumed to learn in a way comparable to that of scientists. This is not to say that the learning activity in school should be completely identical with the activity of professional scientists. Activities are flexible to a certain degree. They can be accommodated to the varying situational conditions without losing their identity. For educational purposes the learning activity must be tailored to the educational aims, the institutional conditions of schools, and to the psychological properties of the participating pupils (Fichtner, 1985). The most important rule that must be maintained here is that the shared activity is recognized as a genuine discursive learning activity by all the participants (including the teacher). Therefore, at least the dynamics of this learning process must compare to the process of constructive learning of scientists. That is, pupils will be allowed to ask their own questions, seek answers in many places, consider different perspectives, exchange views with others, and add their own findings to the existing understanding. The most important didactical point here is that pupils are encouraged to gather their own meanings in discussion with others (including culturally more experienced people). It is the teacher's task now to insert traditionally approved insights into the negotiations and to try to bring the pupils discursively to the reconstruction of the culturally shared meanings. This teaching—learning strategy provides both meaning and sense in the pupils' learning process.

Symbol Formation as a Semiotic Process

Learning processes as conceived of here heavily depend on the use of symbols. Indeed, symbols are the carriers of meaning and as such are the main vehicle in the enculturation process. Summarizing the foregoing argument, we can ascribe three important functions to symbols:

1. Symbols refer to a particular stock of related actions.
2. Symbols replace actions; they enable the thinker to accomplish a particular act not by performing a particular action, but by merely thinking of this action.
3. Symbols underpin the development of shared meaning; that is, they provide the tools for the negotiation of the meanings concerned.

Specifying the process of learning activity first of all amounts to gaining further insight into the process of symbol formation. The abundant research on this issue has made it clear that symbol formation is not a once-for-all event of association of meanings with a particular symbol (sign) (see, e.g., Glotova, 1990; Luria, 1976, 1981; Werner & Kaplan, 1963). Although association may be involved in the first phases of symbol formation, when actions within a particular context are performed in close relationship with a particular symbol, the development of the meaning of this symbol is an ongoing investigative activity of hypothesizing, testing, and negotiating related to what might be represented by the symbol involved. Reference is conceived of here not as a universal fact, but rather as an aspect of the regulation of social practices. The main process in the symbol formation, then, is the activity of figuring out and refining its meaning structure in communication with others. As such, we must characterize the symbol formation process as a semiotic activity aiming at the development of meaning (see also Hodge & Kress, 1988; Walkerdine, 1988; Wertsch, 1991). This is essentially a social, discursive enterprise.

As Vygotsky (1982) has already shown, this development of meaning is always based on the meanings already available for the learning person. Semiotic activity is initially focused on the development of word meanings toward socially shared, more elaborated, generalized and systematized forms. In fact, this developmental process of systematizing and generalizing word meanings constitutes the core of scholarly concept formation. In this process the real character of concept formation is revealed: Concept formation is the ongoing human activity of learning how to speak systematically about some part of (physical or cultural) reality (van Oers, 1987, in press). Considering this argument, it should be clear now that this is not an individual process but a sociocultural learning activity. As such, it may also be characterized as the mastery of a speech genre (Bakhtin, 1986; Wertsch, 1991) or the appropriation of a particular speech register (Halliday, 1978) in a particular domain of culture. In an abstract sense we can also say that concept formation is actually an activity of text-formation.

Viewing symbol formation in terms of semiotic activity directed at the development of word meaning into conceptual meanings brings to the fore the role of symbols (signs, words, and terms) as communicative instruments. A further specification needs to be given in this connection. From a Vygotskian perspective, it is not enough to learn how to use the symbols involved in a direct verbal communication (dialogue). There is more to symbol–concept formation than achieving consensus among social partners. Symbols also must assimilate the historically gathered insights in a certain domain of culture. Symbol–concept formation, therefore, strongly depends on interactions with meanings textually represented in written form (i.e., on "intertextuality;" see Carpay & van Oers, in press).

As Vygotsky (1978) and Luria (1981) stated, written symbols form a necessary element in a cultural-historical approach to literacy. With regard to this issue, Luria (1978, p. 193) contended, "The further development of literacy involves the assimilation of the mechanisms of culturally elaborated symbolic writing and the use of symbolic devices to simplify and expedite the act of recording." Even more important is the fact that this symbol formation transforms the whole process of cognitive functioning itself. With the use of symbols it becomes possible for the child to objectify meanings, compare and change them deliberately, exchange them with others, and purposefully reflect on the organization of the argument (see also Olson & Torrance, 1983; Scinto, 1986). Obviously, the use of (systems of) written symbols ("texts") is indispensable in the realization of a polylogue (see preceding section), certainly when we take seriously the communication with historical precursors.

The fully fledged process of symbol formation now turns out to be closely related to the process of concept formation. Both encompass the formation (and use) of symbols as spoken signs, as well the formation (and use) of symbols as written signs (Scinto, 1986) in relation to object-transforming (practical or mental) actions. Thus the process of symbol formation has to be founded in the act of making the transitions between object transforming actions, spoken language related to those actions, and (textually organized) written symbols, as shown in Fig. 7.1. In the process of symbol formation, all these elements (levels) must be

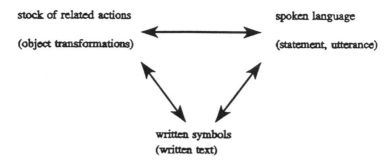

stock of related actions   spoken language

(object transformations)   (statement, utterance)

written symbols
(written text)

FIG. 7.1.   Relationships between actions and symbol systems.

provided and practiced. Special attention must be given to the possible and actual transitions from one level to the other (see also Dyson, 1990).

Developmental Issues

It is important to point out here that, in order to be meaningful, this kind of learning should constitute a zone of proximal development for the pupils in the sense already defined. Hence, one important educational concern should be the formation of the need for the participation in this kind of learning. It is not possible in the present context to dwell on this issue in great detail. Recent research, however, has revealed that this motive for learning is probably rooted in the play activity of young children (see Hakkarainen, 1985; Matjuchina, 1984). In the section on relevance I briefly return to this issue.

One consequence of this approach to symbol formation is that the activities of reading and writing become an essential part of semiotic activity (and mathematics learning as well). Several developmental issues are involved here.

Reasoning from our conception of the zone of proximal development, we can assume that the different tasks to be accomplished are at first socially distributed. In the beginning, such acts as organizing the discussions, providing historical information, critically evaluating the results of the negotiations, and writing results down may be put in the hands of the teacher.[2] Gradually, however, all these functions must be interiorized by the participating pupils. In fact, the teacher must organize the interactions so as to encourage pupils to take over these functions in due course of time. Wertsch (1985, pp. 162–164) has structured this interiorization as a process of developing intersubjectivity in which the child's

---

[2]We can add to this list the issue of watching over the cultural standards of an activity. In the long run the exertion of this authority also must be interiorized by the individual pupils. I believe that this learning also has to be dealt with in a discursive way. I cannot go into this thorny issue here in detail (see Wertsch, 1991, pp. 78–83, for a general treatment of this issue).

and the adult's situation definitions gradually match. Little by little the child learns to respond in a personally meaningful way to the regulation of the adult, and eventually to take over responsibility for carrying out the goal-directed task. It is essential to recall here the two kinds of meaning (as were distinguished in an earlier section). During this educative process the adult should never impose traditionally approved insights onto the pupils, regardless of the sense (personal-meaning) they can attach to them. The adult (teacher) should be constantly concerned with the presentation and comparative negotiation of the meanings of both the canonical (scientific) insights and the ideas of the pupils as worked out by their own constructive activities (as discussed earlier).

Another important question here relates to the qualities pupils must possess in order to participate meaningfully in this process of semiotic activity. With respect to this point, there are as yet many issues to be explained here by detailed investigations. One developmental aspect, however, seems to be very important in the light of recent research. In recent years, Russian researchers (Glotova, 1990; Podd'jakov & Govorkova, 1985; Salmina, 1988; Venger, 1986) have produced much evidence showing the importance of encouraging young children (at the age of 5–7 years) to develop some proficiency in schematizing all kinds of real and symbolic situations. These investigations have shown that, within the context of their play activities, children can learn to make schematic representations of the situations or objects they are dealing with. These young children learned, for instance, how to make diagrams of concrete situations, construction plans, schemes of a story, graphic notations of a melody, and so forth. In all these activities children were encouraged to explore the relations between some object (or situation) and the way it is represented. In this context they answered questions such as, what happens to the diagram (plan, design, scheme) when we change the situation (object) in such or such a way, or what should be changed in situation when we change the representation? The children learn in the context of their play activities how to make the transition(s) from object (situation) to some representation and vice versa. The empirical results of these research projects show that young children can learn this kind of semiotic activity, and that the appropriation of this quality provides a very advantageous precondition for the participation in the discursive learning activity in later years. In conclusion, there is some reason to assume that development of semiotic activity can be encouraged by teaching children how to schematize within the context of their play activities (see also van Oers, 1993). As research shows, this need not initially be dependent on domain-specific concept formation (cf. Langer, 1983). This general semiotic ability is probably a very powerful prerequisite for the participation in mathematical activities later on.

Although there are more prerequisites to attend to in an analysis of the beginning of mathematical education, restricted space does not allow us to discuss these here. Instead, we turn to the formulation of our theory of mathematics learning in terms of the theory described earlier.

MATHEMATICS LEARNING AS DISCURSIVE ACTIVITY

Mathematics as an Orientation Device

Considering the preceding sections, mathematical activity now can be characterized in terms of our psychological theory as an act of orientation. Sometimes (as was the case in the early days of mathematics) there is orientation on concrete actions in a problem situation (e.g., geometry problems, constructing a calendar, or distributing money or food), resulting in mathematical knowledge. At other moments, however, the thinker is often oriented on his or her own mathematical thinking with the help of mathematical means.

In any case, orientation is basically an act of exploration of the material or mental situation within the perspectives of the actors involved. Mathematics education, then, should assist pupils in the formation of their orientational actions with the help of the generally accepted mathematical method. Ultimately, the outcomes of this process must contribute to the process of personal and cultural development of the individual. To put it in terms of the present Vygotskian approach, we can say that mathematics education is basically founded on a process of developmental teaching within the domain of mathematics.

In accordance with the realistic view on mathematics we espoused earlier, we can now give the following general outline of a theory of mathematics learning.

Mathematical Apprenticeship

All mathematical learning should take place in the context of a sociocultural activity in which the pupils want to participate and in which they are able to participate given their actual abilities. The next step in the process of mathematics education is to provoke those actions within this activity that require orientation. For that reason, it is necessary to elicit actions that form a meaningful part of this activity, but that are problematic with regard to the way they should be carried out. Imagine, for example, a situation in which pupils (about 8 years of age) in a classroom are introduced to the activity of furnishing a new room. To save money we consider the possibility of using the floor covering of our old room (which we bought last year). The first question then will be, will it be large enough? And if so, how can we cut it in such a way that it will indeed fit in our new room (which has a different shape), and with as few joints as possible? It goes without saying that this problem needs careful orientation. Mathematical methods might be helpful here.

Essential in this approach is that the pupils and the teacher can pool their ideas by offering various solutions to the problems. Subsequently, the solutions offered have to be compared with one another. It is the teacher's task—if this is to be a mathematics lesson—to see to it that this problem-solving activity will become (or will remain) really mathematical. The teacher must organize the shared activity in such a way that it contains all the aspects of the activity that he or she considers to be necessary for a real mathematical activity. On the basis of our general learning theory, we must assume that the organizational features of the mathematical activity eventually determine the qualities of the individual mathematical thinking. If we want pupils to acquire the act of, say, calculating surface areas, or making and using diagrams of the situation, or the attitude and ability to reflect on the nature and use of mathematics, then we should make sure that these actions are systematically included in this shared mathematical learning activity.

It stands to reason that the pupils themselves will initially not be able to accomplish all the aspects of this activity on their own. The teacher thus will have to assist the pupils, and offer suggestions for solutions, give hints for a mathematical method of acting, scrutinize answers as openly as possible, utter objections, propose ways of symbolizing (schematizing!) the different solutions/situations, as well as encouraging symbolic representation of the reasoning process, and so on. Eventually the teacher has to provoke an assessment of the ultimate shared solution(s). In relation to this assessment, it is very important to reveal to the pupils the difference between the correctness of the execution of a mathematical operation and the applicability of that operation for a particular problem (see Lave, 1988). Mathematics is not only a matter of right or wrong, it can also be correct but inappropriate or even abused. It is the teacher's responsibility to establish this insight in pupils by systematically providing the relevant questions in the common mathematical activity.

Through communication between teacher and pupils, a pool of shared knowledge, strategies, and experiences is built up (compare Edwards & Mercer, 1989, for further details). In terms of the previously described psychological theory of learning, we can say that pupils gradually learn what utterances (about possible actions and methods) can and cannot be maintained in relation to the problem at hand. By negotiating on the meaning of their problem solutions they actually learn a pool of systematically related propositions that can be validly used in the process of orientation on the solution of a problem. Basically this system of related statements forms some kind of mathematical text, which can be retrieved by means of a "label" (a symbol, rule, or "opening metaphor;" Walkerdine, 1982). The text-like character of concepts is essential in our approach to concept formation. As argued by van Dormolen (1986) and Otte (1986), this approach can easily be applied to mathematical symbols/concepts as well. It should be clear by now that concept formation—being a discursive activity aiming at the formation of both culturally and personally meaningful constructs—should not be reduced to the formation of text-based procedural operations.

In the course of this discursive activity it will become clear what aspects of the activity are not yet mastered by the pupils involved. Incidentally, the teacher must focus the pupils' attention on the kinds of action they do not master yet and encourage them within the activity setting to try to master them. When embedded in a sociocultural activity setting, special practice programs can even be set up, as long as the pupils know how to act and why this effort makes sense in the context of their sociocultural activity. Special care must be taken to keep this meaningfulness clear to the pupils. As research has made clear, even automatization processes can be taught in this way (see Sabel'nikov, 1982; van Oers, 1990) without devastating effects on the motivation of the pupils (e.g., Markova, 1986).

The basic didactical rule for this approach of mathematics learning is that of trying to get pupils involved in a mathematical activity:

1. That is recognized as "real" by the mathematical community of our days (as we tried to sketch earlier).
2. That makes sense for the pupils within the context of their activity (i.e., is "real" for the pupils as well).

The main concerns of the teacher then should be:

3. That the shared mathematical activity abides by the rules, methods, and conventions (not necessarily the current results of modern mathematics!) that are acceptable to present-day mathematicians.
4. That the mathematical activity is embedded in a sociocultural activity that makes sense for the pupils (an activity in which they can and want to participate).
5. That symbolic representations of the solutions and reasoning processes are introduced and explored.
6. That the pupils start to negotiate on the meaning of the symbols used in order to change or multiply their already available meanings and actions (verbal actions, mental actions and utterances).

Only then is this mathematics learning a meaningful activity in the double sense described earlier. Like Rogoff (1990), we can now truly characterize the pupil's role as that of an apprentice. It should be clear at this moment that this does not necessarily mean that pupils must be introduced immediately to some sort of high-brown mathematics. This would only be possible when such an activity makes sense to the pupil. In most cases, however, the cooperation of pupils and mathematicians (personified in the teacher) is embedded in and given sense by the children's ongoing activities in a regular classroom. It is the mathematician who must try to become involved in the pupils' activities (not the other way around). The mathematician's task is not primarily to evaluate the results from the perspective of the current mathematical body of knowledge, but only to control the dynamics of the learning process the same way that mathematicians do with each other (see also Bishop & Goffree, 1986).

ASSESSING THE RELEVANCE OF A THEORY
OF MATHEMATICAL LEARNING

Corroborating Evidence, Practical and
Theoretical Value of a Theory

There are several ways to assess the relevance of this theory of mathematics education. The first is the method of empirically testing parts of the general psychological theory or its elaboration for mathematics learning. In the description of my general theory of learning, I already referred to relevant supporting studies. Many other, more specific studies could be cited here as supporting my view on mathematics learning (see, e.g., Davydov, 1990; Lave, 1988; Nelissen, 1987; Saxe, Gearhart, & Guberman, 1984). Supporting arguments can also be found in studies which do not start from a cultural-historical approach (see, e.g., Bishop & Goffree, 1986; Collins, Brown, & Newman, 1989; Gravemeijer et al., 1990; Hughes, 1986; Walkerdine, 1988). It would, however, require more space than is allowed here to elaborate on these studies and scrutinize their evidential power.

Another way of estimating the relevance of this theory is to test its power in the realm of teacher education. Assuming (for the sake of my present argument) that this theory is reliably underpinned by empirical evidence, it would be of additional value when this theory would be formulated in such a way as to assist teachers in the innovation of their practice of mathematics education. This is, however, a tricky field that does not easily give us an unequivocal indication of the practical relevance of the theory. The complexities of this research should not, however, restrain investigators from trying to assess the relevance of this theory by exploring its applicability, failures and successes. More space would be needed to rate the available data at their true value (see, e.g., van Oers, 1991).

A special merit of a theory would be its power to provoke and help forward the debate between competing theoretical approaches towards mathematics education. Elsewhere I pondered on the issue of comparison between the action-theoretical and the information-processing approaches (van Oers, 1990). I think it would be useful to broaden the discussion and compare the view espoused here with the primarily didactic approaches (like Freudenthal's view) as well as with constructivistic approaches. No doubt there are several issues these approaches agree on. But there are also striking differences. It would be, I suppose, very fruitful to concentrate on the differences (see, e.g., Cobb, Perlwitz, & Underwood, in press). One obvious point on the agenda is the conception of the individual and the social. In espousing the idea of cognitive apprenticeship, constructivism nevertheless seems to adhere to some kind of individualism, as appears from its focus on the conditions for facilitating individual learning. Constructivism often seems to stick to the view that children build and develop their own mental structures through interaction with the (social) environment. Cognitive apprenticeship from a Vygotskian perspective, on the other hand, implies that the qualities of mental development are derived from the distinctive properties of the sociocultural organization of the activity.

Finally, the discussions should be directed toward the new issues generated by each of the competing approaches. By putting new issues on the agenda, the competing approaches challenge each other for an elaborate treatment of that issue and for a clarification of the (differing?) practical consequences. By way of finishing my account of mathematics learning as a meaningful activity, I next briefly sum up a few points of concern in the future debate on the improvement of mathematics education.

Theoretically Based Suggestions for Improvement

In some respect, my view on mathematics education does not seem to diverge very much from the already available points of view. Pimm (1987) argued convincingly for the view of mathematics as a language. He also stated that "part of learning mathematics is learning to speak like a mathematician, that is, acquiring meaningful control over the mathematics register" (Pimm, 1987, p. 76). Various other writers could be cited here (see among others Bauersfeld, 1991; Bishop & Goffree, 1986; Freudenthal, 1978). However, for elaboration of the theory more detailed information is needed about how mathematical knowledge is negotiated during classroom discourse. (The importance of research on this issue of classroom discourse analysis—see for example Forman, Chapter 8, this volume—can hardly be underestimated.)

These approaches all seem to espouse the idea that mathematics learning somehow comprises a process of learning to speak mathematically (although "mathematics" should not be reduced to merely copying mathematical speech, as this would lead to "idle talk"). Valuable as they are, they are also restricted as a way of improving mathematics education. In general, there are a few issues that are often overlooked in the current debate about the improvement of mathematics education. Reasoning from our psychological theory, there is more to mathematics learning than learning to speak the mathematical language. The following issues are to be considered as necessary for the further improvement of mathematics education for all pupils. Each of them needs further elaboration. However, I confine myself to short comments.

1. Implementing mathematics as a written language (referring to the activity of reading and writing math): The widely accepted view of mathematics learning as a process of constructing private mathematical representations or discussing about problem solutions in mathematical terms should be extended to a conception of mathematics as semiotic activity related to sociocultural written discourse. The process of acquiring proficiency in symbol manipulation is traditionally too often treated as an isolated act of formal (abstract or decontextualized) and sometimes mechanical learning.

It should (and can) be taught, however, as a deliberate activity of "dressing up" symbols (including models) with shared meaning, which after a process of abridgement turns into a psychological event of instantly recognizing a symbol's "field of meanings." The work of Hughes (1986), Walkerdine (1988), and Scinto (1986) can be of particular value here.

2. Improving the early development of semiotic activity: The development of semiotic activity in the domain of mathematics is to be based on the formation of an ability for semiotic activity in young children. As research has shown, the activity of making, interpreting, and using schematic representations can be started in a meaningful way with very young schoolchildren (see van Oers, 1993). As evidence shows, these general semiotic experiences provide a favorable basis for the participation in discursive learning activity within the disciplinary domains of school learning. The improvement of the foundation for mathematics learning is certainly not to be found in the further advancement of mathematics instruction toward infant school, for example, by making it less threatening for young children (as suggested in Preston, 1987). Rather, the improvement of mathematics education by innovations in the early school years must be based on a general introduction to semiotic activity that can be accomplished by giving these children (from 4 to 7 years of age) assistance in and opportunities for practice with the activity of forming, exchanging, and negotiating all kinds of meaning within everyday practices.

3. The promotion of a mathematical attitude: In a Vygotskian approach to education it is essential that the subject matter taught will become a personally meaningful instrument for the pupil. The pupil eventually must be able to regard the subject matter as his or her own attainment. At least he or she must be prepared to use it independently at the appropriate moments and must see it as a reasonable method, as well as to be prepared to argue for its usefulness. In other words, the pupils must acquire the appropriate attitude to act in accordance with the knowledge obtained. No doubt, this is a long-term learning process, presumably related to the development of the learning motive and personal sense (discussed earlier). Recent research on motive and attitude development (e.g., Harré, Clarke, & De Carlo, 1985; Markova, 1986; Matjuchina, 1984; Nuttin, 1984) provides a firm basis for the hypothesis that the development of a mathematical attitude depends on the condition of being involved in a public mathematical-communicative activity with significant others within a clearly defined community (e.g., the class community). Furthermore, as far as motive development is concerned, there is some reason to assume that the recognition of the usefulness of a particular method of acting, combined with the feeling of mastery of that method promotes the development of the appropriate learning motive (Markova, 1986). As a hypothesis I propose here that, in the context of semiotic activity within play and

learning activity, the conditions required for the development of a (mathematical) attitude are optimally fulfilled. Further research, of course, should substantiate this part of the theory.

CONCLUDING REMARKS

Deliberately, I do not want to be too elaborate here in my conclusions. Starting from the assumption that a theory of mathematics learning must be primarily of a psychological nature, I have tried to show how the action-psychological theory from the Vygotskian cultural-historical point of view can be employed to explain mathematics learning. Theoretically based suggestions for the organization of mathematics teaching can be obtained from this description, as well as suggestions for the further improvement of mathematics education. In part these improvements must be sought outside the mathematics lessons. Although there is already a mass of empirical corroboration of this approach (as I tried to indicate in this chapter), further research and debate are needed.

REFERENCES

Bakhtin, M. M. (1986). In C. Emerson & M. Holquist (Eds.), *Speech genres and other late essays.* Austin: University of Texas Press.

Barabašev, A. G. (1983). *Dialektika Razvitija Matematičeskogo Znanija* [The dialectical development of mathematical knowledge]. Moscow: Izd-vo Moskovskogo Unta.

Bauersfeld, H. (1991). What works? Research in the primary mathematics classroom. In M. Dolk & E. Feijs (Eds.), *Deskundigheid. Panamacursusboek 9* (pp. 9–16). Utrecht: OW & OC.

Bishop, A. J. (1988). *Mathematical Enculteration. A Cultural Perspective on Mathematics Education.* Dordrecht: Kluwer.

Bishop, A. J., & Goffree, F. (1986). Classroom organization and dynamics. In B. Christiansen, A. G. Howson, & M. Otte (Eds.), *Perspectives on mathematics education* (pp. 309–365). Dordrecht: Reidel.

Bruner, J. S. (1985). Vygotsky: A historical and conceptual perspective. In J. V. Wertsch (Ed.), *Culture, communication, and cognition* (pp. 21–34). Cambridge: Cambridge University Press.

Bruner, J. (1986). *Actual minds. Possible worlds.* Cambridge, MA: Harvard University Press.

Carpay, J., & van Oers, B. (in press). Didactic models and the problem of intertextuality and polyphony. In Y. Engeström, R. Mietinen, & R.-L. Punamäki (Eds.), *Research on activity theory.* Cambridge: Cambridge University Press.

Cobb, P. (1990). A constructivist perspective on information-processing theories of mathematical activity. *International Journal of Educational Research, 14*(1), 67–92.

Cobb, P., Perlwitz, M., & Underwood, D. (in press). Constructivism and activity theory: A consideration of their similarities and differences as they relate to mathematics education. In H. Mansfield, N. Pateman, & N. Bednarz (Eds.), *Mathematics for tomorrows young children: International perspectives on curriculum.* Dordrecht: Kluwer.

Cole, M. (1990). Cultural psychology: A once and future discipline? In J. J. Berman (Ed.), *Cross cultural perspectives. Nebraska Symposium on Motivation* (Vol. 37, pp. 279–335). Lincoln/London: University of Nebraska Press.

Collins, A., Brown, J. S., & Newman, S. E. (1989). Cognitive apprenticeship: Teaching the crafts of reading, writing, and mathematics. In L. B. Resnick (Ed.), *Knowing, learning, and instruc-*

tion. Essays in honor of Robert Glaser (pp. 453–494). Hillsdale, NJ: Lawrence Erlbaum Associates.

Davydov, V. V. (1988). Problems of developmental teaching. *Soviet Education, XXX*(8), 9, 10.

Davydov, V. V. (1990). *Psichičeskoe razvitie mladšich škol'nikov: eksperimental'noe issledovanie* [The psychological development of pupils in the lower grades: Experimental investigation]. Moscow: Pedagogika.

Davydov, V. V., & Radzikhovskii, Z. A. (1985). Vygotsky's theory and the activity-oriented approach in psychology. In J. V. Wertsch. (Ed.), *Culture, communication, and cognition* (pp. 35–65). Cambridge: Cambridge University Press.

Dijksterhuis, E. J. (1990). *Clio's Stiefkind* [Clio's stepchild]. Amsterdam: B. Bakker.

Dyson, A. H. (1990). *The word and the world: Reconceptualizing written language development, or do rainbows mean a lot to little girls?* Tech. Rep. No 42. Berkeley: University of California and Pittsburgh: Carnegie Mellon University.

Edwards, D., & Mercer, N. (1989). *Common knowledge. The development of understanding in the classroom.* New York: Routledge.

Fenstermacher, G. D., & Soltis, J. F. (1986). *Approaches to teaching.* New York: Teachers College Press, Columbia University.

Fichtner, B. (1985). Learning and learning activity. In E. Bol, J. P. P. Haenen, & M. A. Wolters (Eds.), *Education for cognitive development. Proceedings of the Third International Symposium on Activity Theory* (pp. 47–63). Den Haag: SVO.

Fischer, W. L. (1990). Mathematisch-naturwissenschaftlicher Unterricht. In H. K. Beckmann & W. L. Fischer (Eds.), *Herausforderung der Didaktik. Zur Polarität von Schüler- und Sachorientierung im Unterricht* [A challenge for instructional theory: The dilemma of pupil orientation versus subject matter orientation in education]. Bad Heilbrunn: J. Klinkhardt.

Freudenthal, H. (1973). *Mathematics as an educational task.* Dordrecht: Reidel.

Freudenthal, H. (1978). *Weeding and sowing.* Dordrecht: Reidel.

Gal'perin, P. Ja. (1969). Stages in the development of mental acts. In M. Cole & I. Maltzman (Eds.), *A handbook of contemporary Soviet psychology* (pp. 249–273). New York: Basic Books.

Glotova, G. A. (1990). *Celovek i Znak. Semiotiko-psichologičeskie Aspekty Ontogeneza čeloveka* [Man and sign. Semiotic-psychological aspects of human ontogenesis]. Sverdlovsk: Izd-vo Ural'skogo Un-ta.

Gravemeijer, K., van den Heuvel, M., & Streefland, L. (1990). *Contexts, free productions, tests and geometry in realistic mathematics education.* Utrecht: OW & OC.

Greer, B., & Mulhern, G. (Eds.). (1989). *New directions in mathematics education.* New York: Routledge.

Griffith, H. B. (1978). *The structure of pure mathematics. Mathematical education.* New York: Van Nostrand Reinhold.

Hadamard, J. (1945). *The psychology of invention in the mathematical field.* New York: Dover.

Hakkarainen, P. (1985). Learning motivation and instructional intervention. In E. Bol, J. P. P. Haenen, & M. A. Wolters (Eds.), *Education for cognitive development. Proceedings of the Third International Symposium on Activity Theory* (pp. 136–151). Den Haag: SVO.

Halliday, M. A. K. (1978). Sociolinguistic aspects of mathematical education. In M. A. K. Halliday, *Language as social semiotic. The social interpretation of language and meaning* (pp. 194–204). London: Edward Arnold.

Harré, R., Clarke, D., & De Carlo, N. (1985). *Motives and mechanism. An introduction to the psychology of action.* London: Methuen.

Hodge, R., & Kress, G. (1988). *Social semiotics.* Cambridge: Polity Press.

Hughes, M. (1986). *Children and number. Difficulties in learning mathematics.* Oxford: Basil Blackwell.

Jackson, Ph. W. (1986). *The practice of teaching.* New York: The Teachers College Press, Columbia University.

Lakatos, I. (1976). *Proofs and refutations. The logic of mathematical discovery.* Cambridge: Cambridge University Press.

Lamon, W. E. (Ed.). (1972). *Learning and the nature of mathematics.* Chicago: Science Research Associates.

Langer, J. (1983). Concept and symbol formation by infants. In S. Wapner & B. Kaplan (Eds.), *Towards a holistic developmental psychology* (pp. 221–234). Hillsdale, NJ: Lawrence Erlbaum Associates.

Lave, J. (1988). *Cognition in practice. Mind, mathematics and culture in everyday life.* Cambridge: Cambridge University Press.

Lave, J., & Wenger, E. (1991). *Situated learning. Legitimate peripheral participation.* Cambridge: Cambridge University Press.

Leont'ev, A. N. (1975). *Dejatel'nost', Ličnost', Soznanie.* [Activity, personality, consciousness]. Moscow: Izd-vo Političeskoj Literatury.

Luria, A. R. (1976). *Cognitive development: Its cultural and social foundations.* Cambridge, MA: Harvard University Press.

Luria, A. R. (1978). The development of writing in the child. In M. Cole (Ed.), *The selected writings of A. R. Luria* (pp. 145–194). White Plains, NY: Sharpe.

Luria, A. R. (1981). *Language and cognition.* New York: Wiley.

Markova, A. K. (Ed.). (1986). *Formirovanie Interessa k učeniju u škol'nikov.* [The formation of learning interest in pupils]. Moscow: Pedagogika.

Matjuchina, M. V. (1984). *Motivacija Učenija Mladšich škol'nikov* [The learning motivation of pupils in the lower grades]. Moskou: Pedagogika.

Nelissen, J. M. C. (1987). *Kinderen leren wiskunde. Een studie over constructie en reflectie in het basisonderwijs* [Children learn mathematics. A study of construction and reflection in elementary school]. Gorinchem: De Ruiter.

Nuttin, J. (1984). *Motivation, planning, and action. A relational theory of behavioral dynamics.* Leuven: Leuven University Press/Lawrence Erlbaum Associates.

Olson, D. R., & Torrance, N. G. (1983). Literacy and cognitive development: A conceptual transformation in the early school years. In S. Meadows (Ed.), *Developing thinking. Approaches to children's cognitive development* (pp. 142–168). London: Methuen.

Otte, M. (Ed.). (1974). *Mathematiker über Mathematik.* Berlin/New York: Springer.

Otte, M. (1986). What is a text? In B. Christiansen, A. G. Howson, & M. Otte (Eds.), *Perspectives on mathematics education* (pp. 173–203). Dordrecht: Reidel.

Pimm, D. (1987). *Speaking mathematically. Communication in mathematics classrooms.* New York: Routledge.

Podd'jakov, N. N., & Govorkova, A. F. (1985). *Razvitie Myšlenija i Umstvennoe Vospitanie Doškol'nika* [The development of thinking and cognitive education of preschool children]. Moskou: Pedagogika.

Preston, M. (Ed.). (1987). *Mathematics in primary education.* London: Falmer.

Roegholt, S. (1993). Towards a concept of multiperspective education. *Journal of Curriculum Studies, 25*(2), 153–167.

Rogoff, B. (1990). *Apprenticeship in thinking. Cognitive development in social context.* New York: Oxford University Press.

Sabel'nikov, V. K. (1982). *Formirovanie Bystroj Mysli* [The formation of fast thinking]. Alma Ata: Mektep.

Salmina, N. G. (1988). *Znak i Simvol v Obučenii.* [Sign and symbol in education]. Moskou: Izd-vo Moskovskogo Un-ta.

Saxe, G., Gearhart, M., & Guberman, S. R. (1984). The social organization of early number development. In B. Rogoff & J. V. Wertsch (Eds.), *Children learning in the "zone of proximal development"* (pp. 19–30). San Francisco: Jossey-Bass.

Scinto, L. F. M. (1986). *Written language and psychological development.* Orlando, FL: Academic Press.

Struik, D. J. (1948). *Concise history of mathematics*. New York: Dover.

Struik, D. J. (1990). *Geschiedenis van de Wiskunde* [the history of mathematics]. Utrecht: Spectrum.

van Dormolen, J. (1986). Textual analysis. In B. Christiansen, A. G. Howson, & M. Otte (Eds.), *Perspectives on mathematics education* (pp. 141–171). Dordrecht: Reidel.

van Oers, B. (1987). *Activiteit en Begrip*. [Activity and concept]. Amsterdam: Free University Press.

van Oers, B. (1990). The development of mathematical thinking in school: A comparison of the action-psychological and information-processing approaches. *International Journal of Educational Research, 14*(1), 51–66.

van Oers, B. (1991). *Talks to teachers on mathematics education*. Internal paper. Department of Psychology and Education, Free University, Amsterdam.

van Oers, B. (1993, September). *Semiotic activity in young children in play: The construction and use of schematic representations*. Paper presented at the Third European Conference on the Quality of Early Childhood Education, Kriopigi, Greece.

van Oers, B. (in press). The dynamics of school learning. In J. Valsiner & H.-G. Voss (Eds.), *The structure of learning*. New York: Ablex.

van Parreren, C. F. (1954). A viewpoint in theory and experimentation on human learning and thinking. *Acta Psychologica, 10,* 351–380.

van Parreren, C. F. (1978). A building block model of cognitive learning. In A. M. Lesgold, J. W. Pellegrino, S. D. Fokkema, & R. Glaser (Eds.), *Cognitive psychology and instruction* (pp. 3–11). New York: Plenum.

van Parreren, C. F. & Carpay, J. A. M. (1980). *Sovjetpsychologen over Onderwijs en Cognitieve Ontwikkeling*. [Soviet psychologists on instruction and cognitive development]. Groningen: Wolters-Noordhoff.

Venger, L. A. (Ed.). (1986). *Razvitie Poznavatel'nych Sposobnostej v Processe Doškol'nogo Vospitanija*. [The formation of cognitive abilities in early education]. Moscow: Pedagogika.

Vygotsky, L. S. (1978). *Mind in society. The development of higher psychological processes*. Cambridge, MA: Harvard University Press.

Vygotsky, L. S. (1982). Myšlenie i Reč [Thinking and speech]. In L. S. Vygotsky, *Sobranie Sočinenij*. T.2. [Collected works, Vol. 2]. Moscow: Pedagogika. Translation: L. S. Vygotskij (1987). Thinking and speech. In *L. S. Vygotsky, collected works* (Vol. 1, pp. 39–285). New York: Plenum.

Walkerdine, V. (1982). From context to text: A psychosemiotic approach to abstract thought. In M. Beveridge (Ed.), *Children thinking through language* (pp. 129–155). London: Arnold.

Walkerdine, V. (1988). *The mastery of reason. Cognitive development and the production of rationality*. New York: Routledge.

Wardekker, W. (1991). Meaning and context in education. *Activity Theory, 9/10,* 36–41.

Werner, H., & Kaplan, B. (1963). *Symbol formation. An organismic-developmental approach to language and the expression of thought*. New York: Wiley.

Wertsch, J. V. (1985). *Vygotskij and the social formation of mind*. Cambridge, MA: Harvard University Press.

Wertsch, J. V. (1991). *Voices of the mind. A sociocultural approach to mediated action*. London: Harvester/Wheatsheaf.

Wilder, R. L. (1968). *Evolution of mathematical concepts*. London: John Wiley.

Yaroshevsky, M. (1989). *Lev Vygotsky*. Moscow: Progress.

Young, R. (1989). *A critical theory of education. Habermas and our children's future*. New York: Harvester Wheatsheaf.

Zinchenko, V. P. (1985). Vygotsky's ideas about units for the analysis of mind. In J. V. Wertsch (Ed.), *Culture, communication, and cognition* (pp. 94–118). Cambridge: Cambridge University Press.

8

Learning Mathematics as Participation in Classroom Practice: Implications of Sociocultural Theory for Educational Reform

Ellice Ann Forman
University of Pittsburgh

Educational reformers in the United States are calling for sweeping changes in instructional practices, such as the new standards for mathematics instruction from the National Council of Teachers of Mathematics (NCTM, 1989, 1991). They argue that students need to be actively involved in practicing mathematics by working in small groups, negotiating ways to define and organize the data in open-ended problems, arriving at multiple solutions, and explaining their ideas to each other. These practices are in contrast to what is seen in more traditional North American mathematics classrooms in which whole-class, teacher-dominated didactic instruction and individual seatwork are the norm. In addition to changes in the processes of instruction, the reform movement is also calling for new instructional goals: from the memorization of number facts and the accurate use of computational algorithms to greater understanding of mathematical concepts and more effective use of problem-solving strategies. Enhancing students' abilities to communicate and to collaborate with others is also emphasized. In addition, the reform movement is interested in changing students' attitudes toward learning mathematics: from anxiety and passive obedience to authority to enthusiasm, confidence, and active involvement in problem solving. Although the reformers call for change in practice as well as content, the new standards for mathematics instruction, for example, contain more information about the latter than the former. More seriously, there is very little justification provided for the connections between changes in practice and desired instructional outcomes.

A number of North American educational reformers have based their proposals on a family of psychological and anthropological theories referred to as sociocultural theory (Brown, Collins, & Duguid, 1989; Forman, Minick, &

Stone, 1993; Lave & Wenger, 1991; Lemke, 1990; Moll, 1990; Newman, Griffin, & Cole, 1989; Saxe, Gearhart, Note, & Paduano, 1993; Tharp & Gallimore, 1988). Sociocultural theory traces its roots to the work of the Soviet psychologists Vygotsky, Luria, and Leont'ev, who began writing in the early part of the 20th century. As this work became more widely available to a North American audience in the 1980s, important expansions, modifications, and applications of the theory were made.

The purpose of this chapter is to show how sociocultural theory can provide a basis for the hypothetical connection between the proposed changes in instructional processes and the desired goals of the reform movement. A secondary purpose is to explicate three crucial constructs: legitimate peripheral participation, activity setting, and instructional conversation, which play a central role in understanding and evaluating educational reform from a sociocultural perspective.

In order to accomplish these purposes, I show how the three constructs relate to the broader theoretical framework provided by van Oers (chapter 7, this volume) and outline some of the extensions and applications of sociocultural theory that have occurred in North America in the past 15 years. Then I use the theory to discuss some observations that were made in two middle school mathematics classrooms taught by Ms. Hanes.[1] The observations were collected during the first 2 years of an educational reform project aimed at fostering high-level reasoning and problem-solving skills for students from economically disadvantaged backgrounds. The goal of this analysis is to illustrate the value of a sociocultural approach for understanding how changes in social practices in the classroom can affect the learning of mathematics. In the final section of the chapter, I discuss the practical significance of sociocultural theory for guiding our analysis of the processes and outcomes of educational reform.

SOCIOCULTURAL THEORY

A complete presentation of sociocultural theory is beyond the scope of this chapter. Interested readers are encouraged to look at other sources for a fuller treatment of this perspective (Forman et al., 1993; Leont'ev, 1981; Luria, 1976; Rogoff, 1990; Saxe, 1991; Vygotsky, 1978, 1987; Wertsch, 1981, 1985a, 1985b, 1991).

The discussion of the Vygotskian approach in van Oers' work (chapter 7, this volume) provides a useful introduction to the constructs to be presented here. There are four key ideas in van Oers' work that are central to the sociocultural approach to learning mathematics. First, social, cultural, and institutional con-

---

[1]All the student and teacher names used in this chapter are pseudonyms.

texts do more than merely facilitate or impede learning. Social organizational processes are an inherent characteristic of learning—whether or not it occurs in an overtly social context. Second, learning needs to be viewed as a form of apprenticeship or a means by which novices become experts through participation in activities within a community of practice. Third, learning mathematics is a discursive activity. Fourth, learning involves the negotiation of meaning within the context of situated activity.

Van Oers traces the source of his action-psychological approach to Russian scholars and educators such as Vygotsky, Leont'ev, Luria, Galperin, Davydov, and Bakhtin. In addition to these sources, North American theorists have been influenced by cross-cultural research conducted by Cole, Lave, Rogoff, Saxe, Scribner, B. Whiting, J. Whiting, and others and by studies of the social context of instruction by Bruner, Wood, and Wertsch (Minick, Stone, & Forman, 1993). Three constructs discussed by North American theorists provide a framework for examining mathematics learning that is compatible with van Oers' action-psychological approach. They are legitimate peripheral participation (Lave & Wenger, 1991), activity setting, and instructional conversation (Tharp & Gallimore, 1988). Each concept and its relevance for understanding learning in reform mathematics classrooms is discussed in this section.

Lave and Wenger described learning as a process by which a newcomer is integrated into a community of practice. They called this process legitimate peripheral participation. Legitimate peripheral participation is used instead of apprenticeship to avoid the restrictive connotations of craft apprenticeship (see Lave & Wenger, 1991, for a more complete explanation).

Unlike many psychologists and educators, Lave and Wenger did not depict learning as internalization, transmission, absorption, or assimilation of information from the "external world" to create some form of "internal" representations. Relying upon Marxist theory (e.g., Bourdieu, 1977, cited in Lave & Wenger, 1991), they denied the dichotomy between the internal and the external. They also argued that learning is not an individual accomplishment and therefore the unit of analysis should not be the individual. Instead of learning as internalization, they proposed "learning as increasing participation in communities of practice" (p. 49). Thus, what matters for learning is not the availability of instructional resources such as computers, small class size, content-rich textbooks, and so on, but access to meaningful practice in a community. Goodnow agreed with this position when she claimed, "it is the nature of one's positions, of one's participation in the social life of the group, that influences the extent to which one picks up, and appropriates as one's own, the skills and ways of thinking valued by the group" (1993, p. 373).

All participants in a community of practice are legitimate, but some (such as newcomers) are more peripheral than others (such as old-timers). Old-timers differ from newcomers in having more power in the community as well as more knowledge of its valued skills. Newcomers can become old-timers, at least in principle, by increasing their range of practice in the community over time. As their range of practice increases, their knowledge increases.

In summary, Lave and Wenger presented an alternative way of conceptualizing learning. Instead of learning as internalization, learning is seen as participation in the activities of a community. Thus, the ideal conditions for learning mathematics would involve access to meaningful activity within a community of mathematical practice. This community could occur outside or inside the institution of school (Saxe, 1991; Saxe & Bermudez, chapter 3, this volume; Schliemann & Carraher, chapter 5, this volume). If learning is to occur inside school, then the classroom teacher has an important role to play as the old-timer in the classroom community. Some of the responsibilities of the old-timer involve the communication of the norms, values, and discourse practices of the community to the newcomers and the design of meaningful mathematical activity settings.

Both Vygotsky and Leont'ev also attempted to redefine learning using some basic constructs from Marx. They argued, like Lave and Wenger, that one needed to identify a unit of analysis in psychological research which integrated the thoughts and actions of individuals with their goal-directed, culturally specific activities (Cole, 1985; Leont'ev, 1981). Activity setting, as defined and used by Tharp and Gallimore (1988), is one approach to comparing and contrasting learning activity in context. Gallimore and Goldenberg (1993) defined five variables that determine an activity setting: "1) personnel present during an activity, 2) salient cultural values, 3) the operations and task demands of the activity itself, 4) the scripts for conduct that govern the participants' actions, and 5) the purposes or motives of the participants" (p. 316). By focusing on activity settings, one is forced to recognize the connections between what a person does, feels, thinks, and believes; the constraints and supports provided by other people and artifacts in that particular setting; and cultural rules, norms, and values.

Activity setting and legitimate peripheral participation provide complementary and necessary tools for the study of learning in sociocultural context. The concept of activity supplies a unit of analysis for the study of educational reform, and the concept of legitimate peripheral participation permits one to infer something about learning from differences in participation patterns. These two constructs emphasize that learning is synonymous with socially situated activity. What they do not include is the notion of learning as a discursive practice, which is also central to sociocultural theory. That is why the third construct, instructional conversation, is also needed.

If, as van Oers and others have argued, learning involves the negotiation of both cultural and personal meaning, then classroom discourse must allow this kind of negotiation process to occur. Tharp and Gallimore (1988) used the term *instructional conversation* to refer to classroom discourse that permits the coconstruction of meaning between teachers and students. They contrasted instructional conversations with the more typical kind of classroom talk known as the recitation script. The recitation script consists of three parts: an initiation or query by the teacher, a student response, and an evaluation by the teacher. The recitation script assumes that learning is a process of internalization, not one of negotiation of meaning. It restricts students' activity to accepting (or rejecting) the interpretation implicit in the teacher's query. There is no opportunity within this script for students to redefine the problem being presented or to offer alternative explanations, unless specifically requested to do so. It also privileges the teacher's evaluation of an answer. In contrast, instructional conversations are modeled after everyday conversations in which the more experienced members of a culture instruct the less experienced via talk. An example of this kind of conversation is the young child learning a first language through interacting with family members, neighbors, and friends.

Instructional conversations involve the integration of concepts from school (i.e., Vygotsky's scientific concepts) and everyday concepts (Tharp & Gallimore, 1988). They serve a similar function in Tharp and Gallimore's theory of learning as does the notion of discursive learning activity in van Oers' approach. Instructional conversations go beyond concept learning to involve the mastery of specialized speech genres such as the mathematics register (Forman, 1992; Halliday, 1975, 1978; Pimm, 1987; van Oers, chapter 7, this volume). In the mathematics register, words may be given new meanings (e.g., "similarity", "identity"), syntax reflects the timeless and impersonal nature of propositions (e.g., there may be no subject in a sentence or the subject may be an impersonal "you"), and particular modes of argument are valued (e.g., precision, brevity, logical coherence).

The three constructs, legitimate peripheral participation, activity setting, and instructional conversation, allow us to ask a number of questions about reform classrooms. For example, how do reform classrooms and traditional classrooms differ in the opportunities each offers for social participation? Within any particular classroom community or activity setting, do individuals differ in their participation? What do these participation patterns tell us about learning mathematics?

APPLICATION OF SOCIOCULTURAL THEORY

In the analyses described next, three different comparisons of participation in activity settings are made with reference to two of Ms. Hanes' middle school mathematics classes. First, the range of activity settings available in traditional and reform classrooms[2] is contrasted. Second, student participation across activity settings within a single classroom is described. Third, student participation within a single activity setting is illustrated by focusing on differential use of the mathematics register. The aim of this analysis is to use data from these classes to

---

[2]The distinction between traditional and reform classrooms used here is similar to Paul Cobb's distinction between the school mathematics tradition and inquiry mathematics tradition.

illustrate how sociocultural theory could be employed to describe instructional processes in particular classroom settings and to make predictions about instructional outcomes in those settings. No attempt is made to generalize the results of this analysis to other reform classrooms or even to the entire corpus of data on Ms. Hanes' classes.

A Comparison of Activity Settings in Traditional Versus Reform Classrooms

In traditional middle school mathematics classrooms, students are participants in a limited range of activity settings. For example, Stodolsky (1988) found that fifth-grade mathematics classrooms devoted 40% of the instructional time to independent seatwork and 29% to whole-class recitations lead by the teacher. In contrast, she found that fifth-grade social studies classes devoted only 28% of the time to seatwork and 18% to recitations. Work in small groups comprised less than 1% of the observed time in the mathematics classrooms in her study but 34% of the time in the social studies classrooms. Thus, fifth graders in Stodolsky's sample participated in a broader range of activity settings in their social studies classes than in their mathematics classes.

In reform classrooms, students may participate in a wider range of activity settings than in traditional classrooms. In addition, students may be asked to follow a different script for conduct in these activity settings.[3] Traditional classrooms are more likely to use the recitation script than are reform classrooms. Thus, in traditional mathematics classrooms, students have limited opportunity to initiate topics, redirect discussion, provide elaborate explanations of their own, or debate issues. Students who deviate from the official recitation scripts or independent seatwork scripts by talking to their peers can be sanctioned for failing to accept their rights and obligations as students in a traditional classroom.

In contrast to this picture of a relatively restricted range of activity settings

---

[3]The notions of activity setting and script have been oversimplified in order to make abstract contrasts between "typical" traditional mathematics classrooms and "typical" reform mathematics classrooms. One oversimplification concerns the intended structure of a particular activity setting versus its actual structure. For example, small group work may be intended to stimulate creative thinking but may, in fact, suppress creativity. A second oversimplification concerns scripts. The recitation script and instructional conversation discussed here do not have an independent existence apart from their context of use. That is, although the rules for these scripts have been identified in previous research, their actual use in any setting needs to be empirically documented. Finally, this analysis presents educational practice, in any form, as if it were a static instantiation of abstract categories like activity setting, script, or community of practice. These static characterizations are antithetical to the dynamic nature of learning in context as articulated by sociocultural theory. Future analyses, both empirical and theoretical, need to emphasize the emergent properties of social participation in communities of practice.

and official scripts in traditional classrooms, reform classrooms can provide opportunities for students to assume a variety of participatory roles. In Ms. Hanes' classroom, the following types of activity settings and interactional scripts were observed: whole-class recitation led by the teacher, whole-class presentations led by one or more students, small group work led by one or more students with the teacher's intermittent assistance, individual seat work, and unofficial peer group activities. By providing a greater range of activity settings, reform classrooms also present a wider diversity of task demands and scripts. For example, students presenting their work in front of the class have to learn to communicate their ideas effectively to others through multiple representational formats. They also need to listen to the ideas of other students, even when they do not agree with them, to support their own positions with evidence, and to reconcile the differences between positions. Students can no longer rely on their understanding of the recitation script.

One script employed in mathematics classrooms follows the rules for the specialized speech genre specific to mathematical talk, the mathematics register. Although the mathematics register can be found in traditional classrooms as well as in reform classrooms, students have less opportunity to become fluent in its use in traditional classrooms because their participation is more restricted. That is, in traditional classrooms, students are asked to absorb this register by reading the text and listening to the teacher. In reform classrooms, students are asked to employ the register in more active and creative ways: to explain and contrast different solutions to a problem or to compare multiple representations of a problem. Therefore, students in reform classrooms have more opportunities to use the mathematics register as both a tool for their own thinking and an object for reflection.

These new task demands and new scripts also bring new purposes and values. Instead of just rewarding accurate and automatic use of algorithms, reform classes may also reward effective problem-solving strategies and communication practices. Students need to view themselves and each other as intellectual resources instead of relying solely upon the authority of the teacher and the text. The aim of this more collaborative approach to learning is to establish a community of learners—with all members having differential but important roles to play in assisting each other's learning (Tharp & Gallimore, 1988).[4]

Table 8.1 gives an outline of the values, task demands, scripts, and purposes associated with the different activity settings in traditional versus reform mathematics classrooms. In this figure, the contrasts between the different activity

---

[4]In this chapter I focus on the rights and obligations of students without giving sufficient attention to the rights and obligations of teachers. This one-sided picture is a deliberate distortion of the system of rights and obligations that teachers and students share in any community of practice in order to emphasize student participation patterns. Obviously, a fuller treatment of this issue would need to give equal attention to teachers' rights and obligations.

TABLE 8.1
Characteristics of Official Activity Settings in Classrooms

Activity Settings and Personnel	Values	Task Demands	Scripts	Purposes
Traditional Mathematics Classrooms				
Teacher-led recitations	Teacher or text are sources of learning Automaticity and accuracy	Internalize mathematics facts and algorithms	Recitation script	Introduce basic skills
Individual seatwork	Teacher or text are sources of learning Automaticity and accuracy	Practice mathematics facts and algorithms	Work independently	Individual mastery of basic skills
Reform Mathematics Classrooms				
Student-led presentations	Multiple sources of learning Multiple solutions Effective strategies and explanations	Pedagogical and communication skills	Instructional conversation	Establish community of learners
Small group work	Multiple sources of learning Multiple solutions Effective strategies and explanations	Cooperation and communication skills	Instructional conversation	Establish community of learners Foster collaborative problem solving

settings are made as distinct as possible. In reality, any one activity setting may have several, sometimes contradictory, purposes. This is especially true for classrooms in the process of change from traditional to reform.

Interviews with small samples of students from Ms. Hanes' class revealed their awareness of the results of changing instructional practices on their learning opportunities. One theme that emerged from the interviews was that students did view themselves and each other as intellectual resources. They cited the advantages of working in small groups for allowing you to offer and receive help, to share frustrations, and to expose yourself to a variety of ideas. They also seemed to view the small group as a supportive community: a place where you can count on people to listen to you. Another theme was the importance of explaining your ideas. The students understood how difficult it is to communicate ideas in oral or written form. Nevertheless, they recognized that it was crucial to get the members of their group to explain their work, not just to share answers. Finally, contrasts between traditional and reform classrooms (and the contradictions within a classroom in the process of change) formed another theme in the student interviews. Many students seemed to feel that Ms. Hanes' class involved too much work, too much homework, too much writing and explaining. One student complained that the work took longer to do than last year because Ms. Hanes did not show them the shortcuts.

Changing classroom practice from traditional to reform activity settings can involve contradictions and confusions between the old system and the new one. One of the contradictions mentioned by the students involved grading. They saw a contradiction between offering open-ended problems, accepting multiple solutions, and assigning grades. Another contradiction they discussed had to do with their confusion about allowable small group behavior. Sometimes helping another student was encouraged, but sometimes it was viewed as off-task behavior.

A Comparison of Student Participation Across Activity Settings in Ms. Hanes' Classes

Reform classrooms, like those taught by Ms. Hanes, provide both opportunities and challenges to students. Some students seem to benefit from having a greater chance to learn in collaboration with their peers whereas others seem confused by the demands of learning alternative scripts. For example, students who are much more comfortable negotiating with their peers than with the teacher are given an opportunity to use their peer networks to participate in the officially sanctioned small group activities of the reform classroom. One student in Ms. Hanes' seventh grade class, Dan, was observed to repeatedly turn away from the overhead projector in the front of the room. Ms. Hanes at one point asked Dan to turn his chair around so he could watch the student presenting at the overhead. When Dan ignored her request, she moved his chair herself. However, he continued to face other students in his group and to avoid looking at the person in authority (who happened to be a student). In a traditional classroom, Dan's active resistance to authority would have resulted in his being excluded from much of the instructional activities. In Ms. Hanes' classroom, however, several other students in Dan's group studiously followed the teacher's instructions and helped him participate in the group's problem-solving work. Thus, Dan's resistance to authority may have been less of an impediment to his learning mathematics in this classroom than in a traditional one.

An example of the challenges of these new activity settings could be seen when other students in Ms. Hanes' class tried to apply the rules for the recitation script to their small group or student-lead activity settings. Some students spent much of their time during small group activity waiting for Ms. Hanes to initiate group activities or to evaluate their work. They were frequently frustrated and confused when Ms. Hanes encouraged them to ask questions of each other and to evaluate each other's work.

These new classroom activity settings with their unfamiliar scripts also result in new task demands, values, and purposes. In Ms. Hanes' classroom, where there was no official textbook and where the teacher shared the responsibility for explaining complex mathematical concepts and procedures with her students, students were required to be effective communicators and collaborators. Any one idea could be presented using a variety of representational formats. No one format was privileged, as it would be in a classroom where seatwork from a textbook and the recitation script predominate. Solutions to problems were achieved through a process of negotiation between the teacher and students or among the students as in an instructional conversation.

In summary, observations of students in Ms. Hanes' seventh-grade class illustrate what a comparison of individual student's participation patterns across activity settings can show. Dan was most active and task-focused when he was able to participate as a member of a small work group. When he was asked to participate as a member of the whole class, either during teacher-led recitations or student-led presentations, he acted in ways that demonstrated his opposition to the person he viewed as an authority.

Other students, such as Betsy and Diana, were more comfortable than Dan when they were given an opportunity to interact directly with Ms. Hanes. However, they found it difficult to sustain task-focused small group activity without frequent assistance from the teacher. Betsy and Diana showed that they relied upon the recitation script, even when Ms. Hanes was not using it, to organize their work. These students tended to be confused by Ms. Hanes' open-ended problems with multiple solutions and frustrated by her unwillingness to evaluate their work. They showed a pattern opposite to that of Dan: resistance to small group work and compliance with teacher-led recitations. All of these students were partial participants in the classroom community of practice. Their participation patterns indicated what skills and ways of thinking valued by the community they were able to appropriate.

A Comparison of Several Students Within a Single Activity Setting

Within any single activity setting, each student may participate in a different way. In the example to be discussed here, three students, at different times, presented their work on the problem at the overhead. Only the presentations of two students, Allen and Ulysses, are discussed here. The problem that all three students were asked to explain is as follows: "During the month of April (30 days), there were eight more rainy days than dry days. How many rainy days were there?" Allen's solution to this problem was 23 rainy days and 7 dry days and Ulysses' solution was 19 rainy days and 11 dry days. Ms. Hanes read the problem to the class and called on Allen to explain his solution.

(1) Allen: [Makes slashes on the overhead to represent 30 days—as
(2) two groups of 15 slashes.] Then, first I took thirty and split
(3) it in half and got two—fifteen and fifteen. And, um, so you
(4) said there was eight more so I put one side was rainy and one
(5) side was dry. So, wait, rainy, wait, yeah, rainy, dry [labels
(6) transparency]. And there was eight more rainy days than dry
(7) days, so I took eight off of the 15 [crosses out eight slashes
(8) on dry side] and put over here [adds eight slashes to rainy
(9) side] and said how many more rainy days were here? So, then,
(10) so I had first I added the eight that were here. And, um, that
(11) equalled . . . 20, 20, 3, 23. And I said how many more so and
(12) there was [counts aloud one, two, three] seven. So, and then
(13) take away from the 23 is 16.

At this point, Allen stopped. Instead of evaluating his answer, as the recitation script would require, Ms. Hanes asked Allen to reread the problem (perhaps hoping that he would notice that his answer was wrong).

(14) Allen: During the month of April (30 days), there were about
(15) eight more rainy days—there were eight more rainy days than
(16) dry days. How many more rainy days were there?

Following this exchange, Ms. Hanes tried to get Allen to reflect on what he had done so that he could identify where his strategy of transferring days from the dry to the rainy group got him into trouble. Unfortunately, Allen did not seem to understand what Ms. Hanes was asking him to do. First, he appeared to think that her lack of explicit evaluation of his solution implied that he was correct. Then, when he realized that she did not think he was correct, he seemed to lose confidence in his ability to provide a correct strategy or answer. Ms. Hanes asked other students to help make Allen's system work. Two other students volunteered but only one of them, Ulysses, actually began with the same system as Allen.

(17) Ulysses: The only thing that made, well Allen's ide—, well
(18) Allen's idea was right. It's just that there's two so you
(19) divide the eight by two so you only add four instead of adding
(20) eight because when you take away four from the dry days, then
(21) it makes it four lower and makes the other one four higher.
(22) So that would make it, still make it a difference of eight
(23) instead of . . .

There are several differences between the explanations of Ulysses and Allen, other than the difference in their solutions. Some of these differences have to do with each student's mastery of the mathematics register. First, Ulysses' explanation is more concise than Allen's. Ulysses assumed that the class understood how Allen had laid out the problem: as two groups of days, rainy and dry (lines 4–5).

He briefly reminded them of these groups in line 18 and then proceeded to work on the problem from there. Second, the syntactic subjects of Ulysses' statements were in the form of the second-person impersonal pronoun or it. In contrast, the subjects of Allen's statements were personal pronouns. Also, Ulysses' verbs were in the present, timeless tense except where he referred to Allen's previous work, whereas Allen's verbs were in the past tense. Third, Allen tended not to use mathematical terms. Instead, he was as likely to use everyday language to represent mathematical operations, such as "split it in half," as he was to use words that have specific mathematical meanings. Ulysses' explanation is full of mathematical terms with precise meanings. One could easily rewrite Ulysses' verbal explanation into mathematical notation.

Finally, Allen's misreading of the problem (lines 14–16) further indicates his difficulty distinguishing mathematical and everyday story problems. That is, in everyday language, it would be considered appropriate to reply to the question, "Did it rain a great deal in April?" by saying, "Yea, there were *about* eight more rainy days than dry ones." However, this is a mathematical story problem that requires a precise mathematical answer—not an approximate one. Thus, it would be important to know whether the problem states that there were exactly or approximately eight more rainy days than dry ones. In addition, Allen's misreading fundamentally altered the problem when he changed the final question posed from "How many rainy days were there?" to "How many *more* rainy days were there?" because the latter question was answered in the original problem, which stated that there were eight more rainy days than dry days.

There is another interesting issue that can be raised about the different explanations provided by Allen and Ulysses. Allen's explanation was a direct report of his personal experience with a homework problem. Ulysses' explanation was very academic; he described a procedure that should work no matter when, where, or who did it.

Together, these two forms of explanation (the everyday and the academic) need to be interwoven in an instructional conversation, according to Tharp and Gallimore. The ability to integrate the mathematics register and the everyday register is not just a linguistic skill; it is also a cognitive skill. When one is capable of integrating the two speech genres, one demonstrates an understanding of the relationship between multiple representations of a problem. This example illustrates the notion of learning mathematics as a discursive activity. Full participation in student-led presentations requires the mastery of two speech genres. Students who participate in these presentations are assisted by each other and Ms. Hanes in the use of the genres.

CONCLUSIONS

This chapter has focused on describing the range of activity settings, participation patterns, and speech genres of students in Ms. Hanes' classes. I have argued that reform classrooms provide a greater diversity of activity settings for students than do traditional classrooms. In addition, I have proposed that this diversity brings with it new task demands, scripts, values, and purposes. Finally, I have shown that the diversity of activity settings is matched by a diversity of participation patterns within and across them.

What can an analysis of activity settings and participation patterns tell us about learning mathematics? For sociocultural theory, learning is inherently related to social activity and discourse; learning is a process by which newcomers are integrated into a community of practice. Before newcomers understand the valued skills of this community, their participation must be peripheral. As the important skills, norms, and ideas of the community are appropriated, the former newcomers move toward greater participation, thus demonstrating their learning.

Ms. Hanes' classrooms can also be seen as communities of practice that are embedded in and create other communities of practice. These communities would include other educational reform projects in the United States and around the world. As a teacher in a school that is part of an educational reform project, Ms. Hanes is trying to foster the skills being promoted by the NCTM standards. Because teaching in accordance with these standards represents a change in instructional practice for Ms. Hanes, she is a legitimate peripheral participant in the community of mathematics reformers. Increased participation would mean that she can help create and sustain the types of activity settings in her classroom and school that are capable of fostering the skills valued by this community. In principle, the student presentations and small group work activity settings that were observed in her classroom should promote the communication, collaboration, reasoning, and problem-solving skills consistent with those standards. However, ensuring that those new activity settings function as they need to do is no easy matter. Ms. Hanes is only one participant in the activity settings observed in her classroom. Her students bring their own values, feelings, and expectations to those settings. In addition, other participants in the reform project, parents, and school district personnel influence what occurs in her school.

Allen, Ulysses, Dan, Betsy, and Diana are all legitimate peripheral participants in the community of practice within Ms. Hanes' classroom. Although Ms. Hanes may be a newcomer in the wider reform community, in her classroom she is the old-timer: the person who has the most authority to determine the skills needed for greater participation. The process by which her students increase their participation in her classroom would be identical to the process by which the full range of knowledge available would be learned. Greater participation would involve the ability to take an active role in creating and maintaining the desired activity settings, to use the scripts or genres required in an effective manner, to meet the task demands, and to embrace the necessary values and purposes of the community.

Throughout this chapter, I have focused on social practices within Ms. Hanes' classrooms. I have tried to argue, using sociocultural theory, that variations in social participation patterns and in discourse practices, within and across activity settings, provide a basis for comparing reform and traditional mathematics classrooms. They enable one to compare students as well. Observing social participation and classroom discourse is rarely viewed as the primary means for evaluating the success of an educational project. If one were working from a cognitive science perspective, then one would want evidence that changes in outward behavior index changes in internal representations. This evidence would most likely come from independent problem-solving activities. Cognitive scientists might view the activity, talk, and collaborative environment of a reform classroom as a stimulating context for fostering change in internal representations. Yet they would still want to focus on the effect of that environment on the performance of individuals.

In contrast, the sociocultural perspective would not make the same distinctions between "outward" behavior and "internal" representations. Instead, the continuities, not the discontinuities between intermental and intramental activity, would be emphasized (Wertsch, 1985b, 1991). Thus, indices of learning are as much present in classroom discourse as they are in individual problem-solving protocols. The establishment of a community of practice—with a common communication system, norms, and values—would also be evidence of learning.

In conclusion, sociocultural theory takes as two of its guiding premises the notions that learning is a form of participation in the activities of a community of practice and that learning is a discursive activity. Thus, it suggests that educational programs that change social practices, activity settings, and classroom discourse in ways designed to support students' active engagement in solving meaningful mathematical problems in collaboration with others should foster learning. The theoretical justification for the reform movement in mathematicss in the United States requires further elaboration, however, if it is to be used to evaluate the success of that movement. I have tried to argue that notions such as activity setting, legitimate peripheral participation, and instructional conversation can be used to conduct the studies of classroom practice that would be needed to provide the necessary empirical evidence. Models for this work are available in a small but growing body of educational research being conducted from a sociocultural perspective (Forman et al., 1993; Moll, 1990; Newman et al., 1989; Tharp & Gallimore, 1988). The collective result of this activity should provide the educational research community with an alternative framework for conceptualizing and assessing the processes and outcomes of reform.

ACKNOWLEDGMENTS

This research was supported, in part, by a grant to the author from the School of Education Faculty Research Fund, University of Pittsburgh and by a grant to Edward Silver, Learning Research and Development Center, University of Pittsburgh from the Ford Foundation (grant 890-0572). I would like to thank Paul Cobb, Linda Davenport, Richard Donato, Jorge Larreamendy Joerns, Dawn Mc-Cormick, Leona Schauble, Edward Silver, May Kay Stein, and Addison Stone for their comments on earlier drafts of this chapter.

REFERENCES

Brown, J. S., Collins, A., & Duguid, P. (1989). Situated cognition and the culture of learning. *Educational Researcher, 18*, 32–42.

Cole, M. (1985). The zone of proximal development: Where culture and cognition create each other. In J. V. Wertsch (Ed.), *Culture, communication, and cognition* (pp. 146–161). New York: Cambridge University Press.

Forman, E. A. (1992). Discourse, intersubjectivity and the development of peer collaboration: A Vygotskian approach. In L. T. Winegar, & J. Valsiner (Eds.), *Children's development within social contexts: Metatheoretical, theoretical and methodological issues* (Vol. 1, pp. 143–159). Hillsdale, NJ: Lawrence Erlbaum Associates.

Forman, E. A., Minick, N., & Stone, C. A. (Eds.). (1993). *Contexts for learning: Sociocultural dynamics in children's development.* New York: Oxford University Press.

Gallimore, R., & Goldenberg, C. (1993). Activity settings of early literacy: Home and school factors in children's emergent literacy. In E. A. Forman, N. Minick, & C. A. Stone (Eds.), *Contexts for learning: Sociocultural dynamics in children's development* (pp. 315–335). New York: Oxford University Press.

Goodnow, J. J. (1993). Afterword: Direction of post-Vygotskian research. In E. A. Forman, N. Minick, & C. A. Stone (Eds.), *Contexts for learning: Sociocultural dynamics in children's development* (pp. 369–381). New York: Oxford University Press.

Halliday, M. A. K. (1975). Some aspects of sociolinguistics. In *Interactions between linguistics and mathematical education* (pp. 64–73). Copenhagen: UNESCO.

Halliday, M. A. K. (1978). *Language as social semiotic: The social interpretation of language and meaning.* Baltimore, MD: University Park Press.

Lave, J., & Wenger, E. (1991). *Situated learning: Legitimate peripheral participation.* New York: Cambridge University Press.

Lemke, J. L. (1990). *Talking science: Language, learning, and values.* Norwood, NJ: Albex Publishing Company.

Leont'ev, A. N. (1981). The problem of activity in psychology. In J. V. Wertsch (Ed.), *The concept of activity in Soviet psychology* (pp. 37–71). Armonk, NY: M. E. Sharpe.

Luria, A. R. (1976). *Cognitive development: Its cultural and social foundations.* Cambridge: Harvard University Press.

Minick, N., Stone, C. A., & Forman, E. A. (1993). Introduction: The integration of individual, social, and institutional processes in accounts of children's learning and development. In E. A. Forman, N. Minick, & C. A. Stone (Eds.), *Contexts for learning: Sociocultural dynamics in children's development* (pp. 3–16). New York: Oxford University Press.

Moll, L. C. (Ed.). (1990). *Vygotsky and education: Instructional implications and applications of sociohistorical psychology.* New York: Cambridge University Press.

National Council of Teachers of Mathematics. (1989). *Curriculum and evaluation standards for school mathematics.* Reston, VA: National Council of Teachers of Mathematics.

National Council of Teachers of Mathematics. (1991). *Professional standards for teaching mathematics.* Reston, VA: National Council of Teachers of Mathematics.

Newman, D., Griffin, P., & Cole, M. (1989). *The construction zone: Working for cognitive change in school.* Cambridge: Cambridge University Press.

Pimm, D. (1987). *Speaking mathematically: Communication in mathematics classrooms*. New York: Routledge and Kegan.

Rogoff, B. (1990). *Apprenticeship in thinking: Cognitive development in social context*. New York: Oxford University Press.

Saxe, G. B. (1991). *Culture and cognitive development: Studies in mathematical understanding*. Hillsdale, NJ: Lawrence Erlbaum Associates.

Saxe, G. B., Gearhart, M., Note, M., & Paduano, P. (1993). Peer interaction and the development of mathematical understandings: A new framework for research and educational practice. In H. Daniels (Ed.), *Charting the agenda: Vygotskian perspectives* (pp. 107–144). London: Routledge.

Stodolsky, S. S. (1988). *The subject matters: Classroom activity in math and social studies*. Chicago: University of Chicago Press.

Tharp, R. G., & Gallimore, R. G. (1988). *Rousing minds to life: Teaching, learning, and schooling in social context*. New York: Cambridge University Press.

Vygotsky, L. S. (1978). *Mind in society*. M. Cole, V. John-Steiner, S. Scribner, & E. Souberman (Eds.) Cambridge, MA: Harvard University Press.

Vygotsky, L. S. (1987). *The collected works of L. S. Vygotsky, Vol. 1: Problems of general psychology*. R. W. Rieber & A. S. Carton (Eds.). (N. Minick, Trans.) New York: Plenum.

Wertsch, J. V. (Ed.). (1981). *The concept of activity in Soviet psychology*. Armonk, NY: M. E. Sharpe.

Wertsch, J. V. (Ed.). (1985a). *Culture, communication and cognition: Vygotskian perspectives*. New York: Cambridge University Press.

Wertsch, J. V. (1985b). *Vygotsky and the social formation of mind*. Cambridge, MA: Harvard University Press.

Wertsch, J. V. (1991). *Voices of the mind: A sociocultural approach to mediated action*. Cambridge, MA: Harvard University Press.

9 Cultural Processes and Learning: Expectations, Actions, and Outcomes

Kathryn Crawford
University of Sydney

It is now generally accepted by a large group of researchers that knowledge is constructed by individuals as a result of their experience (Cobb, 1988; Crawford, 1986a, 1986b, 1991; Duckworth, 1983; Engestrom, 1989; Harel & Papert, 1990; Lave, 1988; Resnick, 1987; Sachter, 1990; von Glasersfeld, 1987). Experience occurs as a result of acting, even as an observer, in a cultural context. Van Oers presents a cultural-historical picture of mathematics as an active human pursuit deeply embedded in a history of human activities. His Vygotskian position focuses on the importance of social interaction or "interactions among adults and children" in the interiorization of culturally approved meanings and symbols— he posits a process in which "meaningful learning is made dependent on pupils' opportunity to evaluate their own insights and ideas in critical comparison with culturally available concepts, norms and methods." However, peoples' engagement with culturally approved ideas and procedures involves taking action— intellectually at least. Perceptions about the relevance, meaning, and motivation to engage depend on both the comparisons just discussed and the extent to which the ideas and insights are perceived to empower people to act in functional ways not possible before.

In the wider cultural arena outside schools, there is some evidence that mathematical activity, the ways mathematics is used and experienced, and the people who use it are changing. In the past, mathematics was generally used by an elite to assist in understanding of the physical environment. More recently, mathematics has been used to interpret, describe, and define the social environment. In addition, electronic machines now carry out many of the routine algorithmic procedures that used to occupy the minds of people in the past. These changes imply a change in the quality of the mathematical knowledge needed by learners for active participation in technologically based cultures, and in the quality of the cognitive activity that occurs as part of the learning process.

In spite of widespread acceptance of recent theories of socially mediated and personally constructed learning, schools and universities are very stable institutions and many have persisted with a craft of instruction and a mathematics curriculum that has changed little in the past generation. As a result there is a often gap between "espoused theories" and "theories in action" (Argyris, 1993) among educators. When activity is considered as an important factor in the construction of knowledge, a number of questions are raised. How does a learner subjectively experience, or interpret, his or her own action, and the actions of others, in an educational setting? What are the relationships, if any, between the cultural context of a learning activity, the behavior of the learner, the learner's subjective experience of the action, and the qualities of the cognitive and affective activity that occur?

This chapter explores the dynamic interconnectedness of learning activities, the sociocultural arena in which they occur, the cognitive processes that are initiated, the cognitive artifacts that are used, and the quality of the resulting learning outcomes. The systemic approach to learning as an activity in context is taken in order to elaborate the practical relevance of theory—a theory of practical action.

CULTURAL CONTEXT AND COGNITION

Despite a history of disagreement and debate, Vygotsky (1978) and his compatriots Luria (1973, 1982) and Leont'ev (1981) have, among them, developed a basis for a comprehensive theory of human development in terms of intra- and interpersonal activity in the course of collective and individual actions in a historical and cultural context. Vygotsky's emphasis on signs as the means of mediation between the objects of experience and mental functions has aroused much interest. His focus on social interaction and language is in keeping with most educational practice. Vygotsky (1978) suggested that the wider cultural forces shape intellectual development and are in turn shaped by the products of human activity. He used the term *coknowledge* to stress the sociocultural basis of knowing. He also stressed the nonabsolute nature of consciousness. That is, people form a culture and are formed by it through the process of socially mediated meanings. Luria's theory of brain action provides an interactive neuropsychological explanation of intrapersonal activity. His theory provides a powerful explanation of the cognitive processes associated with different learning activities. Leont'ev and other researchers have, with the theory of activity, developed an explanatory model of the process of cognitive development in context through the activity of people—of the relationships between knowledge and action. They have proposed a dynamic relationship between human activity of all kinds and cognitive development.

The Russian theorists, particularly Leont'ev and other activity theorists, claim that "higher order mental functions" are complex functional systems that are formed during the course of an individual's development as the result of social experiences and activity. In other words, higher order abstract knowledge, ideas and processing capacities develop in situations where these are functional in terms of the needs, expectations, and goals of the individual or cultural group. Their theoretical position presents major challenges to philosophical and psychological assumptions underlying the organisation and practice of most educational institutions and much educational research.

First, Western psychologists have traditionally limited their consideration of human development at the skull, or skin, of an individual. Educational assessment focuses on individuals without reference to the context of their activity. There has been tendency for differences in experience and action to be interpreted as differences in ability. The early research on girls and mathematics achievement is an example (e.g., Fennema & Sherman, 1977). For the activity theorists the relationships between the elements of an activity system, both people and cultural artifacts, are the focus of attention in an analysis of human activity. Valsiner (1992, p. 7) presented a similar point of view when he suggested that:

> A social nature assumption of the developmental psychology would seem to require that these boundaries be drawn at points that incorporate relevant aspects of the social environment into the system. Finally, this systems approach would seem to require that attempts are made to understand the interdependent relationships between constituent parts rather than searches for cause and effect.

Second, a separation between mind and body, or cognitive and physical action, has been evident in the thinking of educators since the time of Aristotle. It was also the basis of a major point of disagreement between Vygotsky and Leont'ev. This separation is reflected in definitions of culture in western literature. Harris (1968, p. 16) defined culture in terms of "patterns of behavior," whereas Goodenough (1957, p. 167) describes culture in terms of "things people have in mind." For the activity theorists, physical action, thinking, and feeling are all part of human activity.

Finally, the notions of nonabsolute consciousness, multiple points of view, and the lack of separation of human activity from its context fly in the face of the positivistic notions of objectivity, universality, and generalizability that are such important underpinnings of the discipline of mathematics and also underpin much psychological research. For example, Cattell (1971), who acknowledged the role of culture in cognitive development, described tasks that involve visual perception of complex relationships as "culture free" on the basis that the opportunities to see were equally available to all.

The implications of the important contribution of Vygotsky is the focus of van Oers' chapter (chapter 7). He refers to Leont'ev's (1975) term *cultural meaning* (znacenie) and suggests that it can be expressed by symbols (mostly language), transformed into curriculum content, and taught—the major focus of school teaching and learning. For the Russian theorists, "culture" is generally synonymous with education. Although van Oers also mentions the importance of Leont'ev's notion of personal meaning (sense; smysl'), he focuses on the processes of mathematical enculturation and meaning formation—the importance of negotiation between experts and novices as they are initiated into culturally significant forms of mathematical knowledge. In the discussion to follow, the focus shifts away from the traditional school task of negotiating culturally approved meanings to examine the relationships between knowledge and action.

LEARNING AS ACTIVITY

Cognition, Objects, and Activity

Activity theory and the research based on this view of human activity and learning in context suggest the importance of a more systemic model of the process of learning in which the past experience and opportunity of learners, their present conceptions of the educational context, their consciousness or awareness, their feelings, and their approaches to specific tasks are taken into account.

Mathematics is often described as a way of thinking or understanding the world—the process of reasoning with variables and their relationships. Categorical thinking is important in the development of early ideas of number and measurement and in most mathematical applications. The term *categorical thinking* as used by Luria (1973, 1982) and Vygotsky (1978) refers to the process by which previously internalized complex categorical concepts are used as the objects of conscious intellectual activity. Vygotsky was particularly interested in the developmental processes that occur as concepts are gradually internalized through communication with significant others (parents, peers, and teachers).

Perhaps because of a historical need to align themselves with the official ideology, the activity theorists and Luria have investigated a more global view of human activity and communication as the basis for human development and a sharper focus on the relationship between the knower, or learner, and the known. Luria referred to the resulting complex and abstract knowledge about meaningful categories and the relationships between them as *matrices of community relations*. Knowledge derived from past actions and emotions, expectations, social roles, behaviors, and relationships, as well as formal knowledge, is embedded the matrices and embodied in later action. It is highly personal and, in the sense that the history of activity and of the settings in which activity has occurred, is different for each individual, highly subjective.

Schooling is only a small part of the cultural experience of children, of the shared community actions that draw their attention to culturally significant categories. Luria (1976) presented evidence of the shaping of awareness of categories by culturally significant activities. He also noted that without formal schooling many people describe attributes of objects in terms of related activity.

Clear examples of the nonabsolute nature of consciousness and differences in categorical thinking and internalized action occur in bicultural schools for children from traditionally oriented Pitjantjatjara communities in central Australia. Anthropological research (e.g., Rudder, 1983) suggests substantial differences between Aboriginal and non-Aboriginal categorical thinking even about such perceptually grounded concepts as color. For the Pitjantjatjara children the primary colors that are commonly used to distinguish counters and other manipulative materials used in school were not immediately evident as a means of classification. They found the colored plastic counters, commonly used in early number activities, indistinguishable in meaningful terms. This difficulty is in sharp contrast to non-Aboriginal Australian children for whom color is usually a significant, if not overriding, basis for the classification of sets of objects.

In mathematics education it seems important to recognize that shared actions and cultural experience form the basis of the cultural "sense"—the shared personal sense of groups of people. More abstract meanings and insights are created on this basis. Most importantly, the motivation of learners to act mathematically and the quality of their mathematics will depend on their personal perception of the cultural meaning of such actions, of the cultural significance for them of mathematical ways of thinking, as well as their knowledge of mathematical meanings and techniques. Sometimes the value conflict is acute. Adult students of the Anangu[1] Teacher Education Program (ANTEP) among the Pitjantjatjara people of Central Australia often asked: "Why do you compare things all the time and need to know how many there are of everything?" They then explained that comparisons, particularly those made about people, were highly censured in their community. In addition, the very high priority given in Western culture to quantity and to quantifiable variables was not supported by everyday activities and modes of categorical thinking in traditional Aboriginal communities. For them, learning mathematics was a serious decision because of the values and priorities implicit in mathematical activity. One woman stated, "If we learn this stuff we will not really be Anangu any more."

A Paradigm for the Construction of Knowledge Through Activity

The activity theory proposed by Leont'ev (1981) is a powerful paradigm that describes the process through which knowledge is constructed as a result of personal, and subjective, experience of an activity. In contrast to much Western

---

[1]Anangu means people in the local Aboriginal language.

psychology, Leont'ev stresses the inseparability of human mental reflection from those aspects of human activity that engender it. He uses the term *activity* to describe conscious intellectual and other behavior that is stimulated by a motive and subordinated to a goal or expectation. This inclusiveness stretches to include affective factors. For example, Fel'dshtein (1983, p. 22) made a distinction between object-oriented activity and activity directed toward the development of interrelations with people and society. However, he stressed that the distinction is provisional "since the process of activity is one."

Leont'ev (1981, p. 61) gave a microanalysis of activity and describes actions and operations as the basic components. He distinguished between actions and operations as follows:

- An *action* involves conscious behaviour that is subordinated to a goal.
- An *operation* is an action that has been transformed as a means of achieving a result under given conditions.

Leont'ev suggested that operations may be thought of as largely unconscious operational responses that have been included in another action and thus become technical means to an end. He described the process of changing gears in a car as an example of the transformation of an action into an operation. Initially, shifting gears is an action consciously subordinate to a goal. Later, with more experience, this operation is performed unconsciously as a means to the action of changing the speed of an automobile or some other aspect of the driving process. Luria (1973) proposed that different functional units of the brain are involved in conscious actions and routine operations. Research by Crawford (1986b) supported the claim and indicated that operations are a major aspect of the cognitive demands of teacher assessment at all levels of schooling, whereas actions are involved in problem solving and inquiry.

As well as stressing that operations, in contrast to goal subordinated actions, are unconsciously performed, Leont'ev (1981, p. 64) suggested that "It is generally the fate of operations that, sooner or later, they become the function of a machine." For example, when one uses a calculator to solve a mathematical problem the action is not broken by this "extracerebral link." Rather, the arithmetic computation has become a "technicalized" operation: the function of a machine.

A particular activity is necessarily defined by both a motive and a goal or expectation. That is, a single motive may stimulate different actions depending on individual perceptions of the goal or object of the motive. Conversely, a single goal may be reached by different actions depending on the motive. For example, an open-ended question in a secure student-centered learning environment may stimulate a variety of responses as students with different needs and perceptions of the goal of the task seek a solution in different ways. In a more authoritarian setting, the goal of achieving "the answer" to a mathematical problem may be achieved by copying from a friend, working it out from first principles, or remembering the solution from a previous experience. Apparently identical actions may have different meanings and involve qualitatively different thinking, and learning, for people with differing needs and goals.

Davydov, Zinchenko, and Talysina (1983, p. 33) explained these ideas in some detail, suggesting that "activity" involves the following:

1. A need that impels a subject to search for an object or goal.
2. The discovery of an object or goal. Once the object is discovered, intellectual activity is no longer guided by the characteristics of the object itself but by its (subjective) image.
3. The generation of an "image" is seen as a bilateral process between subject and object.
4. The conversion of activity into objective results.

Because the perceptions of needs and goals are subjective, the ideological framework of values, expectations, and beliefs and the knowledge resulting from past activity play an important role in determining the thinking processes that are used. Davydovv et al. (1983, p. 33) emphasized the difference between the above process and stimulus/response theories in which the state of the subject is determined directly by objects. "Activity" in Leont'ev's terms is described as a process in which subject and object reciprocate.

Earlier forms of activity appear to be predominantly externally oriented. Internal activity is perceived as secondary and is formed in the process of internalization of external object related activity. Davydov et al. (1983, p. 34) suggested:

> First, in the process of internalization, there is not only a transition from the external plane to the internal plane but also a transition from collective activity to individual activity (collective activity takes place as joint practical activity and in the form of communication and language). Second, internalization does not consist in a shift of external activity to the internal plane of consciousness that precedes it, but in the very formation of that plane.

Activity theory as proposed by Leont'ev describes the cognitive dynamics of the *setting* described by Lave (1988, p. 150). She conceived of a setting as a *"relation*ship between acting persons and the arena in relation with which they act." When the dynamics of the cognitive consequences of different settings are explored, a number of new questions about learning in a cultural setting are raised. What have students learned from their previous cultural experience? Why do they need to do a particular mathematical task at school? Is there a contradiction or tension between teacher needs and student needs? Are teacher intentions shared by students? What are the students' interpretations or expectations about the "setting" of their activity? How do they perceive culturally significant objects in the environment such as computers? How do they perceive the object (goal) of their efforts?

Engestrom (1989) extended Leont'ev's theory and used the term *activity system* to describe the situation, common in educational contexts, where a group of people act together to develop and use expertise. For Engestrom the activity system involves the community, rules of behavior, division of labor, instruments, subjects, shared objects (goals), and outcomes. It is an interacting system that is always in a state of imbalance as a group works through the tensions and inconsistencies to achieve a goal. The shared meanings are created through a shared history of action.

Applications of Activity Theory in Mathematics Education

Activity theory has been used as a basis for research in mathematics education by Russian researchers. Under the influence of Leont'ev's theory of activity, these researchers investigated aspects of information processing (about objects in the physical world) from a more phenomenological perspective. The connections between such factors as role, mode of coding, and self regulation were their main interest. As a result of this interest, cognitive activity was considered within a social context. This approach added considerably to the explanatory power of the model as a theoretical basis for investigations of the relationships between cognitive abilities and problem-solving behaviors—between thinking and acting.

For example, Semenov (1978, p. 3), in a study of arithmetic problem solving, suggested that "the human problem solver is viewed as bringing a complex system to the task situation and this system plays just as important a role in the resulting outcome as does the information from the environment." He stressed the importance of actions, in Leont'ev's terms, as well as operational behavior in the problem-solving process. According to Semenov, actions involve two planes of intellectual behavior. The way in which the situation is perceived by the subject is referred to as the *person–object plane* or *intellectual plane* of thinking. The cognitive processes involved in the monitoring and evaluating of the ongoing problem solving effort are referred to as the *personal plane* of thinking. That is, conscious goal-subordinated cognitive activity, involving self-regulatory processes, occurs both in reflection about objective information and in reflection about problem-solving strategies. It is only when considering a third "operational plane of activity" that Semenov considered factors such as the logicomathematical, deductive processes that are associated with cognition in most Western research.

Semenov (1978, p. 5) described the different roles of the personal and intellectual planes of cognitive activity in the following way: "The intellectual plane of thought pertains to the development of the content of the problem; the personal plane refers to the extent to which the problem becomes *part of the individual's own consciousness*" (italics added).

In Semenov's detailed descriptions of problem-solving performance, the object-related and "personal" components of cognitive activity are mediated by reflection. That is, subjects switch from reflection of the objects of the problem to consideration and evaluation of their own actions and strategies during the process. The amount of object-related cognitive activity is increased in response to semantically complex novel problems. According to Semenov, a subject's past social experience and perceived role in the problem-solving situation are important factors that determine qualitative aspects of intellectual activity. In particular, the inhibition of immediate responses to allow for reflection and self-regulation in any plane of intellectual activity occurs only to the extent that the subject values the resulting activity.

In my own research on children's approaches to verbally formulated arithmetic problems (Crawford, 1986a, 1986b), data supported the claims made by Semenov. In particular, children's use of conscious intellectual activity or the person–object plane (using simultaneous processing according to Luria's model of brain function and metacognitive processes in the personal plane) were particularly associated with the interpretation of the problems and the selection of strategies for a solution. The results suggested that the actual implementation of algorithmic procedures to achieve a solution (generally well automated for the sample studied) placed less demand on intellectual capabilities. However, interviews with the children revealed the strong impact of the "setting" in which they found themselves. Teacher demands for speed in working were internalized to the extent that most students when solving the problems in a normal classroom context moved immediately to an operational plane of thinking and generally misinterpreted semantically complex questions. In the interview situation, when the expectation that they consider the meaning of the problem prior to attempting a solution was explicitly conveyed many were able to interpret the problem correctly without further assistance. None of the sample ($n = 210$) spontaneously checked their solutions. Several informed me during the interview that "that is the teacher's job." When explicitly asked to check that their answer "made sense" all children checked the operational procedure used and none reviewed the meaning of the question posed. Similarly, although all children were aware of the teacher's instructions to use estimation as a means of avoiding computational errors, none used the technique unless an estimate was required as part of the written answer. Even students who volunteered comments about further encouragement to estimate from parents explained that in reality there was no advantage since estimates were unrecognized by the teacher and because, in their experience, "speed" was so important in mathematics: "If you estimate you don't get the work finished." It was clear that the children's perceptions of their role as learners and the teachers' role, derived as tacit conclusions from the actions of everyone in the context, had a powerful impact on their behavior and overrode verbal instructions and explanations that were not consistent with the dynamics of interpersonal activity.

The results of the study suggest that in an instructional context student cognitive activity in mathematics is often unduly constrained to operations and operational planes of thought. Further, decisions in the personal plane about priorities and choices about the actions to be carried out were generally covert, and strongly influenced by the characteristics of the context—the roles adopted by members of the activity system, the time constraints, and the tacit values and priorities that were interpreted from the past actions of other members of the group. Without prior experience of decision making about actions and opportunity to communicate about them in a group, many students had neither the language development nor the mathematical understanding to tackle semantically complex tasks.

NEEDS, EXPECTATIONS AND GOALS: CHANGING THE QUALITY OF LEARNING

Innovation is also associated with tensions and inconsistencies. Changes in pedagogical style and technological innovation are each associated with situations that highlight inconsistencies in the needs, expectations and goals of the different participants in an activity system and provide insight into the dynamics of the learning process.

Activity in Teacher Education

The relationship between a person acting and the arena in which they act has powerful consequences in terms of learning outcomes. Lave (1988, p. 187) reported that "the classroom with its authoritative program of knowledge to be transmitted and separation from the aspects of life it purports to prepare pupils for, with its discipline and tests, has a powerful impact on embodied knowledge . . . many years later." It signifies the ideology that adults act upon in relation to mathematical activities. She reported that the algorithmic forms of "real math" that were discursively transmitted in the school setting seem far less powerfully embodied in later practice. Johnston (1991) found a similar outcome in her work exploring the memories of adult professional women about how they came to be "mathematized" as women in a Western culture. The memories were of feelings of success, images of topping the class or of failure, of their status or position in the social setting in which they learned, and of how it felt to be a girl doing mathematics. There was a notable silence in their accounts about the actual mathematics they were learning. The memories were almost exclusively of the "setting" in Lave's (1988) terms or in the "personal plane" of Semenov (1978). They described the relation between themselves as acting persons and the context in which their activities were carried out.

Teachers are important actors in context for mathematics education. The experience of learning mathematics in a school setting is also deeply embodied in teachers' later professional practice. Ball (1987) wrote of the necessity to "unlearn to teach mathematics." Crawford (1992) found that preservice primary teachers entered mathematics courses with strongly held attitudes and beliefs about how mathematics is learned and the role of the teacher that were derived from their own educational experience. These beliefs about learning mathematics—about what teachers and students do—shaped their perceptions of classroom events and their behavior as beginning teachers. Although the student teachers had extensive declarative knowledge about recent theories of learning, this form of knowledge was of little help when they were asked to work in groups in schools to develop a student-centered context for mathematical inquiry. Writing essays about theories of learning did not empower them with knowledge about how to act in the classroom. Almost all students experienced difficulties in the early practical sessions because of the belief that they needed to "teach the children something" before they could expect them to enquire or investigate. This need took priority over the imposed goal of the course. Many were surprised when confronted by their strongly held beliefs that the children were "empty vessels." Nevertheless, they reported that they spent most of the time in the early sessions "telling" the children about mathematics. One student wrote: "Often I felt compelled to tell the children the answer or to show them how to do it . . . having always found mathematics easy. However, I realized that I don't enter the classroom empty headed—I was able to restrain my own thoughts and feelings and focus on developing the children ability to think."

In addition to the tensions between their deeply help beliefs about how teachers act and their knowledge of learning theories, another major difficulty emerged. The student teachers had all completed mathematics courses at the matriculation level and had been successful in learning axioms and algorithms. However, few of them had any experience of using mathematics to solve novel problems or of talking about and explaining mathematical concepts. This gap in their mathematical knowledge was only revealed as they attempted to think mathematically in a new setting.

Student teachers were required to assess the needs, expectations, and goals of the children as they worked. They were also asked to allow children to experience active and responsible decision making about the goals of their projects and the ways in which those goals might be achieved. That is, they were to create a setting in which children could be involved in self-directed activity. Many found this difficult. It required a completely new way of looking at children's learning.

Only toward the end of the course did the student teachers begin to differentiate between their own intentions and goals and those of the children. As they began to act on this new awareness they began to see a change in the dynamics of the classroom. As goals were clarified and new expectations for children were negotiated, student teachers changed their position in the classroom and began the process of "seeing" the setting differently. One student talked excitedly about "going through a gate and coming out in a place I never knew existed." Most expressed surprise and amazement at the knowledge and creativity of the children as they responded to the new conditions. In addition, for the student teachers, the action of creating a new setting for mathematics learning had deepened their understanding of the processes of teaching and learning in ways that had not occurred as a result of conventional courses.

It appears that expectations, knowledge, attitudes, and beliefs internalized as the result of previous activities, including the cultural process of schooling, are powerfully embodied in later related activities whether they have been formally discussed and negotiated or not. These "theories of action" (Argyris, 1993) are highly personal and usually tacit and operational. They are not easily available for review, possibly because reflection and discussion about the dynamics of action are not a major component of formal education. There is some evidence that this metacognitive knowledge influences the quality of activity in the "personal plane" for both teachers and students and that it is more powerfully embodied in later action than declarative knowledge of learning theories, advice, or instruction.

Acting and Learning with New Tools

New tools also highlight tensions in an educational activity system (Engestrom, 1989). The presence of a cultural artifact such as a computer in an educational activity system changes the context—the possibilities for roles, relationships, and cognition. For the Russian theorists, cultural sense, or cultural tools in thinking, were considered to be developed through education. In practice they generally ignored the "primitive" learning that occurred outside the education system. However, the impact of different cultural priorities on the approaches of Aboriginal children to school learning tasks has already been mentioned. Computers are a particular kind of tecchnicalized cultural tool that now forms as increasingly important and pervasive part of human activity and social organisation. Papert (1980, p. 20) suggested that "school math" is a social construction from a time before computers. He went on to say that "The metaphor of computer as a mathematics-speaking entity puts the learner in a qualitatively new kind of relationship to an important domain of knowledge." There is a tension between the traditional ways of learning and teaching mathematics in schools and the quality of learning activity needed for functional numeracy in a computer age. At present there is little evidence that computers have fulfilled the educational potential envisioned by Papert.

Engestrom's (1989) notion of an activity system was a useful framework for an analysis of the activity of a group of year six girls who were introduced to Lego/LOGO materials as part of their mathematics and science education (Crawford, 1991). The project provides an excellent example of the tensions and contradictions between traditional modes of instruction and a traditional school

culture and the more active learning environments suggested by recent constructivist theories. The project also provided some insight into reasons behind the
ambivalence that many teachers feel about the use of computer applications in
the mainstream curriculum.

The school culture was extremely conservative. Classroom observations revealed highly teacher-centered modes of instruction. Good behavior, order, and
neatness were most valued. The girls themselves perceived compliance with
specific instructions and production of the "correct" outcome as the major teacher expectations. The students always worked alone, and "cheating" was avoided
by close supervision and censure. Paper-and-pencil tests and percentage marks
were the only forms of assessment and reporting used in mathematics. The girls
correctly interpreted their role as passive and applied themselves in what Semenov (1978) would describe as the personal plane of action, to producing the
learning products that were required by teachers in any way possible. The cognitive demands of the setting were largely operational.

In this culture, learning in mathematics consisted of imitation, following
instructions, remembering, learning set routines until they were efficient "operations" (Leont'ev, 1981), and being evaluated by the "expert" teacher. Learning
was done alone. The quality of the girls' mathematical knowledge was typical of
the outcomes of such traditional educational settings. The girls were extremely
efficient at computation algorithms. Most knew the multiplication tables by rote.
Their books were very neat and filled with carefully laid out calculations or
geometry information that they "copied from the board." When given a task
requiring an explanation of their solution to a verbally formulated mathematical
problem, most responded at a unistructural level in terms of the SOLO taxonomy
of student responses (Collis & Biggs, 1982). Only a very small minority were
able to discuss their solutions in terms of all the relevant variables and the
relationships between them.

In their homes, blocks and mechanics were things for boys to think about.
They were sent to music lessons, ballet lessons, and other more "suitable"
pursuits. Most had never paid very much attention at all to the many electronic
gadgets in their homes, to the gears and pulleys in machinery, or to other features
of their environments that might have given them a basis for some insight into the
possibilities of the Lego Technic building materials and the necessary logic for
designing LOGO programs for the models they made. The girls came from
affluent families, but their experience of family activities had left them conceptually impoverished in three-dimensional geometry and mechanics.

The girls were grouped and provided with Lego/LOGO materials. After some
initial discussions about the building materials, the girls were encouraged to
experiment. They were almost completely paralyzed by anxiety about the responsibility of defining a project for themselves. Project staff provided an initial
input about programming in LOGO and some assistance about the names of
various gears and sensors that formed part of the Lego kit. The girls found
building three-dimensional objects very difficult.

Imagine a group of girls looking suspiciously at a pile of Lego materials. Eventually one comes across to the project staff holding a small model in her hand. "Is this correct?" she asks tentatively. A girl from another group approaches to look at the model. It is snatched away and hidden with cries of "Don't copy!" Eventually, because it is the first session, each group is allowed to choose a card from the Lego/LOGO set to *copy* a model. With sighs of relief they all settle down to a familiar task. The teacher also looked very relieved as order was restored. She commented in a rather puzzled tone that the girls had "done" lots of "work" on three-dimensional shapes in mathematics lessons. She was surprised by their apparent difficulties.

The new context for learning made very different demands on the girls. They needed to experiment, pose problems, investigate, reason about the relationships between the parts of their models and how they moved. They needed to physically organize the materials to build three-dimensional objects—to engage in actions both mental and physical. Each group needed to define their own project and evaluate progress. Their activities were in the personal plane not the operational plane that they had experienced in formal lessons. They needed a conceptual understanding of the three-dimensional geometry of even the simplest models. To work effectively in groups they needed to be able to articulate their thinking, explain their strategies and describe their difficulties. They were inexperienced in these activities, and the need for them was in conflict with their expectations.

Papert (1980) and Sachter (1990) wrote about the potential of LOGO as an active learning environment. The setting in which LOGO is used is an important determinant of the extent to which the potential is realised. For the girls in the project the unaccustomed intellectual activity and responsibility was a new experience. They found discussions about their mechanical models initially difficult as they had neither the vocabulary nor the logico-grammatical structures to explain their problems. A new quality of mathematical understanding was necessary. It became clear that the "work" they had done in class on three-dimensional shapes and gears had not provided them with a knowledge base that they could use in this new context. The class teacher found the facilitative role of the adults in the project quite difficult. She grew anxious that she should be "helping the children . . . so they can get on with it . . . and finish in time." The students adjusted quite quickly to the new demands. By the end of the term most felt secure and proud of the work they had done. They explained the resolutions to the their problems at a relational level in the SOLO taxonomy (Collis & Biggs, 1982). The quality of their responses reflected their ownership of the activities they were undertaking and a clearer understanding of their goals.

One student wrote in her dairy:

> I worked with Nadine and our project was a tower with a flashing light and three gears with smaller gears that go faster and a big gear that goes slower. This tower had a helicopter like top and if it had no gears to make it go slower. It would spin

off which we experienced last week. The gears are like wheels with spiny edges (diagram) with poles on them so that they join to the tower. Our new thing that we did was make gears like the drawing above. We made gears to make the helicopter (top) not fly off. It was fabulous that we made gears. I feel fabulous and proud that we made this creation. We put our fabulous creation on disk 11.

Lego building blocks and LOGO language are both good examples of new cultural artefacts that have substantial mathematical knowledge embedded in them. However, the quality of student learning through the experience of using the blocks to model and of interacting with a computer through programming in LOGO depends on the quality of the setting of the activities. Activity theory suggests that the quality of the thinking of students in such new contexts will be delimited by their subjective perceptions of needs, expectations, and goals. These in turn interact with those of the teachers, parents, and other members of the educational community. The perceptions of each group are shaped by their past experience and learning through cultural processes. As Salomon, Perkins, and Globerson (1991, p. 8) indicated, "this means it is not technology alone affecting minds but a whole 'cloud of correlated variables'—technology, activity, goal, setting, teacher's role, culture—exerting the combined effect."

CONCLUSIONS

Activity theory suggests a need to pay attention to the quality of internalized actions, emotions, and social expectations during learning as well as to issues associated with the processes of acculturation of students into the meaning of culturally approved mathematical ideas, symbols, and techniques. Students' cultural experiences, their intentions, their needs, and the kinds of mathematical activity that they experience all shape the quality of their mathematics learning and the ways that they are later able to feel, act, and think mathematically.

The cultural activities associated with the use of mathematical knowledge have changed significantly with the advent of information technologies. Computers have made possible, and accessible, new mathematical ideas such as those associated with chaos theory and the related fractal geometry. These ideas have changed the way in which large numbers of people think about their environment and their position wwithin it. In addition to changing the nature of mathematics, computers now carry out many of the set routines and algorithms that were once learned through drill and practice (and still occupy a large part of most school curricula). Such a change in cultural tools implies changes in the quality of intellectual activity when most humans act mathematically—perhaps less focus on known techniques and more attention to more creative acts such as interpretation of mathematical information and modeling. Certainly, the traditional focus in schools on operational planes of thought and paper-and-pencil techniques now seems anachronistic.

Like the Pitantjatjara people, mentioned earlier, we need to recognize the seriousness of the choices that are possible. We could choose to maintain the traditional cultural processes of schooling. In particular, we could choose to maintain the authoritative setting in which mathematics is learned, with the social dimensions of the context, the emphasis on paper-and-pencil techniques, and marginal role for computers. However, there is now sufficient understanding of the relationships between the sociocultural environment in which learning activities occur, the qualities of the cognitive processes that are functional for the activity at hand, and the quality of the resulting learning outcomes to suggest a need for some changes in educational practice. We could choose to organize educational contexts in such a way that, in addition to negotiating the meanings of culturally approved ideas, categories, and techniques, attention is paid to the activity of members of educational communities—to the isomorphism between the learning activity and the embodiment of internalized actions in later mathematical activity. Choosing to pay more attention to the actions of learners and teachers, and to how mathematical knowledge is embodied in action, may involve questioning the differences between the quality, aims, and goals of the actions of teachers and learners in school and the actions of mathematicians and users of mathematics in the wider culture.

REFERENCES

Argyris, C. (1993). *Knowledge for action: A guide to overcoming barriers to organizational change*. San Francisco: Jossey Bass.

Ball, D. (1987). Unlearning to teach mathematics. *For the Learning of Mathematics, 8*(1), 40–47.

Cattell, R. B. (1971). *Abilities, their structure, growth, and action*. Boston: Houghton Mifflin.

Cobb, P. (1988). The tension between theories of learning and instruction in mathematics, *Educational Psychologist, 23*(2), 87–104.

Collis, K., & Biggs, J. (1982). *Evaluating the quality of learning outcomes*. Hillsdale, NJ: Lawrence Erlbaum Associates.

Crawford, K. P. (1986a, July). Cognitive and social factors in problem solving behaviour. *Proceedings of the Tenth Conference of the International Group for the Psychology of Mathematics Education* (pp. 415–421). London.

Crawford, K. P. (1986b). *Simultaneous and successive processing, executive control and social experience: Individual differences in educational achievement and problem solving in mathematics*. Unpublished doctoral dissertation, University of New England, Armidale, New South Wales, Australia.

Crawford, K. P. (1991). Playing with Lego/Logo: School definitions of work and their influence on learning behaviour. In L. Nevile (Ed.), *Proceedings of the Logo in Mathematics Conference—LME5* (pp. 45–55). Melbourne, Victoria: Australian Council of Educational Research.

Crawford, K. P. (1992). Applying theory in teacher education: Changing practice in mathematics education. In W. Geeslin and K. Graham (Eds.), *Proceedings of the Sixteenth PME Conference* (pp. 161–167). Durham, NH: University of New Hampshire.

Davydov, V. V., Zinchenko, V. P., & Talysina, N. F. (1983). The problem of activity in the works of A. N. Leont'ev (1). *Soviet Psychology 21*(4), 31–43.

Duckworth, E. (1983). Teachers as learners. *Archives de Psychologie, 51*, 171–175.

Engestrom, Y. (1989). *Developing thinking at the changing work-place: Towards a redefinition of expertise* (Tech. Rep. No. 130). San Diego: Centre for Human Information Processing, University of California.

Fel'dshtein, D. I. (1983). Characteristics of the development of activity in the child in ontogeny. *Soviet Psychology, 1*(3), 18–38.

Fennema, E., & Sherman, J. (1977). Sex-related differences in mathematics achievement, spatial visualization and affective factors. *American Journal of Educational Research, 14*(1), 51–71.

Goodenough, W. (1957). Cultural anthropology and linguistics. In P. L. Garvin (Ed.), *Report to the Seventh Round Table Meeting on Linguistics and Language Study* (pp. 167–173). Washington, DC: Georgetown University Press.

Harel, I., & Papert, S. (1990). Software design as a learning environment. In I. Harel (Ed.), *Constructionist learning* (pp. 19–50). Cambridge, MA: MIT Media Laboratory.

Harris, M. (1968). *The rise of anthropological theory.* New York: Thomas Cromwell.

Johnston, B. (1991, September). *Memory work and the mathematisation of women.* Paper presented at the postgraduate Education Forum, University of Sydney.

Lave, J. (1988). *Cognition in practice.* New York: Cambridge University Press.

Leont'ev, A. N. (1975). *Dejatel' nost, Licnost', Soznanie* [Activity, personality, consciousness]. Moscow: Izd-vo Politiceskoj Literatury.

Leont'ev, A. N. (1981). The problem of activity in psychology. In J. Wertsch (Ed.), *The concept of activity in Soviet psychology* (pp. 7–71). New York: M. E. Sharpe.

Luria. A. R. (1973). *The working brain.* Hammonsworth, England: Penguin.

Luria, A. R. (1976). *Cognitive development: Its cultural and social foundations.* Cambridge, MA: Harvard University Press.

Luria, A. R. (1982). *Language and cognition.* J. V. Wertsch (Ed.). New York: Wiley.

Papert, S. (1980). *Mindstorms: Children, computers and powerful ideas.* London: Harvester Press.

Resnick, L. (1987). Constructing knowledge in school. In L. S. Liben (Ed.), *Development and learning: Conflict of congruence?* (pp. 19–50). Hillsdale, NJ: Lawrence Erlbaum Associates.

Rudder, J. (1983). Qualitative thinking: An examination of the classificatory systems and cognitive structures of the Yolnu people of North-East Arnhem Land. Unpublished thesis, master's Australian National University.

Sachter, J. (1990). Explorations into children's understanding of space in 3-D computer graphics. In I. Harel (Ed.), *Constructionist learning* (pp. 217–248). Cambridge, MA: MIT Media Laboratory.

Salomon, G., Perkins, D., & Globerson, T. (1991). Partners in cognition: Extending human intelligence with intelligent technologies. *Educational Researcher 20*(3), 2–9.

Semenov, I. N. (1978). An empirical psychological study of thought processes in creative problem solving from the perspective of the theory of activity. *Soviet Psychology, 16*(1), 3–46.

Valsiner, J. (1992). A cultural-historical context for social "context." In L. Wineger and J. Valsiner (Eds.), *Children's development within a social context* (pp. 1–18). Hillsdale, NJ: Lawrence Erlbaum Associates.

von Glasersfeld, E. (1987). Learning as a constructive activity. In C. Janvier (Ed.), *The problems of representation in the teaching and learning of mathematics* (pp. 3–17). Hillsdale, NJ: Lawrence Erlbaum Associates.

Vygotsky, L. S. (1978). *Mind in society.* In M. Cole, S. Scribner, V. John-Steiner, & E. Souberman (Trans.). Cambridge, MA: Harvard University Press.

10 Traditions of School Mathematics in Japanese and American Elementary Classrooms

James W. Stigler
Clea Fernandez
Makoto Yoshida
University of California, Los Angeles

The superior mathematical achievements of Japanese children have engendered great interest in the methods used to teach mathematics in Japanese schools. In our current research we are collecting videotapes of math lessons in both Japanese and American classrooms and attempting to characterize the differences. Because so much of teaching and learning is domain specific, we have tried to compare lessons in which Japanese and American teachers are teaching similar topics. For example, we are collecting tapes of 20 Japanese and 20 American fifth-grade teachers teaching a lesson on how to find the area of a triangle. In this chapter we report some preliminary analyses of four fifth-grade lessons, two Japanese and two American, dealing with two topics: the area of a triangle, and the concept of equivalent fractions.

Our aim in this chapter is to begin characterizing two contrasting traditions of classroom mathematics instruction. Although we find Japanese and American lessons to differ on a number of dimensions, we also find that these dimensions cohere to form two distinct systems or cultures of classroom instruction, resembling what Cobb, Wood, Yackel, and McNeal (in press) called traditions of classroom mathematics. What, in general, it means to teach and learn mathematics differs across these societies in a way that resembles the distinction drawn in the American mathematics education community between school mathematics and inquiry mathematics (Richards, in press), or between teaching for understanding and not (cf. Cobb et al., in press). What is perhaps most impressive about the Japanese case is that the inquiry-based or problem-centered tradition of instruction is apparently widespread and not restricted to a few illustrative cases. Thus, it provides us with an opportunity to analyze empirically the various forms such instruction can take.

Our own view is that the key difference between the Japanese and American classroom traditions is in the emphasis placed on students' thinking and problem solving during instruction. Recent trends in American mathematics education have emphasized "constructivist" approaches to teaching. The student is not an empty vessel into which knowledge must be loaded but an active participant in the process of knowledge construction. Instruction, in this view, must be evaluated in light of what students can make of it, what they can construct. Learning mathematics results from students' thinking, not from the training of behaviors. Yet despite the popularity of these ideas and their endorsement by the National Council of Teachers of Mathematics, our major conclusion is that American students have very few opportunities to think during classroom instruction, whereas Japanese students have many such opportunities.

In this chapter we present evidence for this conclusion, using both qualitative examples and quantitative analyses. Our emphasis is on describing the techniques that Japanese teachers use for promoting student thinking during instruction. Although constructivist approaches to teaching in the United States often emphasize small group and individualized instruction, Japanese teachers, surprisingly, combine the almost total use of whole-class instruction with their strong emphasis on students' thinking. Similarly, although American teachers increasingly introduce manipulatives into their classrooms because they wish to promote student thinking and enhance understanding, we find that the use of manipulatives in and of itself does not lead to these outcomes. The ways that Japanese and American teachers use manipulatives in instruction differ markedly, again, we argue, around the issue of student thinking.

We compare two lessons—one Japanese, the other American—on how to find the area of a triangle. By describing these two lessons we illustrate the differences we have found. We also describe some quantitative variables we have constructed that provide new indicators of student thinking in the classroom. These measures are applied both to the triangle lessons and to two other lessons on equivalent fractions, with similar results. Finally, we discuss possible reasons for the differences in instruction that we observe between Japan and the United States.

METHODOLOGICAL CONSIDERATIONS

This chapter is limited, based on an analysis of only four lessons, two Japanese and two American. The lessons were selected from a much larger dataset, however, that we are just now beginning to analyze. It is helpful to briefly discuss our methods for collecting the data and our methods for analyzing them. Although much of this chapter is based on our qualitative comparisons of the taped lessons, some quantitative analyses are presented as well. We want to say something, therefore, about our methods for coding the tapes.

As we have mentioned, our project involves collecting videotapes of teachers teaching selected topics that we have tried to match as closely as possible between the Japanese and American curricula. Matching of topics is difficult, but we have achieved some success. At the second-grade level we are taping lessons on geometric shapes and on multidigit subtraction with borrowing. At the fifth-grade level we are focusing on the area of a triangle and on equivalent fractions. We also have collected some tapes on the introduction to multiplication, a topic that comes in the second grade in Japan but in the third grade in the United States. We have tried to tape an introductory lesson on each topic, one in which the teacher is presenting new material, instead of a lesson that consists primarily of practicing what has been previously learned. Our goal is to tape 20 teachers in each country for each topic.

Our procedure is simple. We establish contact with the teachers early in the year and work with them to identify the lesson they will teach that best fits our comparative framework. We then keep in touch, and as the time approaches we set an appointment to videotape the lesson. These are not surprise visits, so the resulting tapes may not accurately reflect a given teacher's typical way of teaching. Further, the teachers themselves are not typical: Especially in the United States, it is exceedingly difficult to find teachers who are willing to be studied in this way. Thus, the teachers who agree to participate are probably "good" teachers, both in their own view and in the view of their colleagues. School principals often will recommend a teacher to us because they think she or he is good. These teachers tend to be the ones who are willing to be videotaped.

The Japanese teachers may be more representative. In any case, our previous research indicates that Japanese teachers, like Japanese students, vary less than American teachers, so problems of sampling bias may not be as great. But let's assume, for now, that we are studying above-average teachers in both cultures. The tapes we analyze in this chapter are typical of the tapes we have collected thus far.

In addition to taping the lesson, we also collect any additional materials that the teacher can provide us that are relevant to the lesson. In particular we ask the teachers for copies of their lesson plan (if they have one) and of any worksheets and other materials that they hand out to the students.

Quantitative Coding

Recently we have begun to develop a system for objectively coding the differences between Japanese and American lessons. As we have said, the overall differences in instruction are assumed to result from different traditions or cultural models for classroom instruction. Although the cultural model itself would be difficult to code objectively, the consequences of this model in terms of classroom characteristics can be coded. We think it is important to develop techniques for objective coding so that we can assess quantitatively the degree to which instruction approaches the different cultural ideals. It also will allow us, eventually, to discuss variability within a tradition in addition to the prototypical differences across traditions.

Our first step is to transcribe the lessons from the videotapes. American lessons are transcribed verbatim, along with just enough contextual information to render the verbal transcripts interpretable. The Japanese lessons are translated and transcribed into English by bilingual undergraduate research assistants.

The transcripts are divided into different units for analysis depending on the specific question to be asked. For most analyses we have conducted thus far we restrict ourselves to *public discourse*, that is, the talk that goes on between teacher and students when everyone in the class is intended to hear.

We are developing our coding system first in the context of a small number of tapes, starting, for example, by comparing the two lessons on area of a triangle that are discussed later. We view the tapes and study the transcripts, develop intuitions about the differences, and then try to devise ways of coding these differences. Once we have devised some codes we try them out on additional lessons. Once we have the kinks worked out we plan to apply them to our full sample of tapes. In this chapter we present results for two pairs of lessons, the pair on area of a triangle and an additional pair on working with equivalent fractions. All four lessons are from fifth-grade classrooms. We add this new pair to ascertain the degree to which findings generated from two lessons in geometry will obtain as well on lessons on a very different topic.

THE AREA OF A TRIANGLE: TWO LESSONS

One topic that appears in both Japan and the United States at the fifth-grade level is the method of finding the area of a triangle. Students in both cultures have been introduced to the concept of area, and they know how to compute the area of a rectangle. In the lessons we taped, both Japanese and American teachers used children's understanding of how to find the area of a rectangle in order to develop a method for finding the area of a triangle.

Overview of a Japanese Lesson

The Japanese lesson can be divided into four segments (see Table 10.1): presentation of the problem; students attempting to to solve the problem on their own; class discussion about the solutions that students came up with; and students working alone on further practice problems from the textbook. This sequence of activities is prototypical of the Japanese lessons we have observed. The teacher almost always begins the class by posing a problem, and the rest of the lesson is oriented toward understanding and solving that problem.

In this lesson, the teacher begins by asking students to name the kinds of triangles they have studied. As they name them—right, equilateral, isosceles,

TABLE 10.1
Overview of the Japanese and American Lessons
on Finding the Area of a Triangle

Segment	Length	Description
		Japanese Lesson
1	3.5 min	Presentation of the problem
2	14.5 min	Students attempting to solve the problem on their own
3	29.0 min	Class discussion about the solutions that students came up with, leading up to the general formula
4	5.0 min	Doing further practice problems from the textbook (students working on their own)
Total	52.0 min	
		American Lesson
1	1.0 min	Review concept of perimeter
2	8.0 min	Area of a rectangle: explanation, formula, and practice problems
3	25.0 min	Area of a triangle: explanation, formula, and practice problems
4	11.0 min	Students begin homework assignment, teacher walks around and helps
Total	45.0 min	

and so on—the teacher puts the corresponding shapes cut out of paper on the blackboard. She then says, "We have various kinds of triangles on the board, and today I would like you to think about how to find out the area of a triangle." She hands out to each student sheets of paper that are printed with outline drawings of the various kinds of triangles. She instructs the students not to find the area of the shapes, but just to think about what would be the best way to find the area. She suggests to the students that they can cut, fold, and draw.

Students then spend 14.5 minutes working on the problem on their own, during which time the teacher circulates, mostly observing what the students are doing. Students are actively engaged at this point, and though they are not formally divided into groups there is a great deal of discussion and interaction among students seated in proximity to each other. At the end of this time the teacher reconvenes the whole-class discussion by asking a student to go to the board and explain her method for finding the area of a right triangle.

For the next 29 minutes a succession of students go to the board to explain their methods for finding the areas of the various kinds of triangles. All of the students use cutout shapes and chalk drawings to explain their approaches, and the solutions that they have devised are often quite ingenious. After each student explains his solution the teacher and the rest of the class discuss the viability of the solution. The teacher then, in collaboration with the students, writes a formula on the board that summarizes the student's solution, for example, "base × height/2." A total of nine students present solutions. At the end, the teacher directs attention to the formulas on the board and asks the students if they notice any kind of pattern. A spirited discussion ensues in which students observe and then confirm that the different informal formulas that resulted from the different solutions are really the same across the solutions, regardless of the kind of triangle involved. In the final 5 minutes of the lesson students use the formula to solve some problems in their textbook.

Overview of an American Lesson

The American teacher begins his lesson by reviewing the concept of perimeter: What does it mean, how do you find it? He then makes the transition into area:

> So we dealt with perimeter. Today, we are going to deal with area and we are going to deal with the area of two things, we are going to deal with the area of a rectangle and the area of a triangle. Area is how much space is inside a flat shape.

The rest of the lesson is divided into three segments (see Table 10.1), one on the area of a rectangle, one on the area of a triangle, and finally a period of seatwork.

The segment on area of a rectangle starts with the teacher holding up a series of rectangles that have been divided into square units. As he holds each one up he asks the students to tell him the area, which they figure by counting the squares. After several of these, the teacher asks the students for a formula: "Now find me a mathematical way of doing it so that I don't have to count all the time; Brian?" Brian responds: "Times the width times the length." The teacher writes the formula on the board, $A = l \times w$, and then gives the students two practice problems that require them to multiply the length times the width to get the area.

The teacher them moves on to the area of a triangle:

> Now, let's take off some of this (erases board) and see if we can go on to our next thing which is we want to find the area of a triangle. We are going to start out with the same thing, we are going to start out and talk about what we find the area of a triangle we are still finding units, square units like this (holds up a small square). Well here is a triangle (holds up triangle with grid drawn in) and we have units. Now when you get to triangles what's the problem? Sue?

The "problem" the teacher is referring to is that square units are difficult to count with a triangle because they don't fit exactly over the area. Having pointed out this problem the teacher then introduces a solution, giving a demonstration that involves fitting two pre-cut right triangles together to make a rectangle, and showing that the area of each triangle is half the area of the resulting rectangle. The demonstration itself is accomplished quickly, within a matter of seconds, and there is virtually no response—either questions or discussion—on the part of the students. The teacher gives a second demonstration in which he cuts one of the triangles in two and places the pieces adjacent to the other triangle to make a rectangle. Again, he receives no feedback from the students. He then tells the students the formula for the area of a triangle, $A = \frac{1}{2} \times b \times h$.

After giving them the formula, the teacher poses three problems and has the students apply the formula. He then starts them on the assignment.

THREE DIFFERENCES BETWEEN JAPANESE AND AMERICAN LESSONS

Using these two lessons as points of reference we can discuss the differences we have observed between Japanese and American lessons. As we indicated already, we have increasingly focused on the role that students' thinking plays in instruction. We argue that (1) Japanese teachers, in contrast to American teachers, place students' thinking at the core of their lesson-planning process; (2) Japanese lessons provide students with more opportunities to think during instruction than do American lessons; and (3) Japanese lessons create an atmosphere in which students' thinking is valued and legitimized to a far greater extent than do American lessons.

The Role of Students' Thinking in Teachers' Planning

Lesson plans can provide insight into how teachers conceive of and plan their lessons. In our current project we ask all of the teachers we videotape to provide us with written lesson plans. The lesson plans provided by the Japanese and American teachers for the lessons just described are very different from each other. However, they are typical of ones we received from teachers in the two countries. The American lesson plans almost always look like outlines or lists of activities that will constitute the lesson; the Japanese lesson plans are far more detailed (see Fig. 10.1).

Japanese Lesson Plans Stress Coherence of Lesson Activities. The Japanese lesson plan places the current lesson in the context of lessons that precede and follow it and in the context of the mathematics curriculum. The plan begins by stating that this lesson is the third of six lessons in a unit on the area of quadrangles and triangles. The previous lesson was on the application of the formula for finding the area of parallelograms. The objective of the current lesson is to learn that triangles can be transformed so that the formula used for finding the area of quadrangles can be applied to the problem of finding the area of triangles. The next lesson, we are told in the lesson plan, will be on application of the formula for finding the area of triangles.

Planning lessons to be coherent with those that precede and follow facilitates students' thinking by providing them with opportunities to infer connections

American Lesson Plan

1. Correct assignment

2. Review - perimeter

3. Area of a rectangle / square
    A. Introduction
    B. Region marked - find area - counting -3
    C. Mathematical way - multiply Length x width
    D. Examples
    E. Formula   A = L * W - recipe
    F. Examples Note: Answer square centimeter / inch

4. Area of a triangle
    A. Introduction
    B. Region marked - count - difficult
    C. Double triangle - put together - rectangle
        find area - find 1/2
    D. Other examples (2) - find 1/2 (multiply by 1/2
                                    or divided by 2)
    E. Formula   A = 1/2bh
    F. Examples

5. Assignment

FIG. 10.1. Lesson plans for class session to teach the area of a triangle: first shown are American, then Japanese lesson plan.

between different topics in the mathematics curriculum, and between different pieces of knowledge that are relevant to the topic being taught. A student who is striving to make sense of the world must be working in a sensible world. Otherwise the task is impossible. Japanese teachers work in their planning to assure that the most important links can be made by students.

American teachers place little emphasis on coherence across lessons. In the American plan for the triangle lesson the teacher writes down nothing about how this lesson relates to those that precede and follow it. He may be thinking about such relationships, but they are not written down in the lesson plan. In fact, the American teacher does begin his lesson by reviewing the concept of perimeter, which they apparently covered last time. But because there is no direct link between perimeter and the area of a triangle this order of events renders the American lesson less coherent than the Japanese one, which begins with a review of the different types of triangles that exist—events within the American lesson are less connected to each other, and the lesson itself is not seen as connected to the surrounding lessons. (The relative coherence of Japanese lessons is a characteristic we have described elsewhere [e.g., Stevenson & Stigler, 1992; Stigler &

Japanese Lesson Plan

1. Lesson: Area of quadrangles and triangles (the 3rd lesson of 6 lessons)

2. The Principal objectives: In order to find the area of a triangle, if the students cut a triangle, move it around, fold it, multiply it by 2, etc., they will notice that they can use the formula for finding an area of quadrangles that they learned in a previous lesson. Thus, the students will be able to find the area of a triangle.

3. Context of the Lesson:

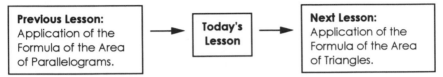

| **Previous Lesson:** Application of the Formula of the Area of Parallelograms. | → | **Today's Lesson** | → | **Next Lesson:** Application of the Formula of the Area of Triangles. |

4. Important Points for Instruction:

- Ask the students to work on the problems that they think they can solve by themselves.

- Make sure that the students do not make mistake to identifying the bottom lines and the heights of the triangles.

5. Expansion of the Lesson:

Steps	Learning Activities	Expected Student Reaction	Time	Guidance/Advice
Understanding the problem	1. Let's find out the area of various types of triangles. - right angle triangle - equilateral triangle - isosceles triangle - the triangle in which the height is located inside of it. - the triangle in which the height is located outside of it	- if the triangle is right angle triangle I think I can do it. - Let's try cutting them. - Let's try folding them. - Let's try drawing a grid on them. - Let's try drawing a line for height.	10min.	- if I see the students who are having difficulty, ask them to think about the right triangle first. - for the students who can not finish completely, encourage them to try as hard as they can.

FIG. 10.1. *Continued*

Steps	Learning Activities	Expected Student Reaction	Time	Guidance/Advice
Investigation	2. Let's present your own ideas and listen to the friends ideas. (1) right triangles	 - multiply by 2 to get a rectangle. - Bottom ¥ height ∏ 2	30min.	- ask the students to think about the formula
	(2) equilateral and isosceles triangles	- cut to half and move them to make a rectangle 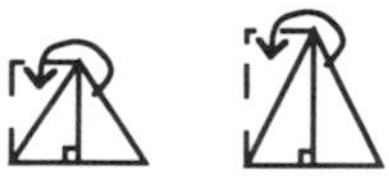 - Bottom ∏ 2 ¥ height - fold and make a rectangle  - Bottom ∏ 2 ¥ height ∏ 2 ¥ 2 - draw a grid and count the squares in it		- ask the students to think about if there is any way to simplify the formula.
	(3) triangles that contain height inside of it.	- draw the height line and multiply by 2 to make a rectangle. 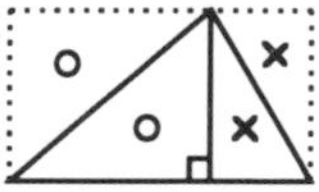 - They will realize that if you divide the bottom line by 2 by drawing the height it is difficult to come up with a formula. - multiply by 2 to make a parallelogram. 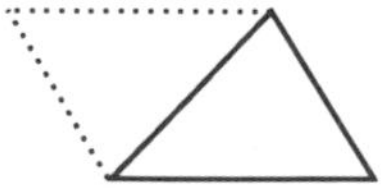 - Bottom ¥ height ∏ 2 - draw a grid and count the squares in it.		- hinting the triangle is half of the rectangle and then asking the formula.

FIG. 10.1. *Continued*

158

Steps	Learning Activities	Expected Student Reaction	Time	Guidance/Advice
Investigation	(4) triangles that contain height outside of it	- They will realize that if you draw the height to make a right triangle, then subtract the part that is not needed that it is very difficult to find a formula. - multiply by 2 to make a parallelogram. - Bottom ¥ height ∏ 2		- the formula will be very difficult even if symbols are used so it is not necessary to go any farther
	3. Let's find out the formula of area of triangles	- all triangles' area are found by the formula of "Bottom ¥ height ∏ 2."		
Generalization	4. Let's find out the area of various triangles.	- if you plug the numbers in to the formula "Bottom ¥ height ∏ 2" the students can find the area of the triangles.	5min.	- Make sure that the students do not make mistakes in identifying the bottom lines and the heights of the triangles.

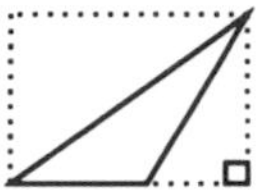

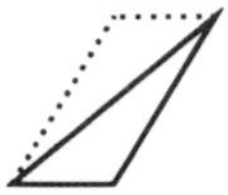

FIG. 10.1. *Continued*

Perry, 1988]). This lack of coherence in the way the American lesson is planned probably renders it harder to interpret than the Japanese lesson.

Japanese Teachers Anticipate Student Thinking.   Children's thinking also plays a central role in Japanese teachers' planning of the activities that comprise the lesson, but not in the American teachers' planning. As evident in Fig. 10.1, the American lesson plan lists the points the teacher plans to make, or things he plans to do. Correct assignment, review perimeter, area of a rectangle. He has laid out a sequence of activities, and also a sequence of discoveries or insights that he wants to impart to the students. He has them count square units to find the area of a rectangle, and then introduces the formula (what he calls the "mathematical way"). He makes a note to himself that he wants to explain to the students that a formula is like a recipe. He wants to demonstrate that the method of counting square units is difficult to apply to the case of triangles.

The Japanese lesson plan emphasizes what students will think, not what the teacher will say or do. Using a format that is commonly used for lesson plans in Japan, the teacher divides the lesson into three steps: understanding the problem, investigation, and generalization. For each step she enters, in a chart, four kinds of information: the learning activities that she will lead the students through, the expected student reactions to the activities, the approximate time that will be spent on the step, and the guidance or advice that she might offer in response to the students' reactions. In the column labeled expected student reaction the teacher carefully lists the solutions—both good ones and not so good ones—she expects students to propose. This fascinating exercise in planning primes the teacher to listen to what students have to say, and allows her to think ahead of time about how to facilitate students' understanding. The American teacher has planned what he will do, but has not, in his plan, started to think about what effect his actions might have on students' understanding.

Opportunities for Student Thinking During Instruction

The concern with student thinking that guides the Japanese teacher's planning of her lesson also manifests itself in the way she teaches the lesson. We have identified a number of ways in which the Japanese lesson provides more opportunities for student thinking than does the American lesson. We discuss these differences next.

The Role of Problem Solving.   One striking difference between the two triangle lessons is in the role played by problem solving. As we saw earlier, the Japanese teacher—and this applies to almost every Japanese lesson we have observed—begins by posing a problem and then having students work to solve it one their own. Only after students have worked on their own does the teacher begin the more directed part of the lesson, that is, the public discussion of students' solutions. Often, and this is the case in this lesson, the problem posed at the beginning of a Japanese lesson is the one on which most of the lesson is focused, with the problem thus serving as a theme around which the subsequent activities are organized.

The American lesson starts with a series of short-answer questions, first about the concept of perimeter, then about the area of a rectangle. The lesson consists primarily of a series of these teacher–student exchanges designed to lead students to an understanding of the formula for determining area. Only after the teacher has presented a formula does he ask students to solve problems on their own, in a period of seatwork at the end of the class.

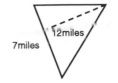

7miles   12miles

A = 1/2 x _ x _
A = 1/2 x 7 x 12
A = 1/2 x 84
A = 42 sq. miles

FIG. 10.2.   A problem from the American lesson.

In general, American teachers put seatwork at the end of the lesson, Japanese teachers at the beginning. This placement corresponds to the different roles seatwork is assumed to play in instruction. American teachers view seatwork as an opportunity to practice what has been learned in the lesson; Japanese teachers view it as an opportunity for students to try solving problems on their own before being exposed to other students' solutions. Our Japanese colleagues point out that the Japanese teachers have the luxury of forgoing the use of seatwork for practice because homework and juku (after school programs) provide ample opportunities for practice outside of class, opportunities that American teachers cannot depend on (see Stevenson & Stigler, 1992).

Partly because problems are not posed until the end of the lesson, they take a very different form in the American lesson than they do in the Japanese lesson. In the Japanese lesson students are given shapes without markings or dimensions and asked to find the area. In the American lesson students are presented with shapes like the one shown in Fig. 10.2. Because the base and the height are clearly labeled, students never really grapple with the problem of how height should be defined in order to use the formula. Thus, what actually is a challenging conceptual problem is simplified to become a simple calculation problem.

Time to Think.   We have noted before that Japanese lessons appear to move at an extremely slow pace (Stigler & Perry, 1988). Part of this perception is due to the organization of the lesson. As noted earlier, Japanese lessons almost always begin with a single problem, the solution to which becomes the focus of the entire lesson. This concentration on a single problem lends coherence to the lesson, and allows a thorough explanation of the problem. Students in American lessons work many more problems than do their Japanese counterparts, and come to emphasize quantity rather than quality of solutions.

Thinking in classrooms takes time. A lesson planned in reference to what the teacher will say instead of what the students will think will inevitably leave some students behind. In the American lesson described earlier, little time was set aside for students to ponder the derivation of the formula for finding the area of a triangle. When the teacher did the demonstration with the two cut-out triangles it happened quickly. The students were expected to follow the demonstration, but were not given enough time to discover the relation for themselves. In the Japanese lesson, students spent the entire time thinking about and discussing how to derive the formula for finding the area of a triangle. The expectation was that

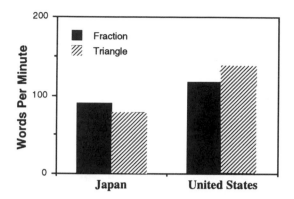

FIG. 10.3. The pace of instruction in Japanese and American class-rooms: average number of words (English translation) spoken by teachers and students during a minute of instruction.

the derivation would take time for students to construct, not be understood by students in a momentary flash of insight.

We have tried to develop ways of objectively coding the pace at which instruction proceeds. One way, of course, is to count the number of problems students solve during a lesson. When we do this we find the pattern we have already described: Japanese students solve far fewer problems than do American students during the course of a lesson. Another variable we have tried to measure is the rate at which talk proceeds during the lesson. In Fig. 10.3 we present a count of the average number of words per minute spoken, by teachers and students combined, during public discourse in the four lessons we have analyzed. This is a very rough measure, comparing number of words spoken in the U.S. classrooms with number of words in the English translations of the Japanese transcripts. Yet we believe that it corroborates one of our recurring observations: Japanese students are less hurried during the lesson, and are allowed more time to construct meaning for the mathematics that goes on around them.

Opportunities to Discuss Mathematics.   Aside from providing time for students to think, the Japanese teacher also provides many opportunities for children to describe their thinking and to hear other students describe their thinking. Just as most Japanese lessons begin with a period in which students work to solve a problem on their own, most also follow the problem solving with a period in which students describe and then debate their various solutions to the problem. Students are heard from more, and at greater length, during the Japanese lessons.

It is also important to note that the emphasis in Japan is on public discourse (as opposed to private one-on-one interaction). The American teachers do not emphasize public discourse to the same degree, as evident in the ways teachers and students interact during seatwork. The American teacher views this as a time to work with individual children and to evaluate their work. He walks from student to student, saying such things as, "Well you are almost right, but you've got to find half of 90 correctly," "You got it," and "OK, now you're substituting OK now . . . You have to go out and put in one half and put in your base and your height." His talk is private, intended only for the student whose desk he is passing by, and not for the other students in the class. He functions as a tutor, going from child to child.

The Japanese teacher talks much less than the American teacher as she walks around the room. When she does talk to individual students her remarks are brief and vague: she might offer a suggestion—for example, a student having difficulty working with the acute triangle might be encouraged to "try working with the right triangle first." But she never directly instructs a child, and never tells children their solutions are correct or incorrect. Her role is not that of tutor but of researcher, studying the children's thinking about the problem. Discussion of answers—both correct and incorrect—is public, after the class has been reconvened. Everyone is thought to benefit from these discussions; to have them privately would be to deprive most students of valuable opportunities for thinking and learning.

We have developed three ways to objectively code the quantity of student talk within a lesson. Results of these three measures, for the four lessons we have analyzed, are shown in Fig. 10.4. In panel (a) we have coded the percentage of total words spoken during public discourse that come from students (as opposed to the teacher). Approximately twice as much student talk is observed in the Japanese class discussion as in the American discussions, across both the triangle and fraction lessons. We also can see, in panel (b), that the average length of the

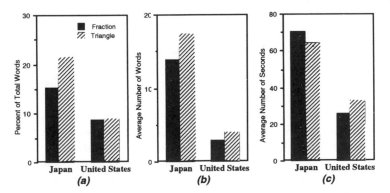

FIG. 10.4.   Quantity of student talk: (a) Percent of total words spoken during public discourse that were spoken by students; (b) average number of words spoken by individual students during a teacher–student exchange; (c) average number of seconds in public discourse before teacher calls on a new student.

public conversations engaged in by students and teachers is greater in the Japanese than in the American lessons. Our unit of comparison here is the *teacher–student exchange,* a subunit that we have defined within periods of public discourse. When a teacher asks a question and then calls on an individual student to answer, everything from the initiating question through the last utterance of the student is considered part of a single teacher–student exchange. Panel (b) shows the average number of words spoken by individual students during one of these teacher–student exchanges. Finally, we see in panel (c) of the figure that having lengthier conversations with students leads to another result: American teachers call on new students during public discourse more frequently than do Japanese teachers (once every 20–30 sec in the American lessons vs. every 60–70 sec in the Japanese lesson).

The Goal of Asking Questions.   Japanese and American teachers appear to have different goals for asking questions: The American teacher asks a question to get an answer, and the Japanese teacher to get students to think (Stevenson & Stigler, 1992). Analysis of the two triangle lessons provides rich confirmation of this general point. The Japanese teacher poses a problem, then asks students to explain their thinking about the problem. The explanations she elicits are lengthy and involved. The teacher interrupts as needed to help the student continue, to draw the student out, but never cuts the student off. Incorrect or less efficient solutions are given as much time and focus as are the correct ones.

The American teacher, in contrast, has a clear idea of where he wants the discussion to go. The kinds of questions he asks are almost all of the "answer known" variety: There is a single correct answer, the teacher knows what it is, and the student's job is simply to produce that answer. An excellent example of what we mean by this is contained in the transcript of the lesson. Recall that the American teacher, in his plan, had written "Region marked—count—difficult" to guide the beginning of his segment on the area of a triangle. We see from the transcript that his strategy is to show students that counting square units is difficult in the case of triangles: as can be seen in Fig. 10.5, problems arise in counting the fractions of square units that inevitably line the hypotenuse of the triangle.

Now, what happens when the teacher tries to implement his strategy? He shows the triangle in Fig. 10.5 and asks a student to tell him the area. His plan is that the student will be stumped, which will then motivate the need for an alternative solution, at which point he can launch into the demonstration he has prepared in which two right triangles put together become a rectangle. But the students are not so quick to give up on the method of counting square units. Instead, they keep trying to do it, despite the teacher's desire to move on. Here is an excerpt from the transcript:

Melissa: I have a question.
Teacher: Go ahead ask.

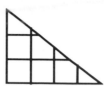

FIG. 10.5. Figure presented by the American teacher to illustrate difficulty of counting squares method for finding the area of a triangle.

Melissa: Like 'cause under there is like, uhmm, two like parts of a square, and one is like missing a little corner, and one is missing like a bigger corner, and there is like a bigger corner, and then there is a little corner over there.

Teacher: OK so it has to be more than three doesn't it?

Melissa: Yeah (looks confused).

Teacher: That's a problem we are going to find.

John: There is 6.

Teacher: There is 6.

Eric: I think that, hmmm, 'cause we have to add a half together to get a whole.

Teacher: That's right but the question: are they halves? This one is not a half is it? This one is not a half, this one is way more than a half (pointing at different pieces of squares drawn along the hypotenuse of the triangle).

Mary: There are 6, right, if you take the little corner like the triangle off the third one form the bottom.

Teacher: OK, there.

Mary: No. Yeahh and you add it to the second one.

Teacher: Here.

Mary: Yeah, that one. Where does the littler one go?

Teacher: Yeah, ok, where . . . (laughing) hold on a minute. Lets go, here is the same triangle (he produces a paper cutout of an identical triangle without the squares). OK, now it is very interesting, in fact I have two of them, it is interesting when you take two triangles that are identical like these are, they are exactly the same and you take and you put them together, what do you end up with (demonstrates), David?

David: A square.

What is evident in this portion of the lesson is that the teacher had no interest in students' answers to the question he posed: he was looking only for the response that would lead him into his demonstration. Students were actively trying to solve the problem by mentally combining the partial square units, but the teacher was thwarting them at every turn, even though the students in fact had correctly solved the problem (getting the answer, six).

Coding Types of Questions Asked.   What kinds of questions do Japanese teachers ask in order to provoke the long and drawn-out discussions that we observe? We began our coding by listing every teacher question that was asked during public discourse. A teacher question is defined as an attempt by the teacher to elicit a student response. Because it is often difficult to distinguish between rhetorical questions and genuine questions that students are unable to answer, only questions that actually elicited students' responses are included in this coding. Questions need not be in the form of an interrogation. They can be, for example, an instruction such as "please go to the board and show us how you solved the problem."

Once we listed all of the questions asked by teachers, we coded them into one of four categories (plus "other").

1. *Name/identify* questions are those where the teacher asks a student to name an answer without asking for any explanation of how the answer was found. Questions like "What kind of triangles have we studied so far?" or "What is the length on this shape?" would fall into this category.

2. *Calculate* questions are those where the teacher asks for the solution to an explicitly stated calculation. Questions like "So to find the area we do 9 times 12 which is?" or "What is 90 divided by 2?" would fall in this category.

3. *Explain how or why* are questions where the teacher asks for an explanation for answers given or procedures carried out. Questions like "How did you find the area of this triangle?" or "Why is the area here 17?" would fall in this category.

4. *Check status* are questions where the teacher is trying to monitor what everyone else is thinking or doing. Questions like "Who agrees?" "How many people found this?" or "Is anyone confused?" fall into this category.

We then determined what percent of the questions asked by each teacher fell into each of the above categories.

In Fig. 10.6 we have graphed the percentage of questions in each lesson falling into each of the four categories. The two Japanese lessons are represented in the upper panel and the American lessons in the lower. First, it is interesting to note the similarity of patterns in the graphs across the two lessons within each culture, but the striking difference in patterns across the two cultures. In both American lessons the most frequently asked type of question was name/identify, followed by calculate and then explain. In the Japanese lessons the most frequent type of question was explain, followed by check status. Neither of these two Japanese teachers asked a calculate question, and neither of the American teachers asked a status question.

These patterns of teacher questioning help us to understand why students might talk more and at greater length in the Japanese classrooms than they do in the American classrooms. If students are asked simply to name, identify, or calculate, then their answers would be expected to be brief. Asking students to explain how or why they solved a problem in a certain way, on the other hand, should lead to lengthier answers. We investigated this possibility by graphing the number of words students said in response to two types of questions: name/identify and explain. The results are shown in Fig. 10.7.

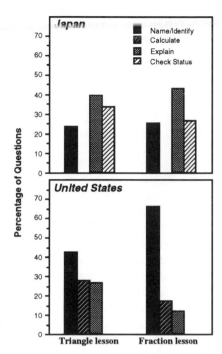

FIG. 10.6. Types of questions asked by Japanese and American teachers.

As we would predict, there is no appreciable difference in length between Japanese and American students' answers to name/identify questions: The average answer, in both cultures, is less than five words. Explain questions, in both cultures, lead to lengthier answers, but the effect is much greater in the Japanese lessons, where students' answers average approximately 20 words in length. We

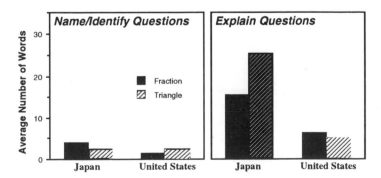

FIG. 10.7. Length of Japanese and American students' responses to questions asking students to name/identify vs. explain.

can think of two reasons for these lengthy answers: First, Japanese students are more accustomed to hearing teachers request explanations than are American students, and they've had more practice answering such questions. Another reason has to do with the nature of the explain questions that teachers ask: In Japan, most of the explain questions ask students to explain new material or novel solutions to problems. In the American lessons the majority of such questions ask students to explain material that already has been explained, either by the teacher or by another student.

The Use of Errors.   Another indication that American and Japanese teachers have different goals in asking questions comes from the way they deal with incorrect answers. As we have noted elsewhere, Japanese teachers treat errors or incorrect answers quite differently than do American teachers (Stevenson & Stigler, 1992). American teachers go to great lengths to keep errors out of the mathematics classroom, and especially out of the public discourse. This may be because of behaviorist learning theories that emphasize the importance of success for learning, or because teachers fear damaging children's self-esteem by exposing their inadequacies. But for whatever reason, American teachers tend to quickly correct mistakes when they do occur, and almost never ask children with incorrect solutions to problems to display their solutions to the class.

Japanese teachers take a very different approach to errors. Instead of seeing errors as indicating lack of ability or potential on the part of the student, Japanese teachers see errors as a natural part of the learning process and as important sources of information about children's mathematical thinking. They believe that discussion of incorrect solutions can play an important role in children's developing conceptual understanding of mathematics. Japanese teachers also think errors should be discussed publicly—not privately, one-on-one—so that all students can benefit by analyzing them.

In our tapes we have observed two strategies that American teachers employ to deal with incorrect responses to questions. One of these is simply to ignore the response and go on to let another student answer. This is consistent with the idea discussed earlier that the American teacher's goal for asking questions is to get the answer she needs to move the lesson along. The same purpose is accomplished as well in the second strategy, that of reinterpreting incorrect or inappropriate answers so that they fit the teacher's expectations. Our Japanese colleagues hasten to point out, however, that these strategies may make sense within a cultural system such as the American one in which mistakes may be interpreted as revealing underlying physical or immutable deficits. If errors arouse anxiety or threaten self-esteem, it may be impossible to use them the way that Japanese teachers do.

The Use of Manipulatives.   Finally, it is fascinating to note the different ways that manipulatives are used by these two teachers. The Japanese teacher gives students paper triangles to work with from the beginning, then has them continue to use the cutouts throughout the lesson as they explain their solutions. The manipulatives in the Japanese classroom are used as tools for thinking and as objects for reflection. The American teacher uses the manipulatives for a demonstration: When he gets to the point in the lesson where he wants to explain the derivation of the formula, he pulls out two right triangles, fits them together, and shows the resulting rectangle. In this particular lesson, students do not get any chance to work with, or even touch, the concrete representation.

The Value Placed on Students' Thinking

It is not surprising that in the Japanese classroom an atmosphere is created in which student thinking is valued and legitimized; in the American classroom a very different atmosphere exists. This difference is seen clearly in the way students' solutions are used in the American and Japanese lessons, the way authority is referred to, and the way mathematical formulas are introduced in the two classrooms.

The Role of Students' Solutions.   The way the Japanese lesson on area of a triangle proceeds is like virtually every Japanese lesson we have observed in one crucial respect: After students are posed a problem to work on in the beginning of the lesson, much of the rest of the lesson involves whole-class discussion of the various solutions—correct and incorrect—that students came up with. In this particular lesson, nine students come to the board, one by one, to explain their solutions to the problem. Inherent in all of these interactions is the value attached to students' solutions. The teacher almost never evaluates the solutions, but simply asks the class to comment on them. She constantly refers to the importance of discovering alternative solutions to the same problem, and relies on students' discussions of the procedures to determine whether each will, in fact, lead to the correct answer. Students themselves learn that much of the content of the class is carried in these student-centered discussions, so they show great patience in listening to lengthy descriptions of sometimes highly idiosyncratic solutions.

Reference to Authority.   Implicit in the way American teachers ask questions is that the teacher knows the answer and is the authority on what is right or wrong. The view that mathematics is a field in which there are definite answers, and that someone always knows what the answers are, is communicated to children in these patterns of discourse. Thus, it is not important what the child thinks, but whether or not the child's answer is correct. Japanese teachers, in contrast, rarely tell students they are right or wrong, leaving any such evaluation to the children's classmates. (Not that students don't care how their teachers feel about their work: Our Japanese colleagues tell us the Japanese students are very sensitive to their teachers' implicit evaluations.) Japanese teachers place great emphasis on asking students to explain how they solved a problem, and promote the view that there are multiple ways of solving a problem. Correct solutions, in the Japanese classroom, are those that make sense and are convincing to the students in the class.

One striking characteristic of the American tapes we have viewed is the frequency with which American teachers refer to authority to justify their mathematical assertions. One example of this is in the quote earlier, when the teacher, in response to a student's suggestion that the width be multiplied by the length to get the area of a rectangle, states that "in mathematical" the order is reversed, that is, the length times the width. In another example from the triangle lesson the teacher refers to "they" in explaining the proper formula for the area of a triangle:

Teacher: So now we can go back and find out what we are going to do. We know that the area of a rectangle equals length times width. OK, that's a rectangle. What are we going to do for a triangle? What would be your guess?

Jack: Take the length and the width of the rectangle and divide that into half.

Teacher: You got it. You got it. You're going to take the length and the width and divide into half.

Now we have to do a couple of things here cause it changes just a little bit. Area equals $1/2$, that's what you said, times, now instead of using length they use base times the height. OK so b stands for base. (Writes height under the h). OK when a triangle is like this and it has a square corner on it (holds up right triangle) then we have what we use to . . . what on a rectangle we call the length and the width. *But on the triangle they are going to call this the base and they are going to call this the height.*

We have never observed the Japanese teachers referring to outside authority, or to their own authority, as justification of a mathematical conclusion or procedure. Common to the Japanese lessons is the technique of giving students the authority to decide the validity of mathematical conclusions or procedures. As in the world of "real" mathematics, the ultimate test of validity for a mathematical argument is how convincing it is to your peers. In the triangle lesson we see the common practice of students, after answering a question or proposing a solution, asking their classmates if the solution is correct or not. This ritualistic aspect of the lesson is probably just that, yet the implicit message is clear: The teacher is not the judge; the community is. We also see the habit, on the part of both teachers and students, of maintaining the link between an idea and the person who generated it. Teachers and students alike refer to "Kei-kun's solution," "Nozomi-san's approach," and so forth. This practice highlights the fact that any particular solution that is proposed is just one of many alternative solutions, and that its validity must be tested. Having more of the crucial information in a lesson come from students—as opposed to the teacher—means that students attend more seriously to what their peers have to say. American students know that whatever is important will come from the teacher, not from other students.

The Use of Formulas.   It is interesting to note the different ways that formulas are used in these two lessons. Both teachers want the students to know that the formula for the area of a triangle is $A = \frac{1}{2} b \times h$. But the point at which they introduce the formula and the manner of introduction are quite different. In the Japanese lesson informal formulas are written to describe each student's solution as they propose it at the board. The goal is to record, in convenient notation, the method that the student used; the form is allowed to vary. Thus, for one student the teacher wrote the formula "base/2 × height," and for another, "base × height /2." The focus is on the problem and the solution; the formula is introduced merely as a summary of what was done. At the end of the lesson the teacher has students look at the nine formulas that remain on the blackboard, and lets them notice the similarity among them: For all the triangles, no matter what kind, the formula for finding their area is essentially the same.

The American teacher introduces the formula early, and immediately tries to get it in the canonical form. After the students count the square units in a rectangle the teacher asks for another way to get the answer, and a student answers with the formula:

Brian: Times the width times the length.
Teacher: OK, if I multiply, and in mathematical we are going to turn it around, we are going to say we are going to multiply the length times the width, so the area of a rectangle equals the length times the width [writes $A = l \times w$ on the board]. Now from just looking at our three samples here you know it works every time: you multiply the length times the width and you end up with finding the area of a rectangle and we could also say a square; the same thing would work on a square wouldn't it?

Notice how the teacher takes a perfectly reasonable answer—times the width times the length—and insists on turning it around into the more conventional order of length times width. This amounts to subtle invalidation of the student's thinking, and at the same time invokes outside authority to justify the move: "in mathematical we are going to turn it around." Note also the speed with which the teacher states the generalization, "from just looking at our three samples here you know it works every time." This is in marked contrast to the Japanese teacher, who lets the children ponder, at the end of the lesson, the generality of their solutions.

We also see in the American lesson plan the note: "Formula $A = l \times w$— recipe." In fact, the teacher refers more than once to this analogy, giving students a very different conception of formulas than is conveyed by the Japanese teacher.

Teacher: 15 sq cm (writes this on the board) now here's how we do that. We say area = length times width; now that's a formula or an equation right? What did I tell you? I said a formula was like a recipe. When you are doing a recipe what do you do with it? You are at home and you are baking cookies and you have a recipe; what do you do?

Miriam: Mix them all together.
Teacher: Yeah, and if it says, if it says one half cup of flour what do you do?
Miriam: Add in one half cup of flour.
Teacher: You put a half cup of flour, you don't put in 2 cups of sugar. So when it talks about area = length times the width you put in what it calls for, so you say area = length, 5 cm, times the width, 3 cm. Now you have a times sign so you go 5 times 3 = 15, and notice that they said square cm. [Teacher wrote formula down while speaking.] They remembered 'cause if they just said 15 cm that's a line measurement; square cm says that is an area measurement.

The teacher goes on to bring in the recipe analogy four more times in the lesson. Near the end of the lesson he says:

Now that is finding the area of a triangle. One thing you want to get use to is, as we go along we are going to end up with more and more formulas. Tomorrow we are going to work with volume and we are going to have a formula for a recipe for finding the volume of something, and once you learn to just to substitute—find the base, plug it in; find the height, plug it in—you won't have any trouble with formulas.

If the Japanese children are learning that formulas are tools to guide thinking, and to represent the results of their thinking, the American children are learning that formulas are things given them by the teacher so they will know what to do in certain situations. The epistemological outlooks that are being socialized in the two lessons differ greatly.

CONCLUSION

In this chapter we have presented preliminary analyses of part of a new set of data consisting of videotaped mathematics lessons in Japanese and American elementary schools. The most salient differences between the Japanese and American traditions of classroom mathematics are in the degree to which student thinking is stressed. We found three major ways in which Japanese lessons emphasize student thinking: First, Japanese teachers take student thinking into account in their planning of instruction. Not only are their lesson plans structured to facilitate students' coherent representation of the lesson, but Japanese teachers actually anticipate—in writing—students' responses to instruction. Second, Japanese teachers use a number of techniques to give students opportunities to think during instruction. These techniques include providing time for students to solve problems during the lesson, not hurrying students to solutions, providing opportunities for public discourse about mathematics, asking students the kinds of questions that will elicit lengthy and thoughtful responses, using students' errors as opportunities for reflection and discussion, and using manipulatives as tools for representing mathematics ideas. Finally, Japanese teachers go to great lengths convey a view of mathematics in which authority lies not in the teacher but in the methods themselves, there are multiple ways to solve a single problem, and the methods of solving problems must be evaluated by mathematical discourse and argumentation.

Why do Japanese teachers teach this way, and American teachers, by and large, not? Surely there are a number of reasons. One might be the mathematical preparation of American elementary school teachers. There is no question that American teachers, like the rest of the American population, are less mathematically competent themselves than are the Japanese teachers. Letting students influence the direction of the lesson, as inevitably happens in the Japanese-style lesson, may provoke anxiety in American teachers who may not be sure themselves if children's novel solutions to mathematics problems are justified.

Similarly, the mathematical preparation of the students may affect the quality of classroom discourse. The kinds of open-ended requests for explanations that appear so common in the Japanese classrooms may only be possible because Japanese students have the knowledge required to answer the questions. A study of social studies instruction by Schneider, Gallimore, and Hyland (1991) lends validity to this possibility. In that study the kind of short-answer "recitation" type instruction was more prevalent in a class for remedial students than in a class for gifted students, even when the teacher was the same. Clearly, the kinds of discussions found in Japanese classrooms depend on both teachers and students to occur.

Another reason American teachers teach the way they do may be the relative lack of resources available to them. Specifically, there is a good deal of research that goes into being able to predict what students' problem solutions will be, as for example was seen in the Japanese teacher's lesson plan above. It is important to note that the Japanese teacher did not have to come up with the anticipated student responses by herself. There are reference books and publications available to Japanese teachers that detail students' thinking about all of the topics in the mathematics curriculum. A teacher who is unsure about a particular topic, or a beginning teacher, has many sources to go to for help.

This point may be far more important than anyone has realized. In fact, one American teacher development program that is apparently achieving results similar to those we have seen in Japanese classrooms seems to work in just this way. The program, called Cognitively Guided Instruction, is based at the University of Wisconsin (Carpenter, Fennema, & Franke, 1992; Frank, Fennema, Carpenter, & Ansell, 1992; Peterson, 1992; Stigler, 1992). Although there are other components to the program, the major one provides teachers with information about the different methods students themselves come up with to solve various kinds of problems.

Finally, what we see when we observe in Japanese elementary classrooms looks quite different from what apparently goes on in Japanese secondary schools, where students talk little and where the focus is on rote memorization

(Rohlen, 1983). This is an important qualification. It also raises the interesting question of why teaching techniques should change so radically over this age range. One factor is no doubt the intense competition associated with entrance exams into college that shape, in a major way, the high school experiences of Japanese students. Another factor is that the kinds of values we see embodied in elementary mathematics lessons—values such as the importance of each individual expressing his point of view in public class discussion—are generally not valued in adult Japanese society. Having good ideas is important, but expressing those ideas in public is often frowned on. Elementary teaching in Japan may thus make more sense when viewed in a life-span perspective. Perhaps elementary lessons are the way they are in order to explicitly teach young Japanese students how to think, analyze problems, and invent solutions. Once they have learned these skills, however, it is no longer necessary to display them publicly, and thus there is the shift in high school. Americans tend to see talking and acting as evidence of thinking. Japanese see thinking as something that goes beyond talk and action. Thinking involves reflection, and reflection is what characterizes instruction in Japanese elementary mathematics classrooms.

ACKNOWLEDGMENTS

The research reported in this chapter is part of a collaborative research project with our Japanese colleagues Giyoo Hatano, Shizuko Amaiwa, and Hajime Yoshida. The project is funded in part by the Spencer Foundation. We are grateful to Giyoo Hatano and Paul Cobb for comments on an earlier draft. Another version of this chapter has been published as Stigler, J. W., Fernandez, C., and Yoshida, M. (in press). Cultures of mathematics instruction in Japanese and American elementary classrooms. In T. Rohlen and G. Le Tendre (Eds.), *Teaching and learning in Japan*. New York: Cambridge University Press.

REFERENCES

Carpenter, T. P., Fennema, E., & Franke, M. L. (1992, April). *Cognitively guided instruction: Building the primary mathematics curriculum on children's informal mathematical knowledge.* Paper presented at the annual meeting of the American Educational Research Association, San Francisco.

Cobb, P., Wood, T., Yackel, E., & McNeal, E. (1992). *Characteristics of classroom mathematics traditions: An interactional analysis. American Educational Research Journal, 29,* 573–602.

Frank, M. L., Fennema, E., Carpenter, T. P., & Ansell, E. (1992, April). *The process of teacher change in Cognitively Guided Instruction.* Paper presented at the annual meeting of the American Educational Research Association, San Francisco.

Peterson, P. L. (1992, April). *Using teachers' and learners' knowledge to transform teaching.* Paper presented at the annual meeting of the American Educational Research Association, San Francisco.

Richards, J. (1991). Mathematical discussions. In Ernst von Glasersfeld (Ed.), *Radical Constructivism in mathematics education*. Dordrecht, the Netherlands; Boston: Kluwer Academic.

Rohlen, T. P. (1983). *Japan's high schools*. Berkeley: University of California Press.

Schneider, P., Gallimore, R., & Hyland, J. (1991). Assisting narrative performance in two eighth-grade classrooms. *International Journal of Dynamic Assessment and Instruction, 2*(1), 14–28.

Stevenson, H. W., & Stigler, J. W. (1992). *The learning gap: Why our schools are failing and what we can learn from Japanese and Chinese education*. New York: Summit.

Stigler, J. W. (1992, April). *Transforming teaching by focusing on student thinking: Similarities between CGI and Japanese classrooms*. Paper presented at the annual meeting of the American Educational Research Association, San Francisco.

Stigler, J. W., & Perry, M. (1988). Mathematics learning in Japanese, Chinese, and American classrooms. In G. Saxe & M. Gearhart (Eds.), *Children's mathematics* (pp. 27–54). San Francisco: Jossey-Bass.

COGNITIVE SCIENCE THEORIES AND THEIR CONTRIBUTIONS TO THE LEARNING OF MATHEMATICS

Brian Greer, Editor

11 Theories of Mathematics Education: The Role of Cognitive Analyses

Brian Greer
Queen's University, Belfast

THE COGNITIVE REVOLUTION AND BEYOND

Throughout this century, there has been a sporadic relationship between theoretical schools in psychology and the emerging field of mathematics education. In the course of this relationship, there has often been tension arising from divergent conceptions of the nature of mathematics and of the aims of mathematics education. To differing degrees, and with honorable exceptions, the psychologists who have worked on mathematics have been open to the charges of viewing mathematics selectively as a convenient domain to supply grist for their theoretical mills, and of having insufficient regard for the implementation of their theories within effective instructional environments.

Progressive exposure of the limitations of behaviorism (dominant as a theoretical school in the United States but much less so elsewhere) culminated in a sequence of events and publications during the second half of the 1950s that Gardner (1985) dubbed the "Cognitive Revolution." From the point of view of those involved in mathematics education, this paradigm shift had many positive aspects. The complexity of tasks used in problem-solving research increased, means for dealing with complex knowledge structures were devised, and links between the psychology of learning and school instruction were restored. Moreover, as time went on, there was a swing away from general theories of knowledge processing toward an emphasis on the domain specificity of the knowledge being processed.

During the 1960s and 1970s it looked as if cognitive psychology was in a relatively stable state with a unifying framework provided by the general concept of information processing, represented by a group of approaches bearing a family resemblance to one another, and mostly sharing the following characteristics (Greer & Verschaffel, 1990a):

- the analysis of complex task performances in terms of knowledge structures and information-processing steps
- the assumption that mental processes are constrained by human memory architecture
- the allocation of a central role to organizing schemata
- a penchant for the implementation of models as computer simulations

A paradigmatic example of computer-based modeling was the analysis of "buggy algorithms." It is a familiar observation that students' errors in multidigit subtraction are often systematic, one of the most common being to subtract the smaller digit in a column from the larger, regardless of position. A theory to explain the development of such error patterns as "buggy algorithms" was developed by Brown, Burton, and Van Lehn (e.g., Brown & Burton, 1978; Van Lehn, 1990). As well as classifying common errors, the analysis suggests how bugs can be predicted as constructions of the child faced with an impasse when conditions are encountered beyond the scope of currently effective procedures.

This body of work was commended recently by Boden (1988, p. 263), who singled it out as one of the few examples of a domain modeled in enough detail to be useful to pupils or teachers, adding, "but there is significant scope *in principle* for pedagogic applications in many different areas" (emphasis added). Even more recently, Newell (1990, p. 368) stated that:

> it is critically important to find some cases where cognitive theory can predict long stretches of behavior—long stretches that are relatively unconstrained, during which humans can be assumed to be freely thinking. Even one or two such instances would go a long way toward convincing us of the essential correctness of cognitive theory.

Newell cited the buggy algorithm analysis as a good candidate (along with modeling of solutions of cryptarithmetic puzzles).

The reaction to such work from within the field of mathematics education stands in stark contrast. Thompson (1989, p. 138) asked, "In what way does a detailed understanding of how students perform tasks mindlessly help us to improve mathematics education?" (see also Fischbein, 1990b; Ridgway, 1988). Hennessy (1993) showed that, in fact, specific "bugs" are very unstable over time and concluded (p. 335) that "the outcome of remediation at a purely syntactic level is the very limited arithmetic competence of a considerable number of both children and adults in our society." This echoes the fundamental criticism made by Cobb (1990) in relation to the explanation given by Van Lehn (1983, p. 5) of the choice of children's multidigit subtraction algorithms as a topic for investigation:

Its main advantage, from a psychological point of view, is that it is a virtually meaningless procedure. Most elementary students have only a dim conception of the underlying semantics of subtraction. . . . This isolation is the bane of teachers but a boon to the psychologist. It allows one to study a skill formally without bringing in a whole world's worth of associations.

From this quotation may be inferred a characterization of the goals of mathematics education in terms of skills in symbol manipulation. Kaput (1992, p. 545) made a parallel point in relation to ICAI (intelligent computer-assisted instruction) systems, which, he observed, "were applied to teach the syntax of formal notations—which is the only inherent content of such notations. [They] did not, because they could not, deal with what the formalisms are used to represent and what they evolved to do in the first place. . . . But this competence has come to be pedagogically inappropriate and curricularly superfluous."

More generally, people involved in mathematics education have found information-processing characterizations inadequate to account for the complexity and richness of mathematical activity, unless such characterizations can be reformulated much more widely (Greer & Verschaffel, 1990b).

Gardner (1985) described the emergence of a multidisciplinary field of study that came to have the label "cognitive science." Among its key features, he included "de-emphasis on affect, context, culture, and history" (p. 41). Moreover, he identified as a central problem the "computational paradox," namely, the insight gained through the use of computational models that "the kind of systematic, logical, rational view of human cognition that pervaded the early literature of cognitive science does not adequately describe much of human thought and behavior" (p. 44).

In reaction to these and other perceived weaknesses, what might be seen as a second wave of the Cognitive Revolution began, the main thrust of which has been to resituate intellectual functioning within a much wider human context. A strong reaction against formalism, in accord with the computational paradox identified by Gardner, has been one of the most salient characteristics of this movement. Prominent examples from the general psychological literature include the description of expert decision making proposed by Dreyfus and Dreyfus (1986), and the radical changes in theories of categorization initiated by Rosch (1973) and others.

In parallel with the attack on what Cobb (1987, p. 11) dubbed "psychological formalism," there have been strong critiques of formalist approaches to the philosophy of mathematics (Tymoczko, 1986b), exemplified by this statement from two mathematicians who have reflected on the practices of their discipline:

The definition–theorem–proof approach to mathematics has become almost the sole paradigm of mathematical exposition and advanced instruction. Of course, this is not the way mathematics is created, propagated, or even understood. . . . Mathematics is a human activity, and the formal-logical account is only a fiction. (Davis & Hersh, 1981, p. 306)

Another major theme has been the development of the Piagetian view of cognition as grounded in perception and action, and in human experience in general (Cobb, 1987; Johnson, 1987; Thompson, chapter 15, this volume; Varela, Thompson, & Rosch, 1991). In a philosophical analysis, Hamlyn (1990) argued that cognitivism inherited from behaviorism the aim of delimiting the subject matter of psychology, and also some of behaviorism's defects. He criticized the concentration on explaining central mental processes while underplaying the complexities of "input" and "output" grounded in the experience, beliefs, and intentions of an agent living in a society.

The first two sections of this book amply testify to the extent to which the deemphasis on social and cultural contexts identified by Gardner has been addressed. A much richer and more complex view of intellectual functioning has been developed, one consequence being that the boundaries of cognitive psychology have become unclear. At one extreme, there are still people working within what Cobb (1990, p. 68) called the "strong information-processing program"; Newell's (1990) "Unified theories of cognition" is a prime example. On the other hand, Cobb (1990, p. 85) identified others whose positions have radically changed. For example, he pointed to the contrast between Brown's previous work on buggy algorithms (discussed earlier) and the highly influential paper on situated cognition he coauthored (Brown, Collins, & Duguid, 1989). Contributors to Greer and Verschaffel (1990b) suggested that information-processing theories might be open to enrichment to address aspects such as affect (McLeod, 1990) and intuition (Fischbein, 1990b). Thus there is likely to be uncertainty and disagreement for some time about how the scope of cognitive psychology should be delimited.

Moreover, in contrast with the period when research in the information-processing tradition could be said to have at least approximated to Kuhn's (1970) idea of "normal science," there is no unifying theoretical framework visible on the horizon. Likewise, current research is characterized by methodological diversity, and a certain lack of agreed conventions and systematicity in the communication of experimental findings.

In summary, the current situation is one of complexity as well as excitement, as reflected in this volume. Against this background, my aim is to make the case for the continuing role of cognitive analysis within attempts to construct theories of mathematical education.

QUESTIONS OF BALANCE

In the ferment of new ideas, liberalization of methodology, and openness to concepts from many disciplines, there are risks of losing balance through overcompensation. Comments by Cobb (1994) on the complementarity rather than opposition of constructivist and sociocultural perspectives have general applicability, as he suggests that "claims that one perspective or the other captures the essence of people and communities should be rejected in favor of pragmatic justifications that consider the relevance and usefulness of a perspective for the issues and purposes at hand" (p. 13).

Here I discuss three broad issues where there are indications of pendular movement, namely, the appeal to constructivist principles (variously interpreted) as the sole authoritative source of guidance for mathematics education, the swing from the individual learner to the social context as the primary focus of attention, and current emphasis on everyday cognition and experience as opposed to formal and abstract knowledge.

Clarification of Constructivism

Constructivists have been particularly prominent and effective in the critique of the first wave of cognitive theories (see, especially, Cobb, 1987, 1990) and in the ongoing attempts to reformulate the philosophical and epistemological bases of mathematics education. However, comparable contributions have been made by others coming from positions not identified as constructivist, such as Freudenthal (1991) and his successors at the Freudenthal Institute (Streefland, 1991; Treffers, 1987). Likewise, Goldin (1990), endorsing a set of ideas on teaching mathematics that are widely identified with constructivism, argued that precisely the same principles could be derived from an empiricist epistemology. Moreover, constructivism does not offer clear guidelines at the detailed level of instructional design; indeed, according to Janvier (chapter 25, this volume), constructivism is not concerned with teaching.

Constructivist analysis raises the question of the balance between guidance by the teacher and (re)invention by the student. Freudenthal (1991) suggested that the learner does not have to repeat in full the learning process of mankind— indeed, it seems implausible that this would ever be possible if advanced mathematics is to be reached. Freudenthal (1991, p. 49) recommended that "the learner should reinvent mathematising rather than mathematics; abstracting rather than abstractions; schematising rather than schemes; formalising rather than formulas; algorithmising rather than algorithms; verbalising rather than language." This key shift to process as what needs to be reconstructed legitimizes the idea that mathematical content may be transmitted—subject to the qualifications set out by Hatano (chapter 12, this volume), namely, that what is transmitted is merely the "raw data" for interpretation by the student. The point is that a student with a good understanding of what it means to algorithmize, say, is thereby well equipped to assimilate information about algorithms. More generally, I feel that constructivists have overcompensated in reaction to simplistic theories of language, meaning, and communication; it is noticeable that the limitations of language do not inhibit them from promoting their theoretical position, at length, through writing and speaking.

A major area of theoretical dispute between constructivist theorists and cognitive psychologists has concerned the concept of representation (Cobb, Yackel, & Wood, 1992; von Glaserfeld, 1987). Goldin and Kaput (chapter 23, this volume) address these criticisms and argue that the notion of representation is theoretically useful in attempts to organize and explain observations of student behavior. It is not clear that this is incompatible with the view that the teacher or experimenter must build up a model of the student's conceptual world (von Glasersfeld, chapter 18, this volume). In the construction of such models, we must have some conceptual tools to work with, and the elaborated view of representations in mathematical cognition offered by Goldin and Kaput must remain a major candidate, in the absence of strong competition.

Only a few issues have been briefly touched on here in order to point to the need for continuing debate and clarification of constructivism, its implications for mathematics education, and its relation to other perspectives. In particular, a major debate, to which I now turn, concerns the balance between individual and social construction of mathematical knowledge.

Individual Cognition and Social Interaction

Voigt (chapter 2, this volume) outlines the antithesis between two theoretical traditions. The first, largely founded on Piaget's theory and developed as radical constructivism (e.g., von Glasersfeld, chapter 18, this volume), focuses on the individual as the constructor of knowledge. The second, which emphasizes the social and cultural origins of knowledge, has been very strongly influenced by Vygotsky and his successors. Voigt proposes an interactive synthesis.

As Voigt points out, the influence of Piaget was such that, for a long time, most research addressed the cognitive development of individual children, often using the methodology of clinical interviews (e.g., Steffe, von Glasersfeld, Richards, & Cobb, 1983). Piaget has been criticized for paying insufficient attention to social, cultural, and educational (in the broadest sense) factors. Even Youniss and Damon (1992), in arguing that ideas about social construction are essential to Piaget's genetic epistemology, admitted that there is some justification for the caricature of a Piagetian "apocryphal child who discovers formal properties of things, such as number, while playing alone with pebbles on the beach" (p. 268).

Attacks from numerous quarters have undermined the characterization of cognitive development in terms of universal, context-independent structures within individual minds. For example, anticipating recent emphasis on situated cognition, Donaldson (1978) effectively critiqued Piaget's focus on "disembedded" rather than "embedded" thinking in children. As Hatano (chapter 12, this volume) points out, evidence suggests that cognitive competencies are not content independent; children with extensive knowledge of a particular domain demonstrate more advanced forms of reasoning within that area of expertise. Likewise, Crawford (chapter 9, this volume) argues that knowledge is culturally relative. A further considerable body of criticisms of Piagetian theory relates to interpretations of interactions with children, such as clinical interviews, which fail to take account of the child's construal of the social situation within which the interaction takes place.

In recent years, often under the influence of Vygotskian ideas, the emphasis has shifted dramatically. Manifestations of this trend include reconceptualizations of cognition as situated (Brown et al., 1989; Lave & Wenger, 1991) and distributed (Salomon, 1993a), and of cognitive development as enculturation within a mathematical community (Solomon, 1989). The parallel methodological shift in research on mathematics education has been to the observation of classroom interactions (Voigt, chapter 2, this volume).

No doubt these shifts represent an appropriate reaction to previous concentration on the individual cognizer, but there is a danger of overreaction. For example, Salomon (1993b, p. 111) described the idea of distributed cognition as novel and provocative, but warned that, like many other newly coined terms, it "strongly illuminates one facet of an issue, sending to dark oblivion others." He characterized the strong version of distributed cognition as the view that "while individuals' cognition are not to be dismissed, cognition in general should be reexamined and conceived as principally distributed" (Salomon, 1993a, p. xv); this view was attributed to some of the contributors to his book. By contrast, he and other contributors put forward a less radical view that "'solo' and distributed cognition are still distinguished from each other and are taken to be in an interdependent dynamic interaction" (p. xvi). Specifically, Salomon argued that "distributed cognitions . . . interact with those elements one traditionally attributes to the mind of the individual: mentally represented knowledge and skill" (Salomon, 1993b, p. 120).

The strong version of distributed cognition, as characterized by Salomon, seems seriously unbalanced. Consider Poincaré's famous description of a moment of insight while engaged in a completely unrelated activity: "the idea came to me, apparently with nothing whatever in my previous thoughts having prepared me for it, that the transformations which I had used to define Fuchsian functions were identical with those of non-Euclidean geometry." (Poincaré, 1960, pp. 2044–2045). I find it difficult to see how this could be classified as a distributed cognition (or a situated cognition, come to that) or how it could be analyzed without taking into account mental activity within Poincaré's individual mind over an extended period. Likewise, in accounting for the development of mathematical cognition in a child, an analysis of a series of participations in social situations needs to be complemented by some account of the coherent development and restructuring of that individual's knowledge and conceptualizations over extended periods of time.

An emphasis on the importance of social factors rather than individual intellectual achievements is also to be found among some current philosophers of mathematics. Representative of this view is the statement by Tymoczko (1986a, p. xvi) that "any serious attempt to understand the evolution of mathematics should begin by locating the practicing mathematician in a sociohistorical context." Although agreeing with this statement in a review of the book that Tymoczko (1986b) edited, Wells (1988) argued that the account is incomplete if it does not also consider the psychology of individual mathematicians and asserted that the history of mathematics makes it clear that psychological and social factors interact. Again, the need for complementary perspectives seems clear.

Formal Education Versus Everyday Learning

Elshout (1992, p. 5) commented that "Educational philosophy seems to be locked into a pendular motion, in some periods favoring formal schooling as its ideal, then swinging to the position that the best of learning is to be found in everyday life."

Several lines of research have contributed to this swing (which, perhaps, it should be pointed out is located in certain academic circles, and rarely in educational systems). Within experimental psychology, a wide range of findings effectively demolished naive normative theories of rational thinking. Among these findings, those from the extensive literature generated by Wason's "selection task" (Wason, 1983; see also discussion by Elshout, 1992) may be taken to be prototypical (see also the earlier references to Dreyfus & Dreyfus, 1986, and Rosch, 1973). Empirical investigations showed that in many areas people's thinking, decision making, and so on simply do not conform with formal normative models. A different broad group of studies has been concerned with the reasoning processes of various cultures and subcultures, such as occupational groups, and of children engaged in authentic activities involving mathematics (e.g., Nunes, Schliemann, & Carraher, 1993).

How relevant are these studies to education in general, and mathematics education in particular? One suggestion has been that education should be modeled on the forms of learning that take place in apprenticeship (Brown et al., 1989). A case may be made that certain aspects of apprenticeship learning could be adapted with advantage to classroom teaching, but the idea that apprenticeship is appropriate as the sole model for mathematics education is untenable. Typically, apprenticeship leads to reproduction and maintenance of the status quo, which is incompatible with any progressive philosophy of education. For example, Greenfield (1993), in a study of weaving among Mayan people in Mexico, observed that the apprenticeship learning common in 1970 resulted in a limited and unchanging repertoire of patterns. In contrast, 20 years later, as a consequence of economic and social changes, a more independent exploratory type of learning resulted in a wide variety of figurative and geometric patterns. Perhaps we should bear in mind Levi's (1988, p. 77) warning: "Beware of analogies: for millennia they corrupted medicine, and it may be their fault that today's pedagogical systems are so numerous, and after three thousand years of argument we still don't actually know which is best."

Mathematics (and science) transcend everyday cognition (and it is just as well that they do for people who like to fly to conferences and type their papers on word processors). Chevallard (1990, p. 18) referred to "the intrinsic *cultural discontinuity* between mathematical and everyday cultures." Resnick (1987) highlighted a number of key differences between (mathematics) learning within and outside of school:

1. Learning and performance in school is primarily individual, whereas out-of-school activities are much more often carried out in groups.
2. School activities are often carried out with limited use of tools. Cognitive activities outside school typically use tools (materials, books, calculators).
3. School stresses decontextualized learning, whereas out-of-school activities are situated.
4. School stresses general knowledge and skills of wide (potential) applicability, whereas knowledge and skills outside school are situation specific.

Two comments may be made on this list. The first is that, at least in some instructional environments, the differences Resnick refers to are significantly reduced. The second is that education is not, nor is it intended to be, like learning in everyday contexts; if it were, why would it be necessary? (I assume, for the purposes of this discussion, that it is necessary.) The theory of didactic transposition (Chevallard, 1985) may be invoked here. This theory is based on the observation that knowledge is normally developed originally to be used, not to be taught. Didactic transposition refers to the process of transforming such knowledge so that it becomes teachable.

None of the foregoing should be taken as denying that education, and mathematics education in particular, should be made more relatable to everyday experience, reflecting the grounding of mathematics in the description of aspects of reality and in the solving of practical problems (Vergnaud, chapter 13, this volume). More specifically, I have argued elsewhere (Greer, 1993) that people in general need to have a discriminating appreciation of the nature of mathematical modeling and of its limitations.

One salient theme of the critique of formal knowledge has been a questioning of the effectiveness of decontextualized knowledge as transferable across situations (see, e.g., Dettermann, 1993; Lave, 1988, chap. 2). This debate is particularly important for mathematics, because, as argued in Greer and Harel (in press), the detection and exploitation of structural similarities underlying superficially different situations is one of the most powerful strategies used by mathematicians. (This is illustrated by the earlier quotation from Poincaré—who once defined mathematics as "the art of giving the same name to different things.") More generally, Hatano (chapter 12, this volume) suggests that gaining expertise may be a process of desituating knowledge, so that problem-solving competence becomes less context bound.

Greer and Harel (in press) argued that the considerable body of psychological research on transfer is mostly of limited relevance to mathematics education for several reasons, including the questionable motivation of subjects and the limited time-span typical of such experiments (see also the comments by Elshout, 1992, pp. 15–16). It is suggested that transfer is only to be expected within a sustained instructional environment in which the analysis of structural relationships is nurtured (Maher, Martino, & Alston, 1993).

MATHEMATICS AS INTELLECTUAL ACTIVITY

In the previous section, I suggested some issues on which there is a danger of taking one-sided positions; this section continues on that theme. Although recent emphasis on social, cultural, and historical contexts has been entirely appropriate, there has been a tendency to forget that being human, both individually and culturally, also includes being intellectual. I agree with Thompson (1993, p. 283), therefore, when he declared that "I consider it imperative that the mathematics education community regain the sense that mathematics is a deep and abstract intellectual achievement."

In this regard, I consider it perverse to argue that what I will call "academic mathematics" (the term "Western mathematics" that is sometimes used seems a clear misnomer) has no special status among the multiple forms of ethnomathematics (the mathematics practiced within identifiable sociocultural groups). Important features of academic mathematics that differentiate it from localized mathematical activities and practices include the length and complexity of its historical development, the multiplicity of cultures that have contributed to that development, the degree of recording and communication and thereby criticism and negotiation of meaning between mathematicians (particularly in modern times), the technological advances that have generated problems stimulating new mathematics, the creation and codification of abstract mathematics, and—perhaps of the greatest significance—the degree of reflection on the nature of mathematics. Chevallard (1990, p. 13) proposed that "At some point in the history of the world, for unknown reasons, people came to take a *reflexive*—not only conscious—view of what can now be thought of as *proto*mathematics.

In reading a recent chapter in a book on language, I was struck by a passage in which it is stated that there was during the 1980s "a boom in those disciplines which study the language-system in a state of formation (child language acquisition, creolistics), or in a state of variability (dialectology, sociolinguistics), or in a state of spontaneous, informal performance (pragmatics, conversation analysis)" (Adamson, 1990, p. 504). The parallel with recent mathematics education research is inviting. Adamson continued by saying that "at the end of the decade, these separate studies are beginning to come together to foster a revitalized historical linguistics which aims to establish the relation between language as a system and language as an activity of speakers."

The claim that it is meaningful and useful to speak of mathematics, like language, as a system is based on the existence of organized knowledge within mathematics, and on identifiable mechanisms for growth within mathematics; these structural aspects of mathematics markedly distinguish it from other cultural constructions (e.g., etiquette). The systemization of mathematics will never achieve completeness; rather, it is partial and forever evolving, as Freudenthal's comments (1991, p. 24) on the Bourbaki codification of mathematics makes plain. Nevertheless, there is inherent organization of knowledge within academic mathematics as structures and structures of structures, and so on.

There have been many attempts to define psychological structures underlying the development of mathematical cognition—most notably Piaget's. Piaget perceived a striking parallel between his structures and those of Bourbaki, which Freudenthal (1991, p. 28) interpreted as Piaget's assimilation of the Bourbaki system to his theory. A more local organizing framework is provided by Vergnaud's concept of conceptual field, which combines mathematical and psychological aspects: "A conceptual field is a set of situations, the mastering of which requires several interconnected concepts. It is at the same time a set of concepts, with different properties, the meaning of which is drawn from this variety of situations" (Vergnaud, chapter 13, this volume).

Freudenthal (1991, p. 15) commented that "in no other field does organising display itself in such purity, impose itself with such force and infiltrate so profoundly as it does in mathematics. Mathematics grows, as it were, by its self-organizing momentum."

Some of the mechanisms of growth may be identified. Mathematics is generative; for example, from any set a more complex structure can be derived by analysing its power set (i.e., the set of subsets of the original set). Mathematical concepts characteristically evolve by restructuring so that they apply to broader and broader domains. The driving force of disequilibrium and the restoring of local equilibrium through restructuring can be seen, par excellence, in the development of number concepts (e.g., the lack of closure of the natural numbers under subtraction and division being resolved by extension to directed and rational numbers, respectively). In such processes, symbols and notation are often key facilitators, as is strikingly examplified by the following statement of Laplace quoted by De Morgan (1910, p. 185):

Newton extended to fractional and negative powers the analytical expression which he had found for whole and positive ones. You see in this extension one of the great advantages of algebraic language which expresses truths much more general than those which were at first contemplated, so that by making the extension of which it admits, there arises a multitude of new truths out of formulae which were founded upon very limited suppositions.

Another characteristic tendency is what Freudenthal (1983, p. 81) termed "anontologisation", by which he meant cutting the bonds with reality (cf. Hatano, chapter 12, this volume).

A further set of mechanisms may be broadly classified as evolutionary. Rav (1993) outlined an interesting theory of the interaction between biological and cultural evolution; as he pointed out (p. 89), "Given [its] remarkably long history, mathematics has been subjected to a lengthy cultural molding process akin to an environmental selection." Prominent among the evolutionary pressures have been problems—both external, practical problems and internal problems relating to incompleteness, inconsistency, refinement of definition, and so on.

Above all, there is in mathematics an interplay between the grounding in reality, human experience, and cultural creativity, on the one hand, and development of abstract systems on the other. This interplay is beautifully illustrated in Weyl's (1952) classic discussion of symmetry, which begins with the recognition of symmetry in biological form and cultural artefacts, finds applications in scientific fields, notably crystallography and quantum mechanics, and leads "up the ladder from intuitive concepts to abstract ideas" (p. 145).

The relationship between the historical development of mathematics and the development of mathematical cognition in a student may be considered of interest for many reasons. Piaget and Garcia (1989) suggested broad parallels between psychogenesis and the history of science. Indeed, the earlier reference to disequilibrium within mathematical structures was intended to invite analogy with the role postulated for it within Piaget's theory of cognitive development. Increasingly, scholars are turning to the historical record for possible indications of the ways in which concepts may develop, the types of cognitive obstacles that may hinder learners, illumination on the relationship of knowledge to problems, and so on. Examples are Kaput's (1994) analysis of early ideas of calculus, and Carraher's (chapter 14, this volume) appeal to conceptualizations of rational number that can be traced back to the Greeks.

A major area for development in the coming years is likely to be the broadening of the domain beyond its current disproportionate focus on early conceptions; in this regard, the book *Advanced Mathematical Thinking* edited by Tall (1991) is an early milestone. As commented by Thompson (1993, p. 278) in reviewing Tall's book, "If in the distant future an archaeologist were to build an image of mathematics education based on artifacts from the educational research community, she might conclude that, as late as 1990, mathematics had not progressed past proportional reasoning." Thompson argued that it is not just a matter of studying more advanced topics, but of conceiving of long-scale development so that as early as possible, mathematics is taught with a view to its long-term goals (Vergnaud, chapter 13, this volume). This means building in advanced ideas early, a fine example of which is the work on proof in an elementary school in New Jersey described by Davis (chapter 16, this volume).

The analysis of mathematics as organized intellectual activity raises questions about the goals of mathematics education. As argued by Davis (chapter 16, this volume) students—irrespective of whether they are going to study mathematics to an advanced level—should have a appreciation of what mathematics is about and what it is for, and a sense of its value within human cultures. Moreover, for responsible citizenship, it is important to have an understanding of the ways in which mathematics is used to model social as well as physical phenomena, and the limitations of such models (Greer, 1993).

THE CONTINUING RELEVANCE
OF COGNITIVE ANALYSIS

In setting the scene for this section of the book, I have tried to sketch the immediate historical background to the present state of ferment within the field, to identify important issues currently being hotly debated, and to provide a framework for the remaining chapters in the section. Many of these issues are dealt with at much greater length in De Corte, Greer, and Verschaffel (in press).

Improving mathematics education is a massively complex human problem, in the cause of which all relevant forms of knowledge need to be mobilized. In pursuit of the (perhaps unattainable) goal of a comprehensive theory of learning mathematics, multiple contributions are required. As pieces of that jigsaw, essential roles will continue to be played by efforts that:

- Relate to general theories of cognition and cognitive development whose primary focus is on the mental processes of individual minds.
- Analyze the structure of mathematics and the processes of development characteristic of it in relation to the development of mathematical cognition in students.
- Are aimed at understanding intellectual functioning within planned instructional environments.

General Theories of Cognition

In recent years, there has been a strong move toward recognition of the importance of domain-specific learning and thinking. Mathematics, in many ways, has been a prime example. In fact, the process can be taken further by recognizing mathematics as a federation of subdomains, within each of which there are specific forms of argument, specific cognitive obstacles, and so on—the most obvious example of a subdomain with its own characteristics being probability.

Nevertheless, Hatano (chapter 12, this volume) argues the case for continuing utility of general accounts of aspects of cognition, notably expertise and knowledge representation. As he points out, the conclusions of comparative analysis are of interest whether they point to commonalities or contrasts across domains. General post-Piagetian theories of cognitive development are of considerable relevance to mathematics education, including those that emphasize the grounding of cognition in action, perception, and experience (Thompson, chapter 15, this volume).

Davis (chapter 16, this volume) argues for the utility of a general theory of mathematical thinking, which he characterizes as based on information processing and using analogies from computer science (although he does not consider computer simulation a necessary tool). However, his approach (see especially Davis, 1984) is much more based on detailed analyses of children's mathematical behavior, and on recourse to multiple sources of metaphors and other explanatory resources, than is typical of mainstream information-processing studies.

Analyses of Mathematical Cognition

There is a vast amount of research on specific areas of mathematics, such as geometrical and spatial reasoning, number concepts and arithmetic, and algebra (e.g., Grouws, 1992; Nesher & Kilpatrick, 1990). Of all the subdomains, probability is a particularly interesting case and deserves attention for many reasons, including its relatively late historical development as a branch of mathematics, the general difficulty of reasoning about probabilistic phenomena, and the continuing profound philosophical problems in its foundations; moreover, probability is arguably the branch of mathematics that most demands an explanation in constructivist terms.

As discussed earlier, a major need is to spread the effort more evenly over the full range of mathematical education, up to the most abstract mathematics. As Fischbein (1990a, p. 5) commented, "most of the more complex mathematical concepts are still insufficiently investigated from the psychological point of view." This is not to deny the crucial requirement to understand, and so improve the teaching of, early mathematical developments such as the extension of number concepts beyond the natural numbers to rationals (Carraher, chapter 14, this volume).

Observation and documentation of the construction of knowledge through social interactions in classrooms need to be complemented by detailed studies of the cognitive processes of individuals in relation to specific mathematical topics and by studies of the development of mathematical understanding of individuals over considerable periods of time (Vergnaud, chapter 13, this volume).

Intellectual Functioning Within Designed Environments

The concept of the environment within which an individual learns has been substantially elaborated beyond the essentially biological conception of Piaget. Certainly, any idea that other people can be considered as just another part of the environment has been rejected. The recent work on situated cognition and distributed cognition may be considered as further elaborations of the role of the immediate physical and social environment, and of the social activities being enacted within that environment.

A further very general aspect is the notion of "designed environments," implying designers who create environments with specific educational goals in mind. There are many examples of detailed studies of the cognitive effects of learning within such environments, including the work of Cobb, Wood, and Yackel (1991) and projects at Rutgers University described by Davis (chapter 16, this volume) (for other examples, see De Corte et al., in press). Recently Collins (1992, p. 15) called for a "design science of education which must determine how different designs of learning environments contribute to learning, cooperation, and motivation."

A final highly significant aspect is that computer software, as exemplified in the software described by Carraher (chapter 14, this volume) and Thompson (chapter 15, this volume), makes possible the design of environments with features previously impossible to implement. If we accept the basic premise of Piaget that mathematics arises through reflective abstraction on actions performed in the environment, then extensions of cognitive theory are needed to take account of the new types of action that have been made possible, and what Thompson (chapter 15, this volume) refers to as the "dialectic between intention, action, and expression."

REFERENCES

Adamson, S. (1990). The what of the language? In C. Ricks & L. Michaels (Eds.), *The state of the language (1990s edition)* (pp. 503–514). London: Faber & Faber.

Boden, M. A. (1988). *Computer models of mind.* New York: Cambridge University Press.

Brown, J. S., & Burton, R. R. (1978). Diagnostic models for procedural bugs in basic mathematical skills. *Cognitive Science, 2,* 155–192.

Brown, J. S., Collins, A., & Duguid, P. (1989). Situated cognition and the culture of learning. *Educational Researcher, 18*(1), 32–42.

Chevallard, Y. (1985). *La transposition didactique* [The didactical transposition]. Grenoble, France: La Pensée Sauvage.

Chevallard, Y. (1990). On mathematics education and culture. *Educational Studies in Mathematics, 21,* 3–27.

Cobb, P. (1987). Information-processing psychology and mathematics education—A constructivist perspective. *Journal of Mathematical Behavior, 6,* 3–40.

Cobb, P. (1990). A constructivist perspective on information-processing theories of mathematical activity. *International Journal of Educational Research, 14*(1), 67–92.

Cobb, P. (1994). Where is the mind? Constructivist and sociocultural perspectives on mathematical development. *Educational Researcher, 23*(7), 13–20.

Cobb, P., Wood, T., & Yackel, E. (1991). A constructivist approach to second grade mathematics. In E. von Glasersfeld (Ed.), *Constructivism in mathematics education* (pp. 157–176). Dordrecht: Kluwer.

Cobb, P., Yackel, E., & Wood, T. (1992). A constructivist alternative to the representational view of mind in mathematics education. *Journal of Research in Mathematics Education, 23*, 2–33.

Collins, A. (1992). Toward a design science of education. In E. Scanlon & T. O'Shea (Eds.), *New directions in educational technology* (pp. 15–22). NATO ASI Series F: Computers and Systems Sciences, Vol. 96. Berlin: Springer-Verlag.

Davis, P. J., & Hersh, R. (1981). *The mathematical experience.* Boston: Birkhauser.

Davis, R. B. (1984). *Learning mathematics: The cognitive science approach to mathematics education.* Norwood, NJ: Ablex.

De Corte, E., Greer, B., & Verschaffel, L. (in press). Mathematics teaching and learning. In D. Berliner & R. Calfee (Eds.), *Handbook of educational psychology.* New York: Macmillan.

De Morgan, A. (1910). *Study and difficulties of mathematics.* Chicago: University of Chicago Press.

Detterman, D. K. (1993). The case for the prosecution: Transfer as an epiphenomenon. In D. K. Detterman & R. J. Sternberg (Eds.), *Transfer on trial: Intelligence, cognition, and instruction* (pp. 1–24). Norwood, NJ: Albex.

Donaldson, M. (1978). *Children's minds.* London: Fontana.

Dreyfus, H. L., & Dreyfus, S. E. (1986). *Mind over machine.* New York: Free Press.

Elshout, J. (1992). Formal education versus everyday learning. In E. De Corte, M. Linn, H. Mandl, & L. Verschaffel (Eds.), *Computer-based learning environments and problem solving* (pp. 5–17). NATO ASI Series F: Computer and Systems Sciences, Vol. 84. Berlin: Springer-Verlag.

Fischbein, E. (1990a). Introduction. In P. Nesher & J. Kilpatrick (Eds.), *Mathematics and cognition: A research synthesis by the International Group for the Psychology of Mathematics Education* (pp. 1–13). ICMI Study Series. Cambridge: Cambridge University Press.

Fischbein, E. (1990b). Intuition and information processing in mathematical activity. *International Journal of Educational Research, 14*(1), 31–50.

Freudenthal, H. (1983). *Didactical phenomenology of mathematical structures.* Dordrecht: Reidel.

Freudenthal, H. (1991). *Revisiting mathematics education.* Dordrecht: Kluwer.

Gardner, H. (1985). *The mind's new science.* New York: Basic Books.

Goldin, G. A. (1990). Epistemology, constructivism, and discovery learning mathematics. In R. B. Davis, C. A. Maher, & N. Noddings (Eds.), *Constructivist views on the teaching and learning of mathematics* (pp. 31–47). Reston, VA: National Council of Teachers of Mathematics.

Greenfield, P. (1993, July). *Cultural historical studies in cognition.* Paper presented at a Workshop on Culture and Mathematical Cognition, Maragogi, Brazil.

Greer, B. (1993). The mathematical modeling perspective on wor(l)d problems. *Journal of Mathematical Behavior, 12*, 239–250.

Greer, B., & Harel, G. (in press). The role of isomorphism in mathematical cognition. *Journal of Mathematical Behavior.*

Greer, B., & Verschaffel, L. (1990a). Introduction. *International Journal of Educational Research, 14*, 3–12.

Greer, B., & Verschaffel, L. (Eds.) (1990b). Mathematics education as a proving-ground for information-processing theories. *International Journal of Educational Research, 14*, 1–100 (thematic issue).

Grouws, D. A. (Ed.). (1992). *Handbook of research on mathematics teaching and learning.* New York: Macmillan.

Hamlyn, D. W. (1990). *In and out of the black box: On the philosophy of cognition.* Oxford: Blackwell.

Hennessy, S. (1993). The stability of children's mathematical behavior: When is a bug really a bug? *Learning and Instruction, 3,* 315–338.

Johnson, M. (1987). *The body in the mind: The bodily basis of meaning, imagination, and reason.* Chicago: University of Chicago Press.

Kaput, J. J. (1992). Technology and mathematics education. In D. A. Grouws (Ed.), *Handbook of research on mathematics teaching and learning* (pp. 515–556). New York: Macmillan.

Kaput, J. J. (1994). Democratizing access to calculus: New routes using old roots. In A. H. Schoenfeld (Ed.), *Mathematical thinking and problem solving* (pp. 77–156). Hillsdale, NJ: Lawrence Erlbaum Associates.

Kuhn, T. S. (1970). *The structure of scientific revolutions* (2nd ed.). Chicago: University of Chicago Press.

Lave, J. (1988). *Cognition in practice: Mind, mathematics, and culture in everyday life.* Cambridge, MA: Cambridge University Press.

Lave, J., & Wenger, E. (1991). *Situated learning: Legitimate peripheral participation.* Cambridge: Cambridge University Press.

Levi, P. (1988). *The wrench.* London: Abacus.

Maher, C. A., Martino, A. M., & Alston, A. S. (1993). *Children's construction of mathematical ideas.* New Brunswick, NJ: Rutgers University.

McLeod, D. B. (1990). Information-processing theories and mathematics learning: The role of affect. *International Journal of Educational Research, 14,* 13–29.

Nesher, P., & Kilpatrick, J. (Eds.). (1990). *Mathematics and cognition: A research synthesis by the International Group for the Psychology of Mathematics Education.* Cambridge: Cambridge University Press.

Newell, A. (1990). *Unified theories of cognition.* Cambridge, MA: Harvard University Press.

Nunes, T., Schliemann, A. D., & Carraher, D. W. (1993). *Street mathematics and school mathematics.* Cambridge: Cambridge University Press.

Piaget, J., & Garcia, R. (1989). *Psychogenesis and the history of science.* New York: Columbia University Press.

Poincaré, H. (1960). Mathematical creation. In J. R. Newman (Ed.), *The world of mathematics* (Vol. 4, pp. 2041–2050). London: George Allen & Unwin.

Rav, Y. (1993). Philosophical problems of mathematics in the light of evolutionary epistemology. In S. Restivo, J. P. Van Bendegem, & R. Fischer (Eds.), *Math worlds: Philosophical and social studies of mathematics and mathematics education,* (pp. 80–109). Albany, NY: State University of New York Press.

Resnick, L. B. (1987). Learning in school and out. *Educational Researcher, 16*(9), 13–20.

Ridgway, J. (1988). Of course ICAI is impossible . . . worse though, it might be seditious. In J. Self (Ed.), *Artificial intelligence and human learning* (pp. 28–48). London: Chapman & Hall.

Rosch, E. (1973). On the internal structure of perceptual and semantic categories. In T. E. Moore (Ed.), *Cognitive development and the acquisition of language,* (pp. 111–144). New York: Academic Press.

Salomon, G. (Ed.). (1993a). *Distributed cognition: Psychological and educational considerations.* New York: Cambridge University Press.

Salomon, G. (1993b). No distribution without individual's cognition: A dynamic interactional view. In G. Salomon (Ed.), *Distributed cognitions: Psychological and educational considerations* (pp. 111–138). New York: Cambridge University Press.

Solomon, Y. (1989). *The practice of mathematics.* London: Routledge.

Steffe, L. P., von Glasersfeld, E., Richards, J., & Cobb, P. (1983). *Children's counting types: Philosophy, theory, and application.* New York: Praeger Scientific.

Streefland, L. (Ed.). (1991). *Realistic mathematics education in primary school. On the occasion of the opening of the Freudenthal Institute.* Utrecht: Freudenthal Institute, Utrecht University.

Tall, D. (Ed.). (1991). *Advanced mathematical thinking.* Dordrecht: Kluwer.

Thompson, P. W. (1989). Artificial intelligence, advanced technology, and learning and teaching algebra. In S. Wagner & C. Kieran (Eds.), *Research issues in the learning and teaching of algebra* (pp. 135–161). Hillsdale, NJ: Lawrence Erlbaum Associates/Reston, VA: National Council of Teachers of Mathematics.

Thompson, P. W. (1993). Yes, Virginia, some children do grow up to be mathematicians [Review of *Advanced mathematical thinking*]. *Journal for Research in Mathematics Education, 24,* 279–284.

Treffers, A. (1987). *Three dimensions: A model of goal and theory description in mathematics education: The Wiskobas project.* Dordrecht: Reidel.

Tymoczko, T. (1986a). Introduction. In T. Tymoczko (Ed.), *New directions in the philosophy of mathematics* (pp. xiii–xvii). Boston: Birkhauser.

Tymoczko, T. (Ed.). (1986b). *New directions in the philosophy of mathematics.* Boston: Birkhauser.

Van Lehn, K. (1983). On the representation of procedures in Repair Theory. In H. P. Ginsburg (Ed.), *The development of mathematical thinking* (pp. 201–252). New York: Academic Press.

Van Lehn, K. (1990). *Mind bugs: The origins of procedural misconceptions.* Cambridge, MA: MIT Press.

Varela, F. J., Thompson, E., & Rosch, E. (1991). *The embodied mind.* Cambridge, MA: MIT Press.

von Glasersfeld, E. (1987). Learning as a constructive activity. In C. Janvier (Ed.), *Problems of representation in the teaching and learning of mathematics* (pp. 3–17). Hillsdale, NJ: Lawrence Erlbaum Associates.

Wason, P. C. (1983). Realism and rationality in the selection task. In J. St. B. T. Evans (Ed.), *Thinking and reasoning: Psychological approaches* (pp. 44–75). London: Routledge and Kegan Paul.

Wells, D. (1988). Proof, social process, and Thomas Tymoczko. *Studies of Meaning, Language, and Change, 21,* 13–26.

Weyl, H. (1952). *Symmetry.* Princeton, NJ: Princeton University Press.

Youniss, J., & Damon, W. (1992). Social construction in Piaget's theory. In H. Beilin & P. B. Pufall (Eds.), *Piaget's theory: Prospects and possibilities* (pp. 267–286). Hillsdale, NJ: Lawrence Erlbaum Associates.

12
A Conception of Knowledge Acquisition and Its Implications for Mathematics Education

Giyoo Hatano
Keio University, Tokyo Japan

In this chapter I discuss characterizations of knowledge acquisition offered by recent cognitive studies, how these characterizations can be applied to mathematical cognition, and what implications for mathematics education can be derived from them. Such an attempt may no longer be appealing to the mathematics education community, who may contend that:

- General theories of learning or acquisition, of either the behaviorist or cognitivist varieties, have not been as informative to mathematics educators as approaches specifically focused on mathematics.
- So-called general theories of learning are in fact about the acquisition of knowledge regarding aspects of the actual world (e.g., physics, biology, and psychology), and thus not relevant to the acquisition of logicomathematical knowledge.
- The course and process of development in the domain of mathematics are unique, so that studies in other domains of expertise cannot be instructive.
- What one has to acquire to become an expert or master in mathematics is radically different from other domains, and also the domain of mathematics is expected to embody a different set of innate constraints.

However, most, if not all, mathematics educators would agree that students' mathematical cognition constitutes a theory-like knowledge system, that is, an organized body of knowledge that concerns a specific set of objects or entities and that, like scientific theories, involves coherent explanations. The acquisition of a mathematical knowledge system will share, at least to some extent, features common to all other theory-like knowledge systems, such as naive physics, everyday biology, and a developing theory of mind. Thus, we can expect that characterizations of the acquisition of theory-like knowledge systems advanced by cognitive studies will provide mathematics educators with some clues for better understanding the development of mathematical cognition and trying to enhance mathematics education. Davis (chapter 16, this volume) argues forcefully that characterizations of the acquisition of knowledge advanced by cognitive studies *are* relevant to mathematics education; able mediators like him are needed urgently to facilitate communication between cognitive scientists, mathematicians, and teachers.

Even if the acquisition of the mathematical knowledge system is unique and the characterizations offered give few direct suggestions for mathematics education, examining that knowledge system in relation to general features of knowledge acquisition can illuminate its unique aspects, and can thereby provide a more solid basis for designing mathematics education.

KNOWLEDGE ACQUISITION AS CHARACTERIZED BY COGNITIVE STUDIES

Let me summarize in a short list of five interrelated characterizations what we cognitive researchers know about the long-term acquisition of knowledge by humans. As a whole, the list represents a coherent conception of knowledge acquisition, although it is decidedly short of being a "theory." (Any adequate theory would have to include a process model of knowledge acquisition, from which these characterizations can be generated, and also explanations for the model in terms of human information processing.) In deriving these five characterizations, I have relied primarily on studies in expertise, everyday cognition, and conceptual development, rather than on experimental studies in the laboratory, because the former types of study have usually been concerned with the acquisition of a body of knowledge prevalent in our society, the prototype of which is a theory-like knowledge system, whereas the latter type deals mostly with the learning of fragmentary pieces of knowledge of an artificial nature. I must admit that the selection of these characterizations reflects my personal biases. It is virtually impossible to construct a list of characterizations of knowledge acquisition that would fully satisfy most cognitive researchers. However, I believe a majority of them will agree that each of the characterizations selected is important as well as tenable, although they may want to add some others that they regard as equally or more important. In other words, although conceptions of knowledge acquisition vary considerably among cognitive theorists, many of them concur with at least most of the characterizations listed next.

The first characterization indicates that knowledge is acquired by construction; it is not acquired by transmission alone (e.g., Resnick, 1987, 1989b). Human acquire knowledge richer than the knowledge they are presented with, or even invent knowledge that has never been presented, often as a by-product of their problem solving and/or comprehension activity. This characterization is self-evident when there is no teacher or when the teacher cannot verbalize (or encode in another symbolic form) the target knowledge. However, knowledge must be constructed, at least partially, even when the teacher gives the learner the target knowledge in a verbalized form, or when she carefully monitors the learner so that his behavior can come to approximate the model behavior. Knowledge can be transmitted to some extent, but transmitted knowledge becomes usable in a variety of problem-solving situations only after it has been reconstructed—that is, interpreted, enriched, and connected to the prior knowledge of the learner. Needless to say, this process of reconstruction is not a purely individual enterprise, because, as will be seen, it is constrained socioculturally.

The second characterization states that knowledge acquisition involves restructuring; that is, not only does the amount of knowledge increase but also one's body of knowledge is reorganized as more and more pieces of knowledge are acquired (Rumelhart & Norman, 1978). Conceptual change in the history of science and in cognitive development (Carey, 1985b, 1988) is the best known example of the restructuring of knowledge. Knowledge systems before and after restructuring are different in organization; for example, one piece of knowledge may become differentiated, while other separate pieces of knowledge may become amalgamated. Historically, powerful ideas in mathematics, such as group theory, integrated many previously disparate pieces of knowledge. Relationships between pieces of knowledge may also change as restructuring takes place; for example, the same phenomenon may be explained differently, some instances may become prototypical whereas others may become marginal, and so forth.

The third characterization indicates that the process of knowledge acquisition is constrained (Gelman, 1990; Keil, 1981). The construction and successive revision of knowledge take place under a variety of constraints so that the acquired knowledge is often similar, if not identical, between different individuals. Because of those constraints, which eliminate in advance a large number of logically possible hypotheses and interpretations in human problem solving and knowledge acquisition, people can reach a reasonable choice readily and quickly in most cases. Needless to say, the same constraints may have negative effects, because they make it extremely hard for some correct hypotheses to even come to mind. The construction process is constrained both internally (by innate tendencies and by acquired prior knowledge, i.e., cognitive constraints) and externally (by culture as a set of artifacts including language and notation, and by other persons, i.e., sociocultural constraints).

The fourth indicates that knowledge is usually acquired domain by domain (Chi, Glaser, & Rees, 1982). The entire body of knowledge humans have is divided into a number of domains, that is, more or less self-contained knowledge systems within which problem solving or comprehension usually takes place. Knowledge acquired through problem solving and comprehension activity is, in turn, stored within the domain. To put it differently, the acquisition of knowledge is basically domain specific.

Domain specificity certainly serves for cognitive economy, because it allows one to examine only a portion of one's stored knowledge in problem solving and comprehension, and also in appending and ultimately integrating a new piece of knowledge. What is acquired in a domain may be transferred to another (e.g., through analogy) or generalized to a variety of domains (e.g., by abstracting structural commonalities), but this is rather exceptional. It is hypothesized that there are distinct "disciplines" or universal theory-like knowledge systems, a dozen or so in number (Carey, 1987), which constitute domains.

The fifth and final characterization specifies that knowledge acquisition is "situated" in contexts (Brown, Collins, & Duguid, 1989). Human activity, through which all knowledge is acquired, occurs in particular contexts, or is coconstituted between a person and contexts (Greeno, 1991), and thus is associated to (or situated in) them. Some contextual features—for example, what goal the activity is directed toward—are inseparable from the acquisition of the target knowledge. The growth of theory-like knowledge systems typically occurs in the context of argumentation (Kuhn, 1991) and in the course of using conceptual resources productively and enjoyably (Greeno, 1991).

Acquired knowledge is also situated; that is, it reflects how it was acquired and how it has been used. The knowledge humans "possess" in their heads includes not only public and abstract representations of "collective" experiences, such as laws, formulas, and rules described in textbooks, but also representations of experiences that are of a personal, concrete nature. Using the terminology adopted by Thompson (chapter 15, this volume), human knowledge involves "imagery" in the widest sense. Many contextual features are irrelevant to the target knowledge in its mature form. Accordingly, gaining expertise may be a process of decontextualizing or "desituating" knowledge (Hatano & Inagaki, 1992). This makes one's problem-solving competence less context bound, and weakens its associations with contextual features—for example, reducing a bias based on particular personal experience.

I next elaborate each of the characterizations in a little more detail. To support them, I refer to empirical findings from studies of expertise, everyday cognition, and conceptual development, as well as our informal daily observations. Although many of the best known findings in these areas are about mathematical cognition, I do not refer at this stage to mathematical examples, because they are discussed in the following section.

Knowledge Is Constructed

Here the constructivist view of the knowledge acquisition is contrasted only with the empiricist (transmissionist) view. The nativist view is not considered as an alternative to the constructivist view, because (a) they are not necessarily incompatible (Karmiloff-Smith, 1991), and (b) a radical nativist position does not seem tenable for (advanced) mathematics.

That knowledge is constructed is a corollary of the "zeitgeist" among contemporary cognitive theorists that human beings are active agents of information processing and action. Humans often explore tasks beyond the demands or requirements of problem solving, and environments that do not permit active exploration are experienced as unpleasant. Humans may create problems to solve rather than solve problems that are imposed. Thus, they often construct knowledge as a by-product of their spontaneous or required problem solving. More specifically, they acquire strategies for avoiding bad consequences and attaining good consequences (e.g., Scribner, 1984; Siegler & Jenkins, 1989; see Anzai, 1987 for fine-grained analyses of these processes). Humans also construct knowledge through comprehension activity (Hatano & Inagaki, 1986). They try to find the "meaning" or a plausible interpretation of their observations of facts and effective procedures, and this enterprise sometimes results in the construction of knowledge of a more conceptual nature (e.g., what the target object is like). Procedural bugs and misconceptions are taken as the strongest pieces of evidence for the constructive nature of knowledge acquisition, because it is highly unlikely that students have acquired them by being taught.

That knowledge is acquired by construction does not deny that it can be transmitted to some extent. Most knowledge we have, as D'Andrade (1981) put it, has been learned from other people. A recipe for cooking or a manual for assembling a kit is useful because the knowledge described there can be transmitted. When a piece of procedural knowledge is coded in the verbal form that refers to external objects and actions, it can be conveyed more or less "accurately." Even a piece of conceptual knowledge can be transmitted to the extent to which it is adequately coded and the code systems of the sender and receiver are alike. Experts in science, who share a large amount of knowledge and terminology, can exchange quite complicated conceptual knowledge through verbal or symbolic communication.

However, transmission cannot be perfect, because any language or other symbol system is able to describe only part of the target knowledge, involves some ambiguity, and allows somewhat different interpretations. Even in the case of procedural knowledge, a transmitted version may not be applied in the same way as the original. More importantly, active humans almost always try to interpret and enrich what is transmitted—in other words, to supplement it by construction. Even when the target knowledge is transmitted effectively, its acquisition is not a once-and-for-all process. It is gradually incorporated into the existing body of knowledge.

Knowledge Acquisition Involves Restructuring

As one gains expertise in a domain, one's knowledge becomes not only richer but also better organized. In other words, the process of knowledge acquisition involves restructuring as well as enrichment. Conceptual change can be regarded as a form of restructuring, probably the most radical one, in the sense that knowledge systems before and after the conceptual change are incommensurable; that is, some pieces of knowledge in one system cannot properly be translated into the other (Carey, 1988). However, "restructuring" includes milder and more subtle forms.

Reorganization of the knowledge system takes place at a number of different levels, from individual to societal, and also in various forms. Constituent pieces of knowledge, and/or concepts included, can change; for example, a few pieces of knowledge are amalgamated into a unitary piece. As children learn biology, they combine the data that animals have babies and that plants have seeds to produce the knowledge that living things reproduce. Relationships between pieces of knowledge and/or component concepts, such as which instances are prototypical, can also change. The perceived status of humans changes as students acquire more and more biological knowledge. Humans are regarded as a typical living thing by the less knowledgeable, but they are a very special species for the more knowledgeable. Finally, there can be general, metacognitive changes in the knowledge system, such as those of patterns of inference, modes of explanation, and so forth. For attributing unknown properties to an animate object, young children rely on similarity-based inference, whereas older children and adults use category-based inference (Inagaki & Sugiyama, 1988).

The Process of Knowledge Acquisition
Is Constrained

According to contemporary cognitive theorists, knowledge acquisition can be concisely described as the process of constructing and reorganizing knowledge under a variety of constraints. Here the term *constraints* refers to conditions or factors that facilitate the process of acquisition as well as restrict its possible range. Cognitive theorists differ widely in the importance they assign to each of the constraints. For example, whereas investigators of expertise emphasize prior knowledge in the target domain, those who focus on conceptual development take innate constraints to be more critical. Nevertheless, most of these theorists would agree that the construction process is constrained both internally (by cognitive constraints) and externally (by sociocultural constraints).

Innate or Early Cognitive Constraints.   Recent cognitive studies have shown that preschool children are more competent than used to be hypothesized (Gelman, 1979). In other words, preschool children, due to innate and early cognitive constraints, possess some knowledge and can learn quickly in several specific areas. The existence of innate or early cognitive constraints is best known in language acquisition, but we can see good examples of early acquisition due to such constraints in a few other areas as well, including the domains of physics

(e.g., Spelke, 1990), psychology (e.g., Wellman, 1990), and biology, partic
ularly that concerning the human body. In this last domain, young children
recognize the mind–body distinction at early ages and thus they do not rely on
intentional causality for biological phenomena inside the human body (Inagaki &
Hatano, 1993). For example, children of ages 4 and 5 years recognized that the
activities of their bodily organs are relatively independent of their intention. In
addition, a great majority of these children clearly understood that weight change
is caused by food intake rather than intention or desire. This early distinction of
mind and body may be facilitated by their innate tendency to establish certain
causal connections between external events and human physical reactions.

Prior Knowledge as Cognitive Constraints.   Recent cognitive studies have
reported that young children show more advanced modes of reasoning in any
domain where they have much experience, in other words, where they possess
substantial knowledge and can use it. Domain-specific knowledge can help problem solvers aptly represent a given problem so that they can readily handle it.
Domain-specific knowledge has also been shown to enhance the acquisition of
new pieces of knowledge within the domain (Glaser, 1984; Kuhara-Kojima &
Hatano, 1991).

Chi, Hutchinson, and Robin (1989) found that children of 4–7 years of age
who know a good deal about dinosaurs have hierarchically structured knowledge
about them, and, using that knowledge, they can make deductive inferences that
Piaget's theory assumed only older children would make. For example, "dino-
saur expert" children assigned unobservable attributes to novel dinosaurs, using
category-based inference (e.g., "He's prretty dangerous.. 'Cause he's a meat-
eater").

Shared Artifacts as Cultural Constraints.   By *cultural constraints* we mean
artifacts that are shared by a majority of people of the community or a subgroup,
including physical facilities and tools, social institutions and organizations, documented pieces of knowledge, common sense and beliefs, and more. Because
these constraints virtually eliminate a great number of possible hypotheses and
interpretations in advance, people can usually be expected to find what they
should do quite easily in everyday situations. Moreover, they can acquire needed
knowledge and skill rather quickly (Hatano & Miyake, 1991).

Cultural constraints are basically external to individuals. However, as they
engage in practice by relying on the constraints, people tend to internalize them
as knowledge in their mind. Much of our acquired knowledge is cultural in
origin, and as such involves the internalization of cultural constraints. As people
gain expertise in a given domain, they acquire not only knowledge and skill
needed for solving problems in the domain, but also metacognitive beliefs that
might be called values and evaluative criteria, which are shared by those regarded as experts in the domain.

Social Constraints: Interactions with Seniors and Peers.   The term *social constraints* includes behavior of other people, interactions with them, and social contexts created by them. Most of what we do and acquire in everyday situations is affected by other people. It may be an empiricist idea that we copy knowledge directly from others, but that our learning is constrained by other people is acceptable even for a constructivist.

As aptly pointed out by Vygotsky (1978), a child can do more under adult guidance or in collaboration with a more capable peer than he or she can do alone. Initially a child deals with a problem by taking partial charge of it under adult guidance, then gradually takes on responsibility for the whole, and finally becomes able to solve the problem by himself or herself (cf. Wertsch, 1979). In other words, adult guidance helps children reduce their possible alternatives of what to do next and, as a result, enables them to deal with problems with less uncertainty. Although this formulation can more readily be applied to the acquisition of knowledge through apprenticeship or parent–child interaction (Rogoff, 1990), classroom learning can also be conceptualized in this fashion. Children learn from their peers, who, though not necessarily more capable, may propose innovative ideas at the critical moment (Hatano & Inagaki, 1991).

Knowledge Acquisition Is Usually Domain Specific

Recent cognitive studies have demonstrated that individual competence varies considerably from domain to domain. In research on conceptual development, Piaget's stage theory, which posited that subjects' competence depended on their logicomathematical structures applicable across domains, has been challenged or even rejected by many current investigators (e.g., Siegler, 1978). Investigators in expertise (e.g., Chi et al., 1982) have asserted that the most critical determinant of problem-solving competence is not general intelligence but the relevant domain-specific knowledge and also that one gains expertise or accumulates knowledge only in a domain within which one solves problems repeatedly. Likewise, in research into everyday cognition, it is generally agreed that what is acquired is related directly to (and a function of) activity one engages in and that generalizations from such experience are highly limited (Rogoff & Lave, 1984). Although a scientific inquiry or an everyday attempt to understand the world may use information from all domains, as claimed by Fodor (1983), it usually takes place within a particular domain. Knowledge produced through such an activity is also incorporated in the relevant domain only. Thus, knowledge is usually acquired separately for each domain, although analogical transfer or generalization of knowledge based on the recognized isomorphism across domains may sometimes occur (Holyoak & Thagard, 1995).

In addition, many cognitive theorists believe that the course and process of development vary from domain to domain. This is because what one has to acquire to become an expert or master can be very different in different domains

(Ericsson & Smith, 1991), and each domain is expected to embody a different set of innate constraints (Carey & Gelman, 1991). In other words, knowledge is acquired, in part, in a unique fashion in each domain.

The term *domain* refers to a range of knowledge or behavior that can be explained by a more or less coherent theory. Thus, how domains are divided is in a sense a cultural product (Laboratory of Comparative Human Cognition, 1983). However, how knowledge is divided into domains is determined at least partially on innate bases, too.

Knowledge Acquisition Is Situated in Contexts

Human knowledge acquisition is conceptualized as a process of representing experience with an object, event, or conceptual entity, so that the resultant representation (i.e., knowledge) can readily be used in future problem solving and understanding. Thus, it is situated in contexts in which experience occurs and cannot but be influenced by various features of these contexts. Contextual features of acquisition are not limited to cognitive ones. Knowledge acquisition is more than "purely cognitive," in the sense that it takes place through interaction within social and cultural contexts that are embedded in the larger cultural-historical setting (Saljo, 1991). Knowledge acquisition goes hand in hand with participation in a community in which the target knowledge is shared (Lave & Wenger, 1991) and thus is based on social motivation to become a full member of the community as well as on motivation to understand and/or to be competent.

Acquired knowledge is also situated in the sense that it reflects the history of its acquisition and use, including associations with contexts. Although textbooks for a given domain summarize a body of knowledge as a set of propositions, the knowledge individuals "possess" in their head includes representations of a more personal, concrete nature. For example, knowledge in the form of a rule is often accompanied by some preferred examples, such as those that were used when the rule was first introduced and that the learner was able to solve for the fist time by applying the rule. It may also be flavored by the social context of its acquisition (e.g., how the teacher explained it and other students reacted). Experts' knowledge in a domain is often inseparably associated with beliefs and values that the members of the community of experts of the domain share.

These personal representations are not just useless adjuncts. They serve as clues for retrieving a rule when it is appropriate. Without them, it is almost impossible to retrieve relevant rules promptly. This explains in part why gaining expertise takes so much time.

As humans gain expertise, knowledge underlying their performance becomes decontextualized (or "desituated") in the sense that it is no longer tightly associated with the situation in which it was originally acquired. Qualitatively different progress is made, when people acquire mental models of major objects or entities of the domain, forms of conceptual knowledge that react or change in response to mentally exerted actions and that thus can be used to run mental simulations (Collins & Gentner, 1982). When they possess a mental model of the target object, they can understand the meaning of each step of a given procedure in terms of the change it produces in the object. By running the mental model, they can also predict what will occur in unprecedented situations. The problem-solving competence of experts is no longer context bound in the same sense as for novices. They are able to achieve goals across contexts, and to solve various novel problems in the domain. However, this does not mean that experts have and use public and abstract rules only. On the contrary, experts seem to rely heavily on their accumulated personal experiences (Dreyfus & Dreyfus, 1986). Experts do not solve the whole problem in their heads, either. Often they have acquired knowledge needed to use external constraints; for example, they are able to "offload" part of the computation involved.

ACQUISITION OF MATHEMATICAL KNOWLEDGE

The Dual Nature of Mathematical Cognition

Before trying to apply the preceding characterizations of knowledge acquisition to mathematical knowledge, let me point out its dual nature (de Corte, Verschaffel, & Greer, in press). Although mathematical knowledge is not about the material world as such, it is nevertheless very useful for solving real-world problems accurately and efficiently. This dual nature is reflected in the makeup of the mathematical community. Mathematics is used daily by many people, whereas it is studied professionally by a small number of scholars called mathematicians. However, these two groups constitute a community, because they share, at least to some extent, what is called mathematical knowledge.

For almost all users of mathematical knowledge, it is primarily a set of tools, by which they can solve real-world problems. According to Davis (chapter 16, this volume), most people view mathematics as consisting of "employing a few rote procedures"; I would insert "but magically effective" after "rote." More precisely, it consists of procedures for converting real-world problems into mathematical representations and vice versa, and procedures for manipulating these representations to find mathematical solutions. "Just plain folks," including the weight watcher described in Lave (1988), though often not aware that they are doing so, perform mathematical operations to find solutions for their everyday problems (e.g., divide a "pie" into quarters and take three to change the original recipe for four into that for three). Most scientists also use various forms of mathematics in order to describe, predict or even create phenomena.

For most users, either laymen or scientists, acquiring mathematical knowledge is subjectively not different from acquiring other procedures for problem solving. They want to learn, primarily, how to use, and when to use, ready-made procedures. The acquisition of a procedure depends on its usefulness as a tool, in other words, how promptly and accurately it leads to a solution. However, as they use the procedures, they may try to understand, adjust, or elaborate the procedures, that is, they may try, like mathematicians, to *do,* and not merely use, mathematics.

Mathematicians deal with patterns or structures and their relationships. They may invent new pieces of mathematical knowledge by endlessly applying operations on operations (Piaget, 1970). What mathematicians do with abstract entities is analogous to, and is in fact derived from, human actions on physical objects (Piaget, 1970), but is often driven by the pure pleasure of intellectual exploration. The truth of mathematical knowledge is based not on its empirical confirmation or practical utility, but on its rigorous derivational or proving steps. Its significance is dependent on what kind of a new structure is introduced, how much the nature of the structure is specified, and so on. However, mathematicians may want to apply mathematical knowledge to real-world problems, or to help others who are trying to apply it. Even when they remain "pure mathematicians," they usually will be willing to admit that the mathematics they do is potentially relevant to real-world problems.

Mathematics education programs take into serious consideration this duality. Good programs try to enhance the acquisition of mathematical knowledge through solving practically significant and/or intellectually challenging problems. For example, Gimbayashi (1982), a current distinguished leader of the Association of Mathematics Instruction in Japan, emphasizes both the practical utility of mathematics and understanding of the meaning of mathematical procedures.

Applying the Characterizations
to Mathematical Knowledge

How well do the five characterizations described in the first section fit the acquisition of mathematical knowledge? Are any modifications, qualifications, or reservations of the characterizations necessary?

First, can we be sure that mathematical knowledge is acquired by construction, not by transmission alone? Some may wonder if, although mathematical knowledge is a human construction, it can be transmitted once it is constructed (by mathematicians), because of its rigorous, formal nature. Others may wonder if mathematical knowledge as a set of tools can be transmitted, like other kinds of procedural knowledge. I admit that mathematical knowledge expressed in terms of laws or formulas can apparently be transmitted. However, before learners become able to use a given law, they have to understand it, that is, interpret it in relation to their prior knowledge—in other words, reconstruct it in their mind. For example, they have to judge which terms are constants, and which are variables.

That students construct mathematical knowledge by themselves can clearly be seen in procedural bugs and misconceptions they reveal. In other words, procedural bugs and misconceptions are produced because students do not swallow a given rule or algorithm but try to construct something subjectively tenable by induction. It is well known that lower grade children show a variety of buggy algorithms for multidigit subtraction (Brown & Burton, 1978). Whether necessitated by the impasse caused by a missing or erroneous production or more spontaneously induced to reduce mental effort, these procedural bugs are certainly students' inventions. Similarly, misconceptions are invented by learners themselves, through their attempts to make sense of their limited experiences. For example, the often observed misconception that division makes the dividend smaller (Greer, 1988) seems to be a result of repeated experiences of division with a divisor larger than 1, but never (before fractions are introduced) with one smaller than 1.

Thus, the first characterization of knowledge acquisition holds with mathematical knowledge. Mathematical knowledge that can be used in a variety of situations as an intellectual tool is acquired by construction, not by transmission alone. This implies that we might adopt a version of the constructivist position for mathematics instruction, either a radical one or a more realistic one.

Second, does mathematical knowledge acquisition involve restructuring? The history of mathematics as an academic discipline reveals something more than mere incremental processes. When revolutionary ideas were presented, reorganizations of the entire discipline have occurred. Old and new versions of mathematics would not be incommensurable, but more often than not, the new included the old as its part. Likewise, when students learn mathematics, their progress is often discontinuous. When they achieve some key insight, their ways of solving a variety of problems may change, which suggests at least local restructuring.

It is an interesting conjecture that some restructuring is needed in order to proceed to a more advanced version of mathematics, and that many dropouts in mathematics are due to failure to restructure. For example, some students have great difficulty in understanding multiplicative structures including fractions, ratio, proportion, and so forth, probably because they stick to mathematics based on additive composition. Another impressive shift in the development of mathematics is that from empirical to logical orientation. Although younger students judge a mathematical procedure to be invalid solely based on the fact that it does not predict the reality, older ones may refer to inconsistency or contradiction with known mathematical facts as the basis for its rejection. The former orientation is similar to the "empiric" orientation found among the Kpelle in Liberia by Scribner (1979).

Thus, although we may not observe conceptual changes therein, it is obvious that the development of mathematical cognition involves restructuring. Mathematics educators should not expect students to show a monotonic increment of mathematical knowledge. Moreover, students' initial understanding of a mathematical concept could be considerably different from its mature, if not final, form.

Third, that the process of mathematical knowledge acquisition is constrained is evident. However, the constraints that play a more critical role in the acquisition of mathematics may be different from those for other domains. For early and universal competence in mathematics, such as counting (Gelman & Gallistel, 1978) and protoquantitative reasoning schema (Resnick, 1989a), innate or early cognitive constraints seem to be critical. For example, as suggested by Gelman and Gallistel (1978), five principles underlying counting, which even children 3 and 4 years of age understand, help them acquire a general procedure of counting from a small number of observations, by restricting the range of possible interpretations. More advanced mathematical knowledge can easily be acquired only when students are helped by prior knowledge in mathematics (Mack, 1990). This implies that a teacher should pay close attention to what students know before formal instruction. Here students' prior world knowledge that can constrain the range of possible operations and answers, as well as their understanding of mathematical entities, such as how to formulate a given problem mathematically, is important for mathematical knowledge acquisition.

The acquisition of mathematical knowledge is also constrained by sociocultural contexts. The most salient example here is information provided by teachers and textbooks, including terminology, notation, and graphical resources in mathematics. Thanks to those constraints that work in human mathematical problem solving and knowledge acquisition, both in external and internalized forms, a large number of possible hypotheses and interpretations are excluded in advance, so that people can reach a reasonable choice readily and quickly in most cases.

It should be noted that by emphasizing cultural constraints in the acquisition of knowledge, current cognitive theorists are at a distance from the radical or "romantic" constructivist position, although they do not favor didactic teaching, either. These theorists claim that human capabilities are inherited not only in the form of innate constraints (or in a genetic form) but also as artifacts. The competence of learners in any domain varies with how well they incorporate or appropriate the artifacts. For example, even a talented student cannot solve problems without mastering the mathematical notation and graphical representation as well as acquiring basic mathematical knowledge like axioms in advance.

Fourth, it should be emphasized that mathematical knowledge is unique because of its domain-general character. It is true that mathematics as a discipline constitutes a separate domain. A talented mathematician may be very poor at other domains of knowledge, such as the interpersonal. Expertise in mathematics not only is relatively independent from that in other domains, but also may have distinctively different features. However, mathematics as an intellectual tool can be applied to a large number of domains, though when thus applied it is not content-free.

Carey (1985a) has already suggested that knowledge about measurement (or quantification in general) may produce a somewhat domain-general difference between young children and adults. Piaget (1950) repeatedly claimed that log-icomathematical knowledge could be applied across domains, creating a uniform stage in problem solving within individuals. Although post-Piagetians tend to doubt this claim, they too will admit that logicomathematical knowledge can form "a domain across domains." Mathematics is powerful as an intellectual tool mainly because it enables us, through formalization, to detect structural com-monalities in apparently very different domains, and thus to apply general prob-lem-solving algorithms to them more or less consciously (Greer, 1984).

Finally, that mathematical knowledge acquisition is situated in contexts seems tenable. As described earlier, it is obvious that the mathematical knowledge novices have is closely tied to the context of its acquisition, such as how a new mathematical concept is introduced. Even when two or more students know a mathematical formula in common, how it is represented may vary among them. Rumelhart (1979) proposed that how fractions are taught influences students' understanding of fractions, as reflected in differential patterns of performance. More specifically, when fractions are introduced by using the pie analogy, stu-dents can learn pretty easily how to add and subtract them, but multiplication or division involving fractions is much harder (see Carraher, chapter 14, this vol-ume). In contrast, when fractions are introduced as a form of division, learning to multiply or divide them is easier than addition or subtraction.

How fractions are introduced is critical, as claimed by Rumelhart, for fifth and sixth graders, but its effect will be much attenuated for high schoolers. Speaking generally, mathematical knowledge that experts (experienced users with mathematical understanding as well as mathematicians) possess is no longer associated tightly with the situation in which it was originally acquired. This is partly because experts' knowledge reflects the long history of its use as well as its original acquisition—that is, it has been used in varied situations. Their knowl-edge may be "desituated" in the sense of being useful even outside of the situations experienced, because experts can adapt known procedures or even invent new ones based on their understanding of a set of conceptual entities. Thus, how a new mathematical concept is introduced in instruction is critical, but even more important is to try to develop students' conceptual understanding, unless the goal of instruction is to teach routine procedures that are useful only for limited problems.

IMPLICATIONS OF THE COGNITIVE CONCEPTION OF KNOWLEDGE ACQUISITION FOR MATHEMATICS EDUCATION

What practical implications for mathematics education can be derived from the characterizations of knowledge acquisition applied to mathematical knowledge? I briefly discuss this question in this final section.

Students' Active Participation.   This stems directly from the first item on the list, that mathematical knowledge is acquired by construction. It is important, but is not very distinctive; Educational methods recommended by the current cognitive conception may vary, from those that have many features in common with previous constructivists' (e.g., Piaget's) to those emphasizing students' meaningfully incorporating mathematical ideas as given by a teacher. Constructivism generally emphasizes that students construct knowledge by themselves, not by swallowing ready-made knowledge from the outside. Thus, those methods that merely require students to practice given algorithms or those that do not allow students to explore various possible ideas are considered to be less effective.

However, what is taken as critical in this characterization is students' understanding, that is, how they interpret a given mathematical idea in relation to their prior knowledge. Therefore, current cognitive theorists, like Piagetians, encourage students' active participation, but unlike Piagetians, do not necessarily expect students to invent mathematical knowledge by themselves. Instead, they expect students to examine a given process or product of mathematical inference against that of another inference as well as with reality, and to use their prior knowledge as much as possible for making sense of their "observations." Needless to say, the contemporary conception of knowledge acquisition recommends teachers not to impose their ideas nor to present an overwhelmingly large amount of information.

Inducing Successive Reorganizations of Mathematical Knowledge.   Because restructuring seems necessary for mathematical cognition to advance, mathematics educators should try to facilitate its occurrence. They should allow students to take time to reflect and reorganize, neither expecting nor desiring them to show a monotonic mathematical development.

As our knowledge about specific features of restructuring in the development of mathematical cognition increases, such as from what knowledge state to what state students tend to shift, we can better design mathematics education programs as well as better predict their progress. This will allow us to make more sensible decisions about teaching, for example, where teachers might slow down and spend much time, and conversely, where they might speed up to save time. Students may need a large amount of time for initial understanding when new entities, like "variables," are presented, and for reorganization when new mathematical structures, such as multiplicative ones, are introduced.

Use of Students' Prior Knowledge as a Constraint.   The cognitive conception of knowledge acquisition, especially the idea of constraints, suggests a number of instructional strategies to facilitate the process of students' mathematical knowledge construction, although it does not assume that students' progress in the domain can be totally under the control of educators. It is recommendable for educators to focus upon constraints over which they have control. They can intervene through social constraints, and they can manipulate a variety of cultural constraints as well. Moreover, although the body of acquired domain-specific knowledge in mathematics is internal and not directly subject to educators' control, modifying it prior to the target lessons is often not too hard. As mentioned earlier, cognitive studies have indicated that acquired rich and well-organized knowledge in a specific domain enables students to process information effectively (acquire new pieces of knowledge as well as reason in advanced modes).

Using Sociocultural Constraints to Facilitate Students' Learning.   Mathematics educators should consider how to make maximal use of sociocultural constraints. Unlike Piagetian educators, who at most try to set up a generally stimulating environment, educators inspired by the cognitive conception might involve themselves more actively, by organizing and directing the process of students' construction of mathematical knowledge. For example, they can (a) present various models to enhance students' understanding, (b) use tools for inducing initial success, (c) amplify conceptions generated by students, and (d) ask students to reflect on what they actually do.

Encouraging students to share ideas is also recommended. Even elementary school children can judge the plausibility of ideas proposed by their peers, and learn a lot by discriminatingly incorporating them (Morita, Inagaki, & Hatano, 1992; see the impressive case described by Davis, chapter 16, this volume). Here too an educator plays a critical role, first by setting up situations where a group of students are able to engage in their collective inquiry, and second by taking the role of a "more capable peer" in their attempts at knowledge acquisition. For instance, she can give an example that will stimulate the students' thinking or help them clarify ideas they have put forward.

Teaching Mathematics in Relation to a Domain of Students' Interest.   That the acquisition of mathematical knowledge may not be domain specific has an important implication for mathematics instruction. It does not exclude the possibility of teaching pure mathematics within its domain or teaching mathematical procedures to solve problems only in a specific content domain, but a wiser alternative seems to teach how to solve problems in relation to a variety of real-world problems in domains other than mathematics, by mathematically representing and transforming them, and then to develop mathematical knowledge itself, through reflection and abstraction, so that it can readily be generalized to other domains as a set of tools for problem solving (Greer, 1984). Placing mathematical solution in the context of the real-world problems that interest students highlights its significance. Moreover, looking afresh at the real-world problems through "mathematical eyes" will enhance their understanding of the problems. What Gimbayashi and his associates have attempted is exactly in this direction.

Choosing Proper Contexts for the Acquiring and Desituating of Knowledge. Three implications emerge from the situated nature of the acquisition of mathematical knowledge. First, a teacher should arrange proper contexts for the activity that will lead to the acquisition of the target mathematical knowledge. The activity should not just be preparation for tests, because students tend to acquire knowledge readily applicable only to a limited range of problems, not usable productively and enjoyably, through such an activity. Second, because mathematical knowledge that novices have is closely tied to the context of its acquisition, a teacher must be very careful in organizing instruction, especially how a new mathematical concept or skill is introduced. Third, he or she must organize a sequence of instruction so that students can experience varied contexts for using the concept or skill, and come to acquire mathematical knowledge that is useful even outside of the experienced situations. In other words, mathematics education should aim at helping students become adaptive experts (Hatano & Inagaki, 1986), that is, experts who can adapt known procedures or even invent new ones based on their understanding of a set of conceptual entities.

Some Suggested Principles for Mathematics Education

Let me propose several guidelines for designing lessons in mathematics by summarizing the preceding discussions. They can be taken as embodying the cognitive conception of the mathematical knowledge acquisition mentioned above. They are admittedly very tentative, and also must be enriched by mathematics educators' intuition. However, I hope they are stimulating and suggestive, if not of immediate practical use.

1. Pose interesting problems. If possible, encourage students to pose problems of their own. The problem should induce a variety of ideas from students, and also motivate them to understand presented relevant ideas, especially those about mathematical representations and their manipulations. Davis (chapter 16, this volume) argues that students should tackle novel problems that no one has told them how to solve, leading to the invention of mathematics. In other words, the problem should arouse epistemic curiosity or motivation for understanding, and lead to the construction of significant mathematical ideas.

2. Place a problem in pragmatic or familiar contexts, unless students are mature enough for pursuing a purely mathematical problem. This strategy, by situating the problem within students' domain of interest, motivates them to explore various ideas intensively. It also makes them recognize the power of mathematics in solving practical problems.

3. Encourage students to bring in their prior skills and ideas. Students are more competent than one might realize and may well know quite a lot even before any systematic instruction is given. Try to develop students' confidence in

their competence by respecting their ideas. They will try hard to construct knowledge themselves only when they have confidence.

4. Suggest that students use tools that enable them to do easily what they want to. Tools here include such things as a calculator and also mathematical symbols and graphics.

5. Use peer interactions for motivating students as well as for constraining the process of their knowledge construction. Students may solve collectively a problem that individually they are unable to solve.

6. Intervene in peer interaction whenever appropriate, as long as it does not endanger students' spontaneous construction of knowledge.

7. Give ample opportunities to reflect after successful performance so that students can acquire mathematics in more or less disembodied forms. I fully concur with the proposal made by Davis (chapter 16, this volume) that students should reflect at length on what they did *after* they have invented solutions. Time pressure often makes it impossible for students to pursue the meaning of mathematical formulations and transformations involved in problem solving.

8. Metacognitive beliefs enhancing mathematical cognition should be established through solving and reflecting on the series of interesting mathematical problems. Although it is very important for students to develop good taste and evaluative criteria of their own for judging whether it is an interesting problem, whether it is an acceptable solution, what kinds of problems might be handled mathematically, and so on, these should not be imposed on students through the teacher's authority.

9. Put problems in order so that students' solutions and justifications can gradually be refined into formal, mathematical ones, and so that they can fully participate in the culture of experts in the domain of mathematics.

10. It may be necessary to require students to do some exercise that will enhance the consolidation of important component skills of mathematical problem solving. The exercise should be engaging to students. Avoid as much as possible relying on mechanical drills, which may weaken students' search for sense making.

ACKNOWLEDGMENTS

I am grateful to Brian Greer for his invaluable comments on earlier versions of the chapter, and to Kayoko Inagaki for her constructive criticisms.

REFERENCES

Anzai, Y. (1987). Doing, understanding, and learning in problem solving. In D. Klahr, P. Langley, & R. Neches (Eds.), *Production system models of learning and development* (pp. 55–97). Cambridge, MA: MIT Press.

Brown, J. S., & Burton, R. R. (1978). Diagnostic models for procedural bugs in basic mathematical skills. *Cognitive Science, 2,* 155–192.

Brown, J. S., Collins, A., & Duguid, P. (1989). Situated cognition and the culture of learning. *Educational Researcher, 18,* 32–42.

Carey, S. (1985a). Are children fundamentally different thinkers and learners from adults? In S. F. Chipman, J. W. Segal, & R. Glaser (Eds.), *Thinking and learning skills* (Vol. 2, pp. 486–517). Hillsdale, NJ: Lawrence Erlbaum Associates.

Carey, S. (1985b). *Conceptual change in childhood.* Cambridge, MA: MIT Press.

Carey, S. (1987). Theory change in childhood. In B. Inhelder, D. de Caprona, & A. Cornu-Wells (Eds.), *Piaget today* (pp. 141–163). Hillsdale, NJ: Lawrence Erlbaum Associates.

Carey, S. (1988). Conceptual differences between children and adults. *Mind and Language, 3,* 167–181.

Carey, S., & Gelman, R. (Eds.). (1991). *The epigenesis of mind: Essays on biology and cognition.* Hillsdale, NJ: Lawrence Erlbaum Associates.

Chi, M. T. H., Glaser, R., & Rees, E. (1982). Expertise in problem solving. In R. Sternberg (Ed.), *Advances in the psychology of human intelligence* (Vol. 1, pp. 7–75). Hillsdale, NJ: Lawrence Erlbaum Associates.

Chi, M. T. H., Hutchinson, J. E., & Robin, A. F. (1989). How inferences about novel domain-related concepts can be constrained by structured knowledge. *Merrill-Palmer Quarterly, 35,* 27–62.

Collins, A., & Gentner, D. (1982, August). Constructing runnable models. *Proceedings of the Fourth Annual Conference of the Cognitive Science Society* (pp. 86–89). Ann Arbor, MI.

D'Andrade, R. (1981). The cultural part of cognition. *Cognitive Science, 5,* 179–195.

de Corte, E., Verschaffel, L., & Greer, B. (in press). Mathematics. In D. Berliner & R. Calfee (Eds.), *Handbook of educational psychology.* New York: Macmillan.

Dreyfus, H. L., & Dreyfus, S. E. (1986). *Mind over machine.* New York: Free Press.

Ericsson, K. A., & Smith, J. (Eds.). (1991). *Toward a general theory of expertise.* Cambridge: Cambridge University Press.

Fodor, J. (1983). *The modularity of mind: An essay on faculty psychology.* Cambridge, MA: MIT Press.

Gelman, R. (1979). Preschool thought. *American Psychologist, 34,* 900–905.

Gelman, R. (1990). Structural constraints on cognitive development: Introduction to a special issue of cognitive science. *Cognitive Science, 14,* 3–9.

Gelman, R., & Gallistel, C. R. (1978). *The child's understanding of number.* Cambridge, MA: Harvard University Press.

Gimbayashi, H. (1982). *Mathematics as human behavior.* Tokyo: Meiji-Tosho. [In Japanese].

Glaser, R. (1984). Education and thinking: The role of knowledge. *American Psychologist, 39,* 93–104.

Greeno, J. G. (1991). Number sense as situated knowing in a conceptual domain. *Journal for Research in Mathematics Education, 22,* 170–218.

Greer, B. (1984). Cognitive psychology and mathematics education. *Journal of Structural Learning, 8,* 291–300.

Greer, B. (1988). Nonconservation of multiplication and division: Analysis of a symptom. *Journal of Mathematical Behavior, 7,* 281–298.

Hatano, G., & Inagaki, K. (1986). Two courses of expertise. In H. Stevenson, H. Azuma, & K. Hakuta (Eds.), *Child development and education in Japan* (pp. 262–272). New York: Freeman.

Hatano, G., & Inagaki, K. (1991). Sharing cognition through collective comprehension activity. In L. B. Resnick, J. M. Levine, & S. D. Teasley (Eds.), *Perspectives on socially shared cognition* (pp. 331–348). Washington, DC: American Psychological Association.

Hatano, G., & Inagaki, K. (1992). Desituating cognition through the construction of conceptual knowledge. In P. Light & G. Butterworth (Eds.), *Context and cognition: Ways of learning and knowing* (pp. 115–133). Hemel Hempstead, UK: Harvester.

Hatano, G., & Miyake, N. (1991). Commentary: What does a cultural approach offer to research on learning? *Learning and Instruction, 1,* 273–281.

Holyoak, K. J., & Thagard, P. (1995). *Mental leaps.* Cambridge, MA: MIT Press.

Inagaki, K., & Hatano, G. (1993). Young children's understanding of the mind-body distinction. *Child Development, 64,* 1534–1549.

Inagaki, K., & Sugiyama, K. (1988). Attributing human characteristics: Developmental changes in over- and underattribution. *Cognitive Development, 3,* 55–70.

Karmiloff-Smith, A. (1991). Beyond modularity: Innate constraints and developmental change. In S. Carey & R. Gelman (Eds.), *The epigenesis of mind: Essays on biology and cognition* (pp. 171–197). Hillsdale, NJ: Lawrence Erlbaum Associates.

Keil, F. (1981). Constraints on knowledge and cognitive development. *Psychological Review, 88,* 197–227.

Kuhara-Kojima, K., & Hatano, G. (1991). Contribution of content knowledge and learning ability to the learning of facts. *Journal of Educational Psychology, 83,* 253–263.

Kuhn, D. (1993). Science as argument. *Science Education, 77,* 319–337.

Laboratory of Comparative Human Cognition. (1983). Culture and cognitive development. In W. Kessen (Ed.), *Mussen's handbook of child psychology: Vol. 1. History, theory, and method* (4th ed., pp. 295–356). New York: Wiley.

Lave, J. (1988). *Cognition in practice.* Cambridge: Cambridge University Press.

Lave, J., & Wenger, E. (1991). *Situated learning: Legitimate peripheral participation.* Cambridge: Cambridge University Press.

Mack, N. K. (1990). Learning fractions with understanding: Building on informal knowledge. *Journal for Research in Mathematics Education, 21,* 16–32.

Morita, E., Inagaki, K., & Hatano, G. (1992, October). *Effects of organized whole class discussion on learning mathematics: A case of addition of fractions with different denominators.* Paper presented at the 34th Annual Convention of the Japanese Association of Educational Psychology, Nagano. [in Japanese]

Piaget, J. (1950). *The psychology of intelligence.* New York: Harcourt Brace.

Piaget, J. (1970). *Genetic epistemology.* New York: Columbia University Press.

Resnick, L. B. (1987). Constructing knowledge in school. In L. S. Liben (Ed.), *Development and learning: Conflict or congruence?* (pp. 19–50). Hillsdale, NJ: Lawrence Erlbaum Associates.

Resnick, L. B. (1989a). Developing mathematical knowledge. *American Psychologist, 44,* 162–169.

Resnick, L. B. (1989b). Introduction. In L. B. Resnick (Ed.), *Knowing, learning, and instruction: Essays in honor of Robert Glaser* (pp. 1–24). Hillsdale, NJ: Lawrence Erlbaum Associates.

Rogoff, B. (1990). *Apprenticeship in thinking: Cognitive development in social context.* New York: Oxford University Press.

Rogoff, B., & Lave, J. (Eds.). (1984). *Everyday cognition: Its development in social context.* Cambridge, MA: Harvard University Press.

Rumelhart, D. E. (1979). *Analogical processes and procedural representations* (CHIP Tech. Rep. No. 81). La Jolla, University of California, San Diego.

Rumelhart, D. E., & Norman, D. A. (1978). Accretion, tuning and restructuring: Three modes of learning. In J. W. Cotton & R. Klatzky (Eds.), *Semantic factors in cognition* (pp. 37–54). Hillsdale, NJ: Lawrence Erlbaum Associates.

Saljo, R. (1991). Culture and learning: Introduction. *Learning and Instruction, 1,* 179–185.

Scribner, S. (1979). Modes of thinking and ways of speaking: Culture and logic reconsidered. In R. O. Freedle (Ed.), *New directions in discourse processing* (pp. 223–243). Norwood, NJ: Ablex.

Scribner, S. (1984). Studying working intelligence. In B. Rogoff & J. Lave (Eds.), *Everyday cognition: Its development in social context* (pp. 9–40). Cambridge, MA: Harvard University Press.

Siegler, R. S. (Ed.). (1978). *Children's thinking: What develops?* Hillsdale, NJ: Lawrence Erlbaum Associates.

Siegler, R. S., & Jenkins, E. (1989). *How children discover strategies.* Hillsdale, NJ: Lawrence Erlbaum Associates.

Spelke, E. S. (1990). Principles of object perception. *Cognitive Science, 14,* 29–56.

Vygotsky, L. S. (1978). *Mind in society.* Cambridge, MA: Harvard University Press.

Wellman, H. M. (1990). *Children's theories of mind.* Cambridge, MA: MIT Press.

Wertsch, J. V. (1979). From social interaction to higher psychological processes: A clarification and application of Vygotsky's theory. *Human Development, 22,* 1–22.

13 The Theory of Conceptual Fields

Gérard Vergnaud
CNRS, France

INTRODUCTION AND DEFINITIONS

The theory of conceptual fields aims to provide, with a few concepts and a few principles, a fruitful and comprehensive framework for studying complex cognitive competences and activities, and their development through experience and learning. By complex cognitive competences and activities, I understand those that are developed in education, at work, and in ordinary experience, and that are required to face both routine situations that do not demand great adaptation of former knowledge, and nonroutine situations (or problems) that do demand some new combination of former knowledge and ultimately some construction or discovery of new knowledge.

This theory is exemplified here by various examples drawn from the psychology of mathematics education, but it is also fruitful for other domains, including social knowledge and physical education. Several of its ideas have been proposed by other scientists before—notably Piaget (1950, 1971, 1980) and Vygotsky (1962, 1978), and other authors like Russell (1910, 1940), Tarski (1971), de Saussure (1972), Newell and Simon (1972), and Bruner (1966). But this theory puts these ideas together in an original fashion with new definitions for such essential points as:

- What is a concept?
- What is a scheme?
- What is conveyed by the distinction signifier/signified?

One reason for referring to such authors as those just mentioned is that a science that is not cumulative is not a science. According to this criterion, one

219

may wonder whether psychology is a science or not, as psychologists tend to ignore or forget former advances of psychology. For instance, information-processing theories do not offer any theoretical perspective for the distinction between signifier and signified, nor do they propose any view concerning the long-term development of representation and competences. Finally, they do not offer any definition of concepts—in particular scientific concepts, which are most often relational constructs and not simple observable properties and regularities.

An important challenge for a theory is that it should be integrative and make it possible to study phenomena at different levels: long-term development as well as short-term construction and learning, implicit knowledge contained in action as well as explicit and articulated principles, widely automatized competences as well as problem-solving behavior, percepto-gestural activity as well as intellectual operations, perception of ordinary objects as well as understanding of sophisticated theories.

This may appear overambitious, but all these phenomena have to be dealt with in mathematics education. Therefore weak theories of cognition, like behaviorism, can only die if they do not provide us with a rich understanding of what a concept is, of what constitutes long-term development and experience, and of the part played by language and symbolic activities in the formation of scientific competences and conceptions.

Representation, as a psychological function, is aimed at providing humans and animals with better and better adapted behaviors. The link between action and representation is essential. It is therefore in the behaviors progressively developed by students that researchers must look for mathematical concepts and theorems, and they must try to identify different behaviors in terms that make the connection with mathematics, that is, with mathematical concepts and theorems. There is no room in the theory of conceptual fields for procedural knowledge as opposed to declarative knowledge, because the concept of purely procedural knowledge is behavioristic, nonrepresentational, and therefore meaningless for a theory of representation. Nor is there room for a description of mathematical knowledge in nonmathematical terms such as semantic networks, because they are associationistic in nature and do not characterize the specific knowledge involved in specific competences. Knowledge is knowledge, even if it is implicit. And mathematics is mathematics. Therefore the concepts of scheme, theorem-in-action, and concept-in-action are essential to the theory of conceptual fields, which is a theory of representation and cognitive development. This explains why I propose hereafter rather strict definitions. But I start with examples.

Example 1.   Counting a set of objects is a basic competence that is originally shaped by the counting of small collections such as candies, marbles, toy cars, persons, or animals. But it is not fully developed until children can count large quantities, and organize their numbering behavior in a sequence of phases, by subdividing collections into smaller ones (of the same size eventually) and adding the cardinals; also they identify some multiplicative groupings, as is the case when one has to count the number of windows on the facade of a building, or the number of seats in a theater.

For 3- to 6-year-olds, numbering a small collection requires two important mathematical concepts—the concept of one-to-one correspondence and the concept of cardinal. It also requires a sophisticated sequence of gestures to control the one-to-one correspondence between the objects, the hand-and-finger gestures, the eye gestures, the number-words pronounced. It also requires some principles such as those identified by Gelman and Gallistel (1978), the most essential of which is the invariance of the cardinal over the order of counting. Neither the concepts of cardinal and one-to-one correspondence nor the principles are usually made explicit by children. They are concepts-in-action and theorems-in-action. Their existence is proved by the observed differences among children's behaviors, especially by the failure of some children to control the one-to-one correspondence or the failure to cardinalize.

But when they have to count a large quantity of marbles, of stamps, of dots on a sheet of paper, older children learn how to separate smaller collections, count them, and add the cardinals. If one calls card(X) the function that maps collections into whole numbers, and repres(x) the function that maps whole numbers into their decimal representation, then children apply three different theorems:

- Card($X \cup Y$) = card(X) + card(Y), provided X and Y have no common part.
- Repres($x + y$) = repres(x) **+** repres(y)
- The combination of both, repres(card$X \cup Y$)) = repres(card(X)) **+** repres(card (Y)), provided X and Y have no common part.

($\cup$ union   + sum   **+** addition algorithm)

A sound psychological analysis demands a clear distinction between different kinds of elements: objects, collections, numbers, symbols. One can use words and sentences to talk about the objects, about the collections, about the numbers, but the place-value notation represents only numbers. It relies on the base-10 polynomial decombination of numbers, and it demands a clear distinction between the signifier and the signified. Symbols are not numbers—the addition algorithm **+** and the sum + are different operations.

The sequence of actions required to count a large collection of marbles requires operations on the marbles, on the collections, on the numbers as cardinals, and on the decimal representations of these numbers. Conceptual difficulties, misunderstandings, and errors may lie at one or several corners of this complex scheme. For instance, students may have difficulties with the addition theorem, or with the place-value notation, quite independently.

Definition: A *scheme* is the invariant organization of behavior (action) for a certain class of situations.

A scheme is a functional and dynamic totality that enables the individual to deal with some class of situations. A scheme usually emerges to deal with a restricted class of situations (small collections of small objects for the numbering scheme in young children). In the beginning, it is made up of just a few concepts-in-action, theorems-in-action, and rules. From this initial structure, a scheme develops by extending its scope of relevance to larger and larger sets of situations and by enriching its contents. Schemes are complex organizations of sub-schemes.

A scheme contains rules of action, but it would be wrong to characterize it as purely procedural. There are also strong representational ingredients in it, which I call "operational invariants," mainly concepts-in-action and theorems-in-action. There are also inference possibilities, which make it possible for the subject to infer what to do and what to control as action and time go on. Last, but not least, there are goals and subgoals to be reached and subresults and phases to be expected. In summary, a scheme is composed of four different kinds of ingredients: operational invariants, inference possibilities, rules of action, and goals. The representational part is essential.

Algorithms are schemes, but not all schemes are algorithms—far from it. The effectiveness property of algorithms (the guarantee of reaching a solution, if there is one, in a finite number of steps) is due to the character of necessity that affects the relationships between the conditions and the actions. Schemes are only efficient, not effective. For instance, most of our gestures are not algorithmic, nor are most of our reasonings.

Example 2. Solving a system of two equations graphically is not a basic competence like counting, but it is an essential competence in the learning of mathematics, and students need to master it even outside mathematics. They have to follow a sequence of phases: Draw a system of graduated axes, draw the graph corresponding to the first equation (linear or not), draw the graph corresponding to the second equation, and interpret the point(s) of intersection as solution(s) of the system, when there is one (or several). If there are no points of intersection they need to be able to think of something intelligent, such as to change the scale, or try to explain the reason for the lack of intersection.

This scheme is obviously composed of several different schemes, which I do not analyze in detail here. I only stress a few conceptual problems underlying these schemes.

What is an axis? What is a graph? A graduated axis is a straight line on which numbers are represented by dots, according to their distance to some arbitrary point taken as origin. Several pieces of research show that many students have difficulties in understanding numbers as represented by dots, and in understanding intervals.

Other observations show that it is not obvious for students that a graph can represent an equation. A graph is supposed to represent the variation of some magnitude as a function of some other magnitude—for instance, distance or speed as a function of time, or cost as a function of the quantity of goods to be bought. In an equation, for instance, a linear equation like $ax + by = c$, there is no natural functional relationship between y and x; on the contrary, x and y may be viewed as two independent variables, on the basis of which one can compute the value of a third variable z, which happens to be given: $z = c$.

$$z = f(x, y) \qquad f(x, y) = ax + by \qquad z = c$$
$$\Rightarrow ax + by = c$$

It is impossible for a student to understand the scheme for solving systems of equations graphically if, at least implicitly, he or she is not able to see the connection between the concepts of equation, unknown, and given on the one hand, and the concepts of function, variable, and parameter on the other. This is crucial in seeing how the function $y = f(x)$ can be derived from the equation $f(x, y) = c$.

It is only after a few years of work with graphs that students can understand graphs as representations of any sort of relationship between two variables, even if this relationship is not a function, as is the case for the circle: $x^2 + y^2 = k$.

It is a problem for researchers to understand how much explication is needed to teach students how to solve systems graphically, which concepts-in-action and theorems-in-action they may rely upon, what kind of control they are able to master, and so on. Once again, a sound cognitive analysis requires a clear distinction between the signified (functions, variables, equations, systems, solutions) and the signifier (axes, dots, graphs, intersection points), and also between concepts of different ranges and levels. It also seems obvious that both long-term and short-term perspectives are needed for the study of learning and teaching algebra.

WHY CONCEPTUAL FIELDS?

Several motives have led me to develop the theory of conceptual fields as an indispensable framework for research in mathematics education and psychology:

1. The need to establish strong connections between situations and schemes, between operational invariants contained in schemes and explicit mathematical concepts and theorems, and between conceptual activities and symbolic manipulations.

2. The need to organize the hierarchical complexity of cognitive tasks (met by students and progressively mastered by them) into a manageable classification, so as to be able to describe both the variety of these cognitive tasks and the development of the schemes and thinking operations needed to deal with them.

3. The need to give an account of the long-term development of students' competences and conceptions, and the continuities and discontinuities that characterize that development, and also to give an account of the short-term emergence (by discovery, invention, or learning) of new competences and conceptions when confronted by new situations.

4. Last, but not least, the need to develop a theory that would make conceptualization the keystone of cognition.

The domain specificity of learning is now recognized by many authors, but the theoretical reasons for this are not clear for most cognitive psychologists, even in the field of mathematics education. The essential reason, for me, is that cognition is first of all conceptualization, and conceptualization is specific to the domain of phenomena to be dealt with—more precisely, to the domain of situations to be mastered.

This specificity is more easily recognized in physics, biology, or technology than in mathematics, because mathematics is supposed to be content-free and structural in essence. This is not totally true even for advanced mathematics, and it is wrong and misleading for the kind of mathematics that students have to develop at the primary and early secondary levels. Children's mathematics is part of the knowledge that emerges from such cognitive processes as identifying objects, their properties, their relationships to other objects, and their transformations, or comparing quantities and magnitudes, and combining them in a variety of ways. The conceptualization of space and time is essential, but several other kinds of qualitative and quantitative dimensions are also important, such as color, weight, cost, and so on.

Not only is cognition mainly conceptualization, but the conceptualizing process lies mostly beneath the surface, like an iceberg. Concepts and theorems are first developed—through experience—as operational invariants. Therefore the concept of *scheme* is essential, as it is those components of the scheme that I have called operational invariants that constitute the core of an individual's conceptual or preconceptual representation of the world, however implicit these invariants may be.

Everybody recognizes today the importance of consciousness, language, and symbols in the formation of scientific concepts, as stressed by Vygotsky over 50 years ago, but Vygotsky pointed out that thought consists also of nonexplicit concepts and even "unconscious concepts." Piaget stressed that point even more strongly in many books, although he did not emphasize the narrow connection between schemes and operational invariants as much as theory requires.

WHAT IS A CONCEPTUAL FIELD?

Schemes refer to situations; therefore it is essential to see the world of our experience as a set of situations, and not merely as a set of objects, qualities and relationships. Actually, both perspectives are necessary—science views the real world as a set of objects at different levels, whereas experience views it as a set of situations progressively mastered. Experience and knowledge comprise both mastering more and more complex situations, and identifying more and more complex objects and their properties. A situation involves a variety of objects and properties; therefore the cognitive analysis of a situation involves several concepts. Reciprocally a concept does not draw its meaning and scope from just one kind of situation. This is the reason why one must study learning in a variety of situations and also use a variety of concepts in conjunction to analyze those situations and to make a reliable description of schemes.

> Definition: A *conceptual field* is a set of situations, the mastering of which requires several interconnected concepts. It is at the same time a set of concepts, with different properties, the meaning of which is drawn from this variety of situations.

The study of cognitive development is more fruitful if one takes it as a network of conceptual fields being developed over a long period of time, analyzed both from the perspective of the situations in which students' activity takes place, and from the perspective of the concepts involved in the analysis of these situations. The first scientific advantage is that it gives us a way to identify the similarities and differences between situations, their hierarchical structure, and also the continuities and discontinuities that organize the repertoire of schemes that is progressively developed to master these situations.

The second scientific advantage is that it provides us with a straightforward possibility of describing the implicit representation of the world underlying schemes in terms of operational invariants, namely, concepts-in-action and theorems-in-action.

> Definition: A *theorem-in-action* is a proposition that is held to be true by the individual subject for a certain range of the situation variables.

It follows from this definition that the scope of validity of a theorem-in-action can be different from the real theorem, as science would see it. It also follows that a theorem-in-action can be false. But at least it can be true or false, which is not the case for concepts-in-action.

> Definition: *Concepts-in-action* are categories (objects, properties, relationships, transformations, processes, etc.) that enable the subject to cut the real world into distinct elements and aspects, and pick up the most adequate selection of information according to the situation and scheme involved.

Concepts-in-action are, of course, indispensable for theorems-in-action to exist, but they are not theorems by themselves. They cannot be true or false, but only relevant or irrelevant. Only propositions can be true or false. Concepts-in-action can be involved in theorems as predicates or arguments. But the same concept can have different cognitive status, as we see later in this chapter.

The challenge is to offer a classification of situations and a set of concepts and theorems that can give a fair account of the most important phenomena observed with children and students, as they progressively master these situations. It is essential to show the hierarchy of complexity that exists between classes of situations, between procedures, and between linguistic and symbolic representations of the objects and relationships involved (especially if such representations are used in the classroom).

I now discuss four different examples of conceptual fields, those of additive structures, multiplicative structures, elementary algebra, and number and space.

Additive Structures

Initially, there are two different situations of addition for children:

- The part-part-whole relationship: knowing the cardinal of the parts, find the cardinal of the whole.
- The state-transformation-state relationship: knowing the cardinal of the initial state and the value of the increase, find the cardinal of the final state.

These two situations are not modeled by the same mathematical concept. Although the first is adequately described by a binary combination that is commutative and associative, the second is adequately described by a unary operation that is neither commutative nor associative.

There is only one initial situation of subtraction, the state-transformation-state relationship: knowing the cardinal of the initial state and the value of the decrease (loss, expense, consumption, . . .) find the cardinal of the final state. From these initial meanings of addition and subtraction, children have to develop a understanding of a wide variety of problems, far away from such primitive, intuitive meanings (Fischbein, 1987).

I do not repeat here the classification I have presented several times elsewhere (Vergnaud, 1981, 1982, 1983, 1988). There are six fundamental relationships and a large number of classes of situations associated with them. It is interesting to study the first three relationships (combination, transformation, and comparison), as has been done by many authors since the Wingspread Conference in 1979 (Carpenter, Moser, & Romberg, 1982); it is also important to study the last three: combination of transformations, transformation of a relationship, and combination of relationships. There are two main reasons for this:

1. Young children do meet these last three relationships in some situations. Three more and two less is one more. If I owe you four marbles and give you one back I owe you only three. Such computations cannot be theoretically handled

within the framework of the first three relationships: combination, transforma
tion, comparison.

2. It is important to offer students situations in which they can find it meaningful to reason and compute with negative and positive numbers. Many 12- to
15-year-old students behave as if numbers could only be positive. They have
great difficulties in subtracting numbers of different signs and they don't know
how to interpret negative solutions of equations. The main reason for this lies in
their conception of numbers—for them, numbers measure some quantity or
some magnitude. As all measures are positive, negative numbers are meaningless.

Yet elementary school students can deal successfully with some situations
involving transformations and relationships, adequately represented by directed
numbers. The theory of conceptual fields provides the interpretation that the
concept of negative number does not emerge all at once, but piece by piece, like
many other concepts. Negative numbers can be taught at different levels, provided one takes care to use situations that stay within the range of reasonings that
students can deal with. There is not much meaning in facing 9-year-olds with
problems in which they would have to subtract transformations or relationships
of different signs, as such problems are still difficult for a majority of 14-year-
olds. But they can handle problems in which they need to combine positive and
negative transformations, such as a win of 7 and a loss of 12 amounting to a
loss of 5.

The complexity of additive structures can be easily summarized by a few
ideas:

1. The same relationship can be mastered for one class of problems but not
for another. A typical example is the state-transformation-state relationship.
Most 7-year-olds are able to find the final state knowing the initial state and the
transformation, but are unable to find the initial state knowing the final state and
the transformation. Although they can discriminate between the transformation
and the states, and between the initial and final states, they do not master equally
well the two corresponding theorems-in-action:

$$F = T(I) \quad \text{and} \quad I = T^{-1}(F)$$

2. Some relationships are simpler than others, and there is no doubt that the
combination of transformations, the transformation of a relationship, and the
combination of relationships are more difficult than the combination of measures, the transformation of a measure, and the comparison of measures. However, it is surprising how easily young students can deal with some complex
relationships when the numerical values make it possible for them to use simpler

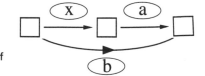

FIG. 13.1.   Decombination   of
additive transformations.

models. For instance, in the decombination of transformations, 9- to 12-year-olds can find easily the first transformation *x*, knowing the second one *a*, and the combined transformation *b*, when *b* and *a* have the same sign and $|b| > |a|$, but not so easily when $|b| < |a|$; most of them fail when *b* and *a* have different signs (Fig. 13.1).

3. Different domains of the students' experience also offer different levels of difficulty—for instance, in physics, geometry, and accountancy. This means that the domain specificity of concepts is not only mathematical but has to do with the domain of experience it refers to—physical, technological, social. It is not the same thing to subtract time coordinates and to subtract two states in a marble game, although both tasks may appear isomorphic at first glance.

4. The same class of problems can usually be solved by several procedures, depending on the numerical values, the domain of experience, and the schemes available for each individual student.

> Definition: The *conceptual field of additive structures* is the set of situations that can be generated by the six basic relationships mentioned earlier, or by a combination of them. From each of them, one can generate two, six, or more classes of cognitive tasks, which demand different theorems-in-action. The conceptual field of additive structures is also a set of interconnected concepts: cardinal, measure, order, part, whole, state, transformation, relationship, combination, inversion, abscissa, difference, and, of course, addition, subtraction, natural number, and directed number.

Multiplicative Structures

As with additive structures, the complexity of multiplicative structures has been recognized in recent research and analysis (Greer, 1992; Harel & Confrey, 1994).

The initial relationship that makes multiplication meaningful for children is the simple proportion between two variables, when a certain value can be iterated a small number of times (Fig. 13.2).

Multiply *a* by *n* and *n* by *a* are not conceptually equivalent, as multiplication by *n* can be introduced as the iteration *n* times of *a*, whereas there is no meaning in iterating *n*, *a* times. Take the example of *a* = 3 dollars and *n* = 4 toy cars. The price of 4 cars is the price of one car, plus the price of one car, plus the price of one car, plus the price of one car, but will never be 4 cars, plus 4 cars, plus 4 cars.

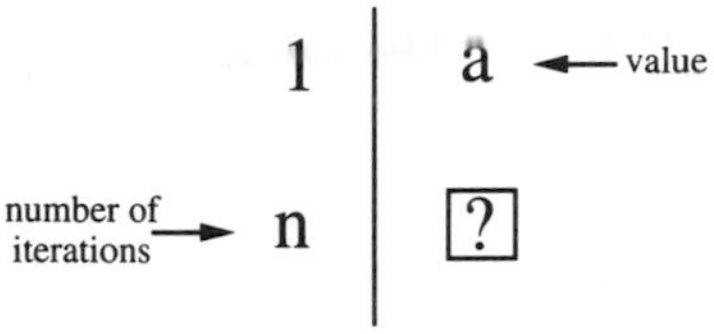

$$1 \quad \Big| \quad a \;\longleftarrow\; \text{value}$$

$$\text{number of} \atop \text{iterations} \;\longrightarrow\; n \quad \Big| \quad \boxed{?}$$

FIG. 13.2. Initial multiplicative relationship.

From the very introduction of multiplication, children's schemes discriminate between the two basic theorems of the linear function:

$$f(n) = n \cdot f(1)$$

$$f(n) = an$$

There are two cases of division:

Type 1: find $f(1)$, knowing n and $f(n)$

Type 2: find n, knowing $f(1)$ and $f(n)$

In Anglo-Saxon countries, type 1 is commonly called *partition* and type 2 *quotition* (Greer, 1992). There has been a lot of research on these divisions, mainly because the change of the numerical value plays a different role for partition and quotition (Fig. 13.3). Further, "n times less" in the partition case is different from inverting the rate, or from finding the ratio between b and a in the quotition case.

Although the constant coefficient property is very useful, and very easy for students who thoroughly understand the invariant rate of the co-variation,

$$f(x) = ax \qquad x = (1/a)f(x)$$

it is remarkable that most students use more spontaneously the isomorphic properties of the linear function:

$$f(nx) = n \cdot f(x)$$

$$f(x) = (1/n)f(nx)$$

$$f(n_1 x_1 + n_2 x_2) = n_1 f(x_1) + n_2 f(x_2)$$

as if it were conceptually easier for them to consider scalars and linear combinations than quotients of dimensions and linear mappings. This can be easily seen

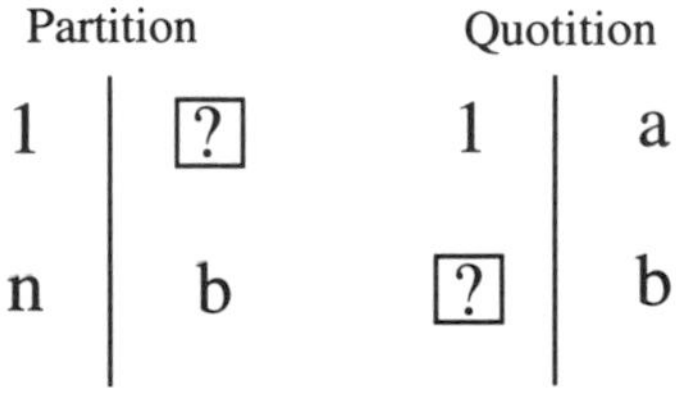

	Partition		Quotition	
	1	$\boxed{?}$	1	a
	n	b	$\boxed{?}$	b

FIG. 13.3. Two cases of division.

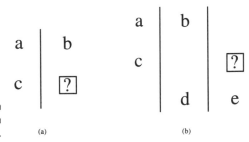

FIG. 13.4. Simple proportion general case (a); concatenation of two simple proportions (b).

when students have to deal with problems of the form shown in Fig. 13.4a or with simple proportions concatenated (Fig. 13.4b).

Inverting a function is more difficult than inverting a scalar ratio. Dimensional analysis provides a reasonable explanation for this difference, namely, that students, like scientists of the past (e.g., Galileo), are reluctant to divide a magnitude of one kind by a magnitude of a different kind (e.g., distance by time, mass by volume). It is even more counterintuitive to do the inverse operation (e.g., dividing time by distance). This is so general that, in natural languages, quotients of dimensions are named one way but not the other way. There is no word for the inverse of speed, nor for the inverse of price. Inverting a function means inverting a quotient of dimensions, whereas inverting a scalar ratio only means inverting "a times more" into "a times less" and reciprocally.

There are two different ways of combining two simple proportions:

- The concatenation, as mentioned earlier, when three variables are covarying:

$$y = ax \qquad z = by \qquad \Rightarrow \qquad z = bax = kx$$

- The product: One variable is proportional to each of the others, when the third is held constant. It is therefore proportional to the product of the other two:

$$z = ax \quad \text{(when } y \text{ is constant)}$$
$$z = by \quad \text{(when } x \text{ is constant)}$$
$$\Rightarrow \qquad z = kxy$$

The product case $z = f(x,y)$ is more difficult than the concatenation case $z = f'(f(x))$. This is a very important result of research as the product happens to be an essential structure for such concepts as those of area and volume, and for many concepts in physics. It requires such concepts-in-action as those of bilinearity, product and quotient of dimensions, and independence. A very specific theorem-in-action can be used:

$$f(a_1x_1, a_2x_2) = a_1a_2f(x_1,x_2)$$

The teaching and learning of fractions, ratios, rates, and rational numbers should be more strongly connected with the teaching and learning of simple and multiple proportion. It is impossible to offer students a comprehensive view of rational numbers as mathematical objects without getting such numbers to work as tools in problems of proportion.

The variety of meanings that rational numbers may have in problems is as wide as the variety of meanings of positive and negative numbers. But there is hardly any common point between the two varieties. The conceptual field of multiplicative structures is very different from the field of additive structures. The theory of groups, which shows that addition and multiplication are structurally very similar, is not at all adequate to theorize about students' learning of elementary arithmetic—it is even misleading. The reason is that elementary arithmetic does not deal with pure numbers but rather with situations involving magnitudes and quantities, states, transformations and relationships.

> Definition: *The conceptual field of multiplicative structures* is the set of situations the solution of which involves a multiplication, a division, or a combination of such operations. This set is generated by different cases of simple proportion and double proportion that can be combined in a variety of ways. The conceptual field of multiplicative structures is also a set of interconnected concepts: measure, scalar ratio, quotient and product of dimensions, fraction, rate, rational number, vector space, linear and *n*-linear function, constant coefficient, linear combination and linear mapping, and of course multiplication and division.

Elementary Algebra

Algebra would be meaningless if students were not able to rely on their previous knowledge in elementary arithmetic. But the relationship between algebra and arithmetics is different from the relationship between multiplicative and additive structures. The new thing with algebra for students is that it uses symbols and operations on symbols to calculate certain unknowns, without the need to control at every moment the meaning of the equations. The arithmetical solution of a problem relies on the choice of adequate data and adequate operations, and on the adequate order of such choices, whereas the algebraic solution relies on the adequate symbolic representation of the relationships involved and the adequate application of rules to generate new equations and calculate the values of the unknowns.

Children are faced with early forms of algebra at the elementary school, but it is only at the secondary level that they have to learn it as a systematic body of knowledge. One needs to identify the operations of thinking in different learning situations and sort out under which conditions one can consider that it is algebra that is learned. Such sentences as $3 + 5 = \Box$, $\Box = 3 + 5$, or $12 - 7 = \Box$ look like equations, but they can also be considered as the mere writing of calculations. There is no algebraic handling of symbols in them.

A different cased is offered by equations like $\Box + 5 = 8$, $6 + \Box = 13$, $12 - \Box = 5$, or $\Box - 8 = 4$, but the symbolic manipulations that would be theoretically needed to transform them are not usually explained to elementary

Sequence of manipulations	Theorems-in-action required
6 + ☐ = 13	
6 - 6 + ☐ = 13 - 6	conservation of equality when subtracting 6 from both sides
	6 - 6 = 0
☐ = 7	0 + ☐ = ☐

FIG. 13.5. Symbol manipulation and theorems-in-action.

school children, because they would require theorems that are beyond the understanding capacities of most of them, as exemplified in Fig. 13.5.

The same remarks hold for several prealgebraic systems of representation such as Euler–Venn diagrams and arrow diagrams, or the simple proportion and double proportion tables. Such diagrams and tables are helpful for children at the elementary and early secondary levels (under certain conditions), because they offer the possibility to categorize and organize information more easily, and also to manipulate symbols, as illustrated by the two examples in Fig. 13.6.

Such prealgebraic representations are useful, but their scope of application is specific and limited. Therefore, it is important to introduce algebra as a powerful way to solve problems as soon as it is possible to do so meaningfully. In France, algebra starts being taught to students at the sixth and seventh grades, but it is not until the eighth and the ninth grades that they have to deal with several unknowns

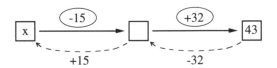

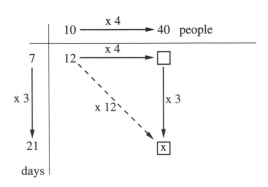

FIG. 13.6. Diagrams and tables: a help to categorize and organize information.

and several equations. This is too late, as the very first functionality of algebra for students should be enabling them to solve problems that they would be unable to solve by ordinary arithmetic. This functionality can be best exemplified when there are several unknowns.

In situations that can be represented by equations of the form $a + x = b$, $ax = b$, or $ax + b = c$, the algebraic solution relies entirely on the arithmetic solution, step by step. It is only with the unknown on both sides of the equality sign that algebra shows its superiority to the arithmetic solution. Actually, in that case, two implicit functions take the same unknown value:

$$ax + b = a'x + b' \quad \text{is equivalent to} \quad \begin{array}{l} y = ax + b \\ y' = a'x + b' \\ y = y' \end{array}$$

Most systems of two equations with two unknowns actually express functions of two variables taking given values.

$$ax + by = c$$
$$a'x + b'y = c'$$

The teaching of algebra cannot be organized properly if the teacher does not see, in a single glance, the whole set of situations, and the whole set of concepts and theorems-in-action that can make symbols and symbol manipulation meaningful for students.

Before algebra is taught per se, without any reference to ordinary arithmetical problems, its function as a powerful mathematical tool has to be exemplified. Many students do not understand the function of algebra. But the use of algebra as a tool does not mean that one can overlook the concepts that make algebra consistent. Such concepts as those of function and variable are essential for students to understand the concepts of equation and unknown, and the concept of function of two (or more) variables appears to be central for linear systems, although it makes graphic representations difficult, as I have shown earlier.

Definition: The *conceptual field of elementary algebra* is a complex set of situations:

- The set of arithmetical problems that can be more profitably solved by algebraic means than by usual arithmetical ones.
- The set of algebraic problems that can offer students a fair idea of the variety of manipulations needed to solve equations and systems of equations.

At the same time, the conceptual field of elementary algebra is the set of interconnected concepts that make it mathematically consistent: equation, unknown, function, variable, given, parameter, inequality, system, independence, directed number and rational number, monomial, and polynomial. It is also the set of several symbolic systems like those used in prealgebraic representations and in graphical representations.

Number and Space

This conceptual field requires some theoretical clarification. Space and number are the main roots of mathematics and also the main tools for us to think about the physical world. The position, displacement, and movement of objects in space and time offer a major source of situations to be mastered by babies and young children. Our percepto-gestural schemes are almost entirely constrained by such situations. Our first experience of necessity, as opposed to contingency, is spatial. Space lends us many metaphoric ideas for thinking about physical and social phenomena, even though they may be nonspatial. It would be a great epistemological mistake to minimize the part played by the properties of space in symbolic representations.

It would also be a mistake not to analyze carefully which properties of space and which spatial operations are used in such representations. They are usually different for different symbolic systems, and there are not many common points between:

- The representation of order in time (initial state, first transformation, intermediate state, second transformation, final state) by a sequence of squares and arrows from left to right (Fig. 13.7a).
- The representation of simple proportion by the correspondence on the same line (or the same column) of the values taken by two or more variables (Fig. 13.7b).
- The representation of dates on a line (Fig. 13.7c).
- The representation by a graph of the variation of speed over time (Fig. 13.7d).
- The representation of two movements and the solution of the classical meeting-point problem of two vehicles going from A to B and B to A (Fig. 13.7e).

Among all symbolic representations using space and drawings (lines, dots, arrows, squares, circles, figures, and other symbols), the number line is certainly the most important and powerful one, because it makes it possible to draw graphs and histograms on the one hand, and to analyze geometrical objects and transformations on the other. But it takes several years for students to understand how to read the number line as a set of numbers, and to use the numberline to place data or find the value of unknowns.

For example, it is rather easy for fifth or sixth graders to use the order properties of space (from left to right, or right to left, or bottom to top, or top to bottom) to represent the order properties of quantities, magnitudes or dates. But it is more difficult for them to use the measure properties of space (length, area, volume) to represent the measure properties of phenomena and objects.

Measures are usually associated with disjoint sets or objects. Therefore the

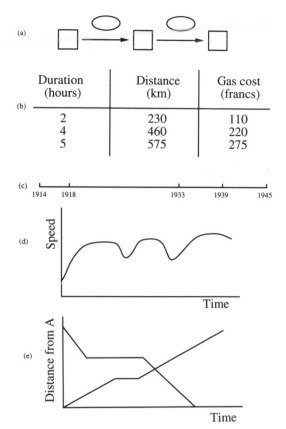

Duration (hours)	Distance (km)	Gas cost (francs)
2	230	110
4	460	220
5	575	275

FIG. 13.7.   Different   uses   of spatial representation.

natural way to use the measure properties of space—length, for instance—is to represent different objects by disjoint segments of different lengths, either separate, or end to end (Fig. 13.8a). In contradiction of this view, the number line takes it for granted that segments start from the same origin. Different ends correspond to different segments, placed at a certain distance from the origin, proportionally to the number represented (Fig. 13.8b). A further step is to identify the number with the endpoint instead of the segment starting from the origin (Fig. 13.8c).

The number line is therefore a high-level concept for many early secondary school students, because they have to give up well-established views concerning measure. In contradiction with their primitive views, they must understand two principles:

1. The punctualization principle: Although points are not measurable, numbers are identified with points

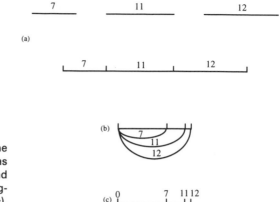

FIG. 13.8. Four steps in the understanding of lines as numbers: separated or end to end (a), included segments (b), and finally dots (c).

2. The inclusion principle: Although measures can usually be added, and are therefore associated with disjoint objects, the implicit segments that join the origin and the endpoints are included in one another.

Another important step is the possibility of dealing with the number line even when the origin is not represented. It is then necessary to work with segments that represent differences and are proportional to them (Fig. 13.9a). It is then possible to represent any number in an infinite set of numbers (e.g., decimals, rationals, irrationals), provided the segments on each side, to the next units or sub-units, are proportional to the differences (Fig. 13.9b). It is no easier to do this, for most students, than to understand interval scales.

In algebra and calculus, graphs must be interpreted quickly. The reading of graphs is different when the tasks are different. It is easier to read a graph to find when a function is increasing, decreasing, maximum or minimum, than to find the solutions of a system of equations and inequations. The perceptual properties of graphs, as spatial objects, must not hide the fact that the reading of these perceptual properties involves high-level concepts and theorems.

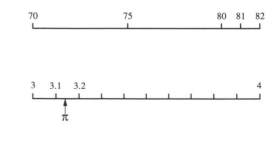

FIG. 13.9. Most difficult cases: The origin is not represented.

CONCLUSION

Mathematics teaching and learning present both long-term and short-term problems. On many occasions a teacher has to find the appropriate situation, the appropriate explanation, the appropriate comment, the appropriate question, and sometimes the appropriate silence. But this short-term management would be unintelligible if it were not related to the long-term process of learning mathematics, which is characterized by slowness and diversity. The theory of conceptual fields offers a framework to conceptualize this long-term process and this diversity.

The theory also considers that the conceptual contents of mathematics provide the best tool to characterize the cognitive processes and competences of students. No cognitive psychology of mathematics is likely to be fruitful without a sound epistemology of mathematics (Vergnaud, 1990), provided that epistemology itself is not based solely on the mathematician's sophisticated knowledge of mathematics, but also pays attention to the process of learning mathematics, and to students' difficulties and errors.

The theory also uses several psychological concepts such as behavior, competence, representation, scheme, rule of action, goal, expectation, operational invariant, signifier, signified. Most other concepts used are mathematical and not psychological.

The concept of scheme is the keystone of the whole construction, as it relates behavior (action, competence, rule, . . .) and representation (operational invariant, expectation, signified, signifier, . . .). It conveys the thesis that there is no procedural knowledge without some conceptual or preconceptual knowledge—operational invariants.

There are different kinds of operational invariants. Most important are concepts-in-action (the function of which is to provide ways of picking up, selecting, and categorizing relevant information), and theorems-in-action (the function of which is to make possible inferences and calculations on the ground of the information available). The domains of availability and reliability of such theorems and their degree of consciousness and explicitation are variable. They depend on the individuals, and on the frequency with which they have to be used. Moreover, theorems-in-action are not always true, but only held to be true. Concepts-in-action are also diverse and they can have different cognitive status, depending on whether they are predicates or objects, and depending also on the way they are put into words and symbols.

The main argument, still, in favor of the theory of conceptual fields is that it enables us to understand filiations and revolutions in the long-term appropriation process of new competences and conceptions. All theories of stages have failed upon the problem of domain specificity. Therefore the theoretical priority is to take the conceptual contents of knowledge as a basis.

Some theories try to explain how similarities and differences are progressively selected, and how analogies and metaphors convey new ideas. They usually deal with very poor empirical phenomena and low-level concepts. Psychology must deal with science, technology, and high-level competences. Conceptual fields are the best framework to trace complex analogical and metaphorical processes.

The learning of mathematics and other sciences involves not only the selection of similarities (empirical invariants) but also the construction of nonempirical concepts, as illustrated by the history of sciences. The thesis that there are filiations and revolutions in learning, and that some of them go far beyond the ideas of similarity, empirical invariant, and analogy, is also essential.

Finally a theory of learning and cognitive development must offer at the same time a way to understand how knowledge is developed in situations, owing to the subject's activity and to other subjects' cooperation, and how it can ultimately take the shape of natural language texts, and of highly formalized representations.

Piaget and Vygotsky are certainly the best sources of inspiration I can quote for my own work, but there are also important differences between the theory of conceptual fields and the Piagetian and Vygotskian perspectives, mainly because neither Piaget nor Vygotsky referred as much as I consider necessary to the ideas of class of situations and scheme, to their conceptual contents and to the overall organization of the different domains to be mastered.

Definition: A concept is a three-tuple of three sets:

$$C = (S, I, S)$$

where S is the set of situations that make it meaningful, I is the set of operational invariants contained in the schemes developed to deal with these situations, and S is the set of symbolic representations (natural language, diagrams, graphs, algebra, . . .) that can be used to represent the relationships involved, communicate about them, and help us master the situations.

Neither Piaget nor Vygotsky offered such a definition of what a concept is from a developmental point of view, nor did they fully consider situations as the main reference for knowledge. But they provided us with the most impressive considerations on schemes and symbolic tools.

REFERENCES

Bruner, J. S. (1966). *The process of education.* Cambridge, MA: Harvard University Press.

Carpenter, T. A., Moser, J. M., & Romberg, T. A. (Eds.). (1982). *Addition and subtraction: A cognitive perspective.* Hillsdale, NJ: Lawrence Erlbaum Associates.

de Saussure, F. (1972). *Cours de linguistique générale.* Paris: Payot, publié par Ch. Bally & A. Sechehaye.

Fischbein, E. (1987). *Intuition in science and mathematics.* Dordrecht: Reidel.

Gelman, R., & Gallistel, C. R. (1978). *The child's understanding of number.* Cambridge, MA: Harvard University Press.

Greer, B. (1992). Multiplication and division as models of situations. In D. A. Grouws (Ed.), *Handbook of research on learning and teaching mathematics* (pp. 276–295). New York: Macmillan.

Harel, G., & Confrey, J. (Eds.). (1994). *The development of multiplicative reasoning in the learning of mathematics.* Albany, NY: SUNY Press.

Newell, A., & Simon, H. A. (1972). *Human problem solving.* Englewood Cliffs, NJ: Prentice Hall.

Piaget, J. (1950). *The psychology of intelligence.* London: Routledge & Kegan-Paul.

Piaget, J. (1971). *Genetic epistemology.* New York: Norton.

Piaget, J. (1980). *Adaptation ad intelligence.* Chicago: University of Chicago Press.

Russell, B. (1910). La théorie des types logiques [The theory of logical types]. *Revue de métaphysique et de morale, 18,* 263–301.

Russell, B. (1940). *An inquiry into meaning and truth.* London: Allen & Unwin.

Tarski, A. (1971). *Introduction à la logique.* Paris: Gauthier-Villars. (Translated from the Polish original version, 1936. English version published in 1941: Introduction to logic and to the methodology of deductive sciences)

Vergnaud, G. (1981). *L'enfant, la mathématique et la réalité.* Berne: Peter Lang.

Vergnaud, G. (1982). A classification of cognitive tasks and operations of thought involved in addition and subtraction problems. In T. P. Carpenter, J. M. Moser, & T. A. Romberg (Eds.), *Addition and subtraction: A cognitive perspective* (pp. 39–59). Hillsdale, NJ: Lawrence Erlbaum Associates.

Vergnaud, G. (1983). Multiplicative structures. In R. Lesh & M. Landau (Eds.), *Acquisition of mathematics concepts and processes* (pp. 127–174). New York: Academic Press.

Vergnaud, G. (1990). Epistemology and psychology of mathematics education. In J. Kilpatrick & P. Nesher (Eds.), *Mathematics and cognition* (pp. 14–30). Cambridge: Cambridge University Press.

Vygotsky, L. S. (1962). *Thought and language* New York: MIT Press.

Vygotsky, L. S. (1978). *Mind in society.* Cambridge, MA: Harvard University Press.

14
Learning About Fractions

David William Carraher
Universidade Federal de Pernambuco, Recife, Brazil

My aim here is to consider a fraction as a psychological concept, explore how it relates to what students already know, and suggest ideas regarding the teaching of fractions, bearing in mind what we have learned about students' thinking.

WHAT IS A FRACTION?

The View from Mathematics

In mathematics a fraction is a number of the form a/b (where a, b are integers and b is not zero) with a set of well-defined and well-known operations and properties, such as commutativity and association of addition and multiplication, identity operations, and so on.

For the present purposes this conception of fractions is relevant but misleading. Fractions are indeed numbers. However part of the concept of fraction is nonnumerical. A narrow mathematical conception disregards the role physical quantity plays in the meaning of the concept and consequently obscures the psychological origins of fractions, for there is little doubt that number concepts, including rational number concepts, are developed through acting and reflecting upon physical quantities. The view that "a fraction is simply a number" may make sense in discussions among mathematicians but it is pedagogically naive as well as historically and psychologically inaccurate.

The View from Classrooms

Traditional approaches to fractions in mathematics education do not suffer from this fault but raise another set of issues. In relying upon concrete materials such

241

as pizzas and cakes in the teaching of fractions, mathematics educators implicitly recognize, wisely so, that children develop number concepts on the basis of their knowledge of the physical world. (This does not mean that the concept of fraction is "abstracted" from objects in the classical empiricist view of abstraction of knowledge as a direct transcription or "reading off" of reality). Just as integer addition and subtraction are introduced through operations on discrete objects, fractions are introduced through the actions of breaking up wholes into sets of units of equal magnitude. Many students and some teachers seem to think that a fraction is a part of a whole and the fractional numeral (e.g., $^2/_3$) is its "name." The idea that a fraction is material substance is, of course, incorrect. If we adopt such a view we must be willing to conclude that any person, regardless of age, who works with parts of wholes is working with fractions. No mathematical concept can be reduced to a physical embodiment. A fraction entails relations, and relations are not palpable, physical objects.

In mathematics education we have no alternative but to steer away from the extreme views that "fractions are simply numbers" and "fractions are simply material substance." In doing so we cannot simply disregard number and quantity. Learning about fractions entails becoming aware of special relations between numbers and quantities and learning to express these relations in diverse ways.

In this regard, it is instructive to reflect on how students are taught to identify fractions. Students are shown a set of elements, some of which are shaded, marked, or selected. They are told to count the marked units and to use the obtained cardinal number as the numerator; likewise, they are instructed to count the total number of (marked plus unmarked) elements and use the total as the denominator of the fraction (Carraher & Schliemann, 1991; Ohlsson, 1988). Fractions are thus tied to the activities of counting and matching.

Later students are given rules for carrying out the multiplication, division, addition, and subtraction of fractions. The rules for multiplication and division are taught as computational recipes. Few students understand, for example, why one inverts a fractional divisor before multiplying. It is hoped that students will later make sense of these operations for themselves. Most of them never do.

These and other shortcomings of traditional instruction regarding fractions can be subsumed under several categories:

1. Part–whole fixation. Students are taught to associate fractions with parts of wholes. This impedes transfer to other cases and makes improper fractions seem mysterious (how can the part be greater than the whole?).
2. Cardinal sin. Counting and matching tasks mislead students to focus on cardinal number while ignoring the ratio meaning of fractions.
3. Missing links. The links of fractions to integer multiplication and division are missing or misleading. Furthermore, fractions are treated as unrelated to ratio, proportion, functions, and other concepts.

4. No challenge. Authentic problems and puzzles are absent in instruction, and "exercises" given to students are merely computational tasks.

These shortcomings constitute a challenge for any alternative approach to teaching about fractions.

The Present View

Over the last two decades, much discussion has been brewing regarding the learning and teaching of fractions (Behr, Harel, Post, & Lesh, 1992; Behr, Lesh, Post, & Silver, 1983; Braunfeld & Wolfe, 1966; Dienes, 1967; Kerslake, 1986; Kieren, 1976; Streefland, 1991). These works have attempted to render a rich account of fractions and rational numbers and to provide a theoretical and empirical footing that will guide curriculum development and teaching. The field still lacks a coherent account of how fractions fit into students' mathematical understanding, beginning from early childhood and extending into late adolescence. However, it seems reasonable to suppose that fractions are tightly interwoven with ratio and proportion concepts, as well as multiplication and division. These reference concepts will be closely linked to representations, schemes, ideas, and concepts such as decimal number, percent, relative increase and decrease, slope, the Euclidean algorithm and maximum common divisor, linear equation, constant of proportionality, intensive quantities and rates, functions and operations, and measurement, to mention several. Clarifying these relations is a long-term enterprise for the field of mathematics education (Vergnaud, 1990, chapter 13, this volume). A general theoretical framework is necessary for giving overall direction to these efforts. But a general framework is not enough because we need to work out the issues unique to the learning of ratio and proportion in the domain of mathematics. It is easy to accept the general notion that all of the aforementioned concepts are interrelated. But when we focus on particular relations, there is much to work out. Consider, for example, the relations between the concept of fraction and integer multiplication and division. Learning studies (see the section on the arithmetical basis of fractions) sometimes give the impression that the student's knowledge about integer operations impedes learning about fractions. So, precisely how integers are related to fractions is a problem for many students. It is not sufficient simply to treat them as separate topics. If instruction is to be successful, it must contend with what students already know about whole numbers and their operations. It must provide conditions for students to build on what they already know, where possible. However, it must also provide opportunities for students to reorganize and advance their knowledge, where necessary. This requires that we think about very specific classes of learning situations that may be useful for helping students come to grips with diverse relations and concepts. What sorts of learning activities can be useful in engaging students in reflection about these relations? What sorts of evidence, demonstration, or proof could students draw on to raise their own hypotheses and to derive their own conclusions?

Here I raise ideas relevant to such a project. First I discuss two kinds of competences that must play a major role in the emergence of the concept of fraction. Next I describe a model and some associated learning activities that draw on these competences and serve to establish links between fractions and diverse related concepts. I hope to make a case for the view that, from the very start, fractions should be treated as "shorthand" for certain functions. Taken seriously, these considerations redefine what a fraction is, assigning to the concept an important role in the transition from arithmetic to algebraic thinking.

HOW FRACTIONS MESH WITH WHAT STUDENTS ALREADY KNOW

In order to situate the concept in the student's long-term development, we must look for the roots of the fraction concept in activities engaged in, and knowledge acquired, long before the student can handle expressions such as $2/3$. The concept of fraction will rely on former knowledge as well as embody new ideas; it reflects a continuity as well as a break with the past. Two sources of continuity are discussed, namely, (a) students' implicit knowledge regarding ratio and proportion, and (b) their knowledge regarding the arithmetic of whole numbers. Both sources of knowledge are highly relevant to learning about fractions.

The Perceptual–Judgmental Basis of Fractions in Ratios of Quantity

A *proportion* is an equivalence of ratios. A typical example is

$$3:4 = 6:8 \tag{1}$$

Because the colon expresses the operation of division, we may alternatively write

$$3 \div 4 = 6 \div 8 \tag{2}$$

or even

$$3/4 = 6/8 \tag{3}$$

This means that a proportion can be expressed as an equivalence of fractions. Two points need mentioning:

1. Equations 1, 2, and 3 are by no means equivalent to students. (This exemplifies a widespread phenomenon, that two expressions that are "obviously equivalent" to mathematicians are not seen as the same by students.) For example, Kerslake (1986) found that most 11- to 15-year-old

students do not think that $3 \div 4$ expresses the fraction $3/4$, By extension, they would not accept the equivalence of Equations 2 and 3.

2. All situations involving ratio and proportion are potentially relevant to the concept of fraction. We must therefore look toward how students reason about ratio and proportion in order to understand how the concept of fraction fits into their prior knowledge.

The psychological literature is replete with evidence suggesting that ratio and proportion concepts develop slowly throughout childhood and that children come to understand proportions only during adolescence. For example, Bruner and Kenney (1966) found that 5-year-olds use the terms "full" and "empty" correctly to describe glasses totally full or empty, but they take the "fuller glass" to mean the glass with more water or a higher water level. Only over several years do they shift towards the interpretation that "fuller glass" means having more water relative to its capacity. The Piagetian school has long argued that the concept of proportional reasoning is a characteristic of formal operational thought. Indeed, much empirical evidence (e.g., Hart, 1984; Karplus, Karplus, Formisano, & Paulsen, 1979) can be found to support this view. But there is now convincing developmental evidence that the concepts of ratio and proportion begin to develop far earlier than normally supposed. In order to understand this we must distinguish the sort of ratio mentioned in the preceding equations from another sort of ratio.

A *ratio of numbers* or numerical ratio entails a comparison of two numbers (which could be rational or real numbers as well as integers). It corresponds to expressions such as 2:3, $2 \div 3$, or $2/3$. A *ratio of quantities* concerns a comparison of two quantities. For example, if A refers to the length of one object and B refers to the length of a second object, then $A:B$ and A/B express the relative magnitude of the two lengths. In general, I use the term *quantity* to refer to a scalar quantity, namely, a property or quality that varies in intensity, magnitude, or duration, susceptible to ordering along a single dimension or continuum (Fridman, 1991). I prefer to reserve the term *measure* to refer to the description of a quantity according to a certain number of units of measure. As quantities become expressed as multiples of other quantities, a ratio of quantities can be treated as a ratio of measures (e.g., $2A:3A$ or $5A:7B$); in this sense a formerly unmeasured quantity (e.g., A) becomes a unit of measure according to which other quantities are measured.

In a psychological investigation of ratio and proportion, Spinillo and Bryant (1991) asked 5- to 7-year-old children to compare a model figure, part of which was blue and the rest of which was white, to two other figures, one of which had the same ratio of blue to white (see Fig. 14.1). The child was told that each of the figures was a photograph of an object made from little blue and little white blocks. The child's task was to decide which of the two remaining figures had the same ratio of blue to white blocks as the model.

Model

FIG. 14.1. Figures used by Spinillo and Bryant (1991). The task is to decide which comparison figure has the ratio of blue to white as the model figure.

Comparison figures

Because the individual blocks used to construct the figures could not be discerned, and hence could not be counted, the child had to rely upon non-numerical information for solving the task. Considering that the total size of the figures varied across trials independently from the ratio of blue to white, responses based on the absolute size of the figures could be separate from those based on proportions. Furthermore, because in some conditions the configurations of blue to white was rearranged, the child could not solve the problem by mentally "rescaling" one of the figures in order to make it look like the model figure. In order for the child to solve the tasks successfully, she would have to use the ratio of colored regions.

The results showed that children as young as 6 years of age were responding at better than chance levels. The children distinguished three types of first-order comparisons between parts A and B of one figure: $A > B$, $A < B$, and $A = B$. Furthermore, they successfully made second-order comparisons equivalent to the following:

$$\text{If } A < B \text{ and } C > D \text{ then } A{:}B \neq C{:}D$$
$$\text{If } A > B \text{ and } C = D \text{ then } A{:}B \neq C{:}D$$
$$\text{If } A < B \text{ and } C = D \text{ then } A{:}B \neq C{:}D$$

The above comparisons can be regarded as special cases of ratios. The comparison $A = B$, for example, corresponds to the equation $A{:}B = 1$. The inequality $C > D$ corresponds to the case $C{:}D > 1$.

The young children were not successful in comparing a pair of inequalities in the same direction. For example, if they were shown figures corresponding to the conditions $A < B$ and $C < D$, they were not able to decide, at better than chance levels, whether or not $A{:}B = C{:}D$.

The authors interpreted the findings as showing the importance of half in children's proportional judgments. In doing so, they recognized that ratio and proportion bear directly on the concept of fraction (one half). It should be emphasized, however, that the children had no understanding of notation regarding fractions.

Lovett and Singer (1991) found similar results in a series of studies using a completely different methodology. There was also evidence, in their studies, that by kindergarten children were beginning to order ratios correctly within logical categories; that is, they were beginning to differentiate among ratios on the "same side of one-half."

The foregoing results suggest that children begin to develop a rudimentary understanding of ratios of quantity long before they reach adolescence and well before they can understand numerical ratios such as 2:3. The concept of ratio emerges in the context of perceptual judgments, and initially bears no relation to calculation skills and knowledge of arithmetic.

The Arithmetical Basis of Fractions

On the basis of their experience with integers, students tend to associate multiplication with increase, and division with reduction in amounts (Bell, Fishbein, & Greer, 1984; Greer, 1990). The operation of multiplying by n is related to the physical action of taking n instances of something. Division is related to the action of taking a part of something.

In tasks where subjects are asked to select the appropriate operation to model a word problem, many students—even at secondary and university levels—select the incorrect arithmetical operation when the operator corresponds to a proper fraction. For example, given the task of determining how much one pays for $3/4$ kg of meat if 1 kg costs \$2, many will say that the answer will be given by dividing 2 by $3/4$. By contrast, it makes virtually no difference whether the operand measure corresponds to an integer or to a decimal fraction (Bell, Greer, Grimson, & Mangan, 1989). Bell et al. also reported a second study in which 15-year-old students either estimated the size of the answer or indicated which operation was to be selected in order to solve the problem. Dramatic differences occurred in performance under the two conditions. Generally, students estimated the sizes of results with a high degree of accuracy, indicating that they understand from the context the effect that the operation must have upon the operand. They select the wrong operation due to a misconception regarding which operation produces the intended effect. The authors concluded that "the estimate is made directly by a semiqualitative ratio comparison, without explicit identification of the . . . operation" (p. 447).

In the problems of Bell et al., quantities were expressed indirectly through written values. Even so, it seems reasonable to suppose that students are working with internal representations of quantities. The students appear to understand interrelations of the quantities well enough to expect a resultant measure greater or less than that of the operand quantity. For example, if 1 k of meat costs $2 and they wish to purchase $3/4$ kg, they know that they will pay less than $2, but do not understand which arithmetic operations will produce the desired effects. Their representations of quantity do not mesh with their representations of number operations.

Students' difficulties with rational operators do not simply reflect a failure to master the computational procedures (e.g., integer multiplication transfers very easily to decimal multiplication), but have to do with making sense of how numerical operations relate to transformations upon associated quantities. Although students' understanding of integer multiplication and division commonly interferes with the concept of a fraction as an operator, this very understanding must constitute a resource for introducing fractions as operators. We know that student's knowledge about fractions must build upon what they already know about whole numbers. Yet integer knowledge is likely to lead them astray when it comes to understanding a fraction as an operator. How can students make use of what they already know without being misled?

To address these questions we must first look closely at the interplay between number and quantity in certain mathematical tasks.

Fractions as Shorthand for Equations Describing Relations Among Quantities

I noted earlier that fractions are closely linked to ratios and proportions. Let us explore this with regard to Fig. 14.2. There is something strange about this figure. The figures and corresponding notation appear correct. The fractions written below are in accordance with textbook conventions. But why is one-half of a whole less than two-fourths of a whole? How can one-half be equal to one-fifth? Does this mean that $1/2 = 1/5$?

The fractions in Fig. 14.2 refer to several "wholes." Perhaps one should not compare fractions derived from different units. On the other hand, perhaps we can set things straight by clarifying what is being compared. Traditional notation regarding fractions does not explicitly represent units. But let us see what happens if we label the units and then try to describe the relations once more (Fig. 14.3).

If A refers to the region occupied by one square, B to two squares, C to three squares, D to four squares, and E to five squares, we can state the relations more explicitly through an equation:

$$A = 1/2 B$$

The other cases can be expressed in a similar fashion:

$$B = 2/3 C$$
$$B = 2/4 D = 1/2 D$$
$$A = 1/5 E$$

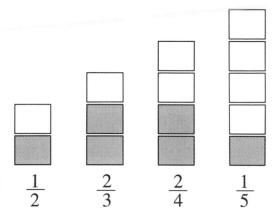

FIG. 14.2. Illustration of the need to consider units when comparing fractions.

$$\frac{1}{2} \qquad \frac{2}{3} \qquad \frac{2}{4} \qquad \frac{1}{5}$$

Consider once again the question "How can one-half be equal to one-fifth?" We now have a clearer means of representing the relations, namely $\frac{1}{2}B = \frac{1}{5}E$, which corresponds to the sentence "one-half of B equals one-fifth of E." This has clear advantages over the potentially confusing $\frac{1}{2} = \frac{1}{5}$.

When working with a physical model of fractions, a fractional numeral such as $\frac{1}{2}$ is actually shorthand for a more complete description such as $A = \frac{1}{2}B$, or $Y = \frac{1}{2}x$, where the parameter, $\frac{1}{2}$, is a constant of proportionality. *Fractional numerals are shorthand for functions involving ratio and proportion.* (It may look as if each letter designates only a single quantity rather than a variable quantity, so that we are not talking about relations between variables. However, even if the notation is initially used to describe relations between particular quantities, it opens the way for talking later about relations between variables and hence functions.) Each "longhand" algebraic statement expresses a special sort of proportional equivalence of a ratio of quantities to a ratio of numbers. For

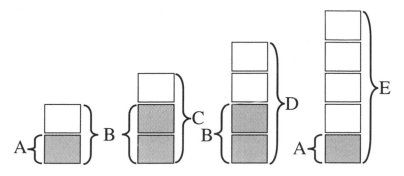

FIG. 14.3. Comparison of fractions, taking account of units.

example the expression, $A = \frac{1}{2}B$ expresses the proportion, $A{:}B = 1{:}2$. Algebra thus provides a means for expressing the interrelations of number and quantity.

It is commonly held that algebra instruction should begin in early adolescence after students have studied fractions. Some would argue that algebra should be postponed until students had mastered arithmetic. I am distinguishing here between arithmetic and algebra according to the psychological criterion of whether there is extensive manipulation of variables in problem solving. According to this reasoning, one works with unknowns in arithmetic, but variables are not symbolically manipulated to a great extent (cf. Vergnaud, chapter 13, this volume). But studies conducted in the former Soviet Union (Davydov, 1991) have provided compelling evidence that students in early grades at school can meaningfully use algebra provided they are oriented in how to represent physical quantities through letters. In short, there are good reasons for placing fractions, ratios, and proportions in an algebraic context at a much earlier point. When letters are used to refer to physical magnitudes, as we suggest here, the longhand, algebraic description is clearer than the shorthand version. Algebraic notation potentially may help establish clear links between fractions, ratios, proportions, functtions, and other concepts that appear otherwise unrelated in traditional instructtion on fractions.

DIDACTIC SUGGESTIONS

The analysis to this point suggests two potential resources students can draw on when learning about fractions. Students bring with them perceptual judgmental skills regarding ratios of quantities. And they have considerable experience with integer arithmetic. Now let us consider some ideas regarding the teaching of fractions that could make use of this knowledge.

Eudoxus' Conception of Proportion

Euclidean mathematics offers itself as a useful point of departure because the Greeks of antiquity had not yet invented fractions, but they were able to handle ratios and proportions through integer operations on quantities. This case may provide insights for instruction regarding fractions, because students acquire intuitive knowledge regarding ratio and proportion before they become familiar with fractions.

Mathematicians of ancient Greece adopted a "constructive" approach to problem solving—for them, a problem was solved when the solution was demonstrated geometrically. Such proofs rely upon actions on physical quantities rather than the manipulation of formal symbols. Number was conceptualized in terms of line segments. This (con)fusion between number and quantity enables properties of numbers to be explored through operations on line segments; in the process, line segments are imbued with arithmetical meaning.

The definition of proportion attributed to Eudoxus, found in Book V of Euclid's *Elements,* has been translated as follows (Heath, 1956, p. 114):

> Magnitudes are said to be *in the same ratio,* the first to the second and the third to the fourth, when, if any equimultiples whatever of the second and fourth, the former equimultiples alike exceed, are alike equal to, or alike fall short of, the latter equimultiples respectively taken in corresponding order.

In modern notation, this is tantamount to asserting that:

Given the line segments A, B, C, D, $A:B = C:D$ is true if and only if, for any positive integers m and n, one of the three following conditions holds:

1. $mA > nB$ and $mC > nD$
2. $mA = nB$ and $mC = nD$
3. $mA < nB$ and $mC < nD$

$A:B \neq C:D$ if there exist positive integers m and n such that any of the following conditions holds:

4. $mA > nB$ and $mC < nD$
5. $mA < nB$ and $mC > nD$
6. $mA = nB$ and $mC < nD$
7. $mA = nB$ and $mC > nD$
8. $mA > nB$ and $mC = nD$
9. $mA < nB$ and $mC = nD$

Figure 14.4 shows how the definition is embodied as a task. The goal is to decide whether $A:B = C:D$.

Figure 14.5 shows the result of multiplying the first segment of each ratio by 3 and the second segment by 2. Think about it for a moment. What can be concluded from the results shown in Fig. 14.5? Is $A:B$ equivalent to $C:D$?

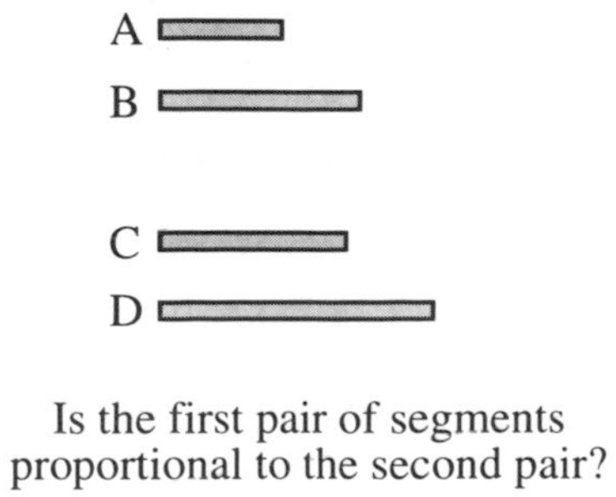

A ▭

B ▭

C ▭

D ▭

FIG. 14.4. Embodiment in a task of the Eudoxean conception of fractions.

Is the first pair of segments proportional to the second pair?

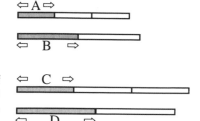

FIG. 14.5. Exploration of whether *A:B* = *C:D* through multiplication of segments. What can be inferred?

The result conclusively demonstrates that *A:B* is not equivalent to *C:D* (see condition 5). If the ratios had been equivalent, the same effects should have been observed in each case. This did not happen: 3 *A*'s fell short of 2 *B*'s, whereas 3 *C*'s surpassed 2 *D*'s.

The Eudoxian definition of proportion provides a test of whether one ratio of segments, *A:B*, is equivalent to another ratio, *C:D*, by "multiplying" (*n*-folding) the antecedents and consequents by *m* and *n*, respectively, and comparing the results. The test results are not always conclusive. Two conditions, 1 and 3, do not allow one to conclude that the ratios are proportional, but only that they have *not* been shown to be nonproportional. Condition 2 alone allows one to conclude that the ratios are proportional. Conditions 4–9 conclusively demonstrate that the ratios are not proportional.

The historical importance of this definition lies in the fact that it allowed Greek mathematicians of antiquity to represent ratios of incommensurable quantities, that is, quantities that have no common measure, such as the ratio of the diagonal to the side of a square. Such ratios were known to exist but were inexpressible as numbers, which for ancient Greeks were restricted to positive integers.

The importance of Eudoxus's definition for the present discussion lies elsewhere. The definition places ratio and proportion squarely in the context of perceptual judgment. This is precisely the context in which children begin to develop the concepts of ratio and proportion, as suggested by studies of psychological development mentioned earlier (see also Piaget, Inhelder, & Szeminska, 1960; van den Brink & Streefland, 1979). The definition specifies actions students can actually carry out on quantities (*n*-folding). They can then judge for themselves what conditions hold, by visually comparing the lengths of the resultant segments.

It is noteworthy that the Eudoxian approach expressly involves integer operations on physical quantities. As the preceding analysis suggests, this appears to be how children originally understand multiplication and division (before they understand integer operations on integers).

Algebraic Relations in Eudoxian Proportion

Labeling the results of the preceding example can lead to some important insights. The first pair of multiplications shows that $3A < 2B$. The second pair establishes that $3C > 2D$. The results can be rewritten as $A:B < 2:3$ and $C:D > 2:3$, respectively. These results can be joined as $A:B < 2:3 < C:D$. This means that the ratio 2:3 falls between the ratio $A:B$ and the ratio $C:D$. So we have learned much more from the results than the mere fact that the ratios are not equivalent. We know a ratio that falls between them (and conversely, we can only prove them nonequivalent by finding multipliers that yield such a ratio).

Because only two ratios are necessary to make a proportion, we can eliminate one of the ratios of quantities. The Eudoxian task is now redefined as the problem of discovering what ratio of integers corresponds to a given ratio of quantities (Fig. 14.6). Each time we carry out scalar multiplications on the line segments, we obtain more information regarding the "correct" ratio. By cleverly choosing the multipliers we should be able to move closer and closer to a correct answer.

In Fig. 14.6, the results of each multiplication are equal in length (we are ignoring for the moment the practical problems of visually deciding whether segments do or do not have the same length). When this occurs the information provided constitutes not an inequality but rather an equation ($5A = 3B$, in the example). In such a case, we can infer the correct or true numerical ratio corresponding to $A:B$. The ratio of quantities, $A:B$, corresponds to the numerical ratio, 3:5, or any equivalent ratio such as 6:10 or 1.5:2.5.

In the modified Euxdoxian task, with one ratio of quantities and one ratio of integers, there are three possible conclusions based on three possible outcomes of any trial:

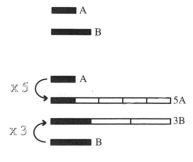

Problem: What is the ratio of A to B ?

FIG. 14.6. Inference of the ratio $A:B$ through equality of multiplied segments.

Solution: 5A = 3B therefore A : B = 3 : 5

1. $mA = nB$ implying $A{:}B = n{:}m$
2. $mA < nB$ implying $A{:}B < n{:}m$
3. $mA > nB$ implying $A{:}B > n{:}m$

Condition 1 is the only one that clearly informs us about the numerical ratio between A and B. The remaining two conditions merely allow one to conclude that the correct ratio is less than or greater than the tested ratio. In Fig. 14.6 condition 1 is satisfied. One can correctly conclude that the proportion $A{:}B = 3{:}5$ is true. It follows that $A/B = {}^3/_5$ and $A = {}^3/_5 B$. So the modified Euclidean test of proportionality is indeed related to fractions.

But here we must tread with caution. Notation involving fractions only makes sense to those already familiar with it. We cannot presume that students would draw the appropriate conclusion from observing the results in Fig. 14.6. For that matter, they are not likely to conclude even that $A{:}B = 3{:}5$. The present analysis, directed to mathematics educators, presumes a familiarity with certain ideas and notation. Students are likely to have their own views on how to explain and interpret situations such as that depicted in Fig. 14.6. In describing the task, they may use concepts entirely different from those of mathematicians or mathematics educators. So what to the experienced mathematics educator looks like a "simple demonstration" may appear to students as a perplexing situation that calls for considerable reflection.

This is not necessarily bad. Overcoming perplexity may be any important part of acquiring new concepts (Hatano & Inagaki, 1992). Besides, students are likely to learn little from tasks they immediately understand. Nevertheless, we should be careful not to appraise tasks simply according to the degree of perplexity they generate in students. Notation does not necessarily become intelligible as students see it again and again. What evidence can students encounter, in the tasks themselves or in ensuing discussions, for making sense of the notation? Where can students borrow meaning from situations they already understand? Where are ruptures or breaks in continuity being introduced?

As a first step in dealing with the problem of making formal notation intelligible, we should note that the present approach is based on the idea that there are important parallels between physical actions and mathematical operations. As we noted earlier, the mathematical operation of multiplying by an integer n is like the physical action of taking some object n times (as reflected in the use of the word "times" to describe multiplication). Division by an integer m is like taking an mth part of some object. These parallels can and should be made explicit to students in order to make sense of hypotheses expressed mathematically.

Mathematical operations can be represented in notation either implicitly or explicitly. Multiplication of the quantity A by 3 can be expressed either as $A \times 3$ or as $3A$. Although these expressions ae mathematically equivalent, there are important differences between them. The explicit form, $A \times 3$, is more appropriate for highlighting the tie between the mathematical operation (multiplication) and the physical action (n-folding, i.e., taking n of some quantity). It represents, better than the implicit form, $3A$, an action that has not yet been undertaken. This can be easily appreciated by simply examining the forms, $A \times 3$ and $3A$. "$A \times 3$" conveys the idea of a multiplication that has not yet been carried out; it is likely to represent to students a "problem," an operation to be carried out in the future. On the other hand, "$3A$" conveys the idea of a measure; it may better represent the result of multiplication rather than the operation itself. Thus we could say that $A \times 3$ yields $3A$, but not the converse. The distinction between instances "before" and "after" an operation is technically irrelevant in mathematics but psychologically important.

Discovering Fractions in a Eudoxian setting

Integer Multiplication and Common Multiples.   A hypothesis is a prediction about what will be observed under certain conditions. What is a hypothesis for the modified Eudoxian task? How can it be expressed in notation?

The modified Eudoxian task challenges one to find a numerical ratio that corresponds to a ratio of segments given in visual form. To be more precise, the task entails a search for a "common product" or "common multiple" of two line segments. In natural language, a hypothesis might be represented as follows: "[I believe that] if one multiplies A by 3 and B by 2, then the resulting segments will be the same length."

The same hypothesis can be expressed mathematically by the following equation:

$$A \times 3 = B \times 2?$$

The hypothesis is tested by carrying out the operations on each side of the equation and observing the results. We saw in the example that $A \times 3$ yields $3A$; $B \times 2$ yields $2B$. The inequality $3A < 2B$, which describes the fact that the line segment $3A$ is shorter than the line segment $2B$, informs us that the hypothesis is incorrect.

A similar analysis can be made of the correct hypothesis:

$$A \times 5 = B \times 3?$$

The hypothesis was tested by multiplying segment A by 5, multiplying segment B by 3, and comparing the resultant segments, $5A$ and $3B$. Because $5A$ was found to have the same length as $3B$, the conclusion is that $5A = 3B$ and, by substitution, $A \times 5 = B \times 3$. In other words, the hypothesis has been confirmed by experimental test.

The following steps show how the diverse notation might be linked to the testing of the hypothesis:

$A \times 5 = B \times 3?$ The hypothesis raised by the student. It can be read as a question: "If I multiply A by 5 and B by 3, will they yield equal results?

$A \times 5 = 5A$	The operation is carried out, yielding the first product segment $5A$.
$B \times 3 = 3B$	The second operation is carried out, yielding segment $3B$.
$5A = 3B?$	By substitution, the original hypothesis now becomes: "Is $5A$ equal to $3B$?"
$5A = 3B$	The segments are experimentally found to have the same length; the variation of the original hypothesis is confirmed.
$A \times 5 = B \times 3$	Therefore the original hypothesis is confirmed.

Understanding the task requires recognizing how a ratio of numbers can compensate for a ratio of quantities. The numerical ratio should correspond to the reciprocal of the ratio of quantities.

Although a correct answer entails numbers, there is no way to solve the task straight away by doing calculations (as there would be if A were broken into 3 units and B into 5 units of the same size). Because the segments have not been broken up into sets of equal units, it is impossible to "count" the length of the segments and perform a calculation on the measured lengths. Some educators would undoubtedly complain that leaving the segments unmeasured in "unfair." They may say: "Shouldn't there be a direct way to *compute* the answer? No one will solve such a problem on the first try." But this is precisely the point. By leaving the numerical ratio of the segments implicit, the students are forced to reflect upon the relative magnitude of the segments (i.e., the ratio of quantities) in order to discover a solution to the task. No amount of counting, matching, or calculating can by itself produce a correct answer. Instead, students must engage themselves in hypothesis testing until they gain an understanding of how the pair of operators chosen plays a role, together with the physical magnitudes, in producing the results.

Integer Division and Unit Fractions.   We saw above that a hypothesis such as $A \times m = B \times n?$ addresses the proportion $A{:}B = n{:}m$ from the perspective of a common product. Conversely, a hypothesis of the form $A \div n = B \div m?$ addresses the proportion from the point of view of a common factor or "common measure" (Fig. 14.7). This task relies upon the operation of division rather than multiplication. Even more importantly, it introduces notation for fractions both as operators and as measures—the results of operation by fractions.

There are two general ways of expressing a hypothesis for the present task in natural language:

1. If I divide A by some integer n, and divide B by another integer m, the resulting segments will be equal in length.
2. If I take one nth of A and one mth of B, the segments taken will be equal in length.

Find a common factor for A and B

Problem: Find integers n, m such that $A \div n = B \div m$

Hypothesis to test: $A \div 3 = B \div 5$?

$$\text{or: } A \times \frac{1}{3} = B \times \frac{1}{5} \ ?$$

Algebraic result: $\dfrac{A}{3} = \dfrac{B}{5}$

$$\text{or: } \frac{1}{3}A = \frac{1}{5}B$$

Geometric result:

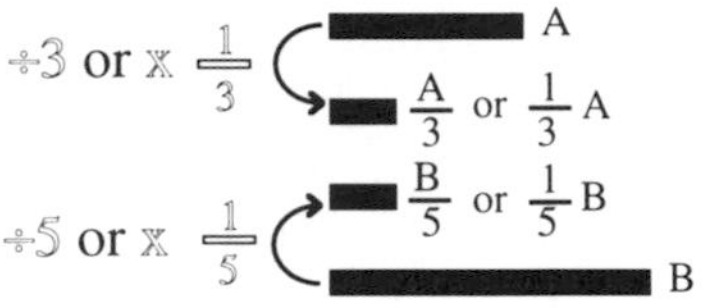

FIG. 14.7. Inference of the ratio *A:B* through equality of divided segments.

These sentences correspond respectively to the operations of division by an integer and multiplication by a unit fraction. They happen to be different ways of describing the same relationships.

It is likely that students do not view "× ¹/₃" as equivalent to "taking one-third" or "dividing by 3." The common measure task may provide a good context for engaging students in discussion about the meaning of such diverse expressions. We need empirical research in order to understand what sense students make of these expressions and how they relate them to actions upon quantities.

A preliminary investigation (Carraher, Heim, & Schliemann, 1994; Heim, Butto, & Carraher, 1993) showed that, when working with concrete materials, some sixth-grade students were inclined to confuse "division by *n*" with "dividing into *n* pieces." The division of a bar of chocolate by 3, for example, is understood by some students as cutting it into 3 pieces. Even when the interviewer drew attention to the written operation ÷ 3, some students maintained that the amount of chocolate was the same as it was before the division. Such observations suggest that the belief that "dividing makes smaller" may be called on or not depending on the context.

It would be foolish to maintain that all mathematical expressions are "really" about actions on physical objects. A statement such as ¹/₄A = ¹/₃B can also be understood as a description of relations. In the present model this can be read as "one-fifth of *A* is equal to one-third of *B*." Such an interpretation lacks explicit reference to actions on quantities. It is different from an action interpretation without being incompatible with it. "One-fifth of *A*" can be legitimately understood as shorthand for the expression "what you get when you divide *A* by 5." In a sense the action interpretation and relational interpretation complement each other.

These ideas do not exhaust how equations and inequalities can be interpreted. There may be other ways of conceptualizing the expressions within the model at hand, and empirical studies with human subjects may be the best guide to determine this. In a community of professional mathematicians there may be a great amount of diversity in interpreting such expressions (Otte, 1993). Some, no doubt, will do so without making any reference to physical objects.

A Fraction as the Result of Multiplication and Division.   Another way of approaching the relation between quantities is to consider what pair of integer operations would transform one quantity into the other. There are essentially two ways, namely, (a) through addition/subtraction, and (b) through multiplication/division. The latter case provides us with very special conditions for learning about fractions.

If the quantities A and B stand in the numerical ratio $n{:}m$ then A can be transformed into B by multiplying it by m and dividing the result by n (Fig. 14.8). The hypothesis in this problem can be written in two different ways:

$$B = (A \times 5) \div 3? \qquad \text{or} \qquad B = A \times {}^3\!/_5$$

A skeptic might be inclined to argue that the latter expression would be meaningless to students who do not already understand what a fractional operator is. There is some truth to this claim. Students certainly cannot be expected to understand at first glance what the expression $A \times {}^3\!/_5$ means. But this is like arguing that parents should not talk to their infant until it has learned what the words mean. The real issue is not whether the learner understands the expressions in the beginning but rather whether, over time, contexts provide support for the learner to come to understand what the expressions mean. What sort of

Problem: Operate on A so that the result has
the same magnitude as B

Hypothesis to test: $B = (A \times 5) \div 3$?

or: $B = \dfrac{5}{3}A$?

Algebraic result: $B = \dfrac{5A}{3}$

or: $B = \dfrac{5}{3}A$

Geometric result:

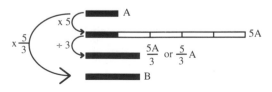

FIG. 14.8. Inference of the ratio *A:B* through combined multiplication and division of segment *A*.

feedback in the multiplication–division tasks could be made use of by students over a series of trials?

Consider first the effects of the integer operations. It should become clear over a series of trials that the multiplier makes the operand segment "grow," and the larger the multiplier, the greater the growth. The integer divisor makes the operand segment "shrink," and the larger the divisor, the more it induces shrinking. When the multiplier and divisor are equal, they nullify each other. In this case they are inverse operations. The relative size of the multiplier and divisor determines the net effect. This is another way of saying that the ratio of the multiplier to the divisor determines the net outcome. These ideas stand in harmony with students' intuitive beliefs that "multiplying makes bigger" and "dividing makes smaller." Let us now look at the case of multiplication by a fraction.

In multiplication by a fraction, the numerator behaves precisely as an integer multiplier. The denominator behaves exactly as an integer divisor. The numerator and denominator act in opposition, exactly as an integer multiplier and divisor do. When the numerator has the same value as the denominator, the effect of one agent is canceled by the effect of the other. The case corresponds to that of multiplying and dividing by the same integer. Multiplication by a fraction of the form n/n is an identity operation; it is just like multiplying by the number 1. A fraction-operator can be thought of as a succinct way of doing multiplication and division (Braunfeld & Wolfe, 1966; Dienes, 1967; Dörfler, 1988; Freudenthal, 1983; Griesel, 1970; Weckesser, 1970).

Although a fraction can derive considerable meaning from multiplication and division, there are still substantial adjustments to be made in students' thinking. Formerly, multiplication by (natural) numbers always led to increase. Now, in the case of fractions the student must consider the net effect of the numerator and the denominator to predict the direction of the outcome. With practice, students should come to see that proper fractions result in decrease and improper fractions result in increase (as throughout this chapter, only positive numbers are being considered).

Even greater adjustments in thinking must be made to come to understand the order of fractions. Why does multiplying by $3/5$ produce a result less than that of multiplying by $2/3$? What fractions will produce results between these values? The multiplication and division of fractions by fractions (e.g., what is $1/3$ divided by $2/5$?) likewise require considerable adjustment.

Links to Computational Tasks.   Let us look now at some ideas about how the preceding three tasks might be related to the sort of ratio and proportion problems typically given in schools. Consider the example in Fig. 14.9. The first thing to note is that one can estimate the fraction of income paid in taxes by examining the relative magnitudes of the two line segments without making any numerical calculations at all. Because the issue here involves the ratio of the segments, the length of each segment, taken alone, must be considered irrelevant.

 gross income

taxes paid

1. If the first line segment represents Maria's yearly salary as director of research, and the second represents the amount of taxes she paid, what fraction (or percent) of her income goes to taxes?

FIG. 14.9. Relation to typical school tasks.

2. If Maria's yearly salary is $45000, how much does she pay in taxes?

If multiple instances of the two line segments are available, students can do multiplications—actually, *n*-folding—"by hand" until they have found a common multiple. This is only part of the solution. Remember, the common multiple produces two integers. However, the problem asks for the fraction or percent of income that goes to taxes.

As students do their *n*-folding, the context of the problem will naturally be used in describing what they see. Students may note, for example, that the income in 2 months is approximately equal to the taxes paid over 5 months. In another context, mathematically similar results may lead to what appear to be very different descriptions. For example, in a problem regarding sales of computers, students may be led to the conclusion that 2 months' sales of IBM PCs correspond to 5 months' sales of MacIntosh computers. Or 2 months of rain in Manaus, Brazil, corresponds to 5 months of rain in Boston.

There are advantages in directing discussion toward issues that crop up along the way to the solution of the problem. Once students have found a solution by means of common multiples, one can ask, for example, whether there will be other common multiples. What about near misses? How can one generally express the relationship between Maria's taxes and her income? Are there other means of solving the problem (e.g., through weighing)?

With a straightedge and compass it is possible to break up the line segments into equal units. This corresponds to the common factor method. Students can test hypotheses about the ratio of the quantities by repeatedly testing hypotheses on instances of the segments. What degree of precision is there in such cases? On a computerized version of the common factor task, there are no limits to precision because algebraic feedback is never ambiguous. This is a topic worthy of discussion.

The multiplication–division method can also be used. Results are likely to be more accurate if multiplication precedes division. Even so, results should be close regardless of the order shown. Do the three methods discussed in this chapter (common product, common factor, multiplication–division) produce similar results? Are they based on the same ratio? If there are differences, which are more likely to be accurate? Do the algebraic statements that correspond to each method mean the same thing? For example, does "5 × Taxes = 2 ×

Income" mean the same as "Taxes = Income × $^2/_5$"? Are there in principle, or in practical reality, pairs of line segments for which there are no clear-cut solutions—for example, for which there are no common multiples, no common factors, no pair of integers that makes one magnitude become equal to the other? What are the implications of the conclusions students will draw? What are the relations to the concept of irrational number?

Once students are satisfied that they know the ratio of the line segments, it is possible to determine the unknown value, in this case, of the segment referring to the taxes Maria paid. Hopefully, when students have looked at the relationships from many perspectives, as we have suggested here, they will find the computational side of fractions easier to understand. Another way to approach the problem is to measure the lengths with a ruler and to engage students in discussions once they have obtained their measurements. It may be interesting to suggest using different types of rulers (e.g., in inches and centimeters) and then have students reflect about how the choice of standard may or may not affect the answer to the problem.

Some Questionable Premises Regarding Fractions.   The problem just given entails a part–whole relationship, because taxes are part of one's gross income. As we saw, this type of relationship can be captured in a two-line-segment model. It can also be represented in the classic pie format (Fig. 14.10).

But we cannot represent common multiples, common products, or multiplication–division in a pie representation. Imagine that the ratio of taxes to gross income is 2:5. If we take five instances of the taxes (5 gray slices) and two instances of the gross income (2 whole pies), there is no way to know through visual inspection that these quantities are equal. So we must be told the relation between taxes and income. The problem then reduces to a computational exercise. This is one disadvantage of pie models for fractions.

But there is an even more serious limitation to the pie model, namely, that it cannot depict ratios that are not conceptually part–whole. Consider, for example, the problem of comparing the populations of two countries, for example, Brazil and the United States. A comparison of appropriate line segments permits us to see that Brazil's population is about $^2/_3$ that of the United States. Once we have a

FIG. 14.10. Pie-chart representation of a part–whole relationship.

gross income

notion of the ratio between the two quantities, we can attempt to use it for answering further questions. By what fraction (or percent) would Brazil's population have to increase to equal that of the United States (presuming that the population in the United States remains fixed)? If the population in Brazil doubles in 30 years, by what fraction would the population of the United States have to increase in order to then equal that of Brazil? But this information cannot sensibly be shown in a pie chart. All ratio and proportion problems can be sensibly represented through fractions, but not all ratio and proportions problems can be adequately depicted in pie-chart models of fractions.

The model discussed in the present chapter begins by drawing the students' attention to a relation between two segments, A and B. The quantities could be identified as $1A$ and $1B$, so in the beginning one does work with "units" in the sense of measures assigned the value 1. Fractions first appear as operators that act upon unit segments. These operations produce other measures such as $3B$, $^3/_4A$, $2^3/_5C$. These fractional results can become the operands for subsequent operations. When this occurs students can begin to reflect about what it means to multiply a fractional measure by a fraction. Hopefully such ideas will some day make sense to the majority of students. I believe that this understanding depends in the beginning on students' success in associating mathematical operations with actions on quantities. With time, the mathematical operations may become fairly autonomous of such translations and references to quantity. But I suspect that mental representations of quantities will continue to play an important role in advanced mathematical thinking.

CONCLUDING REMARKS

In order to understand what fractions are, as psychological concepts, we must try to understand how they relate to what students already know. Here we looked at two sources of knowledge that students can draw on in learning about fractions: (a) understanding of ratio and proportion, and (b) knowledge of integer arithmetic.

Investigations of ratio and proportion paint an apparently contradictory picture of students' abilities. Studies in the area of mathematics education (e.g., Hart, 1984) seem to suggest that the greater part of students in the 11 to 15 years age range have difficulty with ratio and proportion. Yet psychological studies show that children develop rudimentary skills in ratio and proportion as early as 6 years old. It is likely that ratio and proportion understanding begin very early but take many years to fully develop. But, more importantly, children seem to grasp ideas about ratios of quantity long before they work with numerical ratios. A fully developed understanding of ratio and proportion, on which the concept of fraction must rest, entails being able to work with both sorts of ratios and their interrelationships. Traditional notation used in instruction about fractions is incomplete and unsatisfactory for bringing out these interrelationships. A fractional numeral such as $^2/_3$ embodies a ratio of numbers but says nothing about a ratio of quantities. Fractional numerals can be understood as shorthand for more general descriptions regarding relations between two quantities. Equations are better suited than fractional numerals for describing the interpenetration of ratios of numbers and ratios of quantity. Equations are special forms of notation that probably do not map directly onto students' natural language descriptions of relations.

One could in principle introduce equations into standard classroom fractions through tasks involving pizzas and cakes, but there are reasons for looking for inspiration elsewhere. To aid students in moving away from analyses based on cardinal number, continuous quantities have advantages over sets of units. Furthermore, comparisons based on length offer advantages over those based on area, because in the former case the students can judge for themselves whether one quantity is equal to the other. This characteristic is important if we want students to use their perceptual judgmental skills in fractions tasks.

An ancient Greek definition of proportion provides a useful context for learning about fractions.[1] Eudoxus' definition of proportion is based on equivalences between ratios of quantities and ratios of numbers. It constitutes an operational definition, a test, about how one can determine whether two ratios of quantities are equal. The test consists in acting on the quantities and observing the outcomes of one's actions.

A modification was proposed in Eudoxus' definition. The modified version provides a means of determining what numerical ratio corresponds to the ratio of two line segments. Three tasks were suggested for discovering ratios. The "common multiples" task is based on the search for a common product segment of the original two segments. The task is solved when the learner chooses integer multipliers that produce equal product segments. This occurs only if the multipliers chosen correspond to the reciprocal of the original ratio of quantities.

The "common measure" or "common factor" task approaches the proportion through division. One solves the task when the integer divisors chosen produce quotient segments of equal length. This occurs only when the divisors stand in direct proportion to the ratio of quantities. Because division by an integer is equivalent to multiplying by a unit fraction, the task provides an opportunity for introducing unit fractions. Mathematically, the "common factor" task is equiva-

---

[1]The approach may require expanding one's notions about mathematical operations. In ancient Greece, multiplication was not confined to numbers. One could multiply upon quantities (or measured quantities). I have encountered mathematics educators who strongly reject this idea, holding that "you can only multiply and divide numbers." This reaction makes little pedagogical sense given that young learners, as we noted earlier, begin to understand number operations in the context of actions on physical quantities.

lent to the "common multiple" task, although they are conceptually quite different.

A third task was described in which the learner attempts to make one quantity equal to the second through multiplication and division by integers. This multiplication–division task corresponds directly to the case of multiplying by a fraction. The numerator acts as an integer multiplier, and the denominator acts as an integer divisor. Although it is often argued that integer knowledge interferes with students' understanding of fractions as operators, the present task makes clear that a fraction can be defined through integer multiplication and division. In this way, previous knowledge can be used as a resource rather than a stumbling block for the development of new concepts. Seen in this light, fractions are much closer to the topics of multiplication and division than one might expect based on an examination of current textbooks.

A software environment based on the present approach, called *Lines of Thought* (Carraher, 1993, 1994), is now under development. The software comprises a dozen tasks and representational tools that students can use to discuss the relations discussed here, as well as many others. The guiding concern has been to create contexts in which students are challenged to think about how one problem can be analyzed and represented in diverse ways. Accordingly, none of the problems can be solved through computational routines, because computational routines rarely encourage reflection, but rather require thinking about the interrelations among numbers and quantities as well as their embodiment in algebraic statements. Further, in *Lines of Thought,* problems continue even after a student has found a correct answer. The tasks call for multiple solutions, including those that require integrating knowledge regarding diverse representations. There are several advantages to embodying the tasks in software, the most important being that students can produce data that may give rise to new ideas as well as to provide evidence for testing their evolving conjectures about relations among diverse objects.

The present tasks are suggested as learning contexts rather than demonstrations. Concepts as rich as fractions are not acquired immediately, because they require reorganization of prior knowledge. In order to improve instruction regarding fractions and related concepts, the field of mathematics education needs empirical research regarding how students make sense of the situations described in this chapter. By analyzing protocols of students as they attempt to solve problems, we can gain fresh insights into what is involved in teaching and learning about fractions.

ACKNOWLEDGMENTS

I am very grateful to Analucia Schliemann, Michael Otte, Gerard Vergnaud, and Brian Greer for their constructive comments on this chapter.

REFERENCES

Behr, M. J., Harel, G., Post, T., & Lesh, R. (1992). Rational number, ratio, and proportion. In D. A. Grouws (Ed.), *Handbook of research on mathematics teaching and learning* (pp. 296–333). New York: Macmillan.

Behr, M. J., Lesh, R., Post, T., & Silver, E. A. (1983). Rational number concepts. In R. Lesh & M. Landau (Eds.), *Acquisition of mathematics concepts and processes* (pp. 91–126). New York: Academic Press.

Bell, A., Fischbein, E., Greer, B. (1984). Choice of operation in verbal arithmetic problems: The effects of number size, problem structure, and context. *Educational Studies in Mathematics, 15,* 129–147.

Bell, A., Greer, B., Grimison, L., & Mangan, C. (1989). Children's performance on multiplicative word problems: Elements of a descriptive theory. *Journal for Research in Mathematics Education, 20,* 434–449.

Braunfeld, P., & Wolfe, M. (1966). Fractions for low achievers. *Arithmetic Teacher, 13,* 647–655.

Bruner, J. S., & Kenney, H. J. (1966). On relational concepts. In J. S. Bruner, R. R. Olver, & P. M. Greenfield (Eds.), *Studies in cognitive growth* (pp. 168–182). New York: Wiley.

Carraher, D. W. (1993). Lines of thought: A ratio and operator model of rational number. *Educational Studies in Mathematics, 25* (4), 281–305.

Carraher, D. W. (1994). *Lines of thought: Ratio, proportions and fractions.* Unpublished software. Recife, Brazil: Universidade Federal de Pernambuco.

Carraher, D. W., Heim, L., & Schliemann, A. (1994, August). From integers to fractions. In J. P. da Ponte & J. F. Matos (Eds.), *Proceedings of the Eighteenth Annual Conference for the Psychology of Mathematics Education* (Vol. 1, p. 34). Lisbon, Portugal.

Carraher, D. W., & Schliemann, A. D. (1991). Children's understandings of fractions as expressions of relative magnitude. In F. Furinghetti (Ed.), *Proceedings of the Fifteenth Annual Conference for the Psychology of Mathematics Education* (Vol. 2, pp. 184–191). Assisi, Italy.

Davydov, V. V. (Ed.). (1991). *Soviet studies in mathematics education* (Vol. 6). Reston, VA: National Council of Teachers of Mathematics.

Dienes, Z. T. (1967). *Fractions: An operational approach.* Paris: O.C.D.L.

Dörfler, W. (1988). Die Genese mathematischer Objekte und Operationen aus Handlungen als kognitive Konstruktion. *Schriftenreihe Didaktik der Mathematik: 16 kognitive Aspekte mathematischer Begriffsentwicklung* (pp. 55–125). Vienna: Hölder-Pichler-Tempsky.

Freudenthal, H. (1983). *Didactical phenomenology of mathematical structures.* Dordrecht: Reidel.

Fridman, L. M. (1991). Features of introducing the concept of concrete numbers in the primary grades. In V. V. Davydov (Ed.), *Soviet studies in mathematical education, Vol. 6: Psychological abilities of primary school children in learning mathematics* (pp. 148–180). Reston, VA: National Council of Teachers of Mathematics. (Original work published 1969)

Greer, B. (1990, July). *Learning to apply multiplication and division of decimals in solving problems.* Paper presented at the 22nd International Congress of Applied Psychology, Kyoto, Japan.

Griesel, H. (1970). Der wissenschaftliche Hintergrund der Bruchrechnung. *Mathematikunterricht, 16,* 5–29.

Hart, K. M. (1984). *Ratio: Children's strategies and errors.* Windsor, England: NFER-Nelson.

Hatano, G., & Inagaki, K. (1992). Desituating cognition through the construction of conceptual knowledge. In P. Light & G. Butterworth (Eds.), *Context and cognition: Ways of learning and knowing* (pp. 115–133). Hertfordshire, England: Harvester-Wheatsheaf.

Heath, T. L. (1956). *The thirteen books of Euclid's Elements* (Vol. 2, Books III–IX). New York: Dover.

Heim, L., Button, C., & Carraher, D. W. (1993, July). *Understanding the links between fractions, multiplication, and division.* Poster presented at the Twelfth Biennial Meeting of the International Society for the Study of Behavioural Development, Recife, Brazil.

Karplus, R., Karplus, E., Formisano, M., & Paulsen, A. (1979). Proportional reasoning and control of variables in seven countries. In J. Lochhead & J. Clements (Eds.), *Cognitive process instruction* (pp. 47–103). Philadelphia: Franklin Institute Press.

Kerslake, D. (1986). *Fractions: Children's strategies and errors.* Windsor, England: NFER-Nelson.

Kieren, T. E. (1976). On the mathematical, cognitive, and instructional foundations of rational numbers. In R. Lesh (Ed.), *Number and measurement* (pp. 101–144). Columbus, OH: ERIC/SMEAC.

Lovett, S. B., & Singer, J. A. (1991, April). *The development of children's understanding of probability: Perceptual and quantitative comparisons.* Paper presented at Biennial Meeting of the Society for Research in Child Development, Seattle.

Ohlsson, S. (1988). Mathematical meaning and applicational meaning in the semantics of fractions and related concepts. In J. Hiebert & M. Behr (Eds.), *Number concepts and operations in the middle grades* (pp. 53–92). Reston, VA: National Council of Teachers of Mathematics.

Otte, M. (1993). *O pensamento relacional: Equações.* Unpublished paper, Rio Claro, Brazil, Department of Mathematics, UNESP-Rio Claro.

Piaget, J., Inhelder, B., & Szeminska, A. (1960). *The child's conception of geometry.* New York: Harper.

Spinillo, A. G., & Bryant, P. E. (1991). Children's proportional judgment: The importance of half. *Child Development, 62,* 427–440.

Streefland, L. (1991). *Fractions in realistic mathematics education.* Dordrecht: Kluwer.

van den Brink, J., & Streefland, L. (1979). Young children (6–8)—Ratio and proportion. *Educational Studies in Mathematics, 10,* 403–420.

Vergnaud, G. (1990). La théorie des champs conceptuels [The theory of conceptual fields]. *Recherches en Didactique des Mathématiques, 10*(2–3), 133–170.

Weckesser, H. (1970). Die Einführung von Brüchen mit Hilfe von Modellen. *Mathematikunterricht, 16,* 30–77.

15

Imagery and the Development of Mathematical Reasoning

Patrick W. Thompson
San Diego State University

I feel somewhat constrained in attempting to focus on the topic of theories of mathematical learning, for I am unable to separate matters of learning from matters of reasoning. I suppose this is for two reasons. First, in talking about learning, we immediately bump into the question "Learn what?", and that brings us into the arena of concepts, methods, schemes, and so forth that learners always express within occasions of reasoning. Second, any cognitive theory I know of postulates that learning happens by way of action—some theories focus on habituation of overt behavior, some focus on assimilation and accommodation, others focus on compilation of propositions. These various theories' constructs all call for explicit attention to events that occasion learning; I tend to think of such events as necessarily entailing students' reasoning in the context of problems. So, in addressing the issue of mathematical learning I find it rewarding to orient the discussion toward the development of mathematical reasoning—purposeful inference, deduction, induction, and association in the areas of quantity and structure.

The idea I put forward is this: Mathematical reasoning at all levels is firmly grounded in imagery. I ought to say something about what I mean by imagery and why I take interest in imagery. This will take a while.

IMAGERY

By "image" I mean much more than a mental picture. Rather, I have in mind an image as being constituted by experiential fragments from kinesthesis, proprioception, smell, touch, taste, vision, or hearing. It seems essential also to include the possibility that images can entail fragments of past affective experiences, such as fearing, enjoying, or puzzling, and fragments of past cognitive experiences, such as judging, deciding, inferring, or imagining. In regard to this last item, imagining, Tom Kieren and Susan Pirie (Kieren, 1988; Kieren & Pirie, 1990; Kieren & Pirie, 1991; Pirie & Kieren, 1991; Pirie & Kieren, 1994) make it evident that the act of imagining can itself inform our images.

I admit that this meaning for the word *image* is too broad, but that is where my thinking is now, and it has afforded me the ability to hear much more in students' expressions of their reasoning than I used to. Nevertheless, this formulation does suggest that a person's actual images can be drawn from many sources, and hence individual's actual images are going to be highly idiosyncratic.

The roots of this overly broad characterization of image go back to Piaget's ideas of praxis (goal-directed action), operation, and scheme. I discuss this connection more fully in other papers (Thompson, 1985a, 1991, 1994a). For this chapter I focus on Piaget's idea of an image and its relationship to mental operations.

Piaget distinguished among three general types of images. The distinctions he drew were based on how dependent on the image were the actions of reasoning associated with it. The earliest images formed by children are an "internalized act of imitation . . . the motor response required to bring action to bear on an object . . . a *schema* of action" (Piaget, 1967, p. 294; italics in original). By this I take Piaget to have meant images associated with the creation of objects, whereby we internalize objects by acting upon them—we internalize them by internalizing our actions. His characterization was originally formulated to account for object permanence, but it also seems especially pertinent to the creation of mathematical objects.

A later kind of image people come to create is one having to do with primitive forms of thought experiments:

> In place of merely representing the object itself, independently of its transformations, this image expresses a phase or an outcome of the action performed on the object . . . . [but] the image cannot keep pace with the actions because, unlike operations, such actions are not coordinated one with the other. (Piaget, 1967, pp. 295–296)

It is advantageous to interpret Piaget's description broadly. If by actions we include ascription of meaning or significance, then we can speak of images as contributing to the building of understanding and comprehension, and we can speak of understandings-in-the-making as contributing to every more stable images.

A third kind of image people come to form is one that supports thought experiments, and supports reasoning by way of quantitative relationships. An image conjured up at a particular moment is shaped by the mental operations one performs, and operations applied within the image are tested for consistency with the scheme of which the operation is part. At the same time that the image is shaped by the operations, the operations are constrained by the image, for the image contains vestiges of having operated, and hence results of operating must be consistent with the transformations of the image if one is to avoid becoming confused.[1]

> [This is an image] that is dynamic and mobile in character . . . entirely concerned with the transformations of the object. . . . [The image] is no longer a necessary aid to thought, for the actions which it represents are henceforth independent of their physical realization and consist only of transformations grouped in free, transitive and reversible combination. . . . In short, the image is now no more than a symbol of an operation, an imitative symbol like its precursors, but one which is constantly outpaced by the dynamics of the transformations. Its sole function is now to express certain momentary states occurring in the course of such transformations by way of references or symbolic allusions. (Piaget, 1967, p. 296)

Kosslyn (1980) characterized images as data structures that result from the processes of perception. He, along with Piaget, dismissed the idea of images as mental pictures.

> These organizational processes result in our perceptions being structured into units corresponding to objects and properties of objects. It is these larger units that may be stored and later assembled into images that are experienced as quasi-pictorial, spatial entities resembling those evoked during perception itself. . . . It is erroneous to equate image representations with mental photographs, since this would overlook the fact that images are composed from highly processed perceptual encodings. (p. 19)

On the other hand, he took issue with Piaget's notions of early images emerging by way of internalized imitation.

> Even if it were clear what was meant [by imitation], this sort of treatment would seem closer to describing what is taking place than to explaining it. I do not want to deny the value of describing a phenomenon; rich descriptions facilitate theorizing, and there is no more astute observer than Piaget. But in my view explanations of cognitive phenomena should specify the ways in which functional capacities operate. Piaget and Inhelder's account is more on the level of intentionality, and hence is open to multiple interpretations at the level of the function of the brain. They do not specify how interiorized imitation operates, nor have they specified the format or content of the image. This level of discourse will never produce process adequacy, and hence seems of limited value. (p. 411)

---

[1]The Latin root of "confused" is *confundere*, to mix together. Thus, one way to think of being in a state of confusion is that we create inconsistent images while operating.

Kosslyn's objection seems to have three sources. First, his is a correspondence theory whereby images represent features of an objective reality. Piaget's theory assumes no correspondence; it takes objects as things constructed, not as things to be represented (von Glasersfeld, 1978). Second, Kosslyn's notion of image seems to be much more oriented to visualization than is Piaget's. Piaget was much more concerned with ensembles of action by which people assimilate objects than with visualizing an object in its absence. Third, I believe Kosslyn misunderstood Piaget by separating Piaget's notion of image from its theoretical context, it being one piece of the puzzle in describing the emergence of mental operations. Kosslyn focused on images as the *products* of acting. Piaget focused on images as the products of *acting*. So, to Kosslyn, images are data produced by perceptual processing. To Piaget, images are residues of coordinated actions, performed within a context with an intention, and only early images are concerned with physical objects. In regard to Kosslyn's criticism that Piaget's theory does not specify how the brain manages to create images, I suspect it is less severe than he thought. The strong computational metaphor within which Kosslyn frames his theory may not be as lasting as he thinks. In fact, the notion of imagery may be its undoing (Cobb, 1987).

Piaget's idea of image is remarkably consistent with Johnson's (1987) detailed argument that rationality arises from and is conditioned by the patterns of our bodily experience. Johnson took to task realist philosophy and cognitive science (which he together called "Objectivism") in his criticism of their attempts to capture meaning and understanding within a referential framework.

> Meanings, conceptual connections, inference patterns, and all other aspects of rationality are distinguished, according to Objectivism, by their universality and independence from the particularities of human embodiment. They are supposed to be that which is shared by all of us, that which transcends our various embodiments and allows us to partake of a common objective realm of meaning. The chief difference, then, between the Objectivist view of meaning and non-Objectivist "semantics of understanding" being proposed here can be summed up as follows: For the non-Objectivist, *meaning is always a matter of human understanding, which constitutes our experience of a common world that we can make some sense of. A theory of meaning is a theory of understanding. And understanding involves image schemata and their metaphorical projections, as well as propositions.* . . . . Grasping a meaning is an *event* of understanding. Meaning is not merely a fixed relation between sentences and objective reality, as Objectivism would have it. What we typically regard as fixed meanings are merely sedimented or stabilized structures that emerge as recurring patterns in our understanding. The idea that understanding is an event in which one has a world, or, more properly, a series of ongoing related meaning events in which one's world stands forth, has long been recognized on the Continent, especially in the work of Heidegger and Gadamer. But Anglo-American analytic philosophy has steadfastly resisted this orientation in favor of meaning as a fixed relation between words and the world. It has been mistakenly assumed that only a viewpoint that transcends human embodi-

ment, cultural embeddedness, imaginative understanding, and location within historically evolving traditions can guarantee the possibility of objectivity. (Johnson, 1987, pp. 174–175, italics in original)

Piaget maintained throughout his career that all knowledge originates in action, both bodily and imaginative (Piaget, 1950, 1968, 1971, 1976, 1980). Although Johnson's primary purpose was to give substance to this idea in the realms of everyday life, Piaget was primarily concerned with the origins of scientific and mathematical reasoning—reasoning that is oriented to our understandings of quantity and structure. For example, although Johnson focused on the idea of balance as an image schema emerging from senses of stability and their projection to images of symmetric forces (Johnson, 1987), it requires a nontrivial reconstruction to create an image of balance as involving countervailing twisting actions—where we imagine the twisting actions themselves in such a way that it occurs to us that we might somehow measure them. It seems to involve more than a metaphorical projection of balance as countervailing pushes to have an image of balance that entails the understanding that any of a class of weight-distance pairs on one side of a fulcrum can be balanced by any of a well-determined class of weight-distance pairs on the other side of a fulcrum.

The meaning of "image" developed here is only tangentially related to the idea of concept image as developed by Vinner (Tall & Vinner, 1981; Vinner, 1987, 1989, 1991, 1992; Vinner & Dreyfus, 1989). Vinner's idea of concept image focuses on the coalescence of mental pictures into categories corresponding to conventional mathematical vocabulary, whereas the notion of image I've attempted to develop focuses on the dynamics of mental operations. The two notions of image are not inconsistent; they merely have different foci.

Vinner's distinction between concept image and concept definition arose originally in the work of Vinner, Tall, and Dreyfus (Tall & Vinner, 1981; Vinner, 1991; Vinner & Dreyfus, 1989). In their usage, a concept definition is a customary or conventional linguistic formulation that demarcates the boundaries of a word's or phrase's application. On the other hand, a concept image comprises the visual representations, mental pictures, experiences and impressions evoked by the concept name.

In lay situations, people understand words through the imagery evoked when they hear them. They operate from the basis of imagery, not from the basis of conventional constraints adopted by a community. People understand a word technically through the logical relationships evoked by the word. They operate from the basis of conventional and formal constraints entailed within their understanding of the system within which the technical term occurs. Vinner, Tall, and Dreyfus arrived at the distinction between concept image and concept definition after puzzling over students' misuse and misapplication of mathematical terms like function, limit, tangent, and derivative. For example, if in a student's mathematical experience the word *tangent* has been used only to describe a

$$\text{{\Large\it function}} = \text{{\Large waveform}}$$

FIG. 15.1. A concept image of "function." Something written on the left is "equal to" something written on the right.

tangent to a circle, then it is quite reasonable for him to incorporate into his image of tangents the characteristic that the entire line lies to one side or the other of the curve, and that it intersects the curve only once (Vinner, 1991). Notice that this image of tangent—uniquely touching at one point—has nothing to do with the notion of a limit of secants. It is natural that a student who maintains this image of tangent is perplexed when trying to imagine a tangent to the graph of $f(x) = x^3$ at $(0,0)$, or a tangent to the graph of $g(x) = x$ at any point on its graph.

A predominant image evoked in students by the word *function* is of two written expressions separated by an equal sign (Fig. 15.1). We might think that only neophytes hold this image of function. I suspect it is far more prevalent than we acknowledge. An example illustrates my suspicion and at the same time illustrate how Tall, Vinner, and Dreyfus envision the influence of concept images over concept definitions.

My wife, Alba Thompson, teaches a course designed to be a transition from lower to upper division undergraduate mathematics. It focuses on problem solving and proof. Students are supposed to take it after calculus and linear algebra, but a fair portion of the class typically have taken at least one term of advanced calculus or modern algebra. In the context of studying mathematical induction she asked one student to put his work on the board in regard to deriving and proving a formula for the sum $Sn = 1^2 + 2^2 + \ldots + n^2$. The student wrote $f(x) = n(n + 1)(2n + 1)/6$. Not a single student thought there was anything wrong with this formulation. It turned out, after prolonged probing by Alba, that students accepted it because it fit their concept image of function, which I've presented in Fig. 15.2.

FIG. 15.2. Students' acceptance of an ill-formed function representation because it fit their concept image of function.

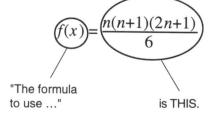

"The formula to use ..."

is THIS.

Why Imagery is Important

There are two aspects to imagery that I suspect have a significant influence on the development of mathematical reasoning. The first has to do with students' immediate understandings of the situations they encounter during schooling. The second has to do with more global aspects of their development of mental operations.

INFLUENCES OF IMMEDIATE IMAGERY

I am often in classrooms with children, either as an observer, interviewer, or teacher. Over the past 4 years I have become ever more aware of the difficulties students experience because of insufficient attention being given to their images of the settings in which problems ostensibly occur. Some examples might make this clear.

Restocking the Shelves

A seventh-grade teacher presented this problem to his class.

> A grocer buys Sara Lee cakes from his distributor in packages of 8 cakes per package. Each package costs $4.25. The grocer figures he needs 275 cakes for the next week. How much money should he plan on paying for cakes?

The teacher first reemphasized a theme he had made prominent through the year—that first they understand the situation. One student, Chris, said that he "didn't understand." The teacher, himself trying to understand Chris' difficulty, asked Chris to put himself in the grocer's position, and asked Chris "How will you figure how much it will cost you?" Chris' response: "They'll tell you when you walk out."

It seems Chris did put himself into the situation. But his image of the situation centered around his experience of shopping, where you get what you need, take it to a cashier, and the cashier rings up the amount you owe. The teacher, an ex-businessman, had a much different image in mind—an image of a person sitting at his desk trying to set up a budget for the coming week. The teacher's instructional objectives had to do with bringing out the issue of when it is reasonable to round a calculation up and when to round it down. He was not sensitive to the situation as Chris had constructed it, and the image Chris had made of the context made the situation non-problematic. He quite literally did not understand what the problem was about.

Fractions

A seventh-grade teacher used the problem presented in Fig. 15.3 in a unit on fractions. Students working this problem looked for patterns in number-pairs.

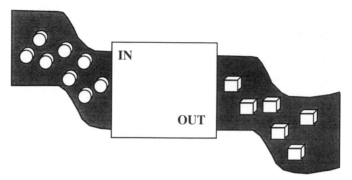

Here is a machine. Eight objects are going in and 6 packs are coming out.

FIG. 15.3. Fraction as operator represented by a machine. The text gives five other in-out pairs for this machine and asks students to complete a table with eight entries, each of which gives a number of pieces going in but does not give a number of pieces going out.

Their conversations were empty in regard to the machine or why the number-pairs were related in a natural way. Instead, students focused completely on filling-out the table as a type of "guess my rule" problem. It occurred to me that there was nothing about the machine that they *could* talk about, for there was nothing imaginative about it except that, as if by magic, things came out of it when other things came in.

I suggested to the teacher that he change the problem's setting and orientation slightly, as in Fig. 15.4.

Following these questions was a problem of filling in a table that was similar to the one given in the original text.

Students' discussions of this situation had a completely different content than their original discussions. Whereas originally they were wondering about what numbers to add, subtract, multiply or divide, in this case they talked initially about the machine (e.g., why would anyone want to turn chunks into packets) and they soon began talking about cutting up an amount of bologna into sevenths versus cutting up the same amount of bologna into eighths, and they ended up talking about turning one-seventh of the bologna into a number of eighths of the bologna. Other problematic matters that came into their discussion were whether or not the bologna on the right was the same stuff as the bologna on the left (that is, could you talk about "filling" a packet with a chunk, or did you need to "reshape" a packet into a chunk), and whether it mattered that there might be any bologna in the machine (and if so, was it the same amount as on either side). I should also point out that this problem was more difficult for many students, in that they experienced difficulties arising from lacunae in their understanding of

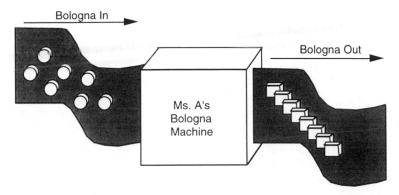

Ms. Allowishus has a machine that turns round chunks of bologna into rectangular packets. All round chunks are the same size and all packets are the same size.

The same amount of bologna comes out of the machine as goes into it. So, if 5 pounds of bologna goes into the machine, then 5 pounds of bologna comes out of it.

Eight packets come out of the machine when seven round chunks go into the machine.

1. Which contains more bologna, a round chunk or a packet? Explain.

2. How many packets does one round chunk make? Explain.

3. How many round chunks of bologna make up one packet? Explain.

4. How many packets will come out of the machine when 10 round chunks go into the machine? Explain.

FIG. 15.4. Revised machine problem.

fractions that they had not experienced in the original problem. One source of difficulty, I claim, is that their images of the situation entailed a severe constraint—the invariance of amount of bologna whether made of a number of chunks or a number of packets.

Someone might argue that it would be better had these difficulties been avoided—that it would be preferable to use the original setting. I would argue in response that the difficulties and issues that these students encountered are among those they will encounter when finding themselves in occasions where fractional reasoning would be appropriate, and that they should encounter occasions to experience these difficulties early in their learning of fractions. Otherwise we enhance the probability that children's school mathematics is useless in their everyday lives (Lave, 1988). The general point is that if students do not become engaged imagistically in ways that relate mathematical reasoning to principled experience, then we have little reason to believe that they will come to see their world outside of school in any way mathematical. On the other hand, we should not think that just any imagistic reasoning guarantees relevance.

GLOBAL INFLUENCES OF IMAGERY

Although immediate imagery always influences direction in a local space of possibilities, present in every moment of reasoning is a cumulative influence of imagery that orients our reasoning. One way this happens is during our uses of notation. Another way this happens is through the mental operations by which we constitute the situations in which we use the mathematics we know. Both aspects of imagery provide a large part of the background for our events of reasoning.

Uses of Notation

When a person applies mathematics skillfully, her uses of notation are largely nonproblematic. It is much like a skilled writer's use of written language; difficulties reside more in deciding what to write than in the writing itself. However, the expression of an idea in notation provides her an occasion to reflect on what she said, an occasion to consider if what she said was what she intended to say and if what she intended to say is what she said. To act in this way unthinkingly is common among practicing mathematicians and mathematical scientists.

Behind the dialectic between understanding and expression is an image, most often unarticulated and unconsciously acted, of what one does when reasoning mathematically. This image entails an orientation to negotiations with oneself about meaning, something that is outside the experience of most school students. The dialectic between understanding and expression just depicted is not the normal stuff of students' experiences in school mathematics, at least in the United States. Instead, the predominant image behind students' and teachers' notational actions seems to be more like "put the right stuff on the paper."

The robustness of the predominant image of acting mathematically—putting it right, on paper—is striking. I observed a senior mathematics major's demonstration lesson on the graphing of inequalities in two variables. The words point, pair, open sentence, and solution never appeared; his entire discussion was about numbers. I asked him where are these y's that are greater than $2x$-3. He waved his hand up and down the y-axis. I asked him, "Where are these x's so that $2x$-3 is less than y?" He waved his hand back and forth along the x-axis. I then asked, "So, if all of the y's are on the y-axis and all of the x's are along the x-axis, why did you draw a graph of $y = 2x$-3 and shade the portion above the graph?" He couldn't say. Now, the fact that this student didn't relate inequalities to open sentences, truth values, or solution sets is not pertinent to my present point. What is pertinent is that he did not feel that he had done anything improper, because his students quickly caught on to his procedure for graphing linear inequalities. From his perspective he taught a successful lesson even though it hadn't made any sense.

A related example comes from students' images of the activity of solving an equation. Their image of solving equations often is of activity that ends with something like "$x = 2$." So, when they end up with something like "$3 = 2$" or "$x = x$" they conclude without hesitation that they must have done something wrong.

These images of mathematical activity and successful teaching, and their concomitant uses of notation, are more like what Johnson addressed than what Piaget addressed. They have to do with normative patterns of activity and what they are supposed to produce, so in this regard one can say they are highly conditioned by social arrangements and interactions (Cobb & Yackel, 1991; Yackel, Cobb, Wood, Wheatley, & Merkel, 1990).

At the same time that images of mathematical activity are conditioned by social interactions, they are personal images that inform students' and teachers' activities. To change the social arrangements that are supported by actions emanating from these images, which thereby reinforce them further, it would seem that students and/or their teacher need to experience a different pattern of intellectual engagement surrounding their use of notation. In (Thompson, 1992), I attempted to design an instructional unit that would support the kind of notational dialectic outlined at the beginning of this section. I hoped that students' experience of a dialectic among intention, action, and expression would enrich their images of notation usage and their understanding of convention.

The unit was on decimal numeration, and it was for fourth-graders. They worked 7 days on it. At the center of the unit was a computer program that simulated base-ten blocks (see Fig. 15.5). Students represented numerical values by dragging copies of blocks into various parts of the screen (with a mouse). They could act on the display by moving blocks around or by "exploding" one block into ten of the next smaller kind or "imploding" ten blocks of one kind into one of the next larger. They implemented these actions on blocks by clicking on an appropriate digit in the value's expanded-notation representation and then clicking Carry or Borrow. Carry caused ten blocks to implode into one. Borrow caused one block to explode into ten.

Part of the instructional design was a continual orientation to the fact that students were free to devise blocks-based methods for addition and subtraction, with one constraint. They were required to devise notational methods by which they could reflect each action and its effect on the current state of their problem.

Instructional tasks and the program were designed to support students' back-and-forth movements between the things they were acting on and notational expressions of the effects of whatever they had done (Fig. 15.6). In fact, "back and forth" from situation to expression to situation was precisely the image of notational use I hoped they would form.

The results of this experiment are available in (Thompson, 1992). What I would like to highlight here is an observation mentioned only in passing in that article. Students at first were highly disoriented by having the freedom (and responsibility) to create their own uses of notation. They would have rather been told what to do, presumably because being told what to do would have fit their

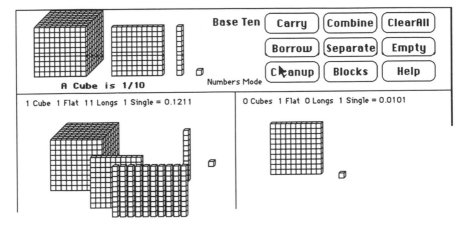

FIG. 15.5. Screen display of Blocks microworld. From Thompson (1992). Reprinted by permission.

image of learning mathematics in school. The students in the control group, who experienced the pattern of engagement illustrated in the left side of Fig. 15.6, remained disoriented by their notational freedom and responsibilities. Students in the experimental group, who experienced the pattern of engagement illustrated in the right side of Fig. 15.6, developed a predilection to speak imagistically about

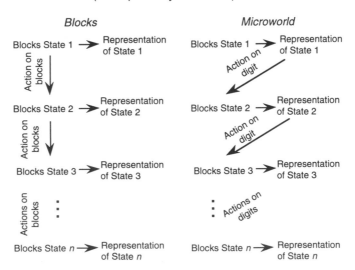

FIG. 15.6. Differences in students' engagement with notation when working with wooden base-ten blocks and with the computer program. From Thompson (1992). Reprinted by permission.

TABLE 15.1
Results for Item Used in Posttest[a]

Statement		Response	Blocks	Microworld
This is the RIGHT way to add		Yes	5	1
8276 and 4185. Other ways	8276	No	2	7
might give the same answer,	$+\ 4185$	Don't know	3	2
but they are not the right way:	12461			

[a]$n = 10$ in each group.
Note. From Thompson (1992). Reprinted by permission.

things happening with blocks *as they spoke about notational actions.* That is, the dialectic nature of their experience when acting notationally supported their synthesis of blocks and numerals as alternative notational systems for representing numerical value.

Table 15.1 repeats one item from the posttest given in (Thompson, 1992). Students who received instruction using wooden base-ten blocks appeared to retain a prescriptive image of notational method, whereas the children receiving instruction in the experimental setting were more open to the validity of alternative, creative uses of notation. An explicit orientation to having students build dialectical images of mathematical activity and its notational entailments seems to be a promising avenue for further investigation and development. The same approach can be taken, in principle, with secondary school and university mathematics.

Although this example focuses explicitly on representations of numerical operations and numerical value, the issue it addresses—teachers' and students' background images of what they are doing while engaged in notational activity— spans all levels of mathematics. For example, if students' image of multiplication is repeated addition, then it is understandable that multiplication of fractions is difficult. But, if their image of multiplication is "make copies of," then there is no built-in incoherence for multiplication of fractions. An image can easily be formed of, say, $3^{2}/_{5} \times 4^{5}/_{8}$, by first constructing something having value $4^{5}/_{8}$, making 3 copies of it, then making $^{2}/_{5}$ copy of it. I suspect this sort of image, if stressed from the outset even with whole numbers, would ameliorate common obstacles, such as "multiplication makes bigger" (Fischbein, Deri, Nello, & Marino, 1985; Greer, 1988, 1992).

Constituted Situations

The previous section focused on students' images of mathematical activity— what it feels like to be mathematically engaged and to use notation to create systematic expressions of that engagement. There is also a kind of imagery that is traditionally aligned with conceptual development. It has been referred to in the past as process-product duality (Gray & Tall, 1994; Sfard, 1989, 1991;

Thompson, 1985b), distinctions between procedure and concept (Hiebert & Lefevre, 1985), and distinctions between operations and figurations in relation to reflective abstraction (Bamberger & Schön, 1991; Dubinsky & Lewin, 1986; Rota, Sharp, & Sokolowski, 1988; Thompson, 1985a, 1991; von Glasersfeld, 1991).

It is in describing the development of images to support operational reasoning-in-context that the power of Piaget's notion of image emerges. In (Thompson, 1994a) I used Piaget's notion of image and mental operation, in support of my own theory of quantitative reasoning, to give a detailed account of one child's construction of speed as a rate. In (Thompson & Thompson, 1992) Alba Thompson and I summarize several years of research on the role of imagery in students' constructions of ratios and rates, as typified by their construction of the mental operations of speed and acceleration. The pertinent aspect of these reports is that they give operational detail to the development of "mathematical objects," and they highlight the important role played by imagery throughout that development. It is through imagery and the operations entailed within images that we constitute situations and act in them.

In many regards these accounts parallel Piaget's (1970) description of children's construction of speed. Children's initial image is of motion—something moving—and their awareness of displacement. They abstract from movement the image of distance traveled and duration of movement, but those images are uncoordinated, and the image of distance dominates in their constituted situations. Children's early image of speed as distance shows up in their inability to reason about completed motion in relation to duration—such as, at what speed must I travel to go 100 feet in 6 seconds? Later images of speed as quantified motion entail the coordinated images of the accrual of incremental distance and incremental time in relation to images of accumulated distance and accumulated time. Images of objects being accelerated entail an image of accumulated accruals of increments to incremental distance in relation to incremental time—the speed of the object "speeds up."

The latter images, accruals in relation to accumulations, are much like what has often been described as proportional reasoning (Hart, 1978; Kaput & West, 1994; Karplus, Pulos, & Stage, 1983; Lesh, Post, & Behr, 1988; Tourniaire & Pulos, 1985). In (Thompson & Thompson, 1992) we made the case that the kinds of images built up in understanding speed and accelerations are foundational for comprehending many areas classically thought of as proportional reasoning. In (Thompson, 1994b), I demonstrated how advanced mathematics students' impoverished images of rate obstructed their understanding of derivative, integral, and relationships between them.

My claim here is that without students having developed images such as these, images that entail both figurative and operative thought, students cannot constitute the situations that their visible mathematics is supposed to be about with sufficient richness to support their reasoning. When this happens they are reduced to forming figural associations between a teacher's notational actions and superficial characteristics of a problem statement's linguistic presentation. Such figural reasoning then orients students and teachers to patterns of activity, and hence images of mathematics, that I spoke of earlier as "get it right, on paper."

CONCLUSION

I have raised the matter of imagery as it relates to four areas of pedagogical and psychological concern. These are:

1. Teachers' and students' images of mathematical activity—the kinds of activities in which they expect to be engaged and the kinds of products these activities should end with;
2. Students' and teachers' background images of situations immediately under discussion frame their understandings of what is being discussed;
3. Students' and teachers' images of notational activity and what might transpire while they are engaged in it;
4. Coordinated images can consolidate in mental operations and can come to provide the conceptual substance by which students constitute situations.

I invite others to expand or alter this list, and to expand the discussion of imagery in mathematical reasoning.

ACKNOWLEDGMENTS

Research reported in this chapter was supported by National Science Foundation grants MDR 89-50311 and 90-96275, and by a grant of equipment from Apple Computer, Inc., Office of External Research. Any conclusions or recommendations stated here are those of the author and do not necessarily reflect official positions of NSF or Apple Computer.

REFERENCES

Bamberger, J., & Schön, D. A. (1991). Learning as reflective conversation with materials. In F. Steier (Ed.), *Research and reflexivity* (pp. 120–165). London: Sage.

Cobb, P. (1987). Information-processing psychology and mathematics education: A constructivist perspective. *Journal of Mathematical Behavior, 6*, 3–40.

Cobb, P., & Yackel, E. (1991). A constructivist approach to second grade mathematics. In E. von Glasersfeld (Ed.) *Radical constructivism in mathematics education* (pp. 157–176). Dordrecht: Kluwer.

Dubinsky, E., & Lewin, P. (1986). Reflective abstraction and mathematics education: The genetic decomposition of induction and compactness. *Journal of Mathematical Behavior, 5*(1), 55–92.

Fischbein, E., Deri, M., Nello, M. S., & Marino, M. S. (1985). The role of implicit models in solving verbal problems in multiplication and division. *Journal for Research in Mathematics Education*, 16, 3–17.

Gray, E. M., & Tall, D. O. (1994). Duality ambiguity, and flexibility: A "proceptual" view of simple arithmetic. *Journal for Research in Mathematics Education*, 25(2), 116–140.

Greer, B. (1988). Non-conservation of multiplication and division: Analysis of a symptom. *Journal of Mathematical Behavior*, 7, 281–298.

Greer, B. (1992). Multiplication and division as models of situations. In D. Grouws (Ed.), *Handbook of research on learning and teaching mathematics* (pp. 276–295). New York: Macmillan.

Hart, K. (1978). The understanding of ratios in secondary school. *Mathematics in School*, 7, 4–6.

Hiebert, J., & Lefevre, P. (1985). Conceptual and procedural knowledge in mathematics: An introductory analysis. In J. Hiebert (Ed.), *Conceptual and procedural knowledge: The case of mathematics* (pp. 3–20). Hillsdale, NJ: Lawrence Erlbaum Associates.

Johnson, M. (1987). *The body in the mind: The bodily basis of meaning, imagination, and reason*. Chicago, IL: University of Chicago Press.

Kaput, J. J., & West, M. M. (1994). Missing value proportional reasoning problems: Factors affecting informal reasoning patterns. In G. Harel & J. Confrey (Eds.), *The development of multiplicative reasoning in the learning of mathematics* (pp. 237–287). Albany, NY: SUNY Press.

Karplus, R., Pulos, S., & Stage, E. (1983). Early adolescents' proportional reasoning on 'rate' problems. *Educational Studies in Mathematics*, 14(3), 219–234.

Kieren, T. E. (1988). Personal knowledge of rational numbers: Its intuitive and formal development. In J. Hiebert & M. Behr (Eds.), *Number concepts and operations in the middle grades* (pp. 162–181). Reston, VA: National Council of Teachers of Mathematics.

Kieren, T. E., & Pirie, S. (1990, April). *A recursive theory for mathematical understanding: Some elements and implications*. Paper presented at the Annual Meeting of the American Educational Research Association, Boston, MA.

Kieren, T. E., & Pirie, S. (1991). Recursion and the mathematical experience. In L. P. Steffe (Ed.), *Epistemological foundations of mathematical experience* (pp. 78–101). New York: Springer-Verlag.

Kosslyn, S. M. (1980). *Image and mind*. Cambridge, MA: Harvard University Press.

Lave, J. (1988). *Cognition in practice*. Cambridge, England: Cambridge University Press.

Lesh, R., Post, T., & Behr, M. (1988). Proportional reasoning. In J. Hiebert & M. Behr (Eds.), *Number concepts and operations in the middle grades* (pp. 93–118). Reston, VA: National Council of Teachers of Mathematics.

Piaget, J. (1950). *The psychology of intelligence*. London: Routledge & Kegan-Paul.

Piaget, J. (1967). *The child's concept of space*. New York: W. W. Norton.

Piaget, J. (1968). *Six psychological studies*. New York: Vintage Books.

Piaget, J. (1970). *The child's conception of movement and speed*. New York: Basic Books.

Piaget, J. (1971). *Genetic epistemology*. New York: W. W. Norton.

Piaget, J. (1976). *The child & reality*. New York: Penguin Books.

Piaget, J. (1980). *Adaptation and intelligence*. Chicago: University of Chicago Press.

Pirie, S., & Kieren, T. E. (1991, April). *A dynamic theory of mathematical understanding: Some features and implications*. Paper presented at the Annual Meeting of the American Educational Research Association, Chicago, IL.

Pirie, S., & Kieren, T. E. (1994). Growth in mathematical understanding: How can we characterize it and how can we represent it? *Educational Studies in Mathematics*, 26(2–3), 165–190.

Rota, G.-C., Sharp, D. H., & Sokolowski, R. (1988). Syntax, semantics, and the problem of the identity of mathematical objects. *Philosophy of Science*, 55, 376–386.

Sfard, A. (1989). Transition from operational to structural conception: The notion of function revised. In G. Vergnaud, J. Rogalski, & M. Artigue (Eds.), *Proceedings of the 13th Annual*

Conference of the International Group for the Psychology of Mathematics Education Vol. 3 (pp. 151–158). Paris: G. R. Didactique, CNRS.

Sfard, A. (1991). On the dual nature of mathematical conceptions: Reflections on processes and objects as different sides of the same coin. *Educational Studies in Mathematics, 22*(1), 1–36.

Tall, D., & Vinner, S. (1981). Concept images and concept definitions in mathematics with particular reference to limits and continuity. *Educational Studies in Mathematics, 12,* 151–169.

Thompson, P. W. (1985a). Experience, problem solving, and learning mathematics: Considerations in developing mathematics curricula. In E. Silver (Ed.), *Teaching and learning mathematical problem solving: Multiple research perspectives* (pp. 189–243). Hillsdale, NJ: Lawrence Erlbaum Associates.

Thompson, P. W. (1985b). Understanding recursion: Process ≈ Object. In S. Damarin (Ed.), *Proceedings of the 7th Annual Meeting of the North American Group for the Psychology of Mathematics Education* (pp. 357–362). Columbus, OH: Ohio State University.

Thompson, P. W. (1991). To experience is to conceptualize: Discussions of epistemology and experience. In L. P. Steffe (Ed.), *Epistemological foundations of mathematical experience* (pp. 260–281). New York: Springer-Verlag.

Thompson, P. W. (1992). Notations, conventions, and constraints: Contributions to effective uses of concrete materials in elementary mathematics. *Journal for Research in Mathematics Education, 23*(2), 123–147.

Thompson, P. W. (1994a). The development of the concept of speed and its relationship to concepts of rate. In G. Harel & J. Confrey (Eds.), *The development of multiplicative reasoning in the learning of mathematics* (pp. 179–234). Albany, NY: SUNY Press.

Thompson, P. W. (1994b). Images of rate and operational understanding of the Fundamental Theorem of Calculus. *Educational Studies in Mathematics, 26*(2–3), 229–274.

Thompson, P. W., & Thompson, A. G. (1992, April). *Images of rate.* Paper presented at the Annual Meeting of the American Educational Research Association, San Francisco, CA.

Tourniaire, F., & Pulos, S. (1985). Proportional reasoning: A review of the literature. *Educational Studies in Mathematics, 16,* 181–204.

Vinner, S. (1987). Continuous functions: Images and reasoning in college students. In J. Bergeron, N. Herscovics, & C. Kieran (Eds.), *Proceedings of the Annual Meeting of the International Group for the Psychology of Mathematics Education* (pp. 177–183). Montréal: Université de Monréal.

Vinner, S. (1989). Avoidance of visual considerations in calculus students. *Journal of Mathematical Behavior, 11*(2), 149–156.

Vinner, S. (1991). The role of definitions in the teaching and learning of mathematics. In D. Tall (Ed.), *Advanced mathematical thinking* (pp. 65–81). Dordrecht: Kluwer.

Vinner, S. (1992). The function concept as a prototype for problems in mathematics learning. In G. Harel & E. Dubinsky (Eds.), *The concept of function: Aspects of epistemology and pedagogy* (pp. 195–214). Washington, DC: Mathematical Association of America.

Vinner, S., & Dreyfus, T. (1989). Images and definitions for the concept of function. *Journal for Research in Mathematics Education, 20,* 356–366.

von Glasersfeld, E. (1978). Radical constructivism and Piaget's concept of knowledge. In F. B. Murray (Ed.), *Impact of Piagetian Theory* (pp. 109–122). Baltimore, MD: University Park Press.

von Glasersfeld, E. (1991). Abstraction, re-presentation, and reflection: An interpretation of experience and Piaget's approach. In L. P. Steffe (Ed.), *Epistemological foundations of mathematical experience* (pp. 45–65). New York: Springer-Verlag.

Yackel, E., Cobb, P., Wood, T., Wheatley, G., & Merkel, G. (1990). The importance of social interactions in children's construction of mathematical knowledge. In T. J. Cooney (Ed.), *1990 Yearbook of the National Council of Teachers of Mathematics* (pp. 12–21). Reston, VA: NCTM.

16 Cognition, Mathematics, and Education

Robert B. Davis
Rutgers University

My purpose in this chapter is to try to build some bridges among three groups:

1. Those who see the world from a perspective of human cognition (and particularly from the psychologists' approach to cognition).
2. Those who view the world from the perspective of specialists in mathematics (and here I mean primarily "mathematics educators" rather than those who create and use mathematics in the fashion of mathematicians, physicists, and engineers).
3. Various interest groups, whose aims are sometimes in conflict, including parents, employers, educational administrators, and politicians.

There is much to be gained from trying to overlap these perspectives. When one tries to examine school or university mathematics programs from more than one perspective, these programs begin to look very different, and important new possibilities come to mind. Indeed, I would argue that the kinds of changes that are desperately needed in mathematics instruction can only be made if we are able to bring these various viewpoints together—the combination would be far more potent than the various parts can be, acting alone.

Lest this orientation seem hopelessly bland, let me point out that, at present, these various perspectives are more different than they are similar. Indeed, the separations in viewpoints are so extreme that, two decades ago, a leading scholar said "It appears that mathematicians and psychologists have nothing to say to one another."[1] Probably no one would say that nowadays; the situation has clearly

---

[1] Readers may wish attribution, but there was some confidentiality that should not be breached. It is no exaggeration to call the person in question a "leading scholar."

improved markedly, and today we do all "have something to say to one another." Contributors to this volume have played a major role in bringing about the improved situation today, as have many others. But, whether in religion, politics, or the study of human behavior, the task of bridging intellectual gaps between alternative belief systems is not simple.

No one can approach this task entirely without prejudice. I should perhaps add a note on my own personal perspective. I have been concerned with two tasks in the area of research and development. The first is to study, and try to improve, instructional programs in mathematics at various grade levels and with different student populations. I spend a lot of time in schools and classrooms, including some where the programs are quite unusual, and may where they are not. The second task is to try to build an abstract model of human mathematical thought that might explain the kinds of behaviors that we observe in teachers, students, and experts. In working on this second task, I often refer to computer models, especially as they appear in the work of Minsky, Papert, and Schank. I would not propose the building of actual computer programs at this time—and probably never—unless there were some particularly contentious point that might be resolved by so doing. In general, computer models are transient things. Good descriptions of what can, and cannot, be accomplished by von Neumann type computers are of greater importance.[2] Better machines come and go, but basic principles of information processing persist.

Perhaps the first questions deal with what we are all trying to accomplish, and why.

WHAT DO TEACHERS AND STUDENTS NEED FROM US?

Although we in this Working Group probably spend most of our time and effort on only one of these, there are in fact two kinds of problem areas that could profit from our attention. The first—which the general public sees as paramount—could be called the social and human needs of students; the second is the general question of how people acquire "mathematical power."

That the social and human needs of students constitutes a problem area is readily apparent, as can be seen from a very large number of recent reports. In fact, this general problem of educational failure can be broken down into various subcases. Probably the best known concerns school drop-outs, people without

---

[2]If this seems strange, consider the situation as regards the task of trisecting an arbitrary angle. The proof that this cannot be done in general has lasted for centuries, and remains unaffected by improvements in measuring instruments, because a good description of the task and an appropriate proof have been given. Minsky and Papert (1972) achieved a similar clarification for some tasks in perception (see also Bobrow & Collins, 1975). And, of course, the work of Turing is classical.

marketable skills, and those who are alienated from society (see, for example, Manegold, 1993, and the special issue of the *Journal of Mathematical Behavior* on "Visions of School Mathematics," Davis, 1994). Within the United States this is a very serious problem, indeed. But in fact there are other groups of students who are also ill-served by existing American educational programs. There are, for example, students of many kinds whose desire to learn is not kindled in the area of mathematics, or is actively thwarted. This includes even those talented students who find nothing of value for them within the area of mathematics, from the people Tobias (1990) studied in *They're Not Dumb, They're Different* to the people C. P. Snow (1964) described in *Two Cultures*. Is it impossible to serve these students? One might imagine that early mathematics courses would have as a main goal giving students a general idea of what mathematics is all about, why it is valuable, and why some people find it extremely interesting—but of course this is not what one does find. Most early math courses seem to have only the goal of preparing students for later math courses.[3] This is not what one sees in courses in history, or economics, or psychology. Introductory courses in these, and most other, areas usually seek to be introductions, not merely providers of prerequisite skills for later courses. In far too many cases, typical precollege and beginning college courses in mathematics do not even come close to meeting either career needs or educational needs for most students.

In summary, providing appropriate mathematical education for various kinds of students provides us with plenty of work that needs to be done, if not with many successes that we can afford to celebrate.

THE GAP BETWEEN PRACTICAL PROBLEMS AND COGNITIVE STUDIES

The second problem area, which probably includes most of what we would call cognitive studies, deals with how small pieces of "information" fit together to become "knowledge" or even "a capability of powerful and flexible performance." How do human beings acquire what the NCTM *Standards* (National Council of Teachers of Mathematics, 1989) refer to as "mathematical power"? Do cognitive studies have anything to offer toward the solution of the desperate practical problems that we, at least in the United States, are currently facing?

I would argue that they do. At present, the practical problems get some scholarly attention, but usually outside a framework of cognitive studies, and outside any questioning of traditional curriculum and traditional forms of pedagogy. This kind of piecemeal approach probably cannot lead to solutions. The

---

[3]This whole question of the goals of various courses deserves deeper discussion than is presented here. See, for example, the special issue of the *Journal of Mathematical Behavior* entitled "Visions of school mathematics" (Davis, 1994).

fact is that traditions, possibly inappropriate expectations, possibly inappropriate methods, and possibly inappropriate methods of evaluation add up to a situation where significant improvement is very difficult to achieve. As one example, some of the students we have been studying in our work at Rutgers are university students who are deficient in algebraic manipulation skills, and although they are adult university undergraduates, they must learn what amounts to ninth-grade algebra. The state of New Jersey has proclaimed this as a requirement. One can see this as merely a problem in getting students to learn what is required to pass the tests, in which case it falls within a familiar area of research. But when one looks at the tests it seems clear that the only thing the students are being asked to develop is skill in a few specific forms of "symbol pushing," often at surprisingly high levels of proficiency, and with no concern for understanding. Do these tests, and these courses, come close to meeting the needs of these students? If not, what alternatives are possible? By splitting our concerns where we often do, such questions get lost in the cracks between categories. "Expectations" and "requirements" and "evaluation" and "curriculum goals" and "the design of learning experiences" simply cannot be dealt with in a piecemeal fashion. They must be studied together, and in relation to one another.

It is, of course, the second problem area, namely, cognitive studies, where most of us in this working group spend much of our energy. How can small pieces of "fact" add up to knowledge, skill, creativity, and good judgment? For many students, existing school programs have at least modest success in teaching small factual items or rote manipulative skills, but do not do equally well in developing mathematical power.

So schools and colleges need help for those "failing" students (and others) who seem very ill-served by our existing mathematics programs. For relatively more successful students (or those who love mathematics despite our instructional programs), schools and teachers also need help in developing a more thoughtful approach to mathematics, with programs that enable students to acquire much more in the way of mathematical power. When we call the first of these a motivational problem, call the second a cognitive problem, and study these two problem areas separately, we end up trying to make failing students succeed in a basically sterile and unpromising educational program. This is not impossible, but it certainly seems to fall short of what is really needed. Presumably, in requiring all college students to pass a test in algebra, the state of New Jersey believed that this would somehow serve the real needs of the students. Does a sterile course in the manipulation of meaningless symbols serve the needs of many students? Few of these students will in fact acquire enough skill to go on in fields such as physics or engineering, nor do they wish to. We need to think through, far more clearly, what might be reasonable goals for these students. Cognitive studies can be valuable here, because they can help us develop a more holistic approach to mathematics for all students, with appropriate programs for students who believe they cannot do mathematics and who in fact will not be going on much further in any mathematical field. I think many contributors to this volume could create a course that would be appropriate for this population. Probably these students should realize that, if they every really need to, they will be able to make use of a typical algebraic formula. This could be a modest, but achievable, goal. I would argue that such a course should avoid the extremely complex algebraic problems in the present course (and in the present tests), but—in one more version of "less is more"—although restricting attention to more modest examples, the course should set the goal of producing very great confidence in the students. They would do easier problems, but they would know that they could do them successfully.

The course should also provide a broader awareness of the many forms that mathematical knowledge can take. I suspect that a "liberal arts" course in mathematics—a true introduction to the subject—should probably include some material on how human beings think about mathematics, as well as why experts have chosen to focus their efforts in the way that they have. Sometimes these two goals fit together remarkably well. Carolyn Maher and Alice Alston have developed a program in an elementary school in New Jersey, in which students as early as fourth grade make original mathematical proofs. The original creative work of these students—in a working-class neighborhood—has been recorded on video-tape.[4] I have watched ordinary people and world-famous mathematicians look at these tapes, and they have all been entranced. Given plastic cubes in two different colors (red and blue), the students were asked to make as many different towers, three cubes high, as they could, and to convince the other students in their group that they had not left any out, and did not have any duplicates.

One group of four children came up with four different proofs. Stephanie's proof (Fig. 16.1) goes as follows. Make all the towers with no blue (clearly only one of these–red, red, red); then all the towers with exactly one blue (the blue must either go on top, in the middle, or on the bottom, so there are three of these); then all the towers with exactly two blues with the blues "stuck together" (the stuck-together blues must be in the top two places, or the bottom two, so there are two of these); then all the towers with exactly three blues (only one of these); and, finally, all the towers with exactly two blues that are "stuck apart" (which must have a red in between, hence filling the entire tower). Jeffrey gives a similar proof, but deals with all the "exactly two blues" cases together, which seems more systematic. Milin gives a still more elegant proof. No blues, and

---

[4]And also analyzed in great detail (see, for example, Maher & Martino, 1992; Maher, Martino, & Davis, in press). Even more minutely detailed analyses are available from the MAPS Project Group, Graduate School of Education, Rutgers University, New Brunswick, NJ. These are part of an extended study of young children solving problems in combinatorics, a study that Carolyn Maher has been conducting for more than 5 years, often following the development of the same individual children for many years.

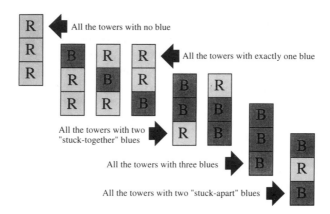

FIG. 16.1. How many different towers three cubes high can be made from red and blue cubes? Structure of Stephanie's solution.

exactly one blue, he handles the same way Stephanie did, but for the troublesome case of exactly two blues, Milin argues: "If you have exactly two blues, since the tower is three cubes tall, there must be exactly one red, and it must be either at the top, or in the middle, or at the bottom." Finally, three of the four children make what is in effect a proof by induction, along the following lines. Make all the towers that are one cube tall; clearly there are two of these. Building upon one of these "one-cube-tall" towers, you can make a "two-cube-tall" tower in either of two ways—by putting a red cube on top, or else by putting a blue cube on top. Hence there are twice as many two-cube-tall towers as there are one-cube-tall towers (and this scheme also tells you how to construct them). This easily extends to towers three cubes tall. In fact, Stephanie, on her own, went on to figure out that there must be exactly 1,024 different towers that would be 10 cubes tall.

Imagine that you had said to these fourth-graders, "Please figure out why the world needs mathematical proofs . . . and, by the way, figure out what a 'mathematical proof' is, anyhow. Find ways to invent proofs, and to criticize proofs, and to fix proofs that need fixing." Nothing good could have come from such an approach. Yet all of this very interesting work, including everything on that list, did take place, in response to the request "Convince the other students at your table that you haven't left any out or put any in twice."

Perhaps what is most striking, in viewing these tapes, is that these children clearly enjoy making mathematical proofs, criticizing one another's proofs, and repairing proofs that aren't quite correct (reminiscent of the processes described by Lakatos, 1976). Their pleasure shows clearly, and so does their self-confidence.

I would use some of these videotapes in this college course for students who are convinced that they cannot do mathematics. It is rather like watching the young female gymnasts in the Olympics. The work—it seems more like play!—

of these fourth-grade children is awe-inspiring, even to world-famous research mathematicians. Yet these are "ordinary" children in an "ordinary" neighborhood in New Jersey. I do not think that watching this videotape would make the college students feel badly. Rather, I think it would begin to open their eyes to the wide range of activities that are "mathematics," and let them see that mathematics is something that human beings invent, and something that one can enjoy. And, when they later become parents, it would help them work with their own children as they go through school.

What else ought to be in this course for college students who "can't deal with mathematics"? I won't pursue this further in the present discussion, but I am confident that we could make a truly valuable course. It may not make the students become engineers, but as a matter of fact they don't want to become engineers. They *do* deserve an education. And for the few among them who might decide that maybe they do want to become an engineer, I think this course could bring them within shouting distance of being able to do so, and what is more, it might give them the inspiration and determination to try.

Before looking at the basic cognitive problem of how the human mind can fit together many small pieces of information, I want to consider a second preliminary question.

WHAT IS MATHEMATICS?

Giyoo Hatano and others in this volume have proposed various distinctions between conflicting views of what mathematics is. This is an important point, and in fact is central to many of the fundamental disagreements about what to teach, and how to teach it.

I would like to propose a different distinction: One view of mathematics is that it consists of employing a few rote procedures, mainly procedures for symbol manipulation, in certain specific predetermined ways. This is the view of most of the people I meet, and I suspect it would not be different in Japan or China or Australia or Argentina. People who believe this will say that adding the fractions $1/2 + 1/3$ to get the answer $5/6$ is "doing mathematics," whereas selecting the best route to drive into the city, making sweet-and-sour pork, dealing a hand of cards, scheduling the use of copying machines in a large office, or packing the luggage compartment of your automobile would not be mathematics.[5] The op-

---

[5]Taking this further, some people would state as the goal that students should be able to carry out the fraction-adding algorithm (probably learned as meaningless rote) from memory; others would argue that it is more important to understand (in some sense) this algorithm. Still others would say we want to educate children so that they can make up these (and other) algorithms for themselves when they need them. Yet others say that the important goal is to be able to look in a book, study a worked-out example, and then imitate it so as to carry out the algorithm yourself. Surprisingly little attention has been given to the different goals that underlie many of today's controversies about what mathematics to teach, and how to teach it.

posing view of mathematics is that it is using some kind of representation to make decisions, or make inferences, or even to ask questions about something that is of interest, and that this tends to be more "mathematical" when it deals with novel problems that no one has told you how to solve. Six examples of mathematics in this second sense are presented in the following problems, which are assumed to be novel problems for the person who is trying to solve them:

Problem 1. The dimensions of a rectangle, measured in centimeters, are whole numbers, and its area, in square centimeters, is numerically equal to its perimeter in centimeters. What does this imply? (And, of course, one is expected to prove the result).

Problem 2. In a certain town, $\frac{2}{3}$ of the adult men are married to $\frac{3}{5}$ of the adult women. What fraction of adults in town are married? (Again, one is expected to prove the result).

Problem 3. You are given the diagram of Fig. 16.2. You must write one of the symbols 0, 1, 2, 3, or 4 in each box with the requirement that when you are done, the number in the box above 0 must be the number of zeros you have written, the number in the box above 1 must be the number of ones you have written, and so on. Can you do it? Is the solution unique? How can you extend this problem? And, again, you are expected to prove your results.[6]

Problem 4. How tall is the flagpole in the schoolyard (assuming that no one has told you how to find out)?

Problem 5. Design a rear windscreen wiper for an automobile.

Problem 6. How many express check-outs for customers with less than 10 items should there be in a supermarket with n check-outs?

The point is that students would come to these problems without prior instruction in how to solve them. It would be the experience of inventing a way to deal with these problems that would enable the students to learn what mathematics really is, and what it means to "do mathematics."

This may seem like an overemphasis on novel problems, but most of the people who hold this view argue that, for students, nearly every new topic in the curriculum involves the solution of novel problems, *for them*. Deciding who has more cookies is a novel problem if you don't know how to count. Videotapes of students dealing with novel problems, by Constance Kamii, by Carolyn Maher, by the Madison Project, by David Page, and by many others (e.g., Corwin,

---

[6]A videotape showing some fourth grade students solving this problem is available from the MAPS Project Group at Rutgers University. The tape is tentatively entitled "Fourth graders solve a problem in thoughtful mathematics". Of course, the students have to invent their own method for solving the problem, and especially for the part dealing with the proof of uniqueness.

FIG. 16.2. Problem 3. Put one of the digits from 0 to 4 in each box so that the number in the 0 box is the number of zeros you have written, the number in the 1 box is the number of ones written, and so on.

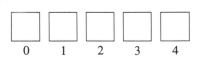

0   1   2   3   4

1989; Erlwanger, 1973; Kamii, undated), show that a very high proportion of students *do* invent their own solution methods, even when the instructional program does try to tell them what to do and how to do it. What may well be the best collection of examples has been assembled by Marilyn Burns (e.g., Burns & McLaughlin, 1990). Some people go even further and pay careful attention to whether students, on their own initiative, go on to pose additional problems, perhaps extending or modifying the original problem that they have just solved— or even posing their own problems to begin with (Brown & Walter, 1993; Silver, 1994).

Perhaps the defining mark of this second viewpoint is that one should not teach "applied mathematics," because this phrase suggests that first you learn some abstraction, and then you look around for somewhere that you can make use of it. This is surely historically wrong, and for those who hold to the second viewpoint under discussion, it is educationally wrong, as well. From this viewpoint, students should spend their time solving novel problems, and after they invent solutions they should reflect on what they have just done. Mathematics as the outcome of such activity—what might be called "My Accumulated Collection of Ways That I Have Invented in Order to Do Things"—stands in stark contrast to "mathematics as something you are taught first and apply second." Such an approach echoes the historical invention of mathematical methods in response to specific practical problems, methods whose power has later become recognized as more generally applicable.[7]

Clearly the two different views of mathematics imply different curricula and different activities in schools. They also imply a different focus on what we need to study in our research. The first view leads to the idea of a prespecified collection of behaviors, and the teacher's task is to cause students to display these behaviors at appropriate times. The second view would see the teacher's task as finding suitable problems that can arouse the students' interest, and that can lead to the invention, by the students, of some of the appropriate concepts, techniques, and habits that constitute mathematics. The contrast between these

---

[7]For example, Fourier set out to study heat flow. In the course of doing this he approximated some functions by a sum of sines and cosines. When he was done, he not only had some results about heat flow, he had a new technique for representing functions by means of what are nowadays called "Fourier functions," but he did *not* set out to "invent" Fourier functions.

two different views of mathematics (colloquially dubbed "the sage on the stage" vs. "the guide on the side") underlies everything else in this discussion.

COGNITIVE THEORIES

Chemists could not have gotten very far just dealing with chemicals. They had to postulate a theory of what was going on "inside" these orange powders and colorless solutions and black precipitates and odorless gases.

I would argue that the same is true for education.[8] Not only do cognitive studies increase our ability to create appropriate learning experiences for students, they give us a lead toward building a postulated theory of how the human mind can deal with the wholeness of knowledge, and not see everything as a large collection of very small pieces (in the way too many curricula do!).

Cognitive theory becomes especially important if we are concerned with mathematics in the second sense. When, using the first meaning, we see learning mathematics as learning to conform to a precisely stated explicit orthodoxy, as something easily broken down into small and largely independent pieces, we can think of the whole enterprise as similar to Skinner training pigeons. By contrast, when we see learning mathematics as a matter of mastering a sizable, interrelated body of knowledge and acquiring mathematical power—even as a matter of achieving membership within a culture—then a different kind of theory is called for.

A COGNITIVE THEORY BASED
ON THE COMPUTER METAPHOR

The one-thing-at-a-time "von Neumann" computer gives us a useful basic metaphor for one kind of postulated model of human mathematical thought. It is far from perfect, but it does represent a beginning.

The basic ingredients for the Euclidean geometry that the Greeks developed were points, lines, and planes. What are the basic ingredients for this computer-based theory?

Clearly there has to be some sort of knowledge representation structure (Davis, 1984). One cannot think about a problem without some mental representation of the problem, and one cannot make use of a piece of knowledge without some representation for that knowledge. One needs, then, a representation of the problem situation, and a (separate) representation of relevant knowledge.

---

[8]The question of mental systems and mental representations is considered elsewhere in this volume (e.g., see chaps. by Maher & Martino, and Davis), and the point of view is accordingly more theoretical.

The representation of the problem situation will often need to be built up gradually, by successive approximations. (One sees this clearly in the case of Problem 3 given earlier. Almost no one seems able to build a correct and complete representation for this problem in the first moments after they read it.) Sometimes representations seem to be retrieved from memory, but clearly they must often be built up from smaller pieces, because the very novelty of the problem implies that one cannot have a complete representation already stored in memory.

As the problem representation is built up, it enables retrieval and construction for a representation of relevant knowledge that may solve the problem. These two representations feed into each other—as one sees potentially applicable knowledge, one gets new ideas of what to search for in the problem itself. All of this construction must also be monitored for appropriateness (although there is evidence that most of us are not very good at this monitoring, and often accept representations that we should have rejected).

It seems useful to postulate some sort of planning space, and to postulate that natural language sometimes plays a role in guiding this planning. (Presumably many heuristics come into play in this way.) Clearly part of what takes place in this planning must have something of the quality of a tree search. One can back up and inquire into the origins of some of the truly basic building blocks from which representations are constructed. Lakoff and others (e.g., Johnson, 1987; Lakoff, 1986) have evidence that these are often perceptual data and were acquired quite early in life. This is of special importance for mathematics education, if one believes that it is important for students to think not primarily in terms of *symbols* but rather in terms of the meanings of those symbols. (It is often easy to determine which way a student is thinking. For example, in Problem 2, given earlier, some students write $2/3 \times 3/5 = 2/5$, and claim this as the answer. This could seem appealing if one focuses on the symbols, but is total nonsense if one thinks in terms of the meanings of those symbols.)

For Problem 1, many solutions have been given (all, of course, coming to the same conclusion), but few of them would seem to have been anything that the ancient Egyptians could have constructed. However, one proof has been given that would have been possible for the ancient Egyptians (Greer, 1993). The secret of its success is that it does not focus on symbols, as most proofs do, but rather on the real objects for which the symbols stand (or on faithful mental proxies for these objects).

The question of mental symbol systems is critical. As we give different answers to what kinds of mental symbols we want students to develop, we must in consequence give different answers to what and how we want students to learn in the area of mathematics. What do we want students to think when they see something like this?

$$3 + 4 = 4 + 3$$

At different stages in their studies the answer will be different, but at early stages I would argue that we want them to think about, say, two stacks of poker chips, one containing 3 chips, and the other 4.

There is abundant evidence for the power of this kind of mental symbolism.[9] The problem 3×5 is easy, in part because we can visualize this as 3 piles of chips, with 5 chips in each pile. The problems 2.1×3.5 is much harder, in part because most people will find it hard to visualize *anything* that is a concrete representation for this problem (such representations do exist, but most people won't know them).

Our present model is not explicit about the forms of processing that must take place in building and manipulating these postulated entities, but clearly this processing is of the greatest importance. Presumably it is this processing capability that is being built up when students invent their own solution methods for novel problems, and that is not being built up when a student is merely following explicit directions.

The building blocks of mental representations, then, are perceptions, past actions, and the results of reflecting on, and abstracting from, already existing representations. A problem representation will often involve identifying and retrieving a "sample" or "prototype" instance; as Hatano (chapter 12, this volume) points out, knowledge of a rule is often accompanied by its preferred examples. Fahlman (cf. Davis, 1984) pointed out that much mental processing probably is based on the identification and retrieval of some kind of typical or relevant example as a basic part of the mental representation. Suppose someone asks you to name a mammal that, in its normal condition, has an odd number of legs. Do you check through the entire catalog of mammals that is stored in your memory? Or do you, as Scott Fahlman suggests, pick one prototypical mammal (perhaps a German shepherd dog) and note that it has four legs. Four is an even number. But one's mental processing does not stop there. Perhaps German shepherds are not typical in this matter. Retrieve some other exemplar, perhaps a cow. Continue in this way until you decide that it seems unlikely that any mammal, in its normal condition, has an odd number of legs.

Anyone who has studied students working mathematics problems in, say, calculus has surely noticed that students are far more likely to look at a worked-out illustrative example, and try to copy it, than they are to read a description of how to go about solving the problem. This would seem to give powerful support to Scott Fahlman's hypothesis.

Crucial to this process is the operation of mapping, which deserves to be on our list of postulated mental mechanisms. One must not only find the illustrative example (or prototypic mammal, or whatever), one must also create a mapping

---

[9]Some recent data provides especially strong evidence in support of student use of this form of mental representation. See Schorr, 1995.

between the illustrative example and the data for the particular problem with which one is concerned.

Continuing in this way, it is possible to relate Hatano's main observations about behavior to internal operations on the entities of this postulated model of mental representations. This includes, in particular, the recent theoretical formulations based on classroom observations that point to successful students being less concerned with learning separate "abstract" facts than with acquiring membership in a viable culture where people deal successfully with mathematical kinds of tasks. (This is spelled out in considerable detail in Davis, 1984.)

REALITY AND EDUCATIONAL REFORM

Before ending, I want to insert a word of caution that is, I think, also a word of hope. I am returning to the question of mathematics courses that do focus on a far broader notion of what behaviors constitute doing mathematics. The need for such courses (or for appropriate learning experiences) is coming to be recognized at every level, from preschool learning experiences through elementary grades, secondary school, and university-level studies (Davis, 1984; Jetter, 1993; Mathematical Sciences Education Board, 1989, 1991; National Council of Teachers of Mathematics, 1989; Toom, 1993; Uhl, 1993; Zvonkin, 1993). Suppose such courses were indeed created (a few actually have been) and offered to students. Would the students be put at risk? In the long run, I think not, and I think that this is exactly what we need to do. But in the short run? On that it is harder to be optimistic, especially if tests continue to be used as deliberate roadblocks to select out many candidates, preventing them from pursuing further educational opportunities or various categories of desirable jobs, and if these tests continue to focus on problems[10] such as:

$$\frac{\dfrac{(x^2 - 1)(x + 2)}{(x + 3)(x - 2)} + \dfrac{(x^3 - 1)(x^3 + 1)}{(x^2 - 4)(x - 1)}}{\dfrac{(x + 2)(x + 1)}{(x + 3)^2} - \dfrac{(x + 7)(x^2 - 1)}{x^2 - 9}}$$

But it is precisely here that a combination of cognitive studies and curriculum studies may be helpful. The reason I dare to speak of hope in this connection is that I believe that cognitive studies, because we look closely at actual behaviors

---

[10]Consider this problem in relation to the version of calculus taught at the University of Illinois by Jerry Uhl. In the Uhl calculus course, the textbook itself is on the computer, based on Mathematica, which means that the full capability of Mathematica is available to all students in this calculus course, as they do homework, do tests, and even as they read the textbook itself.

of students and at what kinds of thought processes are involved in these behaviors, may point the way toward asking whether the kinds of thinking involved in such examples are really what various groups of students need to master. Imagine that this kind of inquiry became common, that courses and topics at every level were carefully scrutinized to determine exactly which kinds of thinking, knowledge, and skills are needed for exactly which categories of students. Suppose we asked whether students planning to be, say, purchasing agents, or writers of advertising copy, actually needed to be able to solve problems such as the one just shown. Suppose we tried to be more explicit in our description of how a course of study, at the level of rather fine detail, would benefit various kinds of students. Would that help us make the kind of changes that many observers are coming to believe need to be made?

Ultimately, the two separate themes of designing learning experiences that meet the needs of students, and understanding more deeply what is involved in the way humans think about mathematics, may indeed be seen as intimately related. Indeed, it is hard to see how those involved in either enterprise can make an optimal contribution if they do not become allies and learn to work together in the closest possible way.

REFERENCES

Bobrow, D. G., & Collins, A. (1975). *Representation and understanding: Studies in cognitive science*. New York: Academic Press.

Brown, S. I., & Walter, M. I. (1993). *Problem posing: Reflections and applications*. Hillsdale, NJ: Lawrence Erlbaum Associates.

Burns, M., & McLaughlin, C. (1990). *A collection of math lessons—Grades 6 through 8*. New Rochelle, NY: Cuisenaire Company of America.

Corwin, R. B. (1989). Multiplication as original sin. *Journal of Mathematical Behavior, 8*, 223–225.

Davis, R. B. (1984). *Learning mathematics: The cognitive science approach to mathematics education*. London: Croom Helm.

Davis, R. B. (1992). Understanding "understanding". *Journal of Mathematical Behavior, 11*, 225–242.

Davis, R. B. (Ed.). (1994). Visions of school mathematics [Special issue]. *Journal of Mathematical Behavior, 13*,(1).

Erlwanger, S. H. (1973). Benny's conceptions of rules and answers in IPI mathematics. *Journal of Children's Mathematical Behavior, 1*(2), 7–26.

Greer, B. (1993). A pre-algebraic solution of the Isis problem. *Journal of Mathematical Behavior, 12*, 175–176.

Jetter, A. (1993, February). Mississippi learning. *The New York Times, Sunday Magazine*.

Johnson, M. (1987). *The body in the mind*. Chicago: University of Chicago Press.

Kamii, C. (undated videotape). *Double-column addition: A teacher uses Piaget's theory*. Available from Promethean Films South, P. O. Box 26363, Birmingham, AL 35226.

Lakatos, I. (1976). *Proofs and refutations*. Cambridge: Cambridge University Press.

Lakoff, G. (1986). *Women, fire, and dangerous things*. Chicago: University of Chicago Press.

Maher, C. A., & Martino, A. M. (1992, August). *Conditions contributing to conceptual change in building the idea of mathematical justification*. Paper presented at the 7th International Congress on Mathematical Education, Quebec City, Canada.

Maher, C. A., Martino, A. M., & Davis, R. B. (in press). Young children's development of mathematical proofs.

Manegold, C. S. (1993). To Crystal, 12, the classroom serves no purpose. In *Children of the shadows*. New York: New York Times.

Mathematical Sciences Education Board. (1989). *Everybody counts: A report to the nation on the future of mathematics education*. Washington, DC: National Academy Press.

Mathematical Sciences Education Board. (1991). *Moving beyond myths: Revitalizing undergraduate mathematics*. Washington, DC: National Academy Press.

Minsky, M., & Papert, S. (1972). *Research at the laboratory in vision, language, and other problems of artificial intelligence*. Cambridge, MA: Artificial Intelligence Laboratory, Massachusetts Institute of Technology.

National Council of Teachers of Mathematics. (1989). *Curriculum and evaluation standards for school mathematics*. Reston, VA: National Council of Teachers of Mathematics.

Schorr, R. Y. (1995). A study of the effect of a teacher development project on children's mathematical thinking. Unpublished doctoral dissertation, Rutgers University.

Silver, E. A. (1994). On mathematical problem posing. *For the Learning of Mathematics, 14*(1), 19–28.

Snow, C. P. (1964). *Two cultures*. Cambridge: Cambridge University Press.

Tobias, S. (1990). *They're not dumb, they're different: Stalking the second tier*. Tucson, AZ: Research Corporation.

Toom, A. (1993). A Russian teacher in America. *Journal of Mathematical Behavior, 12*, 117–140.

Uhl, J. (1993, August 16). *Calculus and Mathematica*. Report presented to the ICTMA-6 meetings at the University of Delaware.

Zvonkin, A. K. (1993). Children and "5-choose-2." *Journal of Mathematical Behavior, 12*, 141–152.

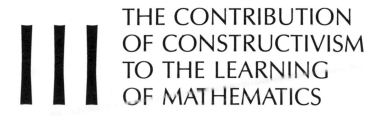

THE CONTRIBUTION OF CONSTRUCTIVISM TO THE LEARNING OF MATHEMATICS

Gerald A. Goldin, Editor

17 Theory of Mathematics Education: The Contributions of Constructivism

Gerald A. Goldin
Rutgers University

It was a great privilege to organize and participate in the working subgroup at ICME 7 devoted to the contributions of constructivism. This section of the volume contains articles based on the presentations during the 3 days in August 1992 that our subgroup met in Québec, substantially revised by the authors. It offers a variety of perspectives to the reader, some mutually supportive and some sharply conflicting.[1]

On the first day of the meeting, our main focus was on the philosophical side of constructivism. Here von Glasersfeld's contribution provides an overview of radical constructivist epistemology, emphasizing the irrevocable subjectivity of the experiential world and reiterating that this experiential reality is necessarily constructed. He stresses that this is not to deny the existence of a "real" world—only to assert its inherent unknowability. The requirement that knowledge be "true" is dropped; knowledge is only required to be "viable," and to "fit into the world of the knower's experience." Von Glasersfeld stresses particularly that in mathematics, "the need for an experiential basis for the abstraction of concepts is often overlooked."

The chapter by Marton and Neuman, which Neuman presented in Québec,

---

[1] I would like to acknowledge Jere Confrey and Ralph Mason, who recorded insightful notes of our subgroup's discussion each day. I wrote a brief summary in August 1992 of those discussions, which appeared in the *Proceedings of the 7th International Congress on Mathematical Education* (Gaulin, Hodgson, Wheeler, & Egsgard, 1994). Unfortunately, some time after that manuscript left my hands, transcription errors led to some rather puzzling ideas being attributed to my colleagues, especially Ernst von Glasersfeld and Paul Ernest. I trust these will be disregarded by posterity, with the present volume taken as the more definitive expression of our subgroup's work.

describes how the research approach termed *phenomenography*—designed to explore differences in learners' experiences—is predicated on some philosophical differences with constructivism, even in its more radical form. Phenomenography adopts a wholly nondualistic position, taking "experience" as "a relation between subject and object" to the point of excluding both subject and object as separate entities. For example, in the study of problem solving, the idea of "the problem as such" is rejected in favor of "the problem as understood (by someone)." The context of this work is that of children experiencing division in mathematics; four "ways of experiencing division" become a basis for discussing children's problem solving.

Ernest then distinguishes among four metaphors for the varieties of theorizing in mathematics education: the computer (information-processing theory), the soft computer (weak or "trivial" constructivism), the evolving, adapting, but isolated organism (radical constructivism), and persons in conversation (social constructivism, the position with which Ernest himself identifies). He identifies the first two varieties with absolutist, neo-positivist research paradigms, and the latter two with fallibilist, relativist paradigms—in parallel with "absolutist" and "fallibilist" notions of mathematics (Ernest, 1991). He also draws general implications from each for the practice of mathematics education.

In Québec a lively discussion followed these presentations, during which (among other major points) the metaphors and epistemological perspectives presented were challenged as inadequate, and the characterization of "trivial constructivism" was vigorously debated. The chapter by Herscovics addresses this issue in the present volume, arguing vigorously for a still-different brand of constructivism that he calls "rational constructivism," which is more eclectic and allows for several different kinds of knowledge and knowledge acquisition.

The second day of the meeting included a series of presentations from the perspective of cognitive theory. All the speakers considered learning to be a constructive process, but not all accepted radical constructivism as their philosophical perspective. Herscovics in his chapter addresses the interface between constructivism, cognition, and developmental theory, describing several models of understanding that can describe children's developing concepts of early arithmetic. These models are of particular interest to me, because at the time of his final illness Herscovics and I had begun to explore them in some depth. We were interested in their relation to my problem-solving model based on five kinds of representational systems (Goldin & Herscovics, 1991a, 1991b). In the course of our discussions I came to appreciate the care with which Bergeron, Herscovics, and their co-workers constructed the theoretical picture of conceptual understanding that is presented so clearly here.

Booker highlights in his chapter two forms that constructivist approaches to learning take—the enlargement or more-or-less continuous restructuring of student thinking, versus a process of cognitive conflict, in which mathematically superior constructions displace less adequate ones. Describing an interaction in which a group of children explore fraction ideas, he identifies tensions between the social conventions that provide a context for the discussion, and the social construction of meaning that is the object of the activity.

In my chapter with Kaput, we present a joint perspective on the notion of representation in the theory of mathematics education—a notion central to our respective theoretical work. We distinguish internal from external representational systems, and explore how the idea of representation fits with constructivism. We also take special pains to respond to radical constructivist critiques, stressing several points: that representations are themselves constructs, that the signification relationship between representations can be two-way, and that internal (cognitive) representations can represent each other as well as external objects or configurations. We go on to discuss various aspects of representational systems and their physical embodiments.

The issue of representation evoked considerable discussion and debate in Québec, some of which is reflected in the chapters here. Von Glasersfeld expresses the view that one cannot validly speak of a representation of something (i.e., an ulterior reality) that is inaccessible; however, he stresses that two meanings of representation are admissible to radical constructivists—"re-presentation (from memory) to an experience one has had at some earlier moment," and "graphic or symbolic structures that provide the cognizing subject with the opportunity to carry out certain mental operations." Marton and Neuman stay away from the notion of representation entirely, relying on the rather different notion of "experience" as their fundamental construct. I think their emphasis on the subject-object "relation" essentially focuses on what Kaput and I call "representational acts." In making the case for the scientific value of the notions of representation, systems of representation, and representational acts, Kaput and I seek to answer radical constructivist objections; we offer a framework that we believe to be "epistemologically independent of the tenets of radical constructivism."

On the third day of the meeting in Québec there were four presentations, of which two are represented by chapters in the current volume. Michael Otte, who did not submit a paper, contributed substantially to a discussion of radical constructivism and radical empiricism, investigating what it is that turns a mental event into knowledge and returning to some of the philosophical questions of the first day.

Maher's presentation included a videotape and analysis of four children discussing a concrete, combinatorial problem, based on her work with Rutgers University colleagues. The analysis is extended in the chapter by Maher and Martino presented here. Excerpts of group problem-solving activity by children that took place over a period of a few years are discussed, allowing an unusual glimpse of the children's mathematical development.

Jere Confrey, whose paper has been published elsewhere (Confrey, 1993) provided our working subgroup with an overview of several key constructivist issues, stressing that we are always building models and seeking to hear the "voice" of the child in the model. She argues for the authenticity that derives from recognizing the child's perspective as we develop the theory of mathematics education.

Finally, Janvier's chapter draws implications for teacher education. He argues that constructive learning *must* occur; it is a necessity, quite independently of the nature of instruction. Thus constructivism as an epistemological perspective does not "tell us what to do" or provide criteria for selecting the best approach to teaching. Considerable discussion followed, with differences of opinion as to how strong the implications of constructivist theory actually are for teaching. Furthermore, it was maintained that implications in the opposite direction (i.e., consequences of classroom practice for the theory of mathematics education) deserve increased attention.

In this brief overview I have sought to highlight a few of the ideas developed in the papers that follow, and to convey in a small way the lively flavor of our working subgroup's discussions.

REFERENCES

Confrey, J. (1993). Learning to see children's mathematics: Crucial challenges in constructivist reform. In E. Tobin (Ed.), *Constructivist perspectives in science and mathematics* (pp. 299–321). Washington, DC: American Association for the Advancement of Science.

Ernest, P. (1991). *The philosophy of mathematics education.* London: Falmer.

Gaulin, C., Hodgson, B. R., Wheeler, D. H., & Egsgard, J. C. (1994). *Proceedings of the 7th International Congress on mathematical Education (pp. 122–124).* Sainte-Foy, Québec: Les Presses de l'Université Laval.)

Goldin, G. A., & Herscovics, N. (1991a). Toward a conceptual-representational analysis of the exponential function. In F. Furinghetti (Ed.), *Proceedings of the Fifteenth Annual Conference for the Psychology of Mathematics Education (PME)* (Vol. 2, pp. 64–71). Genoa, Italy: Dipartimento di Matematica dell'Università di Genova.

Goldin, G. A., & Herscovics, N. (1991b) The conceptual-representational analysis of children's early arithmetic. In R. Underhill (Ed.), *Proceedings of the Thirteenth Annual Meeting of PME-NA* (Vol. 1, pp. 118–124). Blacksburg, VA: Virginia Tech, Division of Curriculum and Instruction.

18 Aspects of Radical Constructivism and Its Educational Recommendations

Ernst von Glasersfeld
University of Massachusetts

In the context of theories of knowledge, the term *constructivism* was introduced by Jean Piaget and became widely known through the publication of one of his major works, *The Construction of Reality in the Child (La Construction du Réel chez l'enfant, 1937)*.

In the United States, Piaget became known mainly for his stage theory of cognitive development. Some thirty years later, when he was being discovered for the second or third time, "constructivism" became a catchword and was used by thousands who had not the least interest in Piaget's epistemological considerations and therefore missed the meaning he intended when he spoke of construction. To most it seemed to mean no more than that the child does not appropriate adult knowledge in one piece and therefore has to construct it bit by bit. Having to teach cognitive psychology at that time, I came to characterize this superficial approach as "trivial," and explicitly differentiated the interpretation of Piaget's neo-Kantian theory of knowledge as "radical constructivism."

This constructivism is radical because it breaks with the Western epistemological tradition. It is an unconventional way of looking and therefore requires conceptual change. In particular, radical constructivism requires the change of several deeply rooted notions, such as knowledge, truth, representation, and reality. Because the dismantling of traditional ideas is never popular, proponents of radical constructivism are sometimes considered to be dangerous heretics. Some of the critics persist in disregarding conceptual differences that have been explicitly stated and point to contradictions that arise from their attempt to assimilate the constructivist view to traditional epistemological assumptions. This is analogous to interpreting a quantum-theoretical physics text with the concepts of a 19th-century corpuscular theory.

It may be useful, therefore, to reiterate some points of our "postepistemological" approach.[1] Let me begin with a term that was brought up several times in our discussion at the meeting, namely, *representation*. Goldin suggested that behaviorism had erred by rejecting the notion of an organism's internal constructs and that constructivism would be making an analogous mistake if it rejected the notion of external constructs (cf. Goldin, 1990). Given the notorious ambiguity of the English word *representation* (cf. von Glasersfeld, 1987), an explanation seems in order. Constructivism does reject the use of the word in the sense of traditional philosophers who intended it to mean a conceptual structure that was in some way isomorphic with a part of ontological reality. However, this leaves at least two meanings of "representation" that constructivism does not reject: (1) the Piagetian sense that refers to a re-presentation (from memory) of an experience one has had at some earlier moment; and (2) the sense that Kaput (1991) has so expertly discussed in the context of "multiple representations," which refers to graphic or symbolic structures that provide the cognizing subject with the opportunity to carry out certain mental operations. Constructivists, too, therefore speak of a certain painting as a representation of a bunch of sunflowers, or of the symbols "$f(x)$" as the representation of a function. It is worth noting, however, that in these cases, the graphic or symbolic structure merely provides an opportunity to replay certain perceptual or conceptual operations.

NO EXIT FROM SUBJECTIVITY

Radical constructivism is an attempt to develop a theory of knowing that is not made illusory from the outset by the traditional assumption that the cognizing activity should lead to a "true" representation of a world that exists in itself and by itself, independent of the cognizing agent. Instead, radical constructivism assumes that the cognizing activity is instrumental and neither does nor can concern anything but the experiential world of the knower. This experiential world is constituted and structured by the knower's own ways and means of perceiving and conceiving, and in this elementary sense it is always and irrevocably subjective (i.e., construed by the cognizing subject). It is the knower who segments the manifold of experience into raw elementary particles, combines these to form viable "things," abstracts concepts from them, relates them by means of conceptual relations, and thus constructs a relatively stable experiential reality. The viability of these concepts and constructs has a hierarchy of levels that begins with simple repeatability in the sensory-motor domain and turns, on levels of higher abstraction, into operational coherence, and ultimately concerns the noncontradictoriness of the entire repertoire of conceptual structures.

The statement that the construction of the experiential world is irrevocably

---

[1] I owe this expression to Nel Noddings, who used it in a review of one of my papers.

subjective has been interpreted as a declaration of solipsism and as the denial of any "real" world. This is unwarranted. Constructivism has never denied an ulterior reality, It merely says that this reality is unknowable and that it makes no sense to speak of a representation of something that is inherently inaccessible.

The insistence on the subjectivity of the experiential world has also led some critics to the rash conclusion that radical constructivism ignores the role of social interaction in the construction of knowledge. This, too, is a misinterpretation, and a rather thoughtless one. If one begins with the assumption that all knowledge is derived from perceptual and conceptual experience, one in no way denies that "others" and "society" have an influence on the individual's cognitive constructing. On the contrary, because others add up to a major part of the individual's experiential environment, they will have a considerable role in determining which behaviors, concepts, and theories are considered "viable" in the individual's physical and linguistic interactions with them. Nevertheless, as a constructivist, one will remain aware of the fact that these others and the society they constitute "exist" for the individual subject only to the extent to which they figure in that individual's experience—that is to say, they are for each subject what he or she perceives and conceives them to be.

In contrast, those who call themselves social constructionists tend to introduce the social context as an ontological given. They are, of course, free to do so, but it does not entitle them to fault another school of thought that endeavors to build a theory of knowing without ontological givens or other metaphysical assumptions. This was seen quite clearly 60 years ago by Alfred Schütz (1932/1974) when he referred to "the immensely difficult problems that are tied to the constitution of the *thou* in each individual's own subjectivity" and added a few lines later that "such analyses belong to the general theory of knowledge and thus mediately to the social sciences" (p. 138). Radical constructivism is indeed intended as a theory of knowing and therefore is obliged to attempt an analysis of how the thinking subject comes to have others in his or her construction of the experiential world (cf. von Glasersfeld, 1986, 1995).

SOME SALIENT CHARACTERISTICS

From the radical constructivist point of view, the basic ideas concerning the questions *what is knowledge and how do we come to have it* can be summarized as follows.

No philosopher in the course of the last 2,500 years has been able to demolish the skeptics' logical arguments that the real world, in the sense of ontological reality, is inaccessible to human reason. In view of this impasse, constructivism, like the pragmatists at the beginning of our century, suggests that we change the concept of knowledge. The pragmatists, however, remained attached to a metaphysical if not material form of realism. Instead, constructivism goes back to Vico, who considered human knowledge a human construction that was to be evaluated according to its coherence and its fit with the world of human experience, and not as a representation of God's world as it might be beyond the interface of human experience. Constructivism drops the requirement that knowledge be "true" in the sense that it should match an objective reality. All it requires of knowledge is that it be viable, in that it fits into the world of the knower's experience, the only "reality" accessible to human reason.

With regard to the cognitive construction, we follow the two pioneers of conceptual analysis, Jean Piaget and Silvio Ceccato. That is to say, we attempt to build plausible models of how, by means of reflection and abstraction, viable concepts could be derived from subjective experience.

This change of view has consequences not just for a few traditional philosophical beliefs but for almost everything one habitually thinks about acts of knowing and the knowledge resulting from them. Here I want to mention only two cases in point.

Inherent in radical constructivism is the realization that no knowledge can claim uniqueness. In other words, no matter how viable and satisfactory the solution to a problem might seem, it can never be regarded as the only possible solution. (Note that this does not contradict the observation that, for instance in mathematics, solutions are often fully determined by the operations one carries out to find them.)

The second is Leo Apostel's admonition that "a system should always be applied to itself" (Inhelder, Garcia, & Vonèche, 1977, p. 61). In our case, this leads to the conclusion that radical constructivism cannot claim to be anything but one approach to the age-old problem of knowing. Only its application in contexts where a theory of knowing makes a difference can show whether or not it should be considered a viable approach.

CONCERNING EDUCATION

In this volume, we are not primarily concerned with philosophical questions, but rather with applications to the teaching of mathematics. In this regard, let me emphasize that although we have promising beginnings (cf. Steffe, 1991; Steffe & Cobb, 1988; Steffe, von Glasersfeld, Richards, & Cobb, 1983; von Glasersfeld, 1981, 1992), the enormous task of analyzing the basic conceptual steps in the construction of mathematics has barely begun.

Teachers at all levels, from elementary school to postgraduate instruction, have to rely on the use of language, and textbooks cannot do without it. Yet in my experience, few language users have given much thought to the question how linguistic communication is supposed to work.

In everyday circumstances, where most of what we say and others say to us does not give rise to obvious misinterpretation, we usually assume that the meaning of words and sentences is the same for all speakers of the particular language. If there are differences, they seem to be insignificant. I have shown elsewhere that, even in the case of the most ordinary objects, the notion of "shared meaning" is strictly speaking an illusion. This is so because we associate the sounds we come to isolate as "words" not with things but with our subjective experiences of things—and although subjective experiences may be similar for different subjects, they are never quite the same (von Glasersfeld, 1990). Sharing meaning, ideas, and knowledge, therefore, is like sharing an apple pie or a bottle of wine: None of the participants can taste the share another is having.

THE MAKING OF ABSTRACTIONS

Here, however, we are concerned with mathematics teaching and thus not with sensory items but with concepts that are abstracted from mental operations. In the case of ordinary sensory objects, the individual gradually learns, by interacting in practical situations with other speakers of the language, to adjust his or her meanings so that they become more or less compatible with those current in the community. In the case of abstract items, however, it is far more difficult to achieve this social adequation, because the occasions where conceptual discrepancies might come to the surface are few and far between. Hence, in order to teach abstract notions, it is indispensable for the instructor to generate experiential situations for the students, such that they themselves can make the necessary abstractions. In order to foster such abstractions, the teacher must be successful in establishing with the students a common language, that is, a language of carefully negotiated and coordinated meanings or, as Maturana has called it, a consensual domain (Maturana, 1980; Richards, 1991).

Mathematics is the result of abstraction from operations on a level on which the sensory or motor material that provided the occasion for operating is disregarded. In arithmetic this begins with the abstraction of the concept of number from acts of counting. Such abstractions cannot be given; they have to be made by the students themselves. The teacher, of course, can help by generating situations that allow or even suggest the abstraction. This is where manipulables can play an important role, but it would be naive to believe that the move from handling or perceiving objects to a mathematical abstraction is easy, let alone automatic. The sensory objects, no matter how ingeniously they might be designed, merely offer an opportunity for actions from which the desired operative concepts may be abstracted; one should never forget that the desired abstractions, no matter how trivial and obvious they might seem to the teacher, are never obvious to the novice.

The same can be said about the use of multiple representations (Gerace, in press; Kaput, 1991). In learning to switch from one representation to another, an act of reflective abstraction may focus on what it is that appears to remain the same. But this abstraction is, again, not automatic, and it may well be precluded if the switch is explicitly presented as the simple exchange of two equivalent items. The point is that the representations are different, but an operative concept or conceptual relation they embody is considered the same.

MEANING AND MISCONCEPTIONS

In contrast, the need for an experiential basis for the abstraction of concepts is often overlooked, because of the formalist myth that all that matters in mathematics is the manipulation of symbols. This ignores the fact that spoken words or marks on paper are symbols only if one attributes to them something they symbolize, that is, a meaning—and meaning is always conceptual. As Hersh wrote, "Symbols are used as aids to thinking just as musical scores are used as aids to music. The music comes first, the score comes later" (1979–1986, p. 19). There is little point in teaching a score to students who have no music to relate to it. In school, however, mathematical symbols are often treated as though they were self-sufficient and no concepts and mental operations had to accompany them. Hence, when students are only trained to manipulate marks on paper, it is small wonder that few of them ever come to understand the meaning of what they are doing and why they should do it.

Because there is no way of transferring meaning, that is, concepts and conceptual structures, from one head to another, teachers, who have the goal of changing something in students' heads, must have some notion of what goes on in those other heads. Hence it would seem necessary for a teacher to build up a model of the student's conceptual world (see von Glasersfeld & Steffe, 1991).

From the constructivist perspective, it is not helpful to assume (maybe on the basis of "wrong" answers) that a student's ideas are simply misconceptions that have to be replaced by the conceptions that are considered correct by mathematicians, physicists, or other experts. In order to become operative in a student's thinking, a new conception must be related to others that are already in the student's repertoire. No doubt there are several ways of establishing such relationships, but the simplest and most efficacious arises when the new structure is built out of elements with which the students are familiar. In other words, students must be shown that there are elements in their experience that can be related differently from the way they habitually relate them; to make such changes desirable to students, they must be shown that the new way provides advantages in a sphere of living and thinking that reaches beyond passing exams and getting good grades.

Besides, when a student has struggled to find an answer to a given problem, it is not only boorish but also counterproductive to dismiss it as "wrong," even if the teacher then shows the "right" way of proceeding. Such disregard for the student's effort inevitably demolishes the student's motivation. Instead, a wiser teacher will ask the student how he or she came to the particular answer. In the majority of cases, the student, in reviewing the path (i.e., reflecting on the operations carried out), will either discover a hitch or give the teacher a clue to a conceptual connection that does not fit into the procedure that is to be learned. The first is an invaluable element of learning: It provides students with an opportunity to realize that they themselves can see what works and what does not. The second provides the teacher with an insight into the student's present way of operating and thus with a clearer idea of where a change might be attempted.

To end this brief list of recommendations, let me repeat a rather unpopular point. From the constructivist perspective, whatever one intends to teach must never be presented as the only possible knowledge—even if the discipline happens to be mathematics. Indeed, it should be carefully explained that a fact such as "2 + 2 = 4" may be considered certain, not because it was so ordained by God or any other extra-human authority, but because we come to construct units in a particular way and have agreed on how they are to be counted.

Radical constructivism, as I have often said, makes no claim to novelty. Its basic ideas can all be found along the wayside of Western philosophy, but to my knowledge, they have never been put together with the intent to create a viable model of the cognitive activity. Claude Janvier was perfectly right when he commented in his contribution that constructivism does not tell us (as teachers) what to do (cf. Janvier, chapter 25, this volume)—and I can only repeat my answer, that in my view, constructivism does tell the teacher a few things that should *not* be done.

REFERENCES

Gerace, W. J. (1994). *Contributions from cognitive research to mathematics and science education*. Research Report, University of Massachusetts, Amherst: SRRI.

Goldin, G. A. (1990). Epistemology, constructivism, and discovery learning in mathematics. In R. B. Davis, C. A. Maher, & N. Noddings (Eds.), *Constructivist views on the teaching and learning of mathematics* (pp. 31–47). Journal for Research in Mathematics Education Monograph No. 4. Reston, VA: National Council of Teachers of Mathematics.

Hersh, R. (1986). Some proposals for revising the philosophy of mathematics. In T. Tymoczko (Ed.) *New directions in the philosophy of mathematics* (pp. 9–28). Boston/Basel: Birkhauser. (Original work published 1979)

Inhelder, B., Garcia, R., & Vonèche, J. (1977). *Épistemologie génétique et équilibration*. Neuchâtel: Delachaux et Niestlé.

Kaput, J. J. (1991). Notations and representations as mediators of constructive processes. In E. von Glasersfeld (Ed.), *Radical constructivism in mathematics education* (pp. 53–74). Boston: Kluwer Academic.

Maturana, H. R. (1980). Biology of cognition. In H. R. Maturana & F. J. Varela, *Autopoiesis and cognition* (pp. 2–62). Boston Studies in the Philosophy of Science. Boston: Reidel.

Piaget, J. (1937). *La construction du réel chez l'enfant*. [The construction of reality in the child]. Neuchâtel: Delachaux et Niestlé.

Richards, J. (1991). Mathematical discussions. In E. von Glasersfeld (Ed.), *Radical constructivism in mathematics education* (pp. 13–51). Boston: Kluwer Academic.

Schütz, A. (1974). *Der sinnhafte Aufbau der sozialen Welt.* Frankfurt: Suhrkamp. (Original work published 1932)

Steffe, L. P. (1991). *Epistemological foundations of mathematical experience.* New York: Springer.

Steffe, L. P., & Cobb, P. (1988). *Construction of arithmetical meaning and strategies.* New York: Springer.

Steffe, L. P., von Glasersfeld, E., Richards, J., & Cobb, P. (1983). *Children's counting types: Philosophy, theory, and application.* New York: Praeger.

von Glasersfeld, E. (1981). An attentional model for the conceptual construction of units and number, *Journal for Research in Mathematics Education, 12*(2), 83–94.

von Glasersfeld, E. (1986). Steps in the construction of "others" and "realty." In R. Trappl (Ed.), *Power, autonomy, utopias: New approaches toward complex systems* (pp. 107–116). London: Plenum.

von Glasersfeld, E. (1987). Preliminaries to any theory of representation. In C. Janvier (Ed.), *Problems of representation in the teaching and learning of mathematics* (pp. 215–225). Hillsdale, NJ: Lawrence Erlbaum Associates.

von Glasersfeld, E. (1990). Environment and communication. In L. P. Steffe & T. Woods (Eds.), *Transforming children's mathematical education* (pp. 30–38). Hillsdale, NJ: Lawrence Erlbaum Associates.

von Glasersfeld, E. (1992). A constructivist approach to experiential foundations of mathematical concepts. In S. Hills (Ed.), *The history and philosophy of science in science education* (Vol. II, pp. 553–571). Kingston, Ontario: Queen's University.

von Glasersfeld, E. (1995). *Radical constructivism: A way of knowing and learning.* London: Falmer Press.

von Glasersfeld, E., & Steffe, L. P. (1991). Conceptual models in educational research and practice, *Journal of Educational Thought, 25*(2), 91–103.

19 Phenomenography and Children's Experience of Division

Ference Marton
Dagmar Neuman
Gothenburg University

Our aim in writing this chapter is to present a research approach, phenomenography, that takes human experience as its subject matter. We make the ontological assumptions underlying phenomenography explicit, and illustrate its application by means of examples that originate from a recent investigation of children's experience of division.

Phenomenography is a research approach that developed during the early 1970s from an interest in studying how learners experience the act of learning on the one hand, and what they learn from reading texts, solving problems, listening to lectures, and so forth on the other hand. What we found above all was that there are qualitative variations in both respects. Our aim became to understand the nature of the variation better (Marton, Hounsell, & Entwistle, 1984).

A common assumption adopted in studies of learning in educational contexts is that different learners read the same text, solve the same problem, listen to the same lecture, and then—because they are equipped differently—do different things with the text, problem, lecture they have somehow internalized. Our studies showed this assumption to be invalid. The conclusion we arrived at was that learners do not really read the same text, solve the same problems, or listen to the same lecture, even if the experimenter sees them bowed over the same text, struggling with the same problem, or attending the same lecture. We found that regardless of what situation or phenomenon people encounter, a limited number of qualitatively different ways of experiencing or understanding that situation can be identified. The driving force of phenomenographic research is to understand better the nature of different learning results. The chosen path is to reveal the nature and structure of differences in how people experience and understand what they are supposed to learn, and the situation in which this learning is expected to come about.

THE DUALISTIC ONTOLOGICAL ASSUMPTION

When doing research aimed at exploring what differences in learning mean, through the experiences of the learners, we face a fundamental ontological question: What kind of thing is an experience?[1]

To begin with, an experience is always necessarily an experience of something: the text read, the problem dealt with, or the learning situation itself. It would be possible to think, to take one such example, of there being a problem, on the one hand, and the learners' different ways of understanding or experiencing it on the other hand. That means that we would be thinking of the problem as existing independently of the learners and independently of the different ways in which they experienced it. Object (the problem) and subject (the learner) would then be seen as two separate entities.

If we develop this assumption we can see the learner as receiving information about the object through her senses, and forming a representation of this object in her mind. Experiences or conceptions are then seen as mental representations making up a subjective world, corresponding more or less well to the objective world. Studying experiences or understandings of a problem then means studying how "the problem as such" is represented in the learners' minds. This way of answering the question "What kind of thing is an experience?" is in accordance with fundamental assumptions made by information-processing theorists, and it rests on a dualistic ontology: Object and subject are separate. As we pointed out earlier (Marton & Neuman, 1990), although radical constructivism aims to study the acts that organize the experiential world, and not to discover an ontological reality, even in that approach there is an assumption of an independent reality. Von Glasersfeld (1990) expressed this view as: "even the most radical form of constructivism does not deny that kind of independent reality. Constructivism merely asserts that it is not accessible to rational knowledge" (p. 37). There is thus, according to these assumptions, the real world beyond our reach and the subjective world that we are locked into, and that is divorced from the "real world." This real world "manifests itself only through the constraints that make some of our ways of acting and thinking unsuccessful" (von Glasersfeld, 1990, p. 37). This is another form of the ontological position of dualism in which subject and object, situated in "ontological reality," are seen as entirely separate entities. As the ontological reality is unattainable, what we are studying are subjective, psychological, mental acts performed on mental objects that are the results of the psychological process of reflection over one's own acts.

When this view is adopted, the focus of interest is on what the individual does

---

[1] In our publications we have mostly used the word *conceptions,* but other synonyms also appear: perceptions, understandings, apprehensions, and others. In this chapter all the synonyms are used interchangeably; when one of them is used it also stands for all the others.

mentally. The study of learning mathematics, for instance, is here tantamount to studying psychological processes.

THE NONDUALISTIC ASSUMPTION UNDERLYING PHENOMENOGRAPHY

Phenomenography, inspired by the phenomenological school of thought and its ontological position, takes a nondualistic view of experience. According to the nondualistic ontological position held by phenomenography, object and subject are not separate, but the subject's experience of the object is a relation between the two. Returning to the learner's experience of a problem, for the phenomenographer there is no "problem as such." A problem is always a problem as it is understood in some way by someone; it does not have an independent existence. From a nondualistic ontological perspective there are not the two worlds of the dualistic ontology (a real objective world on the one hand and, on the other, either a subjective world of mental representations, or a subjective construction of a world beyond our reach). We maintain that there is only one world, a real objective world, which is experienced and understood, however, in different ways by human beings. This one world is both objective and subjective at the same time. An experience is a relationship between object and subject, encompassing both; the experience is as much an aspect of the object as it is of the subject. After all, the expression "how the subject experiences the object" is synonymous with the expression "how the object appears to the subject."

The word "experience" (conception, understanding, perception, apprehension, etc.) is thus used in phenomenography in the sense of being a relation between subject and object, as "something seen in some way by someone." Although the relation is neutral to the distinction between object and subject, someone's way of experiencing something can be seen either in relation to others' ways of experiencing the same thing or in relation to the same individual's way of experiencing other things. When the former relation is studied, interest focuses on variation between individuals, which means stressing the object aspect. When the latter is the focus of interest, we are able to make a more dynamic description of variation or changes within individuals, which means stressing the subject aspect. In the two sections that follow, these two alternative emphases in phenomenographic research are dealt with briefly in general terms and by means of an example.

ON PHENOMENA

We argued earlier that phenomenography rests on a nondualistic ontology and hence contradicts what can be called the commonsense view that experiences are experiences of objectively and independently existing objects. Now, the thesis that an object of experience is not independent of the way in which it is experienced does not imply that the object is identical with the way in which it is experienced. A more reasonable idea is to see the object as a complex of the different ways in which it can be experienced, which are logically related to each other. It is in this sense that they are experiences of the same object. The logically structured complex of the different ways of experiencing an object is what in phenomenography has been called the *outcome space* of the object (Marton, 1981). The outcome space can thus be considered as a synonym for *phenomenon*—the thing as it appears to us—contrasted with the Kantian *noumenon*, "the thing as such." "A way of experiencing something" is then simply one of these different aspects. An experience of an object is thus not a subjective shadow of the real object, but a part of the whole that is subjective and objective at the same time. The experiences are the units of research in phenomenography, and create a picture of the phenomenon they are a part of. All the phenomena together—all the different experiences of how things or events appear to persons in a specific cultural setting—can thus be seen as the "collective mind" (Marton, 1981) or possibly as our "social consciousness" or "our coknowledge" (Vygotsky, cited in Leont'ev, 1981, p. 56). Our individual consciousness is a part of this social consciousness, formed through interaction between the individual on the one hand, and the social and physical world on the other.

ON THE PHENOMENON OF DIVISION

Let us exemplify the foregoing line of reasoning by drawing on a study (Neuman, 1991a, 1991b) of how children in school understand and handle division problems. Two groups of pupils participated in the study. One consisted of second and third graders, most of whom had not yet been introduced to division at school (the second graders not even to multiplication). The other group consisted of fourth and six graders, who had been instructed in these operations.[2] Four problems were involved in the study:

(a) Four boys have got 28 marbles to share. How many marbles does each boy have?

(b) Mum has baked 42 buns. She puts them into plastic bags, 6 in each bag. How many bags does she need?

---

[2]Together 72 pupils from three different communities were interviewed—22 second graders, 21 third graders, 18 fourth graders, and 11 sixth graders. The pupils were chosen so that 2 belonged to those who performed below average, 2 to those who performed above average, and the others to those who performed on average level in mathematics, according to the judgment of their teachers.

In a follow-up study the numbers were changed to:

(c) Seven boys sharing the 28 marbles.
(d) Thirty-two buns of which 4 were put into each bag.

This is a study of different ways of experiencing, understanding, handling "something," meaning the object which is experienced. Let us for a moment try to leave the phenomenographic view that there is no "object as such," and imagine that we want to try to defend the view that the word problems just presented were the "object as such." Clearly, if we think of such a problem as "the problem as such," it cannot be identified with a specific embodiment, with the black print on the white paper, or with any of an infinite number of physical embodiments. It could be printed in any readable style, in any color, on any kind of paper, and it would still be the same problem. It could be shown on an overhead projector, on a computer screen, it could be read, even sung and still remain the same problem. Nor can the problem be identified with its specific linguistic expression: It could be translated into any language and still remain the same problem.

One could argue, of course, that it is precisely the sense of the problem, the meaning of the problem, that is invariant in the various embodiments or through linguistic transformations, and that this sense or meaning is therefore what defines "the problem as such." But then one must raise the question, does meaning always assume a subject, someone to understand? If we answer this question in the affirmative it implies that we are no longer defining the problem in itself— "the problem as such"—but rather "the problem as understood (by someone)."

It is of decisive importance that the aim of the division study was not to describe conceptions of the specific problems that were given, but to describe conceptions of simple integer division in general. It was to reach this goal that the four different problems in the two separate studies were used. So what is it the described conceptions are conceptions of?

We can of course define division as a mathematician would, as the inverse of multiplication. This is certainly one way of understanding word problems on division, but it is certainly not the only way of understanding such problems. As will become obvious from what follows, it was not with division of this kind that most of the children in Neuman's investigation addressed the problems. This is actually the main point we are driving at; we have to find out empirically what problems—in this case what kind of division—the children are addressing, and this is exactly what the phenomenographic approach is all about.

There has been a long debate in Sweden about whether division should be introduced at school as a single or as two kinds of operation. Earlier, a distinction was made between partitive and quotitive division. In the former—illustrated by problems (a) and (c)—the size of the whole and the number of parts are known, and one has to find the size of the parts. In the latter—illustrated by problems (b) and (d)—the size of the whole and the size of each part are given, and one has to find the number of parts. In the 1960s, however, a curricular decision was made in Sweden to introduce division as a single operation, the inverse of multiplication. Nowadays, this is mostly done by setting "naked number problems" when children have been drilled in multiplication for about a year. The pupils are then taught to solve the task 28/4, for instance, by asking, "How many times does 4 go into 28?" They are taught to "measure" the dividend in terms of, or in units of, the divisor.

This way of dividing is readily applicable to quotitive division problems when word problems are introduced later. In problem (b), for instance, you can easily set out from the question: "How many times do 6 buns go into 42 buns?" On the other hand, it is hardly applicable to partitive division problems. In problem (a) the question reexpressed in this way would be, "How many times do 4 children go into 28 marbles," a thoroughly senseless question. Of course, as adults, we might be able to rephrase the question as a more meaningful one, "How many times larger is the number of marbles than the number of children," thus "measuring" between two variables instead of within one variable (Lybeck, 1981; Vergnaud, 1983, 1988). But, as Vergnaud pointed out, measuring between variables is much more difficult than measuring within one variable, and young children would hardly experience partitive division in this way.

The study had two different research questions in focus, one directed at the older and one at the younger children. For the older pupils, the study aimed to reveal the ways in which they experienced partitive division, after being introduced to division as the inverse of multiplication. The research problem concerning the younger children, who had not yet been taught division, was of another kind, and aimed at describing their informal ideas of division. In Sweden there has been a vivid discussion among educationalists (e.g., Kilborn, 1989) about the current formal introduction of division, and it has been emphasized that young children's powerful informal thought models might be destroyed through this introduction. However, questions of the kind "Do there exist any powerful thought models of the two kinds of division before division is taught, and if so, what do they look like?" have actually never been posed. It was questions of this kind that were formulated for the part of the study involving the younger children. It was believed that if those thought models existed and could be identified, they might throw light on the issue whether division should be introduced as a single kind of mathematical operation or whether the distinction between the two forms should be maintained.

The study was carried out by means of open and deep interviews between researcher and child in which the problems of interest were posed. The child was asked to solve the problem, and encouraged to use any method, to talk freely, to write or to draw if they so wished. What they said, did, or produced was discussed in an attempt to probe the child's underlying understanding of the division problem as seen therein.

The interviews, or discussions, were tape-recorded and transcribed. Analysis, following the phenomenographic approach (Neuman, in press), consisted of an immersion in the transcript data together with the children's written and drawn production, as well as listening to the original tape-recordings in conjunction with the researchers' notes. The goal of the analysis was to identify qualitatively distinct ways in which the children experienced division, by a hermeneutic, dialectic process, examining pieces of interview or production against a background of the whole, and reviewing the whole in the light of individual pieces of evidence.

Eventually, an outcome space of four qualitatively distinct experiences were reached, the results of the study. These are:

The dealing out experience, in which the whole is dealt out among the necessary number of parts until it is exhausted.

The dividing up experience, in which the whole is in some way divided up among the number of necessary parts.

The algorithmic experience, in which the child resorts to a numerical algorithm to reach an answer.

The inverse-multiplication experience, in which the child makes use of known multiplication facts to produce an answer.

These four ways of experiencing division are elaborated and exemplified in the rest of this chapter. Further, there is another higher order difference in the children's awareness of division. Their experience can be of a numerical or a situational kind (or both); the former emphasizes the number aspects of division and the problem whereas the latter emphasizes the situation described in the problem.

Neuman's study illustrated that most of the pupils who had not yet been taught division seemed to experience division of both kinds in the same way, as related to "dealing out" situations. For problem (a) they thought of a situation where 28 marbles were dealt out one at a time, or maybe a few at a time at first and later one at a time. And in problem (b) they thought of a situation where 42 marbles were dealt out 6 at a time. They used the two known numbers in the problems, irrespective of which kind of division it involved, and solved them by proportional reasoning. This was built on the constant relationship between buns and bags in problems (b) and (d), for example, 6 buns–1 bag, 12 buns–2 bags, and so on. In problems (a) and (c) it was built on the constant relationship between the number of marbles distributed after each round, and the number of marbles received by each boy after each round, such as 4 marbles–1 marble per boy, 8 marbles–2 marbles per boy, and so on. Thus, even if the divisor had different meanings in partitive and quotitive division (respectively, the number within each part and the number dealt out in each round) the children could in both cases use the two known numbers in the problems to "measure" the dividend in terms of the divisor.

On the other hand, even if both problems were solved in the same way, that did not mean that these pupils experienced division as the inverse of multiplication. As already pointed out, most second graders had not yet been taught to multiply. Rather, the way in which the dividend was measured using the divisor as unit was closely related to primitive sensory experiences of "dealing out" situations, which the children could represent in drawings or describe verbally in their mental calculation acts.

About one-third of the younger children, however, experienced the two kinds of division as dealing out on the one hand, or, on the other experiencing the two kinds of division in different ways. Although even these pupils experienced quotitive division as "dealing out," they understood the partitive problems in terms of "dividing up." For these pupils the divisor did not mean "the number of objects dealt out in each round," in partitive division, but "the number of parts." It had the meaning that the denominator has in a fraction, and the pupils wanted to know directly what $1/4$ of 28 was in problem (a) and what $1/7$ of 28 was in problem (c).

Problem (a) could also be easily solved when experienced in this way. The children could think of it in the terms of "repeated halving"—half of 28 is 14, half of 14 is 7—or in terms of "dividing up the dividend," for instance, first trying to find out what $1/4$ of 20 is and after that what $1/4$ of 8 is. These simple ways, however, are not generalizable; repeated halving can only be used if the divisor is four—or possibly eight—and "dividing up the dividend" carries a similar restriction. Thus none of these simple ways could be used in problem (c). There the generally applicable way of "dividing up"—repeated estimation—was the only one it was possible to use. When repeated estimation was used, an estimate was made of what $1/4$ (or $1/7$ in problem [c]) of 28 might be. This estimation of the quotient was then checked by "building up" to 28 by repeated addition of the estimated number.

For the children who could not yet multiply, the repeated additions, which had to be carried out each time a new estimate was made, were exhausting, and repeated estimation was only used by the second graders, mostly in drawings. Older children seemed to anticipate its exhausting character. On the other hand, they also rejected "repeated halving" and "dividing up the dividend" for their nongeneral character, which might be because they had experienced that these strategies could not be generally applied. The "dividing up" experience thus appeared only rarely after Grade 2 and never after Grade 3. It seemed to demand a binary understanding of multiplication, related to knowledge of the "multiplication table." That was contrary to the dealing out experience through which this kind of understanding and factual knowledge could be developed, which is taken up again later in this chapter.[3]

---

[3]Murray, Olivier, and Human (1992) made similar observations in their longitudinal study of how children develop their own informal division strategies when encouraged to do so at school. Even their pupils abandoned after some time strategies related to the experience Neuman called "dividing up."

The point we wanted to illustrate with this example is that the object of experience or understanding cannot be defined independently of the way in which it is experienced or understood. In actual fact, the different ways in which the object—in this case simple whole-number division—is experienced or understood together constitute the object. The important difference in experiencing division before it is taught is, according to this phenomenographic study, not between partitive and quotitive division, but between experiencing both kinds of division in different ways—quotitive division as dealing out and partitive division as dividing up.

These two types of understanding are some of the possible ways of experiencing division that together constitute the phenomenon of division, and it seems to be of importance for teachers and curriculum designers to know about the possibilities and shortcomings of these primitive experiences.

However, there were two further experiences of division expressed by the pupils in Grades 4 and 6 who had already been taught division, both of which were very different from these primitive ones. The first of these seemed to be an experience of division as "the inverse of multiplication." Problem (b) was then solved by thinking "seven, because 7×6—or 6×7—makes 42," and problem (a) by thinking "seven, because 7×4—or 4×7—makes 28."[4] The second experience could be called "follow the algorithm." The children who could multiply never experienced the quotitive division, for instance, problem (b), in this way. It was still solved by thinking "seven, because 7×6 makes 42." Problem (a), on the other hand, was solved using the long or short division algorithm by five of the nine sixth graders who had instantly solved problem (b) by using a known multiplication. For problem (a), after thinking "Four into 2 goes 0 times; 0 times four is 0 [writing 0]" and then "Four into 28 goes 7 times; 7 times 4 is 28 [writing 7 after the 0, thus 07]," the children who followed the algorithm could answer "Seven."

The problem these pupils experienced was more clearly illustrated by the pupils who arrived at a wrong answer, for instance, by Marita in Grade 6, who put the dividend and the divisor on the wrong places, arriving at the answer 0.14 marbles each. She understands that this cannot be the right answer and supposes she has chosen the wrong algorithm. So she tries the multiplication algorithm, arriving at 112 marbles each, which she also experiences as unreasonable. Finally, for some reason she multiplies 28 by 6. Then she does not know how to handle the carried figure and gives up, saying that she cannot solve the problem. When asked if she cannot find any other way to solve it—instead of bothering with "these" (the column algorithms)—she says "Well, seven . . .", but immediately changes her mind, adding "No, that's not right either. . . ." Asked by the

---

[4]It was not possible, however, through follow up questions to find out any prereflective experiences behind the very automatically given answers identified as "the reverse of multiplication." Some of these answers might thus just have been an expression for the children following the rule "find out how many times the divisor goes into the dividend."

interviewer why it is not right she just again says "No, it can't be like that, can it?" As the interviewer is eager to find out what is behind the correct answer "Seven," she again insists: "But you actually said seven . . . you must have thought it out in some way . . . how were you thinking?"—"I just thought 7 × 4's 28 . . . ," Marita answers, while still rejecting this answer. In this interview it was not possible to come closer to an understanding of why she did not accept it. The interpretation of the answer is that Marita has tried to use the rule for division she has been taught at school, "Find out the number of times the divisor goes into the dividend," translating it to the context of the partitive division problem, but that she is not able to make sense of this rule. How can this problem be solved through working out how many times four children go into 28 marbles?

The algorithmic conception was displayed not only by these six pupils in Grade 6 in partitive, but not quotitive, division.[5] The same phenomenon was observed in Grade 4, and even in answers given by pupils interviewed late in Grade 3. This should have important curricular implications.

ON AWARENESS AND LEARNING

When we discussed division as it can be seen, or experienced, from a mathematician's or an educationalist's perspective, or when we described the ways in which the children in the study understood division, we focused on the object aspect of the experiences. The different experiences of the same object constituted "the outcome space" of the object, tantamount to the phenomenon—the object in the different ways it appears to us. These experiences are interesting in educational discussions concerning the content of the subject matter that should be taught and the sequence in which it should be taught.

If we want to understand how learning takes place, however, and through this the teaching methods that should be used, we have to focus on the subject aspect of experiences. After all, it is always an individual who learns.[6] To focus on the subject means that instead of relating someone's experience of something to other people's experiences of the same thing, as we did in our earlier discussions, we relate someone's experience of something to her experiences of other things or to different experiences of the same thing. The question then becomes, "Is a person experiencing different things simultaneously and if she is, is she experiencing one and the same thing in different ways?"

Phenomenographic data illustrate that a person is able to experience different

---

[5]Two of the 11 pupils in Grade 6 could not solve either of the two problem types, because they could neither multiply, nor carry out repeated addition.

[6]At least in the original sense of the word. We can, as earlier pointed out, also conceive of learning on the level, where the "collective mind" or "social consciousness" is formed.

things simultaneously and that she also can think of each of these things in different ways. The totality of a person's simultaneous experiences, her relatedness to the world, we call her *awareness,* a term that we use interchangeably with the term *consciousness.* A decisive difference between the way in which either of these terms are commonly used and the way in which we use them here is that the usual dichotomic sense of the term is replaced by the idea of structural differentiation of awareness. We are used to thinking of consciousness as opposed to unconsciousness (or to the subconscious), or awareness as opposed to unawareness. We may think that we are aware of one thing or a few things at a time and that all other things are—for the time being—beyond our awareness.

If the stance of information-processing psychology is taken, one may relate awareness to primary memory or short-term store, as "a rather small amount of . . . highly activated, readily available information which is kept alive in the mind—or held in consciousness—while the person is actually making use of it, and which fades out of consciousness or is replaced by new information quite rapidly as soon as the person stops using it" (Carr, 1979, p. 124). Now, even a very limited use of the phenomenological method in the Husserlian sense—that is, to reflect on our way of experiencing things, such as the very situation we happen to be in—should be sufficient to convince us that it is just not right to claim that we are aware of one thing at a time. Let us, for the sake of example, envisage a reader of the present text. When she reads this actual line she is aware of the topic of this chapter, she is aware of what kind of book this is a chapter of, she is aware of—at least to some extent—the line of argument preceding the actual line she is reading. She may have some previous experience of the topic of the chapter, and—to the extent to which that is true—her previous experiences make up a background for her reading. She is aware of why she is reading this chapter, how she feels about it while reading it. She is also aware of who she is, where she is sitting, what time of the year and time of day it is, what she is going to do during the rest of the day. She is aware of her own name, whether she is married or not, if she has any children, if her parents are alive, and so on. Although she is aware of innumerable things simultaneously, she is certainly not aware of everything in the same way. Her awareness has a structure to it. Certain things come to the fore—they are figural, they are thematized—whereas other things recede to the ground, they are tacit, they are unthematized. And again, there are not two categories: figure–ground, thematized–unthematized, explicit–implicit. There are different degrees of how figural, thematized, or explicit things or aspects are in our awareness.

When our reader is reading the text, we hope, but it is not necessarily the case, that the text is in the focus of her awareness. While reading the text things that are related to its content come to the fore in the reader's awareness. Gurwitsch (1964) made a distinction between the object of focal awareness, the theme, and those aspects of the experienced world that are related to the object and in which it is embedded, the thematic field. In the present example the text is the theme and issues such as phenomenography and children's experience of division, phenomenology, and questions of qualitative research methodology in general belong to the thematic field. The same theme can of course be seen against the background of different thematic fields.

Furthermore, there are things that are temporally and spatially coexistent with the reading of the text, such as the room where the reader is sitting, the reader's marital worries, and so on. All that is coexistent with the theme, without being related to it by dint of content or meaning, Gurwitsch called the margin.

Awareness also has a particular structure as far as the theme is concerned. The theme appears to the subject in a certain way; it is seen from a particular point of view. The specific experience of a theme—or of an object, to keep to the terminology we established earlier—can be defined in two ways. First, it can be defined in terms of the way in which it is delimited from and related to a context. And second, it can be defined in terms of the way its component parts are delimited from and related to each other and to the whole (Svensson, 1984).

ON AWARENESS AND LEARNING AND DIVISION

In the division study, described in the previous section, four different ways of understanding what division is were identified: the dealing out experience, the dividing up experience, the algorithmic experience, and the experience of division as the inverse of multiplication.

Previously, we focused on the object aspect of the experiences of division. In this section we focus on the subject aspect. Accordingly, we now illustrate three individual children's ways of dealing with division problems. Daniel, a boy in Grade 2, solves problem (a) saying, "First five each . . . five, ten, fifteen, twenty . . . then one each, and then one each again . . . 28." Daniel has not even been taught multiplication yet, and the written documentation of his thought does not mirror any counting operation at all, he just jots down the numbers he thinks of—a 5, a 1, and another 1.

It is easy to see the similarity between the way in which he solves the problem and the drawings that some of his classmates use to do it. These children first draw five marbles for each boy on their paper, and then one marble for each of the boys, two times. For Daniel, however, it is difficult to know if this experience of a dealing out situation is the only reason why he solves the problem in the way he does. He might also have been avoiding the difficult procedure of adding four seven times, as he would have been forced to do if he had dealt out one marble at a time in his thoughts.

Daniel, not yet instructed in multiplication, already solves the problem with an addition that mirrors the distributive quality of multiplication—an addition that will very soon end up in the "known multiplications" $4 \times 5 = 20$, $4 \times 6 = 24$, and $4 \times 7 = 28$, as soon as he is taught multiplication. It is not possible to say if Daniel is aware of the situational and the numerical aspects simultaneously. But it is possible to see how these two aspects are so closely connected to each other in early division carried out informally that they cannot be distinguished.

In other answers, however, it is more easily seen how the child is simultaneously aware of many different experiences related to the theme that is focused by the division problems. A boy in Grade 3, Mattias, for instance, in solving problem (b) started with "6 × 4 is 24," doubled 24 arriving at 48, and finally subtracted 6. The numerical aspect of the problem is clearly of prime interest for Mattias. To begin with he does not even seem to care that there were 42 buns, 6 in each bag. Instead of thinking of four sixes he seems to think of six fours. (In Swedish 6 × 4 is the written expression of "six times four" meaning six fours.[7]) Then he might have anticipated the difficult procedure of adding several sixes in order to build up to 42, and simultaneously seen the simple way to double 24. It does not seem to bother him that in the latter case he gets 48 buns. He seems to have experienced 48 partly as the double of 24 and partly as exactly "one bag" more than 42, and for the moment neglected the situational experience. Then, however, he again becomes immediately aware of the situation with 42 buns, thus subtracting the difference between 48 and 42: six buns— one bag. Mattias has not yet been taught division, and what he writes is a mixture of relevant figures, words, and symbols, reflecting his thoughts rather than any mathematical expression.

It is not only the relation between situational and numerical knowledge but also the relation between procedural and conceptual knowledge that is mirrored in the thoughts and written documents of these two boys. In the procedures they use it is possible to see that they set out from, or might be beginning to form, a proportional way of thinking. Daniel, for instance, thinks 20, five each; 24, six each; 28, seven each. An embryo of the distributive idea of division can also be observed in both these problem solving acts. Daniel's thoughts, for example, reflect the idea $4(5 + 1 + 1) = 20 + 4 + 4 = 28$. In Mattias' way of solving the problem it is also possible to trace embryonic associative, commutative, and distributive properties of multiplication:

$$(6 \times 4) \times 2 = 6 \times (4 \times 2) = 6 \times 8 = 8 \times 6 = 48 \qquad 6 \times (8 - 1)$$
$$= 48 - 6 = 42$$

One more example is given, illustrating how the child is aware of different experiences of division and how focus is one moment on one of them and the next on another, depending on the dialogue by means of which the interviewer tries to become aware of the experiences from which the child's problem-solving act sets out. In this example, however, the child seems to set out from a solely

---

[7]Yet, of course, Mattias might still have thought "six four times." The correct English expression of 6 × 4—"six multiplied by four"—however, is not taught to Swedish pupils.

numerical experience of the problem, not related to a situational experience at all. However, because the situational experience is in his awareness somewhere in the thematic field, it is possible to bring it into focus through the dialogue.

Kalle, Grade 3, has been introduced to division just some weeks earlier. He solves problem (c), where seven children are to share 28 marbles, by saying "Four marbles each." When asked about how he knew that, he answers:

K: First I do . . . seven and seven, that's fourteen . . . then fourteen and fourteen's twenty-eight . . .

He seems to ask himself: "How many sevens are there in 28?" The interviewer wonders if it is only this question Kalle tries to answer through this sort of addition, which he has made easier through a "doubling," or if he might also think of it in a dealing out way, where seven marbles are dealt out so that each child gets one marble in each round. He can hardly have made a successful estimation when he almost instantly answers "Four each," because then he should have checked that through adding four seven times. Now he adds seven four times. A long dialogue ensues:

I: Why did you take seven?
K: 'Cause . . . it was seven boys that were to share.
I: Now, when you've taken this first seven, what do you do with them then?
K: Mm
I: What happens to them? . . . when you've taken them? . . .
K: When I've taken seven marbles?
I: Mm mm . . .
K: Then . . . well, then they're . . . well, what can I say?

Kalle goes quiet. He does not seem to be aware of what is behind his decision to take—or rather add—seven four times. The interviewer tries to confront his experience of the problem, which possibly is purely numerical, with an experience of a "fair share" situation, trying to find out if he experiences the semantics of the problem at all, and Kalle tries to step away from the abstract numerical division he has been taught and replace it with an everyday experience of fair sharing. It is then natural that he first thinks of a situation where seven marbles at a time are dealt out. Thus, it is a dealing out experience of the kind related to quotitive division that is thematizeed in his mind, and the dialogue goes on like this:

K: Then another's got to take then . . .

Kalle becomes silent for the ssecond time. The interviewer interprets his answer to mean that one boy has got seven marbles and that the next one now gets a similar amount. To keep the dialogue going she says:

I: And then another boy gets to take seven marbles?

K: Ye-es . . . just a minute . . . Ye-es, yes

Kalle might already have continued his thought, dealing out also the "two sevens" left to two more boys, when he says "just a minute. . . ." Then he might have become aware that three boys would not have their shares. He is quiet for a long while. Then he says:

K: But it might be wrong . . .

Kalle becomes silent again. No other experiences seems to be thematized in his mind, and finally the interviewer says:

I: Might it be wrong? . . . You wrote four marbles each . . . And I wonder, how did you know that? . . .

K: Mm m. 'Cause . . . mm mm It can't be that . . .

I: Can't it?

K: Well . . . ye-e-es! 'Cause I've taken seven four times! . . .

Kalle again seems to have found an acceptable point of departure for his thought. But what does it look like? Is it: "Seven marbles four times, one marble to each boy in each round"? Or is it "This is the kind of problem you can solve through working out what makes twenty-eight in the seven-times table"? The interviewer wants to know, and asks:

I: 'N what did you do when . . . Each time you took seven . . . what did you do with them? . . .

K: I put them together.

Kalle is back in the numerical experience of division again, and the interviewer tries to explain what she wants to know a bit more clearly:

I: But now, if you'd really thought that . . . that you'd do like that . . . Here they are, twenty-eight marbles lets say . . . in a little bowl. Then you take seven, and those seven boys are sitting here (points round the table). What did you do with the seven marbles you took?

Again Kalle is forced to turn back to reality. And again the "dealing out" experience related to quotitive division is thematized: "Seven in each part—seven to each boy."

K: I gived 'em to a boy . . .

I: To a boy, all seven? . . .

K: No . . .

Kalle probably remembers that he has already rejected this idea, and a new theme is actualized:

K: No, I'll take four marbles . . .

The new theme is closely related to the "dividing up" experience. But Kalle does not need to make a repeated estimation. He knows that the answer was four when he first solved the problem. Maybe Kalle is trying to check if all the 28 marbles will be used if he takes 4 at a time. In any case, he once again stops speaking. As has already been illustrated, it is difficult to add four seven times. Maybe Kalle thinks this laborious addition is not worth the trouble. Four is still a number that does not appear in the problem, and he has been taught to use the two known numbers in the task of dividing. Again he hesitates over the answer "4" he has written on his paper, asking "'s that right?" And again the interviewer asserts it is correct before she resumes the dialogue:

I: But I just want to know how you can actually think this out . . .
K: Mm m
I: So the seven boys are sitting here . . . Just put them in the middle of the table . . . or what are you doing with them?
K: I'm putting 'em in a pile and I'll take another seven . . .
I: Yes, but these poor boys, they were supposed to share the marbles, they can't be very pleased that the marbles are here in four piles?
[The researcher points to the middle of the table four times.]
K: No. I take one from the pile and give it to one boy . . . [What Kalle now says is impossible to hear on the tape, but according to the protocol maintained by the interviewer, Kalle points to each of the boys in turn, as he imagines them sitting around the table, before again pointing to the middle of the table, saying] 'n' then I take . . . [again impossible to hear] . . .
I: How do you know that then? What do you do to share them out? . . .
K: I'll put 'em . . . mm . . . one to every first like that . . . then I'll do it as long as I can . . . that'll be four to each of them . . .

In the end, the experience of "dealing out one at a time" is thematized. But is it at all related to the numerical experience "7 + 7 = 14; 14 + 14 = 28," the one Kalle expressed from the beginning? The interviewer finds it difficult to formulate more questions, without leading Kalle to an answer expressing the thought "seven in each round." Finally she says:

I: Mm mm . . . I don't really know now . . . really how you mean . . . Because there were all twenty-eight here, weren't there? Did you take them again? Did you put them back in the bowl?
K: No. I take one from the pile and give it to one boy . . . 'n' then I take
[What Kalle now says is impossible to hear on the tape, but according to the protocol maintained by the interviewer, Kalle points to each of the boys in turn, as he imagines them sitting round the table.]

Eventually Kalle relates his numerical experience of division to an experience of "dealing out seven in each round, one to each boy." The interview situation becomes a learning situation for him, causing a change in the structure of his consciousness of division. He becomes aware of there being a relation between fair sharing situations of a certain kind and the calculation he used when he first solved the problem.

CONCLUDING REMARKS

In the examples with the two pupils who had been taught division we observe that—in contrast to the younger untutored children—they no longer seem to relate division to the everyday experiences that gave rise to the need for division, and for which division is to be used in their adult lives.

The sixth grader Marita, for instance, cannot at all relate her purely numerical experience of partitive division to a fair sharing situation of any kind, in spite of the fact that the interviewer tries to make her aware that one can divide intuitively without having to follow a rule. Nor does Kalle, the third grader, who has just some weeks ago been taught division, intuitively relate his numerical thought to a situational experience. Yet fair share situations of different kinds are still within his "thematic field" as something that in an absent way is related to division. Thus, these situational experiences can be brought into focus and thematized through the confrontational discussion between him and the interviewer. On the other hand, Mattias, the third grader, who has not yet been introduced to division, experiences the numerical and the situational aspects of the problem simultaneously, moving freely between them. And finally Daniel, the second grader who has not even been taught multiplication, intuitively solves the problem through a less demanding repeated addition, because that is the result of the less demanding dealing out situation he experiences.

In the three examples of the second and third graders, it is possible to see that they all strive for less demanding problem-solving acts, which will probably result in knowledge of the so-called "multiplication and division facts", but with factual knowledge anchored in—and created in mutual interplay with—conceptual understanding of the three properties of multiplication. However, only the first two of these children, those who had not yet been taught division, relate intuitively the numerical aspects of division to experiences of everyday situations, in the way which they have to be related if they are to be of use in everyday life.

Developing a mastery of division reasonably implies that division problems are understood in terms of numerical knowledge of numbers, certainly anchored in experiences of sharing situations, but no longer focusing on them. Now, what does developing such a capability—or developing any capability of understanding something in a certain way—mean? What does it take to learn in this sense of the word?

The common idea—held by laymen and psychologists—is that capability is developed in the individual and is stored in her head in the form of a scheme or some form of internal representation, which is applied to different relevant cases. This idea of the development and use of a capability rests solidly on a dualistic ontology—subject (the learner) and object (the situation or problem handled) are separate and independent entities. Now, the dualistic line of reasoning, this commonsense idea, runs into logical contradictions and difficulties. Here is one such paradox. According to the dualistic view of the world, something (e.g., a division problem) is understood in a certain way because a scheme or some internal representation that is stored somewhere in long-term memory is applied to that something (e.g., to the division problem). Now in order to retrieve the tool (the scheme or the internal representation), long-term memory has to be searched. But how does the system know what it is looking for before the object has been made sense of by using the tool?

We believe that the nondualistic alternative, based on the view of awareness that we have now introduced, is a more reasonable and productive approach to the study of human experience in all respects. The subject is aware of the object in a certain way. The pupils in the division study, for instance, might be primarily aware of the problem as a "dealing out" or a "dividing up" situation, as a purely numerical problem, or as a problem simultaneously related to numerical and situational experiences. The problem does not exist as such; it is always under-stood in one way or in another. The ways of understanding a problem are always present to awareness; they do not have to be searched for. Either they come into focus immediately when the problem is presented, as for instance was the case when Mattias solved the problem, or they are brought into focus through contra-dictory experiences in a discussion, as in the extract from the dialogue with Kalle, or possibly through discoveries, made in the physical world.[8] The new problem is understood in terms of the subject's previous relevant experiences, which are all present to awareness. And as awareness is always the awareness of something it is a fundamentally nondualistic relation.

Our aim in this chapter has been to demonstrate that phenomenography rests on a nondualistic ontology and that it is only through this realization that we can clarify what kind of entities experiences, conceptions, understandings are. The point we have been making is that experiences, conceptions, understandings, and so forth (terms that we have used interchangeably) refer to subject–object rela-tions. Our world is a world that is always understood in one way or in another; it cannot be defined without someone defining it. On the other hand, we cannot exist without our world.

Still, we can focus on the object or on the subject aspect of the subject–object relations that experiences are. When focusing on the former we ended up with the conclusion that an object is the structured complex of all the different ways in which it can be experienced. When focusing on the latter we came to the conclu-

---

[8]As exemplified in Marton and Neuman (1990, pp. 65–67).

sion that we are always aware of everything, although the way in which we are aware of everything is situationally structured.

Both these conclusions may seem highly counterintuitive to some of our readers. But still, what they imply is that we should explore—without too many preconceived ideas—what the world we experience is like, on the one hand, and what our way of experiencing the world is like, on the other.

And, of course, these are not two things. They are one.

ACKNOWLEDGMENTS

The investigation of children's experiences of division and the preparation of this chapter were supported financially by two separate grants from the Swedish Council for Research in the Humanities and Social Sciences, one to Dagmar Neuman and one to Ference Marton. We have a deep sense of gratitude to Anita Sandahl for carrying out many of the interviews in a most competent way, and to Shirley Booth for her very courageous and able attempts to improve the language as well as the presentation of this chapter.

REFERENCES

Carr, T. H. (1979). Consciousness in models of human information processing: Primary memory, executive control and input regulation. In G. Underwood & R. Stevens (Eds.), *Aspects of consciousness* (pp. 123–154). London: Academic Press.

Gurwitsch, A. (1964). *The field of consciousness*. Pittsburgh: Duquesne University Press.

Kilborn, W. (1989). *Didaktik ämnesteori i matematik Del 1: Grundläggande aritmetik* [Educational theory of mathematics. Vol. 1: Basic arithmetics]. Stockholm: Utbildningsförlaget.

Leont'ev, A. N. (1981). The problem of activity in psychology. In J. W. Wertsch (Ed.), *The concept of activity in Soviet psychology* (pp. 37–79). Armonk, NY: Sharpe.

Lybeck, L. (1981). *Arkimedes i klassen: En ämnespedagogisk berättelse* [Archimedes in the classroom: An account of a subject-specific educational study]. Göteborg studies in educational sciences, 37. Göteborg: Acta Universitatis Gothoburgensis.

Marton, F. (1981). Phenomenography—describing conceptions of the world around us. *Instructional Science, 10,* 177–200.

Marton, F., Hounsell, D., & Entwistle, N. (Eds.). (1984). *The experience of learning*. Edinburgh: Scottish Academic Press.

Marton, F., & Neuman, D. (1990). Constructivism, phenomenology and the origin of arithmetic skills. In L. P. Steffe & T. Wood (Eds.), *Transforming children's mathematics education: International perspectives* (pp. 62–75). Hillsdale, NJ: Lawrence Erlbaum Associates.

Miller, G. A. (1967). *The psychology of communication*. New York: Basic Books.

Murray, H., Olivier, A., & Human, P. (1992, August). The development of young students division strategies. In W. Geeslin & A. Graham (Eds.), *Proceedings of the Sixteenth PME Conference*. University of New Hampshire, Durham, NH.

Neuman, D. (1991a). Barns uppfattningar av innehålls—och delningsdivision. [Children's conceptions of quotitive and partitive division]. In G. Emanuelsson, B. Johansson, & R. Ryding (Eds.), *Tal och räkning 1*. [Number and counting, 1] (pp. 105–129). Lund: Studentlitteratur.

Neuman, D. (1991b, June). Early conceptions of division: A phenomenographic approach. In F. Furinghetti (Ed.), *Proceedings of the Fifteenth PME conference*. Assissi, Italy.

Neuman, D. (in press). Phenomenography: The roots of numeracy. *Journal for Research in Mathematics Education.*

Svensson, L. (1984). Människobilden i INOM-gruppens forskning: Den lärande människan [The view of man in the research of the INOM group: The learning man]. (Rep. No. 3) Pedagogiska Institutionen, Göteborg University.

Vergnaud, G. (1983). Multiplicative structures. In R. Lesh & M. Landau (Eds.), *Acquisition of mathematics concepts and processes* (pp. 127–174). New York: Academic Press.

Vergnaud, G. (1988). Multiplicative structures. In J. Hiebert & M. Behr (Eds.), *Number concepts and operations in the middle grades* (pp. 141–161). Hillsdale, NJ: Lawrence Erlbaum, and Reston, VA: National Council of Teachers of Mathematics.

von Glasersfeld, E. (1990). Environment and communication. In L. P. Steffe & T. Wood (Eds.), *Transforming children's mathematics education: International perspectives* (pp. 30–38). Hillsdale, NJ: Lawrence Erlbaum Associates.

20 Varieties of Constructivism: A Framework for Comparison

Paul Ernest
University of Exeter, England

Following the seminal influence of Jean Piaget, constructivism is emerging as perhaps the major research paradigm in mathematics education. This is particularly the case for psychological research in mathematics education. However, rather than solving all of the problems for our field, this raises a number of new ones. Elsewhere I have explored the differences between the constructivism of Piaget and that of von Glasersfeld (Ernest, 1991b) and have suggested how social constructivism can be developed, and how it differs in its assumptions from radical constructivism (Ernest, 1990, 1991a). Here I wish to begin to consider further questions, including the following: What is constructivism, and what different varieties are there? In addition to the explicit principles on which its varieties are based, what underlying metaphors and epistemologies do they assume? What are the strengths and weaknesses of the different varieties? What do they offer as tools for researching the teaching and learning of mathematics? In particular, what does radical constructivism offer that is unique? And last but not least: What are the implications for the teaching of mathematics?

CONSTRUCTION

What the various forms of constructivism all share is the metaphor of carpentry, architecture, or construction work. This is about the building up of structures from preexisting pieces, possibly specially shaped for the task. The metaphor describes understanding as the building of mental structures, and the term *restructuring,* often used as a synonym for accommodation or conceptual change, contains this metaphor. What the metaphor of construction does not mean in

335

constructivism is that understanding is built up from received pieces of knowledge. The process is recursive (Kieren & Pirie, 1991), so the "building blocks" of understanding are themselves the product of previous acts of construction. Thus the distinction between the structure and content of understanding can only be relative in constructivism. Previously built structures become the content in subsequent constructions.

The metaphor of construction is contained in the first principle of constructivism as expressed by von Glasersfeld (1989, p. 182): "Knowledge is not passively received but actively built up by the cognizing subject." This is the principle of what I term "weak" constructivism, constituting those positions based on this principle alone.

Simple as this basic form of constructivism seems to be, it represents a very significant move from naive empiricism or classical behaviorism, for it recognizes that knowing is active, that it is individual and personal, and that it is based on previously constructed knowledge. Just getting student teachers to realize this, by reflecting on children's methods of doing mathematics or alternative conceptions in science, say, represents a significant step forward from the naive transmission view of teaching and passive reception view of learning with which many arrive. Nor is a passive reception view of learning dead among professionals or administrators in education. Many government-driven curriculum reforms, in Britain at least, assume that the central powers can simply transmit their plans and structures to teachers who will passively absorb and then implement them in "delivering the curriculum." Such conceptions and strategies are deeply embedded in the public consciousness, although it may be no accident that they also serve authoritarian powers (Ernest, 1991a; Freire, 1972).

ROMANTICISM

One danger in all forms of constructivism, which is worth mentioning here, is that it can lead to an overly child-centered, romantic progressivism. Constructivism, conceived in a loose and emotive way, can become associated with a sentimental view of the child (Walkerdine, 1984). "Discovery learning" from the 1960s onward was often bound up with a romanticism that in the end was not wholly productive for learners, and we must guard against constructivism becoming identified with this position. There is an undoubted need to let learners construct their own meanings, but also for the teacher and peers to interact with learners to negotiate a passage toward socially accepted knowledge. However, forms of discovery learning in which teachers always "funnel" learners toward predetermined solutions presuppose that the teacher is in possession of "the truth," rather than someone aware of the conventional nature of knowledge. Elsewhere I have analyzed the ideology of romanticism in progressive education in greater depth, and indicated that it often rests on an absolutist epistemology. In such circumstances there is a perception that there are "right answers" to steer children toward (Ernest, 1991a, chapter 8). Wood, Cobb, and Yackel (1995) and Bauersfeld (1980) referred to this when embodied in classroom behaviors by the teacher as "funneling" the child toward the teacher-desired answer. The epistemological contrast between this absolutist position and the fallibilism of radical constructivism immediately reveals an area where different versions of constructivism make a significant difference in practice.

EDUCATIONAL PARADIGMS

The various forms of constructivism comprise what might be termed an educational paradigm. As such, they might be represented by:

1. An *ontology*: a theory of existence concerning the status of the world and what populates it.

2. An *epistemology* comprising (a) a theory of the nature, genesis, and warranting of subjective knowledge, including a theory of individual learning and (b) a theory of the nature, genesis, and warranting of knowledge (understood as conventional or shared human knowledge), as well as a theory of "truth."

3. A *methodology*: a theory of which methods and techniques are appropriate and valid to use to generate and justify knowledge, given the epistemology.

4. A *pedagogy*: a theory of teaching, the means to facilitate learning according to the epistemology.

Adding the fourth element (pedagogy) takes the specification of an educational paradigm beyond that which is usually admitted as an educational research paradigm, such as in Schubert (1986). However, the addition is justified by mathematics educators' shared concern with keeping educational outcomes, as well as theoretical aspects of research paradigms, in the picture.

Using this conception, I next distinguish four educational paradigms relevant to constructivism. These are information-processing theory, weak constructivism, radical constructivism, and social constructivism. Of course there are others, too. However, such paradigms differ in other ways, too. In particular, their assumed, underlying metaphor for mind and model of the world are very revealing. The mind metaphor indicates much about the epistemology of the position, as well as its pedagogy; the world model indicates much about its ontology. So I focus particularly on these aspects.

For clarity, I ought to state at the outset that my commitment is to social constructivism; what I offer also amounts to a critique of the other three positions from a social constructivist perspective, although I try also to give credit for their strengths.

Information-Processing Theory

Information processing might be regarded as one of the simpler forms of constructivism. It appears to accept von Glaserfeld's first principle, which is common to all constructivist positions, but rejects the second principle, with its far-reaching epistemological consequences (discussed later). However, I argue later that it falls short of being even a form of weak constructivism.

The information-processing paradigm is a broad church that includes the psychology of Ausubel (1968), repair theory (Brown & Van Lehn, 1982, etc.), and many of the positions adopted by researchers in cognitive science and related psychologies. It is largely based on the metaphor and sometimes the conscious model of the mind as computer. This actively processes information and data, calling up various routines and procedures, organizing memorization and retrieval of data. It can even be "heuristically" programmed, that is, modifying its outputs as it learns from experience. The computer metaphor is very fruitful because it has led to important analyses of human problem solving (Newell & Simon, 1972), and to 'buggy' error analysis (Brown & Burton, 1978), with important outcomes for the psychology of mathematics education.

The use of computers as an instructional medium is quite independent from the use of a computer metaphor of mind, and should not be confused with it. A striking example is given by Papert (1980), who is widely regarded as a constructivist. Likewise, the work of Goldin and Kaput (chapter 23, this volume), although concerned with computers and their relationship with representation, relates probably to weak constructivism and not to information-processing cognitivism.

The most common model of the world associated with information-processing theory is that of Newtonian absolute space populated by material objects (scientific realism). In general, information-processing theory represents a shift from the traditional empiricist metaphor of mind as passive to a complex mechanical (or rather electronic) metaphor of mind-as-computer, but there is usually no shift in the underlying metaphor for the world from that of absolute Newtonian space.

In summary, the ontology is the naive realism of science: The world of things we experience is out there. The things are part of an ultimate reality. The epistemology is objectivist—true knowledge of the state of affairs in the world may be possible, as is certainty in mathematical knowledge. However, where this position differs from empiricism is in its theory of learning. It represents a significant step forward from empiricism and classical behaviorism, for it recognizes that knowing involves active mental processing, it is individual, and it is based on previously acquired knowledge. Thus learning is not just a passive absorption of information; rather, it is more interactive, involving the selection, processing and assimilation of information according to the state of mind of the learner.

An important outcome of this perspective in terms of learning theory (and pedagogy) is that it accounts for student "error patterns" in mathematics (Ashlock, 1976), and similarly for misconceptions in science.

Does information-processing theory constitute a form of constructivism? It is evidently close to one, on the grounds that its account of learning seems to satisfy von Glaserfeld's first principle in that knowledge is not passively received but actively built up. However, as I indicated earlier, this principle means that the construction of knowledge is recursive, and builds on previously constructed knowledge, not passively received information or knowledge. But the metaphor of mind as computer means that at a basic level, incoming information or knowledge must simply be received by the cognizing subject, in preconstituted form, and that any complex response or elaboration that may follow its reception builds from this. This is not a recursive process of construction, but assumes instead the existence of objective, preexisting knowledge at a basic level. As one of its exponents says, alongside cognitive science, information processing theory is "the study of how humans process information, and includes the acquisition, storage and retrieval of knowledge" (Mayer, 1982, p. 3) The rhetoric of this quotation reveals the underlying presupposition that some knowledge learned by humans is information that is admitted from the outside, not constructed within. Thus, in the final analysis, information-processing theory contradicts von Glaserfeld's first principle and hence is not a form of constructivism.

Weak Constructivism

Accepting that information-processing theory is not a form of constructivism, it is clear that a weak form of constructivism can be developed from it simply by fully accepting von Glaserfeld's first principle. This is termed *weak constructivism,* and combines the principle that all individual human knowledge is constructed by each individual with the other assumptions of the information-processing paradigm already described. Thus the underlying metaphors of mind and world are almost the same. However, a difference is that the mind is an ideal "soft" computer, namely, the brain. Thus the data it processes is self-constructed, all the way down to the basic level of electrochemical nerve impulses.

There is an epistemological problem—an instability even—built into weak constructivism, for it is difficult for the dual aspects of its epistemology to coexist. On the one hand, all individual knowledge is constructed. On the other, there is a realm of objective knowledge, which, for example, would include the truths of mathematics and facts about the world. But how can such knowledge be known by any individual, if their knowledge is a personal construction? It must be the case that an individual can construct *truths,* to be able to know such knowledge. Thus the individual constructs truths about the world and of mathematics. But in this case, an individual's constructions are in fact correct representations of external states of affairs, via sense organs. This means that knowledge is constructed to match the world, or the eternal verities of mathematics, and not as a recursive construction based on previous constructions, satisfying inner constraints. In short, constructed truths can only be known as such by means of information from the world. Thus there is at the very least an antinomy—if not a direct contradiction—at the heart of weak constructivism.

Weak constructivism deals with this by being a local, as opposed to global, paradigm. That is, it accepts traditional epistemology concerning knowledge, and only tries to account for the knowledge representations of individuals. This is quite legitimate, for not all theories can be theories of everything, and we cannot simultaneously make everything the object of our inquiry.

Another possible way out of this dilemma for weak constructivism is to acknowledge that there is a pregiven world of persons, objects, and conventional knowledge (after all, denying this is problematic), but to adopt an agnostic, tentative position about our knowledge of this world. This is certainly the position of virtually all schools in the modern philosophy of science. Time and again our best theories of the world are shown to be false (Popper, 1959). This is then a defensible position. It is also appears close to that adopted by many of the other contributors to this volume, such as Booker, Goldin and Kaput, and Herscovics. It enables learner's constructions of meanings to be problematized, without having to raise larger ontological and epistemological issues. It does, however, leave the issue of the nature and status of mathematical knowledge unanswered.

Radical Constructivism

Although it originates with Piaget and is anticipated by Vico, in its modern form radical constructivism has been most fully worked out in epistemological terms by von Glasersfeld, in a series of publications over the past 15 years. In methodological terms, the leading figure in the area of mathematics education has perhaps been Steffe (1991).

Definitionally, radical constructivism is based on both the first and second of von Glasersfeld's principles. The second profoundly affects the world metaphor, as well as that of the mind: "The function of cognition is adaptive and serves the organization of the experiential world, not the discovery of ontological reality" (von Glasersfeld, 1989, p. 182). Consequently, "From an explorer who is condemned to seek 'structural properties' of an inaccessible reality, the experiencing organism now turns into a builder of cognitive structures intended to solve such problems as the organism perceives or conceives" (von Glasersfeld, 1983, p. 50).

Although it is controversial, and the caveat is needed that there are a number of different forms of radical constructivism (Ernest, 1991b), my claim is that the underlying metaphor for the mind or cognizing subject is that of an organism underlying evolution, patterned after Darwin's theory, with its central concept of the "survival of the fit (or fitter)." This is indicated in Piaget's notion of adaptation to the environment and his explicit discussion of cognitive evolution, such as in Piaget (1972).

According to the evolutionary metaphor, the cognizing subject is a creature with sensory inputs, furnishing data that is interpreted (or rather constructed) through the lenses of its cognitive structures; it comprises also a collection of those structures all the while being adapted, and a means of acting on the outside world. The cognizing subject generates cognitive schemas to guide actions and represent its experiences. These are tested according to how well they "fit" the world of its experience. Those schemas that fit are tentatively adopted and retained as guides to action. Cognition depends on an underlying feedback loop.

Thus on the one hand, there is an analogy between the evolution and survival of the fitter of the schemas in the mind of the cognizing subject and the whole of biological evolution of species. Schemas evolve, and through adaptation come to better fit the subject's experienced world. They also split and branch out, and perhaps some lines become extinct. On the other hand, the organism itself and as a whole is adapting to the world of its experiences, largely through the adaptation of its schemas.

It is difficult to isolate the underlying model of the world of this position, for it is implicated in that of mind. It is experienceable but not knowable in any ultimate sense, just as the Kantian world of "phenomena" floats above the unattainable substratum of the "noumena." It is like the environment or world surrounding an animal: It is real and resists and constrains the animal, but is not known by the animal (including humans) over and above the ways that the animals schema's fit or fail to fit the world. No match between these schemas and the world is possible; nor could it be verified, if it did exist.

Overall, radical constructivism is neutral in its ontology, making no presuppositions about the existence of the world behind the subjective realm of experience. The epistemology is whole-heartedly fallibilist, skeptical, and antiobjectivist. The fact that there is no ultimate, true knowledge possible about the state of affairs in the world, or about such realms as mathematics, follows from the second principle, which is one of epistemological relativity. As its name implies, the theory of learning is radically constructivist, with all knowledge being constructed by the individual on the basis of its cognitive processes in dialogue with its experiential world. The pedagogy is multifaceted, but at its heart lies sensitivity to individual construction.

Radical constructivism is a rich theory that is giving rise to a whole body of fruitful and innovative research, as this volume indicates. Indeed, it is very important in mathematics and science education, where it might be said to represent the pretending if not yet ruling epistemological theory. Almost uniquely, it represents an educational paradigm—a research program, even—that has been fully developed in that the ontological, epistemological (in both senses), methodological, and pedagogical dimensions have all been extensively treated in the recent literature.

Of course such praise is all the more reason that radical constructivism should be subjected to serious critical scrutiny. One central criticism that might require a clearer exposition of the relevant aspects of the position, or some revision, is as follows. The account of the cognizing subject emphasises its individuality, its separateness, and its primarily cognitive representations of its experiences. Its representations of the world and of other human beings are personal and idiosyncratic. Indeed, the construal of other persons is driven by whatever representations best fit the cognizing subject's needs and purposes. None of this is refutable. But such a view makes it hard to establish a social basis for interpersonal communication, for shared feelings and concerns, let alone for shared values. By being based on the underlying evolutionary metaphor for the mind there is a danger that interpersonal relations are seen as nothing but competitive, a version of the "law of the jungle." After all, this is but another way of phrasing "the survival of the fit." Yet society and its functions, in particular education, depend on articulated and shared sets of concerns and values—values that are most evidently subscribed to by radical constructivists themselves. Thus the paradigm needs to accommodate these issues by balancing knowing with feeling, and acknowledging that all humans start as part of another being, not separate.

Von Glasersfeld has shown in his treatments of aspects of radical constructivism that it is possible to elaborate the position extensively to answer if not rebut much of this criticism. Each individual's knowledge of other persons, and hence, mediately, the realm of the social, can be consistently construed as constructions of the individual knower. Such an epistemology is self-consistent, and does not fall prey to facile critiques. Similarly, being ontologically neutral, radical constructivism is not solipsistic, as some critics have claimed. Nevertheless, it does seem to put up impenetrable barriers between individuals, and between individuals and the social world. Weak constructivism, by adopting a less stringent epistemology, permits both knowledge and morality to enter from the world. No such ingress is easily countenanced by radical constructivism.

A number of researchers, such as Confrey (1995), Cobb (chapter 1, this volume), and Steffe (chapter 27, this volume), are showing how radical constructivism can be elaborated to incorporate some of the social aspects and insights that a strict formulation seems to shut out. So it might be termed a progressive research program, in the sense of Lakatos (1970).

Social Constructivism

Social constructivism regards individual subjects and the realm of the social as indissolubly interconnected. Human subjects are formed through their interactions with each other (as well as by their individual processes). Thus there is no underlying metaphor for the wholly isolated individual mind. Instead, the underlying metaphor is that of *persons in conversation,* comprising persons in meaningful linguistic and extralinguistic interaction and dialogue (Ernest, 1994; Harré, 1989). Mind is seen as part of a broader context, the "social construction of meaning." Likewise, the social constructivist model of the world is that of a socially constructed world that creates (and is constrained by) the shared experience of the underlying physical reality. The humanly constructed reality is all the time being modified and interacting to fit ontological reality, although it can never give a "true picture" of it.

Adopting persons in conversation as the underlying metaphor of social constructivism gives pride of place to human beings and their language in its account of knowing. Following the seminal work of Wittgenstein, Vygotsky, symbolic interactionism, and activity theory, language is regarded as the shaper of, as well as being the summative product of, individual minds. Increasing attention is being given to the impact of language in much psychological research in the psychology of mathematics education, such as the cognitive role of such linguistic features as metonymy and metaphor. It is increasingly recognized that much instruction and learning takes place directly through the medium of language. Even manipulative or enactive learning, emphasised by Piaget and Bruner, takes place in a social context of meaning and is anyway mediated by language and the associated socially negotiated understandings (as Donaldson, 1978, and others have shown).

In summary, the social constructivist research paradigm adopts a modified relativist ontology (there is a world out there supporting the appearances we have shared access to, but we have no certain knowledge of it). It is based on a fallibilist epistemology that regards "conventional knowledge" as that which is "lived" and socially accepted. The associated learning theory is constructive (in the sense shared by sociologists such as Schütz, 1972, and Berger and Luckman, 1966, as well as constructivists), with an emphasis on the essential and constitutive nature of language and social interaction. The methodology is eclectic but recognizes that all knowing is problematic, and that there is no privileged vantage point. Likewise the pedagogy is eclectic, aware of the interactive and inseparable effects of the micro and macro social contexts, and the internal construction of self, beliefs, and cognitions.

COMPARISON

The metaphors for the mind and models of the world of the different paradigms are summarized in Fig. 20.1. One of the major distinctions lies in the underlying metaphor of the world (and the concomitant epistemology). The first two paradigms are based on the model of scientific realism/Newtonian absolute space, for the world and its existents. With it comes an absolutist epistemology and a neopositivist paradigm of research. This locates the "problematic" of epistemology exclusively in the immediate object of inquiry, that is, in the mind of the learner. Thus these research paradigms do not require any reflexivity or doubts about the

TYPE OF CONSTRUCTIVISM	METAPHOR FOR THE MIND	MODEL OF THE WORLD
INFORMATION-PROCESSING CONSTRUCTIVISM	Computer, unfeeling thinking machine	Newtonian Absolute space with physical objects (Scientific Realism)
WEAK CONSTRUCTIVISM	'Soft' computer (brain-as-machine)	Newtonian Absolute space with physical objects (Scientific Realism)
RADICAL CONSTRUCTIVISM	Evolving, adapting, isolated biological organism	Subject's private domain of experience
SOCIAL CONSTRUCTIVISM	Persons in conversation	Socially constructed, shared world

FIG. 20.1.   Constructivist metaphors for mind and world-models.

researcher's constitutive role in knowledge and meaning making. This is a stance that is increasingly questionable in the social sciences.

In contrast, the last two paradigms do not regard the world as something that can be known with any certainty. They problematize the whole relationship between the knower and the known, and accept that no certain knowledge is attainable by humans. This humility with regard to epistemology, knowledge, and the results of the models employed in research process resonates with much of current thinking in philosophy, the humanities, and social sciences. However, it does mean that neither research paradigm nor methodology can be employed mechanically in the quest for knowledge, but that every such approach is fraught with epistemological difficulties and stands in need of justification.

Another important feature that emerges from Fig. 20.1 is that of the varying complexity of the underlying metaphors of mind. The earlier metaphors (following the order presented) offer an inanimate or simplistic model of mind. Simplifying assumptions are essential in science, but so too is the recognition of complexity. If the metaphor of mind adopted accords the cognizing subject something less than human status, there is a risk of neglecting the richness of human thought, feeling, values, reflection, planning, purposes, and goals.

Some of the metaphors of mind and world discussed earlier can be said to be leftovers from successful scientific theories of the past (as Bachelard, 1934, pointed out). By uncovering them, the outcome may be to clear the path to a better evaluation of those theories and to buttress the more powerful and practical forms of constructivism.

Finally, it is clear from the foregoing discussion that one of the crucial

	ABSOLUTIST *EPISTEMOLOGY*	*FALLIBILIST* *EPISTEMOLOGY*
INDIVIDUAL FOCUS ALONE	INFORMATION-PROCESSING CONSTRUCTIVISM WEAK CONSTRUCTIVISM	RADICAL CONSTRUCTIVISM
INDIVIDUAL AND SOCIAL FOCUS		SOCIAL CONSTRUCTIVISM

FIG. 20.2. Classification by epistemology and social/individual focus.

differences between paradigms is in a paradigm's underlying epistemology—whether it is absolutist or fallibilist. Figure 20.2 shows the paradigms classified according to whether the epistemology is fallibilist or absolutist. An increasing number of philosophers (e.g., Rorty, 1979; see also Ernest, 1991a) are adopting a fallibilist position in epistemology, and to mind it is a very great shared strength of radical and social constructivism that they support this position. In addition, another important aspect is shown, the human focus, be it individual alone or a combination of individual with social.

I have not discussed positions, such as the that of "situated learning," that seem to have a wholly social focus; see, for example, Lave and Wenger (1991). However, there are aspects of them that might be consistently combined with social constructivism, and perhaps also with weak constructivism.

Piagetian constructivism seems to emphasize internal cognitive processes at the expense of social interaction in the learner's construction of knowledge (although as always, in Piaget's rich oeuvre it is possible to find discussion of the import of both language and social interaction). However there is a need for constructivism to accommodate the complementarity between individual construction and social interaction. Von Glasersfeld (1995) has shown that mathematical knowledge is taken as shared through agreed rules and conventions, explicitly opening the door to the influence of social interaction. But further elaboration of radical constructivism is needed to recognize the fundamental implication of the social in the construction of the individual (and perhaps to rediscover the notion of "shared" in the "taken as shared").

In my view radical constructivism can be seen to be part of a "progressive research programme" (Lakatos, 1970), evolving to better describe the broad range of phenomena involved. Radical constructivism is adapting to accommodate the criticism it has met, especially concerning its possible neglect of the social and cultural dimensions of learning and knowledge. This development circumvents some of the criticism offered here. Nevertheless, important differences in the underlying model of the mind remain: wholly individual, or a combined individual–social view. I suspect that in further research and debate in the field this difference will prove conclusive.

PEDAGOGICAL IMPLICATIONS

Ultimately, the import of an educational paradigm concerns its implications for practice, notably in pedagogy. However, in my view, there is little in any pedagogy that is either wholly necessitated or wholly ruled out by the other elements of an educational paradigm. (Goldin, 1990, also makes this point with regard to constructivism.) This is due to the fact that pedagogy is predicated on a set of values, those reflected in the following questions. What are the aims of education? What selection from the stock of cultural knowledge is valuable to teach? (Here again, I pause to consider whether radical constructivism is even able to pose this question.) What forms of human organization and interaction fit with the values? What view of the child or person, with what rights and powers, is associated with the values? A pedagogy is merely a theory of techniques for achieving the ends of "communicating" or offering the selected knowledge or experiences to learners in a way consistent with these values. The other elements of a paradigm are consistent with a wide range of pedagogical approaches, so the pedagogy of the paradigm is likely to be eclectic.

All four of the educational paradigms considered earlier suggest as pedagogical emphases the need and value for:

1. Sensitivity toward and attentiveness to the learner's previous constructions.

2. "Diagnostic" teaching attempting to remedy learner errors and misconceptions, with perturbation and cognitive conflict techniques as part of this.

3. Attention to metacognition and strategic self-regulation by learners.

4. The use of multiple representations of mathematical concepts.

5. Awareness of the importance of goals for the learner, and the dichotomy between learner and teacher goals.

6. Awareness of the importance of social contexts, such as in the difference between folk or street mathematics and school mathematics (and an attempt to exploit the former for the latter).

Beyond these, a number of further pedagogical emphases are more strongly suggested by radical and social constructivism than by the other two paradigms.

1. Knowledge as a whole is problematized, not just the learner's subjective knowledge, including mathematical knowledge and logic.

2. Methodological approaches are required to be much more circumspect and reflexive, as there is no "royal road" to truth or near truth.

3. The focus of concern is not just the learner's cognitions, but the learner's cognitions, beliefs, and conceptions of knowledge.

4. The focus of concern with the teacher and in teacher education is not just with the teacher's knowledge of subject matter and diagnostic skills, but with the teacher's beliefs, conceptions, and personal theories about subject matter, teaching, and learning.

5. Although we can tentatively come to know the knowledge of others by interpreting their language and actions through our own conceptual constructs, the others have realities that are independent of ours. Indeed, it is the realities of others along with our own realities that we humans strive to understand, but we can never take any of these realities as fixed.

Finally, a number of further pedagogical emphases are suggested by social constructivism and not by radical constructivism.

1. How is the mind of the learner formed by social interaction? Is the outcome a complex that is very much linked to the specificity of context? How does this impact on the learner's conceptions and activities in the classroom?

2. The focus of concern goes beyond learner cognitions and beliefs, to include her affect and the context-bound nature of her thought.

3. An awareness of the social construction of knowledge suggests a greater pedagogical emphasis on discussion, collaboration, negotiation and shared meanings.

4. As a social construct, mathematical knowledge is irrevocably bound up with texts and semiosis. How can this insight be accommodated in the theories and practices of mathematics education? (This last question indicates the current direction of my research, as hinted in Ernest, 1993.)

CONCLUSION

Because I have been standing outside of a range of educational research paradigms (although admitting that my sympathies lie with one of them), it seems appropriate to conclude with some reflections on my position as commentator. I have offered a schema or comparative framework, and as with any such categorization, the following question arises. How much of the differences and weaknesses indicated in the various educational paradigms is the construct of the schema or framework for comparison? It is clear that there are significant differences between the positions of information-processing theory, weak constructivism, radical constructivism, and social constructivism in terms of the categories distinguished above. However, there is a question to be asked. How neatly can any of the positions of the contributors to this volume be fitted into these categories? I know that I am sometimes uncomfortable when the complexity of my own position is fitted into the Procrustean bed of someone else's comparative framework. One cynical perspective of an aspect of what I offer is that it is a categorization of positions by "epistemological correctness": That is, how fallibilist are the epistemologies offered? This, given my own espousal of fallibilism (Ernest, 1991a), would indeed be ironic—if not self-inconsistent. Just as we (I presume to speak for myself and the others whose views I have commented on) stress the need to understand learner conceptions in their own terms, perhaps educational paradigms also need to be understood in their own terms, too.

Some of the researchers whose work I have identified as weakly constructivist (e.g., Goldin & Kaput, chapter 23, this volume) are making important progress in accommodating the vital issues of representation and semiosis in their educational research, without the inhibitions and obstructions that a radical constructivist position can impose. It is also clear that a number of researchers in the radical constructivist tradition (e.g., Confrey, 1995; Steffe & Tzur, 1994; Wood, Cobb, & Yackel, 1995) are working to accommodate the social aspects of the teaching and learning of mathematics within their positions, and the accommodations are somewhat altering their research paradigm. One well-known social constructivist (Bauersfeld, 1995) is trying to preserve some the strengths of the radical constructivism while working to overcome its weaknesses through admitting the social dimension. How well does he fit with what I have labeled was social constructivism? There is also the question of fruitfulness. Which of the preceding educational research paradigms are providing the greatest pool of empirical knowledge and insights into children's learning of mathematics? Surely this is one of the most important questions to be asked, one that I have scarcely touched upon.

What I have done is to lay bare certain figures of my own conceptual framework. If it suggests certain areas where educational paradigms need to be sharpened up, or if it stimulates further constructive debate about the comparison of such paradigms then it has proved its worth. In all humility I can claim no more.

REFERENCES

Ashlock, R. B. (1976). *Error patterns in computation.* Columbus, OH: Merrill.

Ausubel, D. P. (1968). *Educational psychology, a cognitive view.* New York: Holt, Rinehart and Winston.

Bachelard, G. (1934). *Le nouvel espirit scientifique* [The new scientific spirit]. Paris: Presses Universitaires de France.

Bauersfeld, H. (1980). Hidden dimensions in the so-called reality of a mathematics classroom. *Educational Studies in Mathematics, 11*(1), 23–41.

Bauersfeld, H. (1995). The structuring of the structures. In L. P. Steffe & J. Gale (Eds.), *Constructivism in education* (pp. 137–158). Hillsdale, NJ: Lawrence Erlbaum Associates.

Berger, P., & Luckmann, T. (1967). *The social construction of reality.* London: Penguin Books. (Original work published 1966)

Brown, J. S., & Burton, R. R. (1978). Diagnostic models for procedural bugs in basic mathematical skills. *Cognitive Science, 2,* 155–192.

Brown, J., & Van Lehn, K. (1982). Towards a generative theory of bugs. In T. P. Carpenter et al (Eds.), *Addition and subtraction: A cognitive perspective* (pp. 121–136). Hillsdale, NJ: Lawrence Erlbaum Associates.

Confrey, J. (1995). How compatible are radical constructivism, sociocultural approaches and social constructivism? In L. P. Steffe & J. Gale (Eds.), *Constructivism in education* (pp. 185–225). Hillsdale, NJ: Lawrence Erlbaum Associates.

Donaldson, M. (1978). *Children's minds.* Glasgow: Fontana/Collins.

Ernest, P. (1990, July). *Social constructivism as a philosophy of mathematics: Radical constructivism rehabilitated?* Poster at PME-14 Conference, Oaxaca, Mexico.

Ernest, P. (1991a). *The philosophy of mathematics education.* London: Falmer.

Ernest, P. (1991b). Constructivism, the psychology of learning, and the nature of mathematics: Some critical issues. In F. Furinghetti (Ed.), *PME 15 Proceedings* (Vol. 2, pp. 25–32). Assisi, Italy.

Ernest, P. (1993). Mathematical activity and rhetoric: Towards a social constructivist account. In N. Nohda (Ed.), *Proceedings of PME-17* (pp. 238–245). Tsukuba, Japan: University of Tsukuba.

Ernest, P. (1994, November). Conversation as a metaphor for mathematics and learning. *Proceedings of the British Society for Research into Learning Mathematics Day Conference,* Manchester Metropolitan University (pp. 58–63). Nottingham: BSRLM.

Freire, P. (1972). *Pedagogy of the oppressed.* Harmondsworth: Penguin.

Goldin, G. (1990). Epistemology, constructivism, and discovery learning mathematics. In R. B. Davis, C. A. Maher & N. Noddings (Eds.), *Constructivist views on the teaching and learning of mathematics* (pp. 31–47). JRME Monograph 4. Reston, VA: National Council of Teachers of Mathematics.

Harré, R. (1989). *Social construction of selves as a discursive practice.* Unpublished paper.

Kieren, T. E., & Pirie, S. E. B. (1991). Recursion and the mathematical experience. In L. P. Steffe (Ed.), *Epistemological foundations of mathematical experience* (pp. 78–101). New York: Springer-Verlag.

Lakatos, I. (1970). Falsification and the methodology of scientific research programmes. In I. Lakatos & A. Musgrave (Eds.), *Criticism and the growth of knowledge* (pp. 91–196). Cambridge: Cambridge University Press.

Lave, J., & Wenger, E. (1991). *Situated learning: Legitimate peripheral participation.* Cambridge: Cambridge University Press.

Mayer, R. E. (1982). Implications of cognitive psychology for instruction in mathematical problem solving. In F. K. Lester & J. Garofalo (Eds.), *Mathematical problem solving: Issues in research* (pp. 76–91). Philadelphia: Franklin Institute Press.

Newell, A., & Simon, H. A. (1972). *Human problem solving.* Englewood Cliffs, NJ: Prentice Hall.

Papert, S. (1980). *Mindstorms: Children, computers and powerful ideas.* Brighton: Harvester.

Piaget, J. (1972). *The principles of genetic epistemology* (W. Mays, Trans.). London: Routledge and Kegan Paul.

Popper, K. (1959). *The logic of scientific discovery.* London: Hutchinson.

Rorty, R. (1979). *Philosophy and the mirror of nature.* Princeton, NJ: Princeton University Press.

Schubert, W. H. (1986). *Curriculum: Perspective, paradigm, and possibility.* New York: Macmillan.

Schütz, A. (1972). *The phenomenology of the social world.* London: Heinemann.

Steffe, L. P. (Ed.). (1991). *Epistemological foundations of mathematical experience.* New York: Springer-Verlag.

Steffe, L. P., & Tzur, R. (1994). Interaction and children's mathematics. In P. Ernest (Ed.), *Constructing mathematical knowledge: Epistemology and mathematics education* (pp. 8–32). London: Falmer Press.

von Glasersfeld, E. (1983). Learning as a constructive activity. *Proceedings of 5th PME-NA, 1,* 41–69.

von Glasersfeld, E. (1989). Constructivism in education. In T. Husen & N. Postlethwaite (Eds.), *International encyclopedia of education* (supplementary vol., pp. 162–163). Oxford: Pergamon.

von Glasersfeld, E. (1995). *Radical constructivism: A way of knowing and learning.* London: Falmer Press.

Walkerdine, V. (1984). Developmental psychology and the child-centered pedagogy: The insertion of Piaget into early education. In J. Henriques, W. Holloway, C. Urwin, C. Venn, & V. Walkerdine (Eds.), *Changing the subject* (pp. 153–202). London: Methuen.

Wood, T., Cobb, P., & Yackel, E. (1995). Reflections on learning and teaching mathematics in the elementary school. In L. P. Steffe & J. Gale (Eds.), *Constructivism in education* (pp. 401–422). Hillsdale, NJ: Lawrence Erlbaum Associates.

21

The Construction of Conceptual Schemes in Mathematics

Nicolas Herscovics
Concordia University, Montreal

> *Often, the exclusively behavioral characterization of desirable learning outcomes leads educators to rely on the teaching of discrete, disconnected skills in mathematics, rather than on developing meaningful patterns, principles, and insights.*
>
> (Goldin, 1990, p. 36)

This remark by Goldin reflects a major difference between an exclusively behaviorist approach and a constructivist view of the acquisition of knowledge. Constructivism avoids reductionist attempts to constrict all learning to the appropriation of parcels of unrelated knowledge, and provides instead a structured, organized perspective.

Inherent to a constructivist outlook is the assumption that any learning of higher order concepts involves some kind of integration by the learner into his or her existing cognition. The new knowledge needs to find some anchor points in the learner's cognition in order to maintain some cognitive continuity and relevance. Piaget's theory of equilibration (Ginsburg & Opper, 1979) describes two complementary learning processes: that of assimilation, enabling the learner to fit new knowledge into his or her existing cognitive structure, and that of accommodation, involving the reorganization and expansion of such a cognitive structure.

From an instructional viewpoint, constructivism involves some coherent organization of the knowledge to be acquired by the student. Fundamental mathematical notions, even those as elementary as the number concept, cannot be described by using classical concept formation theory, because they cannot be defined in terms of attributes or in terms of examples and nonexamples. Instead

351

any basic mathematical idea, including the notion of number, can be viewed as a *conceptual scheme,* that is, a network of related knowledge together with all the problem situations in which it can be used (Bergeron & Herscovics, 1990a). The need to relate new knowledge to the learners' cognition requires the identification of a *zone of proximal cognition* that is within their reach. In the context of conceptual schemes the notion of a zone of proximal cognition is not too dissimilar from that of a zone of proximal development suggested by Vygotsky (1978, 1986) in the context of problem solving.

Of course, learning cannot be considered without taking into account the student's cognitive maturation and development. In spite of Bruner's (1960) claim that anything could be taught to a student of any age with some integrity, it is difficult to imagine this applying to more advanced concepts in mathematics because of their formal nature. In his own theory of representation, Bruner suggests a transition from enactive to iconic to symbolic modes, and these can be invoked to justify the avoidance of premature mathematical formalism. Moreover, although Piaget's theory of stages of intellectual development can sometimes be difficult to apply to specific concepts, nevertheless, at a global level, one cannot ignore the very major intellectual changes occurring at the ages of 5 to 7 and 11 to 13 years among most children (Inhelder & Piaget, 1970; Piaget, 1976). Of course, in many countries, these ages correspond to entrance to primary and secondary schools.

This chapter addresses the interface between constructivism, cognition, and developmental theory. It considers this interface through various models of understanding, with understanding being viewed here as the outcome of meaningful learning. In response to some of the other chapters presented, it would appear useful, before proceeding to discuss these models, to situate my approach within a relevant context of constructivism.

THE CASE FOR *RATIONAL* CONSTRUCTIVISM

According to Paul Ernest (chapter 20, this volume), there are now three types of constructivism: radical constructivism, whose metaphor of the mind is the "evolving, adapting organism"; social constructivism, whose metaphor of the mind is "persons in conversation"; and a third type, that of trivial or weak constructivism, whose metaphor of the mind is that of a "soft computer."

Although I consider myself a constructivist, I fail to identify with any of these types. While I cannot suggest a good all-encompassing metaphor for the mind, I still cannot accept the reductionism entailed by those just mentioned. The problem with these reductionist models is that they apply either to a particular aspect of knowledge or to a specific type of knowledge. In my view the existence and acquisition of knowledge are complex phenomena that of necessity require many different but interrelated models. This is essentially the view of what should be considered another type of constructivism, that of *rational constructivism*. It considers learning, the acquisition of knowledge, as occurring in a number of different ways. It regards learning as being somewhat of a probabilistic phenomenon, based on a sequence of gradual approximations.

According to rational constructivism there are many different types of knowledge. Of course, this is not something new—in 1775, Samuel Johnson talked about two kinds of knowledge, the knowledge acquired by an individual and the knowledge of where to find information about the knowledge we wish to acquire.

In mathematics, one way to consider the existence of different types of knowledge is in terms of the different communities under consideration. The mathematics learned in our primary and secondary schools can be considered both from the standpoint of capabilities essential to functioning in our society and also, from a cultural point of view, as a body of inherited knowledge. The mathematics as perceived by the community of mathematics educators can hardly be separated from didactic questions raised in connection with the mathematics. The mathematics perceived by working mathematicians is of yet a different kind, and differs from the mathematics studied by historians who need to tackle difficult questions of epistemology. We have here several different communities, and the mathematics of interest to each one varies according to its specific needs and interests. How can we then expect that restricting ourselves to a single metaphor of mathematical knowledge will suffice?

As a rational constructivist I neither accept the metaphor of the mind as a "soft computer," nor do I seek computer simulation of the human learning process. If anything characterizes my brand of constructivism, it is the refusal to perceive mathematical knowledge and its acquisition as being of only one type. It is, all at once, functional (e.g., numeracy), cultural (e.g., place-value notation), pedagogical (didactic questions), professional (for the working mathematician), and epistemological (for the modern historian). As mathematics educators, we are dealing with a minimum of three of these aspects at any one time, and should not reduce our theories to just one metaphor.

Consider the rejection of the metaphor of "communication," or "transmission" of knowledge, by radical constructivists. As Goldin (1990, p. 35) noted, "In the radical constructivist view, knowledge about mathematics, science, or the everyday world is never *communicated,* but of epistemological necessity *constructed* (and reconstructed) by *unique individuals.*" The question of how far this can actually be taken deserves serious consideration. Does all mathematical knowledge have to be constructed or reconstructed by each learner? Would a positive answer eliminate the possibility of some mathematical knowledge being transmitted, through communication?

Let us take as an example the notion of the (even or odd) parity of natural numbers. Even 6-year-olds still in the process of constructing the conceptual schemes of number and equipartition can be put to work with chips and discover that the numbers they know can be grouped into two distinct classes—those that can be equipartitioned into two equal subsets, and those that cannot. The first subset can be named the set of even numbers and the second one, on remarking that after the equipartitioning one is always left with an odd chip, can now be called the set of odd numbers (Bergeron & Herscovics, 1985; Herscovics & Bergeron, 1985; Nantais, Bergeron, & Herscovics, 1985). Thus, first graders can at an early age construct, with some proper guidance, a notion of parity.

But 9-year-olds in third grade, whose construction of number is far more advanced and who are learning in class about division in arithmetic, are in a very different situation. They can consider any of their known numbers and discover that some are divisible by two, whereas others leave a remainder of one. For these third graders, the construction of the notion of parity followed a very different path. Although the first graders were constructing it at the logico-physical level (see later discussion), a level that involves physical transformations (equipartitions) on physical objects, the third graders were operating at the logico-mathematical level, in which the transformations were applied to mathematical objects, that is, numbers.

Can one "communicate" the notion of parity at a later age? Certainly, by the end of secondary school, a definition such as "An even number is one that is divisible by 2, an odd number is one that leaves a remainder of 1" can be meaningful to most 17-year-olds. The difficulties that occur are no longer at the conceptual level, but at the symbolic or formalization level. Such a verbal definition does not easily translate into, "All natural numbers m are either even, with $m = 2n$, or odd, with $m = 2n + 1$."

What this example shows is that some mathematical knowledge can be communicated, at some times. The difficult task is to determine if this can be generalized to all mathematical knowledge, and if not, what might be the possible conditions for communication. We come back to this question at the end of the chapter, but mention the following points here. The notion is implicit in our discussion that fundamental mathematical ideas constitute conceptual schemes—thus the ideas of number, the four arithmetic operations, fractions, functions, and so on all required several years for their construction. These conceptual schemes involve a network of related knowledge organized in some hierarchical way. This chapter seeks to provide a clear picture of the cognitive matrix associated with a conceptual scheme. It is then my stance that at the procedural and formalization level some communication is possible, if that which is communicated fits into the learner's existing cognition. But abstraction can only be achieved by the individual learner. One must also distinguish between a fundamental conceptual scheme and a derived concept. In the preceding example, natural numbers and divisibility by two are fundamental conceptual schemes. Their juxtaposition is a derived concept. Derived concepts can be communicated in some form if the learner has a sufficiently developed construction of the fundamental concepts that are the basis for the derived concept.

Rational constructivism, in recognizing that the learning of mathematics takes place in many different ways, is neither "trivial" nor "weak." Rather, it avoids making overly reductionist assumptions, and overcomes difficulties inherent in other approaches.

The radical constructivists, who seem to be obsessed with the issue of ultimate truth, concede from the beginning that the real-world environment is "unknowable" and thus that knowledge about it cannot be achieved. But how relevant is this assertion to mathematics education, when all mathematics is in any case made by human beings? How can radical constructivists make absolute statements about an absolute truth that they claim cannot be apprehended? Their stance leads to the position that any "fitting" construction is acceptable—so that in fact, any of the child's constructions seem valid and acceptable to a radical constructivist. In education, this approach can result in a philosophy closer to deconstruction than to constructivism.

Social constructivism has the problem that it is limited by the social acceptability of constructs. Yet Columbus in setting sail found a new continent, despite believers in the "flat earth." The case against social constructivism is epitomized by the observation that one cannot base conclusions about the Earth's curvature either on the simple use of one's senses or on shared beliefs (although space exploration in the 1960s later provided excellent pictures, and few people today believe the earth is flat). In fact, Kuhn's work on the history of scientific revolutions describes how each age adopts new paradigms, eventually rejecting many of the old ones (Kuhn, 1971).

In the context of these ideas, I next consider several models of understanding that fall within a rational constructivist perspective.

MODELS OF UNDERSTANDING

The need to avoid teaching mathematics as isolated atoms of information was, no doubt, the problem that Skemp (1976) was addressing when he distinguished between two specific kinds of understanding occurring in the teaching of mathematics: instrumental understanding (rules without reason), and relational understanding (knowing what to do and why). He duly pointed out their respective advantages. Within its own context, instrumental mathematics is usually easier to understand, so the rewards are more immediate and more apparent, and one can often get the right answer more quickly and reliably. On the other hand, relational mathematics is more adaptable to new tasks, easier to remember, and can be effective as a goal in itself; according to Skemp relational schemas are organic in quality. Skemp's initial work must have struck an important chord in the mathematics education community, for it was followed by a number of papers introducing various models aimed at describing different aspects of understanding mathematics (Buxton, 1978; Byers & Herscovics, 1977; Skemp, 1979, 1982).

These models of understanding became increasingly sophisticated. The Byers and Herscovics tetrahedral model introduced four modes of understanding. It complemented the relational and instrumental modes with intuitive understanding (as evidenced by the solution of a problem without prior analysis of the problem) and formal understanding (as evidenced by the ability to connect mathematical symbolism and notation with relevant mathematical ideas and the ability to combine these ideas into chains of logical reasoning). The very broad scope of these models proved to be their fundamental weakness. Indeed, they did not take into account the specific features distinguishing different mathematical activities, such as the skills needed for problem solving (Goldin & McClintock, 1984), those involved in constructing the notion of proof (Balacheff, 1988; Bell, 1976; Fischbein & Kedem, 1982), and those associated with the construction of conceptual schemes (Herscovics & Bergeron, 1983).

The various models of understanding proved to be deficient when applied to elementary mathematical concepts. They did not provide a coherent frame of reference necessary to describe the construction of these conceptual schemes (Bergeron & Herscovics, 1981). New criteria were needed that would be specific to this particular activity.

A First Constructivist Model

Herscovics and Bergeron (1981) suggested a new model designed to describe the construction of conceptual schemes in elementary mathematics. It involved four levels of understanding:

> *Intuitive understanding,* which takes as a starting point the informal knowledge of the child (pre-concepts, visual perception and estimation, primitive unquantified actions). This knowledge is then coordinated into a procedure leading to a first construction of a concept, a first construction which we consider as a second level of understanding, that of *initial conceptualization.* We speak of initial conceptualization, for at the very beginning the concept is blurred and confused with the procedure leading to its construction (for example, at the beginning, the notion of number is confused with the counting procedure). It is only very gradually that the "outline" of a concept gains precision and that it separates from the procedure, making abstraction possible. *Abstraction* is our third level of comprehension. Detaching the concept from its procedure gives it an existence of its own which can be identified as the "content," a content in search of a "form." This requires a process of *formalization* which we take as a fourth level of understanding. (Herscovics & Bergeron, 1981, p. 69)

In justifying their model, the authors relied on developmental psychology and genetic epistemology. Although the first two levels of understanding were not considered controversial, the acceptability of the last two levels was questionable. As the model was to be used in describing the construction of elementary mathematical concepts, to what extent could one view abstraction as an achievable level of understanding in primary school? Moreover, as the use of symbols could be the result of rote learning and of an idiosyncratic interpretation (Erlwanger, 1973, 1975), under what conditions could the appropriate use of mathematical notation be accepted as another level of understanding?

To answer the first question, one can refer to Piaget's theory of intellectual development identifying three distinct stages, that of preoperational thought (2–7 years), a concrete operational level (7–11 years), and a third stage beginning about the age of 11–12 years at which the child can start building formal operations based on hypothetico-deductive reasoning (Piaget, 1976). At the preoperational stage, children focus on states rather than on their actions. Thus, objects are the only things that are reconstructed internally (empirical abstraction) and not the transformations applied to these objects. Focusing on states prevents children from achieving the reversibility of thought necessary to apprehend the invariance of a mathematical object such as number when one of two equivalent rows of objects is stretched in front of them in the classical conservation of number test. The preoperational child's reasoning reflects a form of "transductive" logic: if A causes B, then B causes A (Mayer, 1977, p. 180). Since experience has taught children that "if there is more, then it is longer," they conclude that "if it is longer, there must be more" when comparing the two rows in front of them. Only later, when they can handle two variables simultaneously (the length and the density of the row), will they perceive a reciprocal relationship.

The model just suggested bears a certain number of similarities to the one Ginsburg and Opper (1979, p. 234) identified in Piaget's theory of intellectual development. It describes three levels of understanding:

> The first of these levels is *motoric* or *practical* understanding. This is the level of action. The child can act directly on objects and manipulate them correctly . . . the child has "understood" objects at the level of motor responses. Another level of understanding is *conceptualization*. Here the child reconstructs internally the actions that were previously performed directly on objects. . . . He organizes the mental activities and provides logical connections. A third level of knowledge involves *consciousness* and *verbalizations*. Now the child can deal with concepts on an abstract level, and can express his mental operations in words. The child can reflect on his own thought.

This model of understanding reflects Piagetian stages because the first level corresponds essentially to the preoperational one, whereas the other two can be linked to the concrete operational stage. At the first level, the child discovers the properties of objects and spontaneously develops notions of classification, seriation, partitioning, bringing together or adding to, and so forth. The second and third levels describe the internal reconstruction and coordination of actions, and thus correspond to the concrete operational stage. Finally, "reflecting on his own thought" implies a prior internal reconstruction of the action and thus leads to a level of abstraction that can be qualified as "reflective." Thus, viewed from a genetic epistemological perspective (in the sense of the child's construction of knowledge), one can definitely conclude that abstraction can be achieved by children learning mathematics in primary school provided their mathematics is rooted in their physical environment.

The fourth level of understanding described by Herscovics and Bergeron, that of formalization, is more specific to the construction of mathematical knowledge and hence does not appear in the more general Piagetian model provided by Ginsburg and Opper. Nevertheless, Piaget's writings indicate that he was quite aware of the importance of mathematical language and notation (Piaget, 1973, p. 87). He even discriminated between mathematical content and mathematical form, and recommended that the representations used should correspond to the "natural logic of the levels of the pupils" (Piaget, 1973, p. 87). Consequently, he suggested that the role of actions should not be neglected by limiting instruction to a verbal form: "Particularly with young pupils, activity with objects is indispensable to the comprehension of arithmetic as well as geometrical relations" (p. 80).

These observations bring into question the role that mathematical notation plays in the understanding of a mathematical notion. Symbolization is essential even in elementary mathematics because it provides the means to detach a concept from its concrete embodiments. However, the introduction of symbols can be premature if an adequate intuitive basis is lacking. In such a case, the child is forced to function at a strictly formal level, which is impossible at the concrete operational stage. Thus, mathematical notation can be meaningful only when it is used in the process of mathematizing previously acquired informal knowledge. It is then that its mastery can be viewed as another level of understanding.

Some Refinements of the Constructivist Model

A year after introducing their constructivist model, Bergeron and Herscovics refined some of the criteria used to describe its four levels of understanding (Bergeron & Herscovics, 1982; Herscovics & Bergeron, 1983). The criteria used to describe intuitive understanding remained unchanged. However, the second level, that of initial conceptualization was now called *procedural understanding*. This was to reflect the fact that intuitive knowledge was to be followed by a process of mathematization involving the introduction of an initial mathematical procedure. For instance, at the intuitive level, the actions of bringing together two sets of objects or augmenting an initial set by a supplementary one were deemed preconcepts of arithmetical addition. Counting the objects in the resulting set enabled the child to answer the question "How many?" and counting from one was the initial mathematical procedure involved. The assimilation of this procedure by the child brought about a procedural understanding of addition.

The third level of understanding, that of abstraction, also underwent some refinement. Although its initial description was limited to a detachment of the concept from the procedure, in their later version Bergeron and Herscovics also took into account another process, that of reflective abstraction. Research on the child's construction of number illustrates the need to distinguish between both abstractive processes. For instance, Greco (1962) found that in the classical Piagetian experiment on the conservation of number, many children between the ages 5 and 6 years could count one row of seven objects and affirm that the elongated row also contained seven objects but "that it had more." These children conserved the numerical label identified with the rows (which Greco called the conservation of "quotity") without conserving as yet the notion of quantity. These children have detached the number seven from the procedure (they can count out a set of seven chips when asked to do so) but they do not as yet conserve number since they do not consider it invariant with respect to a change in configuration. To do so requires the coordination of several variables as well as the reversibility of thought.

Such considerations led the authors to describe abstraction as involving two phases, the first one consisting of the separation of the concept from the procedure, and a second phase characterized by the generalization of the concept, or by some form of conservation reflecting the invariance of the mathematical object, or by the reversibility and possible composition of the mathematical transformations.

The fourth level, formalization, was also subject to greater clarification, taking into account the various meanings the word had acquired (axiomatization, the notion of formal proof) and adding further criteria more relevant to the construction of conceptual schemes. Depending on the notion intended, formalization was evidenced either by the use of mathematical symbolism, or by the logical justification of operations, or by the discovery of axioms. But to avoid these being a reflection of rote learning, formalization could only be construed as a level of understanding if there was evidence of some prior abstraction of the concept.

In 1984, the model underwent another important change (Herscovics & Bergeron, 1984). The second level, that of procedural understanding, specifically mentioned the mastery of an initial procedure. For instance, in the case of addition, the initial procedure could be counting from 1. But how was one to interpret the child's acquisition of more advanced procedures such as counting on from one of the sets, or counting on consistently from the larger set? Because such a pupil had acquired several procedures and could in fact select a more efficient one, this indicated a certain distancing necessary for comparing different procedures and hence could also be construed as a level of abstraction. But then, inevitably, this brought about some confusion regarding the interpretation of the acquisition of some mathematical procedures. To resolve this potential contradiction, it was best to redefine procedural understanding as being evidenced by the acquisition of mathematical procedures that the learners can relate to their intuitive knowledge and use appropriately. The last three words are important, for otherwise the acquisition of procedures represents nothing more than "rules without reason."

A Two-Tiered Model

As useful as the refined model proved to be, there still remained some serious problems. Intuitive understanding had been defined in terms of informal knowledge characterized, as the case may be, by preconcepts (e.g., surface is a preconcept of area), or a type of apprehension based on visual perception (e.g., the nonconservation of number), or unquantified actions (e.g., augmenting a set or joining two sets of objects), or estimation based on rough approximations (e.g., more, less, few, many). But this description did not take into account the fact that well-defined and accurate procedures could be used that did not involve mathematical objects such as number. For instance, most kindergartners can spontaneously use a one-to-one correspondence to determine if one set of objects has the same quantity as another set, or more, or less (Bergeron & Herscovics, 1988). Furthermore, the foregoing description of intuitive understanding did not recognize the fact that the conservation of quantity need not involve number and thus, when no counting was involved, that it was dealing with the invariance of an unquantified set. If abstraction could be characterized in terms of invariance of a concept (under some transformation), then it certainly could be used to describe a level of understanding of the preconcepts.

Such considerations brought about the need to consider the following two-tiered model, with the first tier aimed at describing the understanding of a "physical" preconcept, and the second tier describing the understanding of the mathematical concept emerging from the mathematization process (Herscovics & Bergeron, 1988).

The Understanding of Preliminary Physical Concepts

Intuitive understanding refers to a global perception of the notion at hand; it results from a type of thinking based essentially on visual perception; it provides rough nonnumerical approximations.

Logico-physical procedural understanding refers to the acquisition of logico-physical procedures that the learners can relate to their intuitive knowledge and use appropriately.

Logico-physical abstraction refers to the construction of logico-physical invariants (as in the case of the various conservation of plurality and position), or the reversibility and composition of logico-physical transformations (e.g., taking away is viewed as the inverse of augmenting an initial set; a sequence of increments can be reduced to fewer steps through composition), or as generalization (e.g., perceiving the commutativity of the physical union of any two sets).

The Understanding of the Emerging Mathematical Concepts

Logico-mathematical procedural understanding refers to the acquisition of explicit logico-mathematical procedures that the learner can relate to the underlying preliminary physical concepts and use appropriately.

Logico-mathematical abstraction refers to the construction of logico-mathematical invariants together with the relevant logico-physical invariants (as in the abstraction of cardinal number and ordinal number), or the reversibility and composition of logico-mathematical transformations and operations (e.g., subtraction viewed as the inverse of addition; strings of additions reduced to fewer operations through composition), or as generalization (e.g., commutativity of addition perceived as a property applying to all pairs of natural numbers).

Formalization refers to its usual interpretations, those of axiomatization and formal mathematical proof, which, at the elementary level, could be viewed as discovering axioms and finding logical mathematical justifications respectively. But two additional meanings are assigned to formalization, that of enclosing a mathematical notion into a formal definition, and that of using mathematical symbolization for notions for which prior procedural understanding or abstraction already exist to some degree.

As can be seen from the preceding descriptions, the understanding of elementary mathematical concepts must rest on the understanding of preliminary physical concepts. However, this does not imply that the construction of the second tier must await the completion of the first tier. The nonlinearity of our model is expressed by the various arrows in Fig. 21.1.

To what extent are we justified in distinguishing between a physical precon-cept and the emerging mathematization of that concept? We cannot rely here on Piaget's distinction between empirical abstraction (related to the properties of an object) and reflective abstraction achieved by internalizing one's actions and operations. Indeed, such a simple mathematical concept as natural number can-

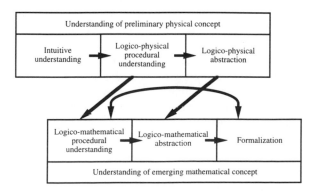

FIG. 21.1.   A two-tiered model for conceptual understanding.

not be construed as the property of an object but of a set of objects. These sets of objects are essential in the initial construction of such conceptual schemes. In fact, this was recognized in Piaget's later work when dealing with the importance of concrete sets:

> We will speak in this case of "pseudo-empirical abstraction" since there is a reading taken on the objects present, but a reading of properties due to the subject's actions, and this initial form of reflective abstraction plays a fundamental psycho-genetic role in all logico-mathematical learning, as long as the subject needs concrete manipulations in order to understand certain structures that might otherwise be too "abstract." (Piaget, 1974, p. 84, translated by N. H.)

This remark indicates that Piaget was well aware of the children's need to build their mathematics through a process of mathematization. However, his distinction between pseudo-empirical abstraction and logico-mathematical abstraction seems to be based essentially on a detachment of the mathematical object or procedure from its concrete support. This corresponds to a classical interpretation of abstraction. The problem with this approach is that it ignores the fact that many mathematical preconcepts can be explored and studied in a qualitative vein, without necessarily introducing quantification. One can perform operations and transformations on unquantified discrete sets of objects and reflect on these, but it is hard to describe the resulting abstraction as being logico-mathematical. This tends to reduce all logic to mathematics. The two-tiered model departs from this tendency and distinguishes between on the one hand logico-physical procedures and abstraction and on the other hand logico-mathematical procedures and abstraction, on the basis of whether or not mathematical objects and operations are present. For instance, augmenting an initial set of objects is a logico-physical procedure, but unless quantification is involved, it cannot be construed as arithmetical addition. The latter necessitates the use of natural numbers.

It is important to stress the nonlinearity of this model. For instance, research on the acquisition of number by kindergartners (Bergeron & Herscovics, 1989a; Bergeron, Herscovics, & Sinclair, 1992; Herscovics & Bergeron, 1989a, 1989b, 1990) has shown that the act of counting based on a one-to-one correspondence between a set of objects and the number word sequence is mastered by nearly all children by the time they finish kindergarten. In a test where the interviewer purposely either skipped an object in a row or counted an object twice, all children were pleased to stop the interviewer and point out her error. Many of these children did not conserve plurality (numerosity) under some transformations of unquantified sets of objects. Thus, some procedural understanding of a logico-mathematical nature can be achieved before logico-physical abstraction is reached. However, there are some limits to this. When these same children counted on (from the sixth chip on) a row of 13 chips and were asked "How many chips are in the whole row?" the success rate varied from 48% for the younger group (average age 5:8) to 69% for the older one (average age 6:2). The

FIG. 21.2.   A transfer of cookies from one set to another.

explanation was quite simple. Unless they had themselves established a one-to-one correspondence between the objects and the number word sequence, they did not consider that all the objects had been "counted."

Another interesting illustration can be found in Piaget's investigation of early arithmetic (Piaget & Szeminska, 1967). At age 6 years, children can add two sets of four objects each and find that the sum is eight. They can also do so by adding a singleton to a set of seven objects. Nevertheless, when they are told the story of a child going to school and bringing four cookies for a morning snack and four for an afternoon snack, and then when faced with a transfer of three cookies from one set to the other set, they no longer believe than the sum remains the same. They tend to focus on the larger of the subsets on the right in Fig. 21.2.

Although the transformation is carried out in front of them, children claim that the right-hand side contains more. Again, a conceptualization similar to the one Greco discovered for the number concept (where he had to distinguish between quantity and quotity) is evident here. How is one to judge this in terms of understanding? Clearly, at the physical level, these pupils have not yet established the invariance of the physical sum. This is why the description of logico-mathematical abstraction requires the invariance of both the physical operation and the arithmetic operation.

The diagram of the model of understanding (Fig. 21.1) shows an arrow relating logico-mathematico-procedural understanding directly to formalization. Again, this is based on the results of research on early number (Bergeron & Herscovics, 1990b). For instance, when asked to leave a written message for a friend telling him how many arrowheads were in front of them (seven), of the 91 kindergartners in this study, 59 (65%) simply wrote the numeral 7, thereby indicating they had apprehended the cardinal meaning of the numeral. However, 19 of the children (21%) wrote out 1,2,3,4,5,6,7, thus indicating a one-to-one correspondence between the objects and the numerical sequence. In effect, this formalization is still a reflection of the counting procedure. Hence, the description of formalization in the two-tiered model needed to include either a prior procedural understanding or some prior degree of abstraction.

Although the arrows in the diagram are unidirectional, this merely reflects the results of prior research. However, there is little doubt that mathematical notation need not await all possible degrees of abstraction before being introduced. In many cases, as for instance with integers, an appropriate notation is essential to introduce mathematical procedures and operations. Quite obviously, this notation has an impact on the logico-mathematical abstraction of this concept. This example also reflects the fact that it is difficult here to conceive of "levels" of understanding. The expression "component of understanding" seems more appropriate to describe each cell in the model and avoids misinterpreting it as a linear model.

APPLICATIONS OF THE MODEL

As with all models, the value of the two-tiered model lies in its use in the analysis of conceptual schemes in elementary mathematics. It is essentially epistemological, because it provides a frame of reference in which to gather all the elements involved in the construction of specific mathematical concepts. Perhaps it should be qualified as "genetic" because it searches for a knowledge basis for the learner's initial construction.

Previously Published Conceptual Analyses

The model has been used to analyze several conceptual schemes and many research results have been published. These are summarized here, followed by an extensive conceptual analysis of unitary fractions.

For their studies on the construction of natural numbers, Bergeron and Herscovics took *plurality* (the distinction between one and several) and the *position of an element in an ordered set* as the two physical preconcepts. It then followed that cardinal number could be defined as a measure of plurality, and ordinal number as a measure of position. For each component of understanding, several criteria were specified and corresponding tasks were developed. These were investigated in experiments with kindergartners in Montreal, in Paris, and in Cambridge, Massachusetts. The results have been reported in several papers (Bergeron & Herscovics, 1989b; Bergeron, Herscovics & Sinclair, 1992; Herscovics & Bergeron, 1989b).

As mentioned earlier, augmenting a set of objects, as well as forming the union of two sets, can be viewed as the physical preconcepts of arithmetic addition. This implies that "taking away" and separating into two subsets are the inverse actions. However, taking away is the only one that corresponds to a preconcept of early subtraction. One should not qualify as "additive" the action of a child who deposits marbles in a cup containing an initial set of five marbles without taking in consideration the pupil's final objective. An adult may perceive it as involving addition. However, to the child it could only involve an action scheme, that of "putting marbles in the cup." An action can be considered as additive only if the whole is perceived as resulting from the addition of elements to a given set or from the union of two sets. The whole–part relationship must be explicit. Criteria for each component of understanding as well as corresponding tasks have been described elsewhere (Herscovics & Bergeron, 1989c).

When applying the two-tiered model in the analysis of early multiplication, one must first answer the question, "What is multiplication?" Most teachers consider this operation as "repeated addition." But this is merely a procedural answer. It is interesting to note that for the other three basic operations of arithmetic, explicit actions can be associated (e.g., augmenting a set, taking away, splitting up into equal parts). But when it comes to multiplication, the associated action is not evident. Yet, quite early, Piaget and Szeminska (1967) related it to the iteration of a one-to-one correspondence between several sets. Later Herscovics, Bergeron, and Kieran (1983) showed that the iteration of a one-to-many correspondence was even more prevalent. Details of this research have been published (Beattys, Herscovics, & Nantais, 1990; Herscovics, Bergeron, Beattys, & Nantais, 1990; Nantais & Herscovics, 1989, 1990).

The model has also been useful in analyzing the concepts of length and measure. One can distinguish between physical length and the mathematization processes leading to the measure of length, just as one can view surface as a preconcept of area (the measure of surface). In his studies of third graders, Héraud (1987) found that the appropriate use of a ruler to measure length involved overcoming a number of cognitive obstacles. In his investigations of area (Héraud, 1989), he found that the children's choice of units selected to measure surfaces was dependent on the shape of the surface. Later (Héraud, 1992), he designed and tested a teaching experiment aimed at overcoming some of the cognitive obstacles previously identified.

That the notion of physical preconcept can be enlarged to include relatively abstract physical ideas is evidenced in Lytle's research on integers (Lytle, 1992). In this research, an "electronic" model was introduced (positive and negative unit values neutralizing each other). Although this model does not extend to multiplication or division, it is conceptually within the learner's reach for the other operations because it retains the meaning of augmenting for addition and taking away for subtraction used with natural numbers. This is particularly important for the subtraction of negative elements, which proves to be the most difficult task with a number-line model. Using charged particles to represent the subtraction of three negatives from two positives ($^+2 - {}^-3$), one simply uses an equivalent representation of two positives by augmenting them with three particles of each charge leaving the value of $^+2$ unchanged; taking away three negatives leaves five positives (Fig. 21.3).

The two-tiered model of understanding has also been used in the conceptual analysis of some algebraic concepts such as points in a plane, the slope of a line, and linear equations in two variables. Dionne and Boukhssimi (1989) have shown that for each of these concepts one could view respectively a geometric point, the steepness of an incline, and the straight line in a plane as the "physical" preconcepts. For instance, Piaget and Inhelder (1977) mention that at the intuitive level of understanding, a point is perceived as a mark left by a pencil on a sheet of paper. As such, it always has a shape and dimension. As a procedural understanding of this point, one can identify a "microscopic" apprehension (in the sense of mental perception) resulting from ever sharper pencils or hypotheti-

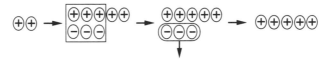

FIG. 21.3.   Charged particle representation of subtraction.

cal subdivisions of an initial point. It is only when logico-physical abstraction is reached that a point loses shape and dimension and simply denotes position in the plane. At the second tier, one could speak of an "algebraic" point in the Cartesian plane. As logico-mathematical procedures, one can consider different ways of determining the position of a point in the plane. Logico-mathematical abstraction is achieved when a correspondence between points in the plane and ordered pairs of reals has been established. Finally, formalization or formal understanding is reached when a generalized point (x,y) can be used to represent any point in the plane.

The Understanding of Unitary Fractions

Research on the child's acquisition of rational number has been extensive. Most of these investigations have dealt with a large range of problems such as the different representations of the number m/n, the notion of equivalence, and the four arithmetic operations. However, few studies have ever raised the fundamental question "what is a fraction?" or the even more basic one, "what is a unitary fraction, $1/n$?" And yet, although m/n can be viewed either as $1/n$ of m or as $m \times (1/n)$, both interpretations involve the prior construction of the concept of unit fraction.

Different Concepts of Measure

Early work by Piaget, Inhelder, and Szeminska (1948) indicated that for the child, "initially, a 'part' is simply a piece detached from the whole, and not an element embedded in the whole, that is, remaining mentally linked to it even after being separated." The tasks designed by Piaget and his colleagues required that the subjects divide the given geometric figures into equal parts. However, success by children in equipartitioning does not imply that the numerical concept of fraction is necessarily present in their mind. In fact, the notion of fraction as a number can only emerge from the quantification of the part–whole relationship involved in equipartitioning.

The arithmetical concept of unit fraction requires more than viewing a piece as part of the whole. It is essential that the learner be in a position to determine what part of the whole is involved. Such quantification requires both a new concept of measure and a primitive sense of ratio. By the time children are introduced to fractions, they have developed a basic concept of measure that can be described as an iterated measure because it involves the selection of a measuring standard or unit, which is then iterated as many times as necessary. This is adequate for all cases that are exact multiples of the measuring unit. However, the measure of part of a unit requires a paradigmatic shift of the very notion of measure and results in the concept of *fractional measure*.

The initial concept of fractional measure does not require any standard unit of measure. It originates from the apprehension of a whole as being divisible. This is why the concept is more general in the continuous case than in the discrete case. For instance, to think of a third of a marble is difficult because the marble as a unit can hardly be equipartitioned without special equipment. In the continuous case, children may have this perception regardless of whether or not they can perform the required equipartition. For instance, it is difficult to cut up a pie into seven equal pieces. Nevertheless, a pie so equipartitioned can be recognized at sight. It is the next step that is essential in the development of fractional measure; the pupils must now quantify the part–whole relationship. "Since the whole has been subdivided into 7 equal parts, each part must be a seventh of the whole." It is in this sense that fraction is a measure of the part–whole relationship resulting from equipartition.

Of course, fractional measure of a whole is not restricted to unit fractions, and these can easily be generalized to multiples of unit fractions of a whole, $m \times (1/n) = m/n$. But even then, children are not necessarily ready to handle the more advanced notion of measure that would involve the use of both units and subunits, which Bergeron and Herscovics (1987) have called *subunitary measure*. Children may very well have acquired the concept of fractional measure, but without fractions having been interpreted as subunits in the sense of measuring standards. In fact, in the construction obtained through the equipartitioning of a continuous whole, a unit fraction denotes the quantification of a single part, and m/n merely a multiple of that part.

The construction of a subunitary measure evolves from a different problem situation, that which involves a measurement exceeding the unit of measure being used (thus requiring at least one iteration of the measuring standard). For instance, if asked to measure a certain length that is not an exact multiple of the unit used, young children will provide approximations, stating that "it measures seven and a bit" or "almost 8." But they do not yet perceive the part left over as being measurable. This is quite reasonable because they do not view the measuring unit as being itself divisible. Even when a unit is apprehended as being divisible, the use of these subunits as new measuring standards is not self-evident, as indicated by Héraud's results on measure (Héraud, 1992). Children who have acquired some knowledge of fractional measure will be able to provide better approximations of the part left over: "It's six and a half," or maybe "six and a third". The apprehension of the relation between inches and feet or between centimeters and decimeters requires some fairly sophisticated thinking.

As mentioned earlier, the quantification of the part–whole relationship also involves a primitive sense of ratio. The general concept of ratio refers to a numerical comparison of two sets, as for example, "The elements in set A and set B are in the ratio of 3 to 7." However, in the case of a unit fraction, the quantification results from a comparison of one part to an equipartitioned whole. The concept of ratio involved here is primitive because the comparison is between one part and the whole, resulting in the ratio $1:n$.

Application of the Model to the Concept of Unitary Fractions

This prior discussion of the different concepts of measure was essential in order to clarify the restricted conceptual scheme resulting from the construction of unitary fractions. The two-tiered model of understanding can now be applied. Corresponding to distinct cells in the model, different criteria are introduced and related tasks are described. Some of these tasks have been used in assessing the understanding of 45 Montreal children in Grades 3–6 (Bergeron & Herscovics, 1987). As described earlier, the physical notion of unitary fraction is the one treated at the first tier; its quantification gives rise to the emergence of the arithmetical concept of fraction.

First Tier: The Notion of Physical Fraction

Intuitive Understanding. As mentioned earlier, at the level of intuitive understanding, Piaget and his associates (Piaget et al., 1948) found that at the beginning among young children (until 5 or 6 years), the very notion of "part" is that of a piece detached from the whole and not at all imbedded in it; it is not mentally connected to the whole after having been separated from it. This is why in tasks assessing intuitive understanding, it is essential not only to denote the parts but also to leave them imbedded in the whole.

The notion of equipartition plays a fundamental role and must be considered as a first criterion of intuitive understanding. The child must be able to distinguish between a partition resulting in equal parts and other partitions. Figure 21.4(a) gives a few examples that can be used.

It should be noted that even in the upper elementary grades, the notion of equipartition is not fully mastered. Among 34 children in Grades 4–6, 10 (29.1%) accepted unequal partitions in selecting a fifth of a rectangle or a sixth of a circle (Bergeron & Herscovics, 1987).

A second criterion at the level of intuition is the apprehension of the equivalence of each part resulting from an equipartition. In the Fig. 21.4(b) the child must consider one part as equivalent to another part within the given form.

A third criterion involves the comparison of different equipartitions of the same form. The child should be able to compare the results of different equipartitions and to determine that a quarter will be smaller than a third but larger than a fifth, as in Fig. 21.4(c).

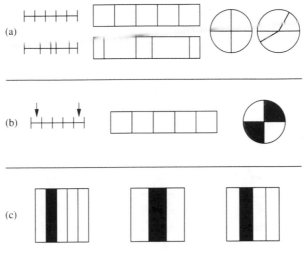

FIG. 21.4

Logico-physico-procedural Understanding. In terms of procedural under-standing, it is no longer sufficient to recognize and compare equipartitions, one must also be able to generate them. Piaget and his associates have found that children master the notion of equipartition in the following order: two, four, three, then five and six pieces. The subdivision of rectangles seems easier than squares, which in turn seems easier than circles.

Some of the Genevans' ideas have been refined by Pothier and Sawada (1983). They studied demarcation procedures that consist in marking off a parti-tion with matches or little sticks that can be used with great flexibility to establish a rough approximation of equipartition. For instance, to divide a circle into six equal sectors, children can use six matches to delineate distinct sectors. They can then adjust them to obtain relatively equal portions (Fig. 21.5).

Of course, this procedure can also be used to partition a length or a rectangle. But there are other procedures one can use depending on the material at hand. For instance, folding is another flexible procedure that can be used with certain shapes to approximate some partitions. A ribbon or a sheet of paper can be folded into five equal pieces whereas a circular form cannot. Once these folding proce-dures have been used, the child can permanently mark off the different parts using a pencil or chalk, and then each part can be cut off.

Logico-physical Abstraction. As a first criterion of logical abstraction, one could consider the invariance of the part with respect to the fractioning mode.

FIG. 21.5

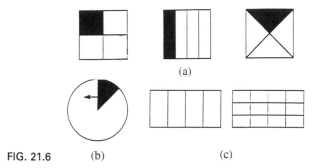

(a)

FIG. 21.6   (b)   (c)

For instance, the part of the square obtained from any of the partitions in Fig. 21.6(a) should provide "the same amount of chocolate." The two leftmost diagrams were used in the Bergeron and Herscovics study. Half of the 10 third graders perceived the quarters as unequal and of the other half, 3 of the 5 children used visual compensation: Splitting up the quarter in the middle square would give the same one as the quarter on the left. Twelve of the 34 upper graders used similar reasoning. For these subjects, the equivalence of the quarters is not based on the equipartitioning of the same square.

A second criterion of abstraction is that of reversibility. Although the previous tasks were concerned with the problem of equipartition, reversibility implies being able to reconstruct the whole starting from one of the parts. In some cases, this can be achieved without prior quantification of the given fraction, but it depends on the shape of the whole. Thus, given a piece of cardboard shaped as a slice of pie, the child can reconstitute the whole by drawing consecutive slices until the circle is completed, as in Fig. 21.6(b). When 10 third graders were given this task, 6 of them spontaneously drew the whole pie. Of course, for linear and rectangular shapes, this reconstruction of the whole is not possible unless the fraction is known.

A third criterion of abstraction can be found in the composition of equipartitions. If at the beginning this is arrived at unconsciously, as in the division of a whole into four parts obtained by a repetition of a division into two parts, this requires more analytical thinking for an equipartition into six arrived at by a division into three parts, each one then split into two. As soon as an equipartition into a higher number of parts is involved and whenever this number is composite, the composition of equipartitions becomes very useful: It is relatively easy to obtain an equipartition into 12 by first dividing by four and then dividing each part by three, as in Fig. 21.6(c).

Second Tier: The Emerging Notion of Numerical Fraction

The first tier of the model is concerned with problems of physical equipartitioning of a continuous whole and focuses on the physical part thus obtained (the

VOICI DEUX RECTANGLES. PEUX-TU ME MONTRER UN
CINQUIEME DU RECTANGLE A GAUCHE ?

PEUX-TU TROUVER UN CINQUIEME DANS L'AUTRE
FIG. 21.7   RECTANGLE A DROITE ?

physical fraction). It is at the second tier that the mathematization occurs through a process of quantification of the part–whole relation. Initially, a problem of vocabulary occurs. The word "moitié" (French for "half") is understood by all third graders. But this is not the case for other fractions. The words "tiers" (third) and "quart" (quarter) are not familiar at that age level. In a task set by Bergeron and Herscovics (1987), French-speaking children were asked if they could find a fifth in the rectangles shown in Fig. 21.7.

Answering the first question, children were pointing specifically to the last part of the rectangle. They did so again with the second rectangle. The explanation was quite simple. They were interpreting "cinquième" (fifth) in an ordinal sense. They were not thinking of a fifth in terms of a fraction but as the fifth region counting from the left of the rectangle. Using the same word for fractions and ordinal numbers causes some misunderstanding. This can be avoided by using expressions such as "one of n equal pieces" or "one of n equal parts." Because definitions have been included in the formalization process, the introduction of appropriate vocabulary is one of the criteria to be listed under formalization.

Logico-mathematico-procedural Understanding. All procedures involved here require both equipartitioning and quantification. For instance, pupils can be given a slice of pie and then asked if they have a way of determining what part it is. To find it, they have to use this slice to draw the full circle and count the number of times they had to use consecutive slices (see Fig. 21.5 for a similar task under logico-physico-procedural understanding). A comparable task can be designed for problems involving length or area. It is essential to present to the pupil both components of the relation, that is, the part and the whole as in Fig. 21.8(a). The procedures invoked by the pupils will depend on the means at their disposal and one can refer to all those mentioned earlier at the first tier. One of the simplest procedures would involve some visual approximation in which segments of length AB in Fig. 21.8(a) are marked off by the tools at hand (matches, pencil marks, etc.), as in Fig. 21.8(b). If instead of licorice or any rigid segment the length involved is a ribbon or a string, folding and cutting techniques can be used.

If the students are provided with a way of "measuring" the whole length by being given another piece A'B', as in Fig. 21.8(c), all they have to do is verify

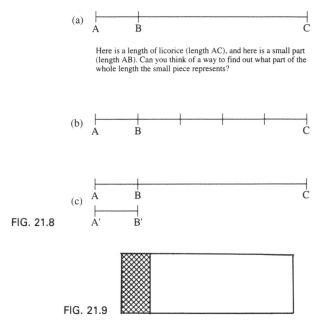

(a)

Here is a length of licorice (length AC), and here is a small part (length AB). Can you think of a way to find out what part of the whole length the small piece represents?

(b)

(c)

FIG. 21.8

FIG. 21.9

that A'B' is the same length as AB and then use it as a measuring standard iterating it as many times as needed.

Another procedure used might be that of conventional measure by finding that the length of AB is 2 cm and that of AC is 10 cm. This results in a ratio of 1 to 5. It should be noted that no subunitary measure is involved here because no subunits are needed.

The procedure selected by the students will vary according to the context and the measuring tools available. Of course, the same problems can be raised with rectangles (Fig. 21.9).

Logico-mathematical Abstraction.   A first criterion of logico-mathematical abstraction might be the students' apprehension of the invariance of a fraction with respect to the mode of partitioning. It is with rectangular and square figures that these problems are interesting. Given two identical squares, these can be subjected to equipartitions resulting in parts of different shapes as in Fig. 21.10(a). One can then ask specifically, "What part of the left square is shaded? What part of the right square is shaded?" Even if the child answers "a quarter" in each case, one still has to verify if abstraction has occurred at the logico-physical level by raising the question, "Do you think that you have the same quantity [amount] of chocolate [or some healthier food] in each of the quarters?" A similar form of questioning can be used with rectangles, as in Fig. 21.10(b).

As a second criterion of abstraction one may use the variability of the size of a fraction in terms of a different whole. For instance, one can ask pupils if two

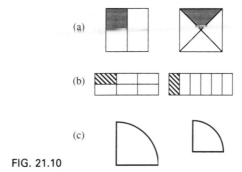

FIG. 21.10

pieces of different size could both be quarters. In fact, this question was used in the Bergeron and Herscovics study using two circular quarters, as in Fig. 21.10(c). Among the 34 children in the upper three grades, all but 2 perceived both pieces as quarters. Among the 10 third graders, only 3 of them did so initially. However, after the other 7 were asked to draw the respective "pies," 2 children changed their mind while the others steadfastly refused to accept both pieces as quarters.

A third criterion of abstraction could be the reversibility of the fractioning process. Can the student reconstitute the whole by knowing what fraction a given piece represents? This is certainly not a trivial question for third graders. After being given a sector and informed that it was a fifth of a pie, only 4 of the 10 students could predict the number of parts needed to get a whole "pie." For the same problem using a "piece that is one sixth of a chocolate bar," only five students could predict the number of pieces needed to reconstitute the whole bar.

A fourth criterion might be the apprehension of a fraction as a number. The problem here is comparable to the transition of natural numbers emerging from counting processes. Eventually, there is a detachment from the counting procedure: The word "three" need no longer be associated with objects. It becomes the cardinality of all triplets. Similarly, one can raise the question, "How does one separate a fraction from an object?" Perhaps this is only achieved when a fraction is perceived as an operator that can be applied to any whole.

Formalization. At first, formalization is achieved in terms of an adequate vocabulary. One must eventually evolve from the expression "one piece out of five equal pieces" to "one fifth." Perhaps one needs to discuss explicitly the problem of using the same word as in an ordinal case, and stress the importance of context.

A second criterion of formalization might be in terms of notation. Rather than immediately introducing the numerical convention, one might let pupils benefit from an intermediate notation, such as x of x x x x. This kind of notation reminds one of tally marks used by young children with natural numbers. It might prove useful for small fractions and motivate a more conventional symbolism by facing the problem of representing one-twenfth as $^1/_{12}$.

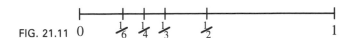

FIG. 21.11

A third criterion might involve the comparison of fractions: ordering the fractions $1/3$, $1/4$, and $1/2$.

A fourth criterion might concern the perception of a fraction as a number. Perhaps, by using fractions to denote positions on a unit line as in Fig. 21.11, one can bring about some detachment from the partitioning procedure.

This conceptual analysis of the notion of unitary fraction is quite extensive without even delving into the concept of equivalence, leading to rational number, or the four operations. This analysis does show the complexity of this conceptual scheme and brings out the many different aspects of the physical preconcept that deserve to be explored. Indeed, what is the sense of teaching students how to add and subtract fractions if they do not have a reasonable intuitive basis to build on? The transition from physical fraction to numerical fraction is far from easy, as shown by Erlwanger's Benny. Care must be taken in this crucial phase, for otherwise the young learner tends to develop idiosyncratic interpretations of the mathematical notation (Erlwanger, 1973).

The tasks presented here may seem trivial to an adult. Nevertheless, results with third graders indicate that they hardly realize at that age that the fraction is an invariant with respect to the fractioning mode. It is by attending to this type of problem that one may be able to avoid an instrumental approach to fraction and induce the learner into a thinking and reasoning mode of intellectual activity. That this is far from the present norm is evidenced by the results of the Fourth Mathematics Assessment of the NAEP (Kouba, Carpenter, & Swafford, 1989):

- Many students appear to have learned fraction computations as procedures without developing the underlying conceptual knowledge about fractions.
- Students in all three grades (3rd, 7th, and 11th) had difficulty with items that did not involve routine, familiar tasks, even when the items tested basic concepts.
- Slightly more than half of the third grade students could identify what fractional part of a figure was shaded.
- An extremely limited knowledge of fraction procedures was demonstrated by about one-third of the 7th graders and one-fourth of the 11th-grade students. (Kouba et al., p. 79)

CONCLUSION

A retrospective overview of teaching practices in mathematics indicates transitions from a prevailing algorithmic approach in the 1950s, to a formalist approach due to the introduction of "new math" in the 1960s, to a "back to basics" trend in the 1970s. The 1980s saw the early stirrings of constructivism, but one cannot claim that it has as yet provided a clear cut alternative. Perhaps one will have to await the latter half of the 1990s for this. But it is most encouraging to find constructivism being a subject of extensive debate and discussion. It is quite likely that this may transform it from a vague philosophy into a pedagogical tool.

Because a constructivist approach to instruction focuses on the learners, and takes as a starting point their existing knowledge and intellectual processes, a discussion of what constitutes appropriate representation in mathematics is absolutely essential. How should one introduce new ideas in mathematics? Of course, developmental questions cannot be ignored, because children in primary school cannot function at a formal level. But neither can students in secondary school start learning more advanced concepts without a strong intuitive basis. This recognition is evidenced by an increasing number of prealgebra courses, aimed at preparing students for a more formal algebra program.

The various models of understanding have addressed some of the issues involved. The two-tiered model of understanding suggests starting explicitly with a search for possible physical preconcepts that can then be connected to standard mathematics through a process of mathematization—that is, the translation into a mathematical language using mathematical objects such as numbers subject to mathematical operations and transformations. Of course, not all topics require a physical support. For instance, once number and division have been acquired, the notion of even number can be introduced in arithmetic without direct physical support. But then, this can be considered a "derived" mathematical concept instead of a "fundamental" one. Whenever a fundamental concept is at stake, it will require grouping all the relevant knowledge into a conceptual scheme.

The two-tiered model of understanding can be used to achieve a conceptual analysis, and thus can be quite helpful in gathering the needed information. The model assembles related knowledge into a cognitive matrix, whose elements are the criteria used to identify the different components of understanding. Because the acquisition of such fundamental concepts requires 2 or 3 years, this cognitive matrix provides an overview and enables teachers to view their pedagogical intervention from a proper constructivist perspective. For instance, teaching counting on in addition is quite important, but it can now be perceived as just one procedure in the more general context provided by a conceptual analysis.

The fact that learners are considered to be the prime elements in the construction of their knowledge does not in any way diminish the importance of the teacher. On the contrary, without proper interventions by the instructor the child is condemned to reinvent all the mathematics that is part of our cultural heritage. It is an impossible demand, and is not necessary. Constructivist teachers can prepare their material and organize it optimally so that their students can reconstruct, not reinvent, the intended mathematics.

This is not an easy task. Teachers, like all adults, have difficulties in assessing the cognitive obstacles faced by their students in learning new topics. This is inevitable for several reasons. Teachers can think at a formal level and have become proficient in using mathematical notation. But thinking at a formal level can blind one to the problems confronting learners who are still at a relatively concrete operational level. For these students, mathematical notation so condenses the ideas at hand that it may be totally meaningless for them. If the ideas are not yet present, they do not yet need to be crystallized and condensed. For these same reasons, the use of the two-tiered model of understanding may be difficult even for experienced teachers asking themselves, "What does it mean to understand" a given mathematical concept. By learning how to apply the model, however, they will become more conscious and sensitive to the difficulties confronting the learner.

EDITOR'S NOTE

The mathematics education community lost an important thinker with the death of Nicolas Herscovics in early 1994, after a long and valiant struggle with cancer. He was also a dear personal friend. The chapter published here can perhaps be considered a summary of some key ideas motivating his work, ideas that Nick continued to develop through the last weeks of his life. Without sufficient time to integrate all his final comments into the book chapter, he asked me to take responsibility for accomplishing this and for necessary editorial changes. I tried to fulfill this request by making only extremely minor changes in Nick's original words, rather than risking inadvertent changes in his meaning. I placed most of his later observations in the section of the chapter entitled The Case for *Rational* Constructivism, and hope that this does justice to his ideas. He will be greatly missed.—G. A. Goldin (July 1994)

REFERENCES

Balacheff, N. (1988). *Une étude des processus de preuve en mathématique chez les élèves de collège*. Thèse d'état, Université Joseph Fournier, Grenoble, France.

Beattys, C., Herscovics, N., & Nantais, N. (1990). Children's pre-concept of multiplication: Procedural understanding. In G. Booker, P. Cobb, & T. de Mendicuti (Eds.), *Proceedings of the Fourteenth PME Conference, 3*, 183–190.

Bell, A. W. (1976). A study of pupils' proof-explanations in mathematical situations. *Educational Studies in Mathematics, 7*, 23–40.

Bergeron, J. C., & Herscovics, N. (1981). Problems related to the application of a model of understanding to elementary school mathematics. In T. Post (Ed.), *Proceedings of the Third Annual Conference of PME-NA* (pp. 24–29). Minneapolis: University of Minnesota.

Bergeron, J. C., & Herscovics, N. (1982). A constructivist model of understanding. In S. Wagner (Ed.), *Proceedings of the Fourth Annual Conference of PME-NA* (pp. 28–35). Athens, GA: University of Georgia.

Bergeron, J. C., & Herscovics, N. (1985). The sequencing of activities for the teaching of the even-odd number notion by primary schoolteachers *without* their prior analysis of this concept. In L. Streefland (Ed.), *Proceedings of the Ninth International conference of PME* (pp. 465–470). The Netherlands: Noordwijkerhout.

Bergeron, J. C., & Herscovics, N. (1987). Unit fractions of a continuous whole. In J. C. Bergeron N. Herscovics, & C. Kieran (Eds.), *Proceedings of the Eleventh International Conference of PME*, Montreal, *1*, 357-365.

Bergeron, J. C., & Herscovics, N. (1988). The kindergartners' understanding of discrete sets. In A. Borbas (Ed.), *Proceedings of the Twelfth Annual Meeting of PME*, Veszprém, Hungary, *1*, 162-169.

Bergeron, J. C., & Herscovics, N. (1989a). The kindergartners' procedural understanding of number: an international study. In C. Maher, G. A. Goldin, & R. B. Davis (Eds.), *Proceedings of the Eleventh Annual Meeting of PME-NA* (pp. 97-104). Rutgers University, New Brunswick, NJ.

Bergeron, J. C., & Herscovics, N. (1989b). A model to describe the construction of mathematical concepts from an epistemological perspective. In L. Pereira-Mendoza & M. Quigley (Eds.), *Proceedings of the 1989 Annual Meeting of the Canadian Mathematics Education Group* (pp. 99-114). Memorial University of Newfoundland.

Bergeron, J. C., & Herscovics, N. (1990a). Psychological aspects of learning early arithmetic. In P. Nesher & J. Kilpatrick (Eds.), *Mathematics and cognition* (pp. 31-52). Cambridge: Cambridge University Press.

Bergeron, J. C., & Herscovics, N. (1990b). The kindergartners' knowledge of numerals. In G. Booker, P. Cobb, & T. Mendicutti (Eds.), *Proceedings of the Fourteenth Annual Meeting of PME*, *3*, 190-198.

Bergeron, J. C., Herscovics, N., & Sinclair, H. (1992). Contribution à la genèse du nombre. *Archives de Psychologie, Université de Genève, 60*, 147-170.

Bruner, J. S. (1960). *The process of education*. Cambridge: Harvard University Press.

Buxton, L. (1978). Four levels of understanding. *Mathematics Teaching*.

Byers, V., & Herscovics, N. (1977). Understanding school mathematics. *Mathematics Teaching, 81*, 24-27.

Dionne, J. J., & Boukhssimi, (1989). La compréhension de concepts géométrico-algébriques dans le curriculum. In A. Warbecq (Ed.), *Actes de la 41e Rencontre internationale de la CIEAEM* (pp. 185-192). Namur, Belgique: Centre technique de l'Enseignement de la Communauté Française.

Erlwanger, S. H. (1973). Benny's conception of rules and answers. In IPI Mathematics. *Journal of Children's Mathematical Behavior, 1*(2), 7-26.

Erlwanger, S. H. (1975). Case studies of children's conceptions of mathematics. *Journal of Children's Mathematical Behavior, 1*(3), 157-283.

Fischbein, E., & Kedem, I. (1982). Proof and certitude in the development of mathematical thinking. In A. Vermandel (Ed.), *Proceedings of the Sixth International Conference for the Psychology of Mathematics Education* (pp. 128-131). Antwerp, Belgium: Universitaire Instelling Antwerpen.

Ginsburg, H., & Opper, S. (1979). *Piaget's theory of intellectual development* (2nd ed.). Englewood Cliffs, NJ: Prentice Hall.

Goldin, G. A. (1990). Epistemology, constructivism, and discovery learning in mathematics. In R. A. Davis, C. A. Maher, & N. Noddings (Eds.), *Constructivist views on the teaching and learning of mathematics* (pp. 31-47). Journal for Research in Mathematics Education Monograph No. 4. Reston, VA: National Council of Teachers of Mathematics.

Goldin, G. A., & McClintock, C. E. (1984). *Task variables in mathematical problem solving*. Philadelphia: Franklin Institute Press. (Presently Hillsdale, NJ: Lawrence Erlbaum Associates)

Greco, P. (1962). Quantité et quotité: Nouvelles recherches sur la correspondance term-à-terme et la conservation des ensembles. In P. Gréco & A. Morf (Eds.), *Structures numériques élémentaires* (pp. 1-70). Paris: Presses Universitaires de France.

Héraud, B. (1987). Conceptions of area units by 8-9 year old children. In J. C. Bergeron, N. Herscovics, & C. Kieran (Eds.), *Proceedings of the Eleventh International Conference of PME*, Montreal, *3*, 299-304.

Héraud, B. (1989). A conceptual analysis of the notion of length and its measure. In G. Vergnaud, J. Rogalski, & M. Artigue (Eds.), *Actes de la 13e Conférence Internationale de PME, Paris, 2,* 83–90.

Héraud, B. (1992). *Genèse de la notion de mesures spatiales: construction de la mesure bilinéaire.* Unpublished doctoral dissertation, Université de Montréal.

Herscovics, N., & Bergeron, J. C. (1981). Psychological questions regarding a new model of understanding elementary school mathematics. In T. Post (Ed.), *Proceedings of the Third Annual Conference of PME-NA* (pp. 69–76). Minneapolis: University of Minnesota.

Herscovics, N., & Bergeron, J. C. (1983). Models of understanding. *Zentralblatt für Didaktik der Mathematik, 2,* 75–83.

Herscovics, N., & Bergeron, J. C. (1984). A constructivist vs. a formalist approach in the teaching of mathematics. In B. Southwell et al. (Eds.), *Proceedings of the Seventh International Conference of PME* (pp. 190–196). Sydney, Australia: University of Sydney.

Herscovics, N., & Bergeron, J. C. (1985). A constructivist vs a formalist approach in the teaching of the even-odd number concept at the elementary level. In L. Streefland (Ed.), *Proceedings of the Ninth International Conference of PME* (pp. 459–464). The Netherlands: Noordwijkerhout.

Herscovics, N., & Bergeron, J. C. (1988). An extended model of understanding. In M. J. Behr, C. B. Lacampagne, & M. M. Wheeler (Eds.), *Proceedings of the Tenth Annual Meeting of PME-NA* (pp. 15–22). DeKalb, IL: Northern Illinois University.

Herscovics, N., & Bergeron, J. C. (1989a). The kindergartners' understanding of cardinal number. In G. Vernaud, J. Rogalski, & M. Artigue (Eds.), *Proceedings of PME-XIII, 2,* 91–98. Paris: Université de Paris, La Sorbonne.

Herscovics, N., & Bergeron, J. C. (1989b). The kindergartner's construction of natural numbers. In L. Pereira-Mendoza & M. Quigley (Eds.), *Proceedings of the 1989 Annual Meeting of the Canadian Mathematics Education Group* (pp. 115–133). Memorial University of Newfoundland.

Herscovics, N., & Bergeron, J. C. (1989c). Analyse épistémologique des débuts de l'addition. In A. Warbecq (Ed.), *Rôle conception des programmes de mathématique, Actes de la 41e Rencontre internationale de la CIEAM* (pp. 155–165). Namur, Belgique: Centre technique de l'Enseignement de la Communauté.

Herscovics, N., & Bergeron, J. C. (1990). The kindergartners' construction of natural numbers: An international study. In L. Pereira-Mendoza & M. Quigley (Eds.), *Proceedings of the Thirteenth Meeting of the Canadian Group for the Study of Mathematics Education* (pp. 115–134). Newfoundland: Memorial University.

Herscovics, N., Bergeron, J. C., Beattys, C., & Nantais, N. (1990). A cognitive matrix describing the understanding of early multiplication. In M. Quigley (Ed.), *Proceedings of the 1990 Annual Meeting of the Canadian Mathematics Education Group* (pp. 79–98). Memorial University of Newfoundland.

Herscovics, N., Bergeron, J. C., & Kieran, C. (1983). A critique of Piaget's analysis of multiplication. In R. Hershkowitz (Ed.), *Proceedings of the Sixth International Conference of PME* (pp. 193–198). Rehobot, Israel: Weizmann, Institute of Science.

Inhelder, B., & Piaget, J. (1970). *De la logique de l'enfant à la logique de l'adolescent,* (2nd ed.). Paris: Presses Universitaires de France.

Kouba, V., Carpenter, T. P., & Swafford, J. O. (1989). Number and operations. In M. M. Lindquist (Ed.), *Results from the Fourth Mathematics Assessment of the National Assessment of Educational Progress.* Reston, VA: National Council of Teachers of Mathematics.

Kuhn, T. (1971). *The structure of scientific revolutions* (3rd ed.). Chicago: University of Chicago Press.

Lytle, P. (1992). *Overcoming difficulties in the learning of integers.* Unpublished master's thesis, Concordia University, Montreal.

Mayer, R. E. (1977). *Thinking and problem solving.* Glenview, IL: Scott, Foresman.

Nantais, N. Bergeron, J. C., & Herscovics, N. (1985). The sequencing of activities for the teaching of the even-odd number notion by primary schoolteachers following their prior analysis of this concept. In L. Streefland (Ed.), *Proceedings of the Ninth International Conference of PME* (pp. 471–476). Netherlands.

Nantais, N., & Herscovics, N. (1989). Epistemological analysis of early multiplication. In G. Vergnaud, J. Rogalski, & M. Artigue (Eds.), *Actes de la 13e Conférence Internationale de PME, Paris, 3,* 18–24.

Nantais, N., & Herscovics, N. (1990). Children's pre-concept of multiplication: Logico-physical abstraction. In G. Booker, P. Cobb, & T. de Mendicuti (Eds.), *Proceedings of PME-14, 3,* 289–296.

Piaget, J. (1973). Comments on mathematical education. In A. G. Howson (Ed.), *Developments in mathematical education, Proceedings of the Second International Congress on Mathematical Education.* Cambridge: Cambridge University Press.

Piaget, J. (1974). *Adaptation vitale et psychologie de l'intelligence.* Paris: Herman.

Piaget, J. (1976). *The psychology of intelligence.* Totowa, NJ: Littlefield, Adams. (Original work published in 1947)

Piaget, J., & Inhelder, B. (1977). *La représentation de l'espace chez l'enfant* (3rd ed.). Paris: Presses Universitaires de France. (Original work published in 1947)

Piaget, J., Inhelder, B., & Szeminska, A. (1948). La géométrie spontanée de l'enfant. Paris: Presses Universitaires de France.

Piaget, J., & Szeminska, A. (1967). *La genèse du nombre chez l'enfant* (4th ed.). Neuchatel, Switzerland: Delachaux et Niestlé. (Original work published in 1941)

Pothier, Y., & Sawada, D. (1983). Partitioning: the emergence of rational number ideas in young children. *Journal for Research in Mathematics Education, 14*(4) 307–317.

Skemp, R. R. (1976). Relational understanding and instrumental understanding. *Mathematics Teaching, 77.*

Skemp, R. R. (1979). Goals of learning and qualities of understanding. *Mathematics Teaching, 88,* 44–49.

Skemp, R. R. (1982). Symbolic understanding. *Mathematics Teaching, 99,* 59–61.

Tall, D. (1978). The dynamics of understanding mathematics. *Mathematics Teaching, 84.*

Vygotsky, L. S. (1978). *Mind in society.* Cambridge, MA: Harvard University Press.

Vygotsky, L. S. (1986). *Thought and language.* Cambridge, MA: MIT Press. (Original work published in 1934)

Constructing Mathematical Conventions Formed by the Abstraction and Generalization of Earlier Ideas: The Development of Initial Fraction Ideas[1]

George Booker
Griffith University, Brisbane, Australia

> *When we talk of students' constructive activities we are emphasizing the cognitive aspect of mathematical learning and would want to complement the discussion by noting that it is also a process of acculturation. As a consequence, we might begin to understand how it is possible for students to construct for themselves the mathematical processes that, historically, took several thousand years to evolve.*
> —Cobb, Yackel, and Wood (1992, p. 28)

CONSTRUCTIVISM AND MATHEMATICS EDUCATION

The assumption that mathematics is learned by the individual construction of ideas, processes, and understanding, rather than through the transmission of preformed knowledge from teacher to student, is now a commonly held belief among mathematics educators. An essential feature of this view is that existing conceptions, whether gained from everyday experiences or previous learning, guide the understanding and interpretation of any new information or situation that is met. As a result, there is often a resistance to adopting new forms of knowledge or to giving up or adapting previously successful thinking. The intuitive conceptions of children may also appear very different from accepted mathematical practice. Yet, much of this intuitive thinking is reminiscent of concep-

---

[1]The data reported here are drawn from Messinbird (1991).

tions that have been observed in the history of mathematics, underlining the fact that there are different possible conceptual frameworks for explaining and acting on phenomena in a consistent manner. In contrast, traditional approaches to mathematics teaching and learning assume that students' everyday and prior conceptions have to be replaced by more mathematical ones. Indeed, there often appears to be no assumption of any prior knowledge or experiences at all. It seems that any existing ideas should simply be erased in the process of inculcating "proper" procedures. Constructivism highlights the fact that old ways of thinking are not usually given up without resistance, and emphasizes that their replacement by or extension to new ways of thinking is guided by already existing conceptions (Duit, 1992). It also reminds us that mathematical concepts are human inventions rather than objective truth.

Much of the support for the belief in constructivism has come from observations of the learning of the elementary mathematics of counting numbers, simple computations, and problem-solving situations that require only whole-number considerations or the use of straightforward ideas of geometry and measurement (Cobb, Yackel, & Wood, 1992; Kamii, 1985, 1990; Labinowicz, 1985; Steffe, von Glasersfeld, Richards, & Cobb, 1983). Further evidence has been drawn from the common difficulties that occur as complex procedures are built with inappropriate or inadequate generalizations of the concepts and processes that gave initial success (Confrey, 1990; Graeber, Tirosh, & Wilson, 1990). It seems a short step from seeing how ill-formed constructions are made to assuming that even "correct" mathematical forms can also be constructed individually. However, seeing how appropriate constructions can be formed is not the same as knowing that they necessarily occur in this way. There is a compelling need to show and explain instances of children constructing for themselves these advanced ideas from among the various possibilities that could arise.

By viewing teachers and learners as active meaning-makers, continually giving contextually based meanings to each others' words and actions as they interact, constructivism also challenges the assumption that meanings reside in words, actions, and objects independently of an interpreter (Cobb, 1988). It suggests that the sharing or exchanging of mathematical thoughts and ideas is dynamic, reflecting a continually changing fit between the meaning-making of active interpreters of language and action rather than as the result of a conduit from teacher to learner. To assist such a process of learning, a teacher needs to have viable models of cognitive development in specific areas of mathematics from which the learners' conceptions can be inferred. With such models, activities that might lead to a restructuring of conceptual understanding toward a particular mathematical goal can be selected or formulated. But this demands of the teacher an awareness of ways in which learners might discuss, negotiate, and resolve their possible constructions, so that much current thinking in mathematics education is directed at the social conditions of learning and the specific activities in which the learning is situated.

These considerations also suggest how constructivism can help to account for the more complex mathematics beyond the counting numbers, that mathematics that has been formed by the processes of abstraction and generalization of earlier ideas rather than simply as a reflection of concrete situations. The conventions that have emerged cannot simply be replaced by the idiosyncratic building of a host of individual learners. Yet, to point out or even lead these learners to the accepted ways of proceeding raises the possibility that whatever is done may be no more than transmission in another guise. Somehow, the conventions that rule mathematics have to be acquired in the same social context from which the mathematical concepts are to be drawn. As Clements (1992) observed, "the dilemma of constructivist teaching is that while educators do not wish to impose 'right' answers, they still feel compelled to teach the subject matter." The need to view the building of mathematical cognition as a process of social (re)construction becomes paramount, and with it, the need to provide a setting in which there are possibilities for discussion, negotiation, and reconciliation of ideas and points of view. In this way, the notion of situated, social knowing can replace the concept of knowledge as the development of routines and strategies that are only viable for coping with reduced complexities, that are nonadaptive, and that have a damaging influence on self-concept and self-confidence (Bauersfeld, 1991).

LEARNING FROM A CONSTRUCTIVIST PERSPECTIVE

Constructivist approaches to learning seem to have taken on one of two forms (Duit, 1992). In one form, conceptual change is avoided to some extent by enlarging or partially restructuring students' thinking (constructivism as enlargement). In the other form, some type of cognitive conflict is involved in the teaching sequence to create a situation where students exchange their initial constructions for something more akin to the mathematical viewpoint (constructivism as cognitive conflict).

From the perspective of constructivism as enlargement, a teacher starts with a learner's existing knowledge and, by means of a continuous chain of development helps him or her "climb up the different steps of the intended construction . . . [so that] each step is an extension of accrued knowledge and this endows the learning process with continuity" (Herscovics & Bergeron, 1984, p. 195). This form of learning sees the teacher's role as a guide and raises the issue as to how much freedom the individual learner will have for her or his own constructions. But, with an orientation toward providing situations in which discussion flourishes and a teacher who sees his or her role as appropriating and utilizing students' constructions as they move toward the mathematical goal the teacher has in mind, this guiding role can be taken to facilitate the student's own constructions of the mathematical ideas that are intended. As long as the formal endpoints that the teacher conceived are seen just as that, endpoints to which the learners might be oriented when they have constructed the essential mathematical meanings themselves, the danger of the teacher becoming simply a transmitter of formal knowledge can be avoided. However, there is also the possibility that the individual student might wish to have the "right" or correct method or notation from the outset. Often, the most influential prior learning that a student brings to the learning of mathematics is a belief that there are exact answers, correct and efficient methods, and that the major, perhaps only, task of the teacher is to give them over to the learner.

The cognitive conflict form of constructivist teaching focuses on situations in which discussion, pertinent examples, and examination of the limitations and advantages of particular points of view lead to the displacement of inadequate or inappropriate constructions by mathematically superior viewpoints. Situations are arranged in which contradictions in the students' own constructions can emerge in contrast to the alternative mathematical view raised by the teacher, text, or some other arbiter of mathematical method. However, this is not as easily achieved as might appear, especially if the student's conception has been successful at some early level, has been practiced for some time and is initially dismissed as some form of "careless" error. Even the situations in which the student's view may be seen to lead to contradictions are not always accepted by the student who may be loathe to change a deeply held belief that is perceived to have considerable power, simply on the basis of one or two instances where it seems to break down or to be less efficient from the vantage point of the mathematically initiated. Indeed, as Confrey (1990, p. 37) wrote, "students cannot see their solution as erroneous until they have constructed a new problem and new solution. Doing this usually means revising their previous belief . . . through reflective abstraction and accommodation."

A cognitive conflict approach also leaves open the extent to which the students' own constructions are valued and whether they might simply perceive an "ideal" learning strategy to be one of waiting for the teacher's examples to point them to what should simply be learned. Access to any independent path to knowledge and to truth may then be denied, giving teachers power over what students learn that could easily be abused (Wheeler, 1987, p. 65). Perhaps the notion of cognitive conflict is more appropriate when an inadequate or inappropriate construction has become ingrained, and thus an aspect of what Bell (1986) has termed "diagnostic teaching." At an earlier stage, what is often called cognitive conflict is really just the process of argumentation and justification that is required to discuss and negotiate the mathematical meanings of a given situation. As Duit (1992) reminded us, the conflict arises first in the various possible constructions that might be formed: "It is a central idea in constructivism that there is a dialectic relation between conceptions and perceptions. Conceptions guide perceptions and perceptions develop conceptions. Where the guidance of perceptions is concerned, one could say that humans tend to see only what their current conceptions allow them to see" (p. 11).

COGNITIVE REPRESENTATION OF
MATHEMATICAL IDEAS

The replacement of the notion of forming a conduit between the teacher's mathematics and the students' mental conceptions as a perspective for the learning of mathematics by a model of individual construction has had profound implications, not only for practice, but also for the relationship between mathematics learning and cognition. No longer is the object to be one of implanting an ideal structure in each student's mind, but to understand the student's conception for what it is. Cognition is necessarily concerned with individual conceptions of mathematical ideas, personally constructed from the experiences to which each individual has been subject but reflected in the particular way of viewing or interpreting these experiences based on prior knowledge and ways of looking at the world. New cognitive structures result from both the social and physical environment, and cognitive development needs to be explained by reference to principles of self-regulated change and interaction. Thus the artifacts and forms of social organization, conceptual, symbolic, or material products that have emerged over the course of social history can be seen to be interwoven with and intrinsically related to the nature of children's intellectual constructions (Saxe, 1991a, p. 4).

This is very different from the view of assimilating and accommodating new ideas to a knowledge structure by simply looking at the structure of the particular aspects to be taught to see how to best represent them so as to replicate corresponding mental structures in the minds of the learners. It draws attention to the need for activity to be in the minds of the students and not merely in their hands if concrete experiences are to be of any help in the processes of acquiring mathematical knowledge. As Cobb (1992) observed, "Manipulative materials can play a central role if we wish students to learn with understanding, but the way those materials are interpreted and acted upon must necessarily be negotiated by the teacher and students." The materials are not "transparent" representations of a readily apprehensible mathematics, but instead are vehicles for the potential meanings that children might construct. But even the theoretical objects of mathematics have a reality akin to the concrete objects once they are produced. These too must be negotiated by teacher and students in the process of interpretation and resolution that gives rise to the "taken-as-shared" meanings that constitute higher mathematics. However, as Matthews (1992) highlighted, too often "constructivism has failed to appreciate the reality or objectivity of human intellectual activity" and mathematics education also needs to be "conceived in terms of the appropriate introduction of individuals into this world of concepts, understandings, techniques and community standards." Saxe (1991a) reminded us of Vygotsky's observations on the critical nature of social interactions in redirecting natural processes in cognitive development to the learning of scientific concepts. Because these are interconnected, comprehensive systems of undertandings that have been elaborated and refined over the course of social history, they cannot simply be internalized. They must undergo a complex transformation in their inward movement from artifacts external to the child's activity to the mental processes that make up an individual's cognition. Knowing is an evolving social practice, continually constituted by constructive activities of individuals, mediated by social interactions that bring about the meaningful adoption of mathematical conventions, and that allows some common perceptions to be taken as shared.

At the same time, by drawing attention to the need to account for cognition in terms of the learner's experiences and interpretations, a constructivist approach reveals the distinctive manner in which ostensibly similar tasks may be carried out in quite different ways or with differing degrees of success. Studies of schooled, nonschooled, and not-so-schooled children and adults have highlighted these differences from situation to situation and the ability or inability of individuals to transfer understanding or methodology from one to the other (Carraher, Carraher, & Schliemann, 1985; Lave, 1988; Saxe, 1991b). This literature shows that the activity and context in which the learning takes place are more than just a pedagogical vehicle for discussion and meaning-making. Rather than being separable from, or ancillary to learning, the situation is integral to what is learned, coproducing knowledge through activity; learning and cognition are fundamentally situated (Brown, Collins, & Duguid, 1989). Knowledge is, in part, a product of the activity, context, and culture in which it is developed and used. Hence, to account for the developing cognitive representations an individual is building, it is necessary to consider sociohistorical precedents for the ideas, the relativity of the context to the learner, and the authenticity of the activity in terms of the experienced culture of the learner.

DEVELOPING FRACTION IDEAS

Fraction ideas are the first abstracted mathematics met by the young learner, and the difficulties experienced by child and teacher alike as the differences and similarities to the earlier whole numbers are met, grasped, and reconciled are well known. Unlike whole numbers, whose development has occurred in all societies, "In the earliest times in all parts of the world there was tendency to avoid fractions by creating a great number of ever smaller units of weights and measure, but the relations of these were in some cases more judicious than others" (Needham, 1970, p. 81). Nonetheless, some elementary knowledge of fractions as parts of things, specifically for halves and quarters, and a background of whole numbers, particularly related to the language and recording of numbers, is brought to the learning of fraction ideas in schools. Consequently, their development offers a rich field for investigating the implications of a constructivist perspective on the learning of mathematics from the points of view of accounting for difficulties and inconsistencies in learning, of drawing up and implementing a sequence of activities that would lead the individual child from an initial conception to a fuller one, and that would allow the efficacy of social interactions in this process to be assessed.

A full understanding of fraction ideas would seem to require exposure to numerous rational number concepts (Behr, Harel, Post, & Lesh, 1992; Kierin, 1988). Kierin's (1988) model of mathematical knowledge building suggests that this development proceeds through four levels, beginning with the basic knowledge acquired as a result of living in a particular environment, such as a recognition of parts and wholes and the names of the elementary fractions in everyday use. At the next level, this is broadened to an intuitive, schooled knowledge built from and related back to everyday experience, as in the case when initial number knowledge is extended to cope with the names of fractions in general. The third level includes the technical, symbolic language that involves the use of standard language, symbols, and algorithms, whereas the fourth and final level consists of axiomatic knowledge of the system. Mature knowledge at this fourth level would allow engagement in "the whole range of thought and action and the [interrelationship of] thought and action at one level with thought and action at other levels" (Behr et al., 1992). Although this provides a viable cognitive model of the overall development of fraction concepts, it does not provide sufficient detail to assess individual children's conceptions, nor does it provide guidance as to the types of activities children might engage in to build their knowledge from one level to the next.

An analysis by Messinbird (1991) fleshed out this framework and led to the developmental sequence for initial fraction ideas that could provide a basis for children's construction of fractional ideas in a classroom setting (Fig. 22.1). Introductory activities were designed in the form of authentic, shared activities involving work with objects such as chocolate bars, cheese, and candies from the children's familiar environment, whereas later instructional situations involved structured activities and games to encourage discussion and the resolution of alternative possible constructions. A decision was made to base this development on the establishment of a part/whole conception first so as to allow a secure, unambiguous conception from which later extensions could evolve and to focus on the development of a mental conception that would allow a meaningful language to emerge and link with the accepted conventions of the formal mathematics of fractions at an appropriate time.

These activities were designed to give situated meaning as opposed to rule-like procedures that often dominate the learning of fractions through the use of models, manipulative materials, and situations involving chance. The use of familiar game formats and characters from their everyday play was designed to allow the meaning-making to resonate with prior out-of-school and in-school experiences. With this conceptual and learning model, it was postulated that the children would "construct and reconstruct their knowledge, returning to earlier

Developmental Sequence

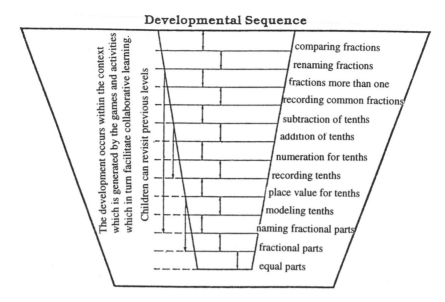

FIG. 22.1.   Contained by the classroom setting.

stages of development as reflection and observation identify areas of incompleteness. The complexity of the situation, with its established social norms, actions and interactions, cognitive conflicts and agreement . . . is best experienced in a collaborative classroom" (Messinbird, 1991, p. 70).

It had been assumed that experiences with forming equal parts, using concrete materials, and establishing a language of shared meanings through activities that required discussion and resolution would generate a need for the recording of fractions. However, while the initial ideas of partitioning and recognizing equal parts appear relatively simple, some children require many experiences over an extended period of time to allow these fundamental ideas to be constructed. Without this conception of a fraction, there is little likelihood of any further building of ideas at anything but a rote level. Thus, the notion of equal parts was often overruled in the rush to simply name the number of parts under consideration. Interestingly, "it appeared more frequently in the upper grades where it is usually assumed that revisiting the idea of equal parts is unnecessary" (p. 158). It is likely that one cause of the difficulties that these children were exhibiting with more difficult fraction concepts and procedures had its roots in the uncertain foundations of the initial fraction idea.

Similarly, the difficulties in having children construct for themselves the representations of simple fractions, as opposed to identifying the correct form from among those given to them, highlights again the pertinence of the comment that concrete representations are not transparent. Perhaps even more than with whole-number concepts, the materials only communicate meaning to those who already have the conception of a fraction. No matter what model or situation is used to introduce the fraction concept, there is always the likelihood that children will see it as the combination of two cardinal numbers, and thus confuse $3/7$ and $7/3$, revealing a difficulty with the fraction concept itself and not just with the naming.

Related difficulties arose with the use of materials used to help in the building up of decimal fraction numeration. When tenths remained as shaded parts on a square which represented ones, the idea could be accepted and worked with in what appeared to be a meaningful fashion. However, when the squares were cut up to form individual tenths to allow for a game that required the trading of tenths for ones, this "understanding" was seen to be shallow and students began to name the ones as tenths, the tenths as ones, or refer to the parts as "oneths." What had seemed to be a very powerful representation was, for some children, simply a set of materials that could be manipulated without reference to any underlying ideas. In fact, upon further probing, it transpired that earlier use of materials to establish place value for whole numbers was just as ineffective, and the rich understanding of whole number numeration that had been assumed as a base for the development of decimal fractions was simply not there.

Nonetheless, many children did manage to construct their own understanding of the fraction concept, including meaningful naming and manipulation of the ideas. But even when this has occurred, there are still problems in trying to provide situations in which children can construct complex mathematical ideas for themselves, as the following extended excerpt from the videotaped record of the interactions of one group illustrates. In the following excerpt, Jo, Lizzie, Rebecca, and Lisa played a game that used cards showing fractions more than one in pictorial form. Each player was required to read a card in two ways: in common fraction and mixed number form.

Jo:	[Picking up a card] Um. Three and . . . yeh, three and one third.
Rebecca:	And what's the other way? You got to say the other way to say it too.
Jo:	Do you?
Rebecca:	[picking up the card and pointing] Yeh, and you got to count how many are shaded and then say the fraction.
Jo:	Okay, one third. [Ignoring the fraction that made up the three completely shaded rectangles]
Rebecca:	No, like count all them that are shaded.
	[Rebecca tries to impose her knowledge]
Jo:	Oh, four thirds. [counting the completely shaded rectangles each as one third instead of as three thirds]
	[Rebecca and the others did not appear to notice. Where does argumentation and resolution enter into the constructive activity when there is not a knowledgeable guide present?]

Rebecca:	Yeh, that's better.
Rebecca:	[picking up a card for her turn, counts] Thirteen eighths or one and . . . one and five eighths. [Jo watches carefully]

[Rebecca models her knowledge for Jo.]

| Lisa: | [Picking up a card] Um . . . one and three fourths or um . . . |
| Jo: | Three fourths. |

[Despite watching Rebecca, her conception persists.]

| Lisa: | Yeh. [seeming to follow Jo's cue and looking only at the partially shaded shape but then reconsidering] |

[Is it her level too, or does she just go along?]

| Rebecca and Lisa together: | No. |
| Rebecca: | Count up . . . |

[Direct instruction again—if a teacher does not try to simply transmit knowledge, children often will!]

[Jo seemed to guess instead of counting as Rebecca had suggested:]

| Jo: | Thirteen fourths? [The fraction under consideration was 1 and 3 fourths.] |

[Or had she? She appeared to have generalized from her recent experiences with decimal fractions, taking one whole as 10 equal parts, then added the three fourths to make thirteen fourths.]

Rebecca:	No, like um . . .
Lisa:	[Looking at Rebecca and asking questioningly] Seven fourths?
Jo:	No, I thought . . . No, it would be three fourths, one and three fourths is three fourths.

[What is a fraction to Jo? Only part/whole? This belief is rife in out-of-school experiences and is situated in the introductory fraction activities with which she had success.]

Rebecca:	Yeh, but . . .
Lisa:	Yeh, but when . . .
Rebecca:	You gotta count up how many to get a four . . .
Lisa:	So there'd be four, five, six, seven, . . .

[Lisa has internalized the relationship of wholes to parts in general (in this case, 1 one is 4 fourths) and counts to show why, rather than counting all like Rebecca.]

| Jo: | Oh, yeh. |

[Jo gives in to the pressure of the other girls' insistent answers.]

| Rebecca: | Four and three . . . seven fourths. |

[However, Rebecca begins to reconstruct her view from Lisa's explanation and by rethinking her own procedure.]

Lisa:	Seven fourths. . . . Yes, that's what I said.
Lizzie:	[Picking up her card] One and three fifths.
Jo:	Or what else?
Lizzie:	Um . . .
Rebecca:	Or . . . [waving her hands]
Lisa:	What's five and three?

[Lisa tries to impose her method on Lizzie in order to get to the social purpose of playing the game.]

Jo: [Answering for Lizzie] Or eight fifths.
                           [Beginning to respond to Lisa's procedure.]
Lizzie: Yeh. [Putting down the card]
Jo: No, it wouldn't. [Picking up the card] No, because . . .
                           [This conflicts with her earlier view. But Rebecca overrules the doubt, now using the thinking she has constructed from Lisa.]
Rebecca: Yeh, because it's five in it and three, five and three is eight.
                           [Jo seldom persisted when she did not understand. Even when she could solve a problem successfully, she was quite prepared to be overruled by the more dominant students. She seemed to regard her social position in the class as very important and rarely created or continued a conflict. To her, capitulation was more acceptable than confrontation, negotiation, and resolution. As a result, Jo's construction of fraction knowledge remained incomplete.]
Jo: [Picking up the card for her turn] Okay [pointing and counting]. Um, one, two, three, four. Four and one third or . . . [pointing and counting again] one, two, three, four, five, six, seven, eight, nine, ten, eleven, twelve and one fifth . . . Oh! . . . or   thirteen   and   three,   thirteen . . . [looking puzzled]
Rebecca: Thirteen thirds if they're equal . . . yeh, thirteen thirds. [sounding impatient]
Jo: Yeh, would it be? [in a questioning tone to Rebecca]

Later, Rebecca used the blackboard as well as one of the card games to show Jo why two and one-fourth could also be called nine fourths. But Jo's attention had wandered and she showed little interest in Rebecca's attempts. As the game advanced, Lizzie and Jo tried to speed up the game by not having answers agreed on by all group members, but interestingly, these children, including Lizzie and Jo, would at times still refer to another for confirmation.

From this transcript and as evidenced in their responses to individual questioning, Jo and Lizzie were apparently experiencing difficulty when renaming mixed numbers as fractions, as shown in Figs. 22.2 and 22.3.

Lizzie's case was typical of many of the less capable children. These children soon realized that in some situations, providing they said "um" or hesitated long enough, one of their peers would answer for them and as a result they neither risked being incorrect nor risked having to apply themselves. This unwillingness

FIG. 22.2. Jo's attempt at renaming fractions shows a restricted notion of the fraction concept.

FIG. 22.3. Lizzie's attempt at renaming fractions reveals that her concept of renaming is related to the decimal fractions just met or perhaps to the earlier whole number work.

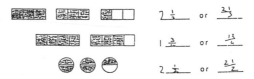

or inability to participate did not go innoticed by their peers. Lizzie, for example, was virtually ignored much of the time. Although this was far from satisfactory, efforts were made to encourage behaviors that would enable all children to participate in constructing their own knowledge through explanation, seeking help from their peers, providing help to others, and gradually taking responsibility for their own progress while simultaneously being aware of the needs of their peers and the growing realization that all members of the class were responsible for facilitating and maintaining a positive classroom culture.

TENSIONS BETWEEN THE SOCIAL CONSTRUCTION OF MEANING AND THE SOCIAL CONVENTIONS OF THE CLASSROOM

Although Lisa and Rebecca constructed appropriate, sophisticated strategies for renaming improper fractions and mixed numbers, Jo and Lizzie often avoided situations where other players checked each person's results, ostensibly to speed up the playing, but actually to avoid the conflict with previous ideas. In this way, the social demands of playing were used to avoid constructing and coming to terms with the social conventions of the more advanced mathematics. This shows how, even with the use of carefully planned materials and engaging activities, children can acquire rote routines for forming answers rather than building for themselves the underlying concepts. Further, not all children will engage in the social actions required for negotiation of meaning, let alone participate in the conflicts needed to overcome cognitive obstacles resulting from inadequate earlier concepts. Indeed, children may well alter the conditions of the situation in which they are placed to avoid perceived difficulties altogether or simply to allow them to achieve their own objectives, which may be very different from those mathematical endpoints the teacher had in mind.

The broader study from which this episode was drawn also suggests that there are many difficulties in introducing the conventions of recording fractions in symbol form. Decimal fractions may be simply treated as whole numbers with a period arbitrarily placed among the digits. In fact, too hasty a move to addition and subtraction seems almost guaranteed to encourage children to focus on procedural definitions of decimal fractions rather than ones based on place value and related to the part/whole notions fundamental to the fraction concept. Indeed, at a later point, the form of recording the two parts of a common fraction, such as seven eighths as $^7/_8$ seems to lead children to writing 7 tenths as 7.10 or

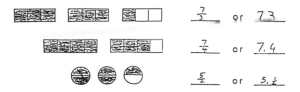

FIG. 22.4. J wrote improper fractions correctly, then transferred these to decimal fraction form.

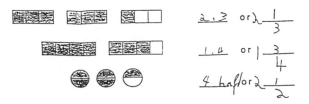

FIG. 22.5. A wrote the mixed numbers correctly, then transferred these to decimal fraction form.

sometimes 10.7. The two different forms often point to a further confusion brought about by seeing $^3/_7$ and $^7/_3$ as representing the same fractional amount. Furthermore, the construction of meaningful conventions for renaming fractions is problematic even with the most careful planning of learning situations that allow for negotiation of new ways of thinking and the resolution of conflicts with earlier ideas. Not only are there potential confusions in the construction of mixed numbers and improper fractions due to the change from a part/whole conception of fraction (that largely goes unnoticed, unannounced, or at least undiscussed), but there are also problems in reconciling the new renaming process between different forms of common fractions and those between decimal fractions and common fractions (Figs. 22.4–22.6).

These points raise concerns about the manner in which we might need to structure a constructivist classroom if the type of learning theoretical considerations lead us to anticipate is going to occur. Our object as mathematics educators is now to provide rich situations and experiences out of which particular mathematical concepts might be able to emerge, then to guide and facilitate the construction of mathematical ways of looking at these situations, and to come to terms with the ways of thinking that each individual has formed in order to do this. In this way we may be able to make sense of each student's mathematical world view and endeavor to assist students to build for themselves the socially accepted concepts, processes, and sometimes even the procedures of what is felt to constitute mathematical knowledge. In time, and with further experience, we may go even further and, taking Bauersfeld's (1991) suggestion, dispense with psychological notions of teaching and learning altogether by adopting a sociological perspective of *mathematizing* as the interactive constitution of a social practice. This would even allow "the outcomes or products, which from a psycho-

FIG. 22.6.   D wrote the parts in the form of a decimal fraction, then transferred this to a common fraction interpretation.

logical perspective are described as 'mathematical knowledge' [to] appear as social accomplishments of the specific culture" (Bauersfeld, 1991 p. 11).

REFERENCES

Bauersfeld, H. (1991). *The structuring of the structures.* IDM Occasional Paper No. 123, Institute für Didactik in Mathematik, Bielefeld Universitat, Germany.

Behr, M., Harel, G., Post, T., & Lesh, R. (1992). Rational number, ratio and proportion. In D. Grouws (Ed.), *Handbook on mathematics teaching and learning.* New York: Macmillan.

Bell, A. (1986, July). Outcomes of the diagnostic teaching project. In L. Burton & C. Hoyles (Eds.), *Proceedings of the Tenth International Conference of the Psychology of Mathematics Education,* London (pp. 331–335).

Brown, J. S., Collins, A., & Duguid, P. (1989). Situated cognition and the culture of learning. *Educational Researcher, 32–42.*

Carraher, T. N., Carraher, D. W., & Schliemann, A. D. (1985). Mathematics in the streets and in schools. *British Journal of Developmental Psychology, 3, 21–29.*

Clements, M. A. (1992, July). *Some pluses and minuses of radical constructivism in mathematics education.* Paper presented at the Fifteenth Annual Meeting of the Mathematics Education Research Group of Australasia, University of Western Sydney.

Cobb, P. (1988). The tension between theories of learning an instruction in mathematics education. Educational Psychologist, *23*(2), 87–103.

Cobb, P., Yackel, E., & Wood, T. (1992). A constructivist alternative to the representational view of mind in mathematics education. *Journal for Research in Mathematics Education, 23*(1), 2–33.

Confrey, J. (1990). A review of the research of student conceptions in mathematics, science and programming. *Review of Research in Education, 16,* 3–56.

Duit, R. (1992, February). *The constructivist view: A both fashionable and fruitful paradigm for science education research and practice.* Paper presented to the Constructivism in Education Seminar, University of Georgia.

Graeber, A., Tirosh, D., & Wilson, P. (Eds.). (1990). Inconsistencies and cognitive conflict: A constructivist's view. *Focus on Learning Problems in Mathematics, 12* (3 & 4).

Herscovics, N., & Bergeron, J. (1984). A constructivist vs a formalist approach in the teaching of mathematics. In B. Southwell & K. Collis (Eds.), *Proceedings of the Eighth International Conference of the Psychology of Mathematics Education,* Sydney, Australia (pp. 190–196).

Kamii, C. (1985). *Young children reinvent arithmetic: Implications of Piaget's theory.* New York: Teachers College Press.

Kamii, C. (1990). *Young children continue to reinvent arithmetic.* New York: Teachers College Press.

Kierin, T. (1988). Personal knowledge of rational numbers: Its intuitive and formal development. In J. Hiebert & M. Behr (Eds.), *Research agenda for mathematics education: Number concepts and operations in the middle grades* (pp. 162–181). Reston, VA: National Council of Teachers of Mathematics.

Labinowicz, E. (1985). *Learning from children: New beginnings for teaching numerical thinking.* Menlo Park, CA: Addison Wesley.

Lave, J. (1988). *Cognition in practice: Mind, mathematics and culture in everyday life.* Cambridge: Cambridge University Press.

Matthews, M. (1992). *Old wine in new bottles: A problem with constructivist epistemology.* Unpublished paper, Education Department, University of Auckland.

Messinbird, B. (1991). *An investigation into the use of structured games and heuristic activities to develop fraction concepts at the year 4 level.* Unpublished BT(Hons) thesis. Brisbane: Griffith University.

Needham, J. (1970). *Science and civilisation in china* (Vol. 3, p. 81). Cambridge, England: Cambridge University Press.

Saxe, G. (1991a). *Culture and development: Studies in mathematical understanding.* Hillsdale, NJ: Lawrence Erlbaum Associates.

Saxe, G. (1991b, April). *Cultural influences on children's mathematical knowledge.* Paper presented at the 1991 Research Presession meetings of the National Council for Teachers of Mathematics, New Orleans.

Steffe, L., von Glasersfeld, E., Richards, J., & Cobb, P. (1983). *Children's counting types: Philosophy, theory and application.* New York: Praeger.

Wheeler, D. (1987). The world of mathematics: Dream, myth or reality? In J. C. Bergeron, N. Herscovics, & C. Kieran (Eds.), *Proceedings of the Eighth International Conference of the Psychology of Mathematics Education,* Montreal (pp. 55–66).

23

A Joint Perspective on the Idea of Representation in Learning and Doing Mathematics[1]

Gerald A. Goldin
Rutgers University

James J. Kaput
University of Massachusetts/Dartmouth

For some time each of us in his own way has been developing the concept of representation in the psychology of mathematical learning and problem solving (Goldin, 1982, 1983, 1987, 1988a, 1988b, 1990, 1992a, 1992b; Goldin & Herscovics, 1991a, 1991b; Kaput, 1979, 1983, 1985, 1987, 1989, 1991, 1992, 1993). In this chapter we explore the compatibility of our ideas, and begin to develop a joint perspective—one that we hope can lay a foundation for future theoretical work in mathematics education based on representations and symbol systems. We believe that the constructs offered here provide a sound basis for further development.

In approaching the issue of representation, we recognize the complexity and magnitude of the challenge. On the one hand, there is a long history of attempts to make sense of the many forms taken by representational activity, attempts that have achieved various degrees of success; on the other hand, some mathematics education researchers reject the construct of representation entirely (e.g., Marton and Neuman, chapter 19, this volume). Nonetheless, we feel that the sharpening of certain notions related to representation, and development of a way to discuss them more systematically and precisely, can greatly benefit the field of mathematics education—and can clarify some of the points of disagreement among researchers.

We also recognize that making a commitment to particular ways of theorizing

---

[1]This chapter was substantially written during 1991–1992, with final revisions in 1994. The authors' current work extends many of the ideas introduced here and will appear in subsequent publications.

entails certain costs. Even the use of a term such as *representation* to describe mathematical activity may presuppose a perspective and set of commitments that some researchers are not willing to make; when we further begin to speak of "internal versus external" representations, the number of participants in the conversation may shrink even more. However, we attempt both to demonstrate the value of these constructs and to answer various objections to them. We know full well that the language we choose to use influences us in turn through the tacit assumptions it may embody; indeed, relationships between thought and language are among the underlying themes of this chapter. Thus we seek to make at least some of our assumptions as explicit as possible, and to offer an approach that is sufficiently flexible to accommodate a reasonable range of epistemological perspectives.

In the first section we describe what we mean by representation, distinguish internal from external representation, discuss relations between representations, and provide an introduction to the systematicity of representational configurations. The second section addresses directly various objections to these ideas, particularly those associated with radical constructivism. In the third section we describe various types of representational systems and media in which they are embodied. This section includes brief discussions of linked external representations, imagistic or analogic systems (external and internal), formal representational systems (external and internal), and psychological models based on various types of internal representational systems. The fourth section is devoted to basic types of representational acts and structures. In the fifth section we discuss the growth of representational systems, followed by a section that characterizes the building of powerful systems of representation as an overarching goal of mathematics learning and development. We conclude the chapter with a brief discussion of how the concept of "representation" is essential to understanding constructive processes in the learning and doing of mathematics, and mention some open issues related to our developing joint perspective.

WHAT DO WE MEAN BY "REPRESENTATION"?

Roughly speaking, a *representation* is a configuration of some kind that, as a whole or part by part, corresponds to, is referentially associated with, stands for, symbolizes, interacts in a special manner with, or otherwise represents something else (Palmer, 1977). We say "roughly speaking" because among other complex characteristics, representations do not occur in isolation. They usually belong to highly structured systems, either personal and idiosyncratic or cultural and conventional. These have been termed "symbol schemes" (Kaput, 1987) or "representational systems" (Goldin, 1987; Lesh, Landau, & Hamilton, 1983). Furthermore, the representing relationship is in general not fixed, nor is its specific nature a necessary feature of the representation. This is because, inevitably and intrinsically, an interaction or act of interpretation is involved in the relation between that which is representing and that which is represented (von Glasersfeld, 1987). Indeed, rather than beginning with "representations" as we do here, we could as an alternative have begun with a discussion of "representational acts."

Internal Versus External Representation

A distinction that is very important for the psychology of learning and doing mathematics, and fundamental to our joint perspective, is that between internal and external systems of representation (see Fig. 23.1). Elsewhere this has sometimes been characterized as a distinction between the *signified* (internal) and the *signifier* (external); thus our approach bears a loose kinship with a similar distinction made by de Saussure (1959). However, we regard the relation of "signifying" not as fixed and unidirectional, but as changeable and reversible.

We use the term *internal representation* to refer to possible mental configurations of individuals, such as learners or problem solvers. Of course, being internal, such configurations are not directly observable. As teachers or researchers we regularly (and necessarily) infer mental configurations in our students or subjects from what they say or do, that is, from their external behavior. Often we make such inferences tacitly rather than explicitly, and sometimes we consciously set out to develop particular sorts of internal representations in our students through teaching activity.

Let us elaborate briefly on this. To some extent an individual may be able to describe his or her own mental processes, as they seem to occur, through introspection. Not only is this "metacognitive awareness" inevitably imperfect and incomplete, but the experience of it is directly accessible only to the person doing the introspecting. We use the term *internal representation* not to refer to the

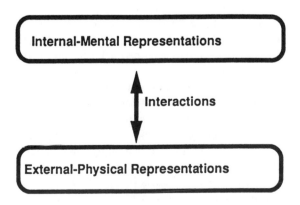

FIG. 23.1. Internal versus external representations.

direct object of introspective activity, but as a construct arrived at by an observer from the observation of behavior (including, of course, verbal and mathematical behavior). Although the experience of introspection is subjective, the descriptions that result from introspection are observable as, for example, verbal and gestural behavior. In developing a theory based on systems of internal representation, it is desirable for the sake of coherence and usefulness that the kinds of configurations that occur in the theory (i.e., internal representations inferred from observations) bear some resemblance to individuals' descriptions of their own subjective awareness. However, it is essential that we clearly distinguish the term internal representation as used here from other perspectives that may involve ontological assumptions about "the mind."

In contrast to internal representation, we use the term *external representation* to refer to physically embodied, observable configurations such as words, graphs, pictures, equations, or computer microworlds. These are in principle accessible to observation by anyone with suitable knowledge. Of course the interpretation of external representations as belonging to structured systems, and the interpretation of their representing relationships, is not "objective" or "absolute" but depends on the internal representations of the individual(s) doing the interpreting.

For example, consider a graph drawn in Cartesian coordinates by a person to "represent" the equation $y + 3x - 6 = 0$. The particular graph is not an isolated drawing. It occurs within a system of coordinate representation, based on specific (socially constructed) rules and conventions, which in turn must be (at least partially) "understood" before the representational act can take place. It is useful for us to consider the graph as an external configuration, and to treat the system of Cartesian coordinate representation as external to any one individual. We thus distinguish the external graph from the internal visual, kinesthetic, or other representations that the graph may evoke in an individual; we further distinguish the conventional system of Cartesian coordinate representation (external) from the individual's internal conceptual/procedural system of representation that may reference and interact with the external system. We stress that we do not regard the relation between such internal and external systems as direct or simple in any way—certainly the internal is *not* to be construed simply as a "mental picture" or "copy" of the external system.

Furthermore, the kind of conceptual entity that the graph "represents" may vary greatly from one context to another—for instance, this graph might be taken to represent a function $f(x) = -3x + 6$ rather than an equation, or it might represent the relation between position and time of an object moving west with a constant velocity of 3 meters per second, beginning 6 meters east of the origin, or it might represent the hypotenuse of a right triangle "facing to the right," whose base is 2 units long and whose height is 6 units, and so forth. The power and utility of the representation clearly depend on its being part of a structured system, and on the degree of flexibility or versatility in what it can represent.

Of special importance are the two-way interactions between internal and external representations. Sometimes an individual externalizes in physical form through acts stemming from internal structures—that is, acts of writing, speaking, manipulating the elements of some external concrete system, and so on. Sometimes the person internalizes by means of interactions with the external physical structures of a notational system, by reading, interpreting words and sentences, interpreting equations and graphs, and so on. Such interpretive acts can take place both at an active, deliberate level subject to conscious, overt control, and at a more passive, automatic level where the physical structures act on the individual as if "resonating" with previously constructed mental structures (Grossberg, 1980); thus natural language or familiar mathematical expressions are "understood" without deliberate, conscious mental activity. Interactions in both directions between internal and external representations can (and most often do) occur simultaneously.

Relations Between Representations

Sometimes when we speak of one configuration representing another, the reference is to two external configurations—a "horizontal" relation, if we imagine the external to be on one level and the internal to be on another as in Fig. 23.1. For example, we may say that the (external) graph represents the (external) symbolic expression $f(x) = -3x + 6$, or that it represents the (external, physically embodied) relation between position and time of a moving object, or an (external) right triangle. In such contexts, of course, the representing relationship is not usually physically embodied; it is the speaker (teacher, student, mathematician, researcher of learning, etc.) who asserts it, and it may range from an idiosyncratic definition, analogy, or metaphor to a widely agreed on mathematical convention.

Alternatively, we may want to stress a correspondence between an internal and an external configuration, the "vertical" dimension of representation in Fig. 23.1. For example, we may talk about whether or not a student, given the (external) configuration $y = -3x + 6$, is able to visualize it (internally) as a straight line. Here, too, the representing relationship is not "preexisting in the situation"; it may be brought to it by the teacher, constructed by the student, and so forth.

Finally, one of two internal configurations can represent the other (again "horizontally")—as when a student mentally relates the (internal) visual image or kinesthetic encoding of a straight line with the (internal) symbolic configuration $y = mx + b$, with m representing the line's slope and b its y intercept in Cartesian coordinates. Such correspondences too do not inhere in the configurations themselves, but involve complex prior constructions achieved through representational acts.

This may be the place to emphasize, in case it is not already clear, that in distinguishing between internal representations ("mental configurations") and external representations ("physically embodied configurations"), we do not in particular intend to assert any sort of profound dualism between mind and matter. We simply regard external configurations as those accessible to direct observation (speech, written words, formulas, concrete manipulatives, computer microworlds as they appear on a screen, etc.), and internal configurations as those characteristics of the reasoning individual that are encoded in the human brain and nervous system and are to be inferred from observation.

Systematicity of Representational Forms

The examples cited—equations, graphs, relations between position and time, right triangles, internal visual and kinesthetic configurations—all illustrate the principle that representations should be seen as belonging to structured systems, whether embodied internally or externally. This systematicity is not a feature confined to mathematical representation. We see it in words, pictures, sculpture, architecture, and many other forms of external human representation. We see it in naturally occurring structures such as the genetic code, where sequences of bases in DNA may be said to represent biological phenotypes through structured biochemical processes. And we see it in internal human representation, as we begin to describe relations among thought structures. Indeed, if we take the goals of mathematics education to include the development in students of powerful representational tools (e.g., visualizing the analytic properties of functions through their graphs), we must certainly see the desired internal representations as belonging to complex systems whose rules and conventions are an essential part of the development.

As we have discussed elsewhere (Goldin, 1987, 1992a; Kaput, 1987, 1991), a representational system or symbol scheme can be understood as constructed from primitive characters or signs, which are sometimes but not always discrete (like spoken words, letters of the alphabet, or numerals). These signs are often embodied in some physical medium. Normally, however, the signs should not be understood literally as being their physical embodiments, but as (imperfectly defined) equivalence classes of embodiments, where equivalence is determined through acts of interpretation. Thus when we discuss "the graph of $y + 3x - 6 = 0$" in the context of mathematics education, we do not usually mean a particular drawing or computer realization of that graph, nor do we usually mean a precisely defined, abstract mathematical construct. Rather we refer to a roughly bounded class of realizations "acceptable" to a community of users of coordinate graphs. In fact, the equivalence classes for an external representation may be thought of as the shared aspects of such a system, with any particular instance being a member of such a class (see Goodman, 1976, for a discussion of this issue).

It is helpful to think temporarily of the signs that form the building blocks of a system of representation simply as characters, without yet assuming them to have further "meaning" (that will come in a moment). In addition to the criteria, either implicit or explicit, that determine whether or not a particular embodiment of a sign or character is an allowable member of a particular system (an "in or out" issue), and if so, which character it is (an "identification" issue), a representational system also has rules for combining the signs into permitted configurations (the issue of operative "syntax"). Typically the system also possesses other "syntactic" structure—relations, networks, rules of procedure, formal grammar, and so on. Inevitably there is ambiguity in defining the characters, the configurations of characters, and the structures of representational systems, as well as the symbolic relationships among them; indeed, it has been noted that without such ambiguity, representations are almost useless (Davis, 1984).

Different Kinds of "Meaning"

Recalling Hilary Putnam's memorable expression "the meaning of meaning," we next discuss some distinct senses in which systems of representation may be said to "engender meaning" as they are interpreted. One of these senses involves interaction with relations within the system—the syntactic rules and other structures that make up the representational system. For example, in this "syntactic" sense, part of the meaning that the symbol "~" in a system of symbolic logic can be said to "have" (for an interpreting individual or system) is expressed in the axiom "(p) $\sim\sim p = p$". This aspect of the structure, although an essential component of the "meaning" of "~", is quite different from and independent of the interpretation that "~" stands for the English word *not*. Thus a second main sense of "meaning," a "semantic" sense, is that experienced by an individual or system interpreting the symbolic relationship *between* two systems of representation—that is, interpreting the correspondence between configurations in one system and configurations in the other (e.g., in the current example, between the symbol "~" and the word *not*). Here the correspondence is drawn between a character in formal logical notation, and a word in ordinary English, and the correspondence becomes part of one's understanding of both. The symbolic relationship between two distinct systems of representation consists of an (experienced or functional) correspondence of some kind between configurations in one, and configurations in the other. As noted earlier, there is no necessary direction to this correspondence; either system can be interpreted to "represent" or "symbolize" the other. And we have already remarked that there is considerable variability in the representing relationships that are possible in this "semantic" sense of meaning.

The decision to regard two systems of representation as distinct from each other, rather than as part of one larger system, is a matter of convenience and convention; thus the distinction between "syntactic" and "semantic" meaning is also conventional—but quite useful in discussions of mathematics, where formal, abstract structures are frequently to be distinguished from particular, concrete instances or interpretations.

There is a certain analogy between the preceding "syntactic" versus "semantic" distinction among kinds of meaning, and the earlier "horizontal" versus "vertical" distinction among representing relationships. The analogy is apparent if we think temporarily of internal representations as forming a single system, and external representations as forming another. Associated with the (vertical) connections between external and internal representations is a symbol-interpretation process where the individual matches prior knowledge (in relation to the external representational system) with what he or she experiences as a result of interacting with the physical environment. Thus an external character is experienced as meaningful or not, according to whether it matches the individual's internal representation of characters in a system that for him or her is operative. Similarly, a combination of external system elements may be experienced as meaningful or not, depending on whether it matches expectations based on existing (internal) constructions of combinations of the system's elements. All this is analogous to the "semantic" sense of meaning. Alternatively, associated with the (horizontal) connections among internal representations is not only a process of the individual's matching prior internal structures of one sort with those of another, but also the processing that takes place within the structured system of internal representation; these are all further aspects of "meaningful" representational activity, analogous to the "syntactic" sense of meaning. Finally, there is a sense in which the (horizontal) connections among external representations, and the structural relationships that exist within external systems of representation, also embody "meaning"—namely, they encode contingencies that are susceptible to experience or interpretation. This too is analogous to meaning in the "syntactic" sense.

Let us illustrate these ideas with some examples. The numerals, letters, and arithmetical symbols of an algebraic system of notation are *signs*. Certain configurations of these signs are permitted (e.g., the equation "$y + 3x - 6 = 0$"); other configurations are not allowed and thus, in ordinary parlance, nonsensical (e.g., "$y3x + = 6\ 0 -$"); and still others are, as expected, ambiguous (e.g., depending on the context the expression "$y = x3 - 6$" might be understood to be a rather sloppy way of writing "y equals x cubed minus 6," or to be a way of expressing the equation "$y = x$ times 3 minus 6"; alternatively, x could be construed in the original expression as a missing digit in a two-digit number; or the expression might simply be rejected as erroneous). In our standard system of algebraic notation there are not only signs and configurations, but considerable further structure that is essential to the utility of algebra, such as rules of procedure for moving from one configuration to another (e.g., for moving from "$y + 3x - 6 = 0$" to "$y = -3x + 6$"), for substituting values for variables (e.g., for determining from the latter expression that "when $x = 1$, we have $y = 3$"), and so forth.

Similarly, consider Cartesian coordinate graphs as a system of representation.

The "signs" of a Cartesian graph might be said to consist of two axes, a set of numerical and alphabetical labels, various geometric forms such as points, lines, parabolas and other curves, segments of arcs, and so forth. The axes must be labeled with letters, and configured to be mutually perpendicular; numerical labels must be appropriately attached to label the units of the axes. In addition there are (geometrical) rules for plotting ordered pairs of numbers as points and interpreting points as ordered pairs. The various constituents of this system can be said to have "meaning" in the (commonly shared, or idiosyncratic) individual experiences of their relationship to the larger structure of the system (e.g., as expressed in the statement, "that vertical line with the arrow pointing up means the y axis").

Let us regard these, the conventional formal notational symbol system of algebra and the system of Cartesian graphing, as two different external systems of representation. Now, associated with the (horizontal) reference relations between them, is a "semantic" sense of meaning in which a coordinate graph is generally understood to represent an algebraic equation—or alternatively, the equation can be thought of as representing the graph. These relations can be, but are not necessarily, represented externally when individual graphs are drawn or equations written.

Within the individual learner or problem solver are (we infer) internal representations, constructs that embody the individual's understandings of formal algebraic notation and of Cartesian graphing. These internal representational systems vary greatly from individual to individual, and vary over time within an individual as learning takes place. In the individual, there is a "semantic" sense of meaning associated with the relations that the configurations in these internal systems have with each other—individuals interpret their own internal representations of graphs by means of their own internal representations of equations, and the reverse. The internal representations, and the semantic relationships between them, are at some level of development needed in order for external representations to be meaningfully interpreted by the individual.

Thus, by means of a rather elaborate development, we are able to talk with some precision about mathematical meanings, mathematical structures, and the ways in which individuals understand them through representational acts.

We close this section by again stressing two points. First, the direction of the correspondence between representations may vary with the representational act. Dugdale (1989) described a teaching experiment involving trigonometric identities, where she reversed the usual referential relationship in which graphs are thought of as the representing entities and the symbolic equations as the represented entities. This reversal led to substantial differences in students' thinking and learning. The reversibility of representing relations depending on circumstances pertains to vertical as well as to horizontal relations. The Piagetian tradition refers to the "signified" as the mental (internal) construct and the "signifier" as the physical (external) one. But we argue that this relation can be inverted whenever an external representation is interpreted by an individual, especially if the external representation is one that was not produced by the interpreter. In that case, the internal construct is acting to represent the external, physical configuration. Second, we note once more that a particular system can in general represent not just one but many others—a notational configuration in mathematics, such as an algebraic equation, can model many different kinds of other configurations drawn from different types of other representations, such as graphs, tables of numbers, physical quantities measured in laboratories, real-life situations, and so forth.

REPRESENTATION AND CONSTRUCTIVISM

External representations permit us to talk about mathematical relations and meaning apart from inferences concerning the individual learner or problem solver. Internal representations give us the framework for describing individual knowledge structures and problem-solving processes. Interactions between external and internal representational systems provide the means for making inferences about individuals, and for describing learning and development as a consequence of the learning environment and contingencies in that environment. Because the construct of representation is so useful in all of this, it is important to discuss at the outset some objections to our approach and to answer them. Many of the points offered in this section are elaborated further by Goldin (1990) and Kaput (1991). We then show how our ideas are compatible with the perspective that knowledge generally, and mathematical knowledge in particular, is actively constructed by learners—a perspective that has come to be known as "constructivist" (Herscovics, chapter 21, this volume).

Answers to Epistemological Objections

A radical constructivist objection to "representation" is that we have direct access only to our worlds of experience, not to any "external" world. Therefore, in this view, it is fundamentally wrong to term internal systems *representational* because there is nothing directly knowable that is being represented. Epistemologically, what is "out there" is not directly accessible; what we have access to is already internal. In this view (von Glasersfeld, 1987, and chapter 18, this volume), internal systems should be considered as systems of "presentation" rather than "re-presentation."

To this we offer two replies. The first is that even within a strictly radical constructivist perspective, the term *representation* is fully justified—because internal configurations can (and do) symbolize or represent each other very flexibly. As already discussed, which configuration is taken as the representing one and which as the represented depends on the circumstances and intentions of the person involved. Usually there is another, "ambient" representational system involved (e.g., natural language), other than the two under discussion, which provides the context for such a decision—for example, a student may conceptualize an internally coded symbolic expression as representing a visualized graph, a visualized graph as representing a symbolic expression, or either one as representing a still different function concept. The choice may depend on the executive planning taking place as a problem is solved. Thus no one such configuration qualifies as purely "presented" without at the same time functioning with representational capabilities. One important consequence of this, as well as of the considerations that follow, is that the framework we offer is epistemologically independent of the tenets of radical constructivism.

Our second reply answers the objection from radical constructivist epistemology more fundamentally. It is that neither the external nor the internal systems we have discussed are intended to explain, to describe, or to "be" a person's world of experience. The distinction that we make between external and internal systems of representation is itself simply a constructed model, developed by an observer or community of theorists to help explain an individual's observed behavior, or the behavior of a population of individuals. Although our model is, in a sense, consistent with human beings' described experience of an "inside" and an "outside," internal "mental" experiences, thoughts, and feelings, as distinct from experiences an external "real" or "physical" world (a dichotomy that has developmental roots very early in the emergence of cognition), the model is not offered as something to be identified with this described experience. Rather it is intended only to organize and explain our observations of complex behavior, including of course the descriptions offered by individuals. Like any other theoretical scientific model, this one embodies several hypothetical constructs and relations, whose value and viability are to be confirmed or disconfirmed, through application and experimentation, based on how well they help others understand mathematical thinking, learning, and problem solving.

Besides the objection to our distinction between internal and external representation, there is a further objection from radical constructivists to our characterization of external representations as "having" structure. Because the only structures of experience are those constructed by a cognizing knower, the concept of a structured system of external representation is considered questionable.

To this we reply in the same vein, that the description of external systems of representation given here is (of course) constructed by the theorist or community of theorists, as is any scientific model or theory. It is not assumed to exist independently of such acts of construction. The "structures" in external systems are conjectured as embodying contingencies, possible interactions, potential relationships with internal systems, and so forth, in a way that is explanatory of behavior. This is the standard method of science: (a) to create structured models that embody relations among selected observables, (b) to use these relations to help generate hypotheses that can be tested, and (c) to explain the outcomes of observations. It is analogous to conjecturing possible structures within atoms and molecules based on observation and experiment, and using such models to understand chemical reactions, although, of course, we have no "direct access" to the structures involved. Thus the structure we ascribe to external linguistic and mathematical representational systems is a feature of an explanatory framework; it fulfills its explanatory role if it adequately describes culturally shared aspects of the internal representations of a community of mathematically experienced people, who interact with these external systems—that is, it is at some level observable within and across individuals. There is a place for it in our theory because shared mathematics is among the things for which we seek to account. Thus our approach is an accepted practice in scientific model-building, whose a priori rejection on philosophical grounds can only impede the progress of research.

The strict radical constructivist objections to our characterization of external systems of representation, or to the view that internal systems can be representational of external systems, are in some sense a mirror image of radical empiricist or behaviorist objections that can be raised against our characterization of internal systems! Such objections, which were taken extremely seriously in the 1950s and 1960s, today seem almost quaint. In a nutshell, the behaviorist position is (again based on a priori philosophical arguments) that external tasks, structures, representations, or environmental situations are recognized as valid constructs, because they are directly observable, and thus susceptible to scientific characterization. Likewise, human behavior (verbal or nonverbal) is directly observable, hence admissible into scientific consideration. But internal states are to be excluded from theoretical models, because they not observable except through introspection—which is a nonreproducible, and not independently verifiable, process. Thus internal representation (or even "presentation") has no place for the behaviorist in a scientifically sound psychology of learning or problem solving.

In reply, we note that again the error has been made of assuming internal systems of representation to describe that which is accessible via introspection, and only that. To us, internal representation, like external representation, is intended to be part of a theoretical model explanatory of phenomena that can be observed. It is not a requirement of a scientific theory that its every component be directly observable, only that it have consequences that are observable. Radical behaviorism has been largely supplanted because models involving internal constructs do better in explaining our observations of behavior than models without them.

To sum up, we see no viable basis for rejecting internal representation, external representation, or the broader concept of representation on a priori philosophical grounds.

Internal Representational Systems as Individual Constructions

Although some of our language and some of our constructs appear to be at odds with certain epistemological claims of constructivism, we are very much in agreement with the perspective that cognitive representations are internally constructed by learners and problem solvers (Steffe, Cobb, & von Glasersfeld, 1988). This position has been termed *trivial constructivism*, although it is in no sense trivial; we prefer Herscovics' characterization of it as a form of *rational constructivism* (Herscovics, chapter 21, this volume). Indeed, in our view one of the major challenges that theories of mathematics learning based on representation should address is that of modeling this constructive process, understanding the characteristics of external and internal representations that affect it, and facilitating its effective occurrence in students. We discuss this further later.

Having laid a foundation, let us now consider some different types of systems of representation that are of interest to the psychology of learning and doing mathematics.

TYPES OF REPRESENTATIONAL SYSTEMS AND THE MEDIA EMBODYING THEM

We begin by discussing some types of systems of representation, as well as the role of the physical media in which representation systems can be instantiated. In our view, characterizing both representational systems and their instantiating media in as much detail as possible is one of the most important means available for describing thought processes in mathematics and discussing how they are influenced.

This is so because thinking itself cannot take place without there occurring, again and again, representational acts—including acts of coordination of internal representations, and acts of interaction between internal and external representations in various media. As noted by Kaput (1991), we see the role of representational systems in organizing thinking as analogous to the role of architectural structures in organizing the activity of people within a working or living space. That is, we follow certain paths of thought (not in a deterministic way) to a considerable degree *because* they have been previously constructed. The representations in which they are encoded are "available" to us. Other paths that have never been constructed are not even considered as alternative thoughts, because they are beyond the realm of present imagination. Sometimes representational systems, like architectural designs, operate without conscious awareness—especially after considerable experience with them—and at other times they are employed quite deliberately. On both sides of the analogy, some are the result of evolutionary processes, whereas others are the result of explicit design efforts. But the central point is that they both are organizers of experience, both physical and mental. And at times, wholly new paths are constructed.

Thus it is essential to get a handle on how different types of systems of representation, in varying degrees, support and constrain different kinds of thinking. What sorts of objects, categories, and relations do they help us construct? What kinds of operations do they afford, and what kinds of efficiencies do they offer? And, just as important, what do they tend to prohibit? In approaching these function-oriented questions, we are beginning a simultaneous attack on the companion questions of "how" and "why."

We next consider some very broad classes of systems, and then distinguish subclasses among these. Each of the classes mentioned can be interpreted in relation to both external or internal representation. Furthermore, some systems may be essentially universal to human thinking (e.g., the object construct), whereas most others come to us as artifacts of our cultures and are widely shared within the respective cultures, but are not universal (e.g., specific natural languages). Still others are specialized and artificial (e.g., various mathematical notations) or largely idiosyncratic (e.g., symbolism drawn from meanings attached to personal memories). We first discuss differences in the physical media embodying external representational systems. Then we single out for discussion the following three dimensions of representational systems, suggested in each case as polar opposites: display versus action systems, imagistic or analogic versus conventional character-based or verbal systems, and formal versus informal systems. We consider both external, physical representation and internal, cognitive representation in relation to these categories. This section concludes with discussions of linked external representational systems, and of various internal systems of cognitive representation.

External Representational Systems, and Differences in Physical Media

Most external systems do not lie at one extreme with respect to the three dimensions just mentioned, and much of their variability results from differences in the physical media in which the systems are physically instantiated. It is possible to regard conventional mathematical representational systems as abstract systems capable of being, in principle, fully captured as systems of rules relative to some other representational system (independent of any particular medium). In this sense, mathematical representations are abstract objects with multiple potential physical instantiations. Practically, however, the differences in the information-carrying capabilities of different media have a strong impact on the features of

actual systems instantiated within them, and, in fact, different features are instan
tiated concretely in different media.

This is easily seen in the example of natural language. Natural language is
regarded as a character-based system (in the case of most western languages)
when instantiated in inert media such as symbols on paper. But when instantiated
as purely spoken language in a sound-based medium as experienced when talking
on the telephone, for example, inflection, tone, and other information-carrying
dimensions come directly into play. And if the spoken language is experienced
visually on a person-to-person basis, the added dimensions of gesture and facial
expression enter. On the other hand, in the inert, two-dimensional spatial medium of symbols on paper, the spatial dimensions afford the possibility of nonserial
processing of the text in a way that spoken language does not! Of course,
considerable learning of the character-based coding system is required before one
can use language in its two-dimensional spatial form, because language is first
learned in the sound-based and visual medium—indeed, studies of infant language learning are illustrating the strong ties between the rhythms of kinesthetic
action and those of spoken language.

The changes in the representational characteristics of systems are so great
when one changes the medium that it can be misleading to try to examine the
properties of systems apart from the media in which they are instantiated. Instead
we seek to understand more fully how the features of media jointly determine the
features of representation systems instantiated within them. To begin, let us
examine some of the differences among physical media that are especially significant to the doing and learning of mathematics. In what follows we largely ignore
many details that are also of significance, but perhaps less so for mathematics—
for example, in two-dimensional static media such as paper, besides the location
and shape of characters based on spatial dimensions, there is the dimension of
color; within color, there are hue and intensity; within the sound-based medium
there are dimensions of amplitude and pitch; and so forth.

What are the fundamental features of media that are critical to mathematical
thinking? We suggest here that one begin with three basic distinctions:

1. Dynamic versus static media.
2. Interactive versus inert media.
3. Recording versus nonrecording media.

These three properties are mainly independent of one another. We regard them as
fundamental because each affects the way in which actions and representational
features are distributed between internal and external representations.

Let us first note how distinctions 1 and 2 differ. Traditional television or video
is a dynamic but not an interactive medium. Although one can adjust features of
the video or change the program one is watching, one cannot interact with the
content of a particular program—the newscaster will not answer the viewer's

questions! On the other hand, a traditional calculator is interactive, but static. Its display responds to the user's inputs, but the displays themselves do not change without that input. Of course, computers can be both dynamic and interactive.

Let us now consider how the relation between internal and external representations may be affected by the characteristics of the physical media involved. Characteristics 1 and 2 have much to do with constraining where actions can or must occur. In the case of static media, dynamic changes must be projected onto static external representations through internal (mental) acts—one imagines the motion of the projectile, the filling of the tank, and so on. Of course, many techniques and conventions have been developed to assist in these mental acts, such as drawing conventions like the use of arrows or "wind marks," the depiction of sequences of states, and others. In the case of a dynamic medium, the change is supplied externally to the interpreter, who, instead of needing to generate the change, can experience it perceptually. Recent work in neurophysiology (Kosslyn & Koenig, 1992) has shown that neurologically, some of the same activity occurs whether one visualizes motion or whether one observes motion; more generally, certain areas of the brain are activated either by external optic stimuli or by internally generated processing described as experienced visualization or production of mental imagery. Further, a key learning development is the ability to produce a version of dynamical phenomena internally, without perceptual stimulus.

In the case of the second distinction mentioned, interactive versus inert media, there is a certain basic sense (according to our "interactivist" account given earlier) in which all external representational systems, in whatever medium, are interactive. But we have a narrower characterization in mind (Kaput, 1992): we mean here interaction that involves a physical contribution from the notation system and the medium in which it is instantiated. We thus characterize a medium as "inert" if the only state-change resulting from a user's input is the display of that input, as when one writes on a piece of paper. The key difference with representations instantiated in interactive media is the addition of something new to the result of a user's actions, something to which the user may then respond. In inert media, the user can only respond to what he or she has directly produced. Any external response to the input must be made by a third party, such as a teacher, tutor, or peer, who happens to be observing, but it does not come from the physical embodiment of the representational system with which the user is interacting. (Note, by the way, that a system may be interactive—e.g., a bicycle—without necessarily functioning representationally.) Among the most interesting kinds of representational interactive systems are those of the type embodying some form of "agent" that performs some task for the person interacting with it, for example, a computer algebra system. This example highlights our basic point about the distribution of actions between the user and the external system. With an inert external system, the user must supply all the strategic direction and any intermediate actions, based on internal activity, or at least based on activity extrinsic to the system, whereas an interactive system can supplant some of that activity—the internal representational activity of the learner or problem solver is redistributed outward.

The third feature of media that we emphasize relates to their different abilities to capture a record of actions taken. This feature's importance is centered in its impact on memory and the subsequent effects on mathematical activity. The redistribution, with a record-preserving medium, is from short- or long-term human memory (internal) to the external record. The profound impact of the development of writing on civilization is mainly rooted in the preservation of long-term records, but various mathematical representational systems developed in part because they help overcome the shortcomings of working memory, such as the placeholder system and the computational algorithms based on it, and aspects of our system of algebraic notation.

Because records are so ubiquitous, the importance of capturing them is easy to underestimate. After all, whenever we write on a piece of paper, we are producing records. This is in contrast to the inputs and states of a traditional hand-held calculator, where each new input overwrites the old and there is no record kept. However, there is now the potential for capturing more than the inert records that are produced with inert media such as paper. It is possible in interactive media to create computationally active records that can be replayed, reused as active components in other procedures, and so on. Computer programs are one version of such external representations, but are not normally created in an automatic way as a record of one's activity. Given that a major factor in conceptual growth involves the "re-presentation" of records of activity (Steffe, von Glasersfeld, Richards, & Cobb, 1983), the ability to create new types of external records can have a major impact on the learning process.

In summary, the three properties of media that we have discussed—dynamic versus static, interactive versus inert, and recording versus nonrecording or ephemeral—have a powerful controlling effect on the representational systems that are encoded in media having those properties. The impact is based on the effects on the interaction between internal and external systems, and how mental (internal) actions are or can be externalized.

Display Versus Action Representations and the Role of Media

We now wish to point to how traditional representational systems can be changed when one changes the medium in which they are instantiated. We refer to an external representation as an *action representation* if it contains rules or mechanisms for the manipulation of its elements, and a *display representation* if it does not. For example, in inert media coordinate graphs are usually used primarily to display quantitative relationships. There are relatively few ways in which one acts directly on such a graph after one has produced it. Likewise, tables are mainly display representations—one produces them initially, but one does not normally transform them in inert media. In contrast, our algebraic system of representation is designed (actually, it evolved) to support actions on the configurations that one produces to generate new configurations. Such actions may, for example, transform a given algebraic statement into other equivalent forms that can better reveal certain quantitative relationships, or may change the quantitative relationships in some systematic way. Although at any given point the algebraic statement acts to display a relationship (or function, series, integral, etc.), the key feature of the algebraic system, as developed mainly in the 17th century, is to provide support for rule-based action on its configurations.

However, the basic underlying characteristic of a representational system, of providing display representations rather than action representations, can be altered when one changes from an inert to an interactive medium! Tables that are instantiated in an interactive computer medium can become highly action oriented, and the actions can be expanded to form a spreadsheet. In the case of coordinate graphs one can again achieve a fundamental change from display to action representations, by moving to interactive media. New coordinate graph systems in the computer medium support direct actions on the graphs—besides rescaling of a graph (which is analogous to making a change in the form of an algebraic expression to a quantitatively equivalent one), one can perform all manner of translations, stretches, flips, and so forth of the graph itself (Confrey, 1993). The point here is that by changing the physical medium in which a representation system is instantiated to one that has additional structure, one can change its basic representational characteristics.

In the case of internal representations there is no issue of instantiating medium; rather, the question is the individual's power to carry out actions within the representational system. Powerful internal representations tend to be dynamic, action representations, in that the learner or problem solver has capabilities of acting on them or transforming them mentally—for example, translating the graph of a function. An individual who can mentally represent a graph, but cannot mentally act on the representation, has more limited mathematical capabilities, and the internal representations are more static in nature. Thus changes in physical media that permit external representations to be action rather than display representations give these representations one characteristic of powerful internal representations.

Imagistic or Analogic Systems

Imagistic or analogic representational systems refer to systems in which the fundamental characters, signs, and configurations are neither verbal nor formal in nature, but bear some interpreted sensory resemblance to what is represented. The term *imagistic* can be interpreted broadly to include internal imagery and image-schematic representation—that which is "imagined", visualized, represented kinesthetically and/or auditorily (e.g., objects and their attributes); it can also include external enactive and pictorial representations, concrete embodiments and manipulatives, computer-generated depictions, and so forth. The term *analogic* is suggestive of the possibility that the way in which the representations carry meaning may be through analogy and even metaphor, rather than through more direct sensory constructions. For instance, cardboard cut-outs of geometrical shapes provide an external, imagistic representational system that relies little on analogy or metaphor; a pictorial representation of data in which larger pictures of objects stand for more objects, or larger areas stand for greater numerical quantities, is more directly analogic.

It is our view that internal, imagistic representation is essential to virtually all mathematical insight and understanding, ranging from the concept of number and "number sense," to the meanings of arithmetical operations and geometrical constructions, to the understanding of equations and functions through Cartesian graphs. Interactions with external, imagistic representations are important to facilitating the construction of powerful internal imagistic systems in students.

Formal Systems

By formal systems of representation, we mean those have been consciously constructed to achieve specific, overt goals, and for which the rules are explicit rather than tacit. Thus what we call mathematical systems of representation— systems of numeration, algebraic systems of notation, and so on—are, in general, formal to a considerable degree. In contrast, informal systems have evolved with predominantly tacit rules—spoken natural language is in large part an informal representational system. Sometimes more or less informal systems are later formalized, and among the important acts of formalization is the explication of formerly tacit rules. It is clear that the process of developing mathematics over the centuries has involved many acts of formalization, such as the introduction of formal notations and the creation of definitions, axioms, and methods of proof.

The introduction of pictorial or iconic systems of writing, followed by character-based syllabaries and alphabets to represent spoken sounds, resulted in increasingly formalized ways of representing language over many centuries. The grammar and syntax of natural language have been increasingly formalized in much more recent times. It is noteworthy, in both the domain of mathematics and the domain of natural language, that the process of formalization has a functional aspect—it serves important purposes, ranging from convenience of communication and use, to economy of description, to problem-solving power. As these functional aspects influence the development of formal systems, the resulting systems acquire structure and can be discussed as structured representational systems apart from the functions that drove their development.

Just as the development of formal external representational systems involves more explicit, less tacit, constructive processes, the development of formal internal systems differs from that of informal systems. To some extent, as children learn mathematics, they will engage in acts of formalization of previously less formal systems, and to some extent, they will construct new systems through formal acts based on increasingly explicit rules. The effective construction of formal internal representational systems (internal representations of numerals, numeration, and arithmetic operations; internal representations of algebraic notation and problem-solving procedures; etc.) depends in large part on the interplay between these systems as formal, explicitly rule-based procedural systems, and other less formal systems that permit the formal systems to be interpreted through representational acts. Thus we seek to make concrete and explicit the distinction between "meaningful" and "rote" learning of rule-based systems.

Linked External Representations

Yet another way in which the medium can affect representational activity is by *linking* representations. It is possible to link representations in nonelectronic media—for example, one can rig physical equipment in such a way that measurements are displayed or graphed as one acts on the equipment, as was done in most instructional physics laboratories for many years. Today, however, a new order of magnitude of sophistication in linking external representations has been achieved in the interactive computer medium.

Let us look more closely at what one might mean by linked representations. If one produces, for example, an equation and its coordinate graph on the same sheet of paper, in what sense might one say that they are linked? Physically, the external representations are not linked at all, except perhaps in the very weak sense of adjacency. Internally, as display representations, they might be linked in the mind of the person who produced them (via internal representations), or they might be linked in the mind of a person who reads them (again, via internal representations), in the sense that the person is able to integrate the cognitive structures for each. A weak form of such an internal integration is that given one of the external representations, the individual is able to predict, identify, or even produce its counterpart. However, a much stronger kind of integration via internal representations is that given an action upon one of the external representations, the individual is able to predict, identify, or produce the results of the corresponding action on its external counterpart, perhaps even providing intermediate representational configurations. It is here, at the action level, that the direct linking of external representations in interactive media plays a role, because the opportunity is afforded to integrate such prediction, identification, or production activity across representations. By acting in one of the externally linked representations and either observing the consequences of that action in the other representational system or making an explicit prediction about the second representational system to compare with the effect produced by actions in the linked representation, one experiences the linkages in new ways and is provided with new opportunities for internal constructions.

Some experience has now been accumulated with such linked systems in the area of algebra and mathematical functions (Confrey, 1993; Yerushalmy, 1991). A promising additional context involves computer-linked manipulatives for elementary mathematics. Up to now there has been no way physically to link manipulatives that represent quantities, quantitative relationships, and (especially) actions on these to other more formal representational systems. Such manipulatives as Dienes blocks, Cuisenaire rods, and Unifix cubes could be treated as external action representation systems in classroom activity—but in order to link manipulative representations cognitively with more formal mathematical counterparts, one was limited to serial translations of actions.

For example, the child learning mathematics could act in one external representational system, say, using Dienes blocks (with the child's actions constrained or supported fairly loosely through instructional text, or the teacher's directions). Then the child could act in a second external representational system, say, written numerals organized in the usual placeholder style. Opportunities for prediction and comparison exist but are rather limited. The child, encouraged by the teacher, could compare the results of the two actions—but to compare all the intermediate actions, overwhelmingly detailed orchestration involving recording intermediate states of the blocks is needed (Thompson, 1992). This example illustrates two intrinsic shortcomings of physical manipulatives: the lack of physical linkability to other representational systems, and the ephemeral nature of actions in such systems. Each action on a state of the external system "overwrites" the previous state to produce a new one, with no record of the prior state remaining. Many pedagogically based attempts have been made to overcome these difficulties over the years, but without convincing success. Computer-linked manipulatives provide a new opportunity to attack the problem but give us no guarantees. Much experimentation will be needed, with computer-based representations, with various forms of records produced, with many different types of linkages, and with accompanying pedagogical approaches, to maximize the utility of the new representational tools (Kaput, 1994a).

Internal Systems of Cognitive Representation

We conclude this section with some comments on five types of mature, internal cognitive representational systems, proposed by Goldin (1982, 1983, 1987) as a model for mathematical problem-solving competency structures, and developed further in the context of mathematical learning, conceptual development, and assessment (Goldin, 1988a, 1988b, 1992a, 1992b; Goldin & Herscovics, 1991a, 1991b). These are (a) verbal/syntactic systems, (b) imagistic systems, (c) formal notational systems, (d) a system of planning, monitoring, and executive control, and finally (e) a system of affective representation. All these types of internal representation are regarded as psychologically "fundamental." They occur universally, not only in mathematical problem solvers, but (possibly excepting formal notational systems) in all normal human beings.

A verbal/syntactic system of representation describes the person's capabilities for processing natural language, on the level of words, phrases, and sentences (only). This system includes verbal "dictionary information" such as common definitions and verbal descriptions, word–word associations such as synonyms, related phrases, and antonyms, word–category relationships, and the parsing of sentences based on grammar and syntax information. Verbal/syntactic configurations can represent configurations in other systems—imagistic, formal, heuristic, or affective configurations are all described in words. There are also self-referential capabilities in natural language, with words and sentences being used to describe words and sentences. It is useful to think of internal, verbal/syntactic representation as partially formal, and not imagistic or analogic. This is a dynamic representational system; it is culturally provided (so that it is meaningful to speak also of external verbal/syntactic systems of representation), but universal in its occurrence as an internal system. It may be valid to regard such internal systems as modeled on a deeper level of internal representation, associated with the Chomskian notion of the "deep structure" of language.

Several different imagistic cognitive representational systems are proposed, the most important of which for describing mathematical learning and problem solving are *visual/spatial, auditory/rhythmic,* and *tactile/kinesthetic* systems. The term *imagistic* here is intended to have the broader connotations discussed earlier. Internal, imagistic systems incorporate nonverbal configurations at the level of objects, attributes, relations, and transformations. Their inclusion in a unified psychological model allows the description of how semantic structures influence mathematical problem solving. Imagistic capabilities are necessary for the meaningful or insightful interpretation verbal statements, and encode students' nonverbal, nonquantitative conceptions and misconceptions. Internal visual/spatial representation corresponds roughly to what Kosslyn (1980) calls "quasi-pictorial." Internal auditory/rhythmic representation in mathematics is evidenced, for example, by children learning to count or recite multiplication tables in rhythm, accenting numbers in groups as they make use of "counting-on" strategies for early addition, and so forth. Internal tactile/kinesthetic representation refers to imagined physical actions by or on the person (distinguished here from imagined sights or spatial transformations)—a kind of internal version of the sort of representation Bruner called "enactive." Comprehension of spoken or written language includes the ability to access or construct internal imagistic configurations that appropriately correspond to verbal/syntactic configurations. Likewise, comprehension of formal mathematical symbols includes quite sophisticated imagistic capabilities. Furthermore, the characters or configurations in verbal or formal representational systems can be treated as "objects" and processed imagistically—for example, in manipulating algebraic symbols, the student may learn to "bring the unknown variable x over to the left-hand-side of the equation" as if the x itself were an object. Internal imagistic representations are in general highly nonformal, action representations (although children often learn, unfortunately, to treat mathematical images exclusively as static displays) Imag ery is highly individualistic, with some apparently universal elements of structure (such as the object construct).

Formal mathematical notations as external representations are typically a major focus of mathematics instruction. The internal systems of competencies associated with the construction and manipulation of such configurations are yet another type of cognitive representational system. Such constructs internal to the mathematical learner or problem solver can be modeled by talking about symbol manipulation, rules, algorithms, bugs in algorithms, searches through formal problem spaces, and so forth. Although some cognitive processing can be seen as occurring within a system of formal notation (e.g., the execution of an algorithm), meaningful understanding in mathematics has more to do with relationships that formal configurations of symbols have to other kinds of internal representation—being able to represent and discuss why an algorithm works, interpreting formal notational descriptions imagistically and visualized situations formally, and so on. Formal notational representations are (mostly) constructed from culturally provided, conventional systems. Typically they have much less redundancy than natural language, and unlike natural language, the formal notational systems of mathematics are not universal in human cultures. Internal formal notational representations may be static or dynamic, and may have imagistic features to them (e.g., the internal construct of a Cartesian graph).

Another cognitive representational system in Goldin's model is taken to plan, monitor, and control mathematical problem solving processes. The configurations of this system are organized into heuristic processes. In a sense this internal system relates metacognitively to the others, as it includes competencies for a number of actions that can be applied to configurations in the other systems, and in itself. These include keeping track of some of the processing, deciding the next steps to be taken during learning or problem solving, as well as modifying other systems—deciding to improve the formal notation, for instance. However, each one of the internal systems in the model can represent information about the others (as well as simply configurations within the others), and each can also represent information about itself. Thus no one system is taken to be uniquely metacognitive. The system of planning, monitoring, and executive control is neither a formal system nor an imagistic one. It is a dynamic representational system, partly provided through the culture and partly individually generated. It is likely that aspects of such a system occur universally in human beings (e.g., some use of "trial and error" or "subgoal decomposition" in problem solving), whereas other aspects are specific to certain cultures or individuals.

A system of affective representation is proposed as a fifth type of internal representational system. This is needed not only to model learning and problem solving effectively, but to allow a discussion of affective as well as cognitive educational goals in mathematics—maximizing enjoyment and positive self-concept, for example. Affective representation is neither formal nor imagistic. It seems to occur universally in human beings, and is highly dynamic, referring not just to relatively stable, attitudinal constructs in relation to mathematics (what Goldin has called *global* affect, and which can be regarded as fairly static), but to the rapidly changing feelings of problem solvers during problem solving (*local* affect), such as curiosity, puzzlement, bewilderment, frustration, anxiety, fear, despair, encouragement, pleasure, elation, and satisfaction, with one mood changing rapidly to another depending on cognitive events. Thus such affect does not occur independently of cognition; it is utilized during learning and problem solving (DeBellis & Goldin, 1991; Goldin, 1988a; McLeod & Adams, 1989). This suggests we consider affective competencies, taking the affect appropriate for problem solving as something learnable and teachable. The interaction between affect and imagery, and between affect and heuristics, is subtle, deep, and worthy of further exploration.

TYPES OF REPRESENTATIONAL ACTS AND STRUCTURES

We have discussed various types and characteristics of representations and representational systems to a considerable extent. Next we consider briefly some basic types of representational structures, and acts that exploit these structures. External, physical systems of representation seem to have evolved at least partly as means for overcoming human cognitive limitations: limitations in memory, and in processing capability. Both personal and social representational acts, whether or not they are deliberately undertaken within the systematic constraints of particular, culturally developed systems (e.g., a system of algebraic notation and manipulation), often amount to efforts to overcome one or more of these limitations. Here we describe a few general features of representational structures and acts from this point of view.

One-for-Many Representing Relationships

An extremely powerful, widely used representational act uses one representational element to stand for many others, or to stand for a sequence of elements. When this occurs internally, it has sometimes been called "chunking." An example involves the concept of counting number, where a single entity (the numeral, represented externally or internally) can stand for a set having that cardinality, or (more abstractly) for an equivalence class of such sets, or for a sequence of physical acts (counting) together with its outcome, and so on. The one-for-many relationship is also used within most numeration systems (Nickerson, 1986), where one symbol often stands for several "lower level" units—as the Roman numeral V stands in a way for IIIII. This representational relationship takes external form in the physical notations we use. It is useful when inscriptions are costly in some way, in time or space, physical effort, and so on. But it has an especially important, complementary function internally, which is to support cognitive activity (e.g., managing working memory load). As is well appreciated, the internal cognitive development of one-for-many correspondences can be initially a laborious process.

One-for-Complexity Representational Substitutions

A related representational structure (actually a more general version of the preceding) is the substitution of a single representational element for a complex web of representational elements. This occurs when a letter or word is used to stand for a possibly elaborate picture or diagram, or when an ordered pair of symbols stands for an abstract mathematical entity: say, (G, *) used to represent a group G under the operation *. Frequently the substitution is based on equivalence, where a single representational element is used in place of an equivalence class, and rules for handling these elements are based on their class representatives, as with fractions in arithmetic, or quotient objects in abstract algebra. Goodman (1976) pointed out that we use such equivalence class exemplars in almost all character-based systems. Besides representing complex objects by simpler symbols, one can represent complex processes by symbols. One might use a single set of symbols to stand for a process, as in Leibniz' notation for derivatives. Such a structure again has complementary functions, both internal and external. It helps to alleviate working memory load, which in turn supports another critical function in mathematics, the building of more complex systems.

Selected Deletion

Many representations involve a process of selected deletion from other representations, with certain kinds of details systematically omitted. Most maps and diagrams employ this approach, as do most practical applications of geometry. This is one important way that representations support the key process of idealization in mathematics and science.

Reification

Some representations provide an external, physical notation, and related internal configurations, for symbolizing entities that are not usually described as physically experienced. This is the case for virtually any abstraction (indeed, it comes close to a possible definition of *abstraction*), and is also the case for environmental or cognitive events that have physical occurrence, but do not leave a trace or do not leave a satisfactory trace. For example, in a computer-based manipulatives environment, one might have the computer create some form of record of the sequence of actions that a user performs (Kaput, 1995). Further, the system could provide means for denoting various strategies for such actions. Psychologically, the introduction of the representing configuration "reifies" the represented entity—according to it a "reality" or "existence" so that it can be discussed or manipulated through its representation. The decision to represent a problem solver's strategy or choice of steps using a computer reifies those entities in this sense, as does the decision to represent a new mathematical or abstract physical construct.

Time-Space Substitutions, and Ordinal Substitutions Generally

Whenever events or changes take place they do so in time-meaning that in the domain of everyday experience, they are inherently ordered. A representational technique used frequently is to represent the time-ordered sequence of events along another inherently ordered instrument, the line in space. Likewise one can order the outcomes of measurements that vary across time by using time axes in various ways, a technique pioneered by the Scholastics (Kaput, 1994b). Such representational techniques provide means of capturing the dynamic aspects of phenomena in static media. They also generalize from the ordinal representation of temporal events, to more general representation of ordering with respect to other sorts of variables.

Additional Representational Structures and Actions

As already noted, computers bring us forms of representation that are not possible in inert media, as most traditionally embodied in interactive computer programs (Kaput, 1992). Here the input of something (like a number or expression), the adjustment of a parameter, or other action on a representational element can result in a certain type of computational processing—a representational element is connected to a response system of some kind or another (e.g., a spreadsheet or other agent). Representations in interactive media also provide constraints and supports for actions on them. Thus they can provide connections between deeply different types of experience. For example, one can superimpose a discrete structure on continuous phenomena by segmenting and counting chunks, or vice versa, by interpolating between points or otherwise embedding individual discrete points in a continuum, and one can do this through external, interactive representation.

One aspect of the power of formal representations is that they can provide common representational configurations that connect or unify not only different kinds of phenomena but also different levels of abstraction. Many different forms of metonymy are used to support generalization in mathematics through formal representations, as when one uses the traditional symbols for addition and multiplication in the definition of an abstract ring or field (Pimm, 1987).

Of course, all of the foregoing representational structures and actions can be iterated, and each takes many different forms. Furthermore, they can be combined with each in various ways—sequentially, in various kinds of networks, and as already discussed, in cross-representational linkages.

We believe that this perspective on the problem of representation—looking at the larger classes of functional structures—can provide a great deal of classificatory and explanatory power.

THE GROWTH OF REPRESENTATIONAL SYSTEMS

Our account thus far has concentrated on the function of representation, especially its mature function, without yet discussing either the long-term development of representational systems or the complexities of their use in actual practice. What are the important processes through which new representations (internal and external, in close connection with each other) develop or emerge, within individuals, short- and long-term, in short-term social contexts, or historically? And how do representations come to be related to one another?

Various researchers have begun to focus attention on such questions, particularly on how representations evolve in shared exploration and problem-solving contexts, identifying the reciprocal role of individuals in modifying socially constructed systems of representation. Microgenetic analyses of representational behavior reveal considerable fluidity and complexity. For example, it is not uncommon for a particular complex of inscriptions to evolve in such a way that the semiotic function of its elements changes dramatically over a short period of time (Meira, 1992). In ongoing work, Kaput is studying these questions with particular emphasis on computational media. Of special importance to the design of appropriate representations in learning environments is how series of representations of varying levels of abstractness can be chained and coordinated, to link students' "common-sense-based" understandings of phenomena with those based in the kinds of abstractions appropriate for scientific and mathematical understanding (White, 1993).

Human beings have a number of very powerful representational capabilities that are reflected in the functional structures just discussed. Many of these seem to emerge, almost automatically, across many different cultures. Among these is the ability to declare or establish an equivalence among many discrete entities, and then to treat the equivalence class as a single entity. We see this with word meanings, for instance; we see it in the use of metonymy, where a single prototypical element acts for the class (e.g., in the example of fractions mentioned earlier). Another related capability important to mathematical understanding is that of taking a complex entity (like a matrix or a function), "packaging it up" and treating it as if it were a (unitary) object (e.g., an element of a vector space of functions or a group of linear operators), then "opening the package up" when necessary to examine its structure or properties.

To whatever degree a theory governing the construction of internal systems can be proposed, we have the beginning of an understanding of mathematical learning and development that goes beyond addressing the acquisition of discrete skills, or particular concepts, or even schemas. One element of such a theory involves identifying stages in their development. Drawing on a variety of ideas, three main stages in the development of representational systems were summarized by Goldin: (a) an inventive-semiotic stage, (b) a period of structural development, and (c) an autonomous stage.

In the inventive-semiotic stage (Piaget, 1969, p. 31), new characters are created or learned, and from the outset are used to symbolize aspects of a prior representational system. The latter is regarded as a kind of template for the development of the new system. The act of assigning meaning or symbolization is called *semiotic* and the prior system serves as a semantic domain for the new symbols. With regard to cognitive representations, the new characters during this stage are often considered not to symbolize, but to actually "be" the aspects of the prior system that they represent; this can lead to cognitive obstacles in the learning of mathematics.

During the stage of a new representational system called structural-developmental, the development or construction is driven principally by structural features of the earlier system. This process makes use of the symbolization that was established in the first stage. In this way configurations are built up from characters, and a syntax for the new system is constructed. Symbolic relationships for the new system other than those already established, or contradictory to those already established, do not in general occur during this stage—as the structure of the new system seems at this point to be a necessary or inevitable consequence of the meanings of the new signs and configurations in the semantic domain of the previous system. Those meanings are typically referred to as the "real" meaning. Over time the new characters and configurations become no longer discrete, unrelated entities, but part of a larger structure (which is the new representational system).

The third stage is called an autonomous stage. The new system of representation, now mature, separates from the old. It can at this point stand in symbolic relationships with systems different from the one that was the template driving its development. As these new possibilities occur, the transfer of "meaning" (or, in the case of internal representations, of competencies) from old to new domains becomes possible.

The development of internal representational systems through such stages requires interaction with external representational structures ranging from spoken language to mathematical constructions. Following this development and trying to trace it allows, in our opinion, the unification of a great deal of cognitive theory. The model has been applied to conceptual development in mathematics, especially children's early arithmetic (Goldin & Herscovics, 1991a, 1991b; Mulligan, Thomas, & Goldin, 1994).

BUILDING POWERFUL REPRESENTATIONAL
SYSTEMS AS A GOAL OF LEARNING

Most often, the goals of instruction in mathematics are defined in terms of the kinds of problems we want students to be able to solve, or the particular skills and concepts we want them to have. But these formulations of learning goals tend to limit the vision we bring to mathematics education. The reason for this is that such goals do not embody capabilities for spontaneous new constructions, for extension to unfamiliar situations, for synthesis of new strategies when necessary, or for creative mathematical acts. One of the major reasons for our emphasis on internal representational systems is that they provide a means for characterizing the outcomes of learning in a much more valuable way.

Instead of traditional learning goals, we propose to formulate educational goals in mathematics in terms of the kinds of internal systems of representation we would like students to have available. We think it is possible to outline a relatively small, manageable set of broad, internal representational capabilities, whose effective interaction makes for powerful problem solving. It is also possible to describe more specialized, internal, mathematical representational systems that have a wide range of applicability. Both of these provide ways of defining what we seek in effective mathematics education.

In the school mathematics curriculum as it is most often implemented, the most attention is paid to formal symbolic systems of representation. Students are expected to "internalize" our base-10 system of numeration and associated procedural rules for addition, subtraction, multiplication, and division of whole numbers written in base 10. They are expected to extend these methods to fractional, decimal, and algebraic systems of formal representation as conventionally developed. Much less attention is given to the (equally mathematical) imagistic systems—techniques of visualization, mental rotation, diagram drawing and interpretation, spatial projection, and so forth. Less attention is also given to heuristic systems of planning and decision making for effective problem solving, and to the development of powerful, helpful affect. Internal representational systems are normally influenced by interactions with external systems in the way they develop. Furthermore, as has recently been stressed (Meira, 1991), the act of construction of external representations is critical to the construction of internal representations. Thus the choices of problems for students to solve, of classroom activities in mathematics for them to participate in, and of external constructions for them to address need to be examined with respect to the kinds of internal representations we want them to develop.

Let us discuss briefly some of the things we mean by "powerful" in this context. One meaning of powerful is that a system of representation has a wide and varied domain of applicability—it can be applied in different contexts, and the system has "meaning" (in the semantic sense discussed earlier) in relation to many different other representations. This aspect of representational power we call *versatility*. Earlier we mentioned, as an example, the different meanings that could be given to a graph. The capability of constructing graphical representation with versatility has to be seen as a major educational objective in mathematics.

Another sense of powerful has to do with efficiency of procedural use. Efficiency can be embodied in the syntax of a system of representation (particularly, in a formal system), so that the system supports transformations with facility from one configuration to another from which insights can be gained. In this sense, the Hindu-Arabic system of numeration is more "efficient" than Roman numerals. This aspect of representational power we call efficiency of syntax. It is easiest to characterize in the case of formal, procedurally oriented mathematical systems of representation, such as the formal systems of arithmetic and algebra, where the syntax and rules of procedure are well defined. It is much harder to describe, but just as important, for less formal systems. For internal systems of representation, efficiency of procedural use is likewise most easily measurable in formal contexts—which is why "skill tests" tend to predominate as assessment instruments in mathematics education, and more authentic forms of assessment are neglected.

Still another kind of power in a representational system has to do with its effectiveness in abstracting essential features from representations in other systems, and encoding these features in a way that makes them accessible, or exhibits essential relationships to some degree. This aspect we call the efficiency of encoding. This can be an especially salient property of imagistic systems, where the abstracted features may be made directly visible (Goldin, 1982). In principle, efficiency of syntax or efficiency of encoding can characterize either formal or imagistic systems, either external or internal.

Other aspects of representational power include the capability of a system to encode general or broad relationships in a very small set of characters (e.g., a characteristic of the representational power of algebraic notation), and the capability of supporting systematic actions on representational elements (Mahoney, 1980).

We thus stress increasing the power of representations as a goal, both in the external representations we use in mathematics and in teaching mathematics, and in the internal representational capabilities that enable individuals to employ all the kinds of functional representational structures described here. For problem solving and learning in mathematics, Goldin's model stresses the special importance of powerful heuristic, imagistic, and affective systems of representation.

CONCLUSION AND COMMENTS

We have seen how many different aspects of mathematical learning and problem solving can be described through the construct of representation. It allows us to talk descriptively about what students can and cannot do, and to discuss prescriptively what capabilities we would like them to develop. It permits considerable careful analysis of structural properties important in mathematics, and a discussion of effects due to the media in which external configurations are embodied. Because the description of how representational systems develop over time involves both semiotic acts (through which representations acquire a certain sort of meaning) and the structural development of new systems (through being built on the "templates" provided by prior representational systems), we see that the notion of representation—far from standing in opposition to constructivist theorizing—is actually an extremely helpful theoretical tool for characterizing constructive processes in the learning and doing of mathematics.

There is certainly a lot more to be said, and many directions in which research can go. One promising direction, in our opinion, is further investigation into what makes systems of representation powerful. With the creation of software for symbol manipulation in mathematical systems, and for visual representation and manipulation of mathematical constructs, we are moving toward the ability to design mathematical representational systems consciously and systematically, rather than inventing them through isolated, widely separated creative acts. Through the invention of new representational systems, mathematics that once was highly complex (e.g., the arithmetic of fractions in ancient notations) is today accessible to children. We believe that the construction of new representational systems will likewise make some of today's complicated mathematics seem very simple in the future, and that an understanding of the psychology of mathematical learning and problem solving based on systems of representations can help to bring that about.

REFERENCES

Confrey, J. (1993). *Function probe*. Santa Barbara, CA: Intellimation.

Davis, R. B. (1984). *Learning mathematics: The cognitive science approach to mathematics education*. Norwood, NJ: Ablex.

DeBellis, V. A. & Goldin, G. A. (1991). Interactions between cognition and affect in eight high school students' individual problem solving. In R. G. Underhill (Ed.), *Proceedings of the Thirteenth Annual Meeting of PME-NA* (pp. 29–35). Blacksburg, VA: Va. Polytechnic University Division of Curriculum and Instruction.

de Saussure, F. (1959). *Course in general linguistics*. New York: Philosophical Library.

Dugdale, S. (1989). Building a qualitative perspective before formalizing procedures; Graphical representations as a foundation for trigonometric identities. In C. A. Maher, G. A. Goldin, & R. B. Davis (Eds.), *Proceedings of the Eleventh Annual Meeting of PME-NA* (New Brunswick, NJ: Rutgers University Center for Mathematics, Science, and Computer Education).

Goldin, G. A. (1982). Mathematical language and problem solving. In R. Skemp (Ed.), Understanding the symbolism of mathematics [Special issue]. *Visible Language, 16*, 221–238.

Goldin, G. A. (1983). Levels of language in mathematical problem solving. In J. C. Bergeron & N. Herscovics (Eds.), *Proceedings of the Fifth Annual Meeting of PME-NA* (Vol. 2, pp. 112–120). Montreal: University of Montreal Faculty of Educational Sciences. Reprinted with minor editorial changes in Janvier (1987, pp. 59–65).

Goldin, G. A. (1987). Cognitive representational systems for mathematical problem solving. In C. Janvier (Ed.), *Problems of representation in the teaching and learning of mathematics* (pp. 125–145). Hillsdale, NJ: Lawrence Erlbaum Associates.

Goldin, G. A. (1988a). Affective representation and mathematical problem solving. In M. J. Behr, C. B. Lacampagne, & M. M. Wheeler (Eds.), *Proceedings of the Tenth Annual Meeting of PME-NA* (pp. 1–7). DeKalb, IL: Northern Illinois University Department of Mathematical Sciences.

Goldin, G. A. (1988b). The development of a model for competence in mathematical problem solving based on systems of cognitive representation. In A. Borbas (Ed.), *Proceedings of the Twelfth International Conference for the Psychology of Mathematics Education (PME)* (Vol. 2, pp. 358–365). Veszprem, Hungary: OOK.

Goldin, G. A. (1990). Epistemology, constructivism, and discovery learning in mathematics. In R. B. Davis, C. A. Maher, & N. Noddings (Eds.), *Constructivist views on the teaching and learning of mathematics* (pp. 31–47). Reston, VA: National Council of Teachers of Mathematics, Journal for Research in Mathematics Education Monograph No. 4.

Goldin, G. A. (1992a). On developing a unified model for the psychology of mathematical learning and problem solving. Plenary talk. In W. Geeslin & K. Graham (Eds.), *Proceedings of the Sixteenth PME Conference* (Vol. 3, pp. 235–261). Durham, NH: University of New Hampshire Department of Mathematics.

Goldin, G. A. (1992b). Toward an assessment framework for school mathematics. In R. Lesh & S. J. Lamon (Eds.), *Assessment of authentic performance in school mathematics* (pp. 63–88). Washington, DC: American Association for the Advancement of Science.

Goldin, G. A., & Herscovics, N. (1991a). The conceptual-representational analysis of children's early arithmetic. In R. Underhill (Ed.), *Proceedings of the Thirteenth Annual Meeting of PME-NA* (Vol. 1, pp. 118–124). Blacksburg, VA: Virginia Tech Division of Curriculum and Instruction.

Goldin, G. A., & Herscovics, N. (1991b). Toward a conceptual-representational analysis of the exponential function. In F. Furinghetti (Ed.), *Proceedings of the Fifteenth Annual Conference for the Psychology of Mathematics Education (PME)* (Vol. 2, pp. 64–71). Genoa, Italy: Dipartimento di Matematica dell'Università di Genova.

Goodman, N. (1976). *Languages of art* (rev. ed.). Amherst, MA: University of Massachusetts Press.

Grossberg, S. (1980). How does a brain build a cognitive code? *Psychological Review, 87,* 1–51.

Janvier, C. (Ed.). (1987). *Problems of representation in the teaching and learning of Mathematics.* Hillsdale, NJ: Lawrence Erlbaum Associates.

Kaput, J. (1979). Mathematics and learning: The roots of epistemological status. In J. Clement & J. Lochhead (Eds.), *Cognitive process instruction.* Philadelphia: Franklin Institute Press.

Kaput, J. (1983). Representation systems and mathematics. In J. C. Bergeron & N. Herscovics (Eds.), *Proceedings of the Fifth Annual Meeting of PME-NA* (Vol. 2, pp. 57–66). Montreal: University of Montreal Faculty of Educational Sciences. Reprinted in Janvier (1987, pp. 19–26).

Kaput, J. (1985). Representation and problem solving: Methodological issues related to modeling. In E. Silver (Ed.), *Teaching and learning mathematical problem solving: Multiple research perspectives* (pp. 381–398). Hillsdale, NJ: Lawrence Erlbaum Associates.

Kaput, J. (1987). Toward a theory of symbol use in mathematics. In C. Janvier (Ed.), *Problems of representation in the teaching and learning of mathematics* (pp. 159–196). Hillsdale, NJ: Lawrence Erlbaum Associates.

Kaput, J. (1989). Linking representations in the symbol system of algebra. In C. Kieran & S. Wagner (Eds.), *A research agenda for the teaching and learning of algebra* (pp. 167–194). Reston, VA: National Council of Teachers of Mathematics, and Hillsdale, NJ: Lawrence Erlbaum Associates.

Kaput, J. (1991). Notations and representations as mediators of constructive processes. In E. von Glasersfeld (Ed.), *Constructivism in mathematics education* (pp. 53–74). Dordrecht.

Kaput, J. (1992). Technology and mathematics education. In D. Grouws (Ed.), *Handbook on research in mathematics teaching and learning* (pp. 515–556). New York: Macmillan.

Kaput, J. (1993). The urgent need for proleptic research in the graphical representation of quantitative relationships. In T. Carpenter, E. Fennema, & T. Romberg (Eds.), *Research in the graphical representation of functions* (pp. 279–312). Hillsdale, NJ: Lawrence Erlbaum Associates.

Kaput, J. (1994a). The representational roles of technology in connecting mathematics with authentic experience. In R. Biehler, R. W. Scholz, R. Sträßer, & B. Winkelman (Eds.), *Didactics of mathematics as a scientific discipline*. Dordrecht: Kluwer.

Kaput, J. (1994b). Democratizing access to calculus: New routes using old roots. In A. Schoenfeld (Ed.), *Mathematical thinking and problem solving* (pp. 77–156). Hillsdale, NJ: Lawrence Erlbaum Associates.

Kaput, J. (1995). Overcoming physicality and the eternal present: Cybernetic manipulatives. In R. Sutherland & J. Mason (Eds.), *Exploiting mental imagery with computers in mathematics education* (pp. 161–177). New York: Springer.

Kosslyn, S. (1980). *Image and mind*. Cambridge, MA: Harvard University Press.

Kosslyn, S., & Koenig, O. (1992). *Wet mind: The new cognitive neuroscience*. New York: Free Press.

Lesh, R., Landau, M., & Hamilton, E. (1983). Conceptual models and applied problem-solving research. In R. Lesh & M. Landau (Eds.), *Acquisition of mathematical concepts and processes* (pp. 263–343). New York: Academic Press.

Mahoney, M. (1980). The beginnings of algebraic thought in the seventeenth century. In S. Gankroger (Ed.), *Descartes: Philosophy, Mathematics and Physics*. Sussex, England: Harvester Press.

McLeod, D. B., & Adams, V. M. (Eds.). (1989). *Affect and mathematical problem solving: A new perspective*. New York: Springer Verlag.

Meira, L. (1992). The microevolution of mathematical representations in children's activity. In W. Geeslin & K. Graham (Eds.), *Proceedings of the Sixteenth PME Conference* (Vol. 2, pp. 96–111). Durham, NH: University of New Hampshire Department of Mathematics.

Thomas, N., Mulligan, J., & Goldin, G. A. (1994). Children's representation of the counting sequence 1–100: Study and theoretical interpretation. In J. Matos (Ed.), *Proceedings of the eighteenth PME conference* (Vol. III, pp. 1–8). Lisbon, Portugal: Univ. of Lisbon Dept. of Education, Faculty of Sciences.

Nickerson, R. (1986). *Technology and education: The evolution of number systems*. Cambridge, MA: BBN.

Palmer, S. E. (1977). Fundamental aspects of cognitive representation. In E. Rosch & B. B. Lloyd (Eds.), *Cognition and categorization*. Hillsdale, NJ: Lawrence Erlbaum Associates.

Piaget, J. (1969). *Science of education and the psychology of the child*. New York: Viking Press.

Pimm, D. (1987). *Speaking mathematically: Communication in mathematics classrooms*. London: Routledge.

Steffe, L. P., von Glasersfeld, E., Richards, J., & Cobb, P. (1983). *Children's counting types: Philosophy, theory, and application*. New York: Praeger.

Steffe, L. P., Cobb, P., & von Glasersfeld, E. (1988). *Construction of arithmetical meanings and strategies*. New York: Springer.

Thompson, P. W. (1992). Notations, conventions, and constraints: Contributions to effective uses of concrete materials in elementary mathematics. *Journal for Research in Mathematics Education 23*, 123–147.

von Glasersfeld, E. (1987). Preliminaries to any theory of representation. In C. Janvier (Ed.),

Problems of representation in the teaching and learning of mathematics (pp. 215–226). Hillsdale, NJ: Lawrence Erlbaum Associates.

White, B. (1993). Tinkertools: Casual models, conceptual change, and science education. *Cognition and Instruction, 10,* 1–100.

Yerushalmy, M. (1991). Student perceptions of aspects of algebraic function using multiple representation software. *Journal of Computer Assisted Learning, 7,* 42–57.

24 Young Children Invent Methods of Proof: The Gang of Four

Carolyn A. Maher
Amy M. Martino
Rutgers University

BACKGROUND

This research is part of a longitudinal study of the development of mathematical ideas in children. We are interested in studying how children build mathematical ideas in classroom environments that support children in creating models, inventing notation, justifying their solutions, and participating in mathematical discussions with others. The children in this report have come from such classroom environments since Grade 1.

Our previous findings suggest that after children have built their own representation of a problem task, they seem ready to listen to the ideas of other students (Maher & Martino, 1992a). In so doing, their original ideas may be challenged or supported. The resulting student interactions may lead students to reject original ideas in favor of others, or may enable students to modify, consolidate, or strengthen an original argument (Maher & Martino, 1991). For this reason, after children have developed their own justifications for their problem solutions, we often ask them to try to convince a partner or another small group that their solution is correct. The opportunity for students to test their ideas and hear the ideas of other students provides a setting for the teacher as a moderator and observer to listen to and assess the thinking of the students involved in discussion (Maher & Martino, 1992b). A sharing of ideas between students sometimes takes the form of a small-group discussion that can often be observed by the teacher.

This report describes one such small-group assessment that was videotaped as four children shared their justifications during a combinatorial problem task. A version of proof by cases and a version of proof by mathematical induction were presented by the children. Important points are highlighted in their discussion and are traced back to earlier work done by the students.

Over the last several years, our work has centered on studying how children build up their ideas when confronted with problematic tasks that promote thoughtfulness about mathematical situations. Tasks are deliberately chosen to challenge children to reorganize or to extend available existing knowledge.

The child, in the process of working out a solution to a problem task, retrieves from memory existing knowledge in the form of mental representations (Davis, 1984). If existing representations are an inadequate match to the problem, the child may find it necessary to reorganize and/or extend his or her available existing knowledge. The process of tackling the problem may trigger the construction of a more adequate representation and provide the individual with incentive to reorganize or extend his or her current knowledge. This process can lead to the development of a new idea (Davis & Maher, 1990).

PRIOR RESEARCH ON METHODS OF PROOF

Much of the research reported on the development of justification and proof has been conducted with older elementary school children, high school students, and adults (Bell, 1976; Galbraith, 1981; Martin & Harel, 1989; Williams, 1980). A considerable portion of this research on older students has focused on the development of formal mathematical proof (Senk, 1985). An exception to this trend is work by Lester (1981) that documented fifth- and seventh-grade students' use of trial and error methods to solve problems and their ability to coordinate multiple bits of information. His work pointed to a marked increase in students' use of a global classification strategy and a dramatic decrease in reliance on trial and error and local classification strategies as children progressed in age. Another study that focused on younger children's development of justification and reorganization of their previous arguments came from Lawler (1980), who indicated that what makes sense to the child dominates what is inculcated as an extrinsic rule. Sometimes it appears that a child has regressed in knowledge; what may at first appear as a decline might instead be interpreted as the result of a struggle between "sense-making" and the input of new information. Lawler's interpretation is the latter. He suggests that when a new "control element" enters the scene, it may subordinate previously independent micro views into a more global and integrated type of knowledge. This process occurs over some time.

Our own observations of children doing mathematics are consistent with Lawler's view. The mathematical strand that we are tracing over time is young children's development of justifications and methods of proof (Maher & Martino, 1991). Balacheff (1988) made distinctions between justifications, proofs and mathematical proofs. He characterized justification as discourse that aims to establish for another individual the validity of a statement, proof as an explanation that is accepted by a community at a given time, and mathematical proof as those proofs accepted by mathematicians. We are consistent with Balacheff's terminology when we refer to justification and proof. The goal of this chapter is to study 9-year-old children's development of methods of justification over time, and to examine how these arguments become refined and accepted by the class-room community to form the basis for a method of proof.

ORGANIZATION OF THIS REPORT

The existence of an extensive library of videotapes and other data on children's performance makes possible a new kind of study, one that enables tracing the development of the details of a child's thinking over several years (Davis, Maher & Martino, 1992). This study comes from such a data collection. Thus, in tracing the development of students' thinking over time, several videotapes are referred to in this report. Analysis of the March 10, 1992, videotape entitled "The Development of Fourth-graders' Ideas About Mathematical Proof," which has also come to be known to many viewers as "The Gang of Four,"[1] provides the major focus. Reference is made to several other tapes (which are outlined in Table 24.1) that were made prior to this March 10 tape in order to trace the early origins and development of these ideas.

TABLE 24.1
Problem Activities and Interviews Used in the Analysis

Grade	Date Recorded	Activity/Objective
2	May 20, 1990	Shirts and Pants Problem: Students find all possible combinations that can be made when selecting from three shirts and two pairs of jeans.
3	October 11, 1990	Tower Problem 1: Students find all possible towers that are four cubes tall when selecting from plastic cubes in two colors.
3	October 12, 1990	Tower Problem 1, Interview 1: Individual children talk about the combinations they found and present any organizations they may have used to arrange their towers.

(continued)

[1]The videotape entitled "The Development of Fourth-Graders Ideas About Mathematical Proof" has come to be identified as "The Gang of Four" since its first presentation by Robert B. Davis at Andrew Gleason's retirement dinner at Harvard University in 1992. This tape is available through Carolyn A. Maher, Rutgers University Center for Mathematics, Science and Computer Education, 10 Seminary Place, New Brunswick, NJ 08903.

TABLE 24.1 (*Continued*)

Grade	Date Recorded	Activity/Objective
4	February 6, 1992	Tower Problem 2: Students find all possible towers that are five cubes tall when selecting from plastic cubes in two colors.
4	February 7, 1992	Tower Problem 2, Interview 1: In this interview, random guess and check methods are replaced by local organizations as students monitor their production of combinations.[a]
4	February 21, 1992	Tower Problem 2, Interview 2: Stephanie, Milin, and Michelle[b] further discuss their organizations for accounting for all possibilities. Stephanie chooses to explore towers that are six cubes tall.
4	March 6, 1992	Tower Problem 2, Interview 3: Stephanie and Milin further explore a partial "proof by cases."[c]
4	March 10, 1992	"The Gang of Four": A taped discussion of four children that provides the focus of this paper. The four students are asked to find all possible towers of height three when selecting from two colors of plastic cubes. In their attempt to justify having found all possible towers to their classmates, Stephanie shares her version of a "proof by cases" and Milin shares his version of a "proof by mathematical induction."

[a]The progression from use of random methods to the use of systematic "local" organizing aids that serve to simplify the task of finding new towers and keeping track of their collections enables children to find new groupings (e.g., by "inverting" a tower and its opposite to produce a new collection, or by arranging a subset of towers that has exactly one blue cube arranged according to some pattern such as having exactly one blue cube but in a different position). These organizations were discussed and students were further challenged to consider whether they had accounted for all possibilities. One student, Jeff, indicated the pattern that the number of towers doubled each time another layer was added to the towers (two towers one cube tall, four towers two cubes tall, eight towers three cubes tall, etc.). While working with these local organizations, some children came to realize that their local organization schemes were inadequate for accounting for all possible towers. In many cases, children came to recognize conflicts between their different local organizations and realized the need for an overall scheme to account for all possible towers.

[b]Michelle, like Jeff in Interview 1, had discovered the doubling pattern that resulted when the height of towers was increased by one cube.

[c]In the course of Tower Interview 3 conducted March 6, 1992, Stephanie developed a "proof by cases" for towers four cubes tall and recognized the "doubling pattern" to predict the number of towers of a given height. Milin developed a "proof by mathematical induction" to predict the total number of towers of any height by understanding how the doubling pattern worked. For more detail on the development of Stephanie and Milin's proofs over time see Maher and Martino (1993) and Alston and Maher (1993).

"The Gang of Four" (Grade 4, March 10, 1992)

We begin this analysis of Stephanie's problem-solving behavior by considering a videotaped small group interaction in which Stephanie tries to convince one of her classmates, Jeff, that she has found all possible towers three cubes tall that could be built selecting from plastic cubes in two colors, one blue and the other red. Two other children, Michelle and Milin, join Jeff and Stephanie in the discussion. The four children sit in a conference-like setting, observed at a distance by their classroom teacher, the school mathematics supervisor, and research staff from Rutgers. Two cameras and microphones are situated to observe carefully the children and their written work.

When presented with the Tower Problem, Stephanie began by immediately drawing a picture of eight towers. The construction of her first drawing showed the following eight different towers. It took her about 30 sec. to make her drawing (see Fig. 24.1).

The swiftness and confidence with which Stephanie retrieved her set of towers comes with little surprise. Stephanie has been involved in a thoughtful approach to combinatorial counting problems since Grade 2. She and her classmates, students in a school where building meaning in doing mathematics is a serious goal, have benefited from several years of reform in teaching mathematics (Maher, Davis, & Alston, 1991; Martino, 1992).

Classroom Problem Solving Prior to March 10, 1992

In Grade 3, the children worked to find all possible towers that are four cubes tall as a classroom activity (see Table 24.1). They were given Unifix cubes in two colors and were videotaped working in pairs to solve the problem. Following that problem activity, the children were individually interviewed about their solution (October 12, 1990). In Grade 4, the same children were given the problem with the variant of building towers of height 5 (February 6, 1992). All of the children were interviewed afterward (February 7, 1992). Thus, several videotaped classroom episodes and individual interviews of the children provided the data for analyzing how Stephanie built up her idea of proof.

"The Gang of Four" (Grade 4, March 10, 1992)

As referred to in Table 24.1, in this particular session, the goal had advanced from finding all possible combinations of towers that could be built, to providing a convincing argument that every possible tower had been found. The students were asked by the instructor, "How do you know that you have them all?" and "Can you convince me that you have all possibilities, that there are no more or no fewer?"

In response to this challenge, Stephanie made a second drawing of towers that

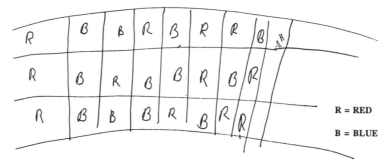

FIG. 24.1. Stephanie's initial drawing of towers.

she used in an attempt to convince her classmates that there were only eight possibilities for towers three cubes tall when selecting from two color choices (see Fig. 24.2).

Stephanie began with the cases of no blue cubes, exactly one blue cube, and exactly two blue cubes that were adjacent.

Stephanie: Alright, first you have without any blues . . . red, red, red [Fig. 24.2, tower 1]. Then you have one blue . . . blue, red, red . . . [Fig. 24.2, tower 2] red, blue, red [Fig. 24.2, tower 3] or red, red, blue [Fig. 24.2, tower 4]. There's no more of these because if you go down another one [She referred to a fourth position in a tower of three.] you have to have another block on the bottom. Then you have exactly two blue . . . yeah, actually that's what I did the last time I was here. You can put blue, blue, red [Fig. 24.2, tower 5] . . . you can put red, blue and blue [Fig. 24.2, tower 6].

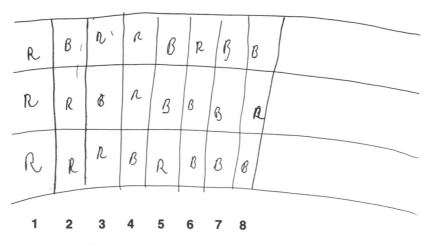

FIG. 24.2. Stephanie's second drawing of towers.

She was then interrupted by Milin, who tried to include the other case of exactly two blue cubes that are separated by a red cube.

Milin: You can put blue, red and blue.

Stephanie reaffirmed her own organization of the data, and was then interrupted by Jeff.

Stephanie: But that's not what I'm doing. I'm doing it so that they're stuck together. [The two blue cubes have no red cubes in between.]
Jeff: You could do one [tower] with one red and then you can do one [tower] with two reds and then one [tower] with three reds and then . . . see, there's all reds, then there's three . . . two reds . . . there should be one [tower] with one red, then you change it to blue.

At this point, the instructor called Milin's organization to Stephanie's attention.

Instructor: Milin said you don't have all two blues, and you said . . . why is that?
Stephanie: [to Milin] Show me another [tower with] two blue [cubes] alright so . . . [She pauses while Milin takes her paper, and then adds the following comment.] with them *stuck together* cause that's what I'm doing.

Milin quickly returned the paper, saying:

Milin: In that case here . . .

Michelle, like Milin, suggested a broader, more all-inclusive organization of cases, that is, all towers with exactly two blue cubes. She added:

Michelle: What if you just had two blues and you weren't stuck together . . . you could . . .

Stephanie again reaffirmed her own organization and responded:

Stephanie: But that's what I'm doing I'm doing the blues *stuck together* [adjacent to each other]. Then we have three blues which you can only make one of . . . then you want two blues stuck apart . . . took apart . . . [separated by a red cube]
Instructor: Separated?
Stephanie: Yeah, separated. Blue, red, blue.

Stephanie had presented a proof for all possible combinations by considering five individual cases (towers with no blue cubes, one blue cube, two blue cubes stuck together, three blue cubes and finally, two blue cubes separated by a red cube.). Another student seated at the table, Jeff, then posed the following question: "Do you have to make a pattern?"

FIG. 24.3. Jeff's use of
patterns which resulted
in "double counting."

■ BLUE

□ RED

Jeff's Prior Experience with Towers Four and Five Cubes Tall (Grades 3 and 4, October 11, 1990, and February 6, 1992)

On October 11, 1990, and February 6, 1992, both earlier classroom problem-solving sessions building towers, Jeff paid attention to patterns, using them to find sets of towers. In doing so, he constructed different categories in which the same tower appeared. For example, Jeff organized his cubes using the above patterns and consequently unknowingly counted the tower with exactly one blue cube in the fourth position twice (see Fig. 24.3). It is possible that due to these prior experiences, Jeff had become somewhat skeptical about the efficiency of looking for sets of patterns.

Returning to "The Gang of Four" (Grade 4, March 10, 1992)

In response to Jeff's question about making patterns, the other students at the table replied that it was not necessary to make a pattern (in the sense that this was not a requirement imposed by the teacher), but it helped them in various ways. Stephanie responded, "It's easier then just going . . . oooh there's a pattern!" As she talked, Stephanie reached up as if she were grabbing something from the air. Her earlier disequilibrium about the efficiency of using various patterns to solve these problems had led her to consider an alternative all-inclusive organization of the possible outcomes. It was at this time that she introduced a new organization of possibilities and built a proof by cases in which she was now able to consider all possibilities with care to avoid counting particular towers twice.

Looking Back at Stephanie Building Towers Four Cubes Tall (Grade 3, October 11, 1990)

Stephanie and her classmates had worked on building towers four cubes tall in Grade 3 and then five cubes tall in Grade 4. In Grade 3, Stephanie found individual towers by trial and error and guess and check. She built what she thought was a different tower, and then she compared it with others to see whether it was a new one or a duplicate. Stephanie also invented descriptive names like "red in the middle" or "patchwork" to identify individual towers. These names were applied to particular towers that were considered individually and were not used to relate the towers to a group or subclass of towers. Also, in Grade 3, Stephanie tried other strategies in her solution. For example, occasionally a tower and its "opposite" would be positioned next to each other, but no explicit reference was made about this pattern (see Fig. 24.4). (Tower A and

FIG. 24.4.   A pair of towers that
Stephanie named "opposites."

■ - RED
□ - YELLOW

Tower B are opposites if, for all n, the cube in position n in tower B has the opposite color from the cube in position n in tower A.) Although Stephanie used a trial-and-error method for generating towers and referred to "opposites" in Grade 3, she did not implement widespread use of this "opposite" pattern in the construction of towers until Grade 4.

Also, in Grade 3, Stephanie noticed another relationship between two towers formed by flipping the first tower to make the second, naming the second tower "cousin" (see Fig. 24.5). (For towers with height h, tower B was the cousin of tower A if for all n, the cube in position n in Tower B had the same color as the cube in position h-n in tower A.)

Stephanie: Let me check. Nope. Nope . . . these must be cousins. [She referred to two towers, one tower with exactly one blue cube in the bottom position and one tower with exactly one blue cube in the top position.]
Instructor: You think they're cousins . . . why do you think they're cousins?
Stephanie: Because this one has one [blue cube] on the bottom and this one has one [blue cube] on the top . . . turn it [the first tower] upside down and they're the same [the two "cousin towers"].

Looking Back at Stephanie Building Towers Five Cubes Tall (Grade 4, February 6, 1992, and February 7, 1992)

In Grade 4, this procedure of constructing a tower and its "opposite" became a primary strategy for both Stephanie and her partner, Dana, as they generated original combinations. They then incorporated the Grade 3 relationship of "cousins" (a tower and its upside-down partner) into their strategy for generating new towers. Stephanie explained how she and her partner would build a tower (call it A), build the opposite of A, build the "cousin" of A, and build the "opposite of the cousin of A." Figure 24.6 depicts the four towers that Stephanie and Dana used to demonstrate their "upside down and opposite procedure" to the instructor for towers five cubes tall.

In grade 4, we see Stephanie applying the "upside down and opposites" pattern to group towers into sets. The patterns initially discovered in Grade 3 now formed a basis for building other more complex configurations in Grade 4.

FIG. 24.5.   A pair of towers that
Stephanie named "cousins."

□ - RED
■ - BLUE

FIG. 24.6.   Stephanie and Dana's use of an "upside down and opposite" procedure.

■ - RED
☐ - YELLOW

The use of "pattern" for Stephanie and her partner, Dana, had two different meanings in Grade 3. One referred to arrangements of cubes within a particular tower ("patchwork," "mixed colors," etc.); the other referred to relationships between two or more towers. To find a new arrangement within a particular tower, Stephanie began by using a guess-and-check strategy. She later found sets of towers that were in some way related. For example, she displayed one pattern among towers five cubes tall that had exactly one blue cube placed in each of the five possible tower positions. Another display illustrated the following arrangement: exactly 1 blue cube in the first position, exactly 2 blue cubes in the first and second positions, exactly 3 blue cubes in the first, second, and third positions, exactly 4 blue cubes in the first four positions, and exactly 5 blue cubes. She soon realized that a tower with exactly one blue cube in the first position was counted twice. This produced some uncertainty and suggested to Stephanie that the production of patterns was not always a reliable way with which to find unique towers. This disequilibrium caused Stephanie to consider an alternative argument.

Returning to "The Gang of Four" (Grade 4, March 10, 1992)

During the group's discussion about the usefulness of patterns, Michelle also responded to Jeff's question about patterns. She explained how patterns provided a system of organization for generating new towers and helped to indicate ways to exhaust all possible combinations. However, she was referring to Stephanie's new organization of considering cases.

Michelle: Because if you just keep on guessing like that . . . you're not sure if there's going to be more.

Stephanie then explained to Jeff that Michelle and Milin had a different system for organizing their combinations:

Stephanie: Like Shelly and Milin's pattern was to put this [a tower with blue cubes in the top and bottom tower positions and a red cube in the middle tower position] in a different category.

In an exasperated tone of voice, Jeff responded, "I *know* their pattern."

Looking Back at Milin and Michelle Building Towers Five Cubes Tall (Grade 4, February 21, 1992, and March 6, 1992)

There was evidence from the earlier interviews that Jeff's conviction as well as Michelle and Milin's argument had merit. For example, after the Grade 3 and Grade 4 problem activities, in a series of subsequent interviews, Michelle and Milin had independently developed a method for computing the number of possible towers with a choice of two colors of cubes when given the number of blocks that could be used in each tower. (If n = the number of cubes in each tower, 2^n is the total number of towers.) Thus, from each tower of two, two towers of three can be made, one with a red cube on top and one with a blue cube on top. Previously, both Michelle and Milin had used patterns like "opposites" as strategies to generate the new towers, but each had independently discovered the shortcoming that this method does not help you decide when you have found every arrangement.

Returning to "The Gang of Four" (Grade 4, March 10, 1992)

Michelle, a problem-solving partner with Jeff building towers five cubes tall, also struggled in dealing with the occurrence of duplicates. She now joined in support of Stephanie as she answered Jeff's question about the advantage of finding patterns.

Stephanie: What I'm saying is it's easier to work with a pattern then to say . . .
Milin: [joined in] Here's another one . . .
Stephanie: [She acted out that she was finding individual towers by reaching out in space to imaginary towers.] Yeah that looks good.
Michelle: Cause you might have a duplicate [arrangement in your set] and you may not know.

Another difficulty experienced by these students as they worked in earlier sessions on variations of this activity (building towers of four, five, and in the case of Stephanie, six) was the formation of duplicate combinations. Until they developed systems for organizing their combinations, they frequently had undetected duplicate combinations.

Stephanie: It's harder to check just having them come from out of the blue.
Jeff: [He further challenged their arguments.] How do you know there's different things in a pattern? [The reader is encouraged to refer back to Fig. 24.3.]
Milin: See. Look at this. [Fig. 24.7]

In an impatient tone of voice, Jeff responded: "I *see* that." Milin continued.

FIG. 24.7. Milin's method for
finding all towers (a).

■ - BLUE
☐ - RED

Milin: These are all different, right? [He was referring to four towers which he drew
            that were two blocks high. He then pointed to his drawing of a tower two
            cubes tall with the red cube on top and the blue cube on the bottom.] From
            this you can make two more, there's a blue, red, and then blue . . . [indicat-
            ing all possibilities for a tower two cubes tall when you add a red or blue
            cube to the top of each tower]

Michelle validated his argument and pointed out that the building up strategy by
multiples of two was indeed exhaustive.

Michelle: Cause there's only two colors [of cubes to place in each tower position] more
            so you know you can't make more.

Milin then drew as he spoke (see Fig. 24.8).

Milin: And then there's blue, red, red [tower with a blue cube in the bottom
            position] and you can't make any more from this one so [he referred to the
            tower with red on top and blue on the bottom] you go on to the next one
            [referred to another tower of height two].

Jeff then questioned Milin: "How do you know you *can't* make anymore?"

Looking Back at Jeff's "Building Up" Strategy (Grade 4, February 7, 1992)

Jeff's question suggested his attempt to reconcile two different systems, the first
to find the total number of towers and the second to account for all possibilities.
In an earlier interview, Jeff had independently noted the pattern of 2^n combinations to which Michelle and Milin referred. He gave no evidence of being able to
imagine what all these towers would look like. For Jeff, this occurred in a
subsequent problem-solving session 2 months after the March 10 session when
he was introduced to a system of recording using a tree diagram when building
upward. At this time, Jeff said:

Jeff: You multiply by two, the last number you got you multiply by two because
            you make branches off of them. [He referred to adding two branches to the
            top of each tower to represent the two possible colors which could be added
            to the top a tower.]

FIG. 24.8. Milin's method for
finding all towers (b).

■ - BLUE
☐ - RED

Returning to "The Gang of Four" (Grade 4, March 10, 1992)

Stephanie, in a second attempt to convince Jeff that all possibilities could be accounted for, discarded her drawing with her first set of towers (see Fig. 24.1) and produced eight new arrangements for her towers, appearing rather confident that all possibilities had been found (see Fig. 24.2). Stephanie had drawn a diagram of towers that she had organized in an attempt to convince Jeff that she had found all possible combinations. She did this case by case. She presented five possible cases for arrangements of towers: towers with no blue cubes, towers with exactly one blue cube, towers with exactly two blue cubes "stuck together," towers with exactly three blue cubes and towers with exactly two blue cubes separated. Note that although adults were present in the classroom and listened to the ideas presented by the students, there was no adult intervention in this episode.

Stephanie: Start here . . . okay . . . you have the three together. [She referred to a tower with three red cubes.] You have the [towers with] one blue . . . how could I build another [tower with] one blue?

Stephanie referred to her drawing of four towers (see Fig. 24.2): one with no blue cubes, one with a blue cube in the top position, one with a blue cube in the middle position and one with a blue cube in the bottom position (Fig. 24.9).

Jeff responded: "You can't." His tone indicated that he had considered the cases with one blue cube and emphatically agreed with Stephanie's conclusion that there were exactly three of these towers. In a tone that demonstrated confidence, Stephanie continued:

Stephanie: Okay, so I've convinced you that there's no more [towers with] one blue [cube].
Jeff: Yeah. [Jeff's affirmation of Stephanie's statement was emphatic.]

Stephanie provided further justification for the case of towers with exactly one blue cube by pointing to the three towers with exactly one blue cube, saying:

Stephanie: Blue, red, red . . . red, blue, red . . . red, red, blue, but then how am I supposed to make another one once the blue [cube] got down to my last block [the bottom position]?

Jeff answered in a tone that indicated that he was convinced, "You can't." Stephanie argued that only three towers could be built with exactly one blue

FIG. 24.9. A model of Stephanie's proof by cases for no blue cubes and one blue cube.

■ - BLUE
□ - RED

FIG. 24.10. A model of Stephanie's proof by cases for towers with no blue cubes, exactly one blue cube, and exactly two blue cubes adjacent to each other.

■ - BLUE
□ - RED

cube, challenging Jeff to create another tower once all three positions had been utilized. Jeff agreed with her reasoning and conceded that all the towers three cubes tall with one blue cube had been considered.

Stephanie: Okay, so I convinced you that there's no more [towers with] one blue.
Jeff: Yeah.
Stephanie: Okay, now [towers with] two blue. Here's one, right? We have blue, blue, red . . . red, blue, blue, but how am I supposed to make another one?

Jeff then suggested another tower with exactly two blue cubes, saying "Blue, red, blue." Stephanie responded with an explanation that she was considering only those towers with the two blue cubes adjacent to each other, saying, "No this is *together*. Milin gave me that same argument." (See Fig. 24.10.)

Earlier, Stephanie had presented two blue cubes separated by a red cube as a separate case. Milin had objected to her choice of grouping and suggested that all the towers with two blue cubes be considered together. During this discussion, it became apparent that Jeff's use of patterns was different from Stephanie's as he suggested that she group towers as follows: "There should be one [tower] with all reds, then one [tower] with two reds then there's one with one red and then you change to blue."

It is interesting that the patterns suggested in this session were the same as those that Jeff made during the Grade 4 problem activity of building towers five cubes tall, which resulted in duplicates from intersecting sets. Michelle, who was Jeff's earlier partner, also had to deal earlier with the occurrence of duplicates from intersecting sets. Now she assisted in interpreting Stephanie's method for grouping towers.

Michelle: She means stuck together.
Jeff: It doesn't matter.
Stephanie: Stuck together.
Jeff: I know.
Stephanie: Okay, so can I make any more of that kind?
Jeff: No.

Jeff quickly looked at Stephanie's drawing (see Fig. 24.2) and agreed that she could make no more towers with two adjacent blue cubes. Michelle then referred to Stephanie's next case of one tower with three blue cubes.

Michelle: Then you have to move to [a tower with] three [blue] which you can only make one. [Fig. 24.2, tower 7]

Stephanie: Yeah, you can only make one. And then you can make without red which is three blue.

Michelle: And then you can make two split apart.

Stephanie continued and included one tower with the two blue cubes separated by a red cube. [Fig. 24.2, tower 8]

Stephanie: Two split apart which you can only make one of and then you can find the opposites right in the same place [She slapped her hand down on the table.]

Jeff: Okay. [His tone indicated that he understood and acknowledged her method.]

Stephanie: So I've convinced you that there are only eight?

Jeff: Yes. [emphatically]

Looking Back at Stephanie Building Towers Six Cubes Tall (Grade 4, February 21, 1992)

Components of the development of Stephanie's argument can be traced over 3 years and across several problem-solving episodes to include classroom small group work and individual task-based interviews. Limitations in space do not permit a more detailed analysis of approximately 8 hours of videotape data. However, some particular aspects are of interest. For example, in Grade 4, Stephanie generated her towers with the pattern of "opposites." In an interview after the problem activity, she initiated work with towers six cubes tall and brought in pictures of towers with height six that she had drawn at home. Her strategy was to group these by a characteristic such as "all towers with exactly one blue cube" and she then immediately built the "opposite" set of this group. This method frequently resulted in the duplication of arrangements. As she built the towers six cubes tall with two red cubes, Stephanie noticed that these were the same intersection of sets as the towers with four blue cubes. Thus, she had discovered that the "opposites" were also within this method of solution by cases. (see Fig. 24.2).

CONCLUSIONS

For Stephanie, we notice that her ideas began to develop when her earlier strategies no longer served her well and the need arose to invent new ones. We saw that her argument using cases was evident in earlier problem-solving activities. Stephanie first had to build up her ideas in her own mind before she was able to retrieve them so confidently to demonstrate her thinking to her fellow classmates. We interpret this as evidence that Stephanie is building up an assimilation paradigm (Davis, 1984) for proof by cases.

Jeff's mental representation for proof is different from Stephanie's. We observe Jeff modifying his own assembled representation in an attempt to make sense of Stephanie's representation (Davis, 1984; see also Booker, chapter 22, this volume; Davis, chapter 16, this volume; Goldin & Kaput, chapter 23, this volume). We also observe Jeff matching Milin's representation to his in the proof by mathematical induction.

Readiness on the part of these students to consider an alternative argument and match that argument against personally held ones was central. All of these children worked hard to reflect on their earlier problem solving and to consider another way of thinking about the problem.

We have learned from our observation and study of the problem-solving behavior of these children that it is possible to get an idea of how children deal with mathematical tasks and how they try to make sense of mathematical situations. These observations help us to learn about how children think about mathematical ideas, and how some children build up their ideas over time. In our work, we have used videotape recordings of task-based interviews, classroom small group interactions, and whole-class discussions to follow, over several years, children's mathematical thinking. Such an approach to evaluation has caused us to focus on how ideas are built up over time as children think about mathematical problems while simultaneously enabling us to support the thoughtful doing of mathematics in classrooms.

ACKNOWLEDGMENT

This research is supported in part by a grant from the National Science Foundation (MDR-9053597) to Rutgers, the State University of New Jersey. Any opinions, findings, and conclusions or recommendations expressed in this publication are those of the authors and do not necessarily reflect the views of the National Science Foundation.

REFERENCES

Alston, A., & Maher, C. A. (1993). Tracing Milin's building of proof by mathematical induction: A case study. In B. Pence (Ed.), *Proceedings of the Fifteenth Annual Meeting for the North American Chapter for the Psychology of Mathematics Education* (Vol. 2, pp. 1–7). Pacific Grove, CA.

Balacheff, N. (1988, April). *A study of pupils' proving processes at the junior high school level.* Unpublished paper presented at the Joint International Conference 66th NCTM and UCSMP Project, Chicago.

Bell, A. (1976). A study of pupils' proof-explanations in mathematical situations. *Educational Studies in Mathematics, 7,* pp. 23–40.

Davis, R. B. (1984). *Learning mathematics: The cognitive science approach to mathematics education.* Norwood, NJ: Ablex.

Davis, R. B. (1992). The Semicolon Curriculum and other weird tales. In E. Rolkor, P. Chernoff, C. Costes, & D. Lieberman (Eds.), *Andrew M. Gleason: Glimpses of a life in mathematics.* Boston: Department of Mathematics and Computer Science, University of Massachusetts.

Davis, R. B., & Maher, C. A. (1990). What do we do when we learn mathematics? In R. B. Davis, C. A. Maher, & N. Noddings (Eds.), *Constructivist views on the teaching and learning of mathematics* (pp. 53–69). Reston, VA: NCTM.

Davis, R. B., Maher, C. A., & Martino, A. (1992). Using videotapes to study the construction of mathematical knowledge of individual children working in groups. *Journal of Science, Education and Technology, 1*(3), 177–189.

Galbraith, P. (1981). Aspects of proving: A clinical investigation of process. *Educational Studies in Mathematics, 12,* 1–29.

Lawler, R. W. (1980). The progressive construction of mind. *Cognitive Science, 5,* 1–34.

Lester, F. K. (1981). A procedure for studying the cognitive processes used during problem solving. *Journal for Experimental Education, 48*(4), 323–327.

Maher, C. A. (1992). Is dealing with mathematics as a thoughtful subject compatible with maintaining satisfactory test scores?: A nine-year study. *Journal of Mathematical Behavior, 10,* 225–248.

Maher, C. A., Davis, R. B., & Alston, A. (1991a). Brian's representation and development of mathematical knowledge: A four year study. *Journal of Mathematical Behavior, 10,* 163–210.

Maher, C. A., Davis, R. B., & Alston, A. (1991b). Implementing a "Thinking Curriculum" in mathematics. *Journal of Mathematical Behavior, 10,* 219–224.

Maher, C. A. & Martino, A. (1991). The construction of mathematical knowledge by individual children working in groups. In F. Furinghetti (Ed.), *Proceedings of the Fifteenth Annual Conference of the International Group for the Psychology of Mathematics Education* (pp. 365–372). Assisi, Italy.

Maher, C. A., & Martino, A. M. (1992a). Individual thinking and the integration of the ideas of others in problem solving situations. In W. Geeslin, J. Ferrini-Mundy, & K. Graham (Eds.), *Proceedings of the Sixteenth Annual Conference of the International Group for the Psychology of Mathematics Education* (pp. 72–79). Durham, NH: University of New Hampshire.

Maher, C. A., & Martino, A. (1992b). Teachers building on children's thinking. *Arithmetic Teacher, 39*(7), 32–37.

Maher, C. A., & Martino, A. M. (1993). Four case studies of the stability and durability of children's methods of proof. In B. Pence (Ed.), *Proceedings of the Fifteenth Annual Meeting for the North American Chapter for the Psychology of Mathematics Education* (Vol. 2, pp. 33–39). Pacific Grove, CA.

Martin, W. G., & Harel, G. (1989). Proof frames of preservice elementary teachers. *Journal for Research in Mathematics Education, 20*(1), 41–51.

Martino, A., & Maher, C. A. (1991). An analysis of Stephanie's justifications of problem representations in small group interactions. In R. Underhill (Ed.), *Proceedings of the Thirteenth Annual Meeting for the North American Chapter for the Psychology of Mathematics Education* (pp. 70–76). Blacksburg, VA: Virginia Polytechnic University.

Martino, A. (1992). *Elementary students' construction of mathematical knowledge: Analysis by Profile.* Unpublished doctoral dissertation, Rutgers University.

Senk, S. L. (1985). How well do students write geometric proofs? *Mathematics Teacher, 78*(6), 448–456.

Williams, E. (1980). An investigation of senior high school students' understanding of the nature of mathematical proof. *Journal for Research in Mathematics Education, 11*(3), 165–166.

25 Constructivism and Its Consequences for Training Teachers

Claude Janvier
Université du Québec à Montréal

The aim of this chapter is to examine the consequences of constructivism for the training of secondary level mathematics teachers. In the first section, I expose my understanding of what constructivism is. This enables me to draw inferences for teaching. It is argued that constructivism is only concerned with learning and not with teaching. As a consequence, it is only possible to specify constructivist conditions that must be respected in order to make "good" learning happen. These conditions lead us, in the next section, to the objectives that constructivism suggests for teachers' training. At this point, the stage is set to proceed to a fair description of the intricate web of cognitive processes underlying the training of teachers who, in short, are taught to learn about learning and teaching. In the final section, I present and analyze the constructivist content and objectives of a few training/learning activities that my colleagues and I, at Université du Québec à Montréal (UQAM), have been developing over the last few years in our program.

CONSTRUCTIVISM: FROM PHILOSOPHY TO COGNITIVE PSYCHOLOGY

For me, constructivism is primarily a philosophical theory or position about knowledge and knowledge acquisition. Its objectives are to rationally explain (by providing a model) knowledge and knowledge acquisition by using a coherent discourse based on major concepts belonging to various branches of philosophy. Its main feature, as I see it, is to acknowledge, as its starting point, the fact that the "knower," in the development of his or her knowledge, is dramatically isolated and individually confronted with his or her experiential contact with reality. It basically means that the notion of truthfulness is challenged in the sense that similarity between what is known and what is at the source of the knowledge is claimed to be unverifiable. As von Glasersfeld (chapter 15, this volume) writes, "Reality is unknowable . . . it makes no sense to speak of a representation of something that is inherently inaccessible." Other authors (Cobb et al., chapter 1; Ernest, chapter 20; and Goldin & Kaput, chapter 23, this volume) have examined this question further.

However, when it comes to knowledge development, concepts of cognitive psychology can be imported because they fit with the initial postulates of constructivism. Indeed, I claim that Piagetian constructivism is basically a philosophical theory complemented with fundamental psychocognitive concepts. As a matter of fact, it is not always easy to draw a dividing line between these contributions. Roughly speaking, knowledge, in this perspective, is regarded as the mental "source" of a series of coordinated actions that are precisely targeted at survival and betterment of an individual being. However, as I understand it, according to strict Piagetian constructivism, there exist forms of superknowledge acting as general mental structures that monitor, so to speak, the acquisition of other pieces of knowledge.

Moreover, the processes by which these mental structures develop are central. Indeed, each structure is constructed in a discontinuous manner because each one substantially differs from the others. Disequilibriun, accommodation, assimilation, and equilibration characterize this development, which is governed by a need to adjust to the environment and may depend on prior genetic capabilities. In fact, Piagetian constructivism (very strongly elaborated from a biological point of view) points to the individual involvement in the acquisition of predetermined schemes that form a series of steps already "programmed" within the necessary evolution of a human mind. Learning in a strict Piagetian sense corresponds to getting adjusted to the environment through interactions with it so that those potential schemes can be actualized. It is more concerned with the development of general mental structures than with the appropriation of knowledge!

The features of this "development learning" have seduced several educators, including myself, since they seem to describe the processes through which subject matters appear to be learned. Actually, as most chapters presented in this volume show, mathematical knowledge ought to be derived from the actions on the environment: listening, talking, manipulating, discussing . . . all sorts of actions that lead to abstractions thanks to the use of representational tools. These abstractions allow reflections and reflections on reflections. These are the basic instruments for developing knowledge considered in a perspective broad enough to encompass a wide variety of entities such as concepts, conceptions, and beliefs.

Nevertheless, it should be understood that I am not personally a strict Piagetian constructivist in the sense that I am not convinced that observations so far substantiate the existence of a general mental structure called formal thinking that would control further advanced reasoning schemes. However, I basically endorse the position according to which knowledge acquisition is a temporal building up of units added to a previously built configuration of other units (Maher & Martino, chapter 24, this volume; von Glasersfeld, chapter 18, this volume). If these new units do not fit the current assemblage, then chances are that rejection will take place. Special events would bring about a transition achieved through a process of accommodation that amounts to a sensible adjustment of the knowledge concerned. In any case, whatever the results are—rejection or assimilation—the learner's initial knowledge is a fundamental factor for the determination of the mind's final state after a learning experiment. Another important point, as mentioned by von Glasersfeld, is the willingness to change on the part of the knower and the conviction that the change is worth a major readjustment. Indeed, the evolution of a person's knowledge is not simply a matter of cognitive competence or capability. Decisions involving affective factors are central in making some basic steps possible. Those two points, in my own opinion, are the essential elements to consider when it is said that the learner is personally involved in the construction of his or her knowledge. First, the subject individually incorporates the new pieces to the previous assemblage; second, there is a form of willingness to do so. It does not mean that the learner discovers knowledge; discovery learning should not be confused with constructivist learning.

As far as research methodologies are concerned, I contend that it is fundamentally important to consider the knowledge of others as unknowable reality (to use von Glasersfeld's phrase). From a real constructivist point of view, other individuals' knowledge can only be approximated through their reactions to external input or solicitations and thanks to a personal observational grid (often implicit).

Finally, any act of knowing, any learning whatsoever, is bound to be constructivist in the philosophical sense of the word if one adheres to the principles of constructivism. In other words, one can only know constructively whatever situation one experiences. Whether subjected to strict Skinnerian behaviorist training sessions or following with difficulty a strict "exposition lecture," the student can not escape the constructivist "rules" of learning. In fact, the building up of basic units of his or her knowledge will take place as a personal appropriation that has to adjust continually to the learner's prior knowledge, which, in turn, is at all times likely to become a source of conflict.

FROM CONSTRUCTIVISM TO TEACHING

As I have pointed out before, constructivism is a theory about knowledge and knowledge acquisition. With Ernest (chapter 20) and Goldin (1990), I believe that constructivism is not concerned with teaching. Teaching regarded as an intervention into the process of other persons' learning is basically determined by several a-constructivist decisions. As Ernest (chapter 20, this volume) puts it, "pedagogy is predicated on a set of values, those reflected in the following questions: What are the aims of education? What selection from the stock of cultural knowledge is valuable to teach? . . . A pedagogy is merely a theory of techniques for achieving the ends of . . . offering . . . experiences to learners in a way consistent with these values" (p. 346). For instance, those values will intervene to establish the needs of the learner or to determine a proper time allocation in the organization of the learning.

As another example, the quality of the knowledge that is appropriated by the learner cannot be solely determined on the basis of a constructivist theory of knowledge. Actually, pedagogues have to distinguish between good and bad ways of teaching on the basis of the quality of knowledge that is "induced" in learners. To appreciate the quality, several other factors must be introduced into the discussion, such as the vague notions of meaning and understanding. Although constructivism stresses the necessary coherence (although limited) of personally elaborated knowledge, meaning and understanding require that external agents be active to judge on some form of efficiency and single out the notion of external coherence. Let me give an example. It is a well-known "constructivist" principle that formulas (e.g., in geometry or in calculus) should be given meaning. This principle, however, can be interpreted in several ways. It may be decided that giving meaning to a formula is equated with the possibility on the part of the learner of mentally associating with each formula a figural prototype. On the other hand, giving meaning to a formula may be interpreted as the possibility of deriving it from a more basic one. The decisions then made are not based on any constructivist agenda that is concerned at a more fundamental level with the way to achieve a stated goal.

But it should be clear to us, at the outset, that learning will always be achieved in a constructivist manner whatever you do. I repeat that it should be accepted as a constructivist principle that even in a typically and purely Skinnerian training the subject cannot do otherwise but learn constructively.

However, as I see it, most constructivist pedagogues have an a-constructivist agenda in that they implicitly value some kinds of knowledge in opposition to others. As soon as they start to judge the quality of an appropriated knowledge (and that is a necessary first step in discussing good teaching), they place themselves in a domain that is not related basically to a specific theory of knowledge acquisition, which is basically value-free. I repeat: The criteria that make the end results of a learning experience rate favorably do not belong to constructivism.

I have not systematically examined the literature with the intention of detecting such tacit criteria. I would not dare in any case to publicly attribute intentions to colleagues! My personal position (which I sketch without going into details) is that the resulting knowledge should be above all generalizable, more easily "recoverable" from memory, more "repeatable." Actually, quality cannot be established per se without any reference to the type of knowledge concerned. It would be necessary to come up with a classification that would be based on the notion of knowledge complexity. For instance, (more a counterinstance, I should say), according to a popular school of thought in cognitive psychology, it is fundamental to separate (in a simplistic manner) types of knowledge into procedural and declarative ones. I do not even try to discuss this classification. My position amounts much more to considering a particular knowledge as a mental organization that allows an individual to react to an external solicitation. Then the complexity of a particular piece of knowledge can be measured either by the complexity of the subject's production that witnesses the existence of this knowledge or by the set of parameters that are needed to trigger its production. Using Pythagoras's theorem, for instance, is most of the time less complex than reacting to a group of students requiring explanations about it.

(Let me mention, in passing, that the strict Piagetian psychocognitive position about teaching is ambiguous and ambivalent and is still as virulently debatable as the existence of generalizable formal thinking. In any case, as Inhelder, Sinclair, and Bovet [1974] "must" see it, a teacher can only speed up the process of knowledge acquisition or mental development. This is an intricate question I have no space to attend to further in this chapter.)

I try in the next section to sort out from the literature some points of convergence about the constructivist conditions that should be respected by "correct" teaching interventions on learning (considered as a process) so that learning can take place. As I mentioned earlier, it is clear that those conditions are always minimally norm-biased.

CONSTRUCTIVIST CONDITIONS FOR TEACHING

All the chapters describe teaching consequences of constructivism or implications for education that amount to no more than "guidelines" that are only partially inspired by constructivist positions for the reasons I have just stated. The following discussion corresponds to the results of a personal analysis enriched with the positions of the other contributors to this volume and to the conference that preceded it.

Acting on the Experiential Reality and Enriching It

All chapters in this volume mention that teaching, as a set of actions intended to guide the knowledge acquisition of someone else, can only be achieved through adequate interventions on this person's experiential reality (von Glasersfeld, chapter 18). All agree that learners should be provided with rich situations. Rich situations seem to refer to complex situations involving the students in problem-solving cycles or inducing reflections based on trial and error. It is indeed very logical to believe that once knowledge has been sufficiently circumscribed, it must be put as efficiently as possible into the experiential reality of the learners. We are then faced with an a-constructivist judgment that leads to distinguishing "genuine" mathematical activities from "nongenuine" ones. This first condition turns out to require a normative position; however, the following conditions detailed focus more on the manner with which to act on the experiential reality and are more solely inspired from strict constructivist positions.

Respecting the State of Knowledge at the Moment of the Intervention

In addition, all the chapters also stress that this intervention will necessarily be carried out on the basis of the existing knowledge in the mind of the individual at the moment of the intervention. There might be a contradiction between the elements to be assimilated and the preexisting state of knowledge. This means that some special actions are necessary. If the input does not fit the student's representation, it can be rejected or distorted (Maher & Martino, chapter 24, this volume). As Booker (chapter 22, this volume) mentions, "Old ways of thinking are not usually given up without resistance, . . . and their replacement or extensive to new ways of thinking is guided by already existing conceptions."

Assimilation and accommodation (with perturbations, conflicts, and adjustments) are often mentioned. It must be understood that these processes, at this point, concern ordinary knowledge more than mental structures. There is consequently a need for the teacher to know the preexisting knowledge and the intended knowledge in the mind of the students. Confrey (1993) insisted on the fact that teachers should identify pupils' schemes and know how they work. Booker (chapter 22, this volume) draws attention to the existence of models of cognitive development while Ernest (chapter 20, this volume) indicates that teachers should be sensitive to learners' previous constructions. Maher and Martino (chapter 24, this volume) mention, as a consequence, that teachers will be faced with numerous students' mental representations to start with. On the other hand, no one has specifically underlined the fact that as far as assessing the results of teaching is concerned, it should be remembered that there is no absolute understood/not understood dichotomy.

Conceptions as a special form of knowledge also have to be considered as an important factor to take into account when it comes to intervening in other persons' experiential reality. In fact, they shape the relations this person will establish with the incoming inputs. Conceptions about knowledge, mathematics, learning, and teaching will all act differently but actively. But the way to proceed effectively to "dislodge" conceptions is not a constructivist issue, even though it can be accepted that the usual process of accommodation through conflicts should work. This question, examined in Borassi and Janvier (1989), is very challenging.

Limits of the Language

The most natural way to intervene in the experiential reality of the learner is manifestly through the use of language. Constructivism has turned this common-place assertion into a central issue. Indeed, according to a dominant point of view that makes a reductionist use of information theory, learning is questionably equated to accumulating information, and teaching is regarded as transferring and sending information. Constructivism stands in total opposition to these positions when it points out to the fact that talking has very limited power in the teaching process. Indeed, the right interpretation depends on the prior knowledge of the subject. And, actually, mathematics and mathematics education are concerned with much more than pure information. I have been very pleased to note that other participants share identical views. For example, von Glasersfeld (chapter 18, this volume), after having noted that working on the educational consequences of constructivism "has barely begun," judiciously adds, "few language users have given much thought to the question of how linguistic communication is supposed to work" (p. 310).

Organizing the Social Interactions

Another aspect of learning singled out by constructivism is the fact that knowledge in general (and it is also the case for mathematics) turns out to be the result of social interactions that bring about convergence towards meaning. Even though mathematics appears as a socio-historical well-defined construction nicely "put together" in books, the constructivist perspective insists on the individualization of mathematical learning processes and on the individuality of the resulting mathematical knowledge. Since there is no transfer of meaning from the teacher to the pupil, most participants insist that a pupil's experiential reality is be more influenced by the other pupils' interaction (not only verbal). Not only are these interactions the main tool for him/her to develop knowledge but moreover, these contacts with others are used to establish a match between their experiential realities. These issues are examined more extensively in the various contributions of Cobb and his colleagues (e.g., Cobb, Wood, & Yackel, 1991).

Exploiting a Variety of (External) Representations

Another element of strong convergence concerns the enrichment of pupils' experiential reality through the use of a variety of representations. From the perspective of a reductionist information theory approach to knowledge acquisition, knowledge stays unchanged or invariable whatever symbolic arrangement is used to represent or encapsulate it. On the contrary, a constructivist theory of knowledge, because of its basic suspicions of the "transmission capacity" of symbolic representation, must coherently put forward that the greater the variety in representation, the easier the knowledge construction. However, it must be mentioned that this trait of constructivism does not belong to the Piagetian orthodox heritage. Indeed, Piaget's schemes or mental structures are basically representation independent. A well-known critique addressed to Piaget's theory is precisely that it does not stress enough the basic role of representations in the construction of knowledge. The notion of décalage (time shift) is admittedly introduced to explain some late appearances of schemes under the disguise of parallel representations but cannot explain their total absence.

The necessity of bringing in variations in the representations of notions to be taught is very questionable and must be, as a principle, applied very cautiously. Let me recall that in my criticisms addressed to Dienes's multiple embodiment principle (Janvier, 1987, p. 102), I have attempted to show that varying the representations must be limited and harmonized with the necessity to dwell on a single representation long enough so as to enrich the experiential reality of the learner and make sure that his or her state of knowledge during the intervention is adequately taken into account. It is interesting to note here that this constructivist condition claiming the use of a variety of representations is not absolute and be must be appreciated relative to other conditions.

TRAINING (EDUCATING) TEACHERS: A SPECIAL FORM OF TEACHING

I have so far examined learning and teaching from a constructivist perspective. However, learning and teaching in a teacher-training program make a formidable web. Indeed, such programs are aimed at one basic goal: get them ready to teach mathematics well and efficiently. In the whole process, prospective teachers will have to learn about how their pupils learn. This should contribute to make them better teachers. They should go through a learning process about learning, as well as an indirect teaching experience corresponding to the more or less systematic interventions of the trainer.

On the other hand, the teachers' trainers are in a parallel position: the trainers teach about learning and teaching. They must know about their students' learning about teaching, and so on. This parallel position implies that the principles I have just stated also apply to the trainer's actions with the prospective teachers.

I next examine how in our teacher training program at UQAM, my colleagues and I have attempted in recent years to respect a few of the constructivist conditions already described. My argumentation will rely on a few basic activities that are proposed to our students inside our curriculum. However, before examining the "how do we do" question, I focus my attention on the goals that can be set in training teachers.

SOME CONSTRUCTIVIST GOALS
IN TRAINING TEACHERS

I repeat that "good" constructivist teaching practice involves respecting some constructivist conditions while taking for granted various normative positions that I have not fully investigated. When those questions are revisited with the training of teachers in mind as a special form of teaching, it becomes possible to formulate goals for the training of teachers. Many suggestions can be found in Confrey (1993). What follows is an adaptation of Confrey's objectives based on my position combined with the goals put forward by von Glasersfeld (chapter 18, this volume) and Maher and Martino (chapter 24, this volume).

The trainer's intervention should aim at:

- Providing the teachers with the abilities required to intervene in the pupils' learning process so that they can listen and observe pupils' production to act efficiently, carefully use tools to introduce conflicts that might provoke accommodation, bring about small changes leading to assimilation, and fruitfully make use of open-ended questions and large tasks unfolding over many lessons.
- Changing their conception or belief about mathematical knowledge, and learning and teaching in general.
- Helping them to note the central role of representations in learning and doing mathematics.
- Making them acknowledge the importance of several affective factors (such as motivations) often resulting from implicit goals.
- Focusing their attention on the importance of social contexts in the process of learning, discussions, and negotiations.
- Making them sensitive to the influence in the whole process of the learner's conception of knowledge and mathematics.

It is, at this point, important to make an essential remark about this ability to observe that we want the prospective teachers to develop. It is impossible to watch and detect everything that goes on in a classroom or even during the production of a single pupil. Observation is always selective and always conceals the implicit presence of a theory in the mind of the observer. As a consequence, any emphasis we would like to put on the development of more adequate abilities to observe should be equated with enhancing the growth of some theory in the mind of the prospective teacher.

No matter how these goals may result from a close analysis of psychocognitive constructivism (enriched after some normative decisions about the values of the resulting knowledge), this same constructivism can be used to organize the learning by the prospective teachers of the abilities concerned with the goals.

COMPLYING WITH THE CONSTRUCTIVIST
CONDITIONS OF INTERVENTIONS
FOR TRAINING TEACHERS

So far, constructivist considerations about learning and teaching mathematics have pointed toward some goals to reach. I now turn to the approach to use in the classroom. In this section, I present and analyze activities that my colleagues and I use in our training of teachers (and that we keep on developing). Within each activity, more that one condition is often respected. But the prevalent condition we want to respect is certainly a constant care in insisting that the students should imagine themselves in a teaching situation.

The Experiential Reality

We see the knowledge our students should construct, develop, and appropriate as a knowledge for actions. We share the view that intervening in a classroom requires complex decision-making processes that are triggered by complex sets of input parameters. That is why we try to enrich their experiential reality (in our classroom) so that the conditions under which they will be required to make decisions in school classroom situations will be partially present in our university class sessions.

Keeping them inside the walls of the university at the beginning of their program is a sheer a-constructivist option; another way to help prospective teachers to develop a theory for actions and decision making could be to initiate them to the actual working conditions by an early immersion in the school environment. However, this sort of "in-the-workplace" organization is not desirable. Our teacher training program must start with a huge enterprise of pedagogical and mathematical "re-orientations." Our initiation courses to the program are basically destabilizing. In fact, most of our students are invited to become a kind of teacher they have never observed before and to work in mathematics as they never did before. This initiation leads to a great deal of frustration and insecurity. This initial reassessment of what mathematics, as well as mathematics teaching and learning, are can only be done by them. They must change. We must provide them with the relevant experiences in the circumstances (keeping them with us and not in school) to generate experiential situations (von Glasersfeld, chapter 18, this volume) so that the prospective teachers construct for themselves several principles for actions. Generating adequate experiential situations for them amounts to bringing the pupils and their productions to the forefront of our training activities during the entire program but more particularly right at the very beginning.

As Herscovics notices rightly in his conclusion (chapter 21) for the teachers (and here I transpose to trainers and adjust everything accordingly), "Constructivist teachers [trainers] can prepare their material or organize it optimally so that their students [the pre-service teachers] can reconstruct, not reinvent, the intended mathematics [the constructivist teaching principles]." This parallel draws our attention to the difference. The prospective teachers do not mainly learn mathematics but rather teaching principles in the perspective of a construction/reconstruction issue.

In our courses (Didactique 1 and Didactique 2), students work on a collection of pupils' mistakes that have been gathered over the years. They are asked to analyze those mistakes, find their source, examine their "gravity" in marking tests involving similar mistakes, and produce short transcripts of interviews where they crop up. Our goal is to help them notice that pupils make mistakes through various kinds of reasoning patterns. Slowly, they should begin to see that mathematics can have more to do with reasoning than memorizing facts. Simultaneously, through general discussions, we hope to lead them to consider alternative approaches to guide their pupils' learning.

In almost all our courses, there are a few activities in which they have to discover and compare pupils' reasoning patterns. Our hidden objective is that they become convinced that all pupils can reason and that they should expect in their teaching a wide variety of methods used by pupils. We also believe that they can come to the conclusion that several mathematical items do not require any specific teaching intervention: They belong coherently to the topics and, as such, are likely to be inferred by most pupils.

Writing up word problem statements on various topics is also another kind of activity we resort to. For instance, we may ask the students to write for their pupils a word problem involving the division of two fractions. Most of them discover that they cannot instantly write such a problem or that they write a multiplication problem. We put them this way in a good mood for fruitful reflections on their momentary incapacity. I think that this is a very powerful way to create a need for them to get involved. As you see, our intentions are not solely "pedagogical" in the sense that it is a sort of activity they are expected to carry out frequently in their future practice. We aim more specifically at helping them appreciate the factors that make problems more or less difficult, that trigger the use of particular right or incorrect solving strategies.

Taking into Account the Actual State of Their Knowledge

The prospective teachers must accept a far greater autonomy in their learning; they must accept, at times, minimal interventions on the part of the trainer. They have to accept being unsettled, and they need to assume difficult periods of instability and insecurity that go with this unsteadiness. Actually, their conceptions or beliefs contradict the constructivist positions exposed so far. At some point, they will be left with indistinct goals to achieve and they will find themselves far off on troubled paths leading to these goals. However, the trainer should be aware of the fact that those periods of tension and conflict are normal. Before those tense moments show up, it is necessary that the trainer has gained the confidence of the students.

In another course on problem solving, students are asked to produce a variety of solutions for a set of hand-picked problems particularly aimed at reviewing the secondary-level mathematics curriculum. In this course, they have many opportunities to change their belief about what mathematics is. They are constantly invited to readjust to new ways of apprehending mathematics. Unfortunately, we continually clash with many of our mathematicians colleagues who teach mathematics in a very traditional expository way. They simultaneously constitute counterexamples in showing how not to teach and how not to do mathematics! Good mathematics teaching should always be a source from which to reflect on mathematical thinking processes.

Social Interactions

Several activities are more closely linked with their foreseeable presence in front of a classroom. In one of our courses (Didactique 1), students are invited to observe colleagues executing exposition tasks at the blackboard or with the overhead projector. They are also given opportunities to analyze several aspects of a video presentation showing real-life interventions in the classroom: questions put to the pupils, answers, conducting pupils' discussions, eliciting good questions, and so on. Clearly, before going to school, they are themselves requested to display their talents in front of a pseudo-class of colleagues who play the role of pupils. Finally, they must also produce a "critique-synthèse" of a colleague's presentation. The outcomes of these different activities are rich and diversified. We want them to be more prepared to cope efficiently with future classroom interactions, to answer questions (and more particularly handle the difficult ones), to elicit questions from pupils, to encourage the pupils to answer their own questions, and so on.

But these activities involve more than just social interactions. Our students learn how to plan their actions in the classroom. They gain a good feeling for the factors that determine classroom dynamics and come across several decision-making strategies. They are confronted with different teaching approaches that they are asked to assess and criticize. They are also provided with opportunities to revise secondary-level school mathematics.

Language

So far it has been very difficult to distinguish between what we do to reach our goals and how we do it. The next point concerns only the "how." As a general principle, I can state that we are very suspicious about the power of language in helping the preservice teachers develop the abilities listed so far. In other words, we avoid talking when we believe that there is no familiarity with a topic that guarantees a right interpretation and an assimilation, and not a rejection. Actually, we consider that trainers should take into account students' knowledge and recognize the limits of language intervention. As the reader may have noticed, the activities described earlier are designed as all sorts of familiarization experience that will eventually make language intervention meaningful. Showing and telling is not enough! Prospective teachers should become convinced of that through their own experience and know what else to do. Prospective teachers should live the fact that teaching is more than talking the theory and asking for practice. If they are sensitive enough, they will discover it in schools, but they can also discover it by themselves and on themselves beforehand. I believe that inducing suspicion about the power of talking and telling and knowing its real limits can be considered as a general constructivist condition permeating all our activities.

On the other hand, language is an important factor that contributes precisely in building up the needed familiarity required from which the interpretation process will be helped. Mathematics is not only learned from books; spoken language is an important buffer, interface. For several other reasons, our students are confronted on a permanent basis with what we call verbalization activities. For example, they are asked to describe in words what they do with manipulatives in an argumentation. They will also be asked to describe in words what a formula or an equation means. For instance, the equation $y = mx + b$ can be verbalized as follows: Every point on the line is such that its ordinate is worth the abscissa times the slope plus the "ordinate at the origin," or alternatively: The ordinate of every point on the line can be obtained when you multiply the slope by the abscissa and add the "ordinate at the origin." Clearly the relevant gestures are expected to accompany or punctuate the flow of words. In the last case, at least the slope would be suggested with a motion of the hands and the ordinate at the origin will be shown. Basically, we regard verbalization as an antidote to meaningless and automatic processing of symbolic representations. Let us take a more general example where our suspicion about language can be observed at work.

One Issue in Practice

In a questionnaire that we once in a while administer to some prospective teachers at the beginning of the session in order to know more about them, we constantly find that many of them believe that the main quality of a good teacher is clarity; a good teacher is clear in giving explanations. How does one tackle this delicate issue of dissuading them of this "pseudo-quality?" It seems plainly ludicrous to insist in the next lesson that despite their opinion, a good teacher must sometimes confuse the students! How can we carry on with a discussion on this theme of clarity? It is precisely at this particular moment that one experiences deeply the real fact that talking has limited powers! Indeed, one cannot explain that a good teacher must sometimes mix students up, must "help" them make mistakes. A constructivist perspective not only points out to the necessity to make sure that preservice students will become convinced of that, but it specifies also that it cannot be done through talking. It provides us with the feeling or the conviction that the relevant experience on which to comment or conduct a debate is absent and some experiential reality must be introduced.

Constructivism contributes a great deal to improve a course or a lecture even though it only specifies that one should be suspicious about language usage. At the end of the year, we consider that our "didactique" course has reached its objectives when the students are able to see for themselves why it is impossible sometimes to be clear and why it is often necessary to provoke a conflict with ambiguous questions. The word "clarity" has then been given a totally different meaning as it now refers meaningfully to activities conducted in the class.

Note that all those activities are utterly classroom oriented in the sense that we have made all possible efforts so that curriculum topics and actual student work will be always the center of attraction and preoccupation.

CONCLUSIONS

I believe that most of what we do in education under a constructivist agenda is governed by some normative decisions, not all of which I have examined and studied. It remains clear, however, that by examining further what is meant by a theory for actions such as the one preservice teachers ought to develop, we could improve our interventions that appear to respect at all times an adequate balance between two extreme positions. Moreover, knowing more about the features of such a theory for action in classroom situations would help us make the delicate choice of examples, of representations, of strategies.

Among the items on constructivism supporters' hidden agenda is the idea that it is always relevant and fruitful to foster as much reflection as possible. It seems, for many "constructivist" pedagogues, that each step from past knowledge to new knowledge is made by an extension through reflection. It leaves no space for the brain to act implicitly via automatic processes. Appreciating the right amount of reflection to provoke on the part of the students is certainly a major aspect teachers should know more about. "The more reflections, the more knowledge" is utterly contradicted, for instance, by the way one learns to ride a bicycle. I often tell my students to be careful about the level of explanations they intend to reach with their pupils. I often use the analogy of the athlete trainer who knows a great deal about physiology, but who will give limited adequate explanations to promote excellence in his protégé's performance. Such comments, however, are not based on any extensive theoretical foundation.

Deriving from this idea of using reflections efficiently, let me point out a good sign that reveals that my course has attained some of its objectives. I am fully satisfied when all students become conscious that the knowledge they construct in their training must not all be explicitly explained or "transferred" to the pupils. I then have the feeling that my preservice students no longer consider themselves as mathematical truth transmitters; they have made an irreversible move. They recognize in themselves and during the discussions among them a special category of knowledge that is used to plan, organize, sustain and support their pupils' learning. They can tell the activities designed for them from those planned for the pupils. They have come to the point where they can distinguish for themselves what is for them from what is for their pupils.

REFERENCES

Borasi, R., & Janvier, C. (1989). Research strategies for pupils' conceptions in mathematics. In L. Pereira-Mendoza (Ed.), *Canadian Mathematics Study Group: Proceedings of the 1989 Annual Meeting* (pp. 71–86). St-Catharines, Ontario: University of Newfoundland.

Cobb, P., Wood, T., & Yackel, E. (1991). A constructivist approach to second grade mathematics. In E. von Glasersfeld (Ed.), *Radical constructivism in mathematics education* (pp. 157–176). Dordrecht: Kluwer.

Confrey, J. (1993). *Function probe*. Santa Barbara, CA Intellimation.

Goldin, G. A. (1990). Epistemology, constructivism, and discovery learning in mathematics. In R. B. Davis, C. A. Maher, & N. Noddings (Eds.), *Constructivist views on the teaching and learning of mathematics*. Journal for Research in Mathematics Education Monograph No. 4. Reston, VA: National Council of Teachers of Mathematics.

Inhelder, B., Sinclair, H., & Bovet, M. (1974). *Learning and the development of cognition*. London: Routledge and Kegan.

Janvier, C. (Ed.). (1987). *Problems of representation in the teaching and learning of mathematics*. Hillsdale, NJ: Lawrence Erlbaum Associates.

IV PERSPECTIVES ON THE NATURE OF MATHEMATICAL LEARNING

Is the Metaphor of Mental Object Appropriate for a Theory of Learning Mathematics?

Willi Dörfler
University of Klagenfurt, Austria

MIND AS A SPACE FOR MENTAL OBJECTS

In many papers, talks, and discussions about mathematical thinking, terms are used like mental objects, mental entities, cognitive constructions, and others. What is the use of such notions? They are used to model and explain thinking and problem solving in mathematics (but also elsewhere). Therefore, they are to be taken as theoretical terms within a psychological theory about how the human mind works and proceeds to produce a behavior that might be judged by an expert observer as mathematical (and correct, i.e., in accordance with established mathematical norms).

According to my interpretation of those papers, the basic tenets and assumptions of that theory are the following points. First, the mind (or cognition) is viewed metaphorically as a kind of space that can contain something and that can be structured. As the product of so-called cognitive or mental constructions in that mental space, mental objects originate or are produced. These mental objects then can be manipulated, transformed, combined, and so on with a kind of mental operation. And, even more importantly, the mental objects are representatives or replicas of so-called mathematical objects. This means they have properties and behave as the mathematical objects do. It is postulated that for an adequate understanding of a part of mathematics, the learner has to construct mentally the mental objects corresponding to the entities of the mathematics in such a way that a kind of isomorphism holds between those two realms. This is viewed to guarantee that the (mental) manipulation of the mental objects produces correct results. Other ways of expressing this model are in the discourse about mental representation of abstract objects (and the mathematical objects are of course abstract objects).

MENTAL OBJECTS SUPPORT UNDERSTANDING

The construction of mental objects/units/entities (also termed cognitive or conceptual ones) is considered a prerequisite for adequately understanding certain mathematical constructions, for instance, addition of functions or quotient structures in algebra and topology. Because those constructions can only be applied to object-like entities, to accomplish them mentally presupposes having constructed the respective mental objects. One must therefore have available a mental object corresponding to a function or to a vector space or to a group. The failure to understand those mathematical constructions is interpreted as being caused by a lack in the corresponding mental objects.

All that is in full congruence with the representational view of the mind. What we know is, according to this position, a sort of a mapping, a picture or a representation of something else, of something outside of the mind, the memory, or the cognition. The working of the mind then consists in manipulating those (mental) representations.

For being able to speak meaningfully and sensibly about mathematical objects of any kind one must have available mental objects as mental representations of those mathematical objects. Those mental objects are, as so-called internal representations, well discerned from the usual representations (as graphs, symbols, etc.), which are termed as being external.

A VERSION OF PLATONISM

In a way, one could call this theory of mental objects a psychological Platonism. If mathematical objects can't be granted an ontological existence and reality, then at the very least they should have a psychological existence and reality. And a prominent goal of teaching and learning mathematics is to guide the novice to construct mentally this psychological reality of mathematical objects, which later get represented as mental objects.

AN EXAMPLE: NATURAL NUMBERS

Let me be a bit more concrete by interpreting this general description by using some examples.

The first example is simple arithmetic of natural numbers. The theory of mental objects would stipulate the existence of mental entities that represent mentally numbers like 2, 3, 4, 5, and so on. At least, this is considered to be necessary for a deeper and adequate understanding of the operations with natural numbers, like 2 + 3, 4*5, and others. In arithmetic, those operations are no longer considered as being general descriptions of manipulations with discrete

468

sets or manifolds, so that 2 + 3 is a symbolic description of combining two units of a certain kind with three others of the same kind. In arithmetic the referents for the numerals are no longer specific discrete sets but (natural) numbers qualified as mathematical objects. And those have to be represented mentally by respective mental objects (constructed by the learner to understand arithmetic). Those mental objects must be able to reflect (isomorphically) the quality of the represented numbers; especially they have to lend themselves to be added or multiplied, to be even or odd or prime or complete, and so forth.

SOME SUBJECTIVE DOUBTS

I feel tempted to formulate some doubts in the ecological validity of the sketched approach to explain mathematical thinking. First, my subjective introspection never permitted me to find or trace something like a mental object for, say, the number 5. What invariantly comes to my mind are certain patterns of dots or other units, a pentagon, the symbol 5 or V, relations like $5 + 5 = 10$, $5*5 = 25$, sentences like five is prime, five is odd, $5/30$, other names for 5, and so on. But nowhere in my thinking I ever could find something object-like that behaved like the number 5 as a mathematical object does. Nevertheless, I deem myself being able to talk about this number, its properties, the relations and operations it takes part in, and I do add 5 and I multiply by 5 quite correctly. In other words, I have a huge amount of knowledge about the number "five" without having distinctly available for my thinking a mental object which I could designate as the mental object "5." Every (almost perhaps) property or relation regarding 5 I can express to myself and others in one way or another, such as by using conventional diagrams or formulas. But according to the common discourse these are just not to be equated with the number 5 itself but only are representations of it. In conclusion, I am constantly treating "five" as an object without having available either an abstract object outside my mind or a mental object inside it that could serve as that object. My knowledge about a (nonexisting?) object is enough to give rise to my feeling of being entitled to talk as if there were such an object. Yet, as my analysis shows, the object itself nowhere turns up; it is not needed, in fact. I can deduce its further properties from those that I already know by deductive reasoning. I can construct material objects ("representations") to exhibit by way of an adequate interpretation at least some of those properties and relationships that are characteristic of the postulated (abstract or mental) object.

MORE OBJECTIVE DOUBTS

Beyond my introspective experience with the number "5" there are other arguments that might question the adequacy of the theoretical discourse about mental objects or entities. For which natural numbers should I have a mental object available? Assuming that the mind has only finite capacity for whatsoever, it will possibly only contain finitely many mental objects. But give me any number as big as you want and I will treat it as an object: I can operate on it (halve it, double it, add it to another one, etc.), I can ascribe properties to it, put it into relations with other numbers, and so on.

This I can do even for a number that I have never thought of before. Or, take very large numbers, like 10^{100}. What could be a mental object representing that number beyond essentially a symbolic or verbal description (10 to the power 100)? But those symbols do not have any mathematical properties; for instance, 10^{100} is neither even nor odd in contrast to the number it is taken to stand for. A similar remark applies to all kinds of (external) representations. Whoever is not yet convinced should take $(10^{100})^{100}$ or the 1000th power of that. Still, by using the common representations we can talk and argue about all these numbers without having access to any kind of object that could be viewed as being the respective number (neither in our mind nor in the abstract realm whatever that might be).

REPRESENTATIONS ARE NOT MATHEMATICAL OBJECTS

Therefore none of the (external) representations can play the role of the intended mathematical object because no single one representation can be ascribed the totality of properties that the mathematical object is viewed to possess. This of course should be substantiated, but just take the various representations for numbers like 5. A point on the number line as such is neither even nor odd; a discrete set will not fit to the order relation. Essentially, all the mathematical properties are—in a Piagetian vein—only the result of our acting upon the so-called representations. Yet the mathematical objects and their mental replicas are stipulated to have the pertinent properties, which are then responsible for their "behavior." In a kind of linear causality those properties will force our thinking like physical properties of physical objects constrain our physical actions. That, of course, holds only provided the adequate mental objects have been constructed!

MORE EXAMPLES

Even worse is the situation with "objects" like $\mathcal{N}$, $\mathcal{Q}$, $\mathcal{Z}$, $\mathcal{R}$, or $\mathcal{C}$. They are infinite and thus cannot have a mental representation, a mental object sharing their constituting properties. But again, I do not have problems treating those sets as objects, for example, by applying certain operations to them or by speaking of the properties and relations to other "objects" (e.g., $\mathcal{N} \subset \mathfrak{X} \subset \mathfrak{Q}$, $\mathfrak{Q}$ is dense in $\mathfrak{R}$, $\mathfrak{C} = \mathfrak{R}^2$ with a specific multiplication, etc.). Of course, for those objects we do not even have a material representation. Any drawn number line by necessity is finite! Only in language and in discourse can we extend it infinitely. To be honest, I cannot imagine (create an image of) an infinite line! Thus, I do not have a mental object corresponding to an infinite line (or plane), and yet, I find it very sensible to talk about those things as objects.

What we do have is material models of a (very) local character that nevertheless are generic in the sense that they convey the general pattern or the general structure. Any finite part of the number line serves this purpose very well, at least if it is interpreted, viewed, and accepted as a local model (for $\mathcal{N}$, $\mathfrak{X}$, or $\mathfrak{R}$). Similarly, a small "window" into $\mathfrak{C}$ instantiated as the Gaussian plane can be used as a generic model for all of $\mathfrak{C}$.

NATURAL NUMBERS AS TYPES OF SETS

Let me return shortly to the natural numbers. One way of thinking of them could be the following. Processes of counting and of establishing one-to-one correspondences yield a kind of equivalence among (finite) sets. Equivalent (equipotent) sets behave identically under the process of counting when applied to them. This leads to the constitution of types of sets that are just the (small) natural numbers. This is a sort of procedure we find in many situations of everyday and scientific discourse. Equivalence there often reduces to similarity and classification. Think of classes of animals and plants or of types of colors. What for me appears to be a significant difference is that in the vernacular we very often use the same noun or word for the specific case (representative) and the type. For instance, "tree" can point in a deictic way to a given visible plant in my garden or I can use it when talking about trees being endangered by pollution, and similarly with animal names and many other general concepts and their names. This way reference is always made to prototypic instance of the type, and discourse about the type mostly is guided by knowledge about the representatives (either directly or mediated). Most importantly, nobody worries about a mental object corresponding to the type (e.g., of the "general tree"; also compare Lakoff, 1987).

Considering natural numbers as types of sets, we have nothing comparable. We do not say: That ***** is a five or a specific instance of five.

We do that in geometry when saying "this is a triangle" and "this is a rectangle, a cube," and so on. There are not many different fives or tens of which the number "five" could be then the type. I do not propose here to change linguistic habits but only want to point to possible sources for common difficulties. But why should we not designate ***** as a five (in German as "Fünf" where the capital letter explicitly expresses the status as a noun and an object)? We have names for other collections (considered as unities): population, class (in school), and so forth. These can have a generic or specific meaning as well. Similarly, as there are many trees, dogs, schools, and so on around us, in such a language there would then be many, many fives around us, of which the number five would be the common type. Therefore it would be the result of our descriminating and uniting what becomes a five (again as with trees, dogs, houses, etc.). In a way, possibly our language makes it difficult to find instantiations and representatives for five. It is nevertheless remarkable that one way of defining cardinal numbers (finite and infinite ones) in mathematics simulates just this procedure: A cardinal number is an equivalence class of equipotent sets.

A possibly German peculiarity in this context is that a coin of 5 or 10 Schilling is called a "Fünfer" or a "Zehner" respectively, and the same with paper money ("Hunderter," "Tausender"). These are nouns referring simultaneously to specific coins and their abstract value (i.e., the type with regard to a distinctive equivalence relation). Here we have a perfect match with the linguistic behavior in geometry (triangle corresponding to Fünfer).

GEOMETRY IS DIFFERENT

With geometric concepts we might have just the reverse problem. There we have the representatives in abundance and rather more often than not the students stick with them and miss the constitution of the respective types (e.g., the concept of "triangle" as the type of all possible triangles or triangular figures). In some sense geometry (of figures and solids) is closer to the vernacular discourse. One stays essentially with operating with the representatives, whereas in arithmetic the types (= numbers) are addressed directly and denoted symbolically. We have a specific symbol (3) for "three" but not for "triangle" (besides the word).

But the symbol "5" and even the word *five* never are understood to refer to instantiations of the type but only to the type, that is, to the "abstract number." In geometry, one mostly argues about the types (e.g., the "general triangle") by way of the concrete cases, and this—as is well known—poses problems for the novice who cannot realize the generality of the arguments. In arithmetic, all too often, the connection to the instantiations (i.e., the concrete sets) is cut off and one stays with the symbols themselves.

ANOTHER EXAMPLE: RATIONAL NUMBERS

Let us return to the question of mental objects and consider some more examples. Notorious are the problems with fractions and rational numbers. As with "5," I have great difficulties with conceiving of a mental object for, say, $\frac{2}{3}$. All kinds of things come to my mind when I see that symbol: part–whole relations, measurements, a point on the number line, many numerical relations (like $\frac{2}{3} =$

0.666. . .), that I can add it to other numbers or symbols or use it as an operator (for taking two thirds), and so forth. I have various so called representations for the number $\frac{2}{3}$, many different instantiations, situations where it gets materialized, but I can't get hold of either an abstract object or a mental object that could serve as the genuine number $\frac{2}{3}$. Thus $\frac{2}{3}$ to me appears rather as a fuzzy system of mutually connected and related situations, and actions (which commonly are termed applications of $\frac{2}{3}$) and of operations with $\frac{2}{3}$. That can't possibly be the mental object for $\frac{2}{3}$! This mental object would have to be of a much more refined and restricted quality, stripped of all these material images and intuitions and just reflecting what counts as the mathematical object $\frac{2}{3}$ (essentially viewed today as being a specific element of $\mathcal{Q}$ with its algebraic and topological structure). Of course here as well the arguments regarding infinity of $\mathcal{Q}$ and others apply as I have made them for the natural numbers. And again one could develop a view of rational numbers as types (of relations and operations), although here the situation is much more complex. It is these types that then can be taken or treated as operands for operations as addition and multiplication. Those operations on the types are compatible with the respective instantiated operations on the respective representatives of the types. This means: (type of $\frac{2}{3}$) $\otimes$ (type of $\frac{3}{5}$) = type of ($\frac{2}{3}$ + $\frac{3}{5}$) and similarly for multiplication. Thereby + is an appropriate instantiation of $\otimes$ (adding of an extensive measure). Thus, no mental object for the rational numbers is necessary to understand the mathematics of them. It appears that it is not the construction (by the way, another metaphor badly needing operative explication) of mental objects that enables me to manipulate comfortably rational numbers as mathematical objects. But for me, there is a decisive shift of my point of view, a deliberate decision and a change of attitude in the sense that I want to, and I make up my mind to, view and treat $\frac{2}{3}$, say, as a symbol for an object that I do not need to know but I only know how I want to handle it.

WHO MANIPULATES MENTAL OBJECTS?

It appears ridiculous to me to pursue a theory of the mind where the mind has or contains mental objects corresponding to the rational numbers. Then the mental objects for $\frac{2}{3}$ and $\frac{3}{5}$ would have to be combinable in ways corresponding to addition and multiplication in $\mathcal{Q}$. How can this be conceived of? Do the mental objects have a kind of extension (length, volume) to be added and, simultaneously, the quality of operators to be multiplied? Who operates on the mental objects? Doesn't that lead to the notorious problem of the homunculus in our head? Thus, even when not regarding the problems with the infinity of $\mathcal{Q}$, the metaphor of mental objects mentally simulating rational numbers and their operations leads to unsurmountable contradictions and inconsistencies. To repeat an earlier remark, I suspect that the theory of mental objects expresses a latent objectivist or Platonist desire to somewhere have existing well-determined objects as the referents of our discourse. Because of the exhibited numerous problems with that theory, I also cannot believe that construction of mental objects—whatever that means—is a precondition for successful mathematical activity.

A MORE ADVANCED EXAMPLE

Let me consider another example. It is argued that for a functional standing of operations on (real) functions (like derivative, intergral) and of spaces of functions [like C(I), L_2] it is necessary to have constructed functions as mental objects (or entities and the like), or to have encapsulated the mapping process, to have reified the process, and so forth. Again, this is the argument that for treating something as an object or for carrying out operations on it that in a common interpretation need objects as operands, one has to have at least mentally available adequate and appropriate objects. Those mental objects are (in theory) viewed to have the pertinent properties which then permit to manipulate and transform them accordingly. In a way in our mind, if trained adequately and extensively, there is to be a kind of imitation or isomorphic simulation of the mathematical processes and objects. Only then can we—it is assumed—genuinely understand the mathematics. What would this mean in our case of functions? Let us take the rather extreme example of L_2 (I), the Hilbert space of (classes of) quadratic Lebesgue-integrable functions on the interval I. Not regarding the infinity of L_2, one does not even have available a structural description of a generic member of L_2. There are various ways to define a limit process that when applied to functions in a certain space (like step functions or continuous functions) will by definition generate all members of L_2. But the latter can be very fuzzy and extremely irregular, which prevents any generic description. How ever then could we have mental objects for the members of L_2? I do not believe that any mathematician has something available that would deserve that name. Yet with relative ease one talks about the set of all those functions, of adding them, of their making up a vector space, of the integral as a linear mapping on that space, of the length or norm of a member of L_2, of the distance of two functions in L_2, and so on. And I repeat, all that is possible without having any kind of mental representation of L_2 and its members, which even appears to be impossible.

MENTAL OBJECTS AS REPLICAS?

Of course, the same argument applies to many (all?) other mathematical constructions that apparently have to be understandable without the support by any mental object or representation mirroring the mathematical structures and processes. To the very last, my arguments and deliberations should make it doubtful to pursue a strict theory of mental objects. Such a theory stipulates a kind of duplication of the mathematics in the sense that in our mind we have available and manipulate mental objects as replicas of the mathematical objects under study. Yet it appears we can get hold cognitively only of specific properties of those objects, but the objects (being abstract, mathematical, or mental) themselves elude our awareness or consciousness. But do we need the objects? All the mathematical reasoning and arguments are exclusively concerned with mathematical properties and relations that, as it is, are mostly formulated as being attached to objects. Proving that differentiability entails continuity, we only use those two properties, and the functions themselves do not occur in any essential way. I could even think of formulations that completely avoid the function concept in a reified form. Maybe it is rather a matter of convenient expression and communication that one uses a language with objects as carriers of the properties and relations. It surely is cumbersome to address properties directly.

It is also in this sense that the so-called (external) representations of mathematical concepts should be viewed not as representing any elusive objects but as material objects (e.g., diagrams, manipulatives) that can be treated as having specific properties. By our (physical or mental) operations on the material objects we present the mathematical properties and relations to ourselves.

AN ALTERNATIVE APPROACH

Having said all that, how then can one explain the well-known difficulties of pupils and students with understanding the talk about mathematical objects, with manipulating them correctly? My thesis, to be substantiated elsewhere, is that this is not a question of the construction of mental objects and the like but that there are involved more general psychological processes and states like those: taking a point of view and changing it, attitudes, beliefs, willingness to accept something, ascribing properties, hypothetical thinking, preparedness to assume that something is the case, imagination, conviction, focus of attention. Part of learning mathematics means to get socialized, to get persuaded that it is meaningful to talk the way mathematicians do, especially about mathematical objects. I think a great part of "understanding" of, say, a nonconstructive proof of the existence of some "object" (e.g., by using the tertium non datur for infinite sets) is not a cognitive question but one of attitude, belief, and so forth. One must accept the argument in a kind of decision (which is open to revision) and agreement and with a curiosity for the consequences of that decision. It is not that the intuitionist does not understand such a proof, but he does not accept it as meaningful!

Mathematics education therefore should be viewed not as a purely cognitive enterprise but as a process of socialization that should lead to appropriate systems of beliefs, attitudes, and convictions and of which students and teachers should become conscious and aware.

A final remark: I am aware that the understanding of mathematical discourse cannot be reduced to a set of beliefs and the like. The main goal of my arguments here was to doubt the sensibility of a theory of mental objects and related notions. In my view, it does not make sense to postulate mental replicas of mathematical objects as a basis for understanding and manipulating the latter ones. In a sequel to this chapter, I will discuss the role of various mechanisms in creating understanding and in the social process of mathematical socialization. Key terms there will be metaphor and metaphoric projection, imagistic thinking, and image schemata (cf., Johnson, 1987, and Lakoff, 1987 see also Dörfler, 1991). For instance, we use our experience with material objects for a metaphoric understanding and affective acceptance of the talk about mathematical objects. Other useful notions will be the concepts of prototype and protocol as used in Dörfler, 1989a and 1989b.

REFERENCES

Dörfler, W. (1989a). Prototypen und Protokolle als kognitive Mittel gegen Bedeutungslosigkeit und Entfremdung im Mathematikunterricht. In *Zukunft des Mathematikunterrichts*, Landesinstitut für Schule und Weiterbildung, Soest, pp. 102–109.

Dörfler, W. (1989b). Protocols of actions as a cognitive tool for knowledge construction. In *Proceedings of the 12th Conference of the International Group for Psychology of Mathematics Education*, Paris, pp. 212–219.

Dörfler, W. (1991). Meaning: Image schemata and protocols. In *Proceedings of the 15th Conference of the International Group for Psychology of Mathematics Education*, Assisi, Vol. I, pp. 17–32.

Dörfler, W. (1995, September). *Means for meaning*. Paper presented at the Conference "Symbolizing, Communication and Mathematizing," Nashville, TN.

Johnson, M. (1987). *The body in the mind*. Chicago: The University of Chicago Press.

Lakoff, G. (1987). *Women, fire and dangerous things*. Chicago: The University of Chicago Press.

27 On the Nature of a Model of Mathematical Learning

Leslie P. Steffe
Heide G. Wiegel
University of Georgia

In mathematics education, we often take for granted that students can and do learn mathematics. But it is quite difficult to specify an account of this process of learning, an account detailed enough for a teacher to recognize particular types of mathematics learning and general enough to provide an orientation for action in future teaching situations. We need a general model of learning and particular models of mathematics learning (von Glasersfeld & Steffe, 1991). Each particular model constitutes a major achievement on the part of the model builder, and we make no pretense to offer such models in this chapter. Our goal is more modest. We focus our comments on the nature of a particular model of mathematics learning: its relation to theory, its constitutive elements, its relation to mathematics teaching, and how it might be built.

Several of the preceding chapters are of a general nature and depict certain world views either explicitly or implicitly (e.g., Goldin & Kaput, chapter 23; Hatano, chapter 12; Marton & Neuman, chapter 19; van Oers, chapter 7; Vergnaud, chapter 13; Voigt, chapter 2; von Glasersfeld, chapter 18). One might say that these chapters have to do with basic theoretical principles that underpin general as well as specific models of mathematical learning. In fact, these authors explicate, in part, what Lakatos (1970) has called hard-core principles of scientific research programs, principles that could be used in building models of mathematical learning. This distinction between a model and theoretical principles used in building the model is not an idle one and goes to the heart of some very old problems in mathematics education.

THE ROLE OF THEORIES IN MODEL BUILDING

Mathematics educators traditionally have borrowed theories from outside of mathematics education to help them understand what they are doing. In the 29th yearbook of the National Society for the Study of Education, for example, F. B. Knight (1930, pp. 145–267) gave an extended treatment of teaching methods based on Thorndike's (1924) theory of connectionism. In more than one-fourth of his chapter, Knight focused on Thorndike's law of exercise as he discussed the drill of basic facts. Wheeler (1935), 5 years later, outlined 12 main principles of Gestalt psychology and, on that basis, provided hints to mathematics teachers. Buswell (1951), writing 16 years later than Wheeler, discussed the influence of association theory and field theory on the teaching of arithmetic. His efforts proved significant inasmuch as meaning theory, a theory compatible with field theory, became influential for the teaching of arithmetic in the 1950s and 1960s (Brownell, 1935; Grossnickle, Brueckner, & Reckzeh, 1968; Van Engen, 1953).

The attitude of mathematics educators seemed to be that theories such as connectionism, Gestalt psychology, or field theory could be applied as extant theories to the practice of mathematics education. In making these applications, they sometimes interpreted the theories in ways that seemed to change the meaning of basic principles. For example, Buswell (1951) pointed out that in applying Thorndike's (1924) connectionism to the theory of arithmetic, "many students did not read Thorndike with . . . care. They read his law of exercise and they read his statements regarding the nature of 'bonds.' They then provided the drills that they thought necessary to 'fix' these bonds . . . for example, Knight's emphasis on mixed drills did not lead to an appreciation of the systematic relationships among number facts" (Buswell, 1951, p. 145). From Buswell's point of view, Knight's emphasis on mixed drills distorted Thorndike's theory. In Buswell's critique of Knight, however, there seemed to be little appreciation that the user of a theory may have purposes outside of the scope of the theory. Moreover, there seemed to be little appreciation that Knight's interpretation of Thorndike's principles would be eventually enacted by teachers, and that such enactments might constitute meaning of mathematical learning not to be found in the theory. Neither Buswell nor other mathematics educators at the time seemed to acknowledge that specific models of mathematics learning are necessary and that the models do not constitute a direct application of a theory.

Conversely, the application of a learning theory like connectionism to the practice of mathematics education can easily distort the experiences and meanings of mathematical learning. This is exactly what happened, according to Buswell (1951), in the case of Wheeler's (1935) application of Gestalt psychology to mathematics education. In our opinion, it also happened in Thorndike's application of his own theory to the learning of arithmetic and algebra. What has been historically ignored by mathematics educators is that the principles of a theory should not be applied naively. Instead, as agents of application, mathe-

478

matics educators should apply the principles of a theory first and foremost to themselves as they engage in the process of application. Theory enters the process of building specific models via self-reflexivity.

Self-Reflexivity in Model Building

As we attempt to build a specific model of mathematical learning within the framework of a theory, the principle of self-reflexivity implies that we apply the principles and constructs of the theory to ourselves in the process of model-building (Steier, 1995). It would be inconsistent to turn to principles or to a language other than the principles and language of the theory one is trying to use. For example, a Gestalt psychologist would hardly use the principles of connectionism to explain how he or she learned to build a model of learning that emphasized Gestalt principles. To illustrate the function of self-reflexivity in the model-building process, we appeal to the chapters by van Oers and by Voigt.

The Vygotskian Approach.   Van Oers (chapter 7, this volume) sees mathematics education predominantly as a process of enculturation. Within this process of enculturation, he distinguishes between cultural and personal meanings and describes mathematics learning as a "process of making sense of mathematics as it is brought to us by cultural history." Van Oers explores the question of meaningful mathematical learning within the context of Vygotskian principles and action-psychological theory.

If we are sensitive to the principle of self-reflexivity we need to ask whether it is sufficient to simply appeal to the writings of such important authors as Vygotsky, Leont'ev, and Davydov as well as to cultural meanings of mathematics in order to account for a process of making sense of mathematics learning. Or might it be necessary for the model builder to learn for him- or herself how students learn mathematics? That is, what does it mean for a model builder to apply the constructs of action-psychological theory to him- or herself in the process of building a specific model of mathematics learning?

In action-psychological theory, action and the qualitative change of action are two central constructs. Action is defined as "an attempt to change some (material or mental) object from its initial form into another form" (van Oers, chapter 7, this volume), and a qualitative change of such action constitutes learning within the enculturational process. In the model-building process, the mental object subject to change is one's concept of activity theory. The model builder can start with activity theory, but the theory cannot possibly account for mathematical experience nor the experience of learning mathematics without there being specific meanings established for principles of the theory. These particular meanings not only deepen the model builders understanding of the theory. They also stand to modify the theoretical principle of action.

The action subject to change is how the model builder uses activity theory in building specific models of mathematical learning. As one uses the theory, the meanings of the principles change, and as the meanings of the principles change, the model builder's use of the theory changes. Neither theories nor models are static, unchanging entities.

The significance of self-reflexivity can be more deeply appreciated if we consider how van Oers views students' mathematical knowledge in relation to mathematicians' mathematical knowledge. For van Oers, "real mathematics" is the "historical developing pursuit of making sense of the quantitative and relational aspects of our physical and cultural world." Van Oers takes this historical account, together with his observations of what mathematicians do when they carry out a mathematical activity, as "a normative basis for instructional practice in the domain of mathematics education." In van Oers' picture of mathematics education, the teacher seems to personify the mathematician, and the mathematical practice of the teacher seems to embody the cultural practice of mathematics. According to van Oers, the cultural practice of mathematics "can be transformed into curriculum content and, as such, it can be taught." Personal meanings students may attach to the "actions, rules, methods, and values as provided by a school subject" are a constitutive part of this normative basis for instructional practice in mathematics education. These personal meanings, however, are left unspecified.

Van Oers' neglect to account for the personal meaning of the learner is evident in his analogy of a child learning to ride a bicycle. Apart from the child's initial desire to learn riding the bicycle, van Oers does not offer an account of the child's personal meaning of bicycle riding. The interpretation of the child's attempts as initial imitation of a cultural activity and as gradual interiorization of "all the functions it could not perform initially" is solely in terms of the observer's concepts. The child is essentially treated as an instructable system (Maturana, 1978):

> If the state a system adopts as a result of an interaction were specified by the properties of the entity with which it interacts, then the interaction would be an instructive interaction. Systems that undergo instructive interactions cannot be analyzed by a scientific procedure. In fact, all instructable systems would adopt the same state under the same perturbations and would necessarily be indistinguishable to a standard observer. (p. 34)

Only if we specify the personal meaning of the child will we see the child as a self-organizing being rather than an instructable system. That is, a model of mathematical learning has to account for and explain how personal meaning "is built up by involvement in an educative relationship" (reference by van Oers to Leont'ev). Van Oers does not provide a model of the students' personal meanings of mathematics nor of the process of interiorization of mathematical processes. It is here that self-reflexivity becomes the most relevant. The general view of learning as qualitative change in action would seem to orient the theoretician to examine his or her own personal knowledge of students' personal meanings of mathematics and of the process whereby he or she, the theoretician, interiorizes the mathematical functions as practiced by students.

Symbolic Interactionism. Voigt (chapter 2, this volume) makes a distinction between the individual's sense-making processes and the interaction process:

> An interactionist approach is preferred [over a Vygotskian approach] because it emphasizes the individual's sense making processes as well as the interaction process. It does not deduce the individual's learning from the social interaction as suggested by theories of socialization and of internalization. From the interactionist point of view, social interaction does not function as a vehicle that transforms "objective" knowledge into subjective knowledge.

In our interpretation, Voigt's emphasis on the individual sense-making process as distinct from the interaction process indicates that self-reflexivity should be a basic principle of symbolic interactionism. Voigt, however, does not explicitly refer to self-reflexivity as part of symbolic interactionism. In the following we elaborate what the principle of self-reflexivity might mean for the model-building process within the interactionist framework. We first address the individual sense-making process.

The principle of self-reflexivity suggests that Voigt, in his attempt to make sense of the students' individual sense-making processes, would also turn his attention to his own sense-making processes. We argue that if it was his goal to develop personal meaning for mathematical learning as well as to build models of the microculture of a classroom, Voigt would naturally construe himself as a participant in interactive mathematical communication with his students and would try to build a living model of mathematical learning within his framework. We base our argument on his comment that "symbolic interactionism views meaning . . . as arising in the process of interaction between people. The meaning of a thing grows out of the ways in which other persons act toward the person with regard to the thing." Thus, although individual meaning is distinct from the process of interaction, it does arise out of interaction. Consequently, the researcher's meaning of students' mathematical learning should arise in the process of interaction among people, that is, between the researcher and his or her students.

We argue that building meaning of mathematical learning implies participation in that learning rather than purely observation. The claim becomes plausible if we compare building a model of mathematics learning with building a model of learning martial arts. In order to develop a model of learning martial arts, one might consider it sufficient to observe a martial arts instructor attempting to teach his art form to novices. However, learning to teach novices is every bit as complicated and involved as learning martial arts for oneself. And this is where self-reflexivity enters. The researcher needs to learn how novices learn, and this learning is similar to the way novices learn—through social interaction. Anyone who has tried to learn martial arts understands that it cannot be learned through observation alone. One has to be an actor as well as an observer and engage in extensive experience produced through interacting with others.

Teaching martial arts involves more than knowing martial arts because teaching is centered on learning those patterns of interaction that yield predictable modifications in the students' art forms. In this, it is essential that the instructor learns the students' art forms. The instructor must learn to move in a way that is in harmony with the movements of the students so he or she will understand how to help the students modify their art forms. It is the students' art forms and the students' modification of those art forms that are of primary concern to the instructor.

Being involved as a participant in the interaction is as important for building a particular model of mathematical learning as it is for building a model of learning martial arts. Learning how students learn is the responsibility of the researcher, and the process of learning is set in motion by interacting with students regardless of whether the researcher focuses on changes in taken-as-shared meanings within a classroom or on individual meanings. In either case, models of learning mathematics are unavoidably a function of the teacher's actions. Without teaching, the researcher is not involved in producing the interactive communication with students that is critical in bringing forth particular meanings of the students nor in sustaining and modifying those meanings. Learning is a living activity and must be experienced to be understood. The researcher needs to be a teacher as well as a model builder (Cobb & Steffe, 1983).

The necessity to base model building on self-reflexivity and thus build living models of mathematics learning is further highlighted by von Glasersfeld (chapter 18, this volume): "This [i.e., the knower's] experiential world is constituted and structured by the knower's own ways and means of perceiving and conceiving, and in this elementary sense it is always and irrevocably subjective (i.e., construed by the cognizing subject)." It seems legitimate to substitute "teacher" for "knower." With that substitution and the understanding that the teacher's experiential world concerns the language and actions of students, von Glasersfeld's comment further clarifies why we consider the experience of the theoretician to be critical for building models of learning of any kind. Theoreticians cannot replace the process of becoming aware—through observation of their interaction—of how their own meanings change as result of interacting with students.

We now turn to the role of self-reflexivity in the analysis of the interactional processes. In commenting on Voigt's chapter, Cobb et al. (chapter 1, this volume) remarked that "an interactional analysis is made from the outside, from the point of view of an observer rather than that of a participant in the interaction." Cobb's comment does not necessarily imply that the researcher, in the role of an outside observer, has to be self-reflexive. We argue, however, that self-reflexivity neoooonrily enters the observation process.

We believe both Voigt and Cobb would agree that observing is a form of interacting in which the operations of the researcher are unavoidably involved. For example, in his interpretation of how students find what must be added to 46 to make 73, Voigt introduces the concepts of abstract composite units and figurative objects. These two concepts—abstract composite units and figurative objects—are concepts the observer attributes to the interaction. Although there is no need for the observer to consider such concepts to be cognitive elements of the students, they are cognitive elements of the observer. Essentially, we agree with Thompson's (1995) rejection of social cognition as an entity separate from an observer: "One notion that I resist strongly is the notion of 'social cognition'— that somehow knowledge, as a socially constructed object, is 'out there,' in between the individuals interacting socially. It is only in the mind of an observer that socially constructed knowledge is 'out there' (Maturana, 1987), and it is 'out there' only as a consensual domain" (p. 128). In contrast, Voigt (chapter 2, this volume) asserts that "from the observer's point of view, the meaning of 'taken-to-be-shared' is not a partial match of individuals' constructions, nor is it a cognitive element. Instead, it exists at the level of interaction."

Taken-to-be-shared meanings apparently are what an observer, who is not a participant in an interaction, makes of the interaction. The claim that these taken-to-be-shared meanings are not cognitive elements seems to be a claim of a first-order observer observing interactive mathematical communication. Such an observer remains essentially unaware of his own processes of observing and of his own interpretations of the interaction. In this, we find it useful to make a distinction between a first-order and a second-order observer (Maturana, 1978). The second-order observer observes the occasions of observing of the first-order observer. It is the second-order observer who is aware of the first-order observer contributing his or her own mathematical concepts and operations to the observations. The first-order observer assimilates the students' language and actions using his or her own concepts and operations and regards the students' language and actions to be taken as shared. The second-order observer includes the first-order observer's circumstances of observing and becomes aware that taken-as-shared meanings are observer abstractions. If the first- and second-order observer are the same individual, then the distinction of the two levels of observing is equivalent to self-reflexivity.

First- and Second-Order Models

In what sense then should social interaction be part of a model of mathematics learning? That is, in what sense should students' mathematics, including changes in that mathematics, be regarded as social? Dörfler's (chapter 26, this volume) view of mathematical meaning of rational numbers opens up the possibility of understanding mathematics learning in both cognitive and social terms.

> As with "5," I have great difficulties conceiving of a mental object for, say, $\frac{2}{3}$. . . . I have various so called representations for the number $\frac{2}{3}$, many different instantiations, situations where it gets materialized, but I can't get hold of either an abstract object nor a mental object which could serve as the genuine number $\frac{2}{3}$ . . . . It seems ridiculous to me to pursue a theory of the mind where the mind has or contains mental objects corresponding to the rational numbers.

In contrast, in Vergnaud's (chapter 13, this volume) representationist theory, mathematical meaning seems basically cognitive: "Knowledge is knowledge, even if it is implicit. And mathematics is mathematics. Therefore the concepts of scheme, theorem-in-action, and concept-in-action are essential to the theory of conceptual fields, which is a theory of representation and cognitive development." Vergnaud makes a further distinction between psychological and mathematical concepts and correspondingly regards mathematics as a given conceptual tool to analyze the cognitive processes and competencies of students. This distinction introduces a dualism between the psychological subject and the mathematical object avoided in Dörfler's nonrepresentational meaning theory.

Marton and Neuman (chapter 19, this volume) also avoid this dualism: "According to the nondualistic ontological position held by phenomenography, object and subject are not separate, but the subject's experience of the object is a relation between the two." Marton and Neuman, however, do not address the problem of the social relations involved in mathematical meaning introduced by Voigt and by van Oers.

To consider social relations, we believe it helps to make a distinction between first- and second-order models. A first-order model concerns "the hypothetical models the observed subject constructs to order, comprehend, and control his or her experience (i.e., the subject's knowledge)" (Steffe, von Glasersfeld, Richards, & Cobb, 1983, p. xvi). Second-order models are the "the hypothetical models observers may construct of the subject's knowledge in order to explain their observations (i.e., their experience) of the subject's states and activities" (Steffe et al., 1983, p. xvi). First-order models pertain, for example, to a student's mathematical knowledge or to the knowledge of a theorist or a teacher who is involved in interactive mathematical communication with students. Second-order models might concern a theorist's or a teacher's knowledge of student's mathematical knowledge, or vice versa, and are necessarily constructed through social interaction. One can legitimately say that they are coconstructed by the observer and the observed. They constitute the primary knowledge of concern in education and could be regarded as what is taken as shared if the constraint that they are purely social is relaxed.

Building a model of mathematical learning involves formulating second-order models of the mathematics of students. The relationship between the students' mathematics—their first-order models are not directly accessible—to the second-order models of the observer is similar to the relationship between cause and effect as described by Hume (1748/1988): "Every effect is a distinct event from its cause. It could not, therefore, be discovered in the cause, and the first invention or conception of it, a priori, must be entirely arbitrary. And even after it is suggested, the conjunction of it with the cause must appear equally arbitrary; since there are always many other effects, which, to reason, must seem fully as consistent and natural" (p. 75).

Similar to Hume's view of the effect being an event distinct from its cause, a second-order model cannot be said to be caused by the students' mathematics. Although the observer constructs a second-order model within the constraints experienced through interacting with students, whatever second-order model is constructed emerges out of the observer's own conceptual elements.

There is a dynamic relationship between first- and second-order models, but it is easy to conflate them in our analyses. For example, does a theoretician who knows ordinal number theory simply give up certain aspects of that theory and form a simplified version in order to understand children's mathematical knowledge? Or does the theoretician use his or her knowledge in living interaction with children and perhaps construct concepts and operations not considered to be a part of ordinal number theory? Ordinal number theory can be orienting when working with children, but we do not regard it as explanatory. In fact, the language of ordinal number theory can be misleading when talking about the numerical knowledge of children. For example, a set of elements arranged in order is a basic element in ordinal number theory. Although children establish composite units and later use these composite units in further operating, they do not constitute the composite units as ordered sets in the sense of ordinal number theory. An observer might regard the composite units as early forms of ordered sets, but to call them ordered sets would be a serious conflation of the observer's knowledge and the student's knowledge. We need to develop new languages and appropriate conceptual constructs in order to form the second-order models that constitute the mathematics of our students. There is no simple transformation of the mathematical knowledge of the adult that can be used in understanding the mathematics of students, and vice versa.

MENTAL OPERATIONS, SCHEMES, AND REPRESENTATION

Dörfler's rejection of the idea of mental objects corresponding to mathematical objects raises the question of what theoretical constructs might be used to formulate models of mathematics learning. Like Vergnaud (chapter 13, this volume), we believe that we need theoretical constructs such as Piaget's ideas of mental operation and scheme to build second-order models of the mathematics of students.

Mental Operations and Schemes

Mental operations form strong connecting links between Soviet activity theory and constructivist approaches. Wertsch (1979) made the following comment in his introduction to Leont'ev's article on the problem of activity in psychology: "According to them [Leont'ev and his fellow researchers], neither the external world nor the human organism are solely responsible for developing knowledge about the world. They argue that the key to the process is the activity in which the human agent engages. This is why the notion of activity has come to play such a central explanatory role in Soviet psychology" (p. 38).

When contrasted with Piaget's (1980b) hypothesis that "the origin of logico-mathematical structures . . . cannot be localized in either the objects or in the subject" (p. 26), we see a fundamental compatibility—but not identity—emerge. The compatibility becomes especially strong when we consider the assumption of the neo-Piagetian's that any knowledge that involves carrying out actions or operations cannot be instilled ready-made into students but must, quite literally, be actively built up. A major difference occurs, however, in the use of the term "operation." Crawford (chapter 9, this volume), for example, refers to Leont'ev's (1979) distinction between action and operation: "The difference between actions and operations emerges . . . in the case of actions involving tools . . . . For example, one can physically dismember a material object with the help of a variety of tools, each of which defines a method (an operation) for carrying out the given action (the dismemberment)" (p. 63). Thompson (chapter 15, this volume), following Piaget, would not call a sensorimotor activity like sawing an operation unless it had been reconstituted by the acting individual as an interiorized activity; that is, as an activity that could be carried out in thought as well as materially. "An operation is an action that can be internalized [in our terminology, interiorized]; that is, it can be carried out in thought as well as executed materially" (Piaget, 1970, p. 21).

Of course, in the context of the citation from *Genetic Epistemology*, Piaget was concerned with logico-mathematical operations rather than with material actions. Whether an action is an enactment of an interiorized operation or whether it is activated only in a particular situation is an essential difference, but it is not the primary difference between the two notions of operation. For us, the essential difference is that in Piagetian theory, operations are part of a system of operations that is goal directed, whereas in Soviet activity theory, operations are a means of carrying out an action. It is the action which is goal directed, not the operations. Operations in Soviet activity theory would be understood in Piagetian theory as the activity of a scheme. Actions, if interiorized, would be understood as the assimilating operations of the scheme.

Logico-mathematical operations are the essential operations we are concerned with as we attempt to formulate a model of mathematical learning. Alone, however, they are not sufficient to build a model of mathematical learning Among other things, we also need to consider representation.

Representation

Many accounts of knowledge representation are misleading because they are based on the assumption that concepts are things—mental objects—"out there" to be represented. Instead, like Dörfler (chapter 26, this volume), we regard mathematical concepts as mental acts or operations, and it is these operations that are represented. We believe that representational elements are constructed as part of the construction of the concept. These basic representational elements are subject to modification and elaboration in that they may become associated with, or a constitutive part of, other representational elements. Image and externalization are two basic aspects in the construction and elaboration of representational elements.

The Concept of Image.   Starting from the Piagetian notion of mental imagery in children (Piaget & Inhelder, 1971), Thompson (chapter 15, this volume) paints a picture of representational elements that involves the representing agent: "By image I mean much more than a mental picture. Rather, I have in mind an image as being constituted by experiential fragments from kinesthesis, proprioception, smell, touch, taste, or hearing." In his study of children's concepts of speed and acceleration, Thompson was interested in the students'—not the mathematician's—images of speed and acceleration. Nevertheless, when Thompson writes about the role of imagery in students' concepts of speed and acceleration, he is writing of how he made sense of what he observed in his interactions with students. The concepts of mental operation and mental image were given meaning in the context of working with the students and were imputed to the students in order to explain their mathematical reasoning. These meanings were Thompson's meanings, not those of his students. All Thompson or anyone else can do when building second-order models is attempt to imagine what the intentions, goals, and mathematical operations and images of students might be like. But there must be very good reasons for imputing certain mental operations or certain mental images to students. The theoretician does not operate fancifully nor capriciously, but from a knowledge of students that is earned through interacting with them over long periods of time.

The Concept of Externalization.   To highlight differences in starting points, we contrast Thompson's understanding of mental image with the idea of representation in the chapter by Goldin and Kaput (chapter 23, this volume). Goldin and Kaput refer to the subjectivity of experience in both of their ideas of internal and external representation systems: "We use the term *internal representation* not to refer to the direct object of introspective activity, but as a construct arrived at by an observer . . . . In contrast . . . , we use the term *external representation* to refer to physically embodied, observable configurations such as words, graphs, pictures, equations, or computer microworlds. These are in principle accessible to observation by anyone with suitable knowledge." The subjectivity of experience with respect to external representations is captured in the phrase "anyone with suitable knowledge." What then, does suitable knowledge mean and how is that knowledge built? How does the knower, in the words of Goldin and Kaput, construct an inside and an outside—internal representational elements, thoughts, and feelings—distinct from external representational elements?

Building on Dörfler's nonrepresentationist view of mathematical meaning, we argue that externalization of mental operations is fundamentally involved in constructing external representational elements. Mental operations are externalized only to the extent that the figurative material on which they operate can be regenerated in the absence of actual sensory material. For example, to claim that one has constructed "$y + 3x - 6 = 0$" as an external representational element means that the mental operations involved in constructing the equation can be used in a generation or regeneration of an image of the equation. In this way, our concept of external representational elements is similar to our more general concept of external objects: An object is external when a knower can regenerate an image of it in the absence of actual sensory material.

The Concept of Symbols.   A claim of having constructed "$y + 3x - 6 = 0$" as a symbol means more than externalizing the operations used to give it meaning. In our formulation of mathematical symbolization, we look to von Glasersfeld's (1991) idea of using a word as a symbol, "A word is a symbol when it brings forth in the user an abstracted generalized re-presentation, not merely a response to a particular situation" (p. 52). So, if the notation "$y + 3x - 6 = 0$" functions in place of representational elements that may be brought forth, the notation would constitute algebraic symbolism. For example, if the interiorized mental operations involved in the construction of a concept of rate of change are included in the representational elements indicated by "$y + 3x - 6 = 0$," the notation would constitute algebraic symbolism. Notation does not have a structure of its own. As Goldin and Kaput point out, it is the individual who constitutes the notational elements as symbols.

The question of what constitutes meaning of conventional notation is informed by what von Glasersfeld (1980) regarded as the basis for a constructivist theory of cognition: "Knowledge is no longer a true or false representation of reality but simply the schemes of action and the schemes of operating that are functioning reliably and effectively" (p. 83). The idea of a scheme provides us with a conceptual construct to model students' mathematical knowledge, and it isn't until we have constructed such schemes can we legitimately claim to understand the students' representational structures. Whether or under what conditions one can impute the observer's representation system along with its structure to students is a matter of great practical and theoretical importance.

Because the mathematical concepts we experience as external and distinct from our own are the mathematical concepts of other people, we have to account for the role of the researcher's sophisticated mathematical knowledge in building models of mathematical learning. Not unlike Vergnaud (chapter 13, this volume), we regard such mathematical knowledge as orienting in our analyses of students' mathematical knowledge. The researcher's mathematical knowledge is centrally involved in interacting with students and in forming images of what the students' mathematics might be or become. Acting in ways that avoid unjustifiably attributing ones own ways and means of operating to students, however, is not always easy. Although Dörfler's nonrepresentationist view of meaning orients one to work self-reflexively and to engage in a conceptual analysis of one's own mathematical knowledge, it does not indicate how one might do such a conceptual analysis nor does it indicate how one might do a conceptual analysis of the mathematics of students. Like von Glasersfeld, we believe that the task of analyzing the basic conceptual steps in the construction of mathematics has barely begun.

INTERACTION AND LEARNING

In introducing the researcher's knowledge of students' mathematical learning as second-order models, we tried to avoid the impression that these models are intended to represent the knowledge of students as if their knowledge was knowable independently of the model builder. We also tried to convey a sense of our view of students as rational, self-organizing beings who have mathematical knowledge of their own. Our view is compatible with Marton and Neuman's (chapter 19, this volume) discussion of learning in children's informal methods of dividing: "The interview situation becomes a learning situation for him, causing a change in the structure of his consciousness of division." In this quotation, Marton and Neuman distinguish between the child's activity of learning and the child's informal methods of dividing. This distinction is compatible with two types of interaction in constructivism, (a) the basic sequence of action and perturbation, and (b), the interaction of constructs in representation or other operations (von Glasersfeld, personal communication). The basic sequence of action and perturbation can be translated into individual-environment interaction if perturbation is not understood as the transferal of information from an environment to the individual. The interaction of constructs in re-presentation or other operations refers to interaction within the individual perhaps, but not necessarily, in the absence of sensory material.

Individual-environment interactions are in the province of empirical abstraction (von Glasersfeld, 1991) because "information is drawn directly from external objects" (Piaget, 1980a, p. 89). Whatever is "out there" (from the observer's point of view) must be assimilated by the individual. "In order to derive information from an object . . . the use of an assimilatory apparatus is indispensable" (p. 90). An assimilatory apparatus for Piaget was endogenic: "We understand by 'endogenous' only those structures which are developed by means of the regulations and operations of the subject . . . . By serving as an assimilatory framework, then, these structures are added to the properties of the external object, but without being extracted from it" (p. 80).

We can now begin to understand mathematics as a contribution of the individual without regarding it as being innate. Piaget postulated a constant interaction between endogenic and exogenic processes, with a gradual replacement of the latter by the former. In this interaction, empirical abstraction never comes into play without there being prior reflective abstractions, and reciprocally, the products of empirical abstraction are always involved in reflective abstraction.

The Concept of Construction

Constructing is based on interaction of endogenic and exogenic processes. In what follows, we distinguish between two general kinds of constructing—assimilation and accommodation.

Assimilation as Construction.   Assimilation, "the integration of any sort of reality into a structure" (Piaget, 1964, p. 18), is based on subject–environment interaction, and items produced by assimilation are constructed items. In von Foerster's (1984) terms, one could even say that such items are invented by the interacting individual. This way of speaking may seem to be inappropriate for an individual who might insist that reality is not a function of the perceiving individual. For a hearing-impaired individual, however, an auditory item may not be constructed even though an observing individual may very well insist that the item "exists" in the auditory field of the individual.

The view of assimilation as based on subject–environment interaction helps to understand assimilation as a fundamental relation of learning: "It is this assimilation which seems to me fundamental in learning, and which seems to me the fundamental relation from the point of view of pedagogical or didactic applications" (Piaget, 1964, p. 18). Note that Piaget called assimilation a relation, which fits well with Marton and Neuman's (chapter 19, this volume) understanding of experience: "The word experience (conception, understanding, perception, apprehension, etc.) is thus used in phenomenography in the sense of being a relation between subject and object, as 'something seen in some way by someone.'" Although Marton and Neuman understand the experience of an observer's object as not being homogeneous across subjects, they describe these differences as they see them rather than explain them in terms of the operations of the subjects. They do not account for the operations that produce relations between the subject and object; they leave out the organism and its structures.

We find Marton and Neuman's notion of experience to be clarified by Piaget's concept of assimilation in another fundamental way. In our view, Piaget did not limit assimilation to any one type of sensory object. Rather, assimilation concerns the integration of any sort of reality into a structure. We interpret the phrase "any sort of reality" as being the observer's reality. Assimilation is based on the subject's sensory signals produced in any sensory channel, especially the auditory, kinesthetic, tactile, and visual channels.

Accommodation as Constructing.   Without assimilation, there would be no constructing. Assimilation, however, does not completely account for constructing. This limitation of assimilation was expressed in a comment made by Konold and Johnson (1991): "If an individual's current set of schemata were always successful in organizing its perceptions to bring about a desired state, there would be no further cognitive development" (p. 8). Accommodation, which we regard as a modification of a conceptual structure in response to a perturbation, is necessary for cognitive development to occur. Perturbation is often interpreted as a synonym for cognitive conflict, which influences how researchers envision teacher interactions in learning situations (Booker, chapter 22, this volume; Janvier, chapter 25, this volume). In contrast, we regard perturbation as referring to any disturbance in the components of an interacting system created through the functioning of the system. A perturbing element can activate or disequilibrate a system at rest or a system in a dynamic equilibrium. For example, if we speak with each other with the intention of carrying out a conversation, the auditory signals activate sound images (de Saussure, 1959) used to recognize words in the flow of auditory signals. This activation constitutes a disturbance in whatever constitutes our auditory records. In this, we can see that perturbation is not identical to cognitive conflict. But it can include cognitive conflict.

If we cast learning as accommodation we acknowledge the learner as a self-organizing being and bring self-regulation into our concept of the learner. The concept of accommodation is powerful enough to explain the modifications that might occur in self-organizing systems as they interact in and with their environments. It can be used in explaining such ideas as negotiated meanings and taken-as-shared meanings, and it can be used to account for the reorganizations involved when an individual solves a problem. Accommodation is more inclusive than problem solving because it accounts for qualitative changes in mental or physical actions, operations, images, and schemes. In fact, accommodation can be used to account for the production of concepts and operations of all kinds. As a result, any model of learning must contain specification of the processes involved in specific accommodations and their products.

Janvier's (chapter 25, this volume) position that "any learning whatsoever, is bound to be constructivist in the philosophical sense of the word" fits our conception of learning as accommodation. Janvier's position is sweeping and needs to be substantiated. Substantiating it involves reformulating learning as it is conceived of in nonconstructivist paradigms in terms of accommodation. Although this is an extensive program of investigation, we believe it is a plausible program because it is possible to reformulate Hume's (1748/1988) principle of association by contiguity.

Association as Constructing.   Guthrie (1942) stated the principle of association by contiguity as follows: "A stimulus pattern that is acting at the time of a response will, if it recurs, tend to produce that response" (p. 23). Hilgard's (1956) comments on the principle of association point to its fundamental and far-reaching importance: "There is an elegant simplicity about the statement . . . . This one principle serves as the basis for a very ingenious and intriguing theory of learning" (p. 53).

If we reformulate the law of association by contiguity, we need to explain first the mental operations involved in the simplest form of an association, the association between two contiguous perceptual items. An association by contiguity occurs when the perceiving individual takes a pair of items together. Shifting the focus of attention back and forth between the items is an elemental act of taking together. While shifting the focus of attention back and forth, the perceiving individual may hold the items still by focusing attention on both items while maintaining a distinction. This taking together is an act of reflective abstraction because the items are experientially united into an experiential composite whole.

In our attempt to reformulate Guthrie's law of association by contiguity, we have to assume that the results of the experiential uniting operation are recorded or registered, forming what von Glasersfeld (1991) has called a recognition template. This recognition template contains records of the pair of perceptual items. If, on some future occasion, the perceiving individual recognizes a perceptual item—the stimulus from the observer's point of view—the whole recognition template would be activated as well as the records of the stimulus item. A disturbance would occur because the records of the response item also would be activated, but there would be no perceptual material available on which this recognition template could act. A regeneration of the response item in the absence of actual perceptual material would be sufficient to neutralize the perturbation. In this case, the perceiving subject could be said to have formed the association, and hence, to have learned.

Mathematics Teaching and Constructivism

Janvier made the comment that any learning is bound to be constructivist, thus separating mathematics teaching and constructivism. He wrote, "I believe that constructivism is not concerned with teaching" (Janvier, chapter 25, this volume). As a model of knowing, Janvier is correct. People who engage in teaching, however, can use the basic tenets of constructivism in building models of the realities of those with whom they interact. If a researcher formulates a model of children constructing mathematical knowledge, the model is an important part of the researcher's meaning of constructivism. Similarly, if a researcher formulates a model of how he or she makes a model of children constructing mathematical knowledge, the model would be a constructivist model of teaching. It too would be an important part of the researcher's meaning of constructivism. Regarding the researcher as a learner in the activity of teaching is essential in an understanding of teaching.

Teaching as Part of a Model of Mathematics Learning.   All of the authors in the preceding chapters seem to agree with Hatano (chapter 12, this volume) that knowledge is acquired by construction, even the researcher's or the teacher's knowledge of students' mathematics. But none of them have explained the process, and if such explanations were offered, we are skeptical that there would be a consensual meaning of the term. Hatano does, however, describe two aspects of constructing that indicate to us that he regards teaching an essential aspect of a model of mathematics learning. The first aspect emphasizes the interaction of previously constructed conceptual items in re-presentation: "Humans acquire knowledge richer than the knowledge they are presented with . . . often as a byproduct of their problem solving and/or comprehension activity." Hatano also points to individual–environment interactions in his comment that "knowledge can be transmitted to some extent, but transmitted knowledge becomes usable in a variety of problem-solving situations only after it is reconstructed, that is, interpreted, enriched, and connected to the prior knowledge of the individual."

Hatano's two comments emphasize the importance of teaching in any model of mathematics learning. Knowing that a teacher cannot transfer mathematics from his or her head into the heads of students orients the teacher to listen closely to students and to learn how to interact in certain ways. Any constructivist model of mathematics learning must be based on what Confrey (1995) has called "close listening" (p. 196). Close listening involves an act of decentering in order to imagine what the experience of the learner might be like. The results of many hours of listening can yield a dynamic, living mathematics of students. But close listening alone is insufficient. Not only must we learn how to listen to our students, we must also learn how to act in ways that bring forth the mathematics of students, sustain it, and modify it. In this, we must include an account of the mathematical activities of the students and how they may or may not change as a result of interacting. Just as students contribute mathematics to experiential situations to establish them as mathematical situations, we adults contribute our concepts and operations to what we observe students do. We then transform our experience of the students' actions and operations into mathematical actions and operations. This is an essential way in which constructivism is concerned with teaching because it is here that the students' mathematical knowledge makes contact with the mathematical knowledge of adults. So, rather than trying to make models of mathematical learning in terms of mathematical practices embedded in the surrounding world, we, as constructivists, try to build models of paths of interactive mathematical communication, paths that cannot be specified a priori. As theorists, we attempt to abstract patterns of interaction that can be used in future experiential encounters. As teachers, we must step out of our actual interactions with students and become consciously aware of ourselves as actors in the phenomic domain of the interactions. As teachers, we must become second-order observers, and it is in this role that a model of mathematical learning can become useful.

Microcultures as Part of a Model of Mathematics Learning.   As a teacher interacts mathematically with his or her students in a medium, and as the students interact with one another, a microculture is built in the immediate here and now. This microculture comes close to what Maturana considers a consensual domain of interactions, which is formed when the individuals of a group adjust and adapt their actions and reactions to achieve the degree of compatibility necessary for cooperation. Building a consensual domain of interactions involves the use of language and adjustments and mutual adaptations of individual meanings to allow effective interaction and cooperation (von Glasersfeld, personal communication). A goal of the interacting individuals is to sustain themselves as viable in the consensual domain, and this is achieved through effective interaction and cooperation. As such, a microculture is not taken as a given, but is produced through the recursive interactions of self-organizing members of a composite unity (Maturana, 1978, p. 47). These microcultures are the sites in which mathematical learning takes place and should be viewed as an essential part of the life of the involved children. The idea of a microculture differs somewhat from the following idea of situated learning: "Knowledge acquisition goes hand in hand with the participation in a community in which the target knowledge is shared . . . and thus is based on social motivation to become a full member of the community as well as motivation to understand and/or to be competent" (Hatano, chapter 12, this volume). In Hatano's characterization, there is target knowledge that is taken as being already shared among the members of some community into which students are to be enculturated. In our interpretation of Voigt (chapter 2, this volume), a microculture is produced by the recursive interactions of the participants in the interaction. There is no a priori target knowledge shared among the members of the composite unity. Rather, whatever constitutes being competent is brought forth through those interactions. This changes the focus from the existing mathematical knowledge and practices of an extant adult community to the mathematical knowledge and practices produced by a community of students and their teachers. We believe that it is crucial to expect pluralism among mathematical classrooms, and this is why we believe that we need models of mathematical learning that are based on the experiential abstractions of the model builders. One of our explicit goals when we immerse ourselves in teaching and learning situations is to become increasingly aware of our own actions as mathematics teachers and of controlling and monitoring those actions. This sense of the self teaching mathematics is crucial in developing models of mathematical learning and in sustaining the motivation to solve the problems that are presented in the context of interactive mathematical communication.

FINAL COMMENTS

In writing this chapter, we tried to indicate what we consider to be essential elements in building models of mathematics learning. First, we regard such models as being based on what students learn. This attitude is based on our experience as mathematics teachers as well as on Piaget's (1980c) understanding of the models he built: "Structures exist in what the children I study 'do' and not only in the semiformalizations that I make of them" (p. 282). Students have an internally consistent and viable mathematical knowledge of their own. Their mathematics is a living and dynamically changing mathematics, and it is the students' mathematics in which we as mathematics educators are primarily interested.

Second, in our frame of reference, we think of students' mathematics as second-order models rather than as first-order models. We make no assumption that our schemes of action and operation represent the students' mathematical knowledge in the sense of forming a match. Rather, our models of students' mathematical knowledge consist of constellations of conceptual constructs we as researchers find useful when interacting with students. We find the construction of second-order models of students' mathematical knowledge and learning challenging because it involves constructing concepts of mathematics not originally part of our own mathematical knowledge.

Third, we see the process of building models of mathematical learning as based on interactive mathematical communication. Here interaction is not understood as interaction between students and mathematical objects existing in an objective, ontological mathematical reality. Instead, there is an "interaction between schemes, sensory elements, and events, but the organism does not get to 'know' the environment in the sense that its own schemes and structures come to resemble or in any sense reflect structures as they might be in the outside world" (von Glasersfeld, 1980, p. 82).

With this understanding of interaction, we distinguish two kinds: individual–environment interaction, and interaction of constructs in re-presentation or other operations involving previously constructed items. Learning through interaction applies to us as researchers who are trying to build models of mathematics learning as well as to students who are trying to learn mathematics. We have found students' learning of mathematics to be a protracted process and our learning of their mathematics to be just as protracted. Confrey (1991) commented that "through the process of the interview, my own conception of exponential functions was transformed, elucidated, and enriched" (p. 129). Confrey's comment highlights the almost inevitable modifications we should expect in our knowledge as we learn the mathematics of our students.

Fourth, we view learning in the context of accommodation. We regard learning as a more or less permanent modification of a conceptual structure in response to perturbation. Our concept of perturbation is not restricted to cognitive conflict. Rather, perturbation refers to a disturbance in the components of an interacting system created through the functioning of the system. This concept of perturbation includes cognitive conflict and the element of surprise.

Fifth, we see teaching as an integral part of model building. As we construct a model of students' mathematics including the modifications of that mathematics, we are also constructing a model of teaching. As constructivists, we try to build models of paths of interactive mathematical communication and abstract patterns of interaction that can be used in future experiential encounters. In this, we as researchers must step out of our actual interactions with students and become consciously aware of ourselves as actors and observers in the phenomic domain of the interactions. As researchers, we need to be second-order observers and focus on the interactive mathematical communication that transpires among the participants.

Finally, in building a model of mathematics learning we also consider the relation of the model to its parent theory. We do not equate constructivism with a model of mathematical learning, but the latter does embody the basic principles of the former. Auerswald (1995) pointed out the difficulties in placing oneself outside of a particular way of thinking and making choices that seem to fit a purpose at hand.

> I am the beneficiary of the epistemological transformation that has been occurring in this century that is allowing us to escape from the exclusivity and perforations, and thus the restrictions, of Cartesian–Newtonian Western thought . . . . This allusion to escape and freedom poses some fascinating ideas/questions. If we have escaped, to where have we escaped? What frame frames my thought as I delineate the choices I have outlined? (p. 453)

Auerswald wrote of a paradigm of paradigms. In constructivist thought, of course, any paradigm of paradigms will inevitably be a model of knowing that cannot possibly attain the status of a supreme or ultimate model. This is why self-reflexivity on the part of the model builders is so important. We cannot simply rely on theory in our efforts to build models of mathematical learning. We must place a high premium on our experiences of the mathematical learning of our students and on our own experiences of learning. We must understand that our models of mathematical learning are a function of our own ways and means of interacting and knowing just as they are a function of our students' ways and means of interacting and knowing. We are striving for models of mathematics learning that can give an account of how students' mathematics might be brought forth, sustained, and modified.

REFERENCES

Auerswald, E. H. (1995). Shifting paradigms: A self-reflective critique. In L. P. Steffe & J. Gale (Eds.), *Constructivism in education* (pp. 447–456). Hillsdale, NJ: Lawrence Erlbaum Associates.

Brownell, W. A. (1935). Psychological considerations in the teaching of arithmetic. In W. D. Reeve (Ed.), *Teaching of arithmetic. Tenth Yearbook of the National Council of Teachers of Mathematics* (pp. 1–31). New York: Bureau of Publications, Teachers College, Columbia University.

Buswell, G. T. (1951). The psychology of learning in relation to the teaching of arithmetic. In N. B. Henry (Ed.), *The teaching of arithmetic* (pp. 143–154). Fiftieth Yearbook of the National Society for the Study of Education. Chicago: University of Chicago Press.

Cobb, P., & Steffe, L. P. (1983). The constructivist researcher as teacher and model builder. *Journal for Research in Mathematics Education, 14,* 83–94.

Confrey, J. (1991). The concept of exponential functions: A student's perspective. In L. P. Steffe (Ed.), *Epistemological foundations of mathematical experience* (pp. 124–159). New York: Springer-Verlag.

Confrey, J. (1995). How compatible are radical constructivism, sociocultural approaches, and social constructivism? In L. P. Steffe, & J. Gale (Eds.), *Constructivism in education* (pp. 185–225). Hillsdale, NJ: Lawrence Erlbaum Associates.

de Saussure, F. (1959). *Course in general linguistics* (W. Baskin, Trans.). New York: Philosophical Library. (Originally published, 1915).

Grossnickle, F. E., Brueckner, L. J., & Reckzeh, J. (1968). *Discovering meanings in elementary school mathematics.* New York: Holt, Rinehart, and Winston.

Guthrie, E. R. (1942). Conditioning: a theory of learning in terms of stimulus, response, and association. In N. B. Henry (Ed.), *The psychology of learning: The forty-first yearbook of the National Society for the Study of Education* (pp. 17–60). Chicago: University of Chicago Press.

Hilgard, E. R. (1956). *Theories of learning.* New York: Appleton-Century Crofts.

Hume, D. (1988). *An enquiry concerning human understanding.* (A. Flew, Vol. Ed.). La Salle, IL: Open Court. (Original work published 1748)

Knight, F. B. (1930). Some considerations of method. In G. M. Whipple (Ed.), *Report of the society's committee on arithmetic. Twenty-ninth Yearbook of the National Society for the Study of Arithmetic* (pp. 145–267). Bloomington, IL: Public School Publishing Company.

Konold, C., & Johnson, D. K. (1991). Philosophical and psychological aspects of constructivism. In L. P. Steffe (Ed.), *Epistemological foundations of mathematical experience* (pp. 1–13). New York: Springer-Verlag.

Lakatos, I. (1970). Falsification and the methodology of scientific research programs. In I. Lakatos, & A. Musgrave (Eds.), *Criticism and the growth of knowledge* (pp. 91–195). Cambridge: Cambridge University Press.

Leont'ev, A. N. (1979). The problem of activity in psychology. In J. V. Wertsch (Ed.), *The concept of activity in Soviet psychology* (pp. 37–71). Armonk, NY: M. E. Sharpe.

Maturana, H. R. (1978). Biology of language: The epistemology of reality. In G. A. Miller, & E. Lenneberg (Eds.), *Psychology and biology of language and thought: Essays in honor of Eric Lenneberg* (pp. 27–63). New York: Academic Press.

Maturana, H. (1987). Everything is said by an observer. In W. I. Thompson (Ed.), *Gaia: A way of knowing* (pp. 65–82). Great Barrington, MA: Lindis-Farne Press.

Piaget, J. (1964). Development and learning. In R. E. Ripple & V. N. Rockcastle (Eds.), *Piaget rediscovered: A report of the conference on cognitive studies and curriculum development* (pp. 7–20). Ithaca, NY: School of Education, Cornell University.

Piaget, J. (1970). *Genetic epistemology*. New York: Columbia University Press.

Piaget, J. (1980a). *Adaptation and intelligence*. Chicago: University of Chicago Press.

Piaget, J. (1980b). The psychogenesis of knowledge and its epistemological significance. In M. Piattelli-Palmarini (Ed.), *Language and learning: The debate between Jean Piaget and Noam Chomsky* (pp. 23–34). Cambridge, MA: Harvard University Press.

Piaget, J. (1980c). Afterthoughts. In M. Piattelli-Palmarini (Ed.), *Language and learning: The debate between Jean Piaget and Noam Chomsky* (pp. 278–284). Cambridge, MA: Harvard University Press.

Piaget, J., & Inhelder, B. (1971). *Mental imagery in the child: A study of the development of imaginal representation*. New York: Basic books.

Steffe, L. P., von Glasersfeld, E. Richards, J., & Cobb, P. (1983). *Children's counting types: Philosophy, theory, and application*. New York: Praeger.

Steier, F. (1995). From universing to conversing: An ecological constructivist approach to learning and multiple description. In L. P. Steffe & J. Gale (Eds.), *Constructivism in education* (pp. 67–84). Hillsdale, NJ: Lawrence Erlbaum Associates.

Thompson, P. (1995). Constructivism, cybernetics, and information processing: Implications for technologies of research on learning. In L. P. Steffe & J. Gale (Eds.), *Constructivism in education* (pp. 123–133). Hillsdale, NJ: Lawrence Erlbaum Associates.

Thorndike, E. L. (1924). *Psychology of arithmetic*. New York: Macmillan.

van Engen, H. (1953). The formation of concepts. In H. F. Fehr (Ed.), *The learning of mathematics: Its theory and practice. Twenty-First Yearbook of the National Council of Teachers of Mathematics* (pp. 69–98). Washington, DC: The National Council of Teachers of Mathematics.

Von Foerster, H. (1984). On constructing a reality. In P. Watzlawick (Ed.), *The invented reality* (pp. 41–61). New York: Norton.

von Glasersfeld, E. (1980). The concept of equilibration in a constructivist theory of knowledge. In F. Benseler, P. M. Hejl, & W. K. Köck (Eds.), *Autopoiesis, communication, and society: The theory of autopoietic systems in the social sciences* (pp. 75–85). New York: Campus.

von Glasersfeld, E. (1991). Abstraction, re-presentation, and reflection: An interpretation of experience and Piaget's theory. In L. P. Steffe (Ed.), *Epistemological foundations of mathematical experience* (pp. 45–67). New York: Springer-Verlag.

von Glasersfeld, E., & Steffe, L. P. (1991). Conceptual models in educational research and practice. *Journal of Educational Thought, 25*, 2, 91–103.

Wertsch, J. V. (1979). *The concept of activity in Soviet psychology*. New York: M. E. Sharpe.

Wheeler, R. H. (1935). The new psychology of learning. In W. D. Reeve (Ed.), *Teaching of arithmetic. Tenth Yearbook of the National Council of Teachers of Mathematics* (pp. 233–250). New York: Bureau of Publications, Teachers College, Columbia University.

Author Index

Subject Index